Fourth Edition

Organized Crime

MICHAEL D. LYMAN
Columbia College of Missouri

GARY W. POTTER
Eastern Kentucky University

PEARSON

Prentice
Hall

Upper Saddle River, New Jersey 07458

Library of Congress Cataloging-in-Publication Data

Lyman, Michael D.
  Organized crime / by Michael D. Lyman, Gary W. Potter.— 4th ed.
     p. cm.
Includes bibliographical references and index.
  ISBN 0-13-173036-3
  1. Organized crime. 2. Organized crime—United States. I. Potter,
Gary W. II. Title.

HV6441.L96 2007
364.1-06—dc21

2006014199

Editor-in-Chief: Vernon R. Anthony
Executive Editor: Frank Mortimer, Jr.
Marketing Manager: Adam Kloza
Assistant Editor: Sarah Holle
Editorial Assistant: Jillian Allison
Production Editor: Linda Zuk, WordCraft, LLC
Production Liaison: Barbara Marttine Cappuccio
Director of Manufacturing and Production: Bruce Johnson
Managing Editor: Mary Carnis
Manufacturing Manager: Ilene Sanford
Manufacturing Buyer: Cathleen Petersen
Senior Design Coordinator: Mary Siener
Cover Designer: Lisa Klausing
Cover Image: James Lauritz, Getty Images
Formatting: Integra
Printer/Binder: Hamilton Printing

Pearson Education LTD.
Pearson Education Singapore, Pte. Ltd
Pearson Education, Canada, Ltd
Pearson Education–Japan

Pearson Education Australia PTY, Limited
Pearson Education North Asia Ltd
Pearson Educación de Mexico, S.A. de C.V.
Pearson Education Malaysia, Pte. Ltd

10 9 8 7 6
ISBN 0-13-173036-3

CONTENTS

Chapter 3 The Evolution of Organized Crime: Urban Beginnings and Major Participants   84

Chapter 4 The Evolution of Organized Crime: Southern Beginnings and Major Participants   127

Chapter 5 The Businesses of Organized Crime   148

Chapter 6   The Illicit Drug Trade   192

Chapter 7   Domestic Organized Crime Groups   222

Chapter 8   A Comparative Perspective   266

Chapter 9   Terrorism as Organized Crime   324

Chapter 10 Organized Crime's Political and Corporate Alliances 376

Chapter 11   Controlling Organized Crime   419

PREFACE

Crime and criminality have been cornerstones for countless movie and book plots and radio and TV talk shows over the decades. Of all the varied types of criminal activity, however, organized crime has proved to be the most intriguing through the years. Images of pinstriped gangsters, police shoot-outs, and flamboyant life-styles emerge whenever the topic of organized crime is mentioned. To a great extent, these images form the basis for stereotyping what the public generally perceives as organized crime. However, these images fail to portray organized crime realistically.

The fourth edition of *Organized Crime* is designed to be an introductory text serving several purposes in the field of criminal justice. First, it gives the reader an understanding of the concept of organized crime—what it is and what it is not—and the necessary historical foundation for understanding the evolution, development, and current status of organized crime. Most important, the book is designed to dispel the myth that organized crime is composed exclusively of Italian American criminal groups. In fact, when considering the overall problem of crime in our communities, other criminal groups, such as the African American, Mexican, Russian, and Nigerian, play an increasingly important role.

Another important component of the book is that drug trafficking plays an important role in the continuing proliferation of organized crime groups. The existence of the illegal drug trade says much about both the groups that traffic in illicit drugs and the members of society who use these drugs, consequently lending support to organized criminals. In addition to a separate chapter dealing with the issue, the topic is discussed intermittently throughout the book.

We have made a great effort to present this material in a logically organized, readable fashion. The problem of organized crime is examined from a social perspective using specially designed pedagogical features. These include chapter objectives, critical thinking projects, chapter summaries, key terms, points of discussion, and suggested readings. All these features are designed to promote scholarly thought and insight into the problem of organized crime, while presenting important thematic questions in each chapter, including these: What is organized crime? Is there really a Mafia? Is terrorism organized crime? Do political machines still exist? Although there are no hard and fast answers to these questions, readers can draw conclusions and perhaps develop probing questions on their own. In many respects the most important pursuit for students studying organized crime is to develop sufficient mastery of the topic to ask the right questions.

Organized Crime, Fourth Edition, incorporates a considerable amount of new material and updates, such as sections on emerging groups, redefining organized crime (OC), drug-trafficking cartels, Chinese OC, Nigerian drug traffickers, Albanian drug-smuggling networks, Dominican drug traffickers, organized crime and the Bushes, Japanese Yakuza, Triborder Area OC activity, as well as updated case studies, statistics, and graphics.

The preparation of this book was a demanding task because it required sifting through an enormous amount of historical data and archives to find and present the most salient aspects of the organized crime problem. The authors' efforts were augmented by numerous individuals and organizations.

In addition to the research offered by well-known experts in the field, information was also culled from government reports generated by organizations such as the Federal Bureau of Investigation, the Pennsylvania Crime Commission, the National Institute of Justice, and the Bureau of Justice Statistics.

In addition to the special people and organizations mentioned, we would like to recognize the efforts of the criminal justice academicians who took time to review this text in its developmental stages. Included are Frank Afflito, University of Tennessee at Memphis; Joseph Andritzky, Concordia University; Paul Becker, Morehead State University; Steven Brodt, Ball State University; David Ferster, Edinboro University of Pennsylvania; Ruth Hefner, Clovis Community College; William Kelly, Auburn University; Ken Mullen, Appalachian State University; and Debra Ross, Grand Valley State University. Their feedback, suggestions, and recommendations are greatly appreciated.

Finally, we wish to thank the many friends at Prentice Hall who helped in the book's production. Special recognition is well deserved for the continued support of Frank Mortimer, senior editor, and Sarah Holle, assistant editor.

The study of organized crime is one of the most fascinating educational endeavors, posing thematic, scholarly, and ideological questions. As we attempt to understand this area of interest, bear in mind that during the past century organized crime became the most insidious form of criminality, involving criminals, politicians, bankers, lawyers, and the all-important users of illegal goods and services. The authors would like to thank you for the adoption of this book for classroom study, and we encourage comments and suggestions regarding this publication for the improvement of future editions. Feel free to contact either of the authors at the following addresses:

MICHAEL D. LYMAN, PH.D.
Department of Criminal Justice
Columbia College of Missouri
1001 Rogers Street
Columbia, MO 65216

GARY W. POTTER, PH.D.
Police Studies
Eastern Kentucky University
410 Stratton Building
Richmond, KY 40475

UNDERSTANDING ORGANIZED CRIME

This chapter will enable you to:

- Understand the various definitions of organized crime
- Contrast the roles of presidential organized crime commissions
- Learn about the Sicilian heritage as it relates to the understanding of the Mafia
- Learn how official investigations into organized crime have contributed to an understanding of the Mafia

- Compare the various theories that have been developed to explain the structure of organized crime groups
- See how organizational constraints affect organized crime groups

INTRODUCTION

On three separate occasions between 1986 and 1991, reputed New York mob boss John Gotti stood trial facing federal racketeering charges. To the surprise and dismay of prosecutors, however, he was acquitted each time. Some say that the acquittals resulted from the furtive trial techniques of Bruce Cuttler, Gotti's attorney; some contend that the government's case, based on plea-bargained testimony, was fatally flawed; others speculate that there had been jury tampering. Whatever the reason, on each occasion the charges against Gotti failed to stick, earning him the nickname "Teflon don." Finally, in 1992, the flamboyant Gotti was convicted and sent to prison for racketeering and for the 1985 murder of his own crime boss, Paul Castellano. This case not only captivated the American people but also helped perpetuate the public's perception of organized crime in America. Indeed, in many ways the image and impression we have of organized crime, whether accurate or not, has been shaped by American "pop" culture.

For example, in 1972 *The Godfather*, starring Marlon Brando, depicted organized crime. Decades earlier movie stars such as Edward G. Robinson, Humphrey Bogart, and James Cagney portrayed tough and cunning gangsters, resulting in an ongoing public fascination with stories about organized crime. Another movie sensation, *The Untouchables*, portrayed Treasury agent Eliot Ness and his nemesis, Al Capone, in the streets of Chicago during Prohibition. The television series of the same name aired for years and is still rerun on many channels around the country. *The Untouchables* provides one example of how Hollywood has managed to keep many of the old gangsters alive in movie reruns and syndicated television, and new ones are being created every year. This fascination with crime, cops, and gangsters still exists and sparks the interest of many people.

Part of the recent concern about organized crime is that it is becoming more and more transnational and, as we will see in Chapter 7, in some cases poses a global threat. This threat is especially evident in the breakdown of the former Soviet Union and the emerging role of opportunist Russian Mafia members. Furthermore, the 1990s and the early twenty-first century, witnessed an increased sophistication in the crimes associated with the global drug trade, an increase in computer-related crime, and the smuggling of radioactive nuclear material.

In addition to those created by the entertainment industry, sensational images portrayed by the electronic and print media tend to present confusing views of organized crime. Consequently, study of this all-important area of criminal justice is laden with misperceptions, distortions, and outright inaccurate information. What is organized crime? How does it relate to other types of crime? In an effort to present the true meaning of the term and clarify the organized crime phenomenon in this chapter, we begin the discussion of organized crime by defining the term and presenting the various theories that are believed to represent contemporary organized crime systems. In subsequent chapters we offer a more specific examination of various aspects of the organized crime problem.

Despite a plethora of literature on organized crime, controversies regarding its definition, structure, functions, and how best to control it continue (Kelly 1986; Bynum 1986; Abadinsky 1994; Potter 1994). The fact that organized crime represents a serious social problem that continues to survive despite aggressive efforts by law enforcement agencies to solve it is certain, however.

The Sopranos Michael Imperioli, James Gandolfini, Tony Sirico, Steve Van Zandt.
(HBO/Picture Desk, Inc./Kobal Collection)

Many issues surround the understanding of organized crime, and many experts and scholars who have studied the topic have interpreted its meaning and social significance differently. Although we have endeavored to present these different views throughout the book, we have chosen to focus on two parallel themes: (1) in addition to widely publicized Italian and Italian American criminal groups, organized crime consists of many other groups for which race or ethnicity may not necessarily play a role, but whose organizational affiliation is based on the special needs of the group, and (2) without the support and assistance of corrupt government officials, legitimate businesspeople, and politicians, organized crime as we know it today would cease to exist.

WHAT IS ORGANIZED CRIME?

For almost 100 years, speculation has flourished regarding the true nature of organized crime in the United States. During that time, countless investigations and governmental studies convinced some members of law enforcement and the media that organized crime is dominated by (but is not exclusively) a single, monolithic criminal organization made up of criminals of Italian descent—the Mafia. In contrast to this view, academics and scholars who have studied the phenomenon have countered that there is no single, dominant crime organization (Italian or otherwise) and that organized crime is composed of numerous ethnic and transnational groups operating together or apart and in conjunction with legitimate businesses and political entities.

In addition to depictions by the entertainment industry and the media, much of the public's understanding of organized crime stems from televised congressional hearings and presidential task forces during the 1950s, 1970s, and 1980s (discussed later). In these hearings, for the most part, organized crime was identified as the Mafia and characterized as a predominantly Italian American phenomenon. This official view was first expounded by Cressey (1969) in an influential work based largely on official data collected by federal agencies. Cressey, who held the view that "if one understands the Cosa Nostra, he understands organized crime in the United States," was criticized sharply for his overreliance on official data, which tended to misrepresent the nature, structure, and function of criminal groups. Both his theory of organized crime and the methodology he employed are still criticized.

In fact, much to his credit, Cressey himself raised questions about his work, pointing out that in exchange for the data he was allowed to use he had to compromise his role as a scientific investigator and become something of a publicist for the federal law enforcement agencies with which he was working. Cressey also pointed to some difficult research issues with regard to organized crime. For example, he noted that the most dangerous hurdle to understanding organized crime is the secrecy surrounding it. Organized crime groups are difficult to identify and harder to scrutinize by virtue of their covert nature. Also, the more violent or well organized a group is, the more difficult it is to examine.

Smith (1990) criticizes Cressey's view of organized crime by suggesting that in understanding only Italian American crime families, one understands only part of the problem—and not necessarily the most important part. He argues that the Mafia mystique was created by headlines crediting law enforcement with crippling many organized crime organizations through the successful prosecutions of its elderly Mafia leaders. According to Smith (1990), "We could almost sleep well, except for the two concurrent crime stories that command our attention: (1) our national failure to control a drug trade in which the major traffickers are not Italian; and (2) the rise in exorbitant white-collar crimes, either proven or still under investigation on Wall Street and the defense industry. Put them next to the Mafia and ask yourself: What is organized crime—really?" Smith summarizes his hypothesis of organized crime by suggesting that the phenomenon be looked on as enterprises occurring along a spectrum of legitimacy. In Smith's view, illicit enterprise, or illegal business, should be the focus of organized crime studies and research. Such focus would avoid stereotypes and emphasize similarities between criminal groups and legitimate enterprises.

Compounding the task of defining organized crime is the serious problem concerning evidence (Morris and Hawkins 1970). Authors of these studies often have little or no direct experience with organized crime, and they focus on events visible to outsiders, such as murders of reputed mob leaders, or material made available by law enforcement agencies, such as transcripts of wiretapped conversations between organized criminals (Best and Luckenbill 1994). Although such evidence is of considerable value in understanding organized crime's activities, it also can be subject to different interpretations. In an effort to clarify the issue, we consider in this chapter both historical and empirical interpretations of what constitutes organized crime.

Media accounts of organized crime can be helpful, but the tendency of journalists to oversimplify the issues and to emphasize the sensational creates problems for criminal justice students who are attempting to understand this phenomenon. Often, the press prepares reports that are not independent in nature, but merely summarize government reports.

Autobiographies by former mobsters suffer from some of the same shortcomings, in addition to questions of reliability. Studies of such works reveal numerous contradictions, a tendency for authors to vindicate themselves, and an inclination for self-glorification (Potter 1994).

In addition, there is no guarantee that government reports, court files, and data collected by regulatory bodies are free of bias or concentrate on the most important problems relating to organized crime. Furthermore, access to such information is not always possible, and law enforcement agents do not always cooperate with researchers seeking information. After all, the primary goal of law enforcement agents is to prosecute offenders, rather than to assist theorists and researchers. In addition, it is highly unlikely that an official law enforcement agency would give researchers information contradicting its official position on organized crime. As a solution, Cressey (1969) has recommended borrowing methods from intelligence sources, geographers, and anthropologists who attempt to understand the present by looking at the past.

Perhaps the greatest problem in understanding organized crime is not the word *crime* but the word *organized*. In fact, although the public, criminologists, and the research literature often agree as to what constitutes criminal behavior, little agreement exists regarding what constitutes organized criminal activity. To illustrate this point, we consider a group of shoplifters who systematically steal merchandise from a particular department store on a regular basis. Can this be considered organized crime? In another case, does a murder spree by two psychopathic killers that takes place over a three-month period constitute organized crime? What about a well-planned bank robbery involving robbers, a professional auto thief to secure the getaway car, a wheelman to drive the getaway car, and a money mover to get rid of the cash? After all, it could be argued that in all these examples the crimes are not only organized, but also well thought out and committed with the explicit intention of avoiding detection.

REDEFINING ORGANIZED CRIME

Traditional arguments about the structure, attributes and characteristics of organized crime have come under even greater criticism in the twenty-first century as the economic, political and social conditions within which organized crime operates are undergoing radical changes. The globalization of the world's economy, the declining importance of nation-states and national sovereignty, along with massively expanded networks of communication and media, have affected organized crime in significant ways.

Letizia Paoli, an Italian sociologist doing some of the most important contemporary research on organized crime, has suggested that the globalization of international markets strongly mitigates against the utility of large hierarchical organizations like the Sicilian Madia, the Yakuza, or Chinese Triads. Paoli argues that these traditional forms of organization seriously hinder successful participation in modern global markets. She suggests that these organizations, whose structure is often predicated on social relations other than market dynamics are no longer efficient structures for the organization of crime (Paoli 2002).

This view is amplified by Manuel Castells who suggests that, in a world of globalized commerce and instant communication, smaller network organizations become the norm for both legitimate and illegitimate business. Castells argues:

> The technological and organizational opportunity to set up global networks has transformed, and empowered, organized crime. For a long time, its fundamental strategy was to penetrate national and local state institutions in its home country, in order to protect its activities. . . . This is still an important element in the operational procedures of organized crime: it can only survive on the basis of corruption and intimidation of state personnel and, sometimes, state institutions. However, in recent times, globalization has added a decisive twist to the institutional strategy of organized crime . . . the high mobility and extreme flexibility of the networks make it possible to evade national regulations and the rigid procedures of international police cooperation. (Castells 1998: 202)

American law enforcement agencies have been very slow to respond to the profound changes in organized crime brought about by globalization. On the other hand, their European counterparts have radically altered their views of organized crime and its structure. In the United Kingdom the National Criminal Intelligence Service (NCIS) has the primary responsibility for analyzing intelligence on organized crime. The NCIS (2005) describes organized crime as having four salient attributes:

1. An organized crime group contains at least three people;
2. The criminal activity the group engages in is ongoing and indefinite in duration;

3. The group is motivated by a desire for profit or power; and,
4. The group commits serious criminal offenses.

This is a very different view of organized crime than the one traditionally employed by law enforcement agencies. But it is a view that reflects the realities of changing illicit markets. Before we explore the elements of this new definition of organized crime, it is important to understand how the globalization of world markets has affected organized crime.

GLOBALIZATION AND ORGANIZED CRIME

Globalization is an immensely complex topic. But, in looking at organized crime, we can discern two major impacts on its activities and structures. First, rather than discrete local markets for goods and services, we now have a single global market. With new computer and communications technology, massively expanded air transportation services, and instantaneous electronic banking services, illegal goods and services can be provided anywhere in the world. The illegal production of these goods and services can also take place anywhere in the world. The legal market provides a good example of this. Today, when you call your bank, telephone company, or credit card company, you are as likely to be talking to a customer service representative in an office in India as to one in the United States. The cost of providing the service is considerably less in India. The same dynamics of cost and profit apply to organized crime.

Second, it is important to understand that the impact of globalization is not the same everywhere. The growth of the globalized economy is uneven. For example, many countries who depend heavily on agricultural exports have been badly hurt by falling prices as their economies have globalized. Similarly, the production of raw materials for manufacturing is much cheaper in some areas of the world than it is in others. Thus organized crime and legitimate business can produce their goods and services more cheaply if they have a wider international reach. At the same time, economic growth is also not stable in the industrialized nations. Inner cities and regions wedded to older forms of industrial production have seen high unemployment, growing poverty, and economic isolation. Good-paying jobs move out of the country and are replaced by low-wage service sector jobs. On the other hand, incomes and wealth are expanding enormously in other parts of these countries, drastically increasing the demand for organized crime's illegal goods and services, particularly in the drug and sex industries.

In accommodating these economic changes, organized crime has moved from traditional criminal activities like extortion to newer forms and has reinforced its role in other activities. For example, there is a massive demand in the globalized world for humans as a commodity. People from areas of the world where globalization has devastated their economies or war has plagued their lives seek to move into more promising social climates in Europe and the United States. Immigrants move from Mexico to the United States, from North Africa to Spain and France, from Eastern Europe to Germany, and so on. Much of this immigration is illegal. Organized crime profits in many ways. It provides smuggling services to illegal immigrants. It supplies illegal labor to sweat shops and factories. It uses immigrants as smugglers. And it provides women and children for the illegal sex trade. Women are trafficked across international borders for prostitution and are often used as mules in the drug trade during transit. Tourists are trafficked across international borders for child sex.

An unstable political world created in the wake of globalization has also created massive markets for illegal arms sales. Organized crime provides small arms and large weapons system for conflicts in Eastern Europe, the Middle East, Africa, and Asia, often supplying both sides of the conflicts and sometimes taking their remuneration in the form of drugs. Drug smuggling itself has become more lucrative as international borders weaken and modes of transportation become cheaper. In the new globalized economy, organized crime can purchase raw materials (coca leaves, opium poppies, etc.) more cheaply and sell the finished product (cocaine and heroin) to more affluent populations at higher prices and in greater quantity than ever before. Business in a globalized economy is very good for organized crime. It is estimated that illegal commerce accounts for about 10 percent of all international trade. But, to take advantage of these opportunities, organized crime must structure itself for the globalized marketplace.

Returning to the issue of redefining organized crime, we must ask what structure best accommodates the realities of a globalized market? We can start our analysis by looking at the criminal group itself.

THE CRIMINAL GROUP

Unlike street criminals or even professional criminals, organized criminals work together on a continuous basis in illegal enterprises. There is a core group of criminals and a much larger group of individuals who work with them, performing specific tasks and providing specific services, but who are primarily legitimate economic and political actors. In the globalized economy, computer experts and financial advisors are every bit as important to organized crime groups as are drug pushers, bookies, and prostitutes. These individuals are brought into a crime network as their services are needed. This kind of peripheral association is highly utilitarian. It makes it extremely difficult for law enforcement to trace specific activities back to a core group of criminals.

A nagging and persistent issue with regard to the structure of the criminal group has been the unfortunate corporate analogy utilized to describe organized crime's decision-making structure. The impression left by the corporate analogy is that organized crime has some kind of board of directors and hierarchical structure that control the operation and transmit orders to line personnel. This traditional definition stresses the role of *bosses*, analogous to corporate CEOs; a *commission*, roughly equivalent to a corporate board of directors; *capos*, who would make up the middle management level of a bureaucracy; and *soldiers*, who are the workers actually carrying out illegal activity. As we have seen, such a traditional view of organized crime is fundamentally flawed.

The newer view of organized crime put forward by European law enforcement agencies totally rejects this view of organized crime. In moving toward this newer conceptualization, we recognize the fact that the older traditional forms of organized crime, such as Mafia-type organizations, if they ever existed, are now an endangered species, no longer useful in a globalized world economy. Just like legitimate corporations, organized crime groups today are actually loose networks of entrepreneurs. In a time of instant communications, the cumbersome forms of hierarchical organization not only are no longer needed, but they also impede the ability to do illegal business, and they are much more susceptible to police infiltration than loose associations of criminal networkers. With instant cash transfers, cellular phones, and the Internet, any small group can purchase and distribute illegal drugs almost instantaneously. The need for a boss is long gone.

Organizing for Profit

In the same fashion as for legitimate enterprises, organized crime exists for one primary purpose: to make a profit. Just like legitimate enterprises, organized crime acquires and makes use of economic and political power to achieve this goal. What has traditionally differentiated organized crime from legitimate enterprises has been the use of illegal means and methods to enhance the accumulation of power and profit. While many scholars argue that this distinction is less important today than in the past, especially in the wake of Enron, Global Crossing, and various banking scandals, the use of criminal means to achieve conventional goals (profit) is still an important definitional attribute of organized crime. These criminal means can range from extortion and corruption to acts of violence, although it should be noted that violence is primarily limited to the lower-level street activities of organized crime groups (e.g., retail drug sales).

Profit-Making Enterprises of Organized Crime

One of the most profound ways in which a globalized economy has changed organized crime is that it has vastly increased the number and types of enterprises from which organized crime may profit. Traditionally, we have thought of organized crime groups as offering vice and racketeering services at a local level. The production and distribution of pornography and drugs, the provision of prostitution and gambling services, loan-sharking, and traditional protection services were seen as the core of organized crime activities.

Globalization has changed all of that. In a worldwide market, organized crime can become involved in virtually any enterprise. Of course, criminal organizations still dominate the sex industry and the drug trade. But even these enterprises have changed dramatically in the past two decades. Immigrants are smuggled across international borders to work in the brothels, strip clubs, and massage parlors owned by the mob, but they are also trafficked to work in manufacturing, agriculture, and personal service industries. Diversification in the drug trade has become possible because of vastly enhanced modalities of transportation and finance. The illegal trade in guns and weapons closely parallels the drug trade and is a worldwide money-maker for organized crime. Luxury automobiles are stolen and transported around the world for resale. Ivory, gems, rare plants, and wildlife are sold in a global marketplace. Even relatively simple and crude forms of organized crime enterprise, such as extortion and protection rackets, have taken on a new importance in a global economy. Instead of shaking down neighborhood bars and restaurants, organized crime in now hired by legitimate businesses to harass competitors, conduct industrial espionage, and intimidate underpaid illegal workers.

In a globalized economy, organized crime's profit-making potential is limited only by the imagination of the actors involved. Geographic scope, dangers associated with long-distance communication, and problems of moving vast sums of money and material no longer limit organized crime to neighborhood rackets.

ORGANIZED CRIME NETWORKS OR GLOBAL MAFIAS?

As we have seen, the issue of the size and complexity of the organization of criminal groups dominated scholarly debate about organized crime through the 1970s and 1980s. Many of the concepts, definitions, and attributes attached to organized crime in this debate were simply wrong and severely impeded our ability to comprehend the vast changes that were occurring in criminal enterprise. For much of the twentieth century, we were thinking like cops and prosecutors, asking who are these people, what did they do, and how do we bust them. These were the wrong questions. The important questions that should have been addressed were these: How does the illegal economy affect organizational size, communications, and coordination of activities? How is organized crime affected by the complex relationships it must maintain with the upperworld (legitimate businesses, politics, the criminal justice system)? What environmental factors impinge on criminal organizations?

In asking the wrong questions we also focused on the wrong issues, often highlighting the most sensational aspects of organized crime, while ignoring the more mundane and far more important day to day activities of organized crime groups. For example, when we looked at the Prohibition Era, we highlighted the relatively brief period of violence at the beginning of that failed social experiment, never looking at the massive and relatively peaceful period of cooperation and profit taking that followed. In looking at the cocaine trade, we focused on the early violence of Cuban, Colombian, and Jamaican traffickers, neglecting the massive, peaceful expansion of the drug trade that dominated the 1980s and 1990s. As the drug trade developed, extensive networks of exchange and trade were created among criminal groups worldwide. Rather than global Mafias, this international trade has stimulated small, flexible, discrete networks. This makes perfect sense. First, smaller networks enhance profitability by reducing production and corruption costs. Second, smaller networks better control the flow of information about what a criminal group is doing and how it is doing it, reducing the risk of law enforcement interference in the daily business of organized crime.

The transition to a globalized economy, as discussed earlier, has made smaller, flexible networks of criminals the preferred method of doing business. A criminal network is better positioned to take advantage of instantaneous communications and financial transactions.

THE FORMS OF ORGANIZED CRIME

In 2002 the United Nations (UN) published the results of a major international study attempting to delineate the various organizational forms utilized by organized crime groups worldwide. The UN research looked at organized crime groups in sixteen separate countries and came up with an organizational typology that defines the various organizational forms found in these countries.

The UN research delineated five ideal types of criminal organization, ranging from the most traditional forms of organized crime to newer, modern organized networks (United Nations 2002):

1. Standard hierarchy
2. Regional hierarchy
3. Clustered hierarchy
4. Core group
5. Criminal network

These are, of course, ideal types. Not all criminal organizations will conform precisely to a specific type, but most will have the predominant characteristics of one these types. The first three types, delineating hierarchical structures, are closest to the traditional forms of organized crime we have been discussing, and the last two, core groups and networks, are closest to the forms of organization we can expect to be most prevalent in an emerging global economy.

Standard Hierarchy A standard hierarchy is a single organized crime group, usually led by an single powerful individual. These organizations have clearly defined roles, a readily identified chain of command, and a hierarchy that is designed to provide a strong system of internal discipline. Standard hierarchies usually have a name by which they are known and often have a strong ethnic or social identity. For example, members usually come from the same ethnic background (e.g., Albanians, Russians, Italians, etc.) or a similar background experience (e.g., prison gangs). Violence is an integral tool of both legal and illegal businesses and these groups usually operate in clearly defined geographical areas.

A particularly good example of a standard hierarchy is an organized crime group in Lithuania referred to by law enforcement officials as the *Cock Group*. This organization has a well-defined hierarchy and common social identity (prison experience). It is primarily engaged in extortion, but also trafficks in heroin, operates prostitution outlets, and engages in motor vehicle theft. The Cock Group engages in the extensive use of violence. It has created a network of corruption that gives it strong local and regional political influence. And it has heavily penetrated into legitimate businesses in the area. In addition to its major criminal enterprises, the Cock Group is also involved in counterfeiting, forgery, fraud, embezzlement, money laundering, armed robbery, trafficking in women and children for prostitution, loan-sharking, arms trafficking, and to a limited degree gambling.

The Cock Group came into existence in 1990 when it was organized by a small group of former prison inmates. The original organization grew quickly, and by 1993 it had splintered into a number of smaller groups operating in competition with each other. A short, but relatively intense period of violent conflict between these smaller groups resulted in the eventual reorganization of the syndicate into two dominant organizations. These organizations have a tight hierarchical structure with a single leader and two deputy leaders. The deputies are in charge of illegal activities. One deputy is responsible for drug trafficking; the other is responsible for other smuggling operations.

In addition, a designated group of members are in charge of security and serve as bodyguards for the group's leader. All members of the Cock Group are Lithuanian or Russian. They are all male and all are former prisoners. The group has an unwritten code of conduct and an initiation test for new members, which usually entails the commission of an act of violence.

At least until 1997, violations of their code of conduct resulted in severe physical punishment, although recently the organization has tried to resolve internal conflicts through means less likely to draw law enforcement attention. Conflicts with other criminal organizations, however, are still resolved by the use of considerable violence, especially bombings and murder.

The Cock Group was able to take advantage of the rapid economic privatization in Lithuania by using its economic resources to penetrate new business enterprises, thereby giving it considerable economic power in that country. In addition, a pervasive system of corruption involving customs and border officials and local police has been put in place. Today this group operates in Germany, Russia, and Spain, as well as in Lithuania.

Regional hierarchies are also tightly controlled groups with strong systems of internal discipline and clearly defined roles and lines of authority. The major difference between these groups and standard hierarchies is that considerable autonomy and independence are granted to local organizations operating within the criminal organization. They have a single leadership structure and a clear line of command. They tend to be regional in their geographic scope and engage in multiple illegal activities. Like standard hierarchies, regional hierarchies have a strong social or ethnic identity and employ violence as a primary means of maintaining discipline and resolving disputes.

Regional Hierarchy

An excellent example of a regional hierarchy is the activities of the Hell's Angels in Canada. The Hell's Angels is a very large, very structured outlaw motorcycle gang (OMG) that derives much of its income from the manufacture and trafficking of illegal drugs. As an outlaw motorcycle gang, the Hell's Angels' members share a strong sense of social identity. Traditionally, this group has been noted for its extensive use of violence. There is strong evidence of localized corruption emanating from Hell's Angels activities, and the group was invested heavily in the legal economy, at least at local levels.

Hell's Angels manufacture a wide range of synthetic drugs and also distribute heroin, cocaine, and marijuana. In addition, at least at the local level, Hell's Angels has been involved in prostitution, money laundering, vehicle theft, and gunrunning.

Like other OMGs, Hell's Angels has an intricate structure based on a national organization subdivided into local chapters. A national president is technically in charge of all chapters, although day to day activities are the responsibility of the chapters themselves. Each chapter has its own president, who has almost absolute power over the chapter; a secretary, who manages financial and organizational details and posts bail for arrested members; a sergeant-at-arms, who is responsible for chapter security and who maintains an arsenal of firearms and other weapons; and a road captain, who is in charge of chapter runs and other motorcycle-related activities. Other criminal organization participants include chapter members; *hangarounds*, who are persons loosely associated with the gang; and *prospects*, who are individuals being considered for potential membership in the gang. Hell's Angels' members are all made with women participating only on the periphery of the gang.

In Canada there are an estimated 280 Hell's Angels gangs. These local chapters cooperate with other OMGs in the area and often absorb smaller clubs into the organization. The Canadian Hell's Angels also cooperate with other Hell's Angels organizations around the world and with other organized crime groups. Hell's Angels members are required to be loyal to the gang, to defer to the president's power, to follow orders, and to avoid drug addiction.

Traditionally, violence has been a key component in maintaining internal and external order for this organization. Deviation from organizational rules can result in death. Canadian law enforcement officials regard Hell's Angels as one of the most violent groups active in Canada, attributing to them 103 homicides in the period from 1994 to 2002.

Hell's Angels chapters and individual members are involved in a variety of legitimate business enterprises, including strip clubs, bars, restaurants, motorcycle shops, and the like. Some organizational members spend most of their time working in legitimate commercial enterprises. Hell's Angels chapters seek to dominate or monopolize drug trafficking and prostitution in their local areas, eliminating or absorbing rival criminal organizations.

The Hell's Angels has been particularly adept at infiltrating and corrupting local law enforcement and government officials. The group has a sophisticated and highly successful intelligence-gathering component that keeps them informed of ongoing investigation by police. In recent years, Hell's Angels chapters have tried to increase their level of social participation in the community by engaging in charitable activities and adopting more conventional dress and appearance codes.

Clustered Hierarchy

A clustered hierarchy is an organized crime group that involves a number of smaller organized crime groups that coordinate their activities and enterprises. Clustered hierarchies consist of a number of criminal groups who have established an arrangement of managing their respective activities in a coordinated manner. As the organization develops, the cluster develops a stronger identity for members than the smaller groups in which they are actual participants.

Mexico's Arellano-Felix Organization, operating out of Tijuana, is a prime example of a successful clustered hierarchy. This group exhibits four major tendencies: (1) it cooperates with a large number of other criminal organization, (2) it is highly penetrated into the legitimate economy, (3) it exercises enormous political influence through corruption, and (4) it has a well-developed reputation for the use of violence. The Arellano-Felix Organization dominated the drug market, particularly cocaine, heroin, and methamphetamines, along the Tijuana–San Diego nexus for much the 1980s and 1990s. Today it is one of the seven largest drug-trafficking organizations in Mexico and is regarded by many law enforcement agencies as the most powerful and dangerous of these organizations.

The transformation of the Arellano-Felix Organization from a localized drug group into a major cartel came with the abolition of the pyramidal structure so often found in traditional organized crime groups. Today the organization is composed of a series of small cells, each protected by the corruption generated by the larger organization, but also independent and autonomous with regard to its own drug-trafficking enterprises and criminal finances. This new form of organization has reduced violence among competitors, increased cooperation in drug trafficking, enabled the sharing of both territories and transportation modalities, and created an intricate system of money laundering and political corruption. All of this is accomplished by organizations who have no direct contact with each other, but who rely on the larger cluster to manage shared activities.

The strength of the organization is found in the fact that it is virtually impervious to law enforcement activities. The arrest of any leader would have no impact on the organization. A large number of individuals referred to as *narco-juniors* exist in the Arellano-Felix Organization who are ready to take on leadership roles at a moment's notice. These are younger, better educated sons of upper-class Mexican families living on both sides of the United States–Mexico border and holding dual citizenship. Everyone in the organization, from drug runners to hitmen, are educated professionals. For day to day high-risk operations, the Arellano-Felix Organization hires local Hispanic gang members.

The organization has a reputation for the extensive use of violence, with several hundred deaths attributed to its activities. The primary reason for the success of the organization, however, is the extensive network of corrupt law enforcement officials it has working for it. In addition, the organization has a sophisticated countersurveillance and intelligence operation in place aimed at police officials in both the United States and Mexico.

One of the most important emerging forms of organized crime readily adapted to conducting enterprise in a global economy is the core group. A core group is an unstructured group of organized criminals surrounded by a larger network of individuals engaged in serious criminal activity. Unlike hierarchies, a core group has a flat organizational structure in which power is shared by all participants. It consists of a small number of individuals, which makes it much easier to avoid law enforcement interference and maintain internal security. Group identity is maintained through their illegal activities, but no strong social or ethnic identities are associated with core group organizations. Rarely is a such an organization known by a specific name or, for that matter, known to the general public or law enforcement at all.

One of the most successful drug trafficking organizations in the world is a perfect example of a core group form of organization. The Juvenal Group operates in Cali, Medellin, and Bogota, Colombia, and is primarily engaged in the trafficking of cocaine to the United States. The Juvenal Group has no shared ethnic or social identity and makes almost no use of violence. Rather it relies on massive political corruption and cooperative ties with other criminal organizations to conduct its illegal activities. In recent years the Juvenal group has expanded its illegal enterprises to include human trafficking and money laundering.

The organization has a horizontal rather than vertical structure, although Alejandro Bernal Madrigal, because of his extensive political connections and financial success, appears to be the most influential of the group's members. Although some participants had previous experience in other Colombian drug-trafficking organizations, the vast majority have no prior criminal records, are professionals or businessmen in their daily lives, and come from Colombia's upper-middle class. It is estimated that the Juvenal Group consists of about 200 members of Colombian, Mexican, Guatemalan, and Ecuadorian descent. The Juvenal group makes extensive use of satellite phones, mobile phones, e-mails, and highly sophisticated

Core Group

encryption software to conduct its business. It also maintains a support network of bankers, lawyers, and other professionals to head off any difficulties with state or law enforcement officials.

The Juvenal Group operates under the cover of its extensive legitimate commercial activities; members avoid conspicuous displays of wealth and exercise great discretion to avoid calling attention to themselves and their activities. The use of violence is strongly discouraged. In addition, the group subcontracts many of its riskier activities to other groups. It makes no attempt to control territories or markets and attempts to avoid conflicts with other criminal organizations. Today the Juvenal Group has extensive cooperative arrangements with organized crime groups in Mexico, Venezuela, and Ecuador. Drugs are purchased in Colombia and then exported to Venezuela, Nicaragua, Guatemala, Mexico, Australia, and Ghana. Drug shipments are usually concealed in bulk exports of fruit concentrate. It is estimated that the Juvenal Group moves 30 tons of cocaine a year, resulting in annual profits of $300 million. This money is then reinvested into legitimate enterprises in Colombia's legal economy.

Criminal Network

The criminal network represents the cutting edge of organized crime in the twenty-first Century. Although localized crime networks have existed throughout history, their utility in a global economy makes them, along with core groups, the most efficient forms of criminal organizations for the new millennium. Criminal networks are loosely organized, highly adaptable, very fluid networks of individual participants who organize themselves around an ongoing criminal enterprise. The membership, shape, and organization of a network is defined by those individuals' participation in it at any given time. Individual attributes, such as specific skills, financial resources, political connections, and the like, determine the importance of network participants. There is no sense of ethnic or social identity—only personal loyalties to the enterprise itself. Networks are created, re-formed, and initiated around a series of continuing criminal projects. Individuals come and go from the network, so the organization is constantly re-forming itself from project to project. Criminal networks maintain a very low public profile and almost never identify themselves by any name or attribution other than the participation of the individuals in the network itself.

A good example of a crime network is the Verhagen Group, which operated in Amsterdam, the Hague, Rotterdam, and Urtrecht in the Netherlands. The primary business of the Verhagen Group was the trafficking of hashish, but it also engaged in large-scale business crimes, including fraud and embezzlement, real estate fraud, and theft.

The Verhagen Group imported hashish from Morocco, Lebanon, and Pakistan and then redistributed it to retail sellers in Switzerland, Belgium, Great Britain, Denmark, and the Netherlands. About 30,000 kilograms of hashish a year was trafficked by this group.

The Verhagen Group had a core membership of only five people, with about forty-five associates engaged in performing contract services for the core group. Associates handled smuggling, transportation, and storage of the hashish, meaning that the core group members were insulated and removed from the actual criminal activities of the organization. All core group members were Dutch and male, and their participation was based on personal relationships and friendships. Associates of the group included German, British, African, Asian, and American participants. The Verhagen Group relied heavily on connections with other criminal organizations to conduct its business. There was no formal code of conduct for group's participants and no violence associated with the group's criminal enterprises.

The organization was built around legitimate automobile sales enterprises and these business contacts throughout Europe were used to create contacts for the criminal enterprise. In addition, the Verhagen group collected intelligence on the activities of law enforcement agencies and personnel, strongly suggesting the existence of a complex system of corruption that operated across transnational borders.

PROBLEMS CAUSED BY ORGANIZED CRIME

Organized crime is more insidious than the preceding examples indicate. Its members are calculating and sophisticated and realize that their actions not only have criminal consequences, but also are constantly under the scrutiny of law enforcement agencies. This scrutiny causes the criminals to be secretive, cautious, and furtive.

If we can assume that every crime has a victim, who are the victims of organized crime activities? After all, crimes such as prostitution, drug trafficking, and gambling involve a buyer and a seller, each of whom is a willing participant. So who is the victim? It could be argued that the public is the most visible victim of organized crime. Whenever the organized criminal makes money through thievery, violence, or swindling, the public loses. Clearly, criminal associates are often victimized by organized crime members, but law-abiding citizens are also victimized in a number of ways. First, citizens are sometimes the direct victims of organized crime enterprises (violence, extortion, intimidation, etc.). Second, billions of dollars of tax revenue from organized crime go uncollected (estimated at $37 billion in lost taxes every year), resulting in higher tax rates for law-abiding citizens. Third, expenses related to law enforcement, criminal prosecution, and imprisonment of convicted members create a substantial drain on the economy of any community.

Organized crime's participation in the realm of legitimate business, which has occurred since the early 1930s, has resulted in an additional economic impact. For example, if the owner of a small business must pay insurance to an organized crime member, this cost is passed on to the legitimate consumer. If organized crime is successful in monopolizing a business or product, the consumer once again must help pay the price. Furthermore, if organized crime members are successful in corrupting public officials, the citizenry's tax dollars support a less effective and less efficient government. These factors suggest the importance of identifying and understanding organized crime. We now consider some common characteristics of many organized crime groups.

UNDERSTANDING THE MAFIA

The organization most commonly associated with organized crime is the **Mafia,** which writers, filmmakers, historians, and others often use as a benchmark for understanding the phenomenon of organized crime. In an effort to appreciate the organizational aspects of what has become known as the Mafia, it is logical first to consider the meaning of the word. By most accounts, the word *Mafia* did not appear in print until the mid-1860s and was thought to be understood by most Sicilians. Part of the dialect used in the poorer districts of Palermo, Sicily, Mafia and mafioso commonly referred to beauty, perfection, grace, and excellence, but when applied to a man, mafioso "connotes pride, self-confidence, and vainglorious behavior" (Hess 1973).

By the mid-nineteenth century, the term *mafioso* had become synonymous not only with crime, but also with a certain type of criminal behavior and attitude. When putting the word to use, Sicilians refer to a "man of honor" or "man of respect" who embodies not only criminal, but also other personality characteristics. These include those of the village strong-arm man, the boss, and the mediator of many conflicts (Hess 1973). Rather than using the term Mafia directly, people speak of the *amici degli amici*, or "friends of friends," to characterize organized patron–client relationships typically controlled by a mafioso. The mafioso was brave and self-reliant: a man of action, one not to be taken lightly. Most important, the mafioso was prepared to become a law unto himself if necessary.

Although there is considerable consensus about the meaning of the word Mafia, its origins are not as clear. Some historians trace it to the Sicilian struggle in the thirteenth century against French rule. "Morte alla Francia, Italia anela!" ("death to France, Italy groans") was their cry, forming the acronym MAFIA. Others suggest that the term originated in 1282 as a battle cry of rebels who slaughtered thousands of Frenchmen after a French soldier raped a Palermo maiden on her wedding day. Whatever the source, the term has become familiar throughout much of the world and is often synonymous with such criminal activities as drug trafficking, gambling, extortion, and murder.

Organized crime is much more, however, than is conjured by the word Mafia. Although experts in the field are somewhat divided regarding components of the organized crime phenomenon, there is a degree of consensus regarding the aspects of an organized crime group. For example, many experts agree that organized crime represents a continuing, profit-motivated, criminal enterprise that employs the use of fear, violence, intimidation, and public corruption to achieve organizational goals and remain immune to law enforcement. In addition, criminal activity is probably restricted to the provision of illegal goods and services (Hagan 1989; Albanese 1983). Debate among experts continues, however, as to the extent to which organized crime is successful in monopolizing any given illegal market.

CATEGORIES OF ORGANIZED CRIMINAL BEHAVIOR

Organized crime is a unique and dynamic phenomenon that permeates virtually all segments of society. It differs from other types of criminal activity, however, in several important ways. These categories of behavior most commonly associated with **organized crime** activities include the provision of illicit services and illicit goods, conspiracy to commit crimes, penetration of legitimate business, extortion, and corruption. An understanding of these categories enables the reader to comprehend the numerous definitions and theories of organized crime that are discussed later in the chapter.

The offering of **illicit services** represents one of the main enterprises of organized crime organizations. Illicit services are those that legitimate businesses do not provide and are proscribed by law. Included are (1) gambling operations that act outside the law and offer a financial tax incentive for those who use this service; (2) protection rackets, a form of extortion by which organized crime members approach owners of small businesses and offer them protection for the business in case of "unforeseen" misfortune, such as fire or vandalism; (3) loan-sharking, the illegal lending of money at usurious rates, whose repayment is enforced through violence and intimidation; and (4) prostitution, the sale of sex acts by persons acting as part of a larger organization.

The provision of illicit services is a criminal enterprise that generates money to further the organization's goals. Also, in many cases illicit services are provided in conjunction with illegal goods.

Provision of Illicit Services

Like illicit services, a second hallmark of organized crime is the provision of **illicit goods,** which are not available from legitimate businesses. In particular, illegal drugs represent a primary product in considerable demand on the black market. Illicit drugs include marijuana, cocaine, and heroin, to name a few, and the sale of these drugs provides organized crime organizations billions of tax-free dollars every year. Pornography is another black market commodity that generates billions of dollars annually. Unregistered guns and stolen goods are other products in considerable demand that illicit dealers can sell at lower prices and with more ease than can legitimate distributors.

Provision of Illicit Goods

Another vital category of organized criminal behavior is **conspiracy,** an agreement between two or more people to violate the law. In most cases, organized crime members work with each other for the purpose of selling drugs or stolen property, loan-sharking, gambling, and other activities. Very seldom is a criminal act committed without the knowledge or approval of the heads of the criminal group. Consequently, managers who authorize criminal acts are guilty of conspiring to commit these acts.

Conspiracy to Commit Crimes

Because organized crime members have no legal way to spend their illicit profits, they must hide as much of their revenue as possible. The ability to penetrate legitimate business gives the organized crime unit both the chance to conceal illicit revenues and an opportunity to hide behind a cloak of legitimacy in the community to avoid the suspicion of citizens and detection by police. An example of organized crime involvement in legitimate business is the well-documented relationship between construction locals, contractors, and the Italian American crime syndicates in New York. In 1986, the President's Commission on Organized Crime concluded that more than a dozen important construction locals in New York had documented relationships with known members of organized crime. The commission observed that organized crime members rely on such relationships for routine extortion of contractors and on elaborate collusive activities within some segments of the construction industry. These relationships are commonly used to benefit contractors and suppliers owned by organized crime groups (President's Commission on Organized Crime 1986a: 226).

Penetration of Legitimate Business

Extortion   Organized crime often infiltrates legitimate business through **extortion.** In its most elementary parlance, extortion is a form of theft and is defined as the use or threatened use of violence or force to achieve a criminal end. For example, organized crime group members could insist that a restaurant subscribe to their linen service by subjecting those who refuse to being attacked. Although extortionate practices may be used in virtually all aspects of organized crime, it has most commonly been associated with loan-sharking and the threat of violence against those who fail to repay debts to the organized crime unit on a timely basis.

Corruption   As discussed in more detail in Chapter 4, **corruption** is another category of organized criminal behavior. Indeed, without the surreptitious aid of public and private figures such as law enforcement officers, judges, prosecutors, mayors, bankers, attorneys, accountants, and elected and appointed political persons at all levels of government, the organized crime unit could not flourish.

DEFINITIONS BY CRIME COMMISSIONS

Over the years, several important commissions have attempted to study organized crime and to offer insight into it.

Chicago Crime Commission   One of the first efforts to explore organized crime in the United States was conducted by the Chicago Commission of Inquiry in 1915. The commission noted that certain traits of criminal groups could be distinguished from other forms of criminality. These traits included special traditions, systematized practices, and a specialized language (criminal argot). Because there was no national focus on organized crime during that time, the commission's findings had limited impact.

The Wickersham Commission   In 1929, the Wickersham Commission studied the impact of Prohibition on criminal activity. It found that organized crime activity prospered around bootlegging activities and that there was a need for a more in-depth national study of organized crime, which did not occur until many years later.

After the highly publicized investigations, arrests, and prosecutions of underworld figures such as Al Capone from Chicago and Lepke Buchalter and Lucky Luciano from New York, the public believed that law enforcement and the entire criminal justice system were effective in combating organized crime. Unhappily, these organizations were not effective. While the country focused nationally on the Great Depression and then World War II, organized crime flourished. By the time Prohibition ended in 1933, gangsters had become more and more involved in gambling, prostitution, and loan-sharking activities.

The Kefauver Committee   In 1950, the Kefauver Committee was formed to investigate organized crime involvement in interstate gambling. In addition to recognizing organized crime's connection to gambling, the committee also noted organized crime's involvement in prostitution, drug trafficking, extortion, and public corruption.

You Decide

Despite nearly a century's worth of investigations by federal and state law enforcement organizations and the findings of several important national commissions, some people still question whether the multinational Italian criminal organization known as the Mafia really exists. For decades, however, high-level criminal conspiracy trials have resulted in the successful prosecution of high-ranking mob bosses such as Al Capone, Frank Erikson, Sam Giancana (not convicted, but jailed for contempt for one year), "Lucky" Luciano, Louis "Lepke" Buchalter, Vito Genovese, Joe Bonanno (jailed for not answering questions about his autobiography), and John Gotti. Police haranguing of suspected mobsters has also had positive outcomes. For example, in the late 1930s "Bugsy" Siegel moved from New York to Los Angeles to avoid capture and prosecution and eventually was killed by fellow mobsters for squandering mob funds. Government prosecutors targeted Dutch Schultz so many times that media exposure and public notoriety resulted in his being killed; and Joe Colombo, the subject of extensive media scrutiny, was shot at the behest of mob superiors.

These are only a few of what could be characterized as successful efforts on the part of law enforcement to dismantle or hinder the mob. Although none of these cases resulted in the total disbanding of organized crime, each case (and hundreds more like them) afforded law enforcement countless opportunities to surveil, monitor, arrest, interview, and work with turncoat members of the Mafia and other organized crime groups (obviously, Erickson, Siegel, and Schultz were not of Italian origin and therefore could not have been members of the alleged Mafia). Some argue that since Joe Valachi's revelations in 1963 about the structure of the Mafia, law enforcement officials have learned that the twenty-five or so Italian gangs throughout the United States known as *families* do indeed work together, communicate regularly, and share many of the same goals, objectives, structures, and rules.

Others claim that there is no single organization known as the Mafia, but a loosely structured consortium of criminal gangs, some of whom happen to be of Italian descent. Pundants reject the notion of a uniform criminal organization known as the Mafia, but adhere to the premise that Italian gangs (or families) do exist, but are not nearly as organized and structured as law enforcement and the media believe. Critics say that popular views of the Mafia are skewed by erroneous police reports that could be attempts to justify the police agencies' existence, to broaden their powers, and to increase their operating budgets.

Is it really important whether we believe in the Mafia? From a policy standpoint, it is always worthwhile to understand the nature and structure of any criminal entity so that appropriate application of laws or the development of new legislation can be considered to eliminate criminal activity. After all, laws addressing conspiracy, such as Racketeer Influenced and Corrupt Organizations Act (RICO), and continuing criminal enterprise are designed to prosecute associates, rank and file members, and management of a criminal organization. If criminal agreements exist between families, if one family aids another in the execution of a criminal enterprise, if there is a national commission whose function it is to arbitrate disputes between families (clearly a management function), if legitimate businesses are involved as fronts or money movers, and if public officials are in the employ of such groups, law enforcement officials, lawmakers, and prosecutors should know this. Is more than 100 years sufficient time to learn of a criminal organization's existence? Is there really a Mafia? If there is a Mafia, is it really the only organized crime group of major importance in the United States? You decide!

Describe your own perceptions of organized crime as you read this chapter. Give specific examples of how your perceptions change. If they remain the same, explain why.

The McClellan Committee

During the early 1960s, the Senate Permanent Subcommittee on Investigations, headed by Senator John McClellan, investigated the organized crime phenomenon. The McClellan Committee convinced a low-level gangster, Joseph Valachi, to testify about life in organized crime.

Through Valachi's testimony, the committee gleaned much information about an alleged organized crime group called La Cosa Nostra (Italian for "this thing of ours"). Valachi testified about some mob leaders and the mob's organizational structure, rules, and rackets, which included loansharking, labor racketeering, extortion, and infiltration into legitimate business. The McClellan Committee proceedings made great contributions to a general understanding of the immense criminal phenomenon of organized crime.

The President's Commission on Law Enforcement and the Administration of Justice

The President's Commission on Law Enforcement and the Administration of Justice offered a definition of organized crime in 1967: "a society that seeks to operate outside the control of the American people and their government. It involves thousands of criminals, working within structures as large as those of any corporation."

In 1968, Congress passed the first comprehensive organized crime bill, the Omnibus Crime Control and Safe Streets Act, which contained the first specific definition of organized crime: "[Organized crime includes] the unlawful activities of the members of a highly organized, disciplined association engaged in supplying illegal goods and services including but not limited to gambling, prostitution, loansharking, narcotics, labor racketeering, and other unlawful activities."

These commissions indicated that awareness of the extent of the organized crime problem in the United States was increasing. Effective action against organized crime was blunted, however, by a continuing controversy between those who believed organized crime was dominated by a Mafia or Cosa Nostra and those who thought that its organization was less well defined, less bureaucratic, far more pervasive, and rooted in public corruption, not ethnic heritage.

Pennsylvania Crime Commission

In 1978, the Pennsylvania Crime Commission (1978) was formed to study organized crime. The statute discussing the commission's powers included this definition of organized crime:

> Organized crime: The unlawful activity of an association trafficking in illegal goods or services, including but not limited to gambling, prostitution, loansharking, controlled substances, labor racketeering, or other unlawful activities or any continuing criminal conspiracy or other unlawful practice which has as its objective large economic gain through the fraudulent or coercive practices or improper governmental influence.

In one of its earlier reports, the Pennsylvania Crime Commission (1980: 2) described organized crime follows:

> a society that seeks to operate outside the control of the American people and their governments. It involves thousands of individuals working within structures as complex as any large corporation, subject to laws

more rigidly enforced than those of legitimate governments. Its actions are not impulsive but rather the result of intricate conspiracies, carried on over many years and aimed at gaining control of whole fields of activity in order to amass huge profits.

THE SICILIAN SEED

One view of the Mafia states that violent crime, organized and ruthless, was transplanted to the United States from Sicily. Much of the research on the Sicilian Mafia is highly speculative, but some compelling research has been conducted during the last two decades to expand our understanding of this organization. Considerable dispute about the basic structure of organized crime in Sicilian society from a historical perspective continues to exist. The official version of organized crime rests on an argument that the Mafia in Sicily was and is a more or less unified group of families operating within a highly organized structure and has dominated the political and social lives of Sicily for at least the last century. The contrary view is that the Mafia as a criminal society never really existed at all, but was and is an apparition created to explain the pervasive corruption and inequity in Sicilian political and social life (Blok 1974).

The Village Becomes Organized

One of the most comprehensive examinations of the Sicilian Mafia comes from Anton Blok (1974), an anthropologist who studied the Mafia of a Sicilian village for the period from 1860 to 1960. He suggests that what we often call the Mafia is in reality an entity that developed from an association between Sicilian bandits and violent peasant entrepreneurs, the *gabelloti,* who had responsibility for the maintenance of order and security on the large estates of absentee landlords. Hiring other local men, they formed something akin to the vigilante groups of the American West.

The gabelloti performed several vital roles in the feudal society of Sicily. One role was as an effective medium of communication among the peasants, the government, and the landlords. Second, gabelloti provided land and jobs to the peasants, thus making themselves vital to economic survival. As mentioned, they also managed estates, thereby providing income for the landlords. Fourth, they in reality provided the only social control on the island, acting as unofficial agents of the state to maintain order.

The final role was to provide the only real official power in Sicily in the absence of an effective police force and military (Hobsbawn 1959: 30–56; Blok 1974). In a very real sense, all elements of Sicilian society depended on the gabelloti. In its genesis from the gabelloti, the Mafia became less a criminal organization and more a business and police organization, providing jobs, social control, and dispute settlements on an island with a poorly organized and ineffective government. In his study, Blok also notes a most important historical and social trend. He suggests, using the Mafia as his prime example, that organized criminals are more often than not allies of the aristocracy to whom they pose no real threat and as a result are inherently conservative and often a reactionary force in society (Blok 1974: 102). Blok's suggestion is supported by the long history of violent conflict between the Mafia and left of center political parties in southern Italy.

In relation to the existence of a hierarchical structure in the Sicilian Mafia, Blok points out that each village had its own *cosca* (a clique consisting of the gabelloti, its employees, and its allies). One becomes a member of a cosca through a long process of socialization within the village structure and the traditions of feudal Sicilian society. Blok suggests that all these local organizations, when viewed collectively, are referred to as the Mafia. He disputes the notion, however, that one centrally organized, united group known as the Mafia existed.

While gabelloti and other members of the village cosca could have occasionally communicated with members from other villages, Blok argues that no single hierarchical organization of mafiosi existed (Blok 1974: 145). A similar study by Hess describes the Sicilian Mafia as a network of *partito*, a series of one on one relationships through Sicilian society. In this system of partito, "clients, individuals seeking jobs, land, or justice, were organized through their connections to a patron in the village" (Hess 1973: 82). He adds an important dimension to the study by Blok. Some recent reports on the Sicilian Mafia have suggested the development of a structure similar to that presented in the official version of organized crime. Hess points out that the urban Mafia in Sicily and Italy, who has been the subject of these reports, has a great deal in common with American urban gangsters precisely because the new urban Mafia in Sicily has copied the model of American criminals presented in the media (Hess 1973: 162–163).

The Camorra

Throughout the nineteenth century no single organization monopolized Italian American crime. Along with the Sicilian Mafia, other criminal societies sprang up in various parts of Italy. In Naples in the province of Campania on the Italian mainland, a powerful criminal brotherhood called the **Camorra** also operated. Stemming from a Spanish word meaning *dispute* or *fight*, the Camorra developed during the 1820s as a self-protection society for inmates in the Spanish-dominated prisons of Naples. The organization soon expanded its operations and influence beyond the prison walls in Italy, and bands of criminals implemented extortion schemes. Although Camorra was once thought to be strictly an Italian phenomenon, some evidence indicates that its members also operated in the United States and even warred over turf with Mafia factions in the United States in the late nineteenth and early twentieth centuries. These disputes centered on immigrant-smuggling schemes and control of extortion rackets in the poverty-wracked, segregated immigrant Italian communities of early urban America.

Camorra members were much more structured and organized than their Mafia counterparts from Sicily. In Naples, twelve Camorra families existed, with a boss as the supreme leader of each family. In addition, each family was subdivided into groups known as *paranze*, which authorized *capos*, or lieutenants, to assign specific tasks, such as robbery, murder, blackmail, and kidnapping, to its members. In Italy, the Camorra and what we now call the Mafia shared two characteristics: (1) total disdain for governmental and official authority and (2) regard for traditional codes of silence, honor, and respect. Over time, Italian criminals in the Camorra and Mafia, despite their differences, learned to cooperate.

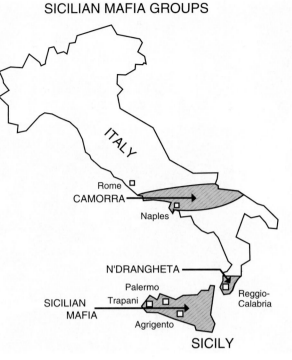

SICILIAN MAFIA GROUPS

Source: President's Commission on Organized Crime, 1986.

INVESTIGATIONS INTO ORGANIZED CRIME

Much of what we now know about organized crime has been gleaned over the years from a series of official investigations by agencies of the Justice and Treasury departments, as well as state and local law enforcement organizations. Although these organizations had different concerns and agendas, they provided invaluable insight into the inner workings, politics, structure, and behavior of organized crime. To understand this criminal enigma further, we now examine notable investigations into organized crime and consider the results of each.

Mussolini's Mafia Purge

The Italian Mafia grew and developed during the reign of fascist dictator Benito Mussolini in the 1920s. As the legend goes, however, local mafioso Mayor Don Ciccio, during the dictater's visit to Sicily in 1924, publicly embarrassed Mussolini. After arriving in the small town of Piana del Greci, Mussolini, who was surrounded by an assembly of his leather-jacketed motorcycle guards, was gently teased by the local Mafia mayor, who exclaimed that "there is no need for so many police . . . your Excellency has nothing to fear in this district when you are with me" (Lewis 1964). It became instantly clear that in Sicily the local mayor had more political and social power than the dictator himself. So Mussolini, a man who saw room for only one absolute power in Italy, was outraged.

Less than one year later, Mussolini installed Cesare Mori as the new prefect of Palermo. Mori's job was to rid the government of all bureaucrats under Mafia control and replace them with loyal Fascists. In doing so, Mori and his small band of agents were granted almost absolute police power in Sicily.

This assignment was not without its problems, however, for Mori soon found many of his new appointees murdered, some in broad daylight but

Italian dictator Benito Mussolini at the height of his power in the 1920s.

with no witnesses. Such murders actually intensified Mori's investigation, which began to wreak havoc on the local Mafia in Sicily as hundreds of suspected mafiosi, including Don Ciccio, were arrested. As the Mafia purge continued, Mori used torture to extract confessions, brought suspected mafiosi to trial for nonexistent crimes, and for a period of four years suspended the legal rights of Sicilians. Almost as soon as the purge began, Cascio Ferro organized a secret route to help hundreds of young mafiosi escape. Every night ships carrying escapees sailed for North Africa and Marseilles, France. From there many traveled to the New World. Some went directly to New York; others traveled to Cuba, Canada, or Florida. Once they arrived, they huddled in the Little Italys of America. From these ranks came many important figures in organized crime in the United States, among them Carlo Gambino and Joseph Bonanno.

In 1928, Prefect Mori declared the Mafia purge a success; it was true that some of those mafiosi who had been driven out had been Mafia leaders in Sicily. However, the timing of the purge was a disaster for the United States. Although the authorities were successful in ridding Sicily of many mafiosi, this resulted in the relocation of these outcasts to the United States during the early years of Prohibition, a time ripe with opportunities for an organized crime group. Moreover, Mussolini's purge of the Mafia failed to provide for economic and social reform in Sicily, so after the fall of fascism, the Mafia reemerged there.

It must be remembered, however, that Mori's investigation was primarily political and dictated by the needs of Mussolini's fascist government. Evidence and data generated by Mori and Mussolini's secret police are highly suspect because of their methods and political goals. It is therefore disturbing that many of the early allegations emanating from the Federal Bureau of Narcotics about the alleged power of the Mafia in the United States were based directly on Mori's investigation. We would certainly treat revelations of criminal wrongdoing by Hitler's gestapo with great caution. That caution should be extended to Mori's findings.

From 1900 to 1914, it has been estimated that about 196,000 Italians, including large numbers of Sicilians, immigrated to the United States (Nelli 1976: 22), primarily for economic reasons. Remember that Sicily was still a society based on a feudal economy. Subsistence living, an inability to own land, and back-breaking work in the fields characterized life for the general public in Sicily. Many of these Italian immigrants chose New York and New Orleans for their new homes. Although the existence of the Mafia was well known by Sicilian and Italian authorities, U.S. police were still unaware of this large criminal organization.

The Hennessey Incident in New Orleans

The first indication of possible Mafia activity on U.S. soil occurred in the late nineteenth century when the police chief of New Orleans, David Hennessey, began to suspect Mafia infiltration into the already thriving underworld of New Orleans. He was correct; a large number of Italian immigrants had immigrated to the Louisiana city, and the Sicilian American community was plagued by Black Hand extortion gangs. These gangs, which directed their activity at newly arrived immigrants, soon gained control of local vegetable markets and dockside shipping and began to exercise power in local politics by controlling the vote in Italian-dominated precincts. It should be made clear, however, that these extortion rings bear no similarity to either the Mafia in Sicily or to the alleged American Mafia of later years. They were organizations that flourished only in the poverty, discrimination, and despair of immigrant ghettos. When these desperate communities of newcomers ceased to exist, so did the Black Hand.

The New Orleans investigation into Italian organized crime began with the murder of a police informer. Vincenzo Ottumvo had been cut out of the organization's profits and then threatened to go to authorities. As he was playing cards one night, his throat was slit. Chief David Hennessey, a tough Irish cop who came from a family of police officers, took particular interest in the murder. Hennessey investigated the case by questioning Italian and Sicilian immigrants of the Italian quarter. He allegedly criticized Italians in general by saying that he had no use for them. Hennessey could have been motivated in his investigation by either anti-Italian prejudice or more self-serving interests. Several other brutal murders soon caused intense public pressure for Hennessey to do something.

Hennessey's Mafia Pact

During the late 1880s, there was an intense conflict for control of the extortion rackets in the Italian community in New Orleans between the Provenzano family and a gang controlled by Anthony and Charles Matranga. The murders that Hennessey was investigating were part of this conflict. After Anthony Matranga was wounded by gunfire when he was driving a horse-drawn wagon, Hennessey investigated and decided that the Provenzano faction was the lesser of the two evils and chose to pursue the Matrangas by making a pact with the Provenzanos: If they would help him stamp out the Matranga gang, he would tolerate Provenzano rackets in New Orleans. A less charitable interpretation was that Hennessey was not an intrepid law enforcer, but merely a corrupt official who engaged with the Provenzanos in alien smuggling. It can be argued from this perspective that the Hennessey investigation was designed to enhance the prospects of one organized crime group at the expense of the others for purely pecuniary reasons.

In any event, Hennessey wrote the police in Palermo, Sicily, requesting names and descriptions of suspected criminals who could be residing in New Orleans. Sicilian authorities complied by sending dossiers on more than 100 Sicilian criminals who had immigrated to the New Orleans area. Hennessey was elated and announced that he would expose this alien organized crime threat at a special upcoming hearing. Unfortunately for him, however, someone had already planned Hennessey's assassination, which was carried out successfully on October 15, 1890, on a dark, lonely street. As he approached his house, Hennessey was caught in a barrage of shotgun blasts. Although he managed to return fire on the dozen or more gunmen, he was hit at least half a dozen times. Overhearing the gunfire in the next block, police Captain William O'Connor came running to find Hennessey slumped on a curb. As the captain held the chief in his arms, Hennessey said, "The Dagoes . . . Billy . . . oh, Billy, they have given it to me . . . and I gave it back the best I could" (*Encyclopedia of Crime* 1993).

An Outraged Community

News of the murder shocked and outraged the community, which was already strongly biased against immigrants in general and Italian immigrants in particular. Civic groups and vigilantes gathered on the streets, crying out for Italian blood. Italian organized criminals immediately went into hiding. The repercussions of the assassination were felt almost at once when nineteen Italian immigrants whose names appeared in Hennessey's files were indicted for his murder. Also indicted was Charles "Millionaire Charlie" Matranga, who, along with several others, had allegedly given the order for Hennessey's murder. The district attorney claimed to have secured a confession from one of the suspects, who said that he was the lone gunman in the murder. However, police believed that the suspect was acting as a sacrificial lamb to protect others who were also responsible. The confession was not accepted so that all those indicted could stand trial.

Of the eighteen Italians tried in the case, nine were exonerated by the jury and the nine remaining suspects remained in prison while their files were slowly processed. The news of the court decision was spread by posters placed all over the city asking "all good citizens to appear at Clay Statue to remedy the failure of Justice in the Hennessey murder." On May 14, 1891, thousands of boiling mad citizens heard W. S. Parkerson, a New Orleans lawyer, address the crowd. "When courts fail, the people must act," he shouted. "What protection or assurance of protection is there left us when the very head of our police department, our chief of police, is assassinated in our very midst by the Mafia society, and its assassins again turned loose on the community?" The citizens of New Orleans were outraged and immediately organized their own brand of justice, dispatching a massive lynch mob to the jail. The lynch mob killed eleven people, some of whom were not connected to the Hennessey murder.

The popular press seized on the assassination and suggested the existence of a secret Italian criminal conspiracy throughout the country. Because no evidence was produced to indicate that such a criminal organization existed and the defendants had not been found culpable in the police chief's murder, why did the press and official police sources so quickly adopt this sinister view of a foreign conspiracy? Smith (1974) provides the following explanation: "Whatever may have been the facts of Hennessey's murder, the trial, and the lynching, we can see in retrospect that the reality of a Mafia had to be pressed as a justification for the lynch mob's action."

The doctrine of necessity, not revenge, became the high-principled defense of the mob's leaders. "What were they to do?" John Wickliffe, third in command of the mob, asked rhetorically in *Truth*, two weeks after the lynching: "Submit to this outrage upon justice, and tamely offer their necks to the yoke of alien criminals, or strike in defense of civilization and organized society?" The mob leaders did not "see" the Mafia of other observers; they had been led to see only violent men whose power, according to the *Illustrated American*, was believed to be dwindling in Italy and who were consequently "transplanting their organization to the United States."

Based on the facts of the Hennessey case, many researchers have argued that at the turn of the century the Mafia existed in the United States primarily in a lynch mob's collective imagination. After the New Orleans incident, however, until the Kefauver Committee hearings in 1950, the single most comprehensive and credible exploration of organized crime was John Landesco's *Organized Crime in Chicago*. In this work he does not mention an American Mafia and refers only in passing to the Sicilian Mafia (Landesco 1929: 108–109, 120).

Landesco's Organized Crime Investigation

The Castellammarese War (also discussed in Chapter 3) is a vital component in understanding the alleged origins of the U.S. Mafia and the important role that the alien conspiracy theory has played in the study of organized crime. This is the juncture at which the modern Cosa Nostra allegedly emerged after the wholesale execution of old-time Sicilian crime leaders. On September 10, 1931, Salvatore Maranzano, "the boss of bosses" in the United States, was assassinated. Cressey (1969: 44) tells us that "on that day and the two days immediately following, some forty Sicilian gang leaders across the country lost their lives in battle."

The Castellammarese War

Cook (1973: 107–108) relates the story as follows:

Within a few short hours, the old-time crime bosses who had been born and reared in Sicily and were mostly illiterates—the "Moustache Petes," or the "greasers" as they were sometimes called—were liquidated by the new breed of Americanized, business-oriented gangsters of the Luciano–Costello–Adonis school. Beginning on September 11 and lasting through the next day, some thirty to forty executions were performed across the nation.

In an attempt to verify this information, Block reviewed newspapers published in eight major U.S. cities for a four-week period surrounding Maranzano's assassination. He reported (1978: 460), "While I found various accounts of the Maranzano murder, I could locate only three other murders that might have been connected." He added, "It is by no means clear why so many scholars have bought a story which so grossly violates historical respectability" (Inciardi et al. 1977: 100).

Nelli (1976) also disputes the official version of the purge. The idea that more than forty top gangsters could have been murdered in a two-day period simply defies logic. First, surely the word that assassinations were underway would have spread like wildfire throughout the underworld or would have resulted in a large-scale counterstrike; second, it took at least four men to murder Maranzano. To wage war against forty veterans of organized crime who were also guarded by their own forces would have required the raising, supplying, and dispatching of an entire army.

Even the *New York Times* failed to see any real significance in the event. On September 11, 1931, the *Times* reported that Maranzano's murder had led to disclosures "regarding operators of a nationwide ring of alien smugglers." Finally, the idea that the Maranzano murder was related to an Italian civil war over the creation of a new corporate hierarchy in organized crime makes little sense considering the participants in the Maranzano assassination included Meyer Lansky and Bugsy Siegel. On the one hand, it is difficult to imagine their interests in an internal Italian feud if it did not have considerable direct benefits for major non-Italian gangsters. On the other hand, if Jewish criminals were part of the organized crime structure that struck out at Maranzano, the idea of a criminal organization made up entirely of Italians must be discarded.

Thomas Dewey and the Mob

Despite millions of dollars of graft and corruption money spread around the country during the early 1930s, Lucky Luciano, Lepke Buchalter, and other major organized crime figures in New York City were unable to entirely deflect government intervention at high levels. Using a variety of charges, including income tax evasion, some federal prosecutors were successful in incarcerating a few organized crime figures.

One of the earliest gangsters to fall to prosecution for tax problems was Al Capone, who was found guilty of tax evasion in May 1932 and sentenced to eleven years in a federal penitentiary. It should be noted that, according to veteran organized crime reporter Hank Messick (1973), the Capone conviction was realized only after Jake Lansky, Meyer Lansky's brother, had suggested a tax prosecution to IRS officials and supplied them with at least some of the data necessary to secure a conviction. Messick alleges that Lansky and others thought that Capone was too public, too visible, and too notorious to be allowed to continue as a major organized crime figure. Arranging for him to be jailed was a far neater solution than having him killed.

Dewey's Mafia War Begins

One of these prosecutors, 34-year-old U.S. District Attorney Thomas E. Dewey gained national attention for convicting "Waxy" Gordon on a similar charge in New York. Perhaps only coincidentally, Gordon's conviction followed his dispute with Lansky, Ownie Madden, Lucky Luciano, and other New York crime figures. After this conviction, Dewey focused on famous Bronx gangster Dutch Schultz, a former ally of Lucky Luciano, who was then involved in a major dispute with Lansky and Madden and who was thought to net $20 million annually from extortion rackets (see Chapter 3).

Despite evidence that Schultz owed literally millions of dollars in back taxes, Dewey charged him with failure to pay $92,103.34 between 1929 and

1931. After evading authorities for over a year, Schultz finally gave himself up in Syracuse, New York. Even though Dewey thought he had an airtight case, Schultz's clever lawyers were able to secure a deadlocked jury in the first trial and, in the second trial, which occurred in the small town of Malone, New York, they obtained a farcical acquittal that shocked the nation. Schultz's acquittal resulted from his arrival in the town several weeks prior to the trial, during which time he seeded the town with money, clearly influencing the jury's decision.

Dewey, now acting as a special prosecutor in New York City, was relentless, however, and pursued Schultz again in 1935. The new charge focused on Schultz's restaurant-protection racket and included the charge of murder. Schultz's problems with Luciano, Lansky, and Madden were reaching a head, however. They had moved in on some of Schultz's rackets, and when Schultz tried to reclaim them, he suspected that he had been double-crossed and responded by killing his own lieutenant with his bare hands. Like Capone, Schultz was too much in the public view and too ready to use violence to solve his problems. Such tactics were not good for business, and other organized crime figures became intensely concerned about the Dutchman. Predictably, Schultz responded to Dewey's investigation in precisely the way his colleagues feared that he might. He asked Albert Anastasia to accept a murder contract on Dewey. Anastasia immediately informed Luciano and Lansky. The only solution to the problem was for the more responsible leaders of organized crime to have Schultz assassinated. Schultz and three of his gang leaders were shot to death while eating dinner at the Palace Chop House in Newark, New Jersey.

With Schultz out of the way, Dewey focused on a new target, Lucky Luciano. After several madams, bonders, and bookers went to Dewey and offered to supply the information necessary to convict Luciano on prostitution charges (discussed later), a special grand jury handed down indictments that carried a maximum penalty of 1,950 years in prison. Dewey's charges against Luciano consisted of sixty-two counts of compulsory prostitution. Sixty-eight of Luciano's associates offered testimony against him, and their testimony ultimately brought him down. The jury found Luciano guilty on all counts, resulting in the stiffest sentence ever handed down by the courts for compulsory prostitution: thirty to fifty years. Despite his incarceration, Luciano remained active in organized crime, transmitting messages from the visiting room at Dannemora State Prison in upstate New York. Most communications were sent through Luciano's trusted ally, Joe Adonis. In his absence, Luciano's management hierarchy consisted of Frank Costello, Vito Genovese, and Meyer Lansky.

Other problems in the New York underworld surrounded Louis Buchalter. Buchalter and his partner, Jacob Shapiro, had been running rackets associated with the garment and foodstuffs business. Word was out that he was going to expand from labor racketeering into drug trafficking. Soon his ostentatious life-style and prolific use of violence attracted the attention of Tom Dewey, who was then the Manhattan District Attorney. By late 1937, Buchalter realized that his prosecution was imminent. For two years, with help from Lansky, Anastasia, and others, Buchalter hid out in Brooklyn. While in hiding he became more and more paranoid. He dispatched hired killers to murder witnesses who were to testify against him. Once again, the excessive use of violence created problems for Lansky, Siegel, Anastasia, and the other gang leaders in New York. Murdering Buchalter would be difficult at best, because he had a coterie of well-trained killers around him and was in hiding already.

So the group made the decision to persuade Buchalter to turn himself in to authorities. Buchalter was led to believe that a deal had been struck with J. Edgar Hoover, over whom Meyer Lansky and Frank Costello exercised considerable power. If he surrendered to the FBI on a federal narcotics charge, he would not be turned over to Dewey for state prosecution. Because Buchalter was terrified of Dewey and was convinced that by the time he finished serving his federal time Dewey's case against him would have dissolved, Buchalter decided to go for the deal and was escorted by Albert Anastasia to a nighttime rendezvous with the FBI chief to whom he surrendered in New York City. Buchalter was then quickly tried and convicted on federal drug charges, which resulted in a fourteen-year sentence. Immediately following the trial, he was turned over to Dewey, who prosecuted him on extortion charges associated with the bakery business. From these charges he received a sentence of thirty years to life. Buchalter was subsequently convicted on a murder charge and became the only organized crime figure in U.S. history to be executed.

The Kefauver Committee

The official, government version of organized crime in the United States begins to emerge most clearly in the report of the Senate's Special Committee to Investigate Organized Crime in Interstate Commerce, chaired by Senator Estes Kefauver of Tennessee. The committee was impaneled in 1950 and was charged with determining the existence of a national crime syndicate using the wire services to transmit the outcomes of horse races to bookies. The committee went far beyond that, however, when it claimed in its interim report that an international criminal conspiracy known as the Mafia, originating in Sicily, was responsible for organized crime in the United States. During the two years of its operation, the committee called more than 600 witnesses to testify about organized crime. The nation watched the hearings on television, then still a new medium, as details of greed and violence surfaced, interspersed with frequent recitations of the Fifth Amendment.

The Kefauver Committee presented valuable information on organized crime, calling before it luminaries such as Meyer Lansky, Frank Erikson, and Nig Rosen. The committee's investigation undoubtedly was invaluable to the study of organized crime. But what the committee did not do in any way was to demonstrate the existence of an international Mafia conspiracy. Senator Kefauver and his colleagues never heard any direct or indirect testimony supporting the Mafia model.

Neither the testimony presented to the Senate Special Committee nor Kefauver in his book (1953) presented any real evidence that the Mafia exists as a functioning organization. Police officials asserted before the Kefauver Committee their belief in the Mafia, and the Narcotics Bureau testified to its belief that a worldwide dope ring, allegedly run by Luciano, was part of the Mafia. When nearly all the Italian gangsters asserted that they didn't know about the Mafia, Senator Kefauver and Rudolph Halley responded incredulously that certain crimes bear "the earmarks of the Mafia" (Bell 1953: 139).

The only information dealing with any national criminal organization presented to the committee came from law enforcement officials. Despite this fact, the committee gave in to the apparently overwhelming temptation to demonstrate that organized crime in the United States could exist only in the context of an alien conspiracy. Even some law enforcement officers found that the Kefauver conclusion strained credibility. Burton B. Turkus, the prosecutor of the Murder, Inc., cases, discounts the Kefauver conclusions (Turkus and Feder 1951) stating:

> If one such unit had all crime in this country under its power, is it not reasonable to assume that somewhere along the line, some law agency—federal, state, county or municipal—would have tripped it up long before this? No single man or group ever was so clever, so completely genius, as to foil all of them forever. . . . In fact, as a factor of power in national crime, the Mafia has been virtually extinct for two decades.

Despite a lack of direct evidence of any kind of national conspiracy such as a Mafia, Senator Kefauver without a doubt had found organized crime and did a valuable job of exposing it to the U.S. public. He made Meyer Lansky, Bugsy Siegel, Frank Erickson, Frank Costello, Nig Rosen, and others household names. As is clear from this list, most of the witnesses, however, were not Mafia members or even Italian. The Kefauver Committee exposed a pervasive network of organized criminals operating in alliances with local politicians, but it never found the Mafia.

Just as the concept of the Mafia began to recede following the sensational disclosures of the Kefauver hearings, new evidence rekindled fears about a national criminal organization. In 1944 Edgar Croswell, a state trooper in New York, arrested an employee of Joseph Barbara, Sr. ("Joe the Barber"), for stealing fuel. When Barbara refused to file charges, Croswell began to suspect that Barbara himself could be a criminal. Accordingly, he began a fourteen-year investigation of Barbara, which included the use of phone taps. On November 14, 1957, Croswell was watching the Barbara home in Apalachin, New York, when he noticed a large number of people arriving there (the **Apalachin incident**). Because of his long-harbored suspicions of Barbara, Croswell set up a roadblock and instituted a check of license plate numbers. New York state troopers and local police raided Barbara's home, and Croswell searched each vehicle and occupant, allegedly for possession of illegal firearms. After netting no contraband in the search and because no law appeared to have been broken, Croswell had no choice but to let the suspects go, although the police arrested a few people for disorderly conduct. They eventually "walked" on this minor charge. The license plate check ultimately enabled Croswell to compile a list of names and addresses of the guests, but it took almost a full week for officials to attach any significance to Barbara's barbecue guests.

The Apalachin Incident

Problems with the Apalachin Incident

The significant question of what between twenty and one hundred leading Italian gang figures were doing in Apalachin remains unanswered. By most accounts, the meeting at Apalachin had been the Mafia's most famous—and most disastrous—summit meeting ever. It was supposedly an assembly of top Mafia dons in the country to anoint Vito Genovese as their new boss of bosses and to cover an agenda of mob business, most notably whether to go into the drug trafficking trade in a major way. Others, including Robert Kennedy, Narcotics Bureau agent Joe Cusack, and later Cressey, described it as a meeting of La Cosa Nostra's National Commission. Senator McClellan believed that the meeting suggested a "lawless and clandestine army—at war with the government and people of the United States" (Morris and Hawkins 1970: 228).

Very few valid and reliable data about the incident at Apalachin are known, however. The following are discrepancies about the incident:

- How many attended? Senator McClellan believed there were fifty-eight guests. Robert F. Kennedy cited more than one hundred, and other estimates ranged from sixty-five to seventy-five (Morris and Hawkins 1970: 225; Albini 1971: 237). However, these estimates included body-guards, chauffeurs, and casual visitors who happened to be Italian. One unfortunate "master criminal" was there to deliver fish.
- Different authorities confidently gave widely varying accounts of the weather that day and the attitudes of the guests. Sondern called it "unusually mild for November" and noted that guests were in "decorous good humor." Buse used the same source to show that the temperature was "just above freezing" and the men were filled with "awkward discomfort" (Morris and Hawkins 1970: 227).

What is remarkable about Apalachin is what we do not know: Who was there? How many were there? What were they doing?

Assuming that we accept the "grand council" view, what had caused such a gathering? Popular theories concerned the future course of narcotics and gambling, the fate of Cuban investments, or the balance of power in the New York underworld. Albert Anastasia had recently been killed, there had been an attempt on the life of Frank Costello, and Vito Genovese appeared to be rising rapidly to a dominant position. Was Apalachin intended to confirm his power and justify his deeds or to condemn him? Much depends on whether we accept the theory that the meeting was called by Genovese himself (Morris and Hawkins 1970: 228).

The wide disparity in possible interpretations should immediately indicate that none of the theorists had any specific information on the matter. Plenty of experts, notably the Narcotics Bureau and, later, Joe Valachi have attempted to prove the importance of Apalachin as it relates to organized crime. We certainly should not reject out of hand the common claim made at the time that the guests were there to visit Barbara during his illness. If more sinister motives are required, possibilities include the McClellan Committee investigation into the garbage-hauling business (Smith 1974: 12), a jurisdictional appeal from Carmine Lombardozzi over control of jukeboxes, and labor problems in the garment industry of New York and northeastern Pennsylvania (Albini 1971: 248–249). This last suggestion is strengthened by the geographical origins of the participants of the meeting. Thirty-one were from New York, eight from new Jersey, six from Pennsylvania, and twelve from other locations. The list bore no resemblance to the supposed distribution of Mafia families, but as a convention of Italian garment manufacturers, it made excellent sense.

Impact of the Apalachin Incident on the FBI

The Apalachin meeting caused considerable embarrassment for J. Edgar Hoover's FBI. Prior to it, Hoover had confidently asserted that there was no such thing as organized crime in the United States, but that the threat of communism was the most important national problem. While the FBI turned out reports on bank robberies, auto thefts, and espionage, it collected virtually no data on organized crime. Once the story of Apalachin surfaced in the news, the bureau's neglect ended. While Hoover's agents were scrambling to collect information on the Mafia, Attorney General Robert Kennedy was demanding access to criminal data dealing with the Apalachin conferees for his McClellan Committee hearings. No such files were available, but, Kennedy received a plethora of information from Harry Anslinger's Federal Bureau of Narcotics (FBN), which had been tracking alleged mafioso for decades.

The following year, 1958, Hoover's demand for immediate action resulted in a two-volume FBI report on the Mafia, but it also embarrassed Hoover because it revealed that the Mafia had been in business during the entire time that he had been denying its existence. In any case, to save face, the FBI began an aggressive effort to build its image as the nation's top Mafia foe. Within days after the Apalachin incident, Hoover initiated the Top Hoodlum Program that asked FBI chiefs to identify the top ten gangsters within their jurisdictions. Next Hoover began an extensive use of wiretaps on suspected mobsters. The technique, which drew considerable criticism from civil libertarians, was an effort to swiftly fill the FBI's intelligence void. It did just that and proved to be one of the most powerful investigative tools ever used against organized crime.

The final piece required to build a conspiracy theory around the Mafia was found in 1963 when Joseph Valachi testified before the McClellan Committee, which was looking into the relationship between narcotics trafficking and organized crime. While a prisoner at the U.S. penitentiary in Atlanta, Valachi beat another prisoner to death. His prison indiscretion proved to be a major break for Attorney General Robert Kennedy as chief counsel for the McClellan Committee. Valachi offered Kennedy testimony out of fear that New York crime boss Vito Genovese had put out a contract to have Valachi killed. This proved to be a miscalculation on Valachi's part, for he was never actually marked for assassination by the mob. Valachi provided the information necessary to construct the operational framework of the mob. His testimony shed light on many questions about the inner workings of the Mafia. He introduced the term La Cosa Nostra and made known the existence of *the Commission*, the mob's supreme council.

The Valachi Testimony at the McClellan Committee

More important, Valachi outlined the mob's hierarchical structure and discussed the geographic distribution of criminal families across the nation. In all, he named 289 specific individuals as members of the Mafia. He described the mob's casual use of murder and violence and the particulars of a Mafia initiation ritual for new members. In exchange for his testimony and breaking the Mafia's code of silence, Valachi was placed in the federal witness protection program. Interestingly, six weeks after Valachi completed his testimony before the McClellan Committee, John F. Kennedy was assassinated in Dallas.

Problems with Valachi's Testimony

Because so much information was gleaned from the testimony of Joe Valachi, it is important that his performance be reviewed and his credibility tested. Valachi's testimony, in all its particulars, has been so thoroughly demolished by Smith (1974), Albini (1971), and Morris and Hawkins (1970) that we need only highlight some of the major problems and inconsistencies with his story.

First, Valachi's testimony must be put into context. Valachi was a small-time, petty hood who, during more than thirty years as an alleged Mafioso,

Joseph Valachi, former Cosa Nostra mobster, is shown October 1, 1963, as he told a U.S. Senate rackets subcommittee of the inner workings of the crime organization. Valachi died at La Tuna Correctional Institution in El Paso, Texas, where he was serving a life sentence for murder.

(*Source:* Associated Press, AP/Staff.)

claimed to have been involved in more than thirty-three murders and to have supervised several different rackets for the Gambino family in New York. During that time, however, none of Valachi's bosses ever saw fit to promote him in the organization or even go out of their way to protect him. Because Valachi's testimony was motivated by the need for protection from his fellow criminals and the desire for revenge, he clearly was not presenting his version of organized crime from an unbiased, objective point of view.

The problems with Valachi's story start with his most basic assertion, the name of the criminal conspiracy of which he claimed to be a part. To this day, it is not clear that the words he actually used in his testimony were La Cosa Nostra. In addition, Valachi denied the use of the word Mafia, saying he knew the organization only by the name La Cosa Nostra (Morris and Hawkins 1970: 213). Beyond the issue of the name, there were other serious problems with Valachi's testimony:

- He contradicted himself several times on the issue of La Cosa Nostra initiations. First, he claimed that they represented a major socialization process in which new "family" members met the veterans, but later admitted that in his thirty-five years as a Cosa Nostra member, he had attended (or even been invited to) only his own initiation. No committee members pursued this issue despite the fact that much was later made of the initiation process.
- Valachi committed a serious error in discussing the death of Murder, Inc., hitman Abe Reles (Morris and Hawkins 1970: 217–281). Valachi claimed that Reles's death was a clear indication of how effective La Cosa Nostra was at silencing potentially damaging witnesses, even those under police protection. However, his assertion was contradicted by the record of a grand jury inquiry into the death, which indicated that Reles had died accidentally while trying to escape. We may or may not choose to believe Valachi; it was a common opinion that Reles had been murdered. But the committee did not pursue the issue of who Abe Reles was. It is obvious

that he was not Italian. In fact, he was an associate of Lepke Buchalter. In no way could an assertion be made that he was part of La Cosa Nostra. Valachi clearly had to reach to come up with this example, or his conception of La Cosa Nostra is not as clear as we have been led to believe.

- Valachi seriously contradicted himself on issues of the actual structure and operations of La Cosa Nostra. The prosecution went into great detail asking about the absolute loyalty, obedience, and fidelity to rules that governed the lives of Cosa Nostra members. This concept of a highly disciplined organization was vital to the official theory. However, in the course of his testimony, Valachi identified at least one area in which "absolute obedience and conformity" appeared to become meaningless: the prohibition against dealing in narcotics. Valachi stated that following the death of Albert Anastasia, the bosses decreed that there would be no further trafficking in narcotics. It was a clear-cut, unequivocal proscription against dealing in dope. However, later Valachi said that the narcotics trade was a financial mainstay of La Cosa Nostra and that even the bosses themselves disregarded their own rule (Morris and Hawkins 1970: 219–220).

- Valachi claimed that La Cosa Nostra provided assistance to family members who were in trouble, specifically providing lawyers, bail, and other services. However, he later testified that he had never received such protection or service from his family, no lawyers, and no bail (Morris and Hawkins 1970: 222). The McClellan Committee made a great deal of this contradiction.

Valachi's testimony was not corroborated by other testimony; it contained serious internal contradictions, and others contradicted it. At the very least, the reliability of some of his recollections and their ex post facto interpretation must be called into question.

Robert Kennedy's Justice Department Task Force

Prior to the presidential election of John F. Kennedy in 1960, it was well known that organized crime had long-standing ties to his father, Joseph P. Kennedy, an associate of many well-known criminals and bootleggers of the Prohibition era. Some evidence, much of it from the recollections of alleged Chicago mafioso Sam Giancana, suggests that the mob played a role in the campaign and election of John F. Kennedy. FBI wiretaps from that period have shown that Chicago organized crime figures put large amounts of money into the general election campaign to get out the vote for Richard Daly's Democratic machine in Chicago. During the 1960 election, one of the more crucial states for the Democratic vote was Illinois, where the Chicago vote had to outweigh the votes from the traditionally Republican rural areas.

Despite allegations of mob assistance to the Kennedy campaign in Chicago and possibly West Virginia, President Kennedy's brother Robert probably played the most significant role in combating organized crime of any government official in U.S. history. As soon as he was appointed United States attorney general, Robert Kennedy made it clear that he had no intention of changing his long-standing opposition to organized crime. In fact, in his first speech as head of the Justice Department, he vowed to root out organized crime. In doing so, he pressured J. Edgar Hoover to collect more intelligence through the use of bugs and wiretaps. In the meantime, Attorney General Kennedy beefed up the Justice Department's Organized Crime Section by adding forty-two lawyers to the staff and opening new field offices in Chicago, New York, Los Angeles, and Miami. Despite his brother John's friendship with Frank Sinatra, Robert ordered a full report of Sinatra's mob connections, resulting in a nineteen-page memo connecting Sinatra with ten high-ranking mob bosses.

Robert Kennedy instructed the task force to prosecute organized crime group members aggressively, which it did. At the end of Robert Kennedy's first year in office, more than 120 mobsters had been prosecuted. This number increased to an impressive 350 during his second year in office. By 1963 the number had soared to 615 organized criminals who had been arrested and prosecuted successfully under Attorney General Kennedy's lead. In addition to winning much support for numerous laws that criminalized interstate travel in support of illegal gambling or racketeering, Attorney General Kennedy also actively solicited information from other federal agencies, such as the Federal Bureau of Narcotics.

Palermo's Maxitrial

During the 1970s, New York police broke up the so-called **French Connection:** the pipeline for heroin shipments to the United States from Marseilles, France. This disruption resulted in a new connection being formed; this time the heroin was traveling to the United States via Palermo, Sicily.

As the fierce competition for dominance of the heroin trade increased in Palermo, Sicily, its crime rate soared, with an average of two murders per week. In 1982, for example, victims of the Mafia included political leaders, two police chiefs, and two judges. According to some estimates, by 1983 approximately 1,000 people had been murdered. As the heroin wars continued, two Mafia dons from Corleone, Salvatore Riina and Bernadardo Provenzano, emerged as victors, and other dons, including Don Masino, otherwise known as Tommaso Buscetta, were marked for extinction by rivals.

Buscetta's Dilemma

Fearing for his life, Buscetta fled Palermo for South America, where he could resume control of his operations in Brazil. However, in October 1983 he was surprised by Brazilian authorities, who arrested him and held him in custody while U.S. and Italian authorities conferred as to who would try him for his role in international heroin trafficking. It was finally determined that Buscetta would receive the harshest treatment from courts in his native country, and extradition proceedings began. After hearing that he was being extradited back to Italy, Buscetta tried to kill himself by swallowing strychnine, for he knew that to return to Italy meant imminent humiliation and eventual death.

After the failed suicide attempt, Buscetta resolved that he would turn state's witness against those who had marked him, his family, and loyal followers. Until then, those who had chosen to testify against Mafia figures were merely low-level actors in Italy's underground. Buscetta's testimony would mark the first time that a ranking don would openly break the sacred code of omerta. As it turned out, Buscetta testified in two major criminal inquiries, Palermo's maxitrial and the Pizza Connection case (discussed next) in the United States.

Palermo's **maxitrial** was like no other in the history of the country: 474 mafiosi were indicted. Of those, about half were jailed and tried, and those not jailed were tried in absentia. In either case, so numerous were the defendants that a special maximum security courtroom was constructed, which included thirty steel cages located behind partitions of bulletproof glass. The indictments were compiled in twenty-two volumes of legal documents consisting of 8,607 pages. Defendants, caged in the courtroom, were known to spit on and threaten journalists and courtroom officials. By the conclusion of the lengthy trial, 254 convictions had resulted, carrying sentences totaling 1,576 years in prison.

The testimonial floodgates were now opened, and significant information about the organizational structure became public knowledge. Buscetta detailed rules, tactics, connections in high places, and networks of both illegal and legal enterprises for the court. Of particular importance, Buscetta named other Mafia dons. Adding to the credibility of his testimony was corroborating testimony from at least a dozen other mafiosi from the losing side of the heroin war.

The most important victories of the maxitrial were the life sentences of all members of the Cupola, a twelve-member commission formed to facilitate the smooth running of Palermo's Mafia families. After providing both Italian and U.S. authorities with invaluable testimony, Buscetta was placed in the witness protection program and whisked away, along with his wife and children, by agents of the U.S. Marshal's Service to assume a new identity somewhere in the United States.

The Pizza Connection

Much of what has been learned about the Italian American crime syndicates and the Sicilian Mafia was gleaned through a major investigation known as the **Pizza Connection.** It addressed several gangland killings, including that of New York's Carmine Galente in 1979, but it primarily involved heroin smuggling, which began with Sicilian Mafia drug shipments from the Golden Triangle (Laos, Burma, and Thailand) to Palermo and then to U.S. cities such as New York and Miami. Once safe in the United States, the drugs were trafficked by the Bonanno crime organization. Bonanno wise guys then sold the drugs at pizza parlors, often utilizing the services of illegal immigrants smuggled in from Sicily. The Bonanno faction also used other retail outlets in the Northeast and Midwest. In fact, it was alleged that between 1979 and 1984, pizzerias in the East and Midwest acted as distribution points for at least 330 pounds of heroin per year, worth an estimated $1.6 million on the street.

The two primary defendants in the Pizza Connection case were Gaetano Badalamenti, the sixty-year-old former Mafia boss in Sicily, and Salvatore Catalano, a power boss with the Bonanno organization, who operated a bakery and pizzeria. According to testimony in the case, Badalamenti and his faction acted as the main supplier of heroin, and Catalano's people were the primary distributors. The prosecution alleged that the Pizza Connection brought massive quantities of morphine base from Turkey to Sicily, where it was refined into heroin and then shipped to the United States. The Sicilian Mafia's share of the drug sales resulted in millions of dollars of profit over a ten-year period. Most of the estimated $60 million profit was hidden by an elaborate international money-laundering scheme, which involved banks in the United States, Bermuda, the Bahamas, and Switzerland.

A key witness for the prosecution was Joseph D. Pistone, known by mobsters as "Donnie" Brasco, a jewel thief. Pistone was an FBI agent who had been undercover with important New York mob figures for more than five years. Pistone's testimony helped secure the convictions not only in the Pizza Connection case, but also in trials of an additional hundred mobsters. Most important, the case demonstrated the effectiveness of government efforts to crack down on organized crime.

The success of the Pizza Connection case can be attributed to a unique brand of interagency communication between police in the United States, Canada, Italy, and other European countries. The case resulted in trials in the United States, Brazil, Turkey, Germany, and Switzerland during the mid-1980s.

Although the trial lasted seventeen months, one of the longest in U.S. federal court history, it resulted in the conviction of eighteen American and Sicilian mob bosses involved in the Pizza Connection, all but one of the defendants charged in the case. Among the guilty were Sicilian mob boss Gaetano Badalamenti, sentenced to thirty years in prison, and Salvatore "Toto" Catalano, of Brooklyn, who received forty-five years for his role in the operation.

Giuliani's Mafia Trials

During the 1980s a new crime buster appeared on the scene. Rudolph Giuliani, the U.S. attorney for New York's Southern District, relentlessly pursued Italian organized crime syndicates in New York by preparing detailed criminal cases for prosecution. Giuliani's rise to fame came in the summer of 1986 when, following an eight-month trial, a federal jury convicted Carmine Persico and eight others for operating labor rackets in New York's Colombo crime family. The case revealed that what is referred to as the Colombo organization controlled several unions, which included the District Council of the Cement and Concrete Workers, and that millions of dollars had been extorted from construction companies in New York. The lengthy trial was successful in showing that even from his cell Persico had been able to direct a pattern of racketeering dating back more than fifteen years. The trial included testimony from more than 100 witnesses and hours of tape recordings of the mob's attempt to gain control over the city's construction industry. A long line of contractors testified that they had paid organized crime to get and keep jobs.

Giuliani's ambition to pursue organized crime was fueled by intimidation suffered by his grandfather, an immigrant from Sicily, who had had occasional run-ins with Italian extortion gangs while trying to run his hot dog stand at Coney Island. Giuliani used two powerful tools in his prosecutions: the Racketeer Influenced and Corrupt Organizations Act (RICO) and electronic surveillance. RICO represented the major legal basis for prosecuting the mob. RICO, mentioned earlier and discussed in greater detail in Chapter 9, enabled the government to prosecute a person simply for being a member of a "criminal enterprise" engaged in a "pattern of racketeering." Even if specific crimes had been committed by other members, all members of the enterprise were guilty.

The FBI and local police acquired court orders that permitted them to bug mob members' telephones and places of business. Stacks of evidence soon resulted from these powerful investigative tools. Included in evidence were photographs of individuals associated with organized crime talking in doorways; the photographs were supported by audiotapes of their conversations, which included detailed discussions of murders, extortion demands, payoffs to corrupt officials, and drug trafficking. The tapes recorded the defendants bragging about being tough and powerful, making money, and the respect they were shown by associates.

The Pizza Connection Case

Couriers of the Bonanno family were to transport U.S. currency, usually in denominations of $5, $10, and $20, out of the country by private jet to Bermuda or Switzerland. These funds were then transferred from Bermuda or Switzerland to their criminal recipients in Sicily. The money was used to pay for the raw opium used in manufacturing heroin in Sicilian laboratories and to finance new laboratory operations. One of these couriers was Franco Della Torre, who in March 1982 deposited more than $1 million in the Traex account at the Manhattan office of Merrill Lynch Pierce Fenner and Smith. He then made four additional deposits totaling $3.9 million in the same account the following month. When making these large deposits, Torre always requested that security personnel accompany him to the Merrill Lynch offices. After Torre consistently refused to enter the *money room* (where there were surveillance cameras) and generally acted suspicious, Merrill Lynch questioned the legitimacy of the transactions and soon closed the account. Torre then moved his laundering operation to the Manhattan office of E. F. Hutton & Company. During the next three months, Torre made seven cash deposits totaling $5.2 million in the Traex account. Eleven additional cash deposits were made by Torre over the following two months, totaling $8.25 million. The last deposit was made in a different account bearing the name Acacias Development Corporation. Torre's deposits totaled more than $18 million (many of which were gym bags full of cash), most of which was either transferred directly to Switzerland or out of the country via a special holding account under the fictitious name P. G. K. Holding. The heroin network of Torre and his Mafia counterparts is estimated to have laundered a minimum of $24.4 million between October 1980 and September 1982.

Another important outcome of Giuliani's investigations was that, for the first time, dozens of organized crime figures, afraid of being convicted and sent to prison, were coming forward and testifying against their superiors. By 1983 the FBI boasted that since 1979 the government had convicted almost 500 predominantly Italian criminals and their associates as the result of organized crime investigations. In 1993 Giuliani was elected mayor of the city of New York, and as part of his campaign platform, he promised to continue his pursuit of organized crime and its related criminal enterprises.

Louis Freeh and the New Mafia War

Sworn in as FBI director in September 1993, Louis Freeh vowed to attack organized crime with "unprecedented dedication of purpose." Freeh had built a reputation for his role in prosecuting the Pizza Connection. As a result of that case, Freeh became well acquainted with investigators on both sides of the Atlantic. In late 1993, Freeh became the first FBI director to travel to Palermo, Sicily, and meet with Sicilian officials as a gesture of goodwill and cooperation in mounting a modern-day attack on organized crime forces in both Italy and the United States. In his speech there, which was delivered at the grave sites of slain judges in Palermo, Freeh stated: "You are not men of honor but cowardly assassins of children . . . we will root you out from under every rock, from the dark places where you hide" (Meddis 1993).

MODELS OF ORGANIZED CRIME

Various theories on organized crime have been presented over the years to help social scientists to better understand this phenomenon. Each theory approaches the topic of organized crime somewhat differently and offers interesting insight for consideration and study.

Report of the President's Commission on Organized Crime on Levels of Membership

In 1983, under the Reagan administration, the President's Commission on Organized Crime (PCOC) was established to study the nature and extent of organized crime in the United States and to develop strategies and recommendations to combat it. Chaired by Judge Irving R. Kaufman, the PCOC was considered the most significant commission of its nature since the Kefauver Committee conducted its hearings on the subject some thirty years earlier. The contribution of the PCOC's investigation of organized crime is likely more significant than those that preceded it because of the commission's ability to subpoena witnesses and compel testimony. In April 1986, the PCOC developed its final report that clearly delineates levels of involvement of members and nonmembers of organized crime. These levels include the criminal group, the protectors, specialized support, user support, and social support.

The Criminal Group

Representing the core of the organized crime unit, the **criminal group** is made up of persons who utilize criminality and violence and are willing to corrupt in order to gain power and profit. The following are characteristics of the criminal group.

- *Continuity.* The group recognizes a specified purpose over a period of time and understands that the organization will continue operating beyond the lifetimes of individual members. This group also realizes that leadership will change over time, that its members work to ensure that the group continues, and that members' personal interests are subordinate to those of the group.

- *Structure.* The criminal group is structured as hierarchically arranged interdependent offices devoted to the accomplishment of a specific function. This means that the group can be either highly structured, like La Cosa Nostra, or extremely fluid, like the Colombian drug cartels. In any case, it is organized by ranks that are based on power and authority.

- *Membership.* The criminal group membership is based on a common trait, such as ethnicity, race, criminal background, or common interest. Potential members of the group must prove their loyalty to the group. In most instances, membership requires a lifetime commitment. Membership rules include secrecy, a willingness to commit any act for the group, and an intent to protect the group. In return, members receive benefits from the group, such as protection, prestige, opportunities for economic gain, and the all-important *sense of belonging* to the group.

- *Criminality.* Like any industry, organized crime is dedicated to the pursuit of profit along well-defined lines. The criminal group relies on continuing criminal activity to generate income. Some activities, such as supplying illegal goods and services, produce revenue directly; other activities, such as murder, extortion, and bribery, are used to ensure the group's ability to make money and gain power. Some groups engage in a number of illicit businesses, and others restrict their efforts to one specific criminal activity, such as drug trafficking. Many criminal groups also engage in legitimate business enterprises that allow the skimming and laundering of money.

- *Violence.* Violence and the threat of violence are integral tools of the criminal group. Both are employed as a means to control and protect members and nonmembers associated with protecting the organization's interests. Members are expected to commit, condone, or authorize violent acts. When the interests of the organization are threatened, murder is commonplace. Violence can be employed either to silence potential witnesses or to punish people as a warning to others.

- *Power and profit.* Members of the criminal group are united in working for the group's power, which results in its profit. Political power is achieved by corrupting public officials. The group is able to maintain its power through its association with criminal protectors.

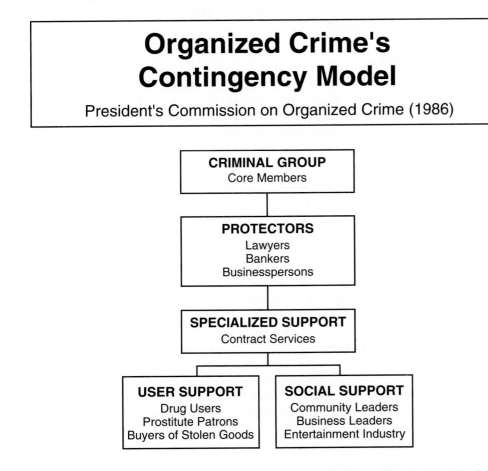

Organized Crime's Contingency Model

President's Commission on Organized Crime (1986)

CRIMINAL GROUP
Core Members

PROTECTORS
Lawyers
Bankers
Businesspersons

SPECIALIZED SUPPORT
Contract Services

USER SUPPORT
Drug Users
Prostitute Patrons
Buyers of Stolen Goods

SOCIAL SUPPORT
Community Leaders
Business Leaders
Entertainment Industry

Protectors

Protectors include corrupt public officials, businesspersons, judges, attorneys, financial advisors, and others who individually (or collectively) protect the interests of the criminal group by abusing their authority. As a direct result of the protectors' efforts, the criminal group is insulated from both criminal and civil government actions. This component of organized crime represents what both police and members of the criminal group have called the *edge*, referring to the advantage that organized crime has over legitimate businesses. Corruption, the central tool of the protectors, relies on a network of corrupt officials who protect the criminal group from the criminal justice system.

An example of this corruption is a law enforcement officer who provides drug traffickers with inside information about police investigations. Another is an attorney who is able to orchestrate the intimidation of government witnesses so that they will change their story. Accountants aid criminal group members by concealing their income in financial institutions, gaming establishments, and other businesses.

Specialized Supporters

The criminal group and the protectors rely heavily on skilled persons known as **specialized support.** These persons, such as pilots, chemists, arsonists, and hijackers, provide contract services that facilitate organized crime activities. Unlike the members of the criminal group and the protectors, specialized support people do not share a commitment to the group's goals, but are still considered part of organized crime.

User Supporters

Another vital component in the success of organized crime is **user support.** This group is composed of persons who purchase organized crime's illegal goods and services, such as drug users, patrons of bookmakers, and prostitution rings, and people who knowingly purchase stolen goods.

Social Supporters

Persons (and organizations) belonging to the **social support** group grant power and the perception of legitimacy to organized crime in general and to specific members of the criminal group. Examples are politicians who solicit the support of organized crime figures, business leaders who do business with organized crime, social and community leaders who invite organized crime figures to social gatherings, and people who portray organized crime or its members in a favorable light.

Just as the criminal group is made up of the members of the crime organization, persons belonging to each of the other categories should be considered members and associates of organized crime. Indeed, without the participation of any of those listed, organized crime could not prosper or succeed in society.

The contingency model, offered by the report of the President's Commission on Organized Crime, provided insight into the hierarchy and physical structure of a crime organization. The following sections present several other perspectives that will help students to consider organized crime as a single comprehensive paradigm.

Like millions of Americans, you may have seen the movie *The Untouchables*, starring Kevin Costner (Eliott Ness) and Robert DeNiro (Al Capone). Although Ness triumphed over Capone, the movie tended to glamorize organized crime. A previous generation flocked to see Marlon Brando in *The Godfather*. If you have seen either of these movies, you could be labeled as a participant in organized crime. Do you qualify as a social supporter of organized crime? You decide!

Cressey's Cosa Nostra Theory

Cressey (1967) has described organized crime as having a bureaucratic structure not unlike that adopted by governmental bureaucracies, such as police departments and federal law enforcement agencies. According to Cressey, the primary unit of **La Cosa Nostra** is the family, which embodies male members of Italian ancestry. The family must abide by a code of conduct that prohibits members from revealing organizational secrets and that authorizes violent punishment for those who violate the code. Cressey has suggested the existence of a hierarchy within the Mafia that facilitates the flow of power and expectations of members. Included in the hierarchy are the boss, the consigliere, the underboss, the caporegime, and the soldiers.

- *The Boss.* A supreme leader known as the boss oversees all organizational endeavors and has the final word on decisions involving virtually all aspects of family business. Bosses are typically older members of the family who have proved their allegiance over a number of years during their affiliation with the family.

- *The Consigliere.* A close associate of the boss is the consigliere or counselor, who enjoys considerable influence on and status in the family. The consigliere, often a lawyer, serves the boss as a trusted advisor.

- *The Underboss.* The next highest position in the family is the underboss, who works at the pleasure of the boss and acts in his behalf when the boss is incapacitated (e.g., sentenced to prison or ill). Underbosses are trusted, older members of the family whose primary role is to relay instructions to those occupying lower positions in the family.

- *The Caporegime.* Rank and file under the underboss begin with the caporegime or capos, who are considered midlevel managers. A primary role of a capo is to serve as a buffer between the lowest-level members and the upper-level members of the family. In doing so, the capo is the trusted go-between through whom all communications from the boss flow to the lowest-level members, and vice versa.

- *Soldiers.* The lowest-level members of the family are the soldiers. Soldiers, also known as wise guys, made guys, or button men, report directly to the capo and often operate at least one specific criminal enterprise, such as loan-sharking, gambling, and drug trafficking. The job of soldiers is to search constantly for new sources of revenue for the family. While doing so, they often become partners with other soldiers or even with nonfamily players in the community. Soldiers are required to pay dues or a percentage of their profits to the family in return for their affiliation with the family. The soldiers direct hundreds of nonfamily associates who work on behalf of the family. Nonfamily members can be anyone who has something to offer the family. Therefore, they are not subject to family membership restrictions, such as being of Italian descent.

The Commission

In 1986, the President's Commission on Organized Crime suggested the existence of a *national commission* that links the most powerful Mafia bosses to one central authoritative body. Commission members are bosses from families in New York, Buffalo, Chicago, and Philadelphia. The purpose of the commission is to arbitrate disputes between families, approve new members for initiation, authorize the execution of family members, facilitate joint ventures between families, and manage relations between U.S. and Sicilian Mafia factions.

A separate commission possibly exists in New York. Made up of the bosses of the five New York families, it settles disputes over criminal enterprises and oversees day to day Mafia operations. Also operating on behalf of the family are specialists or enforcers, who punish betrayal (Cressey 1969). Because the organization goes to great lengths to protect its members against social control efforts, the family maintains a network of informants to warn about criminal investigations, impending raids, and so on. Some organizations also have positions of corrupters who pay control agents (corruptees) and help ensure immunity for the organization and its members (Cressey 1969; Hess 1973).

Although most corruption efforts seem to focus on lower-echelon members of social control organizations, such as patrol officers, it is in the best interest of the crime organization to corrupt any public or political figure. When arrests occur, these corrupted officials can help protect organization members. For example, lower-ranking members are in positions that are most vulnerable to arrest. This separates the organizational leaders from actually committing criminal acts themselves, making it difficult for law enforcement to obtain evidence against them. In the rare event that an organizational manager is arrested, the organization is not crippled since another member simply moves into that position. This policy was followed when Mussolini tried to destroy the Sicilian Mafia by assassinating its families' leaders, who were quickly replaced, allowing the families to survive (Cressey 1972).

Rules of Conduct

Cressey suggests that rules of conduct are indeed an important component in the crime organization, and over time an elaborate set of rules has evolved for members to follow. He admits that, although organizational rules are difficult to substantiate, a parallel can be made between the code of conduct adopted by prison inmates and that adopted by organized crime units. Cressey's (1969) rules of conduct follow:

- Be loyal to members of the organization. Do not interfere with each other's interests and do not be an informer.
- Be a man of honor and always do right. Respect women and your elders. Do not rock the boat.

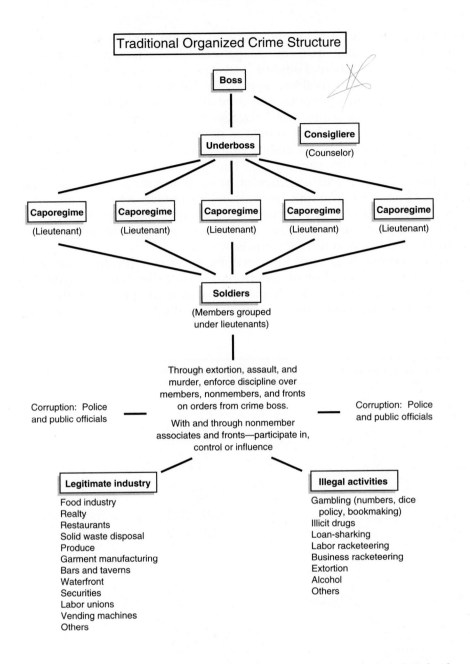

Traditional Organized Crime Structure

Boss

Underboss

Consigliere
(Counselor)

Caporegime
(Lieutenant)

Caporegime
(Lieutenant)

Caporegime
(Lieutenant)

Caporegime
(Lieutenant)

Caporegime
(Lieutenant)

Soldiers
(Members grouped
under lieutenants)

Through extortion, assault, and
murder, enforce discipline over
members, nonmembers, and fronts
on orders from crime boss.

With and through nonmember
associates and fronts—participate in,
control or influence

Corruption: Police
and public officials

Corruption: Police
and public officials

Legitimate industry

Food industry
Realty
Restaurants
Solid waste disposal
Produce
Garment manufacturing
Bars and taverns
Waterfront
Securities
Labor unions
Vending machines
Others

Illegal activities

Gambling (numbers, dice
   policy, bookmaking)
Illicit drugs
Loan-sharking
Labor racketeering
Business racketeering
Extortion
Alcohol
Others

- Be rational. Be a member of the team. Do not engage in battle if you cannot win.
- Be a stand-up guy. Keep your eyes and ears open and your mouth shut. Do not sell out.
- Have class. Be independent. Know your way around the world.

It can be argued that these rules might be a value system, rather than a formally organized set of operating instructions for guiding the bureaucratic organization (Abadinsky 1990). In either case, it is apparent that the success of the organized crime unit depends on some type of prescribed behavior to be profitable and discrete, to ensure allegiance by members, and to endure through time.

Albini's Patron–Client Theory

As a result of his study of organized crime in Detroit, Joseph Albini (1971) concluded that it was made up of criminal patrons who exchanged information, connections with governmental officials, and access to a network of operatives for the client's economic and political support. The roles of client and patron fluctuated, depending on the enterprise, and combinations were formed, dissolved, and re-formed with new actors. Albini suggested that organized crime actually consists of "syndicates" in a "loose system of power relationships" (1971: 229).

Organized crime groups resemble a simple social organization or social-exchange network in the community. The power of organized crime is found in the organizational qualities of loose structuring, flexibility, and adaptability. Organized criminals have strategic contacts with persons who control various resources. Key organized crime figures occupy focal points in social-participation networks that interconnect private and public sector organizations and licit and illicit enterprises.

Organized criminals occupy intersections and are critically positioned facilitators in complex social relationships that permit clients to deal with the larger society. A social network of connections with the police, public officials, and other criminal operatives is at the criminal's disposal. An organized

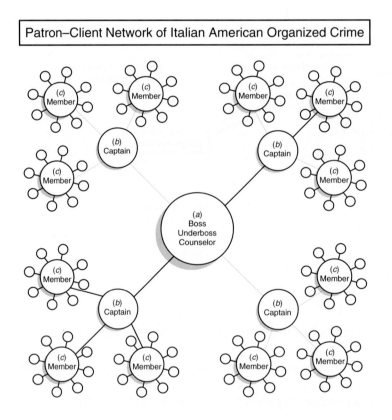

Patron–Client Network of Italian American Organized Crime

(a) At the center of each organized crime unit (*famiglia:* Family) is the boss (*capo*). He is assisted by an underboss (*sottocapo*) and a counselor (*consigliere*).

(b) Surrounding the boss are his clients, the captains (*caporegime*).

(c) Orbiting around each captain are his clients, the lowest-ranking members who have been formally initiated into the Family (*soldati:* "made-guys").
- The members act as patrons to nonmember clients.
- Each unit is tied to other Families throughout the country by the *capo*, whose sovereignty is recognized by the other bosses.

criminal has sufficient contacts to provide coordination and to locate specialized talents and services necessary for criminal entrepreneurship.

Persons involved in organized crime and its operations in this web of social participation are not, in many cases, directly part of an organization. The structure of relationships varies considerably with each participant. Albini (1971: 288) argues that "rather than being a criminal secret society, a criminal syndicate consists of a system of loosely structured relationships functioning primarily because each participant is interested in furthering his own welfare." The patron–client relationship also has been observed by numerous other studies of organized crime (e.g., Block 1979; Reuter 1983; Potter and Jenkins 1985).

In his book *The Mafia Mystique*, Smith (1974) argues that organized crime is nothing more than an extension of normal business operations into the illegal market. Smith maintains that organized crime comes from "the same fundamental assumptions that govern entrepreneurship in the legitimate marketplace: a necessity to maintain and extend one's share of the market." Simply put, he conceives of organized crime as entrepreneurial activity that happens to be illegal. Drug trafficking, loan-sharking, and other illegal enterprises emerge because the legitimate marketplace leaves a large number of customers unserved. As a result, the proper point of intervention for controlling organized crime is not to pursue organizational leaders and notorious individuals, but to attempt to understand organizational behavior in the illegal market. (See Chapter 2 for additional discussion of Smith's enterprise theory.)

Smith's Enterprise Theory

Support of Smith's enterprise theory was offered by Block (1979) as a result of his empirical study of some 2,000 criminals involved in the cocaine trade in the New York City area. Based on his data, Block found that the illegal drug business was not based on a single organizational initiative. His conclusions are contrary, however, to the nationwide criminal theory, which holds that the cocaine trade is controlled by one monolithic criminal organization. Rather, Block suggests that numerous, fragmented, opportunistic criminal groups conduct the sale of drugs and perhaps other illicit commodities.

As a result of two studies of organized crime, one on Italian organized criminals and the other on blacks and Hispanics, Francis Ianni argued that organized crime is nothing more than a traditional social system "organized by action and by cultural values that have nothing to do with modern bureaucratic virtues" (Ianni 1973: 108). Ianni maintains that organized crime is best explained by examining local kinship or ethnic social networks. He argues that organized crime groups are not the formal organizations that have been depicted by the Mafia theory: "Like all social systems, they have no structure apart from their functioning; nor do they have structure independent of their current personnel" (Ianni 1973: 20).

Ianni's Kinship Group Model

In a later work, Ianni (1974) extended his study of organized crime to African American and Puerto Rican criminal organizations. This later work made three important points. First, organized crime was certainly not limited to Italian American crime syndicates. Second, prison friendships, gang associations, and community socialization processes were as important as ethnicity to organized crime's recruiting.

Third, Ianni suggested a theory of *ethnic succession*. In brief, he argued that every new immigrant group faces discrimination, lack of economic opportunity, and blocked pathways to power. One of the most effective means to overcome these blocked opportunities is organized crime because of its profitability and its close relationship with political power. In highly simplified form, Ianni suggests that with each new wave of immigrants the character of organized crime changes as new groups emerge. In addition, he suggests that older ethnic immigrant groups, such as the Irish, gradually move out of organized crime into business and politics. Ianni's theory of ethnic succession provides a valuable tool for understanding the changing nature of organized crime, particularly in relationship to drug trafficking, in the late twentieth century.

Chambliss's Crime Network Theory

William Chambliss's study of organized crime in Seattle depicts an overlapping series of crime networks with shifting memberships highly adaptive to the economic, political, and social exigencies of the community, without a centralized system of control (Chambliss 1978). Chambliss argues that whatever control there is in organized crime comes from far outside the criminal organization itself and is imposed on the illicit market by powerful political and economic forces in the community. Chambliss conceives of organized crime as being a network of individuals, the most powerful of whom are businesspeople, law enforcement officials, and political officeholders who direct the activities of criminal actors involved in prostitution, gambling, pornography, and drugs. As such, Chambliss sees those often called organized criminals to be more appropriately employees of the crime network participants.

Haller's Partnership Model

Mark Haller's (1990) research reveals that organizations such as those surrounding the Capone gang and Meyer Lansky's extensive operations were in reality a series of small-scale business partnerships, usually involving several senior partners (Capone, Nitti, Lansky) and many junior partners, who sometimes conducted business in concert with one another and often conducted business separately. Organized crime was not directed by Lansky or Capone in any bureaucratic sense, but was merely a series of investment and joint business ventures with a wide variety of constantly changing partners.

Block's Description of Enterprise and Power Syndicates

Block's study of the history of organized crime in New York City between 1930 and 1950 offers an additional and very important way to conceptualize organized crime syndicates. He found that organized crime became more centralized and exhibited a greater degree of hierarchical structure during this period, but he found absolutely no evidence of the development of a Cosa Nostra or any other national crime syndicate in that period.

Block found that organized crime was dominated by two different types of criminal syndicates: enterprise syndicates and power syndicates (Block 1983: 13). Simply defined, *enterprise syndicates* are groups of criminal entrepreneurs organized for the purpose of producing and then distributing illicit goods and services, such as drugs, gambling, and prostitution. Block argues that because they had to distribute illicit goods and services to thousands of customers, enterprise syndicates tended to be large in terms of the number of participants, and they tended to have a hierarchy of command, some centralization of authority, and a well-defined division of labor.

On the other hand, *power syndicates* are "loosely structured, extraordinarily flexible associations centered around violence, and deeply involved in the production and distribution of informal power" (Block 1983: 13). They have no clear division of labor because they have no clear production or distribution task to perform. The only organizational goal of a power syndicate is to use extortionate means to maintain power over other organized crime groups. The basic tool of a power syndicate is force, gaining control of the illicit market through the threat of violence. Block argues that several very energetic power syndicates operated during this period, specifically those under the direction of Lucky Luciano, Dutch Schultz, and Louis Buchalter (Block 1983: 129–199).

These men and their syndicates tried to control and exploit the many enterprise syndicates that were actually doing the work of organized crime. What Block found, which contradicts any notion of a centralized, monopolistic Cosa Nostra, was that power syndicates were extraordinarily disruptive in the illicit market, tended to last for only very short periods of time, and made their own demise inevitable, while enterprise syndicates were able to go on and on delivering goods and services to an eagerly consuming public.

As a case in point, he looks in depth at Lucky Luciano's attempt to gain control of the prostitution business in New York. Briefly, Luciano and his associates attempted to centralize prostitution under the control of one syndicate by taking over both bonders (people who provided bail) and bookers (those who placed prostitutes in the various brothels) operations through the use of violence. Luciano started the process by forcing the bonders out of business in 1933 and becoming the only source of legal protection for prostitution operations. The syndicate then changed the rules for bonding operations, exploiting prostitutes, bookers, and madams, by raising fees and decreasing benefits. After taking control of the bonders, Luciano moved on the bookers, using threats of murder and violence to secure protection payments from the bookers (Block 1983: 144). By the end of 1933, the bonders had been entirely replaced by Luciano operatives, and the bookers had been reduced to employee status in the Luciano syndicate.

To realize any profits from this arrangement, Luciano and his minions intensified the exploitation of prostitutes and madams, demanding ever larger payoffs and supplying ever declining services. As Block points out, this quest for increased profits, which were required to make the power syndicate's efforts pay off, led to exploitation of prostitution operators, which "was one of the key disruptive issues under the new syndicate" (Block 1983: 147).

By 1935, only two years after Luciano's power syndicate had succeeded in organizing prostitution, madams and bookers were in open rebellion. They hid brothels from Luciano and his enforcers, and they refused to pay the extortionate protection money. By 1935 Luciano was looking to get out of the prostitution business because the limited profits that he and his syndicate were realizing were simply not worth the expenditure of time, effort, and money needed to keep the prostitution operators in line. In fact, the struggle to maintain control so depleted the resources of Luciano's own syndicate and the rebellion became so strong that in 1936 Luciano was indicted for compulsory prostitution and was subsequently convicted and sentenced to fifty years in prison (Block 1983: 68–69). Block's summary (1983: 147–148) of these events is very enlightening in understanding organized crime and the futility of power syndicates such as a Cosa Nostra.

Luciano took a fairly centralized operation, the booking system, and subjected it to intense pressures that threatened to disrupt the entire trade. It turned on the key personnel in the trade with the exception of the prostitute herself, who was already cruelly exploited, and initiated various methods of financially squeezing both bookers and madams, who resorted to cheating and ultimately to testifying against their bosses. It was clearly an effort at extreme centralization that attacked what was already a stable system of organized prostitution. As neither the price structure nor the volume of trade changed under the Luciano syndicate, profits for the entrepreneurs of violence could only come from the pockets of formerly independent syndicate leaders and madams. Indeed, one might want to argue that, without substantial changes in the economics of prostitution, it had about all the centralization it could take by 1933.

NONTRADITIONAL ORGANIZED CRIME

The term **nontraditional organized crime** emerged during the 1980s and offers a different perspective on the understanding of the organized crime phenomenon. Just as traditional organized crime is associated with Italian American and Sicilian crime organizations, nontraditional organized crime is associated with new and emerging crime groups, such as the Chinese triads, outlaw motorcycle gangs, and California-based youth gangs. Probably the most significant aspect of groups in this category typically involve the drug trade. Although many characteristics of traditional organized crime (discussed later) also fit the nontraditional groups, this category of criminals has unique characteristics that set it apart from traditional groups. To begin, the very genesis of nontraditional organized crime can be attributed to several distinctive factors, most of which became apparent during the early 1970s. According to Lyman and Potter (1991), these factors include the following:

1. Profound social, political, and economic changes in the drug-producing and drug-consuming nations had combined to accelerate and intensify the spread of drugs.
2. Mobility within and between consuming and producing nations, aided by cheap, readily available international transportation, had vastly increased. There was also a huge immigration from South America and the Far East to the United States.
3. In the opium-producing countries, many peasants and urban workers had surplus time for the work needed to sustain the drug traffic.
4. In the consuming nations, old restrictions against many types of behavior, including the taking of drugs, had declined sharply.

With all these factors at work, a new level of drug trafficking with far more sophisticated levels of organization was made possible. When attempting to understand these organizations as a whole, we should first consider that no single nontraditional organized crime group is typical. Rather, there is a collectivity of criminal organizations that demonstrates a few well-defined patterns. Thus, several conditions that seem to lend cohesiveness to modern-day drug-trafficking organizations exist: vertical integration, alternative sources of supply, exploitation of social and political conditions, and insulation of leaders from the distribution network.

1. *Vertical integration.* Vertical integration is illustrated by the major international trafficking groups such as the Colombian cartels and domestic criminal groups such as outlaw motorcycle gangs, which often control both the manufacturing and wholesale distribution of drugs. Also, city-based operations, such as the California street gangs that concentrate on domestic distribution and retail sales, represent an organization with operations that are more directly linked to the end user than are the Colombian cartels or the motorcycle gangs.

2. *Alternative sources of supply.* Among the various types of organizational structures and operational types, most have common distribution channels and

operating methods. Most groups acquire the primary illicit drugs outside the United States. Exceptions are marijuana and certain drugs made in domestic clandestine labs. Consequently, distribution channels are long and complicated. For example, there are numerous links between the coca leaves grown and harvested in the Huallaga Valley of Peru and the destination of the finished product: a U.S. city. Many larger organizations acquire drugs from alternative sources of supply. Thus, the Colombian cartels can purchase either coca leaves or partially processed coca paste in any of several countries in South America. When the Turkish government clamped down on the illicit cultivation of opium poppies, drug organizations shifted their production to regions in the Golden Triangle in Southeast Asia and the Golden Crescent in Southwest Asia.

3. *Exploitation of social and political conditions.* Drug-trafficking organizations today demonstrate a willingness to capitalize on vulnerable social and economic milieus. This occurs, for instance, in inner-city areas and even entire countries where investors in labor markets are willing to take risks to partake in the huge profit potential offered in drug-trafficking operations. Generally, most players drawn into drug trafficking are expendable, provided that the leaders remain untouched. The leaders can then choose from a large pool of unskilled labor those who are willing to take personal risks and who can be taught one or two menial duties in the trafficking system. Certain traffickers have even demonstrated that they can manipulate market conditions to make trafficking more profitable. In particular, the introduction of black tar heroin in the mid-1980s was a response to heroin shortages, and the change from cocaine HCI to crack in the mid-1980s was an effort to permit the nonaffluent drug user to afford cocaine.

4. *Insulation of leaders.* The organizational structure of a drug-trafficking organization can be described as a solar system with the leaders at the center. Only these leaders (or kingpins) see the organization as a whole. Trafficking leaders strive to minimize any contact with drug buyers or the drugs themselves as a strategic effort to insulate themselves from governmental detection. Orbiting the leader are many different individuals who serve various functions (e.g., money launderers, enforcers, attorneys), each of whom has other people orbiting him or her, and the cycle continues.

Although the four preceding operational variables describe the functioning of drug-trafficking organizations, they fail to explain adequately the tremendous growth of such organizations. The growth of a particular organization can be attributed partially to the highly addictive qualities of some drug commodities, such as heroin. This accounts, at least in part, for a degree of return business for many organizations. Here the drug users themselves effectively become salespeople or "ambassadors," working on behalf of the drug-trafficking organization and introducing drugs to new users. Additionally, powdered drugs, such as heroin and cocaine, can be transported (smuggled) much more easily than can a bulkier commodity such as marijuana.

ORGANIZATIONAL CONSTRAINTS

As with legitimate business, **illicit enterprises** also must sustain the criminal organization as a profitable business entity. For example, in the legitimate business world, when a small company is successful, expansion is often considered to maximize profits. Unfortunately, too much expansion too quickly can result in organizational and financial chaos and the ultimate demise of the company. The same is true of organized crime; it is in the best interests of organized crime members to try to maximize profits while avoiding detection by authorities and minimizing competition. We now consider some comments on constraints as they relate to the organized crime unit.

Reuter on Economic Constraints

Reuter's study of Italian organized crime in New York (1983) found that no group exercises control over entrepreneurs in gambling and loan-sharking. He concludes that, rather than the officially depicted view of organized crime as a monolithic conspiracy, it is in fact characterized by conflict and fragmentation. The empirical research clearly reveals that organized crime is made up of small, fragmented, and ephemeral enterprises.

There are very practical reasons for these characteristics. First, small size and segmentation reduce the chances that the enterprise will be caught and members prosecuted. Because employees in illicit industries are the greatest threat to these operations and make the best witnesses against them, organized crime groups must limit the number of people who have knowledge of the groups' operations. This is achieved, in part, by employing persons who know only about their own jobs and their own level of activity in the enterprise. Such arrangements are clear in the gambling and drug industries. In gambling, runners and collectors are distanced from the bank itself (Reuter 1983; Potter and Jenkins 1985). In drug trafficking, the production, importation, distribution, and retail activities are kept as discrete functions, often performed by completely different organized crime groups, most of which are both temporary and small (Laswell and McKenna 1971: 84; Hellman 1980: 148; Wisotsky 1986: Chap. 3).

For the same reasons that organized crime groups choose to limit the number of employees, they also tend to limit the geographic areas they serve. The larger the geographic area, the more tenuous communication becomes, requiring either the telephone (and the threat of electronic surveillance) or long trips to pass on routine information in person, a most inefficient means of managing a business. In addition, the larger the geographic area becomes, the larger the number of law enforcement agencies involved and the higher the cost of corruption (Reuter 1983; Wisotsky 1986). In his study of New York, Reuter found no evidence of centralization in gambling and loan-sharking, and he argued persuasively that drug trafficking has even less permanence and centralization (Reuter 1983: 184).

Mastrofski and Potter on Organizational Constraints

In an examination of the empirical research on contemporary organized crime groups, Mastrofski and Potter (1986) argue that the available literature cites several characteristics of organized crime and that these characteristics are often diametrically opposed to those cited in the official version of organized crime. Mastrofski and Potter argue that the empirical studies have demonstrated that, rather than being a tightly structured, clearly defined, stable entity, organized crime operates in a loosely structured, informal, open system.

Organized crime is made up of a series of highly adaptive, flexible networks that readily take into account changes in the law and regulatory practices, the growth or decline of market demand for a particular good or service, and the availability of new sources of supply and new opportunities for distribution. This ability to adapt allows organized crime to persist and flourish. The inflexible, clan-based corporate entities described by law enforcement agencies could not survive in this turbulent environment. Mastrofski and Potter (1986) cite Albini's study of organized crime in Detroit, Haller's study of Capone's and Lansky's operations, and Chambliss's study of Seattle as supporting this contention.

In addition, Mastrofski and Potter (1986) point to several other pieces of empirical evidence to buttress their point. Block's study of the cocaine trade in New York concluded that it was operated by "small, flexible organizations of criminals which arise due to opportunity and environmental factors" (1979: 94–95). Gardiner's study of corruption and vice in "Wincanton" (Gardiner 1970), Ianni's two studies of organized crime in New York (Ianni and Reusso-Ianni 1972; Ianni 1974), and a study of organized crime in Philadelphia (Potter and Jenkins 1985) reach similar conclusions. Reuter's study (1983) of Italian organized crime in New York found that no group exercises control over entrepreneurs in gambling and loan-sharking. Rather than the officially depicted view of organized crime as a monolithic conspiracy, he concludes that it is in fact characterized by conflict and fragmentation.

Mastrofski and Potter (1986) also take issue with the assumption in the official version that organized criminals act as corrupters of public officials. Available evidence indicates that a more accurate perspective is that organized criminals, legitimate businesspeople, and government officials are equal players in the marketplace of corruption. Each brings to the market things the others want, and a rather routine series of exchanges occurs. The purveyors of illicit goods and services wish to exchange their products, money, and influence for protection, selective enforcement against competitors, and favorable policy decisions by governmental authorities. For venal reasons or in recognition of a need to regulate and constrain illicit activity, public officials put their policy-making and enforcement powers on the market. Who initiates such a deal depends on circumstances, and the initiator is as likely to be the "legitimate" actor as the "criminal."

ORGANIZED CRIME, THE MEDIA, AND POPULAR CULTURE

Studying and understanding organized crime have been perilous endeavors for both scholars and criminal justice policymakers. Organized crime has been both a contentious topic, with widely varying paradigms reflected in the literature, and a troublesome topic in terms of accumulating and interpreting valid and reliable data. The scientific study of organized crime has generally been impossible. Surveys, questionnaires, structured interviews, and experiments are all highly problematic instruments in the world of organized crime. And although historical methodologies and various qualitative methods have been used profitably (see, e.g., Albini 1971; Smith 1974; Block 1983; Chambliss 1988; Haller 1990), their inherent limitations leave much of our understanding of organized crime to popular culture.

Once we wade into the quicksand of culture and media, however, scientific validity and reliability become lost in the shifting sands of words and images—not that there is a dearth of popular cultural sources of information on organized crime. To the contrary, a plethora of images and words are available to us in a kaleidoscope of forms. Organized crime is an immensely popular theme for novels, movies, television dramas, true-crime reenactments, and journalistic presentations both in print and on film. Movies such as *Blood Ties* (1988), *Blood Vows: The Story of a Mafia Wife* (1988), *Crime Lords* (1991), *The Godfather,* Parts 1, 2, and 3 (1972, 1974, 1990), *Mafia Princess*

(1988), and *Scarface* (both the 1932 and 1983 versions) are only a few of the many films portraying organized crime (Ryan 1995: 253–258).

In addition to the "reality" television versions of organized crime often presented on *Hard Copy, A Current Affair, Top Cops, America's Most Wanted,* and the numerous other variations on the same theme, we have seen a blossoming business in "reality" publishing, as alleged Mafia turncoats scramble to cash their royalty checks for recollections often as questionable as they are salacious. Consider the litany of recent tell-all potboilers: "Sonny" Franzese's *Quitting the Mob: How the "Yuppie Don" Left the Mafia and Lived to Tell His Story* (1992), Tony Franco's *Contract Killer: The Explosive Story of the Mafia's Most Notorious Hit Man* (1992), Nick "the Crow" Caramandi's *Blood and Honor: Inside the Scarfo Mob—The Mafia's Most Violent Family* (1990); Joe Cantalupo's *Body Mike: The Deadly Double Life of a Mafia Informer* (1990), Cecil Kirby's *Mafia Enforcer: A True Story of Life and Death in the Mob* (1987), and Jimmy "the Weasel" Fratianno's *The Last Mafioso* (1981), to name only a few (Firestone 1993: 216–217). These organized crime "memoirs" have not only made it into print, and not infrequently onto the bestseller list, but also have been replayed on reality television programs and even network news specials.

Of course, organized crime is also a mainstay of the legitimate news media. Smith points out that during the 1950s the prestigious *New York Times* ran between 5 and 11 pieces on organized crime each year. Following Joe Valachi's testimony in 1963, that number escalated to 63 and rose to 148 in 1967 (Smith 1974: 240–241). Kenney and Finckenauer (1995: 346) report that in 1989 the *New York Times Index* had 27 references to the Mafia, 98 to organized crime, and 175 to racketeers. They also report that in 1989 the *Reader's Guide to Periodical Literature* had 15 references to the Mafia; in 1990 it had 22 to the Mafia and 2 to organized crime. Between January 1988 and July 1991, the *National Newspaper Index,* which indexes stories from the *New York Times, Los Angeles Times, Washington Post, Wall Street Journal,* and *Christian Science Monitor,* had 423 references to organized crime. Organized crime's topical importance to the print media seems obvious.

With all these sources of information—fictional, nonfictional and somewhere between; print, image, and multimedia—organized crime as a social fact becomes blurred in a technological avalanche of impressions. In fact, organized crime as portrayed in contemporary society has been subsumed in a multimedia spectacle (Debord 1970, 1990). There is a plethora of information, and it comes at us at such speed and in such volume that discerning fact from fiction, reliable from unreliable, valid from invalid becomes an almost impossible task. In fact, the modern mass media works as what Reiman (1998) calls a "carnival-mirror."

In presenting information to us, movies, books, newspapers, magazines, and television change our view of social reality. We then reflect this altered view back to the producers of media products, who then sell us products that are familiar, safe, orderly, and predictable, thus creating a perpetual cycle of imprecision, misimpression, and misinformation. This is particularly true of crime-related presentations in which behaviors, places, and people are blended into a composite picture of a threat or danger (Potter and Kappeler 1998). The media create a symbolic "dangerous world" (Cavender and Bond-Maupin 1993; Kappeler et al. 1993), which, in turn, markets predictable, orderly fear.

Several scholars have critiqued media coverage of organized crime, primarily as it has related to print coverage of the subject, specifically newspapers, magazines, and books (Galliher and Cain 1974; Smith 1974; Martens and

Cunningham-Neiderer, 1985; Morash and Hale 1987; Kooistra 1989; O'Brien and Kurins 1991; Potter 1994; Kenney and Finckenauer 1995; Ryan 1995; Abadinsky 1997). In general, these scholars have three overarching concerns with the journalistic handling of organized crime: (1) the superficiality of the coverage (Smith 1974; Martens and Cunningham-Niederer 1985; Morash and Hale 1987; Kooistra 1989; Potter 1994; Ryan 1995); (2) the sensationalism in selecting stories to cover (Martens and Cunningham-Niederer 1985; Potter 1994); and (3) the tendency to create reality and reproduce the state's viewpoints on organized crime (Galliher and Cain 1974; O'Brien and Kurins 1991; Potter 1994).

1. *Superficiality.* Critics see superficiality in the media's handling of organized crime manifested in four different ways. First, Smith (1974: 182) asserts that media coverage provides very little substantive knowledge or analysis of organized crime. A corollary to Smith's criticism of superficiality is the view that news coverage of organized crime is usually treated by the media more as entertainment for popular consumption than as serious news (Smith 1974; Kooistra 1989; Potter 1994). Morash and Hale (1987: 147) have suggested that inadequate sampling of both organized crime groups and activities contributes greatly to the problem of superficiality. Finally, critiques of the superficiality of media coverage of organized crime have suggested a strong tendency on the part of the media to emphasize discrete and isolated events in their coverage, rather than organizational dynamics and interrelationships in the market (Morash and Hale 1987: 142).

2. *Sensationalism.* The second overarching criticism of media coverage of organized crime is that it tends to be sensational and to focus on notorious individuals and events (Martens and Cunningham-Niederer 1985; Potter 1994). Notoriety can relate to a group, clearly demonstrated by the frequency of mentions of Cosa Nostra and Mafia groups in news stories, movies, and books. It can also be related to individuals who are notorious in the tradition of Al Capone or Lucky Luciano. For a while, the mantle of notoriety rested most heavily on the shoulders of John Gotti, the alleged head of a New York Cosa Nostra family.

3. *Creating reality.* Finally, the media has been criticized in their coverage of organized crime for creating their own social reality of notorious gang leaders; conspiratorial, exotic, and alien organized crime; and a world of illicit business controlled by the wanton and often random use of force and violence (O'Brien and Kurins 1991; Potter 1994). Not surprisingly, some critics contend that this is a social reality that closely reflects the state's view of organized crime (Albini 1971; Smith 1974; Potter 1994). Integral to this claim is the charge that the information that journalists generate is suspect because it is not subjected to methodologically rigorous controls (Galliher and Cain 1974; Potter 1994; Ryan 1995).

A key element of this concern is the charge by some critics that journalists uncritically report information provided by state social control agencies (Morash and Hale 1987; Potter 1994). This is of concern for several reasons. First, the state has a genuine interest in promoting an image of organized crime that has close correlation to its enforcement policies and its political interests. If state policy is predicated on investigating, arresting, and incarcerating powerful syndicate leaders, there must be powerful syndicate leaders. If the state has strong political interests in new and expanded law enforcement powers, such as easing restrictions on electronic surveillance, changing the conditions of immunity grants, empowering U.S. attorneys to call grand juries and conduct lengthy investigations, and passing draconian drug laws, the state needs to portray organized crime as secretive, tightly organized, difficult to penetrate, violent, and adhering to strong codes of criminal conduct. If the state has a vested interest in deflecting arguments about domestic markets, indigenous consumer demands, and political corruption, it needs a social reality of organized crime that is both conspiratorial and alien and therefore not affected by market or demand-side tinkering in the United States.

Identifying law enforcement agencies and government officials as sources is troubling for three reasons. First, it affects the credibility of the information in the stories. There is a real question about how much the government actually knows and how much accurate information government sources have at their command. Rubinstein and Reuter (1978: 57) correctly note that the government had virtually no information on the oil industry during the energy crisis of the 1970s, even though it is a highly regulated industry. Additionally, they point to government estimates of illegal gambling revenue, noting the totally unscientific basis for government estimates and suggesting that numbers were created purely for propaganda purposes (1978: 62).

Second, there is a troubling tendency of the state to release information known to be inaccurate as part of disinformation campaigns aimed at specific organized crime groups. A prime example was the media's gullible acceptance of claims about Carmine Galante's alleged attempt to take over heroin trafficking in New York in 1977. The story was leaked by the Drug Enforcement Administration, was demonstrably false, and after being widely circulated in the media may have played a role in Galante's murder (Villano 1978).

Third, of course, it is highly unlikely that the state would release information or its agents would provide sourcing that directly contradicted the state's position on organized crime or that questioned the efficacy of enforcement efforts, support for legislation, and support for funding.

Officials review government reports on organized crime, cull out contrary information, and heavily edit wiretap transcripts before release, and argue the state's position. The lack of external validation of information coming from state law enforcement agencies is troubling at best. As Smith has pointed out, state social control agencies in the United States have a peculiar preoccupation with organized crime conspiracies. In view of the alleged origin of many organized crime groups, Smith refers to this as an *alien conspiracy theory* in the case of organized crime (1974).

The treatment of organized crime by the news media raises concern beyond issues of superficiality, sensationalism, and the replication of state ideology. This treatment creates a social reality of organized crime that is very much in conflict with the data available from scientific studies. More than that, it neglects the complexity of organized crime and paints a simplistic picture of an entity that is at odds with the elegant complexities of the real illicit market and the organizational dynamics of real organized crime groups. Scholars know that organized crime groups are primarily informal, loosely structured, highly ephemeral entities, whose complexion changes rapidly and facilely to meet the demands of the market and the efforts of social control agents (Albini 1971; Block 1979; Block and Chambliss 1981; Reuter 1983; Abadinsky 1985; Potter and Jenkins 1985).

Scholars also know that organized crime operates in a rich tapestry of political, law enforcement, and business corruption, compromise, and accommodation (Gardiner 1970; Potter and Jenkins 1985; Block and

Scarpitti 1985; Block 1986; Chambliss 1988). The sterile still-life snapshots provided by the news media are fundamentally misleading. The network evening newscasts do not even attempt to portray intricacies and overlays of Albini's description of patron–client relations (1971), Chambliss's intricately woven crime networks (1988), Smith's (1974) market-driven enterprise crimes, or Haller's (1990) engrossing discussion of organizational dynamics in his study of organized crime partnerships. Virtually all organized crime portrayals in the news media are characterizations of what Block has called "power syndicates" that specialize in violence and extort resources from other syndicates (Block 1983).

The truth, however, is that enterprise syndicates that deliver illicit goods and services are far more numerous and that power syndicates are notoriously unsuccessful; in fact, none has ever survived (Block 1983). Rather than showing organized crime to be a complex yet integral part of political, economic, and social life, the media reduces it to a caricature. This has stunning implications for policymakers and the public alike, because it is essentially a false image of organized crime that drives public outrage, admiration, envy, and sometimes sympathy and that compels official state action that is doomed to fail because it is based on a flawed presentation.

WHAT HAVE WE LEARNED?

Many attempts to define organized crime have been made, but because of its diverse nature and origins, a definitive definition is difficult to develop. Many experts have agreed that organized crime organizations have certain characteristics that make them similar to one another. These characteristics, discussed earlier in the chapter, are important in developing a framework for defining the term.

It is not uncommon for a series of exchanges between the under- and upperworlds to develop into a long-term corrupt relationship. In fact, studies have shown that in some cases those who occupy positions of public trust are in fact the organizers of crime (Gardiner 1970; Chambliss 1978; Gardiner and Lyman 1978; Block and Scarpitti 1985; Potter and Jenkins 1985). Investigations of police corruption in Philadelphia and New York have demonstrated how thoroughly institutionalized corruption can be among public servants. In the private sector, respected institutions such as Shearson/American Express, Merrill Lynch, the Miami National Bank, and Citibank have eagerly participated in illicit ventures (Lernoux 1984; Moldea 1986; *Organized Crime Digest* 1986). Contrary to popular public opinion, under- and upperworld criminals form close, symbiotic bonds. Public officials are not

the pawns of organized crime; they are part of its fabric, albeit the part found in America's respected institutions. In many cases one cannot operate or profit without the other.

The cases in which organized crime networks demonstrate ethnic homogeneity could simply reflect the exigencies of urban social life, not the machinations of a secret, ethnic conspiracy. It makes sense that vice in a black neighborhood is going to be primarily delivered by a black crime network. Similarly, illicit goods and services in an Italian neighborhood will probably be delivered by entrepreneurs of Italian lineage. This is not an organizational design; it merely reflects the fact that small, geographically compact, organized crime networks will have a membership that reflects their constituency.

On the other hand, literally hundreds of criminal investigations in all levels of government have demonstrated elaborate criminal networks of structure, organizational design, and communication in large ethnically based criminal groups such as Italian, Jamaican, and Hispanic organizations. Although we must not discount the notion that many organized crime groups are small, fragmented associations of criminals, we must be aware that other groups can indeed pose a much more considerable threat to public safety than is generally known.

DO YOU RECOGNIZE THESE TERMS?

Apalachin incident
Camorra
conspiracy
corruption
criminal group
extortion
French Connection
illicit enterprise
illicit goods
illicit services
institutionalized crime

La Cosa Nostra
Mafia
maxitrial
nontraditional organized crime
omerta organized crime
organized crime
Pizza Connection
protectors
social support
specialized support
user support

POINTS OF DISCUSSION

1. Describe the characteristics that make organized crime a unique type of criminality.
2. Explain why defining organized crime is difficult.
3. Discuss the value of organized crime investigations by presidential commissions.
4. Explain what official investigations into organized crime have told us.
5. Explain and discuss the organizational structure of an organized crime group.
6. Discuss the basic qualifications for membership in an organized crime group.
7. What are the advantages and disadvantages of membership in an organized crime group?

SUGGESTED READING

ABADINSKY, H. (1981). *The Mafia in America: An Oral History.* New York: Praeger. The structure, membership, roles, rules, and business of Italian American organized crime are discussed based on interviews with a New York–New Jersey organized crime figure and government witness.

ALBINI, J. (1971). *The American Mafia: Genesis of a Legend.* New York: Appleton-Century-Crofts. The author presents evidence arguing against the existence of a national centrally directed criminal syndicate.

ANDERSON, A. (1979). *The Business of Organized Crime: A Costa Nostra Family.* Stanford, CA: Hoover Institution Press. The scope of a Mafia family's illegal enterprises and legitimate business interests is detailed in this case study of an Italian organized crime group of about seventy-five men, one of twenty-four groups held to be the core of La Cosa Nostra.

CHAMBLISS, W. (1988). *On the Take: From Petty Crooks to Presidents,* 2nd ed. Bloomington: Indiana University Press. This study examines the structural bases of official corruption and how local crime networks are connected to national business and political interests.

IANNI, F. A. J., and E. REUSSO-IANNI. (1972). *A Family Business: Kinship and Social Control in Organized Crime.* New York: Russell Sage Foundation. This book is a field research study of an Italian American crime syndicate in New York City.

REUTER, P. (1983). *Disorganized Crime: The Economics of the Visible Hand.* Cambridge, MA: MIT Press. New York's illegal markets of bookmaking, the numbers game, and loan-sharking do not conform to the orthodox view of domination by the Mafia through violence and the corruption of public officials.

THEORIES OF ORGANIZED CRIMINAL BEHAVIOR

This chapter will enable you to:

- Understand the fundamentals behind rational choice theory
- See how deterrence theory affects crime and personal decisions to commit crime
- Learn about theories of crime

- Learn about social disorganization theories of crime
- Explain the enterprise theory of organized crime
- Learn how organized crime can be explained by organizational theory

INTRODUCTION

In 1993, Medellin cartel founder Pablo Escobar was gunned down by police on the rooftop of his hideout in Medellin, Colombia. At the time of his death, Escobar was thought to be worth an estimated $2 billion, which he purportedly earned during more than a decade of illicit cocaine trafficking. His wealth afforded him a luxurious mansion, expensive cars, and worldwide recognition as a cunning, calculating, and ruthless criminal mastermind. The rise of Escobar to power is like that of many other violent criminals before him. Indeed, as history has shown, major organized crime figures such as Meyer Lansky and Lucky Luciano, the El Rukinses, Jeff Fort, and Abimael Guzmán, leader of Peru's notorious Shining Path, were all aggressive criminals who built large criminal enterprises during their lives.

The existence of these criminals and many others like them poses many unanswered questions about the cause and development of criminal behavior. Why are some criminals but not others involved with organized crime? Is organized crime a planned criminal phenomenon or a side effect of some other social problem, such as poverty or lack of education? As we seek answers to these questions, we are somewhat frustrated by the fact that little information is available to adequately explain the reasons for participating in organized crime. Some might argue that individual characteristics such as greed, opportunism, and a propensity for violence were the primary factors contributing to Escobar's rise to prominence in the criminal underworld. Although there are many causes of individual crime, sociologists have argued that there must be a broad explanation of criminal behavior. But sociologists' explanations have rarely addressed the specific phenomenon of organized crime. Explanations of individual criminal behavior can provide some insight into it.

Criminological theory is rooted in the causes of criminal behavior. Such theory considers the characteristics of individuals and society that result in crime. For example, we know that the cause of a murder could be an individual psychological condition or something in the social environment. Whether a theory proposes an individual personality or social condition, experts agree that no single theory serves to explain all types of crime.

This chapter considers the theories that are most applicable to explain membership in organized crime, and although we use the word *theory*, we should point out that not all explanations discussed are theories per se. Theories are explanations that consist of clearly defined, interrelated, and measurable propositions. Many explanations in this chapter fall short of that definition and can be characterized as organized hypotheses, paradigms, conjectures, and speculations. Nonetheless, in this chapter we offer a glimpse of both empirical and speculative theories that explain different aspects of organized crime.

ALIEN CONSPIRACY THEORY

One of the most widely held theories of organized crime today is known as the **alien conspiracy theory.** This theory blames outsiders and outside influences for the prevalence of organized crime in U.S. society. Over the years, unsavory images, such as well-dressed men of foreign descent standing in shadows with machine guns and living by codes of silence, have become associated with this theory. The alien conspiracy theory posits that organized crime (the Mafia) gained prominence during the 1860s in Sicily and that Sicilian immigrants are responsible for the foundations of U.S. organized crime, which is made up of twenty-five or so Italian-dominated crime families. Also known as the La Cosa Nostra, the families are composed of *wise guys* or *made men* and number about 1,700 members.

Although some skeptics insist that the alien conspiracy theory was born out of hysteria incited by the media, it has received considerable support over the years from federal law enforcement organizations, public officials, and some researchers. It has been argued, however, that federal law enforcement organizations have self-serving reasons to promulgate this theory: It explains their inability to eliminate organized crime, it disguises the role of political and business corruption in organized crime, and it provides fertile ground for new resources, powers, and bureaucratic expansion. In fact, almost a century of criminal investigations, public hearings, and studies by presidential commissions have produced conflicting information regarding the existence of the Italian American group known as the Mafia. That Italians are involved in organized crime is certainly not a point of debate; the degree of interconnectedness between Italian crime syndicates and their overall power in the world of organized crime is considerably more controversial.

Mafia or Cosa Nostra families are thought to control well-defined geographic areas and specific criminal enterprises. Five families are said to dominate New York City: the Colombo, Lucchese, Bonanno, Genovese, and Gambino families, each named after its founder. Also representing a large geographical area is the alleged Mafia family in Chicago, which is known as the *outfit*. Influence from the Chicago outfit reaches to other cities, including Phoenix, Milwaukee, Kansas City, and Los Angeles. In addition to the individual families, a national commission exists whose function is to arbitrate disputes between families and assign territory (discussed later in the chapter).

Ethnicity is a key to the alien conspiracy theory of the organized crime phenomenon. Many criminologists argue, however, that available empirical research indicates that this theory misinterprets and overstates the role of ethnicity in organized crime. Some evidence suggests that many organized crime groups consist of persons of a specific ethnic background who cooperate on a regular basis (Block 1979; Abadinsky 1985; Potter and Jenkins 1985; Pennsylvania Crime Commission 1986), but Haller's (1990) study of Lansky's and Capone's enterprises makes clear that organized criminals who wish to survive and prosper quickly learn the limits of kinship, ethnicity, and violence and proceed to form lucrative partnerships on the basis of rational business decisions and common needs.

An apparent contradiction of the alien conspiracy theory is the simple fact that virtually every U.S. city had well-developed organized crime syndicates long before the large-scale Italian immigration of the late nineteenth and early twentieth centuries. If Italians and other immigrants played a major role in developing organized crime, they were only joining and augmenting widespread crime corruption already native to the United States.

RATIONAL CHOICE THEORY

When we consider theories of organized criminal behavior discussed in this chapter, we consider why some people conduct themselves in a manner that potentially entails risk, personal injury, arrest, or imprisonment. Some theorists believe that regardless of the reason for committing crime, the decision to do so is a rational choice made after weighing the benefits and consequences of the action.

Examples of this theory include a man who discovers that his wife is having an affair and chooses to kill her, her lover, or both; the bank teller who is experiencing personal financial difficulty and decides to embezzle funds from the bank to substantially increase her earnings; and an inner-city youth who decides that social opportunities are minimal and that it would be easier to make money by dealing crack cocaine. These are just a few scenarios in which people make a reasoned choice and exemplify a theory of criminality known as rational choice.

Rational choice theory first emerged in the mid-eighteenth century and was originally referred to as classical theory. It was developed by the **classical school of criminology** through the writings of Cesare Beccaria and Jeremy Bentham. It perceived people as free agents who are able to make rational choices in virtually all aspects of their lives. This school views organized crime members as possessing free will and as being able to make rational decisions regarding their involvement in crime and wrongdoing. Policies stemming from this approach dictate dealing harshly and quickly with offenders in an effort to deter them from making such choices again. Little consideration was given to the offenders' backgrounds or the circumstances surrounding the crimes that they committed.

Because offenders were considered to be rational thinkers, punishment for their crimes was based on the pleasure–pain principle. This meant that the pain of punishment for the offense must outweigh the pleasure the offender received as a reward for committing the crime. So, in theory, the rational offender would realize that it was not worth it to commit the criminal act in the first place. Beccaria also espoused the idea that the punishment should fit the crime.

Rational choice theory suggests that people who commit crimes do so after considering the risks of detection and punishment for the crimes **(risk assessment),** as well as the rewards (personal, financial, etc.) of completing these acts successfully. On the other hand, persons who do not commit crime decide that completing the act successfully is too risky or not worth the benefits. It should be noted that crimes are committed for an array of reasons, which include economic, psychological, physical, social, and even political motivations. In the context of organized crime, financial incentives clearly play an important role in the person's decision to engage in crime. However, it is likely that dynamics other than rational choice can cause persons to commit a crime; for example, although an enforcer for a syndicate has financial interests in his organizational role, he also could act because of the need for acceptance, respect, and trust by other members or the organization. It is likely that the enforcer understands that his actions could result in his arrest and possible imprisonment. However, because he believes that his criminal talents or the resources of the organization will aid him in avoiding detection, he feels confident that the crime can be carried out with minimal risk.

DETERRENCE THEORY

Some theorists believe that crime can be reduced through the use of deterrents. The goal of deterrence, crime prevention, is based on the assumption that criminals or potential criminals will think carefully before committing a crime if the likelihood of getting caught and/or the fear of swift and severe punishment is present. As a rule, deterrents to crime are both general and specific in nature.

General deterrence theory holds that crime can be thwarted by the threat of punishment. If people fear that they will be arrested, they will choose not to commit the criminal act. Capital punishment is an example of general deterrence. Although evidence indicates the contrary, the purpose of capital punishment is to discourage people from committing crime because they fear that the state will put them to death.

Special deterrence theory holds that penalties for criminal acts should be sufficiently severe that convicted criminals will never repeat their acts. For example, if a person arrested on a first-time marijuana possession charge is sentenced to spend sixty days in a boot camp designed for first-time offenders, the punishment is to convince him or her that the price for possessing marijuana is not worth the pleasure of using it.

Although the effectiveness of deterrence is highly debatable and not supported by empirical evidence, some experts suggest that it can be effective. For example, Wilson (1975: 494) points out that most crimes are committed by a small number of people. Because many courts and corrections

---

Critical Thinking Project

Are organized crime groups a presence in your own community? To what extent? Considering the perceived benefits of organized crime to some areas of the country, explain your attitude about organized crime activities in your home town and state.

components of the criminal justice system embrace treatment instead of punishment, criminals are more willing to risk getting caught. He argues that if the expected cost of committing crime goes up without a corresponding increase in the expected benefits, would-be criminals will commit fewer crimes.

PSYCHOLOGICAL TRAITS AND CRIMINALITY

Many different views regarding the connection between psychological traits and crime exist. The term *personality* can be defined as a phenomenon of behavior that is governed by one's emotions and thoughts and that controls the manner in which a person views life events and makes personal choices. Specific personality traits have often been linked to criminals, but whether certain personality traits are present in criminals is controversial.

A person's personality traits do play a role in that person's day to day decision making. When examining criminal populations, a number of personality traits, such as anxiety, conduct disorders, depression, and short attention spans, have been identified (Farrington 1988). Such traits tend to make people especially susceptible to problems such as substance abuse, promiscuity, violence, and sociopathy. However, the same traits have been found among significant populations who have never been arrested for a crime.

The Antisocial Personality

One personality type that has been identified by the research in biopsychology is the **sociopathic** (or psychopathic) **personality.** The sociopath is thought to be a dangerous, aggressive person who shows little remorse for his or her actions, who is not deterred by punishments, and who does not learn from past mistakes. Sociopaths often appear to have a pleasant personality and an above-average level of intelligence. They are, however, marked by an inability to form enduring relationships. Abrahamsen describes the sociopath (also called a psychopath) as someone who has never been able to identify with anyone else. The person lacks fundamental traits, such as the ability to love and care for others and to experience emotional depth, and displays an unusually low level of anxiety. Harvey Cleckley, a leading authority on psychopathy, offers this definition (1959: 567–569):

> [Psychopaths are] chronically antisocial individuals who are always in trouble, profiting neither from experience nor punishment, and maintaining no real loyalties to any person, group, experience, or code. They are frequently callous and hedonistic, showing marked emotional immaturity, with lack of responsibility, lack of judgment, and an ability to rationalize their behavior so that it appears warranted, reasonable, and justified.

Cleckley's Description of the Sociopathic Personality

1. Considerable superficial charm and average or above-average intelligence
2. Absence of delusions or other signs of irrational thinking
3. Absence of anxiety or other neurotic symptoms; considerable poise, calmness, and verbal facility

4. Unreliability, disregard for obligations, no sense of responsibility in matters of little or great importance
5. Untruthfulness and insincerity
6. Lack of remorse, no sense of shame
7. Exhibition of antisocial behavior that is inadequately motivated and poorly planned, seeming to stem from an inexplicable impulsiveness
8. Poor judgment and failure to learn from experience
9. Pathological egocentricity, total self-centeredness; incapacity for real love and attachment
10. General poverty of deep and lasting emotions
11. Lack of any true insight, inability to see oneself as others do
12. Ingratitude for any special considerations, kindness, and trust
13. Fantastic and objectionable behavior—vulgarity, rudeness, quick mood shifts, pranks—after drinking and sometimes even when not drinking
14. No history of genuine suicide attempts
15. An impersonal, trivial, and poorly integrated sex life
16. Failure to have a life plan and to live in any ordered way, unless it be one promoting self-defeat (Cleckley 1976)

For the concept of sociopathic behavior to be useful in understanding criminality, it must be correlated with criminal behavior. Criminality refers to lawbreaking in a given society at a given point in time. The sociopath is viewed as someone who does not respond emotionally after committing an act that generally elicits shame and guilt in most people, which is an element of Cleckleys' definition. Research by Hare (1980) suggests that these two characteristics, no sense of responsibility and no sense of shame, indicate sociopathy. The lack of shame or guilt is presumably linked to the sociopath's inability to learn from experience, in particular the inability to avoid punishment.

Some studies have estimated that about 25 percent of all prison inmates are antisocial, although no data exist on its prevalence in society at large (Rabin 1979: 236–251). One problem in understanding the nature of the sociopath is that most research in the area has been conducted on people who already have criminal convictions. The available literature does not allow us to generalize about the behavior of sociopaths who are successful in avoiding arrest.

The Dependent Personality

Dependent personality is also known as inadequate personality, passive personality, and asthenic personality. There are two particularly important characteristics of this personality type. The first is reflected in the definition of dependent personality as found in the 1987 edition of DSM-III-R, the psychiatric diagnostic guidelines: "pervasive pattern of dependent and submissive behavior beginning by early adulthood and present in a variety of contexts." Persons with this trait have a history of poor social interaction and have been described as being "weak and ineffective, lacking energy, passive and nice but totally inadequate."

The inability to interact successfully with people at an early age is carried into adulthood. Dependent personality types have maintained a relationship with a significant member of the immediate family—typically, the mother or father—well into their adulthood. Of particular interest is the discomfort those with the disorder feel about having maintained the relationship although they did so anyway. In fact, many dependent personality types actually feel resentment and animosity toward their significant other, but often state that they don't know what to do about the relationship. Many significant others had made most, if not all, decisions for persons with this disorder.

The second important characteristic of dependent personalities is the overcontrolled aspect of their personalities. As a rule, individuals falling into this category are unable to control their anger, frustration, and hostility. The emotional life of such people can best be described by comparing them to a very large, expanded steel coil. The coil, at the time of the person's birth, begins to be compressed within the person's psyche. As he or she experiences situations in which frustration, anger, and hostility are involved, the giant coil compresses more and more. Each time the person is involved in circumstances that cause stress or anxiety, the tension of this emotional coil increases. Concomitantly, a button that can trigger that coil to expand develops, and the person runs the risk of an explosive episode. Unfortunately, there is little or no way that one can predict when or how the coil will be triggered. When a situation occurs that is perceived by the person as hostile, he or she reacts excessively and inappropriately, releasing years of anger and frustration.

Closer Look

Case Narrative of an Antisocial Personality Type

Edward is the fictitious name of a person who is responsible for the death of a police officer in the northeastern part of the country. At the time he killed the officer, Edward was 32 years old. He is the oldest of eight siblings, having seven half-brothers and -sisters, and his father had left the household when he was six months of age. Because Edward's mother was very young when she gave birth to Edward, he and his mother continued to live with Edward's grandmother. It was Edward's grandmother who was the dominant person in the household. Over the next several years, Edward's mother worked outside the home as a seamstress.

The grandmother's discipline was reported by Edward as being very inconsistent. There were times when he would be praised for having done something and punished the following day for having done the very same thing. The family's socioeconomic status was reported to have been marginal. Although Edward claims that he was physically abused during times he was being punished, there was no report of sexual abuse. During his school years, Edward claims that he did "average" in elementary school—his definition of average was As and Bs. This changed dramatically during his high school years, when his grades dropped to Ds and Fs. During this time Edward dropped out of school. During his prison term, he completed his GED.

Edward's social encounters were replete with conflict. From police reports it was determined that Edward had a reputation of being threatening and impulsive. His friends, according to newspaper accounts, characterized him as "dangerous because you didn't know what he would do." Frequently, his response to frustration was aggression. Edward had been found guilty of another homicide, which took place prior to the law enforcement officer shooting. The person he had killed had been a friend of his for almost twenty years. The two got involved in an argument concerning a girlfriend, and during the argument, which took place in a car driven by Edward, he shot his friend in the neck. Not certain that he had killed him, he took his friend's pulse to determine if, indeed, he had died. Once Edward was certain

(continued)

his traveling companion was dead, he proceeded to push his body on the floorboard of the car to conceal its presence. As he "drove around for awhile trying to find a place to dump the body," he removed the gold jewelry, rings, and watch from the body since "they weren't no value to a dead man."

According to police and court reports, Edward's reputation also included his ability to use and con others into thinking that he intended to include them in his future plans. What actually happened is that once a person no longer proved to be a means to a desired end, Edward would quickly remove himself from the relationship without explanation. It became apparent to others that the only person that Edward had feelings for was Edward himself. On the afternoon that ended with the law enforcement officer's death, Edward and two associates had decided to "hold up a gambling joint." Prepared to face resistance at the illegal gambling establishment, the three were all well armed with handguns and shotguns. Having completed their robbery, they proceeded to drive away from the building. Edward, the front-seat passenger in the car, reportedly told the driver of the car to proceed without too much speed so that no unnecessary attention would be drawn to them. The driver drove the wrong way down a one-way street, attracting the attention of an officer who was on patrol in his marked vehicle. After the officer stopped the vehicle, Edward opened the door of the car and walked to the officer's car. Asking the officer why he had stopped their vehicle, the officer told Edward to go back to his car and wait there. During this verbal exchange, Edward noted that the officer was "speaking into his radio" and not paying attention to what Edward was doing. When Edward finally returned to the car in which he was a passenger, he told the person in the back seat of the car to "get ready . . . something is going to happen . . . someone is going to get hurt." He then told the person in the back seat to get his shotgun because something "had to be done about this . . . I'm going to shoot him." When asked by the backseat passenger if Edward meant that he was going to kill the officer, Edward responded "You're damn right—I'm going to kill him." Edward quoted himself further as saying, "I'm going to shoot this man because I have a feeling something is going to happen."

Edward reportedly walked back to the officer's car and stood to the side of the seated officer. Edward stated that when he arrived at the side of the car, the officer was "still looking at the radio when he was talking into the microphone. He didn't see me come to the car. Then he looked up out of the corner of his eye for a fraction of a second and saw that I had a gun. I shot him once in the chest and went back to the car." Edward then told the driver of the car to drive away because he had "just shot the officer." They succeeded in their escape.

LEARNING THEORIES

Some learning theories have been used to explain the onset of criminal activity. The body of research on learning theory stresses the attitudes, ability, values, and behaviors needed to maintain a criminal career.

Researchers from a number of disciplines, such as sociology and psychology, have studied how individuals learned deviant values and behavior within the context of family and friends. Experts suggest that how to become criminals and how to deal emotionally with the consequences of such activity are learned.

Miller on Gangs   Miller (1958) argues that participation in youth gangs often provides a training ground for future organized crime participants. During this period of development in a youth gang, useful organized crime qualities are inculcated in apprentices. Miller (1958: 7) identified toughness and smartness (obtaining money by one's wits) as important values necessary for such development. He also suggests that this crime–community nexus creates the "capacity for subordinating individual desires to the general group's interests as well as the capacity for intimate and persistent interaction" (Miller 1958: 14).

According to Sutherland (1973: 5), criminal behavior is learned as a result of associations with others, and the propensity for innovating through criminality depends on the strength of these associations. Sutherland argues that criminal behavior occurs when definitions favorable to violation of the law exceed definitions unfavorable to violation of the law. Sutherland suggests that factors such as deprivation, limited access to legitimate alternatives, and exposure to innovative success models (i.e., pimps, gamblers, or drug dealers) create a susceptibility to criminal behavior.

Sutherland on Differential Association

Sutherland viewed **differential association** as a product of socialization in which criminals are guided by many of the same principles that guide law-abiding people. A study of the tenets of differential association shows that the sources of behavioral motivation for criminals are much the same as those for conformists (e.g., a desire for money and success). The difference is, of course, that criminals pursue their goals through unlawful means.

Sutherland's Principles of Differential Association

1. Criminal behavior is learned.
2. The fundamental basis of learning criminal behavior is learned in intimate personal groups (e.g., gangs).
3. Criminal behavior is acquired through interaction with other persons in a process of communication.
4. The learning process includes the techniques of committing the crime and specific rationalizations and attitudes for criminal activity.
5. General attitudes regarding the respect (or lack of respect) for laws are reflected in attitudes toward criminal behavior.
6. A person becomes delinquent or criminal because of an excess of definitions favorable to violation of law over definitions unfavorable to violation of the law.
7. Differential association can vary in duration, frequency, and intensity.
8. The processes for learning criminal behavior parallel those of any other learning process.
9. Criminal behavior is an expression of general needs and values (as with noncriminal behavior), but is not explained by these needs and values (Sutherland 1973).

According to Sutherland, people learn the specifics of criminality, such as specialized techniques, attitudes, justifications, and rationalization. Learning these specifics develops a favorable predisposition to criminal life-styles.

Suttles on Community History

Suttles (1968: 111) proposes that a "strong sense of history" is an important factor in the development process from participation in juvenile crime to organized crime. Suttles believes that this historical sense of community provides a strong sense of criminal heritage.

SOCIAL DISORGANIZATION THEORIES

Some researchers link criminality to social conditions prevalent in neighborhoods. Many of them believe that the reasons crime rates are high in these areas are urban decay, a general deterioration of the ecology of inner cities, and general social and familial deterioration. Why are these inner-city neighborhoods, which have high poverty, low employment, and many single-parent households, prone to criminality? Some theorists suggest that in these socially ravaged areas, the necessary social services, educational opportunities, housing, and health care are inadequate or totally unavailable, thus exacerbating the problem of disorganization and criminality.

Relative Deprivation

Some researchers attribute inner-city crime to **relative deprivation.** This ecological approach suggests that the inequality between communities where the poor and the rich live in close proximity to one another creates a general feeling of anger, hostility, and social injustice on the part of inner-city inhabitants. Peter Blan and Judith Blau (1982) assert that poor inner-city youths, such as those in Los Angeles, New York, and Detroit, experience an increasing sense of frustration as they grow up and experience poverty, while they witness those who are well-to-do in nearby neighborhoods. These youths are able to witness affluence firsthand, but they are deprived of its benefits through social discrimination, which makes it virtually impossible for them to attain success through conventional means.

Bell's Queer Ladder of Mobility Theory

Bell's essay on the American way of crime (1953), although dated, represents the classic formation of the *queer ladder of mobility.* Bell explained the entry of Italian American criminals into organized crime (1953):

> The Italian community has achieved wealth and political influence much later and in a harder way than previous immigrant groups. The Italians found the more obvious big city paths from rags to riches preempted. . . . The children of the [Italian] immigrants, the second and third generations, became wise in the ways of the urban slums. Excluded from the political ladder . . . finding few open routes to wealth, some turned to illicit ways.

An extension of the queer ladder theory explains that **ethnic succession** develops as one group replaces the other on the queer ladder of crime, while the earlier group moves on to respectability along with legitimate social status and livelihood. According to ethnic succession, Jews replaced the Irish in crime, Italians replaced the Jews, and blacks, Cubans, Puerto Ricans, Mexicans, and Colombians are now replacing the Italians.

Bell's theory seems reasonable, but some critics have argued that it lacks empirical support. Furthermore, it has been suggested that immigrants did not

Critical Thinking Project

Examine at least one highly visible organized crime figure who has appeared in recent newspaper and magazine accounts. Explain how learning theories could explain how the figure became involved in criminality.

choose the queer ladder because of frustration or the few legitimate opportunities that were open to them, but because rare and exciting opportunities to wealth (i.e., bootlegging) were available. In other words, serendipity played an important part in routinizing nationwide syndicated crime.

We know that when Prohibition was enacted, Lucky Luciano was 20, Vito Genovese 19, and Carlo Gambino 17. By the end of Prohibition in 1933, each had acquired capital, organizational skills, and social influence. Perhaps one could argue that Prohibition and personal choice, not frustration and blocked ladders of opportunity, propelled these small-time hoodlums into nationally syndicated confederations of crime (Lupsha 1981).

Merton's Anomie

The process by which organized crime provides a means for social adaptation begins with the basic definition of success. Merton (1938: 673) has argued that an emphasis on specific goals often develops in U.S. society. This emphasis becomes virtually exclusive and ignores appropriate means for achieving these goals. Sacrifices aligned with conformity to the normative order must be compensated by socialized rewards (Merton 1938: 674). Deviant acts become attractive when expectations of rewards are not fulfilled. According to Merton's **anomie theory,** aberrant behavior can be viewed as a symptom of the dissociation between "culturally defined aspirations and socially structured means." He argues that the emphasis on the accumulation of wealth as a symbol of success leads to a disregard for considerations of how that wealth was obtained (Abadinsky 1981: 30–31). Fraud, vice, corruption, and crime become increasingly common means of achieving culturally induced success goals (Merton 1938: 675–676).

Cloward and Ohlin on Differential Opportunity

Patterns of criminal socialization probably have their origins in **socioeconomic stratification,** which relegates some people to environments in which they experience a sense of strain (Abadinsky 1981: 31). The strain is intense in environments that have traditionally spawned organized crime. Subsequent development patterns include identification and association with reference groups that formed as a result of criminal behavior. Sutherland (1973) suggests that factors such as deprivation, limited access to legitimate alternatives, and exposure to innovative success models (e.g., pimps, gamblers, or drug dealers) create a susceptibility to criminal behavior.

This is summarized by Cloward and Ohlin's (1960: 106–107) argument based on **differential opportunity:** Many lower-class male adolescents experience a sense of desperation surrounding the belief that their position in the economic structure is relatively fixed and immutable. As a result of failing to meet cultural expectations of achieving upward mobility, conditions become ideal for socialization functions such as recruitment, screening, and training for organized crime to occur at the community level. Cultural transmission of criminal behavior, due to generations of ecological conditions, has been recognized by several studies of gangs (Abadinsky 1981: 32). Shaw and McKay (1942: 175) suggest that patterns of criminal apprenticeship relative to Chicago youth gangs occurred in the community. They identified consistent patterns of younger boys participating "in offenses in the company of older boys, backward in time in an unbroken continuity. This relationship permits contact with older criminals and allows evaluations of individual potential for criminal success.

Taylor, Walton, and Young on Blocked Opportunity

Taylor, Walton, and Young (1973: 97) argue that when opportunities to succeed are distributed unequally, consequential results include the adoption of illegitimate means of obtaining success associated with definitions of the American Dream. Merton (1938: 678) supports this argument: "the use of conventionally proscribed but frequently effective means of attaining at least the simulacrum of culturally defined success" applies when people select success routes outside normatively prescribed channels.

Considerable precedent for using illegitimate goals to achieve success exists in locations noted for the presence of organized crime. It is not unusual for some communities to have a history of illegitimate adaptation. Numerous families have ancestors who were involved in illegal efforts to organize unions or who were involved in an array of other illicit enterprises.

CULTURAL DEVIANCE THEORIES

Cultural deviance theories assume that slum dwellers violate the law because they belong to a unique subculture that exists in lower-class areas. The subculture's values and norms conflict with those of the upper class on which criminal law is based. The subculture shares a life-style that is often accompanied by an alternative language and culture. The lower-class life-style is typically characterized by being tough, taking care of one's own affairs, and rejecting any kind of governmental authority. This subculture is attractive to many youths in the inner city because role models such as drug dealers, thieves, and pimps are so readily observable. After all, if social status and wealth cannot be attained through conventional means, an attractive alternative is financial success through the lower-class subculture. As a result, lower-class youths who are involved in drug dealing, for example, are not really rebelling against the upper class as much as they are striving to comply with the rules and values of their lower-class culture.

Culture Conflict

Sellin (1938) first developed the concept of a **culture conflict theory,** essentially a clash between the social mores of the middle class and the conduct norms of other groups. These conduct norms are held by groups who live within conventional society, but have not been afforded full membership in it. Conduct norms can be defined as the day to day rules that govern the behavior of these fragmented groups. History has shown that an allegiance to conduct norms often results in a clash with the mainstream culture.

Smith's Enterprise Theory

Smith (1980) has proposed an **enterprise theory,** which explains that organized crime exists because the legitimate marketplace leaves unserved or unsatisfied many people who are potential customers. The theory explains that economic enterprises involve both legitimate business and some types of criminal activity. Smith says that there is a range of behavior within which any business can be conducted. The legality of doing business is an arbitrary variable that can be changed by passing new laws. Doing so, however, does not necessarily result in a change of behavior. In other words, laws merely make legal behavior that was previously thought to be illegal, or vice versa.

A good example of the enterprise theory at work occurred during Prohibition. Passage of the Volstead Act in 1920 restricted manufacturing and distributing alcoholic beverages, but demand for the product remained virtually unchanged. A result was the black market for alcoholic beverages, which resulted in the creation of enormous criminal enterprises to satisfy customers unserved by legitimate enterprises. The thirteen years of Prohibition blurred the line between clearly predatory underworld criminals and a new style of gangster who was quasi-legitimate.

According to Smith (1980), market dynamics operating past the point of legitimacy tend to establish the primary context of the illicit entrepreneur. A high-level demand for a particular form of goods and services (such as illicit drugs or prostitution) combined with a relatively low level of risk of detection and considerably high profits provides the ideal conditions for illicit business groups to enter the market and profit from supplying these goods and services. Clearly, an identifiable market is everything to the illicit entrepreneur. Furthermore, a certain rate of consumption is required to maintain an acceptable profit and to justify risks. Accordingly, competition is the great foe of the illicit entrepreneur and must be discouraged at all costs. To this end, illicit enterprises employ the use of violence, intimidation, corruption, and extortion to expand markets and increase revenues.

At the heart of enterprise theory (Smith, 1980) is the hallmark of economics, the law of supply and demand, which the illicit drug trade can illustrate. With few exceptions, certain drugs are illegal to possess or sell, but a substantial market for them exists. Organized crime groups, which enjoy considerable profits, supply this market. Proponents of drug legalization refer to the enterprise theory by arguing that legalized drugs would put those who sell them out of business and thus would significantly reduce the ranks of organized crime. Although strong arguments on both sides of the issue exist, the fact remains that when a market is altered the dynamics of organized crime (e.g., risk, violence, finances) may be forced to adjust, one way or another.

ORGANIZATIONAL THEORY AND ORGANIZED CRIME

An enormous and increasing body of literature provides empirical data on the organization of legitimate business, but only a handful of empirical studies provides such data on the business of organized crime. To some degree, this lack of information is a function of the nature of criminal enterprise. In addition, the existing body of data on criminal enterprise has been contaminated with misimpressions and outright inaccuracies emanating from myriad journalistic accounts and government reports that lack credibility and are fascinated with a conspiracy model of criminal behavior. Nevertheless, some efforts have been made to explore the organization of criminal enterprise through empirical investigation. From these studies have emerged two consistent themes that can form the basis for further research and exploration:

1. Groups engaged in criminal enterprise are loosely structured, flexible, and highly adaptable to environmental impacts. These enterprises respond readily to the growth or decline of a market for a particular illicit good or service and to the availability of new distributors and manufacturers. For example, when cocaine became an attractive drug of choice in the early 1970s, many drug distribution syndicates responded by adding cocaine to marijuana shipments or by replacing marijuana with cocaine. In recent years,

the glut of cocaine on the market in the United States and the concomitant fall in retail price have led distribution groups to market Dilaudid (a heroin substitute) and heroin in an attempt to stimulate new market demand, which will provide more profit than cocaine trafficking. Similar adaptations can be seen in the sex industry; as a result of the threat of HIV infection, the industry has shifted the emphasis from selling straight sex to selling fantasies, adult conversation, and the like, leaving more routine services to the less profitable street market. As another example, the institutionalization of intertrack wagering has caused bookmakers in Kentucky to shift their betting from horse racing to sporting events.

2. Organized crime is a business and has many similarities to legal businesses. However, because organized crime conducts its business in the illegal marketplace, it is subject to a series of constraints that limits and defines its organizational structure, size, and mode of operation. Small, fragmented enterprises tend to populate illegal markets. Two basic facts of the illegal market cause this. The first is that a small number of employees and organizational segmentation minimize exposure to law enforcement. As Reuter (1983) has pointed out, the employees of the illicit enterprise are the greatest threat to its continuation because they make the best witnesses against the enterprise. The second is that the geographic scope in organized crime is limited. This minimizes the number of law enforcement agencies, that the organization must deal with and provides a more efficient means of communication.

Empirical evidence strongly suggests that the pattern of association in organized crime resembles what has variously been called a network, a partnership, or a patron–client relationship. In his study of criminal enterprise in Detroit, Albini (1971), found illicit business dominated by criminal patrons who exchanged information, connected with government officials, and accessed a network of operatives for economic and political support for their enterprises. He found that these networks of association constantly changed and that the roles of patrons and client fluctuated. Haller (1990) found that criminal enterprise was organized on the basis of a series of separate small-scale business partnerships, involving senior partners (those with money and political power) and an ever-changing list of junior partners. Chambliss (1976) found an amalgam of crime networks conducting criminal enterprise in Seattle with shifting memberships and no central control. Block (1979) depicted the cocaine trade in New York as operated by "small, flexible organizations of criminals which arise due to opportunity and environmental factors."

Reuter (1983) found gambling and loan-sharking industries in New York to be populated by small operators with no organization and having a monopoly or market hegemony and no central control or coordination. He found competition, treachery, communications breakdowns, and other forms of disorganization to be characteristic of the criminal enterprises he studied. Studies of criminal enterprises in Philadelphia (Potter and Jenkins 1985) found dozens of active enterprises with overlapping interests and participants, but no central direction or organization. These studies concur that criminal enterprise does not engage in routine production and distribution, but in a never-ending series of ad hoc projects and deals carried out through small, short-term agreements.

The propositions that can be derived from an analysis of the structure of organized crime support two conclusions that can be drawn from the available empirical evidence. Therefore, both the empirical evidence and the extant body of organizational theory suggest two basic propositions about the structure and conduct of organized crime's illicit enterprises.

1. All criminal enterprises exist in relatively hostile environments primarily as a function of their illegality. As a result of functioning in a hostile environment, criminal enterprises avoid complex technology and stay small in size with little organizational complexity, formality (i.e., formal rules, procedures, chains of command) is lacking, and the organizations are based on mutual understandings and a relatively discrete and concise set of operating procedures.

2. All criminal enterprise exists in relatively uncertain environments, both as a function of the illicit market and of the uncertain and changing nature of law enforcement policies and public attitudes. As a result, the danger of structural elaboration for criminal enterprises increases as the degree of uncertainty increases. However, the uncertainty of the environment requires that organizational structures be informal, with decentralized decision-making authority.

Both of these conclusions result from an analysis of the organizational literature and the commonalties in the empirical evidence on organized crime. The conclusions reached differ markedly from the popular image of organized crime and the model of criminal enterprise used by law enforcement agencies. That model suggests that criminal enterprise is controlled by a single criminal group (La Cosa Nostra) or at least by a body of large criminal conspiracies (Yakuza, the triads, the Colombian cartels, the Cuban Mafia, etc.) that exercise a tightly organized system of control that directs the efficient production of goods and services by organizational members. Inherent in this approach are the assumptions that (1) such a conspiracy or conspiracies exist, maintain a criminal monopoly in the marketplace, and follow a fixed, detailed, operating strategy, and (2) these criminal conspiracies are controlled by bosses at the very top of their hierarchies, with a chain of command that passes orders related to specific criminal tasks down to workers.

Moore (1987) suggests that this is not an unreasonable illusion. He argues that viewed from a distance, outside the world of illicit commerce, criminal enterprises might give the impression of producing a very high volume of illicit activity that, because of its prevalence, seems highly organized and, because of the distance of the observers, appears to be a single organization or several very large organizations. He suggests, however, that the same structure viewed from the inside would look like a series of partnerships organized around specific criminal projects.

Both the empirical evidence on organized crime and the logic of organization theory support Moore's assertions. First, empirical evidence strongly suggests that the internal structure of criminal enterprises is extremely fluid, with little control or direction from a central authority. Second, the logic of the situation demonstrates how unlikely a tightly organized criminal conspiracy is in actual operation.

A monopolistic syndicate would have to provide constant instruction and information to street-level vice purveyors, thereby jeopardizing the continued existence of the organization. Such a syndicate would have to monitor employee performance, keep careful records, and engage in considerable discussion about specific plans, situations that also would jeopardize the organization's existence. If such a conspiracy existed, removing its head or leadership, would cripple the enterprise. Experience demonstrates that this has not happened despite successful prosecutions of syndicate leaders.

Social Implications of the Enterprise Model

We are left therefore with a model of criminal enterprise in which these organizations are not centralized, formalized, or departmentalized. This model has profound implications for both research and law enforcement. This view suggests that scholars interested in unraveling the mysteries of the persistence and prevalence of organized crime should look to market forces at work in criminal entrepreneurship, not to people who have attained some degree of notoriety in the field. The view also suggests that law enforcement policy should attempt to disrupt the organizational environment of the enterprise, rather than jail mythical corporate masterminds believed to be manipulating the criminal enterprise from afar.

The model suggested here is based on the simple truth that criminal enterprises come into existence and are profitable because of strong public demand for their goods and services. A market dynamic is at work that is independent of the criminality of any specific individual or group. It is inevitable that organizations will arise to meet these demands and reap the profits. The impetus behind organized crime is not a criminal conspiracy, but simple market opportunity, which can also constrain organized crime's structure, form, and social perniciousness. Therefore, the market and its environment provide the most appropriate point of intervention in controlling organized crime.

ORGANIZED CRIME AS A COMMUNITY SOCIAL INSTITUTION

An important focal point for understanding organized crime is available in a body of literature viewing the **community** as a social system. Conceptual dimensions of this school of thought suggest that much could be learned by examining local community functions. Warren (1973: 9) defines community as "that combination of social units and systems which perform the major social functions having locality relevance." This definition offers several constituent elements. First, it recognizes a community's organization of social activities, rather than geographic or legal boundaries. Second, it conceptualizes *locality relevance* dimensions of community in terms of access points to the social activities and functions necessary for daily living. Specifically, Warren identifies five major community functions having locality relevance:

1. Production–distribution–consumption
2. Socialization
3. Social control
4. Social participation
5. Mutual support

The failure of the production–distribution–consumption function is the key element for organized crime's existence. The legitimate market's failure to serve sizable consumer populations is responsible for the existence of most vice operations. As a consequence, organized crime capitalizes on market voids and profits from services to these consumers. Several researchers (Merton 1957; Schelling 1976; Smith 1978) have noted similarities between legitimate and illegitimate businesses. Of course, organized crime's provision of consumer goods and delivery of services are defined predominantly as illegal. Nonetheless, demands by certain populations make the creation of such organizations inevitable. The organizing of crime results from the dynamics of the production–distribution–consumption function of the community.

Organized crime groups inevitably seek profitable and safe investments. Therefore, calculated movements into a community's commercial life through ownership of legitimate businesses are expected. Participation in legitimate business dimensions of the production–distribution–consumption process serves several needs (Anderson 1979a).

Alignment with Legitimate Business

First, legitimate businesses offer concealment opportunities for illegal activities. It is not unusual for these businesses to serve as pickup points for gambling operations, as disposal points for stolen goods, and as fronts for other vice operations. Second, these businesses provide money-laundering opportunities for illegal profits. The Pennsylvania Crime Commission (1980: 227–230) provides evidence of laundering operations involving banks, beer distributorships, car dealerships, bars, and nightclubs. Third, legitimate businesses provide sources of reportable and legitimate income. Organized crime groups regularly use bars and restaurants as legitimate reporting mechanisms because the high cash volumes associated with them are ideal for the concealment of illegal profits (Pennsylvania Crime Commission 1984).

Finally, active participation in legitimate businesses enhances the existence of high degrees of integration with members of the business community. Chambliss (1978) reported that distinctions between organized crime and legitimate businesses in Seattle were nearly impossible to discern. In their Morrisburg study, Potter and Jenkins (1985) reported intense intertwinement of legal and illegal businesses serving as gambling collection points, pornographic film distribution points, fencing and loan-sharking operations, and street-level prostitution operations.

Similarly, organized crime provides lucrative services to some businesspeople in a community. This does not imply either that all businesspeople deal with organized crime or that all organized crime activities are favorable for business. What it does indicate, however, is that in a significant number of specific situations businesspeople avail themselves of the services of organized crime. Relationships between fences and retail establishments, such as pawnshops and salvage yards, are particularly good examples.

Benefits for Legitimate Business

Additionally, organized crime's racketeering services provide businesses with potent weapons for harassing competitors or securing favorable employee contracts (Chambliss 1978; Pennsylvania Crime Commission 1980; Block and Chambliss 1981; Potter and Jenkins 1985). Numerous examples detailing this symbiotic relationship have been cited in the literature [e.g., the automobile industry's attempts to suppress unionization (Pearce 1976), local industry's collusion with the Teamsters (Chambliss 1978), the activities of the Roofer's Union (Pennsylvania Crime Commission 1980), and corruption in the garment manufacturing industry (Block and Chambliss 1981)]. Racketeering provides opportunities for collaborating with labor management in

You Decide

Can Law-Abiding People Tacitly Support Organized Crime?

Organized crime groups often supply illicit drugs. Consider someone you know who occasionally uses an illegal drug, such as a college student who smokes a marijuana joint at a party. Is this person guilty of supporting organized crime? You decide!

efforts to gain control of unions and their pension funds. The Teamsters union is an example of this relationship. Organized crime's extensive influence in Philadelphia area union health care plans is another example of this collusional relationship (Pennsylvania Crime Commission 1983).

Finally, businesspeople occasionally utilize organized crime's financial services in joint investment ventures. Numerous case studies have reported instances of local legitimate businesspeople openly engaging in partnerships with reputed organized crime figures, particularly in the trucking, construction, mining, and banking industries. This consensual relationship offers the advantage of stimulating quick capital accumulation for both parties. In addition, some illicit activity fails to supply quick capital needs that must be secured through ancillary legitimate sources. Drug networks offer investment opportunities for legitimate business capital that could subsequently be converted into wholesale illicit drug purchases. Furthermore, legitimate business holdings by gambling organizations have all but eliminated the need for lay-off services and provide avenues for profitable investments in real estate and local service industries.

Organized Crime Provides Benefits to Legitimate Businesses

- Harassment of business competitors
- Extra capital for joint investment ventures
- Opportunities for collaborating with management to control labor unions

Illicit Income for Community Members

Collusional relationships between organized crime groups and legitimate community businesspeople represent only a small part of the picture. Relative to a community's production–distribution–consumption function, organized crime often provides services and jobs for community residents that the legitimate world cannot or will not supply. Doing so is particularly important in depressed or economically declining areas. Laswell and McKenna (1971) identified the numbers business as the single largest employer in Bedford–Stuyvesant. Whyte (1961) reported that gambling operations often provide employment in legitimate business settings. In the Morrisburg study, Potter and Jenkins (1985)

Reasons That Organized Crime Aligns with Legitimate Business

- Collaborative business investments
- Concealment opportunities for illicit activities
- Provision of money-laundering resources
- Sources of reportable legitimate income
- The appearance of legitimacy

determined that the city's largest gambling organization provided full-time employment for at least fifty persons and part-time employment for many others. In addition, the gambling network provided supplemental income for persons who were on fixed or low incomes or who had other economic problems. Many of these participants had no moral or ethical opposition to gambling. Furthermore, these participants came to depend on this vital source of supplemental income.

Organized crime also provides prostitution, pornography, and drugs. Regardless of moral and political issues surrounding it, prostitution often employs women whose primary goal is to support their legitimate incomes. James (1976, 1977) argues that many women enter prostitution as a career choice that is made possible by organized vice operations. Numerous jobs are associated with both the legitimate and illegitimate sides of the production and distribution of pornography. Satchell (1979) and Kirk, et al. (1983) estimate the existence of 100,000 legal jobs in the pornography industry. Drug networks provide employment income for numerous participants occupying various levels in the organization.

An often overlooked aspect of organized crime is its provision of legitimate jobs for waitresses, clerks, technicians, and bartenders. It seems logical to argue that many people thus employed by organized crime operations could be threats to the community in other employment activities. Because many of these people are unskilled, not well socialized, and unemployable, poverty and unemployment could make them amenable to various predatory crimes directed at people within the community if they were not offered the option of taking such jobs in criminal enterprises. Therefore, in a bizarre way, organized crime can be said to reduce conventional criminality.

Legitimate Employment Opportunities

Another contribution relative to the provision of jobs is the economic enhancement associated with money received from organized crime groups. Whyte (1961) described Boston gamblers as free spenders at local businesses who probably use these businesses's legitimate services. Silberman (1978) suggests that gambling profits assist small shopkeepers in competing with chain stores or larger competitors. Although this could seem insignificant, money generated by organized crime can be an important determinant, especially in depressed areas, in the survival of some small businesses.

Organized crime often provides investment capital that would otherwise not be available from other sources. Developments in cities such as Las Vegas; Miami; Newport, Kentucky; and Saratoga Springs, New York, illustrate the power of organized crime's investment capital. Morrisburg gambling syndicates enhanced the survivability of small businesses that ultimately assisted in the revitalization of a sagging economy (Potter and Jenkins, 1985). The Pennsylvania Crime Commission (1980) estimated that mob-owned businesses employ approximately 2,000 persons in Pennsylvania's garment industry.

The **socialization** function is helpful in explaining why organized crime is not regarded as an inherent evil in all communities. Many years ago, Bell (1953: 13) proposed that crime was an American way of life. He argued that the pioneers of American capitalism were not graduates of the Harvard Business School, but amassed fortunes by "shady speculations and considerable amounts of violence." Bell (1953) and Ianni (1974), among others, have argued that crime, particularly organized crime, offers avenues for social mobility, especially in communities where legitimate paths are either blocked or difficult to achieve.

Community Acceptance of Organized Crime

Local studies of organized crime (Gardiner 1970; Potter and Jenkins 1985) lend credence to this argument. The communities studied (Wincanton and Morrisburg, respectively) had large populations of blue-collar, religiously oriented persons who had experienced economic decline and who had, in essence, seen their jobs and accustomed life-styles collapse. Most forms of basic manufacturing either reduced operations or experienced a complete shutdown, leaving residents with limited legitimate options for "success–goal" achievement.

In addition to the dearth of legitimate success routes, some communities have specific conditions that make innovation more likely to result in criminal outcomes (Abadinsky 1981: 30–32). Cohen (1965) argues that community reference groups shape modes of adaptation to social conditions. He suggests that in observing other people who have attained success by innovating, a sense of strain that helps shape future conformity develops. Other community members are influenced by reference groups' actions and means of success attainment (Cohen 1965: 6). Patterns of criminal socialization probably have their origins in socioeconomic stratification that relegates some people to environments in which a sense of strain is experienced (Abadinsky 1981: 31). Subsequent development patterns include identification and association with reference groups that innovated through criminal behavior.

Although empirical studies of organized crime have not specifically set out to evaluate these socialization processes, all have reflected on community socialization functions (Gardiner 1970; Albini 1971; Laswell and McKenna 1971; Ianni 1974; Chambliss 1978; Abadinsky 1981; Potter 1994). In each case, a strong sense of criminal–community history and a consistent reverence for that history have been reported. These studies also identified belief patterns that criminal organization members were not substantially different from their legitimate business and political counterparts. Most studies have reported well-defined systems of ethnic and socioeconomic neighborhood demarcation patterns.

A sense of economic and social desperation in communities that have experienced economic decline has also been identified consistently. Many neighborhoods where organized crime figures are active would have been classified as slums by some researchers. Finally, the existing information lends credence to the idea of the existence of socialization and social bonding processes that serve a recruitment function and ensure a sense of loyalty and belonging among organized criminals.

The Corruption Link

Understanding the social control function of a community is necessary to understanding its accommodations to organized crime. Since organized crime groups' illegal activities are continuous, these groups must seek accommodations from a community's formal social control entities. Hills (1969) argues that a basic characteristic of all organized crime is its collusion with enforcement and political structures. This close symbiosis between vice and political structures has been noted by numerous studies (Dorsett 1968, in Kansas City; Gardiner 1970, in Wincanton; Albini 1971, in Detroit; Haller 1972, in Chicago; Chambliss 1978, in Seattle; Bayor 1978, in New York City; Harring 1983, in Buffalo; Potter and Jenkins, 1985, in Philadelphia).

The compromises of the political and criminal justice systems include more than just graft and corruption; they also involve a subtle interplay among many community forces. These compromises not only make accommodations for organized crime with the criminal justice system, but also allow organized crime to be used as a means of resolving contradictions inherent in the enforcement of pertinent laws.

Selective enforcement of laws prohibiting illicit services provided by organized crime is inevitable (Schur 1965). Cooperation between consumer and supplier of illicit services necessitates discretion in enforcing these laws. This process enables organized crime to influence the processes of justice and social control.

Community members involved in illegal transactions do not perceive themselves as victims and consequently are unlikely to initiate complaints regarding them. In the absence of a complainant or a victim, the police have difficulty prosecuting offenders (McCaghy and Cernkovich 1987). When enforcement does occur, its selective nature invariably strengthens organized crime groups at the expense of individual entrepreneurs (McCaghy and Cernkovich 1987). Stronger organization by a group decreases risk of arrest. Consequently, people apprehended by the police are often those with greatest vulnerability. Highly visible streetwalkers and independent pushers, rather than call girls and middle-level distributors for organized groups, are more likely to become the focus of police activity.

Some argue that selective enforcement of laws is itself a vital control function. The reduction of the strain on the criminal justice system limits organizational strain and reduces the potential for violence, thereby strengthening the community's social control function. The consequences of dysfunctions in the criminal justice system can be illustrated by the mob war in Philadelphia in the early 1980s (Pennsylvania Crime Commission 1983; Potter and Jenkins 1985). Alternatively, cities in which corruption is maximized, as in Newport, Kentucky (Messick 1967); Wincanton (Gardiner 1970); Seattle (Chambliss 1978); and Morrisburg (Potter and Jenkins 1985), experience very rare and brief occurrences of organized crime-related violence.

An equally important consideration is that such an accommodation in enforcement reduces tension emanating from the law itself. Social control functions must decide whether to enforce legislation that lacks consensus. Groups offended by certain behaviors often engage in moral entrepreneurship (Gusfield 1963). Most often, these groups are assisted by law enforcement agencies pursuing their own agendas. Similarly, community elites seeking to expand their base of support often support criminalization efforts. As these groups converge, they create a powerful impetus, resulting in legal proscription against this behavior (Chambliss 1964, Becker 1976; 1963; Harring 1977; Hindus 1977).

Unfortunately, this process is not without contradictions. Powerful community forces that assist in the criminalization processes often are involved in illegal activities and, more important, profit directly or indirectly from them and pressure law enforcement to permit these activities. Hills (1969) proposes that *tolerance policies* are adopted as an effort to accommodate illegal interests. Community members choosing to participate in illegal activities do so under restricted conditions. These restrictions give those who are offended by illegal behaviors the impression that the law is being enforced. Tolerance policies often facilitate control of illicit activities through ecological or geographical confinement. Designated zones (e.g., Boston's Combat Zone or Philadelphia's Arch Street) are highly controlled and monitored, thereby reducing or preventing incidents that could cause illicit activities there to be investigated.

Finally, persons involved in social control functions often benefit directly from the presence of organized crime. High demands for illicit services generate huge profits sufficient to offer substantial inducements capable of encouraging the nonenforcement of these laws. Numerous studies (Gardiner 1970; Knapp Commission 1972; Pennsylvania Crime Commission 1974; Chambliss 1978) have documented this symbiotic relationship. Community members can benefit directly in the form of campaign funds, investment opportunities, assistance in negotiations relative to public service, and so on. A number of years ago, King (1969: 286) estimated that organized crime figures provided $2 billion annually in campaign contributions to public officials. Relationships between organized crime, politicians, and the police represent the ultimate example of the social control of crime in the community. Antagonists, situated at polar ends of the criminal justice continuum, are engaged in functional and profitable collaborative efforts.

Interfacing with the Community

Social participation and mutual support, as community functions, are highly interrelated. These processes of association explain a great deal about the organization of organized crime. As discussed previously, Albini (1971) characterizes organized crime as a **patron–client relationship** emerging from social participation in a community. Individuals involved in organized crime and its operations in this web of social participation are not, in many cases, directly part of an organization. The structure of relationships varies considerably with each participant. Albini (1971: 288) argues that "rather than being a criminal secret society, a criminal syndicate consists of a system of loosely structured relationships functioning primarily because each participant is interested in furthering his own welfare." The patron–client relationship has been observed by numerous studies of organized crime (e.g., Albini 1971; Block 1979; Reuter 1983; Potter and Jenkins 1985).

Organized crime's role in providing assistance to the community in its major functions while taking advantage of opportunities provided by the community makes organized crime a functional community institution. Although some view organized crime from a social pathological perspective, realistically and in reference to the exigencies of contemporary social, political, and economic structures, organized crime is a simple, fundamental fact of community life.

As noted, organized crime occupies a key role in a community's production–distribution–consumption function, which provides the rationale for the existence of organized crime. The community function provides the impetus for the creation of criminal enterprises, dictates their structures and means of operations, and makes profits possible. It is within this community function that interconnections between organized crime and other economic institutions exist, and it is the closeness of connections that creates difficulty in distinguishing between illegal and legal commerce.

Organized crime also occupies an important position in a community's socialization functions. It not only socializes its participants, but also supports broad dimensions defining parameters of acceptable behavior, legally or illegally. Organized crime serves as a model for use of talents, including innovation, in specific social settings and as a means for adapting to exigencies within social, political, and economic environments.

Organized crime frequently complements functions of formal social control agencies. While actively engaging in some forms of violent predatory crime (probably instrumental forms surrounding control mechanisms), it provides protection against other forms of predatory crime in some cases. It sets limits on illegal behavior and controls disruptive activities that the law cannot. An ameliorative influence is provided in response to deficiencies relative to social order maintenance functions.

Organized crime often provides a socially acceptable means for social participation to persons otherwise excluded from community functions. Existing as a massive social network, organized crime is interconnected with numerous segments of a community and provides opportunities for political, social, and economic participation. It services a complementary function to upperworld agencies with important forms of support. Finally, it often serves a cohesive function by strengthening social interaction patterns within some families and other social groupings within a community.

Community is a broad term, encompassing numerous aspects of social and political life. Organized crime serves a functional role in the community. Organized crime often maximizes opportunities and fills voids associated with a community's failure to provide adequate employment opportunities, sufficient retirement benefits, adequate information and assistance in providing and locating adequate housing and consumer goods, and sufficient funding to strengthen legitimate economic enterprises on which many community members depend for survival. In a strange and unique way, organized crime probably serves an effective social welfare function for many segments of some communities. These intricate and interconnected patterns within the community's basic social functions best explain the persistence and durability of organized crime in America.

WHAT HAVE WE LEARNED?

One way to obtain a better understanding of the unique dynamics of organized crime is to understand why persons pursue criminal careers with violent criminal organizations. One could argue that profit is a clear enough motivation, but this fails to explain the ease with which many organized crime members perform their ruthless actions. Rational choice theory is rooted in one perverse aspect of U.S. values: that only suckers work and that in our society people can choose either to be suckers or to seek easy money through exceptional illicit opportunities. This school of thought interfaces with the deterrence theory, which suggests that one reason many people choose not to pursue criminal careers is that they fear being detected, prosecuted, and imprisoned. Of course, if this theory has any relevance, it would apply only to people who perceive the justice system as being at least moderately effective.

Psychologists suggest that the most dangerous criminals are those with antisocial and dependent personalities that persons with these personalities might be predisposed to join the ranks of violent criminal groups.

Enterprise theory suggests that the laws of supply and demand play an important role in the willingness of a criminal group to enter into criminal behavior. Finally, social disorganization theories suggest that a breakdown in social norms and opportunities has occurred and that the resulting frustration causes people to choose criminality as their only source of success.

Social scientists will probably never reach consensus about the exact causes of criminal behavior or the reasons that individuals are attracted to group criminal behavior such as organized crime. What is evident is that organized crime represents one of the most violent and insidious forms of criminality known in the world and that persons belonging to it seem to readily accept its violence, greed, and damage to society. As we explore other aspects of organized crime in subsequent chapters, we encourage the reader to refer to this chapter to identify causes for people to join organized crime groups.

DO YOU RECOGNIZE THESE TERMS?

alien conspiracy theory
anomie theory
classical school of criminology
community
cultural deviance theories
cultural transmission
culture conflict theory
differential association
differential opportunity
enterprise theory
ethnic succession

general deterrence theory
Marxist criminology
patron–client relationship
rational choice theory
relative deprivation
risk assessment
socialization
socioeconomic stratification
sociopathic personality
special deterrence theory

POINTS OF DISCUSSION

1. When considering group and individual organized crime dynamics, which theory of criminality seems most appropriate to you? Why?

2. Explain why you agree or disagree with the premise that organized crime is a social institution.

3. Explain how organizational theory helps us understand the concept and function of organized crime.

4. Discuss the ways in which organized crime complements the functions of formal social control agencies.

5. Discuss the various theories that might help explain a person's attraction to and an involvement in the subcultures of outlaw motorcycle gangs.

6. Consider the patron–client relationship as it relates to organizational theory and explain how groups that appear on the surface to be formalized, such as the La Cosa Nostra, can operate as a social institution as well.

7. Is it possible that criminal organizations that do not have a clearly defined hierarchy of command can effectively operate as an organized crime unit over an extended period of time? Explain.

SUGGESTED READING

CLOWARD, R. A., and L. E. OHLIN. (1960). *Delinquency and Opportunity: A Theory of Delinquent Gangs.* New York: Free Press. This book explores the causes of crime and delinquency in terms of a theory of differential opportunity systems.

CRESSEY, D. (1969). *Theft of the Nation: The Structure and Operations of Organized Crime in America.* New York: Harper & Row. This presents an in-depth review of the methods and organization of the criminal syndicate, which provides illicit goods and services by corrupting officials.

HOMANS, G. C. (1961). *Social Behavior: Its Elementary Forms.* New York: Harcourt, Brace and World.

IANNI, F. A. J. (1974). *Black Mafia: Ethnic Succession in Organized Crime.* New York: Simon & Schuster. This research describes the takeover of crime operation by black and Puerto Rican networks that are replacing the Italian families.

PEARCE, F. (1976). *Crimes of the Powerful: Marxism, Crime and Deviance.* London: Pluto Press. This book discusses the role of the ruling corporate and political interests in the creation of deviance, white-collar crime, and organized crime.

SHAW, C., and H. D. MCKAY. (1972). *Juvenile Delinquency and Urban Areas.* Chicago: University of Chicago Press. This work explores the ecology of crime and delinquency in Chicago, with comparative data for other large U.S. cities.

SMITH, D. C., JR. (1990). *The Mafia Mystique*. Lanham, MD: University Press of America. This book examines the history of the concepts and imagery of Mafia and organized crime, the interaction of the imagery with current events, and the significance of this process.

VOLD, G., and T. BERNARD. (1986). *Theoretical Criminology*, 3rd ed. New York: Oxford University Press. This revised edition of George Vold's 1958 classic work discusses all major criminological theories, from eighteenth-century theories through the more modern sociological, economic, biological, physiological, and Marxist explanations of crime.

WHYTE, W. F. (1961). *Street Corner Society*. Chicago: University of Chicago Press.

—3————————————

THE EVOLUTION OF ORGANIZED CRIME

Urban Beginnings and Major Participants

This chapter will enable you to:

- Appreciate the significance of Irish immigration to the United States at the turn of the century
- Learn the role of the political machine in the early twentieth century
- Learn about various events that led to Prohibition

- Learn about the evolution of criminal organizations in Philadelphia, Chicago, and New York
- Understand the significance of ethnic makeup in the composition of organized crime groups

INTRODUCTION

As we discussed in Chapter 1, Italian crime groups have dominated much of the literature of organized crime for decades. As a result, the public perception of organized crime is that it is solely an Italian American phenomenon. However, history tells us that this is not the case. Nearly a century ago Irish and Jewish criminals also used organized crime to attain wealth and stature in their new country. Organized crime historian Haller (1972) explains:

> Those groups that became most heavily involved in organized crime migrated from regions in which they had developed deep suspicions of governmental authority. . . . Within a community suspicious of courts and government officials, a person in trouble with the law could retain roots and even respect within that community.

Poor immigrants and their children often had vocational choices related to politics, labor unions, sports, entertainment, and businesses such as construction that often relied on political contracts. These businesses had an undercurrent of criminality and corruption, but immigrants were not forced to turn to a life of crime. For example, aspiring politicians often used money (and personnel) from gambling operations to get elected. Also, organized crime figures worked closely with labor racketeers. In some areas, such as Chicago, there was barely a distinction between the worlds of organized crime and the entertainment industry.

Among members of this underworld society, the prevailing attitude was that "criminal justice institutions were just another racket, not an unrealistic assessment considering the degree to which the police, the courts, and prosecutors were, in fact, used by political factions, and often favored criminal groups" (Haller 1972).

In the early twentieth century, the Irish played the dominant role in organized crime in Chicago. They ran major gambling syndicates, were leaders in labor racketeering, and, as an outgrowth of these rackets, became involved in politics and even law enforcement careers. In short, they were at the apex of both the city's political and criminal hierarchy. Also in Chicago during this time, people of Jewish ancestry were also active in criminal enterprises, but made their contribution to organized crime primarily by taking supportive roles, such as bail bondsmen and fences (outlets for stolen goods).

By World War I, Italian criminals had moved into vice as their primary money-making activity, but soon were blocked by Irish competitors. Then Prohibition occurred as the first generation of Jewish and Italian youngsters were reaching adulthood. To a great extent, Prohibition provided Italians and others a major opportunity to break into a major field of organized crime that was not already monopolized by the Irish (Haller 1979).

The immigrant groups were not the only ones who became involved in organized crime, however. As we discuss in Chapter 6, African Americans, who were moving into the urban areas in search of jobs, were just as susceptible to the allure of huge profits and local power as other groups. During the 1920s, running the numbers, policy gambling, and prostitution served as growth enterprises for many African American criminal entrepreneurs. In turn, African American political strength grew in many urban areas as an outgrowth of illicit gambling enterprises. In cities such as Chicago and Detroit, African American criminals seemed to gain more influence and power than they did in other cities. In the 1930s African American gambling operations in many large cities were closely tied to politics. As a result, their gambling operations enjoyed political protection from being taken over by competing criminals until the end of World War II. As the decades passed, African American organized criminals continued their involvement in gambling and increasingly participated in drug trafficking, sometimes securing drugs from Italian and Jewish importers. Since the mid-1970s, African American drug traffickers have also turned to Cuban and Colombian importers for their wares.

As this indicates, a number of ethnic groups participated in what we now know as organized crime. Although it is difficult to draw conclusions and make assumptions about the relationships among these groups, it is important to have a basic understanding of the role they played in the evolution of organized crime.

THE IRISH IMMIGRATION

By most accounts, the first major immigrant group to enter the United States, the Irish, arrived in large numbers between 1820 and 1850. The massive immigration was blamed on the failed potato crop in Ireland during the 1840s, the widespread famine that followed, and British colonial oppression of Irish citizens. During a four-year period in the 1840s, more than 250,000 Irish

Catholics entered the United States, followed by an additional 1.5 million by 1854 (Bennett 1988). In fact, Buenker (1973) suggests that in the largest cities in the northeastern United States, Irish immigrants composed more than two-thirds of the population. They were the first English-speaking immigrants to arrive in the United States who were not predominantly Anglo-Saxon in origin. Like other European immigrants who would come to the United States, however, they were segregated in urban slums. Because of this, most Irish immigrants were precluded from their traditional occupation of farming, and a majority of them sought work as unskilled laborers, the only jobs open to them in the industrial areas of large cities.

An interesting comparison of Irish and Sicilian immigrants later in the nineteenth century can be made. As we observed in Chapter 1, for generations Sicilian people had been oppressed by foreign, absentee landlords, which resulted in an informal social mechanism referred to as the Mafia. As far back as the sixteenth century, the Irish experienced a similar oppression by the British government that imposed Protestantism on the mostly Catholic population and that denied the basic rights of land ownership and means of economic production. The British seized the most valued land in Ireland, which became dominated by a system of excessive rents and taxes focused on the already impoverished native Irish. As with the Sicilian immigrants who came to the United States later, Irish immigrants were met with anti-Catholic prejudice, generally preventing their upward social mobility. Consequently, Irish Catholics huddled close in their Irish-dominated neighborhoods.

Rather than relying on the formal system of government imposed on them by the British, the Irish created an informal social system of negotiating and bargaining to achieve amenable outcomes for social conflicts and concerns. With the rule of Britain upon them, the Irish slowly became a politicized people who joined both secret and public organizations to resist the despotic British government. As with the Sicilians, the Irish grew to resent the government, formal law, and the educational system. Rather than pursuing a formalized education, the Irish thought that employment in politics and government was the most logical and attainable path to social mobility. They viewed the Democratic party as an outlet for voicing their social and political needs. Following this path was easier to accomplish for Irish immigrants than for the Sicilians because the Irish spoke English and had a working knowledge of the British system of government, many aspects of which had been retained in the United States. With larger numbers of Irish becoming involved in politics and government, crime rates dropped dramatically in many Irish neighborhoods, at least until the Prohibition era began in 1920.

The Political Machine (1830–1919)

Urban politics became the route for Irish immigrants to follow to attain local power and upward mobility. In most cases, the local politician was closely affiliated with corner taverns and often some aspects of criminality. Tavern operators frequently doubled as local politicians (machine politician), and the tavern owner and his followers easily influenced the tavern's customers. This became especially important in the large cities, where local government was fragmented into wards, each of which was sectioned into precincts. It was common then for politicians, with the help of local gangs and other supporters, to deliver a lopsided vote on election day to ensure the dominance of Democrats. In exchange for their help in securing votes, the machine politician reciprocated by finding these supporters jobs, housing, and assistance from government agencies in the district. The only thing asked in return was a vote, enabling politicians to become increasingly powerful and wealthy.

The Tammany Hall Machine

The name **Tammany Hall** has become synonymous with political corruption in New York. This political organization controlled New York politics from the early days of the United States until its demise. Tammany Hall, which took its name from the Indian Chief Tammaned, was founded in 1789 to oppose the ruling conservative Federalist party, which failed to represent the interests of less affluent citizens.

Tammany Hall was incorporated as a fraternal society in 1805 and was aligned closely with the newly emerging Democratic party. With the arrival of the Irish immigrants, Tammany Hall was soon in the hands of Irish politicians, who pushed aside traditional political factions while claiming to represent the interests of all other ethnic and religious groups in Manhattan.

The organization's strength was based on its ability to elect candidates to the state legislature in Albany and to the board of aldermen in New York City. Tammany reached its peak of political power during the 1860s when William March Tweed became head of Tammany's general committee. Tweed went on to become state senator in 1868 and facilitated the 1870 passage of a city charter that allowed Tammany Hall the authority to control the city's treasury

At the turn of the century, Tammany Hall, which began as a fraternal organization, became synonymous with New York City's corrupt political machine.

without interference. Soon, the Tweed ring pillaged millions of dollars using bid-rigging schemes, padded payrolls, and overpriced goods and services provided by Tammany thugs.

The spoils of Tammany were plentiful to the politicians who controlled it over the years. For example, Richard "Boss" Croker was a Tammany boss from 1886 until he retired to Ireland with his fortune in 1903. In the following decade, "Big Tim" Sullivan, owner of the luxurious Hesper Club, a lower east side gambling den, dominated Tammany Hall. In the tradition of his predecessors, Tweed and Croker, Sullivan protected vice operators in New York while delivering the Democratic vote at election time. Tammany's power was reduced in 1932 after political factions in Manhattan failed to lend support to Sullivan's candidacy for president. Later that same year, Mayor James "Jimmy" Walker resigned in the aftermath of the Seabury investigations, which uncovered layers of municipal graft in virtually all city agencies. For the next thirty years, Tammany continued its decline at the hands of reform mayors such as Fiorello H. La Guardia and John V. Lindsay.

The Pendergast Political Machine

Just as Irish organized criminals used the political machine in cities such as New York, Chicago, and Boston, other gangsters made good use of it in other U.S. cities. Although researchers suggest that the era of the political machine technically ended in 1919, variations of it continued to proliferate across the United States for more than a decade. In Kansas City, the Pendergast political machine dominated politics for more than five decades. It also can be used to illustrate the power and effectiveness of the political machine in local government.

Thomas Joseph Pendergast operated a typical political machine that ultimately became famous as one of the most powerful, corrupt, and violent in U.S. history. He was one of the few political bosses who participated in meetings during the 1920s and 1930s in which organized crime planned Prohibition and gambling strategies. Tom's older brother, James Pendergast developed the machine around the turn of the century. After his death in 1910, the younger Pendergast, with the help of gang bosses Johnny Lazia, Jake "Cutcherheadoff" Weissman, and city manager Tom McElroy, transformed Kansas City into a nationally recognized center of vice. The machine operated by requiring virtually every tavern and saloon in the city to pay tribute to Lazia's and Weissman's goons, who would, in turn, pay off the police and provide a handsome percentage of the spoils to Pendergast himself.

Lazia and Weissman controlled vice in Kansas City; no illegal rackets operated without their permission. In turn, they welcomed almost every midwestern hood and murderer to Kansas City, which later became known as the crime corridor of the 1930s. The welcome came with a proviso: Outsiders could always find refuge in Kansas City, but could not engage in criminal activities there. All criminal rackets, including gambling and liquor operations, were the province of Weissman's and Lazia's own people. Unlike their vulgar counterparts—Al Capone in Chicago, "Lucky" Luciano in New York, and Ed Fleisher of the Purple Gang in Detroit—the Kansas City crime bosses were sophisticated, charming, and mild mannered. Lazia, for example, dressed like a banker, had impeccable manners, was very soft spoken, and almost never cursed.

Tom Pendergast, posing with his wife, was the boss of Kansas City's powerful and corrupt political machine of the 1930s.

To ensure the promptness of liquor deliveries and the weekly kickbacks on gambling, prostitution, and liquor, Weissman and Lazia employed an army of henchmen. Their power rested in Pendergast's ability to control local politics by using strong-arm squads to ensure that any election turned out to be a victory for him and his cronies.

In 1933 the bloodiest crime event of the decade, the **Union Station Massacre,** occurred in Kansas City. It was a gory event personally orchestrated by Lazia to free bank robber and killer Frank "Jelly" Nash from the custody of FBI agents, who were transporting him to federal prison. The massacre brought Kansas City into national focus as a slaughterhouse safe for no one.

The news of the massacre shook the Pendergast machine as the political boss realized that one of his crime boss allies was no longer able to maintain a low public profile. In addition to encouraging local reform politicians to act against Lazia, Pendergast marked him for elimination. As a result, bootlegging and tax evasion charges were brought against Lazia in 1933. Shortly after Lazia's criminal conviction for tax evasion in 1934, he was machine-gunned down in the street. It was suspected that he might become an informer against the political machine's boss, Pendergast.

In the late 1930s the government began to crack down on crime in Kansas City, partly as a result of the blatantly fraudulent 1936 election. An FBI investigation ordered by federal judge Albert L. Reeves revealed evidence of stuffed ballot boxes, voter intimidation, vote theft, and erasures of votes from ballots in that election. At last, the Pendergast machine was doomed, with the criminal convictions of 256 Pendergast followers charged with vote fraud. Pendergast himself was convicted in 1939 on charges of tax evasion and died in 1945. As a result, the Pendergast machine fell into extinction.

THE EARLY DRUG SYNDICATES (1915–1930)

Gambling, prostitution, and loan-sharking were usually associated with organized crime groups in U.S. cities throughout the nineteenth and twentieth centuries. Vice syndicates allied themselves with political machines in these cities. Large organizations, which extended beyond city neighborhoods, came into existence only if the market required that an infrastructure be created to obtain and distribute illegal commodities over wide areas, especially if the goods had to be imported from abroad.

The importation of bootlegged liquor during the Prohibition years was the most obvious and celebrated example of this market dynamic. Even prior to liquor prohibition, however, a criminal syndication had imported and distributed opiates and cocaine to the U.S. public. As early as the late nineteenth century, W. W. Whaley was identified in the popular press as the King of the Opium Rings, with charges that he controlled the Pacific trade in opiates (Silver 1979: 24–25). For years, opiates and cocaine products had been freely available in over-the-counter patent medicines, soft drinks, and wines in the United States. By the turn of the twentieth century the United States was estimated to have more than 500,000 opiate addicts, most of whom were white, middle-age, middle-class women.

The passage of the Harrison Narcotics Act in 1914 could have provided the additional stimulus that transformed isolated and localized drug rings such as Whaley's into national organized crime groups (Brecher 1972: 48–63). The attempt to control opiate distribution through the Harrison Act and the subsequent outlawing of opiates and cocaine through the bureaucratic machinations of the Federal Bureau of Narcotics left a huge drug market unserved.

Considerable evidence suggests that crime was becoming syndicated prior to the passage of the Volstead Act and the outlawing of liquor. For example, in 1915 an American, Henry Goddard Thomas, went on trial in Paris (Silver 1979: 60). He had formed a narcotics trust modeled directly on the corporate structure of Standard Oil. By 1917, Philadelphia had become a major link in a cocaine-trafficking network, supplying drugs to much of the east coast (Block and Chambliss 1981: 51, 59). By the 1920s the tabloid press noted the existence of tightly organized criminal networks specializing in drugs long before they discovered the operations of bootlegging organizations. The press referred to the opium ring and the international drug ring, headed by an unidentified "big fellow" (Silver 1979: 41). It is probable that this unidentified big fellow of the drug world was Arnold "the Brain" Rothstein.

Much information points to Rothstein's direct involvement in narcotics trafficking. More important, there is abundant evidence that Rothstein also maintained corrupt relations with members of New York City's Narcotics Squad (Silver 1979: 100–103). (We take a closer look at Rothstein's role in organized crime later in this chapter.) The collaboration between criminals, politicians, and law enforcement members seems to have occurred in the drug trade prior to Prohibition. So drug trafficking in the early twentieth century appears to indicate a new intercity, interregional, and perhaps even international dimension for organized crime. Newspaper reports such as those appearing in 1926 declaring that "Drug Bosses Run Buffalo," which alleged that organized criminals dealing in drugs were holding an entire city hostage to permit imports from Canada, could indicate the early shifts in organized crime from localized criminal–politician alliances to the syndicates of the 1920s and 1930s (Silver 1979: 236).

Although moderate drinking was generally accepted during the eighteenth century, by the early nineteenth century some people had begun to perceive an increase in the abuse of alcohol. The American Temperance Society, founded in 1826, began gathering pledges of abstinence, marking the beginning of the **temperance movement.** In the 1840s the Washington Temperance Societies conducted revival-style meetings to encourage similar pledges. As early as 1846 the state of Maine was persuaded to outlaw alcohol, followed by similar attempts elsewhere. However, these efforts were hampered by the Civil War, and despite the passage of many liquor laws, the sale and use of alcohol remained widespread.

The national **Prohibition** movement, also known as the **Noble Experiment,** was spearheaded by prohibitionists, who ostensibly believed that alcohol was a dangerous drug that destroyed lives and disrupted families and communities. Consequently, they believed that it was the responsibility of the government to prohibit its sale. Between 1880 and 1890, a new wave of prohibition sentiment swept the Evangelical Protestant churches. Organized by the Woman's Christian Temperance Union (WCTU), the Anti-Saloon League of America, and the National Prohibition Party, prohibitionists pressured their local politicians for an amendment to the Constitution banning the sale of alcohol.

The sentiments behind the Prohibition movement are vital to an understanding of the development of organized crime in America. In his classic study of the Prohibition movement, *Symbolic Crusade*, Gusfield (1963) argues persuasively that the anti-alcohol movements had less to do with the evils of John Barleycorn than with a pervasive distrust and nativist hatred of recent immigrants. Contrary to the mythology of high school civic books, the citizens of the United States did not open their arms to the "tired and the poor" from foreign shores. In fact, they subjected immigrants, particularly those who were Catholic or non-English speaking, to widespread discrimination; denied them access to jobs, education, and medical care; and at least initially, excluded them from the political system. Immigrants huddled together in ethnic slums similar to the inner-city ghettos of the late twentieth century. Gusfield claims that the Prohibition movement was primarily a nativist reaction to these immigrants.

Prohibition was also an attempt by white rural Protestants to reassert their authority and political power against the growing power of urban immigrants. When we speak of early organized criminals as being Jewish, Italian, or Irish immigrants, we are certainly not pointing to any criminogenic characteristics of these cultures or any moral or intellectual inferiority of newly arrived citizens. The importance of the waves of immigration in organized crime is the reaction of white Anglo-Saxon Protestants to them. The prejudice and discrimination experienced by certain groups attracted some of them to crime, as they do Latino and African American youth today.

The **Eighteenth Amendment** was passed in January 1919 followed nine months later by the passage of the **Volstead Act,** which provided an enforcement mechanism to the prohibition of alcohol. Once in place, the law was enforced sporadically and met with considerable public opposition. Soon, bootlegging, speakeasies (illegal nightclubs), and smuggling flourished under the direction and dominance of local gangsters. It was estimated that Chicago had approximately 10,000 speakeasies in operation at any given time during the Prohibition era. Opponents of the law claimed that it was ineffective and represented an unnecessary restriction of personal choice. As a result, a massive campaign to repeal the amendment was mounted and achieved success in 1933 with the ratification of the Twenty-first Amendment. Thereafter, the temperance movement faded.

Prohibition created a virtual gold mine for crime, which made millionaires out of petty thugs such as Frank Costello, "Waxie" Gordon, Lucky Luciano, Al Capone, Dutch Schultz, and many others. It tainted politics and corrupted police officers. It set the stage for one of the most lawless periods in U.S. history—the roaring twenties. Despite the newly passed law, no one would go thirsty during this period. Flappers, bobbed hair, the Charleston, coonskin coats, the hip flask, and other memorabilia gave this period its distinctive color. However, the glitter and party atmosphere were provided by organized criminal forces that took great advantage of America's preoccupation with the good life.

The need for a massive infrastructure to handle public demand for alcohol soon became obvious to many entrepreneurial criminals. Factories were needed to produce it, a transportation system was needed to ship it in bulk, and an importation system capable of dealing with large, bulk shipments from England, Cuba, and Canada had to be constructed. Prohibition brought with it a demand for precisely the type of organization that Henry Goddard Thomas had envisioned for drugs a few years earlier. This market demand for a more complex organization, combined with subsequent advances in electronic technology that would revolutionize communications and subsequently revolutionize gambling, brought organized crime into the modern age.

Prohibition required a concentration of power in criminal activity at two levels: within individual cities and states and on a national scale. After 1933 the new organizational structure was carried over into other forms of enterprise, such as gambling and labor racketeering (summary based on Messick 1972, 1973; Ianni 1973; Fried 1980; Abadinsky 1981: 100–109).

THE CHICAGO MOB

Prohibition and the political machine in Chicago came together to create one of the most notorious criminal organizations in U.S. history. The political machine was in control of Chicago as well as New York City and Kansas City. Turn of the century machine bosses such as William "Big Bill" Thompson and Mont Tennes changed the history of Chicago forever by creating and fostering a spoils system in which corruption was the common way of conducting daily business. However, it was newcomer Al Capone who caused Chicago to be epitomized as one of the most ruthless and crime-ridden towns in the nation.

Al Capone (1899–1947)   Al Capone's white hat, scarred pudgy face, and complacent sneer became parts of the quintessential caricature of a gangster. Although some thought that Capone was born in Naples, he was actually born in Brooklyn, New York, in 1899. Although he never got past the fourth grade, Capone learned all he ever needed to know by running the streets between Gowanus Canal and the harbor in a street gang known as the Five Pointers.

Frankie Yale, a flamboyant and vicious mob boss who controlled many of the New York street-gang protection rackets, recognized certain talents in

Al Capone was a flamboyant and vicious crime boss in Chicago during Prohibition.

Capone, including both his toughness and willingness to follow orders. Yale put Capone to work as a bartender and greeter at the Harvard Inn, a Coney Island dime-a-dance club, and became young Capone's mentor. Al never questioned Yale's orders or opinions on the rackets, but Capone began to act on his own. At one point he was suspected of committing two murders and nearly killing a member of "Wild Bill" Lovett's White Hand gang. Capone had only two options: leave New York or risk being killed.

In 1920, Johnny Torrio, also Capone's mentor, brought Capone to Chicago to work with crime boss "Big Jim" Colosimo, Torrio's uncle. Colosimo, who was known as the largest operator of prostitution in Chicago, had risen from an immigrant ditch digger to be the owner of a fashionable café and a political power in Chicago's first ward. However, Colosimo was not as progressive as many of his contemporaries. He was aware of the impending Prohibition amendment, but resisted entering into the liquor rackets because he felt that his prostitution rackets were sufficiently lucrative. It became evident to the newer, more aggressive crime figures in Chicago that Colosimo had to go because the potential liquor profits were just too great to pass up. Finally, Colosimo was found shot to death in his office in his Wabash Avenue café.

Capone's Move to Chicago

Torrio, known for his intellect more than his toughness, seized the opportunity to take over Colosimo's rackets and expand them with the help of Capone. Torrio saw all the possibilities of Prohibition even before its enactment and quickly bought breweries to ready his organization for the coming demands of the "big thirst." In addition, Torrio painstakingly convinced other gangsters in Chicago to stop fighting among themselves for turf in the city and to settle for assigned territories. Dion O'Banion, a ruthless killer, was given the north side of the city. Other territories were assigned to several local gangs, but Torrio and Capone claimed the majority of Chicago, including the suburbs. By 1924, they were splitting $100,000 per week after expenses. As Torrio turned his attention to intercity alliances and future prospects, Capone became more involved in the day to day operations of the syndicate.

Capone soon developed a reputation as a benevolent crime king who was providing the people of Chicago what they wanted most: beer and liquor. He began to exert political influence in the city. During 1924, in the aftermath of one of the bloodiest campaigns in U.S. history, Capone's puppet candidate was elected mayor of Cicero, a city that became known as one of the country's most wide-open cities, as well as a power base for Capone. From Cicero, Capone gradually gained control of rackets in virtually all of Chicago. He ruled as defacto mayor, police chief, and fire chief from his headquarters in the Hawthorne Hotel.

Trouble for O'Banion had been brewing for some time because he had been hijacking Torrio and Capone's liquor. It finally came to a head in late 1924. Torrio, Capone, and O'Banion were uneasy partners in a brewery, but the Irishman sold out shortly before a raid (which he knew about beforehand). Torrio was arrested in the raid, and because it was his second liquor violation, he was fined $5,000 and sentenced to serve nine months in jail. Confrontation between Capone and O'Banion was therefore inevitable. On November 2, 1924, O'Banion was shot to death in his northside flower shop.

Succeeding O'Banion as the northside gang leader was Polish-born Hymie Weiss. Weiss and his gang retaliated for O'Banion's murder on January 12, 1925, by ambushing Capone at a street corner in downtown Chicago. Although Capone escaped unharmed, his mentor Johnny Torrio was not so lucky. He was ambushed later that day at his home and was shot five times. Three weeks later, Torrio, wrapped in bandages, began serving his nine-month sentence. When released, Torrio retired from the rackets, supposedly with a $30 million fortune. Upon his retirement, Al Capone became Chicago's new crime boss. The war continued, and Capone finally decided that Weiss had to be eliminated. One day as Weiss was walking from his car to his headquarters, two gunmen blasted the northside gang boss with machine gun and shotgun fire.

The St. Valentine's Day Massacre

With Weiss dead, opposition to Capone fell to another gang leader, Charles "Bugs" Moran. Moran's headquarters were located in a Clark Street garage, which was the site of the **St. Valentine's Day Massacre.** The massacre was ordered by Capone, planned by "Machine Gun" Jack McGurn, and carried out by two of Chicago's most notorious killers, Albert Anselmi and John Scalisi. After ordering the massacre, Capone left Chicago for his Florida home, thus providing himself an alibi.

The hit men, dressed as police officers, were driven to the garage in a black limousine. Believing them to be real police officers, Moran's men offered no resistance and lined up spread eagle on the garage wall. The hit men then opened fire, spraying them with a hail of machine gun bullets from left to right. The massacre left seven dead on the floor of the garage. No one was ever tried for the killings, but Anselmi and Scalisi were murdered later by Capone himself.

The Untouchables

It was becoming apparent among Chicago's business leaders and organized crime leaders that something had to be done about Capone. In March 1929, a group of Chicago citizens visited President Herbert Hoover to urge the repeal of Prohibition and ask for help in controlling Capone. As a result, the Treasury Department assigned Agent Eliot Ness to the Chicago Police Department. Ness, aware of widespread corruption within the police department, selected a special squad of officers with whom to work. In typical mob fashion, efforts were made to bribe Ness and his men, but were unsuccessful.

More in legend than in fact, the personal integrity of Ness and his band of detectives earned them the name the **Untouchables** from journalists. Ness and his men relentlessly pursued Capone and his gang, serving search warrants and conducting midnight raids. Although much liquor was seized and destroyed during these raids, Ness was unable to obtain sufficient evidence to arrest Capone. Finally, someone in the Treasury Department came up with the idea of prosecuting the gangster not as a boss of the rackets, but as an income tax evader. Messick suggests that it was Meyer Lansky's brother Jake who persuaded the government to follow this strategy (Messick and Goldblatt 1976). After inquiries into Capone's business dealings, investigators discovered that he had more than $165,000 of taxable income on which no tax had been paid. Another lucky break came when Ness was successful in placing an informer, "Artful" Eddie O'Hare, Capone's lawyer, within the Capone organization. These innovative approaches paid off in Capone's indictment for income tax evasion in June 1931. Capone was convicted on the charge and sentenced to eleven years in prison and an $80,000 fine by Judge James H. Wilkerson.

Until Capone, law enforcement had not considered the tax evasion angle, but it soon became more widely used against other gangsters. After spending two years in an Atlanta prison, Capone was transferred to the prison island of Alcatraz, off the coast of San Francisco. Suffering from syphilis, he was released in 1939 and spent his final years at his Florida estate. According to many sources, he virtually lost his mind during his final years and finally died on January 25, 1947, at the age of 48.

As a graduate of westside Chicago's old "42 gang," Sam Giancana became part of one of the nation's most notorious criminal syndicates, which became known as the outfit. As parttime chauffeur and "wheelman" for Capone during the 1940s, Giancana dutifully accepted his assignments, regardless of how dangerous they were. He had more than seventy arrests dating from 1925 when a Selective Service interviewer asked Sam what he did for a living. He replied "Me? I steal." The Selective Service classified Giancana as a psychopath and sent him home, preventing his military induction.

Sam Giancana (1908–1975)

After being sentenced to a term in federal prison at Terre Haute, Indiana, Giancana met Chicago gangster Edward "Teenan" Jones, who convinced him that Chicago's southside gambling rackets were the most lucrative enterprises in the city. Released from prison, Giancana moved into the southside gambling rackets.

The aging of Chicago's bosses played the largest role in Giancana's rise to the top of the outfit. Jake Guzik, Sam "Golf Bag" Hunt, Phil D'Andrea, and Louis Campagna were all Prohibition veterans whose retirement paved the way for younger gangsters to move up the hierarchy. By the mid-1950s,

Giancana was acting as manager of operations, and by 1957 he was alleged to be the head of the Chicago outfit a position he enjoyed until 1966 when the government escalated its efforts against him. This increased focus on Giancana was partly due to the seventy-nine mob-related murders during his nine-year rule. This compares to twenty-four murders during the eight years following Giancana's rule.

Giancana was noted for many things during his reign in Chicago, one of which was his resistance to the old ways and traditions brought to the United States from Sicily and commonly practiced by the old-guard mobsters such as Carlo Gambino. Indeed, Giancana was not a native Italian but a product of the streets of Chicago. Anyone who earned income for the outfit automatically earned his respect without regard to ethnicity or tradition.

In the 1960s during the Kennedy administration, Giancana, Santo Traficante, and Johnny Roselli were hired by the CIA to assassinate Cuba's Fidel Castro. The go-between who transferred messages between Giancana and the White House was Howard Hughes's chief of security and former FBI agent, Robert Maher. The botched attempts on Castro's life provided other sources of unwanted media and law enforcement attention on Giancana. This attention highlighted other aspects of his life, including his celebrated affair with singer Phyllis McGuire of the famed McGuire Sisters and his opulent estate in Cuernavaca, Mexico, which were already the subject of gossip columnists. In 1965, Giancana was sent to prison for one year for failing to cooperate with a government probe into organized crime. Upon his release, he went into self-imposed exile in Mexico and South America.

FBI scrutiny of the gangster was relentless, and in July 1974 Giancana was arrested by Mexican authorities and flown to San Antonio where federal agents were waiting. From there, Giancana was taken to Chicago; he appeared before a federal grand jury investigating gambling operations and the 1973 murder of Richard Cain, a former Chicago policeman turned mobster and a Giancana bodyguard. The outfit watched the inquiry closely as Giancana answered questions on how the mob invested its money in South American interests. Informants testified that Giancana had ordered his people

Sam Giancana, who once worked for Al Capone, inherited the role of Chicago's mob boss during the 1960s.

to get the Justice Department off his back by calling in IOUs from friendly congressmen. Witnesses reported Giancana saying "seven out of ten times when we hit a guy we're wrong . . . but the other three times we hit, we make up for it." Finally, mob higher-ups in Chicago decided that there was no choice; Giancana had to go.

In June 19, 1975, after returning from successful gallbladder surgery in Houston, Texas, Giancana was ambushed and shot seven times at close range as he stood at a stove cooking sausage and escarole in the basement of his Oak Park home. Although the assassin must have been a member of Giancana's organization whom he knew and trusted, no one was ever arrested for the murder. In fact, the Chicago Crime Commission classified Giancana's murder as one of more than 1,000 unsolved mob murders since 1919.

Ethnicity and Organized Crime in Large Cities

Chicago is thought of as having a predominantly Italian mob structure. In the early twentieth century, names like "Big Jim" Colosimo and Johnny Torrio were prominent there, and their reign was followed by the Capone era. True, the Capone mob had a preponderance of Italians, including Charley Fischetti, Frank Nitti, Paul Ricca, Tony Accardo, and Sam Giancana. There were also others, however, such as the Welshman Murray "the Camel" Humphries and the Pole "Greasy Thumb" Jake Guzik and later the Dorfmans, who were money movers.

Other cities present a similar picture of ethnic criminal coexistence. In Philadelphia, both Italians and Irishmen operated within the context of a predominantly Jewish leadership. In Cleveland, the domination of the "Four" is clear, with Italians such as the Polizzis and Romanos clearly in a subservient position. In New Jersey, Longie Zwillman worked with Jerry Catena and Willie Moretti; in Kansas City, crime was run by Solomon "Cutcherheadoff" Weissman and Johnny Lazia. The fact is that gangsters of different ethnic backgrounds were coexisting at street level throughout this period of alleged Italian domination (Messick 1967; Fried 1980: 116). The ethnic model employed by advocates of the alien conspiracy theory obscures the true nature of organized crime, as New York clearly demonstrates, with gangsters from Italian, Irish, and Jewish backgrounds.

THE NEW YORK MOB

New York City is probably the best-known example of the emergence of Italian American organized crime in a single city. Prohibition provided significant opportunities for Italian criminals, who had coalesced into two factions led by Joe "the Boss" Masseria and Salvatore Maranzano. Masseria's group, nicknamed the "Young Turks," included many of the later celebrities of organized crime, most of whom had been born in the United States: Vito Genovese, Joe Adonis, Frank Costello, and Charles "Lucky" Luciano. In time, each of these gangsters would become criminal legends as heads of their own syndicates in New York.

The Masseria and Maranzano Assassinations

After Frankie Yale's murder, Masseria achieved new power in New York, challenged only by Maranzano, who had begun hijacking truckloads of Masseria's liquor. Soon, Masseria decided to fight back, and the alleged **Castellammarese War** had begun (see Chapter 1). As it would turn out, at least for Luciano, this conflict paved the way for his rise to the top of organized crime in New York.

The Masseria–Maranzano conflict began in 1930 with an offensive by Masseria that involved several strategic attacks on Maranzano's allies. However, for months Luciano had been steaming over Masseria's old-fashioned management style and dictatorial ways. In fact, Masseria was said to have threatened Luciano because his liquor rackets were taking time away from Masseria's criminal exploits. Masseria demanded that Luciano work for him twenty-four hours a day and that all liquor profits go into the pot. Luciano, at that time in a partnership with Meyer Lansky and Bugsy Siegel, began conferring with his colleagues to decide how to weaken both Masseria and Maranzano. Luciano went to Maranzano, who promised him the top spot in his organization provided that Luciano would personally kill Joe Masseria. Luciano suspected that at best he would be given a secondary role with Maranzano, and he might even be killed in a double cross. In response to Maranzano's offer, Luciano snapped back, "You're crazy."

Suddenly, Luciano was hit in the head from behind by one of Maranzano's men. More than half a dozen men worked Luciano over, slashing his face and chest with knives, whipping him with belts, and burning him with cigarettes. He was tied up, beaten unconscious, revived, and then worked over again. The entire time Maranzano repeated his offer in hopes that Luciano would relent. Finally, after passing out, Luciano was dumped on a vacant street. A passing police car transported him to a nearby hospital where he received fifty-five stitches. The resulting stories about what might have happened to Luciano began to spread. Because most people could not have received such a beating and survived, New Yorkers started to call him Lucky Charlie and Lucky Luciano.

While recuperating, Luciano pondered why Maranzano had let him live. It became evident that Maranzano knew that if anyone were to kill Masseria it would have to be someone on the inside—someone close. Although Luciano was in disfavor with Masseria, he was still close enough to kill him. In a series of bold strokes, Luciano arranged to kill both bosses. Masseria was murdered at Scarpato's on Coney Island in April 1931. After enjoying Italian specialties at the restaurant with Luciano, Masseria played cards for awhile with the young turk. Luciano went to the men's room, and he was there while two men (one of whom was reportedly Bugsy Siegel) entered the restaurant and shot Masseria. Maranzano immediately claimed the title of "boss of bosses," but only enjoyed it for five months. On September 11, four gunmen, again including Siegel, entered the suite of offices maintained by the Eagle Company in midtown New York and sprayed the place with machine gun fire, leaving Maranzano dead.

Lucky Luciano and New York's New Order

Luciano immediately became the most important Italian American crime boss in New York, partly because of his long-term alliance with Jewish organized crime leaders. Lucky sent word to all crime factions that they were welcome in the new order. There would be no more boss of bosses; rather, negotiation and conciliation would characterize all major decisions.

By 1934, Luciano found himself surrounded by a virtual army of discontented operatives who were looking to him for a way to profit in post-Prohibition New York. With the illegal liquor rackets defunct, it was time for Luciano to find new sources of revenue. He was an opportunist who had interests in many different rackets, including bookmaking, casino gambling, the number's rackets, construction, the waterfront, trucking, the taxi business, bail bonds, drugs, bars, nightclubs, and restaurants. These new rackets did not take the place of time-honored ones such as protection, burglary, hijacking, and warehouse robberies, but supplemented them. Under Luciano's management, the mob developed a new racket—prostitution.

Luciano and his syndicate decided that they could take over New York's independent brothels. He permitted the use of his name in this effort, and his syndicate members began to coerce independent prostitution operators into splitting profits with the mob. Ultimately, Luciano put together the largest combination of brothels in history. At the height of his operation, he had more than 200 madams in charge of more than 1,000 prostitutes in his employ. Although this proved to be a big money maker in the beginning, it also proved to be a big mistake as well, for there were simply too many people involved. In addition, Luciano was becoming careless and made damaging remarks and telephone calls in the presence of many of his prostitutes, whom he referred to as "dumb broads." To his chagrin, three such "dumb broads," Nancy Presser, Cokey Flo Brown, and Mildred Harris, became witnesses against Lucky Charlie.

The flamboyance and outrageousness of organized crime in New York spurred the public into demanding action from public officials. Governor Herbert Lehman appointed a special prosecutor named Thomas Dewey (see Chapter 1) to head an organized crime task force. Dewey had already established himself as a crime-buster from his days as an assistant U.S. attorney. This time he vowed to go after New York mobsters one by one. The first on the list was Dutch Schultz, a loud-mouthed, vulgar hood who was not especially popular with other mobsters anyway. He was a powerful, rich mobster who had control of a couple of large breweries, some

Lucky Luciano became famous for organizing New York's criminal rackets.

numbers banks, and a restaurant protection ring. Schultz eventually made the mistake of offending Ownie Madden, Meyer Lansky, and Luciano. One day Luciano and Lansky got word that Schultz had decided that the best way to end Dewey's inquiry was to kill him. Luciano immediately called a meeting of New York's syndicate leaders to discuss Schultz's plot.

The syndicate heads were outraged because they knew that Dewey's murder would result in the biggest organized crime crackdown in history. There was no disagreement; Schultz needed to be eliminated. In October 1935, at the Palace Chop House in Newark, New Jersey, Schultz was gunned down. Unfortunately for Luciano, he was the next mobster on Dewey's list. With the help of prostitutes Presser, Brown, and Harris and dozens of other witnesses, Dewey was successful in building a case and prosecuting Luciano for prostitution in New York. Upon his conviction on these charges, Luciano was sent to prison for thirty to fifty years, the longest sentence ever handed down in a pandering case. While behind bars in New York's Dannemora Prison, Luciano was said to have continued to exert control and influence over day to day mob affairs with Lansky's help until his ultimate release and deportation to Sicily several years later.

Siegel, Lansky, and the New York–Las Vegas Connection

The story of the evolution of New York organized crime is important in the development of big-time gambling. A major player in New York's organized crime was Benjamin "Bugsy" Siegel, a notorious, cold-blooded killer allied with Lansky, Buchalter, and Luciano. Siegel had maneuvered his way into a leadership position in the New York mob through his partnership with Lucky Luciano and Meyer Lansky (also discussed in Chapters 4 and 10). Although Siegel was born into a respectable middle-class home in Brooklyn, he moved to Manhattan, where he met Meyer Lansky, at the time a small-time young hood involved in the stolen car business. Together the boys often found themselves in trouble, and when that happened they would often appear as character witnesses for each other. This amused a judge on one occasion after they had been arrested for running a crap game. The judge was said to have shaken his head and said, "You boys must have bugs in your head. . . . Go home and stay away from this court." From that moment on Ben Siegel was known as "Bugsy," and Lansky became "Bug." Gradually, as Lansky rose to the top of gangland with a reputation as a financial wizard, he lost his nickname, but Ben wasn't as fortunate. He hated the nickname. It became well known that anyone referring to young Ben by using the name Bugsy in his presence would risk getting roughed up.

Siegel's Move to Hollywood

Siegel moved from New York to Hollywood where he fit in well. With his handsome, boyish face, he fancied himself as a likely candidate for stardom—despite his criminal past. Upon arriving in Hollywood, Siegel looked up boyhood pal George Raft, who introduced Siegel around. Raft fancied being a gangster as much as Siegel fancied being a movie star. Siegel enjoyed the good life and soon bought a mansion in Beverly Hills, regularly attended races, and worked out at the YMCA. In time, he began to muscle in on local rackets, which included getting pieces of booking operations, labor racketeering, and even a not so successful offshore gambling operation. He organized the Screen Extras Guild and the Trans-America racing service, which wired odds, entries, results, and pari-mutuel payoffs from tracks around the country. He even became a partner in the fabled, luxurious Clover Club gambling casino.

Benjamin Bugsy Siegel envisioned Nevada's first celebrity casino, the Flamingo.

Siegel's propensity for violence surfaced on the day before Thanksgiving 1939, when he killed Hank Greenberg, a small-time hood who was thought to be an informer. Although the murder raised a ruckus in Hollywood, Siegel saw it as a chance to establish himself as an authority figure on the West Coast. However, in August 1940, things changed when Siegel was arrested for Greenberg's murder. The Greenberg arrest achieved much publicity and, as a result, Siegel was no longer welcome in Hollywood circles. However, he arranged the murder of a witness in New York, colluded with the district attorney, and spread a great deal of money around both Los Angeles and New York, resulting in the murder charges against him being dropped.

Siegel was thought by many to be a visionary. Aside from his own rackets, he had one particularly good idea. He wanted to build a combination luxury hotel and gambling resort in the middle of the desert. He even had a name for his dream: the Flamingo. With input from his girlfriend Virginia Hill, a Hollywood actress, Siegel estimated the cost of the venture to be around $1 million or more. The logical source of the money was somewhere back east. The project was presented to the key New York syndicate heads, Frank Costello, Meyer Lansky, and Lucky Luciano. Lansky understood Siegel's idea, but concluded that it was much too big for private financing and stock

Critical Thinking Project

Assess the performance of the mayors of New York, Chicago, Philadelphia, or any large city with a rich history of organized crime. As part of your assessment, consider the extent to which these mayors represent their constituents or their personal agendas.

would have to be sold. After much finagling and numerous contributions from Siegel's estranged wife, Lansky, and many others, the initial investment capital was raised and the Flamingo project began. However, Siegel became obsessive about the construction, demanding the best of materials and workmanship. Contractors robbed him blind, selling him materials at inflated prices.

Siegel's Downfall

On Christmas Day in 1946, the casino portion of the complex opened with a roster of star-studded guests, including George Jessel, Charles Coburn, and Jimmy Durante. Unfortunately, due to Siegel's reputation as a hood, the new Flamingo had the reputation of a place run by gangsters for gangsters. Rumors suggested that the games were fixed. This situation was exacerbated when Siegel slugged two people who uttered his dreaded nickname, Bugsy. In January, the Flamingo closed until the hotel facilities were completed. In the meantime, Siegel's New York partners met and determined that Siegel had a good idea but was not a manager, and that hotel construction costs could be recouped if the casino were placed under new management. Against the wishes of his childhood buddy Lansky, Siegel was marked for assassination.

The problem was how to get to Siegel, who had several capable body-guards who would have to be neutralized. In addition, the murder needed to be conducted away from the Flamingo to avoid more bad press. Finally, Virginia Hill posed a special problem because she had many influential friends, had a close association with Siegel, and could be angered to the point where she might go to the authorities. In early June 1947, Siegel and

For more than three decades, Meyer Lansky was the financial brains behind New York's Italian organized crime syndicate.

bookie friend Allen Smiley arrived at Virginia's home after dinner. From a car parked outside, a lone figure carrying a .30 caliber carbine rifle walked to the living room window. The murder was quick, with the first shot hitting Siegel in the head, driving his left eye fifteen feet to the opposite side of the room. Of the seven bullets fired, one tore through Smiley's jacket. Benjamin Siegel was dead. Virginia Hill quickly moved to Switzerland, where she later married and retired.

The Black Hand

Contrary to claims by journalists and some law enforcement officials over the years, the **Black Hand** was never a formal organization with any kind of national or international ties. Furthermore, it was never a secret society, nor was it ever tied to organized crime groups. Put simply, it was an extortion racket that preyed chiefly on Italian citizens, first in Italy and Sicily as early as the 1750s and later in the United States. Black Hand members threatened the use of violence to extort money from a well-to-do victim in the community. Threats commonly involved kidnapping a member of the victim's family, blowing up a business, or killing a member of the victim's family. The Black Hand would send the intended victim a note containing a number of horrifying symbols, depicting guns, daggers with dripping blood, bombs exploding, and the skull and crossbones.

The Black Hand flourished between 1890 and 1910 during the mass immigration of thousands of Italian immigrants into New York. The chief Black Hander was Ignazio Saietta, also known as "Lupo the Wolf," who gained a reputation for violence by victimizing Italians living in the Little Italy section of New York City. He was said to have strangled victims in their homes, pulling their bodies out to the street and placing them in a cart to be hauled to his livery stable. There he would hack up the bodies, burning some of the body parts and burying what he did not burn. Saietta profiteered from other Italians for more than three decades until he was arrested for counterfeiting and sentenced to prison for thirty years. Subsequent to his arrest, the Black Hand continued to proliferate and victimize many prominent Italians in New York.

The Black Hand's criminal activities were not restricted to New York, however. For example, the Black Hand's activities drastically increased in Kansas City in 1912 with the arrival of Joseph "Scarface" DiGiavanni from Sicily. DiGiavanni had purportedly murdered more than a dozen Black Hand victims there. Unable to speak or write English, DiGiavanni's nickname resulted from the explosion of one of his stills, which left his face grossly scarred. He and his brother Peter "Sugarhouse Pete" DiGiavanni were quick to take over Black Hand operations in Kansas City. For more than fifty years, these brothers and numerous thugs controlled the protection racket in the Kansas City area. Not until the 1950s was their stranglehold in Kansas City weakened by younger gangsters who were successful in taking over Kansas City's rackets.

The Black Hand also flourished in Chicago. Dating back to 1890 and extending to the 1920s, Black Handers such as James "Sunny Jim" Cosmano operated freely for decades, telling victims to pay up or be killed. Things got so bad in Chicago that during a fifteen-month period between 1910 and 1911, thirty-eight Italian victims were shot to death on one street corner by a Black Hand shooter known only as "Shotgun Man." Word had it that Shotgun Man walked the streets openly carrying his shotgun while looking for Black Hand victims who refused to pay. Prohibition proved to be a blessing for Italian immigrants, because most Black Handers abandoned the extortion rackets and moved into the bootlegging business. By the mid-1920s, the Black Hand was considered a thing of the past.

The Unione Siciliana

The *Unione Siciliana* had its beginnings in the 1880s as a fraternal organization to promote social events and provide life insurance for Sicilian immigrants in New York City (Inciardi 1975). In time, its influence grew and votes cast by its members were sufficient to affect the outcome of major elections in several wards. Gradually, its influence reached to other major cities across the country. The organization slowly became transformed into a criminal group under the leadership of Ignazio Saietta, who manipulated his way to the top spot in the organization shortly after World War II. Once there, he used his official powers to establish rackets in prostitution, extortion, kidnapping, and murder for hire.

In his office he installed meat hooks from which victims were hung, and there were even reports of people being burned alive in the basement furnace. In 1918, Saietta went to prison and the reins of power were passed to Frankie Yale, an equally violent player. Aside from the rackets, in which Yale was also involved, Saietta did manage to broaden the legitimate interests of the organization until 1928, when Al Capone had him murdered.

Capone tried to muscle in on the Unione leadership but was viewed as an outsider because of his Neapolitan background and the fact that he was a Chicagoan, not a New Yorker. During the 1920s the Unione was run by Capone's friend, Mike Merlo, whose death by natural causes in 1924 sparked a bloodbath as various factions competed for leadership of the Unione:

- "Bloody Angelo" Genna proclaimed himself as the Unione's president but was murdered the following year on orders of the northside mob. It was suspected that the hit had been ordered by Vincent Drucci, "Bugs" Moran, or Earl "Hymie" Weiss.
- Samuzzo "Samoots" Amatuna became the next president, but was shot to death by Drucci in a barbershop before the end of 1925.
- With the support of Al Capone, the new president was Anthony Lombardo, who lasted three years. He became well known as a negotiator between families of kidnap victims and members of the Black Hand. Lombardo and his bodyguard were gunned down by two henchmen on September 7, 1928.
- The next president was Pasqualine "Patsy" Lolardo, who lasted only four months until his murder by the Aiello brothers.
- The day following the murder of Lolardo, Joseph Aiello assumed the presidency and remained in the position for a year and a half until Capone had him murdered.

It became clear to possible contenders for the presidency of the Unione Siciliana that the benefits of holding the office were clearly outweighed by the hazards. However, as the Depression of the 1930s began, the Unione Siciliana faded into obscurity.

OTHER NOTABLE FIGURES IN NEW YORK

We now consider some of the more notable gangsters who played important roles in the formation of organized crime in New York.

Arnold Rothstein

Arnold "the Brain" Rothstein (AR) was the epitome of a big-time gambling operator and money-maker for more than twenty years in New York. AR was so successful that he was never indicted for any of the crimes in which he was involved. He accomplished this by remaining distant from his many schemes and never directly handling any criminal operation. In doing so, Rothstein's technique was to employ well-paid lieutenants and front men to do the dirty work, insulating him from detection and prosecution. As a matter of practice, he always dealt with cash and demanded a 90 percent take from all deals. Rothstein's enforcers dealt harshly with those who reneged.

Rothstein was the son of Jewish immigrants who settled in New York. He had a keen mind for mathematics, which he used in figuring the odds in gambling operations. By 1910 he owned a lavish casino in the Tenderloin district, catering to the elite carriage trade and making tens of thousands of dollars.

By 1919 he was a millionaire. That year he bribed eight players on the Chicago White Sox baseball team to throw the World Series. The **Black Sox scandal** implicated Rothstein, who was called to testify in Chicago in 1920. After arriving at the courthouse in a black limousine and acting as an indignant New York impresario, Rothstein convinced the grand jury that he was innocent.

Thereafter, Rothstein's empire of casinos, brothels, and racehorses grew until the mid-1920s, when his interests began to focus on drug trafficking. The drug business proved to be an enormous source of income, making Rothstein additional millions. He dispatched his enforcer, Jack "Legs" Diamond, to set up trafficking routes between Europe and the eastern seaboard.

Rothstein's income grew so rapidly that he could not invest it or gamble it away. Rather, he made loans to politicians, police officials, judges, and prosecutors—anyone who was in debt and who would be willing to repay the debt in a manner beneficial to AR. These loans represented power to Rothstein. Anyone in default received a visit from Legs Diamond. Politicians who could not repay were asked to do a number of things for Rothstein, including releasing fellow gangsters from prison, quashing warrants and indictments, and dismissing charges against him and his gang. By 1928 he was one of New York's most powerful citizens. However, later that same year he began to fall apart.

For no apparent reason Rothstein's health deteriorated, and he became noticeably nervous with shaking hands and twitching eyes. His speech was often slurred, but not from drinking because he did not imbibe. Furthermore, he fell into a spiraling losing streak, often losing tens of thousands of dollars at a time. His racehorses came in last, his gambling casinos were raided, and his crap games were closed down. In an effort to recoup his losses, he entered into a big-time poker game at New York's Park Central Hotel. Rothstein lost more and more, including $50,000 for side bets for high card draws. By the end of the game, he had lost more than $320,000; he later claimed that the game was rigged. For days he was hounded at his nightclubs by George "Hump" McMannus and colleagues, who wanted their money.

Finally, one evening after receiving a phone call from McMannus at one of his clubs, Rothstein left for the Park Central Hotel. He was later found in front of the hotel holding his stomach and gasping for air after being shot. Although Rothstein never identified his assailant to the police, McMannus and associate Nathan Raymond were arrested and charged with the murder. After a lengthy trial, neither was convicted. Rothstein's criminal empire was quickly divided among his lieutenants: Frank Costello took charge of the political and police protection system, Frank Erickson took control of the gambling rackets, Lepke Buchalter was given the garment rackets, and Legs Diamond received the bootlegging business.

Dutch Schultz

Born Arthur Flegenheimer, "Dutch Schultz" grew up in the Bronx and never went beyond fourth grade. He embarked on a career of thievery. At age nineteen, he was arrested for theft and sentenced to serve fifteen months in prison. When he emerged from prison, he purchased a Bronx saloon with the spoils of his robberies. He then announced that his new name would be Dutch Schultz, a name taken from an old-time Bronx gangster at the turn of the century. Slowly he began to assemble some of the toughest Jewish criminals in the area. With Prohibition underway, Schultz quickly realized that he could make a fortune in the liquor and beer business, and he proceeded to purchase several more saloons, which he supplied with bootlegged beer and whisky. Soon Schultz's Bronx empire spread into Manhattan as Schultz's gunmen systematically eliminated rival gang members.

Schultz soon realized that the numbers racket in Harlem was also a lucrative racket. He believed that the best way to break into Harlem's number's rackets was to approach Stephanie St. Clair, the queen of numbers in Harlem. Schultz combined a promise of protection and greater profitability with the implied threat of a gang war. Madame St. Clair not only accepted the offer, but also encouraged the rest of the Harlem policy kings to follow suit and join the Schultz organization. By 1930 Schultz had become a millionaire from his bootlegging and numbers rackets and had decided, along with Frank Costello and associate Joey Rao, that a new racket—slot machines—was worth pursuing. The Schultz gang, which was by then numbering into the hundreds, distributed slot machines throughout New York.

Violent Competition

Trouble began to brew during 1930 when Schultz realized that Legs Diamond, a former employee of the Schultz organization, was behind the hijacking of many of his beer delivery trucks. War broke out between the Schultz and Diamond factions and ended with Diamond's demise. During his criminal career, Diamond had been shot so many times that the press named him the "underworld's clay pigeon." Finally, his luck ran out on December 19, 1931; after celebrating his acquittal on a kidnapping charge, Diamond staggered home drunk and collapsed in his bed. As he slept, he was murdered by killers dispatched by Schultz.

More trouble occurred in 1931 when the Coll brothers, Vincent and Peter, began beating up speakeasy owners who bought their beer from the Schultz mob and insisting that the owners buy beer and liquor from their organization. Although hopelessly outnumbered, the Coll brothers and their gang of ten began systematically eliminating Schultz's lieutenants. One day on a crowded

Manhattan street, Vincent Coll and others were in the process of riddling a rival enforcer with machine gun fire when several stray bullets hit innocent passersby. One victim was a child who later died, thus earning Coll the nickname "Mad Dog."

For some time Coll remained the focal point of concern for the Dutchman. One night Schultz and his body guard Danny Iamascia were walking down a Manhattan street and spotted two persons walking in the shadows close behind. Figuring these men were Coll and company, Schultz and Iamascia pulled their guns and fired. The two figures turned out to be New York City detectives, who returned the fire, killing Iamascia and chasing Schultz into an alleyway. Detective Steve DiRosa was the first to catch up with the Dutchman and to identify himself as a police officer. Schultz immediately pulled out more than $18,000 in cash and handed it to the detective saying, "Here—take it all." By the time the second detective arrived on the scene, DiRosa was reportedly attempting to stuff the money into Schultz's mouth. Schultz was arrested for attempted murder, but through the efforts of his attorney Richard "Dixie" Davis, Dutch was able to have the case thrown out by one of Schultz's mob-connected judges.

Rattled by the notion that Coll might show up at any time, Schultz had Mad Dog followed for several weeks. He soon learned that Coll made regular stops at a drugstore on West Twenty-Third Street to use the pay phone to make blackmail demands from Ownie "the Killer" Madden for kidnapping Madden's partner, "Big Frenchy" DeMange. During one such call, one of Schultz's men spotted Coll in the drugstore and immediately summoned gunmen Abe and George Weinberg. The brothers, accompanied by two additional gunmen, drove up to the drugstore and went inside. As one of the men herded the customers to the back, the other killers pulled submachine guns out from under their coats and sprayed Coll with .45 caliber bullets as he stood at the pay phone.

New Legal Problem

Soon a new problem emerged for Schultz. He was now charged with tax evasion by Thomas Dewey, U.S. attorney and mob-buster (see Chapter 1). With some slick legal maneuvering on the part of Schultz's attorney, the trial venue was changed to upstate New York, where Schultz mingled with the rural population of the town and endeavored to convince citizens that he was being framed. In doing so, Schultz and his wife Frances attended town functions such as bingo games and small-town dances, a strategy that ultimately paid off. Schultz was considered by the townsfolk to be a nice and rather generous guy. The local jury that sat in judgment of Schultz found the gangster not guilty—another victory for the Dutchman.

However, while Schultz was in upstate New York dealing with his legal problems, Luciano, Lansky, and Madden were fast at work taking over his illegal operations in New York City. Ultimately, they left few rackets for Schultz. Rather than go to war with these powerful forces, Schultz chose to relocate from the Bronx to Newark, New Jersey, where he began to rebuild his rackets. During this time, organized crime reoriented itself to post-Prohibition realities. Luciano, Madden, Lansky, Buchalter, and Anastasia believed that Schultz was too powerful a figure in the underworld to be ignored, so he was included in these discussions. In true Schultz fashion, he was argumentative and demonstrated a tendency to ignore the good of other syndicates in favor of his own personal rackets. This made the others feel very uneasy. In addition to Schultz's behavior, Luciano and Lansky were also nervous about Thomas Dewey, who was starting to closely scrutinize Schultz's underworld rackets.

Schultz's Biggest Mistake

At one point, Schultz decided to murder Dewey to end the investigation once and for all. The matter was discussed by the other syndicate leaders. They agreed that the plan was dangerous. "It will bring down all of us," Luciano reportedly declared, even though he had also considered doing the same thing. Schultz exploded and replied, "You guys stole my rackets, and now you're gonna feed me to the law—Dewey's gotta go! I'm gonna hit him myself—in forty-eight hours." Schultz then stormed out of the room, leaving a group of stunned mobsters. Word was sent to Albert Anastasia, head of Murder, Inc., the independent enforcement arm of the mob, whose job it was to eliminate anyone who was collectively viewed as a problem. Schultz's peers decided to kill him and save his rackets, which would no doubt be exposed by a massive investigation if Dewey were murdered. Ironically, to ensure its own continued existence, the syndicate realized that it must preserve the life of one of its archenemies, Dewey.

Schultz and three of his gang members were at the Palace Chop House in Newark, New Jersey, where they discussed the details of Dewey's impending assassination. During this discussion, a car drove up in front of the restaurant. Its occupants were Emmanuel "Mendy" Weiss, Charles "the Bug" Workman, and a third man known only as "Piggy." The men entered the tavern and shot Schultz and each of his associates, all of whom were taken to the hospital where they later died. Schultz lingered for the longest period of time, raving incoherently with bullets in his back and side. While police waited at his bedside, hoping to learn the name of his killer, the Dutchman uttered an engrossing litany of suspicion, power, and fear. By 8:40 P.M. Dutch Schultz was dead. His killer, Bug Workman, was tried for the murder six years later and sent to prison for life, but was paroled twenty years later.

Frank Costello   Of all of the early organized criminals in New York, the cool-headed Frank Costello was probably one of the most politically influential. His rackets were protected by some of New York's most powerful politicians. Even though Costello had a respectable veneer, he was a hardened gangster with Murder, Inc., architects Joe Adonis and Albert Anastasia and the "King of the Bookmakers," Frank Erikson, as his closest friends. Costello was born in Italy and immigrated with his family to New York in 1896, where he was raised in East Harlem. His criminal career began in his youth when he ran the streets as a petty thief. His big break came when he and his brother were recruited into Ownie Madden's vicious Manhattan gang.

Soon Costello opened numerous fruit stands in New York, which served as fronts for gambling operations. He then began to pay off police and politicians systematically for protecting his gambling rackets. The money began to roll in by the tens of thousands, and Costello became a wealthy man. In time, he became associated with bootlegger William Vincent "Big Bill" Dwyer, who then introduced Costello to Tammany Hall associates, including Jimmy Hines. Rather than enter the bootlegging wars, Costello eventually carved out a niche in the liquor distribution business, while associating with some of the most notable gangsters in the business: "Waxy" Gordon, Lucky Luciano, Ownie Madden, Dutch Schultz, and Joe Adonis. He imported some of Canada's highest-quality liquor and used his contacts to furnish the swankiest nightspots in New York.

In addition to being one of Luciano's top advisors during the 1920s, Costello was instrumental in organizing one of the first national crime meetings in Atlantic City in 1929, which was called by Johnny Torrio and Meyer Lansky to introduce a new wire service to future syndicate leaders. At the end of Prohibition, Costello and friend Meyer Lansky concentrated on gambling interests in New York and Miami and eventually developed casinos in Havana, Cuba, with the support and backing of Cuban dictator Fulgencia Batista. By the 1950s, Costello was considered one of the most powerful mob bosses in the United States. His knack for arbitration and negotiation in place of violence earned him the nickname the "Prime Minister."

In time, however, problems developed for Costello. He was one of the first to build gambling casinos in Las Vegas. Although he was not a collaborator with Benjamin Siegel in the building of the Flamingo Hotel, he felt the same pressure that Siegel had when his own casinos showed considerable profits, which he was not willing to share with other mob bosses, in particular Vito Genovese. Genovese's response was typical. In May 1957, a large-framed syndicate enforcer, Vincent "the Chin" Gigante, was sent to kill Costello. As Costello entered his luxury apartment building in New York, Gigante shot several bullets at him, grazing Costello's head. Gigante was later arrested for the shooting, but Costello refused to identify him as the attacker. However, Genovese's message was loud and clear and, in the aftermath of rumors about his instrumental role in the imprisonment of Genovese in 1959, Costello retired from the rackets in the early 1960s.

Frank Erikson

Born in 1896, Frank Erikson was one of the most important organized crime figures in New York, with a career stretching from the 1920s to the 1950s. In addition to his New York operations, he owned "points" in Meyer Lansky's Colonial Inn in Florida; leased the rights to a horse parlor at the Roney Plaza Hotel in Miami; owned a piece of another Florida casino, the Farm; and ran bookmaking operations that covered the Florida race tracks (Kefauver 1951: 811–830).

In addition, Erikson ran an extensive bookmaking operation throughout New Jersey. He also had legitimate holdings, such as the Park Avenue Theater and the Anderson Galleries in New York City. One of his more surprising holdings was Bruil Petroleum, which had vast oil interests in Texas. Moreover, Erikson did well financially. He filed income tax returns showing incomes of $194,000 in 1937, $184,000 in 1946, $169,000 in 1948, and $132,000 in 1949. One can safely assume that reported income was only a small part of his real income, because it is unlikely that he reported income from illegal ventures. In any case, the amounts he did report were substantial sums of money for those years.

Erikson was a close friend and associate of Frank Costello, with whom he probably shared control of New York bookmaking. In addition, Erikson was in business with Meyer Lansky, "Dandy" Phil Kastel, Willie Moretti, Charles Fischetti, Joe Massei (from Detroit), Willie Bischoff, and "Little Augie" Pisano. Despite Erikson's rather successful efforts to shield himself from too much public scrutiny, it is clear that he played a major role in the organizing of crime networks in New York and Florida. He certainly brought considerable financial resources to that organization.

Vito Genovese

Without a doubt, Vito Genovese was one of the most feared and ruthless mob bosses in U.S. history. His climb to power was attributed to his ability to betray friends and associates, while being able to outwit his organized crime counterparts and underworld rivals. Born in Naples in 1897, Genovese arrived in the United States in 1913, and while living in New York's lower east side, he soon fell in with several local street gangs there. His first rackets were the extortionate protection rackets, in which he preyed on local business people and vendors in the neighborhood. Soon, he met another small-time thief who possessed some of the same "qualities"—Charles Lucky Luciano. Genovese soon began working for Luciano while branching out into other criminal ventures, such as burglary and robbery.

Escalating Rackets

Genovese was arrested on several occasions for carrying a concealed weapon, and in one case he served a sixty-day stint in jail. In time, Genovese and Luciano began working for the Jacob "Little Augie" Orgen gang. Along with Joe Adonis and Albert Anastasia, Luciano and Genovese established themselves in the prostitution rackets by organizing several cheap brothels in Manhattan. Although the bootlegging business was a lucrative racket during the 1920s, Luciano and Genovese found the sex-for-hire and narcotics businesses equally as lucrative. At that time, however, mob leaders frowned on drug dealing; they believed that it was a business more appropriately handled by African American gangsters. As time went by, Luciano and Genovese branched out and began associations with other more powerful New York gangs run by Big Bill Dwyer, Ownie Madden, Dutch Schultz, and Legs Diamond.

Overseeing most of these gangs was the crime czar Arnold Rothstein, who was interested in expanding the narcotics rackets through Little Augie's gang. Orgen decided that Luciano and Genovese should control his heroin rackets and in time they became the chief suppliers to New York, becoming rich but still operating under the auspices of Orgen and Rothstein. By 1925, Luciano and Genovese had shifted their allegiances to Joe "the Boss" Masseria's gang while cultivating other associations with non-Italian gangs, such as those of Benjamin Siegel and Meyer Lansky, and Louis Lepke Buchalter and his enforcer, Jacob "Gurrah" Shapiro.

Masseria meant little to Genovese; Masseria was from the old school of so-called "mustache Petes" who clung to old-world customs and preferred some of the older rackets, such as the extortionate Black Hand operations. Genovese had been married twice by 1932. His first wife died in 1929. He spotted his second wife, Anna Petillo Vernotico, at a social gathering in 1932. Two weeks later, her husband's strangled body was found on top of a Manhattan building. In 1963, Joseph Valachi testified that Vernotico's two killers were hired by Genovese, but were later themselves murdered so as not to provide a link between the murder and Genovese. Indeed, Genovese did seem to be prone to violence. Between 1920 and 1930 he was thought to have personally committed six murders.

With the deaths of Joe Masseria and Salvatore Maranzano, Luciano and Genovese united the various factions of Italian American syndicate crime in

A handcuffed Vito Genovese arrives at court in New York City in 1959 on a narcotics conspiracy charge.

(*AP Wide World Photos*)

New York. In the meantime, under Luciano's direction, Genovese's drug-trafficking rackets flourished, earning him an estimated $500,000 per year. Another lucrative Genovese racket was fleecing wealthy Italians in crooked card games. One such event occurred in the back room of a small restaurant owned by Ferdinand "the Shadow" Boccia, where $160,000 was scalped from an unsuspecting victim. After learning of the huge take, Boccia approached Genovese and demanded a $35,000 cut of the spoils. Genovese assured him that he would consider the demand. Instead, five gunmen shot Boccia dead. Genovese soon found out that another gangster, Willie Gallo, had learned of the Boccia killing. As a safety measure, Genovese ordered Gallo killed. The contract went to Gallo's friend Ernest "the Hawk" Rupolo. He and Gallo went to a movie a few days later and just after the end of the film Rupolo pulled a gun, placed it to Gallo's head, and pulled the trigger. Nothing happened—Rupolo's gun had misfired! A shocked Gallo turned and said, "What the hell is this?" Rupolo replied, "It's only a joke." The two men then proceeded to Gallo's home, where Rupolo went to the washroom to examine the gun. He reloaded it and, as he walked back into the living room he fired into Gallo. Gallo was not mortally wounded, however, and lived to identify his assailant, who was arrested and sentenced to a twenty-year sentence.

While in prison, Rupolo brooded because Genovese had failed to provide him adequate legal counsel. He soon talked to prison officials about his boss Vito Genovese and his involvement in the Boccia murder. New York's famous mob-buster prosecutor, Thomas Dewey, became interested in what Rupolo had to say. Rather than wait around to be arrested, Genovese left the country for Naples, where he owned an elegant villa. Over the years he had anticipated the possibility of an emergency move and had moved an estimated $2 million in cash to Italian banks to facilitate his comfortable existence in exile.

Once in Italy, however, Genovese became active in Mafia–Camorra drug-trafficking activities. He was soon able to ingratiate himself with Italian dictator Benito Mussolini by making large cash contributions to Mussolini's personal bank account. Genovese also contributed $250,000 for the construction of a huge monument of Mussolini to be placed in front of fascist headquarters in Nola, Italy. Consequently, despite Mussolini's war on the Mafia, Genovese was allowed to operate drug-trafficking operations in Italy. Genovese's operation established heroin links between the Middle East, Italy, Sicily, and the United States.

It was not long, however, before Genovese was identified as an American fugitive and was brought to New York to stand trial for the murder of Boccia. Two witnesses testified against him in this trial: Ernest Rupolo and Peter LaTempa. LaTempa was later poisoned in his jail cell. No one was ever arrested for the murder. As for Rupolo's testimony, Genovese knew that by itself it probably was not enough to secure a conviction. He was right; a jury acquitted him of the murder.

Genovese operated as a top mob boss in New York until he was indicted there in 1959. At last the government built a strong drug-trafficking case against him, which resulted in his receiving a fifteen-year sentence in prison, where he died in 1969.

Joseph Bonanno

Joseph Bonanno worked for Chicago's Al Capone in the bootlegging business during the 1920s. In the early 1930s he moved to New York and worked for gang boss Salvatore Maranzano, who was in the midst of his ongoing war with Joe Masseria. Following the deaths of both Maranzano and Masseria, Bonanno emerged as a powerful gang boss controlling loan-sharking and gambling operations stretching from Montreal to Haiti. After the imprisonment of Lucky Luciano and Louis Buchalter in 1938, Bonanno fled to Sicily, but he returned in 1945 and became a naturalized U.S. citizen.

One of Bonanno's specialties was his ability to get rid of bodies of persons killed by the mob. He did so by using his many funeral home businesses and developing coffins with false bottoms. When a person was buried, the coffin would also contain the body of an organized crime murder victim under the false bottom. In addition to his funeral parlor business, Bonanno employed an army of henchmen in locations such as California, Las Vegas, Chicago, and New York in loan-sharking operations. He supplied the cash, while local syndicate leaders supplied the muscle to collect the "juice loans."

In the fall of 1964, Bonanno's ambition got the better of him. He called enforcer Joe Magliocco with an order to kill most of the top Italian American syndicate leaders in the United States: Carlo Gambino of Brooklyn, Thomas Lucchese of New York and New Jersey, Steven Magaddino of Buffalo, and Frank DiSimone of California. Because Magliocco was severely overweight and in ill health, he summoned his enforcer, Joe Colombo. Colombo secretly went to a meeting with the syndicate leaders on the hit list and told them of the plan. This resulted in Bonanno's summons by the nine-member "national commission," of which Bonanno was a member. He declined to attend. On the night of October 21, 1964, Bonanno was abducted by his own bodyguard as he was about to enter his apartment house on Park Avenue. For most of a year, he was held prisoner at a Catskills retreat. Eventually, he agreed to retire and turn his drug, gambling, and loan-sharking rackets, worth an estimated $2 billion per year, over to the other syndicate leaders. He was then freed on the proviso that he would leave the country in retirement. Bonanno agreed and moved to Haiti, where he remained for one year.

A short time after his move, Bonanno's son was nearly killed in New York by a botched hit. This was a blatant violation of the agreement reached between Bonanno and the syndicate leaders. As a result, the Bananas War, the greatest inter-Italian war in U.S. history, began in November 1967. Bonanno asked a few gunmen still loyal to him to kill Paul Sciacca, who had taken over Bonanno's rackets and who was thought to have orchestrated the attack on Bonanno's son. The bloody war raged for years, killing some forty gangsters in all. Finally, a truce was called; Bonanno was allowed to remain in the United States and retain control over some rackets. In return, he agreed to stop killing his enemies. In the 1980s Bonanno wrote an autobiography in which he admitted much of his organized crime activities. As a result, authorities questioned him about statements made in the book. When he refused to answer, he was jailed. Bonanno died in 2002, leaving behind a colorful chapter in organized crime's history.

Joseph Colombo

Joey Colombo began his criminal career as a low-level thief until he was ultimately taken into Joseph Bonanno's syndicate. When Bonanno decided to take over in 1964, he reportedly gave Joseph Magliocco a hit list. As a result, Magliocco called Joe Colombo, his top mob enforcer, and gave him the arduous task of killing several mob bosses on the list. Colombo realized that completing this assignment would mean his own death and decided to inform each target on Joe Bonanno's list of the plot. As a result, Bonanno was kidnapped but later released on his promise that he would retire from the business.

For his betrayal of Bonanno, Colombo was rewarded with control of some of the Italian American syndicate operations in New York. He proved to be a better enforcer than a leader. He immediately cut the income of his syndicate members, most of whom had rackets on the side. No longer were they allowed to keep the profits of their own rackets, but had to give most of the money to Colombo. At one point, a full-scale war developed within Colombo's organization after he refused to let the Gallo brothers keep a larger share of the gambling profits they managed for him.

Colombo's Fatal Ego

In the 1960s, Colombo made another serious error by stepping in to the limelight with his newly created Italian-American Civil Rights League. The organization was created to promote the Italian heritage and fight the stereotypical public image, created by law enforcement agencies and the media, of Italian and Sicilian Americans as gangsters. In reality, Colombo intended to provide a smokescreen to conceal criminal activities. However, the organization began to grow, making tens of thousands of dollars for Colombo's mob.

According to Colombo's plan, the power of the police and politicians would be neutralized by the league's brotherhood, which would be able to dictate elections, similar to the goals of the old Unione Siciliana of the early twentieth century, which also had essentially been a front for illegal activities. Colombo's plans, however, were doomed because the Gallo brothers had planned to murder Colombo at the next Italian-American Civil Rights League rally. Joey Gallo knew that, if he personally attempted to kill Colombo, Colombo's bodyguards would recognize him and he would himself be killed. Instead, Gallo hired a killer from one of Harlem's African American gangs, Jerome Johnson.

On June 29, 1970, Colombo's Italian-American Civil Rights League hosted a giant Italian American rally in Columbus Circle against the wishes of other organized crime leaders. The event was an enormous success, attended by an estimated 50,000 people. Wearing a newspaper photographer's badge, Johnson was able to work his way through the crowd and get close to Colombo. Johnson fired three shots, one of which hit Colombo in the head. Before Johnson could flee, Colombo's bodyguards shot and killed him. Colombo was rushed to a nearby hospital where he was diagnosed as suffering severe brain damage. He lingered in a vegetative state for seven years until he died in 1978.

Carlo Gambino

Upon his death in 1976, law enforcement officials widely believed that Carlo Gambino had probably been the most powerful organized crime figure in New York. Gambino disdained publicity, preferring to stay within the Italian community of New York. He deplored the suggestion that drug trafficking should become one of the mob's rackets, fearing that it would allow federal authorities to infiltrate the ranks of organized crime more easily.

Gambino was born in Sicily and moved in 1921 to New York, where he soon began working for Joe Masseria. After the murders of Masseria and Salvatore Maranzano, Gambino and his brothers-in-law, Paul and Peter Castellano, became part of Albert Anastasia's organization. In 1951, Anastasia was gunned down (purportedly at the behest of Lansky), and Gambino was given the chance to take over the syndicate. He expanded Anastasia's organization by making peace with Meyer Lansky and being conciliatory toward the other crime leaders in New York. In time, he extended his operations and eventually exerted great influence on New York's waterfront unions.

Gambino was arrested sixteen times, but went to jail only once (for two months) on a tax-evasion conviction. Shortly before dying of natural causes in 1976, Gambino selected his brother-in-law Paul Castellano and Aniello Dellacroce to take over syndicate operations.

Paul Castellano

Following Carlo Gambino's death, Paul Castellano took charge of the syndicate's Manhattan operations. Due to his conservative politics, the stature of the organization slipped in the following nine years. Castellano's underlings tried to convince their boss that entering into the airport rackets, where a fortune could be made in freight disappearances, was a lucrative proposition. Castellano rejected the notion and chose to continue doing business with legitimate business people, such as Frank Perdue, the chicken mogul. Perdue was having trouble finding shelf space for his products in local supermarkets. After moving his business to Dial Poultry, a business run by Castellano's sons, Perdue's chicken products always received adequate space.

A significant event occurred on December 2, 1985, with the death of Aniello Dellacroce (another Carlo Gambino successor), who died of lung cancer. His replacement was John Gotti. Castellano made plans to replace Gotti with Thomas Bilotti, but two weeks later, Castellano and Bilotti arrived at Sparks Steak House on West 46 Street in New York. No sooner had they stepped out of their Lincoln than three men appeared and gunned them down. Following their deaths, the press accurately speculated that Gotti was the successor to the reins of the Gambino syndicate.

The 1980s introduced a new kind of organized criminal, one who frowned upon the old ways and tended to view the rackets from a new perspective. The new organized criminals were younger men who opted for suburban life and favored large extravagant homes, flashy cars, and expensive clothes. They were less insulated than their predecessors and more open to new opportunities.

John Gotti

Before he was sentenced to prison in 1992, John Gotti was the prototype of the new breed of Italian American criminal. The "dapper don," as the media dubbed him, was known for his limousines and tailored suits and for eating at fine New York restaurants. Gotti rose quickly to the head of the old Carlo Gambino syndicate. His rise in the New York mob began with an incident in 1972 when Manny Gambino (nephew to the all-powerful Carlo Gambino) was kidnapped and held for ransom. After receiving only part of the $350,000 ransom they had demanded, the kidnappers murdered their captive and dumped his corpse in a New Jersey garbage dump. Enraged over the incident, Gambino sent for his top enforcers to avenge the incident. One of the kidnappers, James McBratney, was murdered by three of Gambino's men, including Gotti, in a Staten Island bar. He was arrested, convicted, and sent to prison for seven years.

John Gotti, convicted in 1992 of racketeering and murder, was New York's Gambino family celebrity Godfather.

Upon his release, Gotti was rewarded for his loyalty by being made one of the top managers in the Gambino syndicate. He earned a reputation of being ruthless, even with his own gang members. According to FBI surveillance tapes, Gotti threatened to blow up members' houses if they refused to obey his orders. Gotti was also famous for orchestrating the deaths of his rivals while climbing to the top spot in the New York mob. A short time after Paul Castellano and Thomas Bilotti were gunned down on December 2, 1985, Gotti took control of the Gambino syndicate. His leadership became apparent several weeks after Castellano's murder, when New York City detectives, who were conducting covert surveillance on Gotti's Mulberry Street social club in New York's Little Italy, observed Gotti arriving for a Christmas party held in his honor. At the party, Gotti was greeted with great respect and was embraced by other syndicate members.

During the late 1980s, federal authorities made several attempts to convict Gotti for the murder of Castellano and on other charges. On three different occasions, Gotti was acquitted, earning him another nickname, the "Teflon don," because charges would not stick. Indeed, Gotti's attorney, Bruce Cuttler, was a flamboyant master of courtroom trial tactics. He energetically paraded in front of the jury while suggesting that the Mafia was only a figment of the prosecution's imagination. After the third acquittal, FBI agents observed Cuttler accompanying Gotti to the mob's social club, where electronic surveillance disclosed that illicit business was being decided in Cuttler's presence. As a result, the lawyer was considered too close to his client's criminal dealings, and a federal judge used the social club meetings as a way to ban Cuttler from representing Gotti in future trials. This proved to be a costly setback for Gotti, who was forced to employ a new and less effective attorney. In 1992, after being indicted for the fourth time since 1986, he was finally convicted in federal court on charges of racketeering and murder and sentenced to five life terms in prison and a $250,000 fine.

Perspectives on Gotti

John Gotti died in federal prison in 2002, but his life is one of the most controversial topics in the study of organized crime. Federal prosecutors pursued him with a vengeance, trying him three times before getting a conviction and then only after denying him the services of his preferred attorney. Federal law enforcement officials and the media were quick to declare that John Gotti was "the most powerful criminal in America" and the new leader of the fabled Cosa Nostra. It is interesting to note, however, that a review of the evidence gathered in the massive federal investigation of John Gotti goes a long way toward disputing this claim (Kappeler et al. 1993: 239).

There is no disputing the fact that John Gotti was a criminal. He had an impressive criminal résumé, which included arrests for hijacking, public intoxication, drug charges, murder, assault, theft, burglary, and gambling. Federal wiretaps clearly reveal Gotti threatening underlings and enemies, bragging about his criminal prowess, boasting about his personal attributes, and, interestingly enough, complaining about the dire state of his criminal career. These facts, developed in the course of a massive investigation, are precisely what is so troubling about the official portrait of Gotti as an all-powerful mob leader. "The most powerful criminal in America" had a conspicuously troubled career marked by dozens of arrests and an almost unbroken string of unsuccessful criminal schemes. Simply put, on the basis of official résumé, John Gotti looks much less successful than thousands of other New Yorkers who law enforcement could brand as petty crooks.

The facts about John Gotti paint a portrait of an organized criminal with a somewhat limited career. It is true that he ran a very large dive game in Manhattan, but federal wiretaps reveal that he was a notoriously bad gambler, frequently losing as much as $60,000 to $70,000 a day. At one point on the government's own wiretaps, Gotti is heard exclaiming that his gambling efforts were going so badly that he would "have to go on welfare." It is also true that Gotti was the leader of a den of thieves operating out of the Bergin Hunt and Fish Club. It is equally true that members of his crew frequently complained about Gotti's inability to come up with targets for scores and to create income-producing opportunities in other illicit ventures. This was a very curious problem for someone supposed to be the "head of all organized crime in America," particularly in a city where minor thieves seem to do very well and have no trouble identifying targets. Prosecutors also alleged that Gotti had connections to several drug operations, but the truth is that most of these schemes were planned by associates, failed, and cost Gotti and his syndicate money: once again a very curious outcome for the head of all organized crime.

In addition, the wiretaps show a man who thought little of using intimidation and threats to keep his minions in line. What the government's investigation clearly shows is a man who was frequently out of control, threatening to kill people with regularity—a very expensive and dangerous thing for a major organized crime figure to do. Gotti also pursued a series of personal, nonbusiness-related vendettas, allegedly including the disappearance of a neighbor. His bail was once revoked because of his involvement in a fistfight over a parking space. While federal investigators and prosecutors have been successful in portraying John Gotti as a criminal and as a man with an explosive and dangerous temper, they have not been successful in portraying him as a major organized crime figure.

It is inconceivable that organized criminals such as Meyer Lansky, Frank Erikson, and Lucky Luciano would have gotten into a fistfight over a parking space. One assumes that the "most powerful criminal in America" would have his own parking space. It is also inconceivable that real organized criminals would be so consistently unsuccessful in their criminal exploits, or that they would threaten to "whack" everyone they came in contact with, or that they would be arrested with such shocking regularity for so petty a list of crimes.

John Gotti had a long criminal record and frequent press notices, but they did not make him a leader of organized crime. What they did is make him a candidate for federal prosecution and subsequent exaggeration and embellishment of his status by federal prosecutors (Hampson 2002). Like "Little Nicky" Scarfo in Philadelphia and countless other alleged mafiosi, John Gotti was only a petty hood, but an easy target. There are dozens, if not hundreds,

Critical Thinking Project

In your judgment, was John Gotti the successor to the Gambino syndicate and a major Mafia boss or merely a minor gangster who benefited from media glamorization? Defend your viewpoint with factual support.

of organized crime figures in New York who surpassed Gotti in importance. But like Lansky and others before them, they were beyond the reach of federal prosecutors.

The Gotti case serves only to obfuscate the real nature of organized crime in America. The thesis of the federal prosecutors is that La Cosa Nostra is the single license-granting authority in organized crime. The facts presented in the Gotti trials belie the claim. The criminal enterprises headed by John Gotti were not the results of careful planning and execution by a corporate organized crime operation, but of informal criminal relationships evolving out of social proximity and prior entrepreneurial connections. He did not head a major crime organization, but an informal, loosely structured, ephemeral criminal network. Gotti's alleged heroin operation, for example, was really headed by Mark Reiter and Angelo Ruggiero. They engaged in a series of opportunistic (and unsuccessful) drug deals involving amounts of drugs and money minute in comparison to the activities of dozens of other New York City drug merchants. The Bergin crew was just that; it was not an offshoot of a powerful syndicate; it was an informal social network of hoods. The members came together to rob a drug dealer or to do some muscle work for a loan-shark or to run a dice game. They never formed a cohesive criminal organization.

Gotti's conviction did not represent the end of the "most powerful criminal in America," but one in a series of relatively unimportant victories by federal prosecutors in easy cases. As Reuter (1983) said in his book *Disorganized Crime*, if there ever was a Cosa Nostra, it had become a "paper tiger." Gotti was just another paper tiger trapped by federal investigators.

THE PHILADELPHIA MOB

As discussed previously, much of the history of organized crime is befuddled by media hype, incorrect assumptions by law enforcement investigations, and the acceptance of rumor as fact. Sorting it out is no easy matter. Although it is impossible to confront the many instances of misimpressions and misinformation about organized crime in all cities throughout the United States, it could be instructive to look at one city other than Chicago and New York—the city of Philadelphia (Potter and Jenkins 1985). This city provides a textbook case of a Mafia city in the organized crime literature. Official law enforcement agencies have produced a detailed history of Mafia supremacy in Philadelphia's underworld from Prohibition days to the present.

We are told that from about 1958 to 1980 the Philadelphia family was headed by Don Angelo Bruno, supposedly a model of the conservative Sicilian patriarch, a respected member of the national commission of Cosa Nostra. After the don's assassination in 1980, a gang war began that resulted in twenty deaths in two years. Media and law enforcement officials agreed that this was a classic family power struggle. They differed only in whether it was purely internal or resulted from intervention by the fabled Five Families of New York. The competing parties, whoever they were, were fighting for dominance of the family and hence of the city.

As noted previously, the reality of organized crime is quite removed from the Mafia stereotype. Angelo Bruno may or may not have been the head of a Cosa Nostra family, but even if that group did exist, its power was very suspect. For example, organized crime from about 1917 to 1960 was dominated by a crime network, usually led by men of Irish or Jewish descent. The gambling elite were predominantly Irish at the turn of the century. In the early twentieth century they were joined by Italians and Jews, but the Irish were never wholly displaced.

Prior to Prohibition, Philadelphia played a key role in a massive drug-trafficking network headed by men with names like "Dopey" Bennie Fein. In the days of Prohibition, the bootlegging syndicate was led by Max "Boo Boo" Hoff, and its leadership was predominantly Jewish and Irish. Between 1930 and 1960, Philadelphia's organized crime was dominated by the Rosen mob, a Jewish-led gang with strong Irish and Italian components. The Rosen mob "corporatized" gambling and played a major role in heroin importation in the 1950s. Of course, there were also Italian criminals, but they acted only within the context of these larger crime networks.

Even in this supposed Mafia stronghold, grave historical problems exist in the mere identification of families and leaders, and even greater difficulties arise in assessing their real power. The city of Philadelphia shows a clear history of dominance by powerful organized crime groups, but virtually never by those mentioned in the "official" history of the Mafia. Bruno and his associates were a startlingly recent occurrence, dating from about 1960. When they emerged, it was not as a result of an apostolic succession from the ancient crime lords of Sicily, but within the context of the Rosen mob. It was abundantly clear that Bruno came not from Maranzano or Masseria, but from Nig Rosen and Meyer Lansky. All Bruno's early criminal and legitimate activity occurred in concert with members of the Rosen mob, not with any independent Italian organized crime group. Creating an elaborate history of the Mafia was accomplished by law enforcement officials in the late 1960s. The existence and history of the Philadelphia Cosa Nostra largely represent the work of myth makers.

Starting in the 1960s, Bruno and his associates played a large role in crime, but they had no coordinating role or monopoly on crime. In fact, they held only a small share of organized criminal activity. The Bruno family at most could be described as a South Philadelphia gambling and loan-sharking organization, serving only a small part of the city and without significant influence over the numerous other organized crime groups that were active in Philadelphia.

Although it is true that some Bruno members were active in loan-sharking, gambling, and fencing, they coexisted with many others. For example, if we look at gambling operations, it is clear that by the 1970s and into the 1980s, scores of organized crime groups were in operation. The largest and most successful of these were African American numbers bankers with hundreds of operations scattered throughout the city. In bookmaking it was clear that the major role was played by a handful of Jewish and Irish bookies in the center city. There was still a large Irish role in gambling. Research identified at least a dozen Irish gamblers with volumes in excess of $5 million a year.

The same situation was found with regard to drug trafficking. While several alleged Cosa Nostra associates had been involved in a few disastrous and unsuccessful drug deals, approximately sixty other criminal conspiracies fed Philadelphia's voracious appetite for heroin, methamphetamines, and cocaine. Groups as diverse as the the black Mafia, the Greek mob, the K & A gang, and the motorcycle clubs financed and directed much of the drug trade. The Mafia had no discernible role in prostitution or pornography at all.

Very simply, no ethnic group dominated or dominates organized crime in Philadelphia.

Philadelphia and the National Syndicate

The history of organized crime in Philadelphia contradicts the idea of a Mafia-dominated syndicate at every point. First, the gangs run by Boo Boo Hoff and Nig Rosen were certainly tied into some sort of national confederation, but it was a loose association of bootleggers and gamblers clustered around Meyer Lansky, certainly not an Italian-dominated national syndicate. Second, insofar as Rosen had a family, it was not territorially based, but operated in Pennsylvania, New York, New Jersey, Delaware, and Maryland—at least—and always maintained the closest alliances with former members of the Bugs and Meyer mob. Finally, the Italian organized crime groups, such as those headed by Marco Reginelli in southern New Jersey and the Matteo brothers in Philadelphia, existed within the context of the Rosen mob. Certainly, no Italian national commission tried to tell Nig Rosen what to do.

There is no doubt of Rosen's national connections. For instance, he allegedly supplied the hit man "Chinkie" Rothman, who was believed responsible for killing Bugsy Siegel, which was certainly a Lansky operation. Siegel was supposedly guilty of misappropriating funds earmarked for investment in Las Vegas casinos and of attempting to run a rival wire service to compete with the Chicago mob's operation. Bugsy was treading on a number of sensitive toes: Accardo in Chicago, Lansky, and other East Coast investors. With Anastasia's approval, an old-style Murder, Inc., gangland hit was approved, and Rosen supplied the killer. The FBI believed that "Stromberg [Rosen] was reportedly a member of Murder, Inc.," and that his interests in New York's racket-ridden garment industry linked him with Anastasia, Lepke Buchalter, and Gurrah Shapiro.

Rosen's move out of the rackets and into investment in the decade after 1945 connects him directly to the world of Meyer Lansky. Rosen attempted to finance the French Connection in heroin, invested in Las Vegas, and had interests in Cuba in the 1950s. In 1963 the Senate investigation of organized crime and narcotics placed Rosen at the heart of the old syndicate's move into drugs. It described the activities of Rosen allies the Eliopoulous brothers in the early 1940s as "members of Murder, Inc." It also included Buchalter, Legs Diamond, Saul Gelb, Harry Meltzer, and others in Rosen's heroin importation activities. Rosen's drug ring also included Harry Teitelbaum, a veteran associate of Lansky's.

During the Kefauver investigation into interstate gambling in 1951, Rosen admitted knowing Siegel, Lansky (Rosen set the date for these associations as being prior to 1925), Luciano, Costello, Erikson, Zwillman, Reinfeld, and Carfano. His contacts in Chicago were also pervasive, including Jake Guzik, the Fischetti brothers, and other veterans of the Capone mob. Rosen cited the Fifth Amendment when asked about his business dealings with Erikson and Zwillman.

Rosen was obviously tied to some sort of powerful crime network or confederation, held together primarily by common financial interests. Angelo Bruno, Rosen's alleged successor, was supposedly part of an even closer-knit federation, La Cosa Nostra. It is alleged that he was appointed as Philadelphia boss by this body and was given the right to kill his predecessor (he declined). Bruno then allegedly became a member of the national commission and remained a commission member until his murder in 1980 (Blakey and Billings 1981: 233–236).

This commission has been the subject of inordinate discussion based largely on evidence from mob informants, such as Valachi, and on wiretaps, such as the De Cavalcante tapes. Cressey (1969: 110–123) described the commission as performing these functions:

- Appointing the boss of each family
- Approving new La Cosa Nostra members
- Settling disputes and acting as an interim boss in the absence of the family's boss
- Holding hearings and taking votes on issues

This view suggests that La Cosa Nostra is some kind of alternative state within a state. Some evidence suggests the existence of a commission that plays a role in settling disputes among Italian American syndicates, especially in New York. Incidents frequently cited are the exile of Bonanno and the Gallo–Profaci wars. Beyond existing, what did the commission actually do? As it stands, there are serious problems with the "commission" assertion.

The first problem is that the commission is a body without a plausible history. In essence, it is the Italian product of non-Italian developments. Did a commission really emerge from the Italian–Jewish–Irish bootlegging collaboration? If so, how did it become exclusively Italian? Of course, gang leaders met to discuss problems of common interest. They did so in Cleveland, Chicago, Atlantic City, and New York in the 1920s and 1930s; and there was a grand conference in Havana in 1946. The regular core of attendees—Luciano, Lansky, Buchalter, perhaps Dalitz, Rosen, Abrams (from Boston), or Zwillman (from New Jersey)—could have seen themselves as suited to answering policy questions. By the late 1930s, ancestors of the later Five Families—Adonis, Costello, and the rest—might have felt the urge to be represented (Messick 1973), but all this raises more questions, such as what the commission did before the late 1950s. We know virtually nothing about it before then.

Was the commission a new structure, set up perhaps to thwart Genovese's ambitions? What do we really know about the Five Families of New York? The earliest reference to them comes from the highly inventive speculations of the Bureau of Narcotics in 1952, when they isolated five or six main crime syndicates in New York (Costello, Genovese, Lucchese, Profaci, Anastasia, Buoncuore). But from what period does this structure date? 1950? 1960? Finally, when did the strong Jewish element in the syndicates move out? In 1945, a commission might have included mainly Italians from New York and Chicago, but it also would have included Jews from Cleveland, Philadelphia, and Detroit. What changed, and when?

The second problem is that, as we have seen, a commission does not fit the Philadelphia evidence. It suggests that Bruno was imposed on the city's criminal empire. In fact, Bruno apparently rose through the ranks of the Rosen mob to manage one part of a gambling and loan-sharking operation, and that is all. Could an Italian commission impose Bruno on Rosen, Lansky, and Rosen's successor, "Willie" Weisberg?

A third problem is that if there is a commission, it intervened only at the very highest level. The idea of the commission reflects a New York perspective that is probably not appropriate for other cities. The evidence seems to suggest that the Kefauver Committee, the McClellan Committee, and the Justice Department under Robert Kennedy focused on Italian crime and La Cosa Nostra instead of major organized crime because "the Mafia was small and handy" (Pearce 1976: 161).

THE NEW BREED

Although the concept of nontraditional organized crime is discussed at length in Chapters 5 and 7, a discussion on the development of new-style gangsters is appropriate here. Indeed, a new breed of gangster has emerged since the early 1980s and has redefined the role of organized crime leaders. Whether it be Colombian Cali Cartel leader Gilberto Rodriguez Orejuela, Mexican Gulf Cartel boss Juan Garcia Abrego, or the heroin lord Kuhn Sa from Myanmar, drug kingpins have adopted an approach to organizing and controlling illicit rackets that is very different from that of their traditional Italian and Jewish counterparts of the 1920s and 30s.

In the early days of organized crime, the old-style Sicilian gangsters were unassuming and peasantlike, striving for power to gain respect. Today's new breed of gangster is far more self-serving and flamboyant, still seeking power as did his predecessor, but for the purpose of achieving wealth. As a case in point we consider the rise and fall of one of the pioneers in modern-day drug trafficking, Pablo Escobar.

Pablo Escobar At the end of the late 1970s, one of the most powerful organized crime organizations in history was beginning to develop. Three South American criminal entrepreneurs, Jorge Luis Ochoa-Vasquez, Carlos Lehder-Rivas, and Pablo Escobar-Gaviria, had formed a cocaine trafficking alliance that later became known as the Medellin Cartel. In addition to controlling much of the cocaine trade, the alliance employed business strategies to mass market the drug in the United States. The organization accomplished this by becoming vertically integrated to the point that it controlled virtually all aspects of the business, from manufacturing, to smuggling and wholesale and retail distributing of cocaine in North America. Much of the cartel's success was attributed to extensive political payoffs to key government officials in both Colombia and the United States.

Escobar, who had humble beginnings in the Colombian village of Rionegro, was credited as being the key founder and brains behind the Medellin cartel's operations and one of the richest men in the world. He was arrested in 1976 with thirty-nine pounds of cocaine. The arresting officer was soon murdered, however, and, after receiving death threats, the nine judges refused to hear the case. The official records of the case soon disappeared, and Escobar never went to trial. His wealth was estimated at $2 billion. He built a luxury estate near the Magdalena River, which included a private zoo. In addition, he built housing for the poor and a hospital, all of which earned him favorable media coverage and a reputation as a Robin Hood–type criminal among Colombia's poor. In a strategically brilliant move, he was elected an alternative representative to the Colombian Congress in 1982, giving him immunity from arrest.

Pablo Escobar, cofounder of Colombia's Medellin Cartel, epitomized the new breed of organized crime boss.

In 1982 drug trafficker Fabio Ochoa-Restrepo organized a brutal criminal cartel to force out independent operators from the cocaine trade and to reduce losses resulting from drug seizures by government officials. Escobar's organization controlled distribution into the United States: cocaine laboratories, transportation, and airstrips; Jorge Ochoa provided "muscle" and bribes to officials. Within two years, the Medellin Cartel controlled an estimated 80 percent of all the cocaine trade in the world. Cartel members transported coca paste from Bolivia and Peru to Colombia, where it was converted to cocaine hydrochloride powder in secret laboratories there and in Colombia, Ecuador, and Panama. It was then moved to hidden warehouses in Mexico, the Bahamas, and the Turks and Caicos.

Reacting to pressure by the United States and subsequent to the assassination of the Colombian minister of justice, Rodrigo Lara-Bonilla, Colombia's President Belisario Betancur-Cuartas agreed in 1984 to extradite all drug traffickers to the United States to stand trial. With the support of the Colombian judicial system and numerous newspapers, aerial spraying of marijuana fields was authorized. This resulted in a declaration of war by Escobar's cartel against the Colombian government. Between 1984 and 1987, fifteen judges and numerous other governmental figures were assassinated in the streets of Medellin. In November 1986, indictments of Escobar and nine others were issued in Miami for conspiring to import more than 60 tons of cocaine to the United States. The indictments resulted from information provided by government informer Barry Seal, a former TWA pilot and smuggler for the Medellin Cartel.

In 1991 Escobar offered to surrender to Colombian authorities with two provisos: (1) he would not be extradited to the United States and

(2) he could stay in a prison built according to his own specifications, which included a king-size bed, private bath, and Jacuzzi. Colombian authorities agreed, and the prison was constructed. In July 1992, Escobar escaped from it and eluded a 1,500-man search; they pursued him by secretly moving among his supporters in Medellin and the surrounding countryside. Escobar's hiding places included secret rooms carved out between walls, under stairs, and in underground locations. On at least four occasions when police thought they had trapped him, he escaped into the hills and disappeared.

In December 1993, Escobar's reign came to a violent end. He had been concerned about the safety of his family. His brother-in-law recently had been killed by police and his children's teacher had been murdered by the PEPES, a vigilante group thought to be made up of former colleagues whom Escobar was thought to have betrayed. In addition, hit men from the rival Cali Cartel and rebel police officers also wanted Escobar dead. Fearing that his family would be killed, Escobar sent his wife and children to Germany, where they were refused admittance by German authorities and returned to Bogotá. This action led Escobar to make two fatal mistakes: (1) he called a Medellin radio station to complain about the lack of solidarity by the German government and (2) he phoned his wife to advise his family to stay in Bogotá.

Within 90 minutes the call was traced through a scanning operation set up outside Medellin with U.S.-donated equipment. The equipment pinpointed the source of the call as a house in the western part of the city. Rather than risk a mass operation, a seventeen-man search contingent went to the location, surrounded the building, and cut off any telephone communication. As officers watched, a teenage boy thought to be Escobar's nephew arrived at the house with lunch. Once the door opened, officers entered with guns blazing. From his room upstairs, Escobar and his bodyguard Alvaro de Jesus-Ahudelo returned fire. After thrusting himself through a second-story window, Escobar attempted to pass through a narrow metal grating leading to the roof next door, where, he could leap to the ground and dash to a nearby wooded area. Instead, a shower of machine gun bullets stopped him on the grating. Escobar was dead.

Between 1983 and 1993, Escobar was credited with the assassinations of a Colombian attorney general, justice minister, three presidential candidates, more than 200 judges, thirty kidnapping victims, dozens of journalists, and an estimated 1,000 police officers (Fedarko 1993). Drug enforcement officials have since concluded that, while Escobar's death could have resulted in the end of the Medellin Cartel, it did not end the cocaine trade, because rival cartels such as the Cali Cartel had gained considerable momentum during Escobar's sixteen-month run from the police. (We examine drug cartels and the international organization of drug trafficking in the twenty-first century in Chapter 6.)

WHAT HAVE WE LEARNED?

This chapter discussed the formation and development of a number of historical organized crime groups. Many factors contributed to their development. Immigration of the Irish, Jews, and Italians in the late nineteenth and early twentieth centuries played an important role in this development. Because of their foreign status and sometimes the language barrier, many of these immigrants were not afforded decent housing, jobs, or respectable social status in U.S. communities. Slowly, members of these groups gained representation in local politics through political machines in cities such as New York, Chicago, and Kansas City. As they attained political prominence, local politicians could award jobs and other political favors to people with the expectation of a vote in return.

The Prohibition era was one of the most important periods in the development of organized crime because many immigrants who had been denied legitimate employment opportunities found wealth and prestige in selling bootleg beer and liquor. Prohibition enabled gangsters not only to profit handsomely from illegal liquor sales, but also to acquire the revenue to incorporate their activities slowly into legitimate business, making detection of their rackets much more difficult than ever before. This was the true beginning of organized crime as we know it today. Over the past seventy-five years we have observed that, in its zeal to realize profits and survive over long periods of time, organized crime knows no language, ethnic, racial, or cultural barrier. Although some groups are more homogeneous than others, most organized crime organizations are willing to employ persons from a number of backgrounds.

DO YOU RECOGNIZE THESE TERMS?

Black Hand
Black Sox scandal
Castellammarese war
Eighteenth Amendment
Noble Experiment
Prohibition
roaring twenties

St. Valentine's Day Massacre
Tammany Hall
temperance movement
Twenty-first Amendment
Union Station Massacre
Untouchables
Volstead Act

POINTS OF DISCUSSION

1. Explain the prevailing social philosophy of many of the immigrant groups who migrated to the United States at the turn of the century.

2. Describe the rise of Irish immigrants to political prominence in major U.S. cities during the early twentieth century.

3. Discuss the development of the political machine and its connection with the growth of organized crime.

4. Explain the role of Prohibition and the emergence of organized crime in the United States.

5. Compare and contrast the social and political variables that led to the growth of organized crime in Chicago and New York.

6. Explain the interrelationship between Italian, Irish, and Jewish gangsters during the 1920s and 1930s.

SUGGESTED READING

BLOCK, A., and W. J. CHAMBLISS. (1981). *Organizing Crime.* New York: Elsevier. This book examines organized crime within the context of its history and the political–economic forces that created it, presenting essays and case studies on organized crime and criminals in the United States and Europe.

FRIED, A. (1980). *The Rise and Fall of the Jewish Gangster in America.* New York: Holt, Rinehart and Winston.

JOSELIT, J. (1983). *Our Gang: Jewish Crime and the New York Jewish Community, 1900–1940.* Bloomington: Indiana University Press. This book examines the patterns and personalities of Jewish crime in New York between 1930 and 1940, as well as the effect of the crime and the perpetrators on the New York Jewish community.

LACEY, R. (1991). *Little Man: Meyer Lansky and the Gangster Life.* Boston: Little, Brown.

NELLI, H. (1976). *The Business of Crime: Italians and Syndicate Crime in the United States.* New York: Oxford University Press. This is a comprehensive history of Italians in U.S. crime during the period from the murder of Police Chief Hennessey in New Orleans in 1890 to the end of 1941.

STUART, M. A. (1985). *Gangster 2: Longy Zwillman, the Man Who Invented Organized Crime.* Secaucus, NJ: Lyle Stuart.

4

THE EVOLUTION OF ORGANIZED CRIME

Southern Beginnings and Major Participants

This chapter will enable you to:

- Recognize the significance of rural organized crime development in the South
- Understand the historical role that piracy played in organized crime
- Distinguish between land and river pirates

- Learn the significance of gambling, bootlegging, and prostitution as organized crime enterprises in turn of the century southern U.S. cities
- Understand the development of vice districts and street gangs in the South

INTRODUCTION

Chapter 3 examined the beginnings of organized crime from an urban approach. The urban setting is an important component in understanding the origins of organized crime, but it represents only one piece of the puzzle. This chapter considers organized crime roots from a southern focus. Doing so will provide students of organized crime an important perspective from which to achieve a comparative perspective. This chapter discusses the development of organized crime in the South.

HISTORICAL PERSPECTIVES OF ORGANIZED CRIME IN THE SOUTH

The development of organized crime in the United States has been well documented for major industrial cities of the North and Midwest. New York, Philadelphia, Detroit, and Chicago have been the subjects of numerous histories tracing the roots of organized crime to political machines; gambling, saloon, and prostitution operators; professional thieves; and street gangs made up of newly arrived immigrants. What is less well known is how criminal organizations developed in the southern states. It is clear that such organizations developed and that by the 1940s and 1950s organized crime was as entrenched in southern locales, such as the cities of New Orleans, Louisiana, and Nachez, Mississippi, and in rural areas across the South, as it was anywhere in the country. What is unclear is what pattern of development preceded the establishment of major syndicates in these areas (Albini 1971; Block 1978; Albanese 1989; Abadinsky 1994; Kenney and Finckenauer 1995).

In many ways we would expect the genesis of organized crime to follow similar and consistent patterns everywhere. For example, it is well established in the organized crime literature that citizen demand for illicit gambling, liquor, sex, and other goods and services spurred the development of criminal organizations. It is also a virtual maxim that such groups cannot develop and take hold without powerful support from political and economic entities in the communities in which they operate. The similarities seem, however, to end there. The major cities of the North and Midwest were heavily and densely populated. The South was sparsely populated and predominantly rural in character, although it did have cities with large populations. The North and Midwest were commercialized and in the process of industrializing when organized crime took hold. The South's economy had been based on slavery, which hindered its economic development for centuries.

The northern and midwestern cities had developed strong political party organizations, usually supported by immigrant-populated youth gangs, which often sanctioned and controlled illicit vice. In contrast, the South was a consistently single-party system, first with slavery and then segregation. Organized crime took root in the South, however, within the same general context of vice and corruption that historians have detected in the northern and midwestern cities. The context was the same, but the flavor was distinctly southern, with the early formations of organized crime occurring around some activities that would scarcely be imagined by their northern and midwestern counterparts (Albini 1971; Smith 1974; Chambliss 1988).

Political corruption was, of course, central to organized crime in both the North and South. It had a larger context in the South and therefore provided a more powerful impetus to organized crime. Of course, the sheriff and judge, the mayor and governor were involved in organized crime, but in the southern states these forces were insufficient. For organized crime to take hold, the aristocratic southern planters and the mercantile traders of the great port cities were also integral to organized crime. The vices—liquor, prostitution, and gambling—obviously formed an economic service core in the South, but even these basic vices took new forms.

In the South, riverboat faro games were sometimes part of an organization. River ports were the vice districts of the South. Procuring, kidnapping, or otherwise acquiring young girls for the prostitution trade was in some cases more profitable and more highly organized than the prostitution business itself. The liquor trade involved not just tax evasion and smuggling, but also production in highly organized enclaves. Equally important were crimes not imagined in the North. Slave stealing and land and river piracy were integral parts of the development of southern organized crime.

The basic characteristics of development of organized crime articulated by Albini, Smith, Chambliss, and others applied to southern culture as it did to the great cities of the North and Midwest. These characteristics merely adapted to southern forms of society.

Beginning in the 1990s, one of organized crime's oldest enterprises started making a major comeback. Maritime piracy reappeared as an organized criminal enterprise, particularly in shipping lanes off the coasts of Southeast Asia and Africa. Modern-day piracy is a crime of theft on the high seas that carries the danger of significant environmental damage, because so many ships today carry environmentally hazardous cargoes. In addition, modern maritime piracy is a significant danger to navigation on the high seas because of the common practice of leaving vessels underway with no crew, thereby drastically increasing the dangers of collision and grounding (Gallant 1999).

Direct financial losses from maritime piracy are estimated to be about $450 million a year. Since 1994 the number of reported incidents of maritime piracy has more than doubled to an average of 200 to 300 such incidents per year. Like many crimes, however, officially reported incidents of high-seas piracy severely underestimate the total number of such incidents. Many, if not most, instances of piracy go unreported, particularly those involving coastal fishermen and recreational sailors. In 1999, 185 attacks occurred on ships at sea, at anchor, or in ports. In those attacks, 408 crew members were taken hostage as a result of ship boardings by pirates.

Acts of maritime piracy are most likely to occur in unpatrolled or lightly patrolled waterways. Pirates prefer coastal waterways or narrow straits through which ships must pass. These locations allow for a relatively fast, often well-concealed approach to the target vessel to avoid any warning to the crew. Piracy is a major problem along the coastlines of Indonesia, Malaysia, Thailand, and the Philippines. These nations have heavy concentrations of islands, archipelagoes, and peninsulas from which attacks on shipping can be easily staged. Numerous maritime choke points between land masses slow shipping and make for easy targets by pirates. In addition, similar conditions, along with virtually nonexistent governmental patrolling, have also made the west coast of Africa a prime site for pirate activity, particularly the coasts of Nigeria, Senegal, and Somalia. The east coast of Africa provides a different kind of target for pirates. Heavy volumes of maritime shipping into the ports of Mombasa, Kenya, and Dar es Salaam, Tanzania, make these harbors attractive locations for attacks on anchored or berthed ships. Most pirate attacks are crimes of opportunity, undertaken quickly when an appropriate and easy target is located. However, some of these attacks involve ships that are specifically targeted for the cargo they are carrying. In these cases, pirates often attack as agents for sellers who have already prearranged for black market sales of the stolen goods.

Criminal networks active in piracy usually operate as independent groups, but many have business ties to other organized crime groups, either as specialized agents to conduct the theft or as patrons to use the capabilities of larger organized crime groups to dispose of stolen goods. Current criminal networks involved in piracy are both more sophisticated and more violent than their earlier counterparts. The ever-increasing frequency of pirate attacks has begun to have a chilling effect on maritime commerce, particularly in Asia. Modern-day pirates are more likely than their earlier counterparts to engage in multiship attacks and to disguise their own vessels.

These pirate networks use corrupt officials to obtain shipping schedules and the routes that they use to coordinate their attacks. In addition, pirates today tend to avoid attacks on large shipping companies, concentrating their efforts on small shipping lines that could own only one or two vessels. Finally, modern-day pirates are well armed and show a consistent inclination to use force when seizing the ships they have targeted. In an alarming trend, the number of crew members killed or injured in pirate attacks has increased every year since 1995.

LAND PIRATES, HORSE AND SLAVE THIEVES, HIGHWAYMEN, MARAUDERS, AND TRAIN ROBBERS

In the early nineteenth century, several gangs operated across the southern states as **land pirates.** They were primarily highwaymen who attacked and stole various merchandise. Many land pirates also specialized in slave stealing, a trade that involved kidnapping slaves who had been freed, who were away from their plantations on errands, and, occasionally, who were on plantation grounds. The pirates resold these slaves at auctions or private sales. Slave stealing had a kind of official sanction because gangs specializing in this activity also hired out to slave owners to track down runaway slaves, thus acting in a quasi-official capacity as slave patrols. On occasion, these land pirates also operated as private armies, or mercenaries, for large landowners and as enforcers and boundary patrols on huge southern estates (Rothert 1924; Coates 1930; Sherry 1986).

Micah "Big" Harpe and Wiley "Little" Harpe are among the most notable of the many land pirates who operated along the Wilderness Road in Kentucky and the Natchez Trace in Mississippi. The Harpe brothers were born into a Tory family in North Carolina and fled to the Tennessee and Kentucky areas after the American revolution. The brothers were credited with killing dozens of men, women, and children who moved west on these early settlement trails in the late eighteenth century. Eventually, the Harpes found the Wilderness Road to be slim pickings for profitable robbery and moved to Cave-in-the-Rock at Hurricane Bars, off a dangerous channel on the Kentucky shore of the Ohio River. The cave had subterranean chambers so large it has been alleged that the Harpes hid herds of cattle in them. From Cave-in-the-Rock, the Harpe gang, joining with other outlaws, took part in a syndicated river theft operation that involved luring flatboats and settlers to the shore and then killing them and stealing their possessions.

The Harpe Brothers' gang was broken up by a frontier posse in 1799, when Micah was captured, killed, and beheaded. His head was boiled and his skull placed on a post for passersby to see near the town that is now picturesquely called Harpeshead, Kentucky. Wiley and the other gang members escaped and in 1803 joined up with another land piracy group. The original Harpe gang had simply been rural bandits, but the organization they joined offered a greater promise of success, uniting the bandits with the local constabulary. This new gang was led by Samuel Mason, a Kentucky justice of the peace.

The Mason gang had been operating as horse and slave thieves for almost a decade when Wiley joined them in 1799. Unfortunately, for Sam Mason, Wiley Harpe was not particularly trustworthy. After getting word that a large reward was being offered for Mason in Mississippi, Wiley and another gang member cut off Mason's head with an axe and traveled to Natchez, Mississippi, with the head to collect the reward. They delivered the head to authorities in Natchez and settled down to wait for the reward money. Being no smarter than trustworthy, Wiley and his associate soon got bored and decided to steal some horses to augment the value of their trip. Unfortunately, they were caught and hanged at Greenville, Mississippi, in 1804 before they could collect the price on Mason's head (Rothert 1924; Coates 1930; Marshall and Evans 1939).

Both contemporaneous with and succeeding the Harpe brothers was a gang operated by Bully Wilson from about 1800 to 1824, a land and river piracy gang at Cave-in-the-Rock. The gang, consisting of about 100 men, lured settlers traveling on the river ashore in two ways. Sometimes they would place markers on the river that would guide the rafts and keelboats into the rocks, and then the gang would attack the passengers. Wilson and his cohorts would also lure thirsty settlers to shore with signs advertising liquor and entertainment.

If all else failed, the Wilson gang simply attacked the rafts and keelboats from skiffs or canoes, killing the passengers and shipping their goods to New Orleans merchants who dealt with the Cave-in-the-Rock gang on a regular basis. Cave-in-the-Rock was notable as a sanctuary and hangout for other marauders, robbers, procurers, slave stealers, and criminals on the Ohio River (Rothert 1924; Havighurst 1964; Sherry 1986).

Of all the land pirates and slave stealers, John Murrell (born in 1794) most captured the public imagination of his day. Much of what is written about him is based on rumor, folklore, and southern slave owner hysteria. Although the specifics are vague, it is reasonable to suggest that Murrell was a major figure in early organized crime along the Mississippi (Coates 1930; Marshall and Evans 1939; Sherry 1986).

Murrell owned a very successful plantation in Tennessee from which he directed his criminal activities, the core of which was slave stealing. He raided plantations, mostly in Mississippi, stole slaves, and resold them. If he stole a slave who could not be resold, he simply murdered the slave. Murrell and his gang also operated as highwaymen. They visited the gambling dens and bordellos of New Orleans looking for rich travelers moving north along the Natchez Trace. Murrell frequently offered to travel with a hapless victim, whom he or a member of his gang robbed and killed along the way. Murrel disposed of his victims by disemboweling them, filling their stomach cavities with stones and sand, and sinking them in a convenient river. Murrell is rumored to have murdered 500 men, although this figure is impossible to confirm (Coates 1930; Marshall and Evans 1939).

Murder was a minor infraction, however, compared to what Murrel was accused of conspiring to do. Whether the plot was real, exaggerated, or merely a figment of slaveholders' imaginations will never be known. It has been alleged that Murrel planned to start a slave rebellion. While civil and military authorities were busy putting down the insurrection, Murrel and a group of 500 or so syndicate members planned to sack and pillage the cities of New Orleans, Memphis, Natchez, and Nashville. Murrel planned to stage the insurrection to create a new nation governed by the underworld, with New Orleans as its capital and Murrel as its ruler (Coates 1930; Sherry 1986).

How much of this alleged conspiracy was real and how much fancy and paranoia is difficult to determine. In several jurisdictions, however, authorities heard rumors of the insurrection. They tortured and whipped slaves, who named several white conspirators in their confessions. In addition, Virgil Stewart, an alleged recruit in Murrel's plot, defected and disclosed its plans, and Murrel was arrested. Some activities seemed to support the conspiracy. Disturbances in the red-light districts of Nashville, Memphis, and Natchez occurred on July 4, 1835. In Tennessee, twenty slaves and ten white men were hanged after confessing to complicity in the plot. Murrel served a ten-year prison term and never regained his prominence in the criminal underworld (Coates 1930; Havighurst 1964).

One of the more notorious of the land pirates and one who operated under the protection of the landed gentry was James Copeland. He and his gang, who were active in 1840s and 1850s, were primarily contract "muscle" for the immensely wealthy and powerful Wages family of Augusta, Mississippi. They not only took care of trespassers on Wages's lands, but also tracked down runaway slaves and even carried out murder contracts for the family. For example, the Wages paid Copeland to kill a man named James Harvey, who had shot Gale Wages, one of the heirs to the family fortune. On July 15, 1848, Copeland shot Harvey in the head and collected his $1,000 fee.

Copeland's gang, which consisted of at least three dozen outlaws, was credited with several successful river hijackings and attacks on merchants in southern Mississippi. He was arrested for the Harvey murder, but the power of the Wages family was sufficient to keep him free and off the hangman's platform for ten years. Copeland was finally hanged on October 30, 1857 (Coates 1930; Havighurst 1964).

The outlaw gang headed by the legendary Bras Coupe was something of an anomaly in early southern gangs. Bras Coupe, who started life as a slave named Squire, developed a reputation as a talented dancer and entertainer. His master, General William de Buys, took advantage of Squire's talents and promoted him, making Squire a well-known entertainer. In addition, his master allowed Squire great freedom, taught him to hunt, and took him on excursions into the swamps of southern Louisiana. Despite his fame as an entertainer and the favor he enjoyed with de Buys, Squire ran away several times.

In 1834 Squire was captured after one escape attempt by a planters' patrol, who amputated his right arm as punishment. When his arm healed, Squire ran away again. This time, however, he organized a gang of other escaped slaves and some whites (a shocking development in 1830s Louisiana). He adopted the name Bras Coupe and led his gang on raids robbing plantations and stores. Over the years Bras Coupe's reputation grew as local plantation owners and the press suggested that he possessed superhuman strength and was invulnerable to gunfire. Hunters told tales of bullets flattening against his chest as they shot him.

Stories circulated of slave patrols and soldiers who tried to bring him in but were lost in the mists of the Louisiana swamps, never to be seen again. Eventually, stories of cannibalism and magic embellished Bras Coupe's reputation. His invulnerability to gunfire was apparently overstated because in 1837 he was shot by hunters, but escaped. While he recuperated in the hut of a fisherman ally, Francisco Garcia, Bras Coupe was bludgeoned to death with a club. Garcia then brought the body to New Orleans to claim the $2,000 reward (Asbury 1940; Sherry 1986).

The post–Civil War period also experienced marauding gangs. The Farrington Brothers and their associates had ridden with Quantrill's Raiders during the Civil War and had participated in the particularly infamous raids on Lawrence, Kansas, and Centralia, Missouri. After the war, Levi and Hilary Farrington led their outlaw band back to their native Mississippi. Primarily armed robbers by trade, they engaged in a string of violent and deadly robberies in the small towns of western Mississippi. In 1870 the gang attacked the Mobile and Ohio Flyer at Union City, Tennessee, and stole $20,000 from the train. Hilary Farrington was crushed by the stern paddle on the steamboat *Illinois* while eluding pursuers, and Levi was lynched in Union City after showing up in the town square drunk and challenging the entire town to a duel. The gang disbanded after the demise of its leaders (Sherry 1986).

In late nineteenth century the tradition of robber gangs in the Deep South was carried on by Eugene Bunch, also known as Captain Gerald, and his gang. Bunch had been a schoolteacher, but decided that robbing trains was a more rewarding occupation. The first known robbery by the Bunch gang was of a Southern Express train outside New Orleans in 1888, which netted the gang about $10,000. Over the next few years, the gang hit several more trains in Louisiana, Mississippi, and Texas. Bunch became a criminal celebrity who had frequent notices in the newspapers and carried on a lurid affair with the daughter of the governor of Texas. In the middle of his career, Bunch went straight again for a brief period and served as the editor of a newspaper in Virginia. By the 1890s he had again formed a gang, which included five of the best gunslingers in Mississippi, and resumed robbing trains. Finally, Bunch and two other gang members were killed in a raid on his hideout in the Mississippi delta swamps (Havighurst 1964; Sherry 1986).

VICE IN THE SOUTH

By the time of the Civil War, every major U.S. city and the relatively sparsely populated South had well-established vice districts catering to the trade in liquor, prostitution, and gambling. The organized urban vice trade had developed in the confines of early commercialism and industrialization, with considerable assistance from political organizations. Vice in the South had grown up around a slavery-based economy under the protection of aristocratic landowners and local politicians. Although vice was more geographically dispersed in the South and associated with the commercial life on the major river arteries, it was part of the development of criminal organizations (Albanese 1989; Abadinsky 1994; Kenney and Finckenauer 1995).

Natchez-Under-the-Hill

Outside New Orleans, the major southern port, vice districts had become well established in Nashville and Memphis, Tennessee, and Vicksburg and Natchez, Mississippi, prior to 1850. Natchez was a busy river port in the United States during the nineteenth century. Most of it was situated on a high bluff overlooking the Mississippi River, but below that bluff was Natchez-Under-the-Hill, which became one the most important organized crime entrepôts of the nineteenth century. The geographical separation between Natchez proper and Natchez-Under-the-Hill allowed vice and crime to flourish, because people had little reason to descend the bluff unless they were looking for sin. Gambling dens and houses of prostitution flourished as flatboats and keelboats sailing the Mississippi tied up under the hill on a regular basis. Histories of the time suggest that some prostitutes were actually born in the Under-the-Hill district, grew up in brothels, and never even saw upper Natchez (Roe 1910; Asbury 1938, 1940; Marshall and Evans 1939).

Natchez-Under-the-Hill had many organized vice operators, but two of the most influential were a tavern owner, Jim Girty, and his common-law wife, Marie Dufour. Marie was the most prominent madam operating in the district, and Girty was regarded in popular legend as unkillable. One story professed that instead of ribs, Girty had solid bone protecting him that deflected knives or bullets. Marie was no slouch when it came to brawling and fighting. She frequently took on rivermen in wrestling matches and, according to custom, won far more frequently than she lost. In the end, Girty turned out not to be unkillable and was murdered from ambush after a gambling dispute. Marie, heartbroken at the death of her lover, shot herself and died (Marshall and Evans 1939).

Several attempts were made to clean up Natchez-Under-the-Hill, but all failed. The most spirited attempt degenerated to violence and vigilantism in 1835 when reformers attacked lower Natchez and killed a number of gamblers. Many other gamblers and prostitutes escaped on the rivermen's boats. Curiously, the attack on lower Natchez resulted not from public outrage over gambling and prostitution, but from a widespread and probably false rumor that gamblers were conspiring with slaves to rise up against the Mississippi plantation aristocracy. The vigilante attack did little good, and Natchez-Under-the-Hill was open for business again in short order. Not until the decline of the steamboat as a major mode of transportation after the Civil War did Natchez-Under-the-Hill slowly begin to divest itself of vice, with many gamblers and prostitutes moving downriver to the more promising port of New Orleans (Asbury 1938; Marshall and Evans 1939).

New Orleans   New Orleans had two identifiable vice districts, both operating in full swing from about 1820 to 1840. The Vieux Carré was a high-class gambling, prostitution, and liquor distribution center in the American section of the city above Canal Street. The Swamp, a seedier vice district made up of about six city blocks between Cypress and South Liberty, served as the docking area for flatboat men operating on the Mississippi. By 1840 many of the illicit enterprises in the city had relocated to a smaller enclave within the Vieux Carré on Gallatin Street. This district was known for its bawdy, loud, and raucous dispensing of alcohol, prostitution, and gambling from cheap gin mills, barrelhouses (beer halls), and bordellos. From the Civil War to the end of the century, vice shifted again, this time into three distinct districts, Corduroy Alley, Basin Street, and Smoky Row.

Corduroy Alley was an alleyway populated with cheap bars (gin mills) and lower-priced brothels. Basin Street was the showplace of New Orleans vice, full of saloons, dance halls, upscale bordellos, and gambling dens. African American vice operators working New Orleans were confined to the area known as Smoky Row, a vice district populated by African American-owned brothels and saloons (Asbury 1938, 1940; Havighurst 1964; Donovan 1966).

New Orleans had long had a reputation as a notorious city for prostitution. By the end of the nineteenth century, however, it had become clear that New Orleans was flooded with prostitutes looking to ply their trade and that prostitution had to be controlled, or regulated at least, or it would overrun the city. The problem in doing so was that the proprostitution lobby was very strong, and all proposals to regulate the industry had been defeated when they came before the city council.

In 1897, Alderman Sidney Story seemed to have hit on a workable solution. He proposed that prostitution be allowed in prescribed and contained areas of the city. Despite the opposition of many real estate speculators, who worried that they would lose their incomes if brothel districts and their land-holdings coincided, the city council passed an ordinance creating a quasi-legal district that became known as Storyville. Altogether, thirty-eight blocks were set aside for legal prostitution, brothels, assignation houses, saloons, cabarets, and other vice businesses. These illicit enterprises operated under the benevolent eye of Fourth Ward political boss Thomas Anderson and a political ally, William Struve (Asbury 1940).

Storyville became the prime attraction in the city. Organized tours took tourists "down the line," including the often very elegantly appointed broth-els, arranging for stops in the saloons and cabarets so that visitors could par-take of the lewd and bawdy entertainment offered in New Orleans, and even arranging for tourists to "peek" at the prostitutes and their customers working the inexpensive "cribs" in the bottom-of-the-line houses of prostitution (Asbury 1940).

Storyville offered a wide range of sexual services and prices for any customer. At one end of the trade were the cheap, flimsy shanties where customers could crawl into a crib with a prostitute for 25 cents. More discrim-inating customers could step up to the $2 and $3 houses. For higher-class consumers, the $5 houses in the North Basin area were well-appointed and elegant mansions, which required customers to refrain from the use of foul language and banned drunkenness. These upscale mansions had mirrored walls and ceilings, ballrooms, and stages for elaborate entertainment, includ-ing circus acts, strippers, and what was politely called "indecent displays." The mansion brothels had house bands that entertained customers and played dance music in the ballrooms (Roe 1910; Asbury 1940).

Storyville had several of its own newspapers. Ironically, one of them, the *Mascot*, sold for 5 cents and was one of the major organs of reform in New Orleans, exposing political and police corruption while offering district gossip, which assisted customers in locating their favorite madam or prosti-tute. The most famous publication in Storyville was the *Blue Book*, a kind of social register for prostitutes. The *Blue Book* carried advertisements for broth-els and reviews of prostitution services at the finer establishments (Roe 1910; Asbury 1940).

Storyville's reign as a vice district ended in World War I. Prostitution was banned within five miles of army and naval bases. Federal agents visited Storyville and ordered the brothels closed. The mayor protested vociferously in Washington, but after an appeal to the U.S. Supreme Court failed, Storyville was officially closed. The net result was simply to disperse prostitu-tion throughout the city (Asbury 1940).

Gambling

As with pre-Prohibition organized crime in New York, Philadelphia, Chicago, and other northern cities, gambling and prostitution were the backbones of illicit enterprise in the nineteenth-century South. Prominent gamblers and gambling syndicates plied their trade in vice districts along the Ohio and Mississippi rivers and on the riverboats that traversed these arteries. Some gamblers were independent operators who worked with a small group of con-federates, and others operated as parts of well-established, highly profitable gambling organizations.

One of the earliest organized gambling operators on the Mississippi was John North, who ran a fairly complex crime organization out of Natchez-Under-the-Hill during the 1820s and 1830s. Among other enterprises, North ran a gambling casino, a saloon, and a brothel. In addition, he controlled and supervised much of the piracy, theft, and fencing activity in the port. Along with North, Sam Smith, "Dutch Bill," D. Hullum, and a steerer named McCall ran the group's operation. In 1835, as part of a general panic in Mississippi over the prospect of slave rebellions connected to the activities of John Murrell, rumors circulated that North planned to create an army of runaway slaves, thieves, and gamblers to attack and loot Natchez proper. In the subsequent attack on Natchez-Under-the-Hill, vigilantes captured North and hanged him on a hill overlooking Natchez with a roulette wheel tied to his body (Marshall and Evans 1939; Donovan 1966).

Gambling on the Mississippi River itself was prone to organization, as the case of Elijah Skaggs demonstrates with regard to the high-profit game of faro. Skaggs was born in Kentucky in about 1810 and made a career of as a cardsharp on the Mississippi River. He operated primarily out of the Nashville area, where he made a considerable fortune cheating other gamblers, but his major contribution to southern organized crime was his role in institutionalizing the game of faro along the river. Skaggs served as banker and manager for faro games up and down the Mississippi and in the 1840s was netting $100,000 a month from this organization's faro games. By 1847, he was a millionaire who augmented his faro income by studying other cardsharps on the riverboats and in the gambling halls lining the river banks and blackmailing them into paying him for not revealing their methods of cheating. At the age of 37, Skaggs retired from gambling and purchased a massive plantation in Louisiana (Anthony 1929; Asbury 1938; Havighurst 1964; Donovan 1966).

Other gambling operators also flourished on the Mississippi and Ohio rivers. Some, including James Ashby, were independents and more con men than gamblers. Others, such as George Devol and his partners Tom Brown, Canada Bill Jones, Pinckney Benton Stewart Pinchback, and Holly Chappell, operated with a higher degree of organization. From the 1840s through the 1880s, Devol and his associates banked faro, poker, and seven-up games on riverboats. In his autobiography, Devol claimed to have made about $2 million gambling on the Mississippi. He and his partners operated a syndicate that netted about $200,000 a year running games on riverboats. One of Devol's protégés and partners, Pinckney Pinchback, later became acting governor of Louisiana. Devol was famous for settling disputes by headbutting his opponents. In fact, he frequently engaged in headbutting contests, on which considerable sums would be wagered. In the 1880s, Devol married and settled down in Cincinnati, where he lived out his life in considerable comfort (Asbury 1938).

Many others also plied their trade on the Mississippi and Ohio rivers in the 1840s. James Fitzgerald was a New Orleans–based steamboat gambler. Thomas Mackey, James McLane, "Umbrella Jim" Miner, John Powell, Jules Deveareax, Colonel Starr, and the country bumpkin con man James Ashby made fortunes running games on the riverboats during this time. James Hargeaves, who would have a thirty-year run on the river from 1840 to 1870, reputedly retired with $2 million in his pocket after killing eight or more men in duels over the outcomes of card games (Anthony 1929; Havighurst 1964; Donovan 1966).

In New Orleans itself, the business of gambling was as big or bigger than prostitution, and—if possible—gambling had even more political protection.

One of the earliest casinos was Maison Coquet, an elegant establishment for high rollers that also provided high-class prostitution services. By 1827, the politically powerful John Davis had opened a gambling house. In the 1830s and 1840s, James Hewlett combined all manner of illicit activities in Hewlett's Exchange, a business combining gambling, prostitution, and slave auctions. By the 1850s gambling was in full swing in New Orleans, with much of the illicit business under the control of Augustus Lauraine and his partner, Charles Cassidy, a prominent newpaper reporter, who opened a large keno parlor. Another exclusive and elegant keno hall was opened by Price McGrath in partnership with James Sherwood and St. Louis gambler Henry Perritt. A high-stakes, exclusive casino featuring wagers on chess, Boston, and poker was operated by a mysterious figure known only as Curtius. From 1870 to about 1883, one of the last of the major southern land pirates, Major S. A. Doran, operated a casino and, at about the same time, William Franklin was running a gaming establishment. By the 1880s, New Orleans had all but given up trying to regulate illegal gambling. Mayor Joseph Shakespeare initiated the Shakespeare Plan, which licensed large gambling dens whose proceeds then were funneled into the Shakespeare Almshouse. Subsequent administrations abused the fund. After a grand jury investigation in 1897, the system ceased to work (Anthony 1929; Asbury 1940; Donovan 1966).

One of the most successful of the southern gambling organizations of the nineteenth century operating outside New Orleans and off the rivers was headed by a New Yorker named Zachariah Simmons. During the 1870s, Simmons organized the independent policy gambling operators in New York City into a cooperative confederation that he headed. He was assisted in this venture by an overt alliance with the politicians of Tammany Hall. The Simmons takeover was effectuated by Tammany, which arranged for police raids on all independent policy bankers in New York in the summer of 1870. Those who aligned with Simmons suddenly found that police pressure had eased. Simmons and his three brothers, in cooperation with Boss Tweed, effectively took control of 75 percent of New York's policy gambling action. By 1872 the Simmons syndicate had expanded its operations to Baltimore, Chicago, Philadelphia, Washington, D.C., and Richmond, Virginia. Its annual profits exceeded $1 million (Asbury 1938).

The Simmons empire expanded even more when in 1875 Zachariah was named one of the managers of the Kentucky State Lottery and the Frankfort Lottery of Kentucky—after all, who better to head a state-run racket? Simmons was an effective administrator who profited handsomely from his new position. After taking control of the official lotteries in Kentucky, he presided over a remarkable string of coincidences. It seems that the numbers drawn for the official games in Louisville and Frankfort were almost always the same numbers drawn in the same order as those selected in New York.

Conjecture is that Simmons selected the numbers in New York and wired them to Frankfort and Louisville. The numbers were then announced in Kentucky and wired back to New York through Jersey City and Cincinnati. Simmons was able to keep up this profitable scam until he retired and turned both the legal and illegal operations over to Albert Adams, who had started his gambling career as one of Simmons' policy runners (Asbury 1938).

New Orleans Street Gangs

Much like cities in the North, New Orleans had its share of street gangs, which served both as enforcers for local vice operators and as street workers for local politicians. Just like the Dead Rabbits, the Five Pointers, and the Plug Uglies in New York, the New Orleans gangs played a key role in the development of organized crime (Block 1978; Abadinsky 1994). In the 1850s and 1860s, one of New Orleans' most important gangs was the Live Oak Boys, who derived their nickname from their predilection for using oak truncheons as weapons. The Live Oak Boys were formed in about 1858 by Red Bill Wilson. They operated a kind of protection racket, attacking dance halls and saloons unless the operators paid for protection. They also hired out to the highest bidder when someone wanted a competitor's business disrupted. Their unofficial headquarters was the Fireproof Coffee House run by Bill Swan, a former Live Oaker himself. Prominent Live Oak Boys gang members included "Crazy Bill" Anderson, William Emerson, Michael and William Knuckley, Thomas Lewis, Charles "Lagerbeer" Lockerby, John Lowe, Barry Lynch, Hugh and Jimmy O'Brien and Hugh's son Matthew, and Henry Thompson, who was killed by Jimmy O'Brien in 1867 (Asbury 1940).

The other major gang of the period was the Yellow Henry Gang, named for Henry Stewart, whose visage was defined by a jaundiced look resulting from a bout with malaria. The gang engaged in well-planned burglaries and an extensive protection racket. Stewart and three gang members were sent to prison in 1884 for robbery, and Yellow Henry died of malaria in July 1886. Frank Lyons took over leadership of the gang after he escaped from prison in 1888. He was recaptured and returned to prison, but was quickly pardoned by Governor Francis T. Nicholls in 1890. Lyons was finally stopped when he killed a policeman and was sentenced to prison in 1890 (Asbury 1940).

Professional criminals also organized around some famous gangs in New Orleans in the nineteenth century. Pierre Bertin and Jean Capdeville ran a network of con men and burglars active in the 1860s. By the 1870s, Monk and Thomas O'Brien were heading up a gang of thieves, swindlers, and bunko artists in the French Quarter. Perhaps most important, Philip Oster, a burglar and gang leader, ran a network of thieves and counterfeiters that was one of the most successful counterfeiting rings in U.S. history. The gang came together in 1872 and began a fifty-year stint of counterfeiting money. Finally, William Walla ran a large burglary gang in New Orleans in the 1880s (Asbury 1940).

Procuring

Procuring young girls for the prostitution trade was a major vice industry in New Orleans and throughout the South. The trade, buttressed by chattel laws that also protected slavery, flourished throughout the nineteenth century. As early as the 1780s, Sam Purdy was probably the best known white-slaver in the United States. He usually secured young girls for sale by buying them from their families, usually poor settlers having great difficulty supporting their children.

Occasionally, to augment his supply, Purdy and his gang would use the same tactics as those of land and **river pirates,** stealing young girls off keelboats and rafts and kidnapping them from their families along the wilderness trails. The girls would then be taken to Natchez and auctioned off to prostitution operators or sold to "hogpen" operators on the Ohio and Mississippi rivers. The youngest and most attractive girls were taken to New Orleans, where they were sold directly to high-class madams as part of a contract arrangement with Purdy. The Purdy syndicate was huge, consisting of several gangs headed by other notorious white-slavers, including Lou Evans, Blackie Coe, James Fenney, Johnny Gaines, Joe Bontura, and Tommy McMurren. The Purdy gang had amazing longevity through 1805 or so and great financial success dominating the river slave trade. (Roe 1910; Marshall and Evans 1939).

Better known and more infamous was the procuring business in New Orleans itself. Although prostitution was widely tolerated in a number of open cities in the United States, the complementary racket of procuring young girls for the trade was universally denounced except in New Orleans, where it emerged as a mainstay of nineteenth-century organized crime.

One of the most famous procuresses was Mary Thompson, who in the mid-nineteenth century operated a cigar store, but whose real profits came from selling young girls to houses of prostitution. The prices ranged from $200 to $400 for inexperienced girls, depending on the marketability of their physical appearance. Thompson is famous for having one of her young girls arrested for theft when she escaped the procuress's clutches. The girl, a 15-year-old, had been sold to an elderly gentleman for $350. The girl ran away from him, however. Thompson had the girl arrested and charged with theft of services—the clothes, toys, and candy that Mary had bought for her. Mary was awarded $50 in damages (Roe 1910; Asbury 1940).

By the late 1860s, procuresses were supplying not just the brothels of New Orleans, but also operations in Atlanta, Memphis, Galveston, and other southern cities. At this time procuresses were taking orders and their supplies were divided into "stock" and "fresh stock," depending on virginity and age. Procurers commonly sent out circulars advertising their available stock. One of the best known of the post–Civil War procuresses was Louisa Murphy, a New Orleans schoolteacher who managed prices as high as $800 for a young unspoiled girl (Roe 1910).

By the 1880s, procuring had became a major racket in New Orleans. Miss Carol, Mother Mansfield, Spanish Agnes, Emma Johnson, and Nellie Haley dominated the now very public and very profitable trade in young girls. Spanish Agnes operated an employment agency for prostitutes; throughout the 1880s and 1890s, her agency supplied a steady stream of prostitutes for brothel keepers in Galveston and New Orleans. Not until 1917, when the Navy intervened in New Orleans and shut down the brothels, at least temporarily, did procuring begin to fade as a major source of illicit income (Roe 1910; Asbury 1940).

Prostitution

The organizers of New Orleans–based prostitution were important actors in the development of organized crime in the Deep South. The open toleration of prostitution in New Orleans attracted women from all over the South and the East Coast. At times, competition between prostitutes for available jobs in brothels and dance halls was so intense that many women failed to find employment as part of an organized prostitution operation. Some of these women, who were now relegated to street prostitution, carried mattresses on their heads that could quickly be converted to an open-air bedroom in an alley or vacant lot. The real prostitution trade was run by scores of persons, primarily women, who supervised the operation of small, efficient prostitution networks in the shifting vice districts of New Orleans.

In the early nineteenth century, brothel prostitution in New Orleans was pioneered by women such as Annie Christmas, a free black woman who operated a floating "hogpen" near the New Orleans levee. Mother Colby was running a bordello out of the Sure Enuf Hotel as early as the 1820s. Mother Colby operated with partners, among them Juan Contreras and Bill Sedley. Eventually, Mother Colby sold out her Sure Enuff Hotel operation to Frederick "Crazy Bill" Krause, who operated the bordello and hotel until 1855 (Roe 1910; Anthony 1929; Donovan 1966; Havighurst 1964).

Delia Swift, better known as Bridget Fury, operated a bordello that opened in 1859. Fury was born in Cincinnati in 1837 and by her early teens had developed a talent for pickpocketing, which she turned into a profitable trade at local dance halls. In the 1850s she left Cincinnati for New Orleans, where she linked up with other tough female prostitutes, including the infamous Mary "Bricktop" Jackson, in one of the earliest recorded female street gangs in the United States. Fury supported herself through pickpocketing and prostitution, but in 1858 she murdered one of her johns and was sentenced to life in prison. Her popularity among local politicians, however, allowed her to secure a pardon in 1862. At this point she decided that mugging and pickpocketing had limited potential as occupations. She opened her brothel and combined prostitution with the fairly regular robbing of customers. In 1869 she was arrested for robbing two Texans of about $700 and was sent to prison again. While she was in prison her prostitution operation was taken over by a larger organization and she never regained her prominence in the New Orleans underworld (Roe 1910; Asbury 1940).

In the 1860s the Buffalo Bill House, a dance hall and concert saloon run by Bison Williams, was an anchor of the prostitution business. During the same period, Archie Murphy operated a major prostitution organization, and Harry Rice ran the infamous Green Tree Brothel. In 1865, Mary "One-Legged Duffy" Rice took over the Green Tree operation from Murphy (Roe 1910; Anthony 1929; Asbury 1940).

By the 1870s women such as Leila Barton had opened brothels on Basin Street. Katherine Townsend ran one of the original bordellos on the street until her murder in 1883. Hattie Hamilton, also known as Hattie Peacock, operated the lavish Twenty-One Club on Basin Street. Hamilton is also notable for having shot and killed Louisiana Senator James D. Beares on May 26, 1870. Sweet Fannie (born Mary Robinson) operated a brothel on Basin Street despite a murder charge in 1861. She stayed in business until 1889 when she retired to Florida at the age of 62. (Roe 1910; Donovan 1966).

In the 1880s and 1890s prominent brothel operators on Customhouse Street included Frankie Belmont, Fanny Decker, Anne Deckert, Caroline Freeman, Nettie Gaybright, Nina Jackson, Kitty Johnson, Madge Leigh, Sally Levy, Mattie Marshall, Anne Merritt, Mary O'Brien, and Nellie Williams (Roe 1910; Asbury 1940).

In the 1890s in Storyville, the brothel business was organized by Julia Dean, Eunice Deering, Lulu White, Countess Piazza, and other women.

A man who played a major role in Storyville was Ray Owens, who operated the Star Mansion, one of the most famous brothels in New Orleans in the 1890s. Other noted prostitution operators of the late nineteenth century included Frances Morris; Abbie Reed ("Mary Hines"), who ran two bordellos in Burgundy Street; and "Queen Gertie" (Gertrude Livingston), who took over Reed's operations in 1893 (Roe 1910; Asbury 1940).

Probably the most notable of the women operating prostitution businesses was Mary Deubler, better known in New Orleans as Josie Arlington, whose elegant brothel on Basin Street operated from about 1890 to 1905, when it was destroyed by fire. Without question, Arlington operated the highest-class, most elegantly appointed house of ill-repute in the city. A tough business manager in a very tough business, she had worked her way up from the streets to become one of the most successful purveyors of vice in U.S. history. Starting at the age of 17, she worked as a house prostitute in a series of bordellos under the alias Josie Alton. For nine years she labored as a prostitute, with a reputation for being a very difficult employee. Josie Alton seemed to have a proclivity for brawling; in one incident she is alleged to have bitten off half an ear and the lower lip of Beulah Ripley, another house prostitute, in an altercation over a customer. But in 1888, as Josie Arlington, she opened her own brothel.

Through the brothel operations, Josie Arlington supported her entire extended family and her lover, Philip Lobrano, who co-managed the enterprise. Lobrano apparently objected to sharing the house profits with all of Josie's siblings, and in 1890 during an argument over "family values," Lobrano shot and killed Josie's brother. Of course, in New Orleans in the 1890s, murder was more a matter of inconvenience than of crime, and Lobrano was acquitted of the murder. This incident was sufficient for Arlington to realize that she no longer needed assistance from any man. She threw Lobrano out, fired all the local women acting as prostitutes, and reopened with elegant, well-behaved ladies, whom she claimed to be of foreign descent. She also raised her prices and screened out rowdy customers, entertaining only wealthy, well-mannered gentlemen.

Whether Arlingtons' prostitutes were really foreign countesses is a matter of dispute. For example, one of her prostitutes, La Belle Stewart, who was advertised as being straight from the Czar's court at St. Petersburg, turned out to be a former circus dancer from the Chicago World's Fair. Nonetheless, Josie Arlington's brothels flourished in the quasi-legal environment of the Storyville district. When fire put her out of business, she bought a mansion in the French Quarter, retired, and lived comfortably for another decade (Asbury 1940).

Bridget Fury and Josie Arlington have achieved legendary status. The other women and men who supervised and coordinated the flourishing prostitution business in New Orleans, so vital to the subsequent development of organized crime, are no less important. As the decades passed in the nineteenth century and the focal points for vice shifted from one neighborhood to another, the prostitution business remained as the vital cornerstone of organized crime on the southern Mississippi.

By the pre-Prohibition twentieth century, the well-established brothel operations had passed into the hands of women such as Gertrude Dix (Gertrude Hoffman). She was the wife of Fourth Ward political boss and saloon owner Thomas C. Anderson (Asbury 1940).

One-hundred-pound sacks of grain used to manufacture illegal moonshine alcohol, circa 1928.

(*Evans, Getty Images Inc. -Hulton Archive Photos*)

BOOTLEGGING AND MOONSHINING

The production and distribution of *white liquor* (illegally produced and distributed spirits) and *red liquor* (spirits, usually whiskey, bought legally but sold illegally in dry counties) is a popular legend in southern folklore. The quaint and often amusing portrayals of hillbilly moonshiners and bootleggers conceal an important truth about the illegal liquor industry. Rather than being an illicit business conducted by barefooted country bumpkins with straw in their teeth and young rednecks with greased ducktails and fast Fords, the illicit liquor industry was a highly vital component of southern organized crime integrated economically, socially, and politically. From the initiation of the illegal liquor industry in response to British taxes in colonial America, through the Whiskey Rebellion that protested the first federal tax on alcohol, through Prohibition to a contemporary underground economy evading federal state and local taxes and circumventing local liquor prohibitions, **bootlegging** and **moonshining** have been a well-organized and integral part of southern organized crime.

Throughout the South, local syndicates of moonshiners, bootleggers, law enforcement officials, politicians, local businessmen, and ordinary citizens created and maintained a series of *moonshine enclaves*, some with histories of more than two centuries. In these enclaves, crime organizations effectively and efficiently carry out and profit from the trade in illegal liquor.

In northeastern Alabama, Cleburne County was a stronghold of illegal liquor. In the late nineteenth century, a state law enforcement crackdown on moonshining in the county resulted in the arrest of about three-fourths of the county's population. A little farther to the north, the Paint Rock region of Alabama was even more notorious. Law enforcement officials refused to enter the area after dark, and dynamite blasts signaled the presence of strangers to warn moonshiners and scare off the intruders. The road from Paint Rock north to Huntland, Tennessee, was also a major route for bootleggers. During the height of Prohibition, Lick Skillet (in the same general area on the western side of Putman Mountain) and Lauderdale County also became major sites for the production of moonshine (Griffith 1975).

Georgia is a state with an historically large thirst, stimulated in great measure by the fact that 116 of the state's 159 counties are dry. The center of the illicit liquor trade has been Dawson County (about 50 miles north of Atlanta). Early in the nineteenth century, Dawson County supplied liquor to the major settlement in the area, Terminus, which later became Atlanta. Other moonshine enclaves were in Lumpkin, Gilmer, and Pickens counties. By the end of Prohibition, these counties alone were estimated to be producing about 1 million gallons of whiskey a year. By the 1950s, production had climbed to 1.5 million gallons (Dabney 1974).

As long ago as 1888, bootlegging and moonshining had become highly organized in Georgia. In Murray County the blockade runners (liquor transporters) formed an organization they called the Distiller's Union, in Gilmer they formed the Working Men's Friend and Protective Organization, and in Pickens they organized into the Honest Man's Friend and Protector. These early syndicates were really mutual protection and assistance societies that provided alibis for members, rigged juries, and harassed informers.

Georgia also produced one of the most mysterious of the major moonshiners in U.S. history. To this day he is referred to only by his alias, J. R. Turner. Turner, who was active in the Prohibition era, was never caught. One of his largest operations was in Lumpkin County, where agents sized eighty-one 220-gallon fermenters, which produced about 1,000 gallons of illegal liquor a day. Turner appears to have relied on a network of local informants who would tip him off to law enforcement activity and on a widespread system of payoffs. Turner was famous for having advance information on raids and surveillance operations by federal agents. When one of his operations was endangered, he simply called on the local sheriff and arranged for local authorities to raid him and seize his equipment. The sheriff would then execute the raid with an illegal warrant, and one of Turner's gang would show up at the courthouse to reclaim the equipment after the case was dismissed (Weems 1992).

Kentucky openly brags about its moonshine and bootlegging heritage. Although the illegal liquor industry thrived in most of the state, primarily because a local option kept much of the state dry, two areas stand out as important historical centers for the moonshine trade. The first is one of the most notorious locations in the United States, famous not just for liquor but for what locals refer to *killings*. (Killings are what would be referred to as murders in most states, but in Kentucky are purposeful murders seen as justified by the perpetrator and often not thought of as criminal, immoral, or wrong.)

Critical Thinking

To what extent are modern criminal enterprises similar to some of the old criminal rackets of the 1920s and 1930s? How do current criminals responsible for these rackets parallel their counterparts of 75 years ago?

The place famous for feuds, killings, and the widespread use of violence is Coe Ridge, a rugged seven-mile stretch on the Tennessee–Kentucky border. Just one raid on Coe Ridge during the 1920s seized seven stills, 4,000 gallons of mash, and 40 gallons of moonshine.

The other important moonshine enclave was the Golden Pond area in the Land Between the Lakes, situated neatly between the Cumberland and Tennessee rivers. During Prohibition, Golden Pond whiskey was a highly sought after commodity in the United States. In an area with no more than 300 inhabitants and no airport, it is said that dozens of planes flew in and out of Golden Pond on a weekly basis carrying the prized brew to Chicago and New York. The local moonshiners supplied much of the needs of the Capone syndicate in the early days of prohibition and sold to Meyer Lansky, Bugsy Siegel, and Owney Madden in New York throughout the entire "dry decade." Moonshining was so organized and demand so intense for its products that each hollow had as many as fifteen stills. In addition to producing some of the best illegal liquor, Kentucky also produced the most famous *blockade runner* (a courier who drove the liquor to its destination): Jaybird Philpot of Manchester, Kentucky. He was famous for ramming his way through roadblocks with his tanker car (Kellner 1971).

One pioneer of moonshining got his start in Rutherford County, North Carolina. Amos Owens was born in 1822. Although no doubt involved in small-scale home brewing with his father, Owens did not become a major figure in moonshining until after the Civil War. He enlisted in the Confederate Army at the age of 38. After the war he joined the Ku Klux Klan and, with a little help from his friends, established a moonshine enclave on a 3,000-foot-high mountain. From this enclave Owens produced and sold a potent mixture of corn liquor, honey, and cherry juice, called *cherry bounce*, which his organization distributed to Mississippi River paddle steamers. Owens and his cohorts were a fixture in illegal liquor production for more than fifty years (Dabney 1974).

The Piedmont section of North Carolina was also a hotbed of moonshine enclaves, particularly Wilkes and Ash counties in the northwestern part of the state and Burke County in the west central area. Wilkes County has an unbroken record of continual moonshining dating back at least to the mid-eighteenth century. By the end of the 1940s, estimates placed the production of moonshine in this county at around 500,000 gallons annually. A federal seizure of 7,100 gallons in a raid on a house in Wilkes County is still the largest seizure of untaxed whiskey. Eastern North Carolina also had important moonshine enclaves in Dare County and Robeson County (southeast). During Prohibition, illegal liquor organizations operated thirty steam distilleries producing 50,000 gallons a week in Dare County. Their liquor was shipped almost exclusively to criminal syndicates in Baltimore (Dabney 1974).

A more contemporary moonshining kingpin was Percy Flowers, who operated in the 1950s out of Johnston County, a little south of Raleigh. Flowers established a moonshining empire with an annual income exceeding $1 million. In addition, he owned a 5,000-acre farm, was a well-known local philanthropist, a deacon of his church, and a good friend of local politicians. Between 1929 and 1958, Flowers was indicted ten times at the federal level and eighteen times at the state level for bootlegging and evading income and liquor taxes. All the indictments except one resulted in acquittal, a small fine, or a suspended sentence. In 1936 he was sentenced to three years in jail for assaulting a federal agent, but he was out in one year on good behavior. In 1951 he was found to be delinquent in his 1951 federal income taxes, but he never paid the $285,000 levy (Kobler 1958).

Flowers was not overly sophisticated in his money-laundering methods, usually depositing money in safe deposit boxes around the state rented in the names of relatives. All vehicles used in his bootlegging and moonshining operations had fictitious registrations. Most important, however, Flowers contributed heavily to local charities and political campaigns. In 1957 ATF federal authorities targeted him for investigation and dispatched some of its best agents to Johnston County. Flowers complained bitterly and openly about the investigation, charging that the agents were ignoring moonshiners in neighboring Wake County who were undercutting his prices. At one point he offered the agents twice their federal salaries to work for him.

At the end of the investigation, the agents produced a 216-page report on Flowers and the sixteen other major operatives in his illegal liquor organization. In 1958, the government produced thirty witnesses and sixty-eight exhibits at Flowers's trial, but could only obtain a mistrial. He still faced eleven indictments in Johnston County, carrying a potential sentence of life in prison. Flowers entered a no plea to the charges, and the judge fined him $150 and sentenced him to eighteen months in jail, subsequently reduced to twelve months (Kobler 1958).

In northeastern South Carolina, tucked away in the Glassy Mountains, is the area referred to as the Dark Corner, a moonshine enclave that according to locals had a distillery on every branch of every creek. Just south of Dark Corner was a place called Jugtown where local potters worked to supply containers to moonshiners in South Carolina and Tennessee. Other enclaves in the state included Hogback Mountain and the Winding Stairs. Lewis Redmond was one of the pioneers of the illegal liquor trade, operating out of Oconee County. Redmond lived in a log cabin outfitted with portholes and stocked with weapons on a bluff overlooking the Tennessee River. His moonshining organization operated in a part of the state that as late as 1880 had no roads or incorporated towns. Redmond was as famous for his defiance of law enforcement as he was for his liquor.

In 1877, revenue collectors raided Redmond's stronghold, although he was able to escape. On their way out of the mountains, the collectors were ambushed by Redmond and nine followers, who seized the booty the agents had captured earlier. In another incident, Redmond kidnapped an agent's wife and forced her to cash a check to pay for horses that her husband and other agents had seized in a raid. In 1878, Redmond and thirty other members of his organization stormed the Pickens County jail and freed three of their fellow moonshiners. After being captured while squirrel hunting in North Carolina in 1882, Redmond served two years in jail before being pardoned for being in poor health. Apparently, Redmond went straight after his incarceration and produced liquor legally in Walhalla County, South Carolina, into the 1890s (Dabney 1974; Atkinson 1981).

During the nineteenth century the most important moonshine enclave in Tennessee was the Chestnut Flats area of Cades Cove in Blount County in far eastern Tennessee. This area was a center not only for the illicit liquor trade but also for prostitution and gambling. It served as a kind of "hole-in-the-wall" sanctuary for outlaws of all types. Another sanctuary was the enclave at Signal Mountain. In the northeastern part of the state, the town of Cosby in the Great Smoky Mountains supplied illegally produced whiskey to Lexington, Kentucky; Asheville, North Carolina; and Johnson City, Tennessee.

The moonshine industry in Tennessee was organized in the late nineteenth century by Campbell Morgan, who for years dominated the illegal liquor trade in southern Kentucky and middle Tennessee. Morgan is famous for having led an attack on revenue agents on August 23, 1878, in Overton, Tennessee, resulting in a two-day firefight in which the moonshiners prevailed (Carr 1972; Miller 1991; Weems 1992).

As is clear, federal law enforcement agents experienced violence in attempting to shut down the illegal liquor industry. In 1877 revenue agents seized 596 stills in North Carolina and arrested 1,174 people. In the course of these seizures and arrests, twelve agents were killed or wounded. From 1876 to 1902, thirty-five revenue agents were killed in the moonshine enclaves; another nineteen would die by 1905. Attempts to enforce the liquor tax laws in the South were greeted with perpetual guerrilla warfare (Miller 1991).

Local law enforcement appears not to have faced such grave danger. For example, in Kentucky and Tennessee local sheriffs commonly fired over the heads of moonshiners and then waited, giving the miscreants plenty of time to escape before seizing stills that would later be sold back to the moonshiners (Kellner 1971). Local courts in the South were also rather cordial in their relations with the illegal liquor industry. In fact, it was common practice in the 1870s for local prosecutors to charge federal and even state revenue agents with trespassing, carrying concealed weapons, assault, and even murder. Between 1876 and 1879, 165 federal agents were arrested in the southern moonshine enclaves, with Georgia alone charging forty-eight agents (Kellner 1971).

Moonshiners, on the other hand, got a modicum of mercy from their local prosecutors and judges. In Georgia, moonshiners were usually assessed a $100 fine, which they could evade by swearing a pauper's oath. Those who had to be sentenced to jail usually received thirty-day sentences. Unlike drug users today, moonshiners were well rewarded for their good behavior if they had to go to jail. Most were let out of their thirty-day sentences early. In fact, jailers and judges routinely allowed prisoners convicted of moonshining or bootlegging to visit their homes, walk around town, and drink at illegal saloons (Miller 1991).

Organized crime is one of the most highly adaptable social organisms commonly found in human cultures. Depending on public demand for illicit goods and services, organized crime can adapt to the exigencies of absentee landlords and feudal means of production in Sicily, heavy immigration and industrialization in the northern United States, and slavery-based agricultural production in the southern states. Organized crime's greatest strength is its ability to adapt effectively and efficiently to political and economic obstacles and to create functional alliances with those exercising political, social, and economic power, no matter the mechanisms being employed.

Whether it allies with industrialists, procurers, or landlords, with southern sheriffs, northern police, or the Italian military, whether it profits from feudalism or modern capitalism, the fact is that organized crime persists because it is necessary in the maintenance of power in whatever location or historical era it is found.

WHAT HAVE WE LEARNED?

As the complexion of organized crime changed with the turn-of-the-century immigration of Irish, Jewish, and Italian immigrants, equally as important developments were taking place in the deep South. Predominantly, these developments involved the formation of major criminal vice operations and their accompanying political counterparts.

This chapter begins with a general overview of historical perspectives of southern organized crime and then discusses the little known phenomenon of piracy. This piracy represents an aspect of organized crime that is well deserving of discussion and investigation, because it is prevalent today as it was centuries ago. The subject is treated with regard to modern-day piracy, as well as to historical perspectives on maritime piracy, land pirates, and hijackers in general. It is important for the student of organized crime to understand the historical beginnings of these groups,

diminutive as they are in some cases, because doing so provides a foundation for understanding larger criminal organizations, many of which also began as small splinter groups.

The chapter also discusses the origins of large-scale vice districts in certain southern regions. In addition, examples of criminal organizations, their leaders, and their contributions to organized crime are discussed. Of these, New Orleans is an excellent case study for understanding the interaction between politics and vice operations. Furthermore, New Orleans can be studied with regard to the formation of street gangs and how those gangs were utilized by corrupt public officials before the end of the 1800s.

Finally, the subjects of bootlegging and moonshining are addressed, with discussion of the geographical regions where this criminal enterprise was most common.

DO YOU RECOGNIZE THESE TERMS?

bootlegging
land pirates
moonshining

political corruption
river pirates

POINTS OF DISCUSSION

1. Explain the prevailing social philosophy of many of the immigrant groups who migrated to the United States at the turn of the century.

SUGGESTED READING

BLOCK, A., and W. J. CHAMBLISS. (1981). *Organizing Crime*. New York: Elsevier. This book examines organized crime within the context of its history and the political–economic forces that created it and presents essays and case studies on organized crime and criminals in the United States and Europe.

MESSICK, H., and B. GOLDBLATT. (1972). *The Mobs and the Mafia: An Illustrated History of Organized Crime*. New York: Gallahad. This publication traces the history of organized crime and

discusses the roles played by various actors in shaping the activities and structure of its operations.

PETERSON, V. W. (1983). *The Mob: 200 Years of Organized Crime in New York*. Ottawa, IL: Green Hill. This detailed compendium of East Coast crime builds a massive, factual portrait of the delicate, ever-changing relationship between Tammany Hall politicians, corrupt judges, racketeers, and certain union and labor bosses.

5

THE BUSINESSES
OF ORGANIZED CRIME

This chapter will enable you to:

- Understand the various businesses of organized crime
- Understand the various aspects of the prostitution business
- Realize the importance of drug trafficking to organized criminals
- Learn the various types of gambling operations

- See the relationship between organized crime and legitimate business
- Understand the role of labor and business racketeering in organized crime
- Understand the problem of money laundering

INTRODUCTION

The businesses in which organized crime is involved are as varied as one's imagination. In March 1996, seventeen reputed top figures in Detroit's underworld were arrested, including boss Jack Tocco. The Tocco family was reputed to be involved in numerous criminal rackets, and when its interests were threatened, it resorted to the familiar organized crime tactics of muscle and intimidation. For example, Tocco family members squeezed money as protection insurance from small-time bookmakers, numbers operators, and small-business owners.

In one case, when an illegal lottery operator rebuffed the family's attempts to get him to repay an illegal loan, Tocco gave orders to have him killed. In another case, a local businessman was the target of an extortion attempt, and Frank Whitcher, a Tocco strong-arm, was authorized to inflict as much injury as he wanted without killing the businessman. The Tocco family attempted to acquire interests in both the Aladdin Hotel and Casino and the Frontier Hotel in Las Vegas (Johnson 1996).

Three years earlier, former New York Gambino family underboss Salvatore "Sammy the Bull" Gravano had testified before a U.S. Senate sub-committee about some of the businesses in which organized crime is involved. In his testimony, he specifically discussed the business of prize fighting and stated that organized crime no longer fixes fights, but seeks control of managers, promoters, and prize fighters to cut itself in on a percentage of the substantial championship purses. Along with the infiltration of countless other legitimate businesses, prize fighting represents just one example of the many businesses that organized crime has infiltrated over the years.

Although organized crime is likely to become involved in almost any profitable illegal venture or activity, vice and racketeering services form the core of organized crime's entrepreneurial activities. Because the legitimate market does not provide vice operations, which include gambling, prostitution, pornography, drug trafficking, and loan-sharking, a sizable consumer population is left unserved. Consequently, organized crime capitalizes on these market voids and profits from providing services to these consumers. Several researchers have noted similarities between legitimate and illegitimate businesses, which we discuss later in this chapter. Of course, organized crime's sale of consumer goods and delivery of services are predominantly defined as illegal. Nonetheless, demands by certain populations make the creation of such criminal organizations inevitable.

How much money organized crime realizes from these illegal activities is the subject of considerable and widely varying speculation. In 1986, the President's Commission on Organized Crime (1986b: 423) calculated organized crime's annual gross income at $66 billion. If that figure is even close to being correct, organized crime is one of the largest industries in the United States, with roughly the same income as the textile and apparel industries and the metal industry (iron, steel, and aluminum) and a higher income than the rubber and tire industry. Some authorities have suggested that the commission's estimate is low, however. For example, James Cook, writing for *Forbes* magazine in 1979, estimated organized crime's revenues to be closer to $150 billion. As the President's Commission notes, that would be about $226 billion in 1985 dollars (President's Commission on Organized Crime 1986: 419).

In any event, despite the lack of precision in estimating income and profits, we are able to examine the primary income generators for organized crime groups. This chapter considers not only the illegal commodities and services supplied by criminal syndicates, but also how these organizations interface with legitimate business.

DELIVERY OF ILLICIT GOODS AND SERVICES

Organized crime provides a wide array of illegal goods and services to millions of customers on a daily basis. Although this statement seems to be obvious, it has important implications in understanding the inner workings of the business of organized crime. The scope of organized crime activities and the volume of the businesses engaged in by organized crime require a massive and pervasive series of networks covering the globe. Organized crime groups must be prepared to deliver illegal goods and services on a regular and continual basis. Thus, crime syndicates must achieve a highly efficient and effective level of organization. Organizations dealing in different goods and services are likely to have different forms of organization. For example, the efficient organization of a numbers gambling syndicate probably would not be efficient in the hauling of toxic wastes, nor would the most effective loan-sharking organization be efficient and effective in drug trafficking.

The idea of an overreaching syndicate controlling all aspects of illegal service delivery is, at least, improbable. To deliver illicit goods and services on a regular and continuous basis to millions of customers, organized crime must conduct its business in a public way. People cannot place bets if bookmakers are inaccessible and hidden in the deep recesses of a criminal underworld. Customers cannot find illegal drugs if drug traffickers are so concealed from the police that they cannot be located. Inevitably, this means that where organized crime exists, and it exists and flourishes almost everywhere in the United States, some form of official accommodation must be made. Corruption is integral to the organization of crime. The exigencies of the market and the requirement for political corruption tell us more about the organization of crime than does any rogues' gallery of foreign miscreants.

CORRUPTION

In Chapter 9 we discuss in some detail the nuances of political corruption and its important relationship to organized crime. Although **corruption** is not a business per se, in this section we make a few comments in general about the role of corruption in organized crime enterprises.

On March 18, 1996, the first 1,800 police officers graduated from a new-style New York City Police Academy that focused on anticorruption training. The revamped program is part of New York City's response to the city's worst corruption scandal in a generation that resulted in the investigation of twenty-nine officers in the city's 30th precinct for criminal wrongdoing.

Anticorruption training is thought to be the best test yet as to whether police training academies can prevent corruption or whether character, morals, and the daily temptations confronted on the street are beyond the influence of the classroom. Whether the program works is still to be seen, but one thing is clear: In many cities across the nation, police officers fall prey to the temptations of corruption, a phenomenon that erodes the effectiveness of the police and public confidence in them.

Thus far we have indicated that the primary motivating factor for organized crime groups is profit. To achieve the greatest possible return, members of many organized crime groups have found it expedient to invest some of their capital in government. Essentially, corrupt relationships between organized criminals and public officials occur in two areas.

The first is on the law enforcement level; the second is between the organized criminals who infiltrate legitimate businesses and the public officials who are in charge of regulating these businesses. Cressey (1969) notes that "Cosa Nostra functions as an illegal invisible government . . . its political objective is a negative one: nullification of government." Cressey suggests that each crime organization has had a *corrupter* of law enforcement figures and politicians. This does not mean to suggest that all corrupt public officials are in the control of organized crime, but those who have demonstrated a propensity for corrupt practices in general could be ideal candidates to become organized crime's corrupters.

Once we recognize the importance of corruption in organized crime enterprises, we must consider how prevalent it really is. We must assume that of the tens of thousands of law enforcement officers and public officials, most possess high ethical and moral standards and are not subject to corruption. One carefully placed government source working in behalf of organized crime, however, can allow criminal rackets to go undetected.

Of the many examples of police corruption in the United States, perhaps the most highly publicized investigation in recent history stemmed from charges made in the 1970s by two New York City police officers, Frank Serpico and David Durk. The corruption began to surface when these officers began to protest to fellow officers about corrupt practices in their precinct. The two were told to shut up and mind their own business or go along with the others and their corrupt practices. Out of frustration, the officers complained about corruption to officials high in the police department and were assured that their charges were being fully investigated, but nothing was ever done. Finally, Serpico and Durk took their story to the *New York Times*, and the paper ran a series of stories about corruption in the New York Police Department (NYPD). As a result of widespread public concern, the Knapp Commission investigated these allegations and found widespread corruption throughout the NYPD.

Resulting from the Knapp Commission's final report were reforms, which included the appointment of a special prosecutor to supersede the five New York City district attorneys in all corruption investigations in the city and the creation of a strong internal affairs division within the department.

Despite the Knapp Commission's revelations and recommendations, police corruption has remained a major problem in many major U.S. cities. For example, in 1988 more than seventy-five Miami police officers were under investigation at one time for possible involvement in criminal activities. Allegations included drug dealing, robbery, theft, and even murder. One investigation in particular revealed several officers who had ambushed drug dealers bringing cocaine into Miami. The investigation revealed that officers stole $13 million in cocaine from a boat anchored in the Miami River and loaded it into marked police vehicles. Between 1992 and 1996, dozens of police officers were arrested in New Orleans on charges such as rape, drug dealing, bank robbery, and auto theft. One officer was convicted of murdering another police officer and killing two Vietnamese restaurant workers while she participated in the robbery of the family's restaurant. In New York City, sixteen police officers were implicated in a scandal that broke in 1994 in Harlem, resulting in their pleading guilty to charges that included stealing cash from drug dealers, extorting money from suspects, and lying about arrests.

In 1995, more than fifty criminal cases were dismissed in Philadelphia involving arrests made by six renegade officers who subsequently pleaded guilty to charges of robbery, obstruction of justice, and civil rights violations. Past investigations into the Philadelphia Police Department revealed collaboration between police officers and known organized crime members. Also in 1995, Atlanta was rocked by corruption allegations in its police department when seven officers were arrested on charges of stealing money during drug searches and extorting money from citizens in exchange for police protection.

Some experts have suggested that the public does not really want the laws dealing with organized crime enforced as long as they do not see themselves as being victimized by criminals. Since organized crime provides the public with services, the public does not give law enforcement much incentive to prosecute these criminals. This concept tends to ignore the effects of corruption on the government in its responsibility to the governed. The employment of dishonest public servants results in a dichotomy. Officials paid to uphold the common good instead pursue personal gain and selfish ends through corrupt activities. As a result, the loyalty of the public servant is transferred from the public agency to the private-interest group through which he or she obtains these gains. This results in a reduction of the government's efficiency and effectiveness, an increase in taxes, and the possible generation of more crime and less enforcement.

PORNOGRAPHY

The pornography industry supplies customers with a remarkable range of goods and services, which range from hard-core books, magazines, films, and videotapes to various devices designed to be used in conjunction with sexual activity, to live and interactive encounters in *rap booths* and *live peep shows*. Although the U.S. Supreme Court has had difficulty defining the word *pornography* in recent years, the word seems to have a clear meaning to producers, sellers, and buyers of porn products as a product verbally or visually portraying sexual anatomy and behavior with the main purpose of eliciting sexual arousal. It is useful to distinguish between soft- and hard-core pornography. As a rule, the distinction refers to the degree of the sexual portrayal's explicitness. **Soft-core pornography,** for example, results from the restrictiveness of public policy that prohibits hard-core pornography or from a producer's desire to reach a consumer audience larger than that patronizing porn shops or adult movie theaters. *Playboy* magazine is an example of soft-porn material, featuring suggestive sexual material, compared to **hard-core pornography** magazines, which depict more specific and explicit sexual acts.

Since the 1960s, pornography has become much more visible in society, but the actual size of the industry is difficult, if not impossible, to measure. FBI estimates place the annual profits of the hard-core pornography industry at $2.4 billion (Satchell 1979); the California Department of Justice places that number at closer to $4 billion (California Department of Justice 1976: 21). Still other sources, including people active in the industry, insist that the actual number is closer is $6 billion (Kirk et al. 1983).

What we do know with some certainty is that the pornography industry engages in extensive business activities throughout the country. For example, the industry employs about 100,000 people in its legal activities (Kirk et al. 1983). An estimated 15,000 and 20,000 retail adult bookstores operate in the United States (Kirk et al. 1983), which realize, on average, about $200,000 a year in gross sales. In addition, according to the Adult Film Association, approximately 800 adult theaters nationwide draw 3 million customers a week and generate about $500 million in annual gross receipts (Kirk et al. 1983).

Forms of Pornography

Many forms of pornography exist. In addition to sexually explicit material, pornography includes cartoons, comics, joke books, sensational newspapers, and political satire. Most of these survive with a modest circulation. Some examples are *Screw* magazine in the United States and *OZ* in Great Britain, both of which are more obscene than they are pornographic and both of which have been subject to legal action. The distinction between the words *obscene* and *pornographic* is unclear, which illustrates the courts' difficulty in deciding issues related to the topic. The most widely circulated venues include *Playboy* and *Penthouse* magazines, which combine soft-core pornography with sensational "news stories" about crimes, catastrophes, and scandals. Other forms of pornography include homosexual pornography, addressing both male and female audiences; child pornography, depicting children in sexually explicit acts (now generating the most public attention); and aggressive pornography, portraying violent sexual elements that include sadomasochism, fetishism, bondage, and even *snuff films*, depicting sex and murder.

The pornography business has become an intense political issue in places such as Australia, Great Britain, Canada, and the United States. Controversy exists with regard to whether pornography is dangerous to both society and individuals. Official commissions studied the business of pornography during the 1960s, 1970s, and 1980s, and all came to remarkably similar conclusions: Pornography is not a source of rampant social dysfunction that should be totally suppressed, but is an offensive and dehumanizing expression of speech in need of some restraints.

Organized Crime and Pornography

Any business offering such a large flow of hard cash, little competition from respectable businesses, and a clandestine environment seems perfect for attracting organized crime, and it does. Exactly what form organized crime's interests take in the pornography industry is, however, controversial. For example, investigative journalist Jack Anderson has reported that "the pornography industry is controlled by organized crime. Phony names and dummy corporations are used, but behind them are the crime bosses" (Anderson 1979b). Convicted child pornographer Guy Strait told interviewers that the pornography industry is controlled by "the syndicate," a nationwide cartel that specializes in pornography and narcotics (Linedecker 1981).

The fact is that any cash business is susceptible to organized crime influences. Pornographic bookstores offer the opportunity to skim money off the top, thereby increasing profits and decreasing tax liability. Research showed that some pornography outlets in Pennsylvania instructed their managers to turn off their electronic cash registers during certain times of the day so that their records would not reflect their real sales income (Potter 1986). In other cases where retail establishments were owned by individuals with interests in other illicit enterprises, such as gambling or loan-sharking, the retail sales figures were inflated artificially so that profits from these illegal activities could be laundered through the store (Potter 1986).

In some major cities, motorcycle gangs have made a major move into the commercial sex industry. In Philadelphia, for example, the Pagans motorcycle club has been involved in retail pornography, the production of pornographic films, and the provision of other sexual services, including prostitution connected to live peep shows and rap booth operations in porn stores (Pennsylvania Crime Commission 1980; Potter and Jenkins 1985). A confidential 1978 FBI report on pornography said that "organized crime involvement in pornography, as evidenced by this survey, is indeed significant and there is an obvious national control directly and indirectly by organized crime figures of that industry in the United States. Few pornographers can operate independently without some involvement with organized crime" (Potter 1986: 24). The FBI report went on to detail a series of extortionate tactics prevalent in the illegal porn industry (Potter 1986: 24–25):

- A requirement that film producers distribute through organized crime–controlled companies under threat of piracy
- Burglaries of independent retail outlets
- Strong-arm tactics against theater owners screening pirated versions of organized crime-controlled films

The shadowy outlines of a syndicate in the pornography industry similar to the one described by Guy Strait was uncovered in the FBI's 1980 Miami Pornography (MIPORN) operation. MIPORN was an undercover investigation of the pornography industry, which resulted in the indictments of fifty-five people in ten states (Kirk et al. 1983). Among the key actors indicted in MIPORN were the following (Kirk et al. 1983; Potter 1986): Theodore Rothstein and Robert DiBernardo, both of Star Distributors Ltd. of New York, one of the largest hard-core film, videotape, book, and magazine distributors in the country; Louis and Joseph Peraino of New York, who were involved in financing and distributing the box office hit *Deep Throat*; Kenneth Guarino of Providence, Rhode Island, the operator of Superior News, Inc., the largest pornography distributor in New England; Mickey Zaffarano of New York, considered to be a major distributor of adult motion pictures, with interests in retail pornography operations in Washington, D.C., Boston, and San Francisco; and Reuben Sturman of Cleveland, Ohio, owner of Sovereign News Company, who was known as the King of Porn. Sturman was the largest pornography distributor in the United States and owned or controlled hundreds of retail and wholesale outlets across the country. He also had an extensive production and distribution operations in Europe.

Of those indicted by the federal government in the MIPORN operation, Reuben Sturman was clearly the most important. Sturman presided over his business enterprises from his Sovereign News Company headquartered in Cleveland. Sovereign News was housed in a three-story red-brick building, surrounded by chain-link fences and barbed wire and protected by the most modern and sophisticated electronic surveillance devices that money can buy (Satchell 1979; Potter 1986). Sturman controlled pornography distribution warehouses in Baltimore, Chicago, Pittsburgh, Denver, Milwaukee, Buffalo, Toronto, Los Angeles, and Detroit. In addition, he was the principal owner of between 300 and 800 retail pornography stores around the country (May and Hosenball 1981).

Sturman's empire dominated the pornography industry and created an environment in which small operators and their distributors depended on Sovereign News for their survival. A confidential FBI memorandum on the pornography industry noted that Sturman's business practices included the strong-arm shakedowns of other dealers, distributors, and suppliers throughout the United States, particularly on the West Coast. Sturman accomplished a total takeover with the assistance of Robert DiBernardo (Potter 1986: 136).

PROSTITUTION

One of the more notable prostitution cases involved California-based prostitute and madam Heidi Fleiss. In 1993, Fleiss was arrested on charges of pandering and procuring prostitutes for undercover officers. Fleiss, dubbed by the media as the Hollywood Madam, was thought to be head of Hollywood's most sophisticated prostitution ring, procuring prostitutes for movie stars, politicians, and others. The trial gained national attention because Fleiss's black book reportedly contained the names of Hollywood's rich and famous. Surprisingly, her father, Dr. Paul Fleiss, a pediatrician, was also implicated in the case and pleaded guilty to helping his daughter launder money and hide the income she made from her prostitution service. The Fleiss business is only one of many operations that have been exposed over the years. It represents the ongoing criminal supply of services that many demand.

Heidi Fleiss, reputed Hollywood Madam, leaves federal court in Los Angeles August 1, 1994, after she and her father pleaded innocent to tax evasion and money laundering.

(*AP Wide World Photos*)

Although prostitution has been legalized and regulated in only a few states, it operates in virtually every city in the United States, even those in small rural areas. In the large cities, prostitutes, who refer to themselves as *professionals*, make contacts for paid sexual services on the street. Prostitutes work out of bars, massage parlors, telephone networks, and entertainment services or are represented by agents, known as *pimps*, who in many cases are the prostitutes' boyfriends. A pimp's job is to secure customers and provide protection for the prostitute and to discourage competition by protecting the prostitute's operational territory.

Prostitution has social, moral, and legal implications and can be defined as any sexual exchange in which the reward is neither sexual nor affectional (James 1980). Persons prostitute themselves when they use their bodies as a commodity in exchange for material gain, such as money, clothes, apartments, promotions, or entertainment. The legal definition is narrower, involving four primary social concerns: (1) cash, (2) promiscuity, (3) relationship to a sexual partner, and (4) subtlety (James 1980). The key to understanding prostitution is that the women and men who are typically arrested are overt in the management of their profession; that is, they are **streetwalkers.** The subtler members of the profession, such as **call girls,** are seldom detected by police.

Organized crime's role in the prostitution industry depends on the type of prostitution activity, its location, and the historical period under consideration. Furthermore, various forms of prostitution have existed from the earliest recorded times and depend on the economic, social, and moral values of a society.

The passage of the Mann Act in 1910 forbade the transportation of women across state lines for immoral purposes. During subsequent years, police clamped down on organized prostitution in large cities, but such raids failed to eliminate it, and the business continued to thrive at a variety of locations. Prior to Prohibition, organized crime, along with the political machines in most major cities, played a key role in organizing local prostitution and gambling activities. Lucky Luciano attempted unsuccessfully to consolidate and centralize the prostitution business in New York City in the 1930s (Block 1983). With the decline of the brothel in the early twentieth century and the subsequent closing of the red-light districts, however, the organization of prostitution and organized crime's role in it became more difficult to define (Rosen 1982: 28–32).

Types of Prostitutes

The type of prostitution depends on the customer's desire for protected or unique services, as well as ability to pay. The range of services offered is almost endless. Official estimates place the number of full-time prostitutes in the United States at about 500,000 who engage in an estimated 750 million sex acts a year (Kappeler et al. 1993: 177–179). Prostitution occurs in a variety of formats and venues, including the streets, massage parlors, brothels, bars, and hotels. Rough estimates suggest that about 20 percent of all prostitutes are streetwalkers, about 15 percent are call girls or escort service workers, and the remainder (65 percent) work in an establishment of some kind (25 percent in massage parlors, 15 percent in brothels, 15 percent in bars, and 10 percent in hotels (Simon and Witte 1982: 253).

Streetwalkers

Eleanor Miller's (1986) study of female prostitutes working the street suggests that streetwalkers often operate within informal criminal networks and within the context of a street subculture. These "deviant street networks" (Miller 1986: 35–43) consist of persons who engage in prostitution, auto theft, drug trafficking, burglary, robbery, and other petty crimes. Cohen described a similar structure for streetwalkers in his study of prostitution in New York (Cohen 1980). These informal and relatively small networks more closely approximate support groups than organized crime syndicates.

Massage Parlor Prostitutes

Organized crime is more likely to be involved in prostitution at its higher levels. For example, many massage parlors provide sexual services. In many ways, massage parlors and bathhouses are ideal settings for the provision of illicit sexual services. While the owner of the facility pretends to be unaware of illegal activity, the massage parlor prostitute works off the streets, does not have to solicit customers, has some degree of protection provided by the owners or operators of the business and, if careful, is relatively safe from arrest (Simon and Witte 1982: 244–246).

Critical Thinking Project

Prostitution is an easy-entry business, but much of this business is highly organized. Suppose that you are a local police chief faced with an increasing problem of streetwalkers and call girls working in your city's convention center. Because this is bad for their businesses, hotel and restaurant managers have insisted that the police department do something about it. What course of action will you take?

Streetwalkers often operate within informal criminal networks.

(*Sean Murphy/Getty Images Inc. —Stone Allstock*)

A massage parlor prostitute works for the owner or owners of the parlor, who are responsible for paying the masseuses, keeping the books, collecting the fees, and providing other services. Many massage parlors are small, independent businesses, but some are tied to the activities of larger criminal organizations. Investigations of organized crime have found significant involvement of motorcycle gangs, particularly the Pagans, in both operating massage parlors and supplying prostitutes for these establishments (Potter and Jenkins 1985). In addition, recent evidence has demonstrated increasing involvement in the massage parlor trade by Korean and Chinese organized crime groups (Pennsylvania Crime Commission 1990: 299–304). In many cases these Asian prostitution operations border on sexual slavery, because these prostitutes are brought into the United States and then forced into a period of indentured servitude in return for the costs of their immigration (either legal or illegal).

Stag Party Girls

The majority of stag parties today are sponsored by men's clubs, whose topless waitresses serve drinks and dinner to men while strippers and dancers present a show. If the girls are prostitutes, arrangements can be made with the men for sexual services at a later time. By working such parties, a prostitute can build a lengthy customer phone list. These operations are commonly made through an entertainment agency or through other prostitutes.

Hotel and Convention Prostitutes

In the past many hotels would give prostitutes complimentary rooms in which to entertain their guests. The current typical arrangement is for the prostitute to make arrangements with the bellman or manager to refer customers to her for a finder's fee. Many hotel prostitutes also work conventions for out of town clients. Some even obtain convention lists and travel the convention circuit. These prostitutes claim to know which professions have the biggest spenders and attend these conventions accordingly. The women, posing as secretaries or sales representatives, roam hotel lobbies, product display rooms, and company-sponsored hospitality rooms looking for customers.

Bar Girls

B-girls (bar girls), one step removed from the streetwalker, can also find that they are working for enterprises connected to organized crime groups. The B-girl plays a dual role. First, she attempts to get the customer to buy her drinks (at exorbitant prices, often ranging from $12 to $15 per drink) and gets a commission on each drink she can sell. The cost of the drink pays for personal conversation at the customer's table. When her mark is no longer willing to pay simply for conversation and company, she attempts to engage him in the purchase of sexual services, either on premises or at another location. Although it takes longer for a prostitute to obtain a customer in a B-girl operation, she is far safer from arrest than when she works the street. Many B-girl operations also include table and lap dances, which may cost the customer up to $20 per dance.

In some cities, such as Newport, Kentucky, these bar–prostitution outlets have been controlled by organized crime groups for the past fifty years. In other areas, it is not unusual for organized crime groups to have significant investments in bars and nightclubs or to own the establishment where bar prostitution occurs.

Escort Service Prostitutes

In the call girl or escort service market, a much higher degree of organization is required. At its most complex, these services must have a financial backer, a business or sales manager, drivers or security personnel, and a sales staff of service providers (James 1977; Simon and Witte 1982: 244–246; Potter and Jenkins 1985; Potter 1986). Escort services usually hire attractive, well-educated, and very high-priced prostitutes, although some employ women already working for massage parlor operations. The service charges a fee for supplying an escort, and the customer negotiates the price of additional prostitution services separate from this fee. Call girl escort service operations vary widely in size; some employ few escorts, and others have as many as 500 women working part-time for them (Potter and Jenkins 1985). In any event, the procedures utilized are the same whether one is running a group of six full-time professional call girls or three dozen part-time semipros.

The initial contact is made by telephone; a way to verify the client's identity (a credit card number, hotel room, etc.) is established and the fee established for supplying an escort. The escort sent by the agency checks back with the agency by phone as soon as she arrives in the customer's room. Negotiations for sexual services occur following specified rules of conduct (the customer names the act or the price or preferably both), and the service is provided as expeditiously as possible (James 1977; Simon and Witte 1982: 244–246; Potter 1986).

The manager of the enterprise is a person with sufficient investment capital to establish an office, buy advertising, put in phones, and pay for protection. The call girls sell the organization's services for a profit based on their expertise (and probably their physical attributes). The agency usually collects a fee ($75 to $150 in small cities and $250 or more in major cities) for supplying an escort to a customer. The call girl gets a portion of that fee (33 percent was the usual commission paid in Philadelphia in the 1980s). She is then free to negotiate a tip for her services to enhance that commission.

An escort may negotiate the price of a particular service with each customer on an individual basis, such as the clothes she will wear, the demeanor she will adopt, and the acts she will perform, but usually she cannot negotiate the portion of the initial referral fee paid to the agency.

She can also provide discounts. She is expected to follow the steps necessary to protect the organization from detection by law enforcement. If suspicious, a prostitute will challenge a customer to reveal his law enforcement connections, if any, and will not name either the specific act or the price in negotiations. Failure to follow these procedures will abrogate the responsibility of the agency to supply her with protection, legal services, and money for bail and fines (James 1977; Simon and Witte 1982: 244–246; Potter and Jenkins 1985).

Pimp–Prostitute Relationship

Some prostitutes, particularly streetwalkers, work with a pimp who is also a lover or companion. Although more than one prostitute may work for a pimp, the maximum is about seven. Interactions between pimp and prostitute are often based on profit or friendship. Sometimes such relationships stem from psychologically dependent or coerced affiliations between the two.

In the pimp–prostitute relationship, the woman is the breadwinner and the pimp is a manager who may manage two or more prostitutes. Prostitutes who are able to achieve a relationship with high-class pimps not only elevate their status in their profession, but also earn substantially improved financial dividends. Sometimes the pimp assumes the role of a father figure or uses physical abuse and manipulation to control his prostitutes. Although rarely accompanying her while she works, he manages the money, provides the transportation, and maintains the residence.

Experts believe that some women in the United States are socialized into believing that they need a man to take care of them or to "take care of business." Prostitutes are no exception. Because of the illegal nature of prostitution, some prostitutes must gravitate toward men who are understanding and supportive of their life-style.

The Clients

Customers of prostitutes are seldom examined by social scientists. The lack of research may be due to the perceived deviance of the prostitute compared to the "normal urges" of her male customers in a sexist society. Still, prostitution is a supply and demand business, with dynamics and differing motivations on the part of all parties involved. As a rule, the motivation of a prostitute's customers fall into the category of sexual needs, the most common of which is quantity, expressed by those men who desire access to numerous women. Other motivations include a desire to experience a variety of different women, a variety of sexual services, sexual therapy for a dysfunction, companionship, sexual release, homosexual contact, and relief from temporary deprivation while traveling (James 1980).

You Decide

Is Prostitution Organized Crime?

Consider the famous Madam Heidi Fleiss example from the early 1990s. Was she merely a criminal opportunist who ran a prostitution ring for her own profit, or was she the most conspicuous player in a larger and more complicated organized crime operation? Consider the methods involved in the prostitution ring. You decide!

Organized Crime and Prostitution

In Philadelphia during the 1970s and 1980s, it was revealed that massage parlor owners, escort service operators, after-hours club proprietors, and gamblers regularly paid off the vice squad in the central police district both to avoid arrest and to guarantee prior warnings of impending crackdowns (Pennsylvania Crime Commission 1974, 1980, 1983; Potter and Jenkins 1985). Many escort services and massage parlors advertise openly in adult publications and newspapers and even in the classified pages of the telephone book. Such a public display of illicit business requires the existence of an ongoing understanding with the law enforcement community (Mastrofski and Potter 1986; Potter 1986; Jenkins and Potter 1986).

DRUG TRAFFICKING

A business of significance in organized crime is **drug trafficking.**

Cocaine Traffic

Most of the cocaine, heroin, and MDMA (also known as ecstasy) and much of the methamphetamine consumed in the United States are smuggled into the country by international criminal organizations from source countries in Latin America, Asia, and Europe. Cocaine consumption in the United States, the world's most important and largest market, has declined somewhat since its peak in the late 1980s, but has remained relatively stable for most of the last decade. Cocaine is produced in the South American Andean countries of Colombia, Peru, and Bolivia; Colombia is the source of an estimated 90 percent of the cocaine supply in the U.S. market (United Nations 2000: United States Department of State 2000).

Heroin Traffic

Heroin use in the United States increased significantly in the early to mid-1990s, but has leveled off in recent years. The purity of heroin currently available in the United States is higher than ever. Southwest Asia's Golden Crescent (Afghanistan and Pakistan) and Southeast Asia's Golden Triangle (Burma, Laos, and Thailand) are the world's major sources of heroin for the international market, but Colombia is the largest source of supply for the U.S. market, with Mexico as the second largest source. Together, Colombia and Mexico account for about 75 percent of the U.S. heroin market, with heroin from Southeast Asia making up most of the remainder.

Synthetic Drug Traffic

The worldwide production and consumption of synthetic drugs, particularly amphetamine-type stimulants, including methamphetamine and ecstasy, have dramatically increased since the early 1990s. The majority of methamphetamine available in the U.S. market is produced by Mexican traffickers operating in the United States or Mexico; the U.S. Drug Enforcement Administration (DEA) estimates that Mexican trafficking groups provide 70 to 90 percent of it. There has been a significant increase in methamphetamine production in Southeast Asia in recent years. Although little has found its way to the U.S. market from Southeast Asia, increasing quantities of Thai Tabs have been seized in the western United States.

Most of the ecstasy available in the U.S. market is produced in the Netherlands. Amsterdam, Brussels, Frankfurt, and Paris are major European hubs for shipping ecstasy to the United States; the Dominican Republic, Suriname, and Curacao are non-European shipment points for U.S.-bound ecstasy. Mexican and South American traffickers are becoming involved in the ecstasy trade.

Marijuana remains the most widely used and readily available illicit drug in the United States. Although most of it comes from domestic sources, a significant share comes from Mexico, with lesser amounts coming from Jamaica, Colombia, and Canada. Very little of the cannabis grown in other major producing countries—Morocco, Lebanon, Afghanistan, Thailand, and Cambodia—comes to the United States.

Marijuana Traffic

International drug-trafficking organizations have extensive networks of suppliers, front companies, and businesses that facilitate narcotics smuggling and laundering of the illicit proceeds from it. The evolution of the international drug trade in the last decade has included increased involvement by more players and the production of more synthetic drugs. Criminal organizations whose principal activities have traditionally focused on enterprises of smuggling of contraband, racketeering, and fraud have recently become increasingly involved in international drug trafficking. Although they generally are not narcotics producers themselves, many organized crime groups, including those from Russia, China, Italy, and Albania, have cultivated and expanded ties to drug-trafficking organizations to obtain cocaine, heroin, and synthetic drugs for their own distribution markets and trafficking networks. Traffickers from many countries increasingly are eschewing traditional preferences for criminal partnerships with single ethnic groups and are collaborating in the purchase, transportation, and distribution of illegal drugs.

Taking advantage of more open borders and modern telecommunications technology, international drug-trafficking organizations are sophisticated and flexible in their operations. They adapt quickly to law enforcement pressures by finding new smuggling methods, transshipment routes, and mechanisms to launder money. In many of the major cocaine- and heroin-producing and transit countries, drug traffickers have acquired significant power and wealth through the use of violence, intimidation, and payoffs of corrupt officials.

Importers bring large quantities of cocaine or heroin into the United States. They are responsible for making arrangements for the purchase of the drug at its point of origin: for heroin, probably the Golden Triangle (Laos, Burma, Thailand), the Golden Crescent (Afghanistan, Iran, Pakistan), or Mexico; for cocaine Bolivia, Colombia, or Peru. The importer must employ highly skilled smugglers to transport the drugs and coordinate shipments. Most importing syndicates calculate a certain amount of loss of their inventory to law enforcement interdiction efforts. Once the drug arrives in the United States, the importer's role is finished, and the wholesaler takes charge of the operation.

The Distribution Chain

The drug wholesaler purchases its drugs from an importer. This transaction requires that the person or persons at the top of the wholesale organization have sufficient liquid capital to make discount buys. The importer and the wholesaler represent different organizations or syndicates. The arrangement between the importer and the wholesaler could require the creation of an additional position—*mules* or *runners*—if the wholesaler, in an attempt to hold down cost, agrees to incur the risk of moving the contraband from its point of entry to the sales area or distribution point. The mules are paid by the trip, often as much as $5,000 to $10,000 for a run from Philadelphia to New York or Florida to Kentucky.

Once the drugs have arrived in the area where they will be distributed, the wholesaler again uses mules to deliver the drugs to the retailing organizations that have purchased them. The retailers either pay cash up front (by far the preferred method of doing business) or take the commodity on consignment, agreeing to pay after retail sales are completed. The latter arrangement is obviously far riskier and often requires mules to serve also as collectors and be compensated appropriately for the added responsibility (Simon and Witte 1982: 128–134; Wisotsky 1986).

Wholesalers receive imported drugs of high degrees of purity. Therefore, one of the first things a drug wholesaler must do is dilute ("step on") the purchased drugs by mixing them with a variety of substances, such as mannite, lactose, or quinine, which often doubles, triples, or quadruples the drug's volume and weight. Wholesalers usually dilute heroin and cocaine to a 25 percent level of purity before selling them. Wholesalers must go to great lengths to conceal their criminal activity. The organization must be highly mobile, often without a permanent business address. Communication must be in person or through pager systems, which allow messages to be exchanged from cell phones. The organization must provide a buffer between the wholesalers and the highly visible street dealers. No evidentiary trail linking the pusher and supplier can be tolerated. There can be no payroll checks or inventories (Simon and Witte 1982: 128–134; Mastrofski and Potter 1986; Wisotsky 1986).

The street syndicate or dealers again step on the drug, reducing it to a purity level of 10 to 15 percent and repackaging it in bundles of heroin and eightballs of cocaine for sale to users. A number of studies of retail drug networks have been conducted; among the most recent and most carefully researched is Mieczkowski's (1986) work on heroin street sales in Detroit.

Street Sales

Mieczkowski reports the existence of three primary roles in a street heroin organization. At the top is the crew boss, the manager, who obtains heroin from a wholesaler, supplies it to runners, and collects money from its sale from the runners. Runners are the salespersons who work a specific location in a neighborhood (a corner, a street, a particular building) and sell the heroin to users. Runners carry very little heroin, preferring to return to the crew boss frequently for additional supplies. *Guns,* the third participant in a street syndicate, are heavily armed members who set up surveillance close to the actual points of sale and provide security for the runners. They not only watch out for police, but also intervene if there is an attempted robbery and control other disorders that threaten the conduct of business. According to Mieczkowski, the average crew boss can earn as much as $1,500 a week and the average runner as much as $800.

ARMS TRAFFICKING

Arms Trafficking in munitions (arms, ammunitions, and other weaponry devices) became a major international organized crime enterprise during the 1990s. The relaxation of international tensions between the United States and the countries of the former Soviet Union and the temporary cessation of civil conflicts in Central America and Lebanon created a surfeit of both new and used weaponry on the world market. Among those most valued by international illicit entrepreneurs are spare parts for large weapons systems; small arms, including assault rifles and portable antitank and antiaircraft weapons; and ammunition for both small arms and larger artillery and armor systems. In some rare cases, international organized crime groups have also gained access to larger military systems that have been placed on the black market for resale (Ruggerio 1996).

Most illegal arms transfers occur through the *gray market,* which is dominated by large arms brokering firms. Gray market arms sales use the otherwise legitimate export licensing process that these firms engage in on a daily basis. The true nature of the transaction is disguised in a number of ways: (1) fraudulent documents hide the true recipient of the arms, (2) false papers disguise the military nature of the good, and (3) false declarations hide the true identity of the supplier. Obtaining licenses that are a normal part of the exporting process, even if these licenses are fraudulent, allows illicit arms transactions to appear to be legitimate.

As long as the transaction appears to be legitimate, illicit arms merchants can arrange for payment in typical legitimate ways and use normal methods of transportation to move hundreds of tons of armament valued at millions of dollars. In rare cases, illegal arms shipments brokered by legitimate firms are smuggled as contraband, particularly if the nature of the arms or the identity of the recipient would set off alarms to customs agents around the world. One subterfuge commonly used is to disguise the shipment as humanitarian aid. Millions of dollars worth of illegal weaponry, including helicopters and fighter aircraft, were sold to clients in Afghanistan and the countries of the former Yugoslavia by foreign suppliers disguising the arms caches as humanitarian aid.

Arms brokers acquire munitions from many countries; much of it is U.S. military equipment. In 1999 alone, U.S. Customs seized $4.6 million in arms and ammunition that was being smuggled out of the United States.

Arms transfers on the black market do not use the legitimate export licensing process at all. Black market arms transfers utilize a simple smuggling strategy. Because the goal of black marketers is to hide contraband from government officials, most black market transfers involve small quantities of weapons. These weapons are usually purchased through gunshops or stolen from extant military stockpiles.

CONTRABAND SMUGGLING

Smuggling contraband (cigarettes, alcohol products, and firearms) across international borders has become a highly profitable criminal enterprise for international organized crime groups. **Contraband smuggling** is an attractive criminal enterprise because it typically carries far less severe penalties than does drug trafficking. Smuggling seeks to achieve high levels of illicit profits by avoiding taxes, tariffs, and duties on certain consumer items. The logistics of contraband smuggling has become much easier with the massive increases in international trade at the end of the twentieth century.

Countries such as the United States that engage in high-volume commercial trade provide the perfect cover for organized crime groups that smuggle. The high volume makes the concealment of contraband relatively easy, minimizes the chance that law enforcement will detect the contraband, and usually involves high import duties, which increases the profit in smuggling.

Comparatively light criminal penalties and very high profit margins have made smuggling a major criminal enterprise of organized crime groups in Asia, the former Soviet Union, the Middle East, and Central and South America (Saba et al. 1995; Resendiz and Neal 1998).

Tariffs and excise taxes drive the contraband market. Because they are high almost everywhere on tobacco, alcohol products, and luxury automobiles, these commodities have become the mainstays of the market. Organized contraband smuggling groups cater to consumers who wish to acquire luxury items while avoiding a surcharge that is usually 25 percent or more of the item's value. The contraband market therefore pockets often substantial revenue intended for taxes. Because Russia, China and the countries making up the former Yugoslavia (Bosnia, Serbia, Croatia, Montenegro) have the highest tariffs on luxury imports in the world, they are frequently the targets of international organized crime groups.

Smuggling of U.S. tobacco products is a major secondary market for Colombian drug cartels and costs the Colombian government millions in lost taxes. Smuggling U.S. cigarettes into Europe costs European Union countries more than $3.7 billion in tax revenues. The illegal import of alcohol and tobacco products has a major economic impact in Scandinavian countries, which have not only high tariffs and excise taxes on these goods, but also value-added taxes on tobacco and alcohol products at the point of sale. The United States is also a consumer country for illicit contraband. Smuggling of cheaper and often substandard substitutes for legitimate products produced in the United States causes negative economic impact on manufacturing, high-tech, and retail industries. Products such as imitation pharmaceutical drugs and nonprecision automobile parts often pose a significant threat to U.S. public health and safety.

The United States is a primary transit country for illegal contraband being shipped to other destinations. According to the U.S. Customs Service, more than 1.3 million people, 341,000 vehicles, and 45,000 trucks and cargo containers enter the United States every day. At best, the Customs Service is able to examine only 3 percent of the goods entering the United States every day, and as the volume of international trade increases, the Customs Service estimates that it examined only 1 percent of imports in 2005. Moving illegal contraband through a transit country can conceal its origin, nature, and destination.

In addition to consumer products, the illegal movement of hazardous waste and hazardous chemicals into the United States can harm the environment and therefore public health. One of the largest illegal markets in the United States is the black market for chlorofluorocarbons (CFCs). CFCs deplete ozone from the atmosphere, are illegal or heavily controlled in both Europe and the United States, and provide an extremely lucrative illicit business for international criminals. Obviously, the import of illegal CFCs requires both criminal contraband smugglers and criminal industrial consumers who use CFCs within the United States. Every year almost 20,000 metric tons of illegal CFCs are smuggled into the United States and purchased for use by legitimate businesses. The main source countries for illegal CFCs are Russia, China, Mexico, and India. Organized crime groups in Mexico can purchase Freon, much of it legally imported from China, for less than $2 per kilogram and sell it in Los Angeles for ten times as much. The profit margin for illegal importation of CFCs to Europe and the United States is estimated to be $600 million a year.

The United States is also a major consumer nation for the illicit trade in protected wildlife and rare plants. Illegal trafficking in exotic species threatens biodiversity in source countries and can expose residents of consuming countries to deadly diseases.

The United States is a source of considerable contraband. Commodities include automobiles, alcohol, tobacco products, and cigarettes. Automobiles, including those stolen particularly from the United States, Western Europe, and Japan, are significant contraband items. Luxury vehicles and SUVs are particularly valued by organized crime groups because of their high resale value on the black market, the high excise and luxury taxes attached to them in foreign markets, and the minimal risk of detection by law enforcement. Organized crime groups make profits of about $15 billion a year from the trade in stolen vehicles. For 1997 the FBI estimates that 1.6 million stolen vehicles from the United States were illegally transported out of the country and resold in foreign markets for a total profit of about $4 billion. In addition, European law enforcement sources estimate that 300,000 stolen vehicles in Western Europe, worth about $5 billion, are illegally exported every year. Demand for luxury automobiles is particularly strong in Russia and China, where import tariffs exceed 100 percent of value. The value of stolen vehicles from the United States resold in Europe increases three to four times over their U.S. market value, according to the National Insurance Crime Bureau.

The worldwide trade in stolen vehicles is dominated by organized crime groups from China, Russia, Eastern Europe, and Mexico. They frequently rely on organized crime groups in the United States to obtain the vehicles and arrange for export. Russian and Asian criminal groups commonly cooperate with Mexican smuggling rings that move stolen vehicles across the U.S.–Mexican border for re-export to Russia and China. Stolen vehicles are most commonly shipped out of the United States in maritime shipping containers directly from U.S. seaports or are driven into Mexico.

International car theft rings appear to be increasingly organized and professional in their operations. Typically, these rings alter vehicle identification numbers so that the stolen vehicles cannot be traced.

COUNTERFEITING

United States currency has been counterfeited by individuals and small groups from the time it was first minted. Traditionally, currency **counterfeiting** has been outside the portfolio of organized crime primarily because of the high risk in such ventures, the labor-intensive nature of the process, and the relatively low yield in terms of profits. As technology has advanced and the use of U.S. money has spread worldwide, organized crime groups have been more willing to engage in the counterfeiting of U.S. dollars (Levi 1998; Myers 1995). Advances in reproductive technology have played a major role in the expansion of counterfeiting activities worldwide. New advanced design, copying, and publishing technology, usually linked to computer software, has made the production of high-quality counterfeit currency much easier, less expensive, and less time consuming than in the past. The introduction of these reprographic capabilities has been very rapid. In 1995 about 1 percent of counterfeit U.S. currency was produced with these enhanced technologies. By 2000, this production increased to 50 percent.

Today international organized crime groups produce and use counterfeit U.S. money. Sometimes they sell it; sometimes they use it to facilitate illicit transactions or to finance other illicit operations. The profit margin for U.S. currency is a little less that 40 percent on the dollar on the counterfeit market.

Organized crime counterfeiting schemes are not limited to producing bad money. They also involve illegal reproduction of other financial instruments, such as traveler's checks, commercial bank checks, and money orders, as well as securities, stock certificates, and other negotiable instruments. Counterfeit documents are regularly used as collateral for loans or insurance. Organized crime uses these financial instruments to defraud individuals, financial institutions, corporations, and even the government itself.

Half of all counterfeit U.S. currency is produced within the borders of the United States and about half is produced abroad. The expansion of international trade and the growth of the international financial networks means that about two-thirds of $570 billion of U.S. currency in circulation is being circulated outside U.S. borders.

In recent years the largest source of counterfeit U.S. currency recovered in the United States was Colombia, about one of every three counterfeit dollars. Well-established drug organizations in Colombia are believed to be involved in the distribution of the counterfeit currency.

GAMBLING

Like other forms of vice, **gambling** has been outlawed or regulated for decades because of its perceived ability to erode society's morals. Although many people are responsible gamblers, many others are not. Casinos, dog tracks, and horse tracks often attract people with their potential for becoming rich overnight. This allure sometimes results in big winners, but more often in big losers. Gambling creates distinctive problems that can lead to different crimes, such as loan-sharking at usurious rates. If a debt is not paid back in full within the period designated, the loan-shark can use violence and intimidation to collect.

Organized crime's involvement in gambling is well documented. The 1995 movie *Casino* depicted the real-life involvement of the Kansas City mob and how it skimmed more than $1 million in cash from the Tropicana and Stardust Casinos in the mid-1970s. Organized crime generates roughly $29 to $33 billion in income through its illegal gambling operations each year in the United States (*Business Week*, April 14, 1989: 114). Although organized crime occasionally runs casino-type games, its primary income comes from the numbers game and bookmaking. The numbers game is one of the simplest of all gambling operations (Reuter 1983: 45–54).

The profitability for the syndicate running the numbers game is obvious in that it retains between 40 and 50 percent of the money bet for expenses, salaries, and profit. The number is calculated in a variety of ways. Some numbers are determined by the outcomes of various races at a particular race track (e.g., the winners' payoffs in the third, fifth, and seventh races added together or the last three digits of the track's handle for that day). In contemporary numbers gambling, with the prevalence of state lotteries, most numbers bankers rely on the official daily number to determine winners.

Gambling creates distinctive problems that can lead to different types of crimes. Seen here is the New York Hotel–Casino in Las Vegas.

(*Shaun Egan/Getty Images Inc.—Stone Allstock*)

Betting with an illegal numbers bank rather than the state provides several advantages. First, numbers banks do not collect taxes on winnings. Second, they are more convenient to the bettor and will extend credit. Finally, they provide a daily means for social interaction among friends and acquaintances, rather than a sterile encounter with a state lottery ticket machine. Numbers syndicates work quite easily.

The Process

A numbers organization follows certain procedures. *Writers* write bets on the street, in bars, at newsstands, in tobacco shops, and in luncheonettes, for example. They are paid a commission of 25 percent of their receipts. Customers come to the writer to make their bets, pay their money, and have their transactions recorded. At specified times during the business day, pickup men come to collect the bets from the writers. Pickups are also paid by commission, usually 5 to 10 percent.

The bets are then taken to a central office or bank where they are totaled and recorded. After the winning number for the day has been determined, the winners are identified and their winnings are sent back to the writers through the pickup men. In a small numbers syndicate, these procedures represent the totality of the organization. A single *banker* oversees the entire organization and exercises total authority, since it is his or her money in play. In larger numbers syndicates, the procedure is the same; it is simply replicated.

Many neighborhood *banks* follow the additional step of reporting their daily take to a central bank, which provides overall financial backing to the whole operation. Very large numbers organizations may add another level, a layoff bank. The *layoff bank* covers extraordinarily high betting action on a particular number, providing a kind of insurance against a large "hit," in return for an ongoing percentage of the numbe organization's profits (Rubinstein and Reuter 1978; Simon and Witte 1982, 212–214; Pennsylvania Crime Commission 1987).

Several specific cases may clarify the procedure. For three decades, Caesar Nelson ran a massive numbers gambling organization in North Philadelphia. Nelson's annual wagering volume was estimated to be about $40 million, or $160,000 a day. To achieve this volume, he had about 2,000 writers, making for a very large organization. These writers turned in their betting action to separate neighborhood numbers banks, which in turn passed the daily take to Nelson's central bank. By operating in this way, Nelson was able to run an extensive gambling organization from which he, as the principal financial backer, was buffered. No actual bets ever went beyond the smaller banks. Transactions that involved Nelson were strictly large cash transfers that never involved betting slips themselves, but only daily tally sheets (Pennsylvania Crime Commission 1974, 1980; Potter and Jenkins 1985).

An even more complex operation involved the Baldassari family of Scranton, Pennsylvania. This organization handled bets for numbers, sports, and horse racings. Gambling action was written in a number of local businesses. A series of vending machine companies owned by members of the Baldassari syndicate picked up the bets several times a day. These bets were distributed to a series of banks, each run by different combinations of syndicate members acting in partnership. The profits were then directly deposited (or, more appropriately, laundered) with a series of real estate corporations owned by participants in the gambling syndicate, including apartment complexes and land development companies (Pennsylvania Crime Commission 1980).

The key point, however, is that the nature of the service being provided dictated an efficient means of doing business, which can be found with only minor variations in all gambling syndicates everywhere in the United States, from those handling only a few thousand dollars to highly complex, very large, high-volume gambling operations. They all use the same procedures for conducting business.

In gambling organizations, money is a crucial organizational factor. The banker is a person who has put up the liquid capital needed to establish the business. The officemen, lieutenants, and the like are salaried employees. The pickup men and writers are the rough equivalent of commission salespersons (Simon and Witte 1982: 212–214; Reuter 1983; Jenkins and Potter 1986; Pennsylvania Crime Commission 1987). In a gambling organization, a writer can decide from whom to take bets and whether to take action for more than one bank, but has no power to change the odds, the point spread, or the method of moving the action to a central bank.

Bookmaking

Bookmaking involves the placing of bets on horse races, fights; basketball, football, and baseball games; and so on. The *bookmaker* is a broker who, for a fee known as the **vigorish,** accepts wagers that he hopes will balance one another so that payoffs to winning bettors can be paid from losing bettors' money, with something left over for the bookmaker. *Middlemen*, often known as writers or runners, are usually employed to funnel bets to a bookmaker. These persons typically have access to the general public, such as waitresses, barbers, and bartenders. A bettor who does not go through a middleman or bookmaker can place a bet over the telephone. Most bookmakers use several methods to conceal their whereabouts, including telephone-call forwarding services, senior citizens with no criminal record who answer the telephone, and answering services with which the caller can leave a phone number, often with a code, where he can be reached.

Sports Betting

In the past, horse racing was the primary business of most bookmakers, but the widespread availability of intertrack and off-track betting has resulted in a shift among most bookmakers to sporting events. Sports betting events are handled this way. The bookmakers sets the line, the amount by which a team will win a game. The line on a professional football game involving the Green Bay Packers and the Chicago Bears, for example, could be the Packers by 7.5. This means that for a bet on the Green Bay Packers to win, the Packers must beat the Bears by more than 7.5 points. Setting the line allows bookmakers to guarantee their profit margin. The line can also be adjusted at various times during the week preceding the event to discourage bets on teams that have drawn too much betting action (Reuter 1983: 17).

Bookmaking syndicates, like the numbers syndicates, are fairly simple in organization. The bookmaker provides the capital for the operation. Below the bookmaker are clerks who record the bets and pay the winners. At the bottom of the operation are the writers, who actually take the bets from patrons. Some large bookmaking operations also employ *tabbers* (Reuter 1983: 20), persons who keep track of both the betting action and the information about the game and then adjust the line to guarantee that the bookmaker will not take a major loss on an unexpected outcome of a particular game.

From a gross dollar standpoint, **sports betting** is the king of bookmaking. Unlike numbers and horse wagering, sports betting caters mainly to the affluent. In addition, it is one of the enterprises with the most extensive documentation, in the form of records of betting action, which must be held at least temporarily. Usually, many telephones are required for a large "book," and personal computers are used to store records and run programs calculating bets and payoffs. In the past, the wire services and attendant equipment were required, but they have been replaced by television.

There is widespread public tolerance of sports bookmaking, especially in the areas of the country in which it flourishes (New York, Pennsylvania, California, Florida, Kentucky, and New Jersey, states that allow some kind of wagering on a legal basis and have some legitimate gambling enterprises). Furthermore, police generally believe that the gambling laws are not sufficiently important to enforce with any real vigor. As a result, the bookie can take more business chances than can other criminal entrepreneurs who are likely to be the target of public moral outrage or proactive police campaigns (Gardiner 1967; Simon and Witte 1982: 212–214; Light 1992).

The Effects of Illegal Gambling

The impact of illegal gambling operations on a community can be substantial and is often positive. Laswell and McKenna (1971) identified the numbers business in Bedford–Stuyvesant as its single largest employer. Moreover, Whyte (1961) reported that gambling operations often provide employment in legitimate business settings. In the Morrisburg study, Potter and Jenkins (1985) determined that the city's largest gambling organization provided full-time employment for at least fifty persons and part-time employment for many others. In addition, the gambling network has been found to provide supplemental income for persons on fixed, low-income pensions or who had other economic problems. Many of these participants had no moral or ethical opposition to gambling. Silberman (1978) suggests that gambling profits assist small shopkeepers in competing with chain stores or larger competitors and enable some small businesses to survive, especially in depressed areas.

LOAN-SHARKING

Second to gambling, **loan-sharking** is one of the top money-makers for traditional organized crime and represents one of its most violent enterprises. Also called **shylocking,** loan-sharking provides money at a high interest rate to people who, for a variety of reasons, have little choice but to go to such sources in search of financial support. Loan-sharking has the reputation for charging exorbitant amounts for its loans and for physically assaulting those who delay or never repay their loans.

In contemporary U.S. society, many individuals and businesses have numerous reasons for obtaining capital in illegitimate ways. For instance, a business could have "tapped out" all its capital and be unable to obtain money from a bank or other legal source, which is a rather common occurrence in some industries, including the garment and fur trades. Individuals also can find their sources of legitimate credit overextended when they encounter a financial problem, such as the payment of a gambling debt (Simon and Witte 1982: 229). For these people the loan-shark provides a ready source of cash.

A normal repayment schedule for small loans is twelve weeks at 20 percent interest. This means that $1,000 from a loan-shark involves twelve weekly payments of $100. For larger loans, for example, in excess of $20,000, the interest rate is considerably lower, usually about 1 percent (Reuter 1983: 96–97). In the 1980s in Philadelphia, a man borrowed $1,900, paid $14,000, and still owed $5,000 in late fees and penalties. The loan-shark offered a solution: Sue the owner of a railyard where the borrower's son had been accidentally electrocuted and assign the damages recovered to the loan-shark.

Movies and television programs often depict loan-sharking as a violent, brutish business in which unsuspecting borrowers find themselves in a desperate attempt to repay a loan on which "their body" is the collateral. This can be the case in reality, but most loan-sharks see violence as being counterproductive. Violence inevitably attracts law enforcement attention, which is not good for business, and a disabled or dead borrower is unlikely to repay any part of the loan. Instead, loan-sharks tend to rely on collateral, such as part interest in a business, a car title, jewelry, or even a home deed on a loan, in much the same way a legitimate lending institution does (Reuter 1983: 98–99).

A loan-sharking syndicate, even a complex one, is vertically organized with bankers who supply money to *entrepreneurs* on the street, who make loans to gamblers, businesspersons, and others at usurious rates at street level, essentially the bottom of the organizational pyramid. The financier, the person who supplies money to the loan-sharks, is at the top. The expectation is that at a specified time money will be returned with an appropriate profit (Reuter 1983).

In the 1960s in Philadelphia, three major loan-sharking financiers were "Willie" Weisberg, Frank Jaskiewicz, and Angelo Bruno. They dominated the organization of loan-sharking because they controlled the flow of money. They supplied capital to the loan-sharks and expected a 25 percent return on their investments a year later. These loan-shark bankers, for want of a better term, then supplied money to smaller entrepreneurs on the streets, who made loans to gamblers, businesspeople, and others at usurious rates of interest (Potter and Jenkins 1985). The point is that the supply of capital financing dictates the structure and definition of positions in the syndicates (Rubinstein and Reuter 1978; Jenkins and Potter 1986b).

As the twentieth century came to an end, organized crime involvement in **environmental crime** was becoming one of its most lucrative and fast-growing new markets. Organized crime groups worldwide, particularly those operating in Japan, Russia, China, and Italy, took advantage of the high costs of legitimate waste disposal by opening a new market in illegal disposal of hazardous wastes. In addition, organized crime groups realized that some of the waste that they were supposed to dispose was, in and of itself, highly valued or rare natural resource commodities that could be resold on the black market, thereby circumventing environmental laws and restrictions on the trade or sale of these resources. Organized crime earns about $30 billion annually from illegal dumping and trafficking in outlawed or protected natural resources (Hoser 1993, 1996; Friman and Andreas 1999).

The need of legitimate business to spend enormous amounts to legally dispose of dangerous chemicals and other pollutants has created a growing industry for organized crime. Organized crime groups earn $10 to $12 billion a year from the illegal dumping of hazardous waste materials. Particularly important and profitable activities in this regard are those that mix toxic wastes with recyclable materials, such as scrap metal. In addition, organized crime groups realize large profits in trash-for-cash enterprises that involve shipping hazardous waste to countries in Africa, Asia, Central America, and Eastern Europe, where disposal costs are lower and enforcement of environmental laws are not a high priority.

Illegal waste disposal is a major business of organized crime in Italy, primarily because organized crime groups own and dominate many, if not most, legitimate waste disposal companies. Italian organized crime secures contracts for waste disposal throughout Italy and the rest of Europe through both legitimate and illegitimate companies. Illegally disposing of the wastes that they have contracted to handle greatly increases the profit margin for these companies. Roughly half of the 80 million metric tons of hazardous waste produced each year in Italy simply disappears as a result of illegal dumping.

Italian law enforcement authorities believe that organized crime groups control the majority of Italy's waste disposal contracts. In 1997 alone, 11 million metric tons of toxic and industrial waste was deposited in 2,000 illegal dump sites in the Mediterranean Sea or local Italian waterways. At least 53 Italian organized crime groups are involved in the illegal disposal of hazardous wastes. When they are not dumped into the sea or other waterways, they are frequently shipped to dump sites in eastern Europe and on the west coast of Africa.

Radioactive waste is a particular problem. There are no existing inexpensive, safe disposal options for radioactive waste, a fact that attracts organized crime involvement in a large way. Organized crime groups involved in the illegal disposal of radioactive waste, for the most part, are already involved in drug, arms, or contraband smuggling. Illegal disposal of radioactive waste has become a problem in Austria, France, and Germany, countries with strong environmental enforcement mechanisms requiring the use of costly but effective disposal options. Italian organized crime groups have been diverting radioactive waste from these three countries for illegal dumping in eastern Europe into the Mediterranean and Adriatic seas. In 1998, one Italian organized crime syndicate was accused of dumping radioactive waste off Italy's southern coast.

Stealing and illegally exporting valuable natural resources have also become a major environmental crime of organized crime groups, worth between $5 and $8 billion a year. Organized crime groups in Africa, Eastern Europe, Latin America, China, and Southeast and Southwest Asia are heavily involved, for example, in illegally cutting and trading forest timber. Illegal logging poses a significant threat to biodiversity and has resulted in major deforestation problems worldwide. In addition, Russian and Chinese organized crime networks are heavily involved in the illegal fishing industry, which not only seriously depletes seafood supplies, but also evades the payment of both import and export taxes. Russian organized crime syndicates alone earn $4 billion a year from the illegal exportation of 2 million metric tons of seafood. Much of this Russian trade involves poaching sturgeon from the Caspian Sea and the illegal sale of crab to businesses in Japan. About 85 percent of the seafood exported from Russia to Japan each year is exported illegally and worth about $1 billion.

Illegal international trade in animal parts, particularly from elephants, whales, and hawksbill turtles, along with other endangered species is also large and growing. This trade has become a major illegal enterprise for many Asian criminal organizations. Organized crime groups earn between $6 and $10 billion a year in the illegal trafficking of exotic birds, ivory and rhino horn, reptiles, insects, rare tigers, and wild game.

TRAFFICKING IN GEMS AND GOLD

A highly lucrative international market exists for diamonds, other precious gems, and gold. This market and the availability of stolen gems and gold has created a new criminal enterprise for organized crime groups, particularly those operating in collusion with warlords participating in regional conflicts in diamond-rich areas of Africa. The legitimate diamond industry has never been too concerned about the source of the rough diamonds they purchase. Traditionally, diamond brokers have purchased their supplies from legal and illegal sources without exercising any discernible discretion. Obviously, once precious gems have been converted into jewelry, their source is of little concern to merchants. Almost 75 percent of the rough diamonds on the world market, a market worth roughly $5.2 billion, is mined in Africa. Of that African diamond supply, about 13 percent is mined illegally (Echevarria and Rahe 1993).

A wide variety of organized crime groups, most notably those that originate in Russia, China, Italy, and, of course, Africa, are heavily involved in the illicit gem and gold markets. Russian organized crime groups have successfully moved into the legitimate diamond and gold industries in Russia. These groups use numerous legitimate front companies to conceal their role in obtaining gems and gold and to make it virtually impossible to identify illicit shipments hidden in legal exports. The use of payoffs to corrupt officials allows these organized crime front companies to circumvent the payment of tariffs and customs duties, thereby massively increasing the profit margin when gems and gold are sold at market value to industry brokers. One of the largest illicit gem industries in Russia involves the illegal mining and exportation of amber, a criminal enterprise worth about $1 billion a year.

South African crime syndicates were able to steal 20 metric tons of gold and diamonds in 1996 alone. The value of these thefts was estimated to be about $350 million. In Southeast Asia, gem smuggling provides an important secondary income for drug-trafficking warlords in the Golden Triangle, particularly those operating in Burma.

Recently, the largest source for diamonds has been areas controlled by insurgent groups in Africa. The diamond trade not only is a source of enrichment for crime groups, but also of financing for regional conflicts on the African continent. Among the primary participants in the illegal diamond trade in Africa are rebels in Angola, rebel militia groups in the Democratic Republic of the Congo, and the Revolutionary United Front (RUF) in Sierra Leone. These groups loot diamond mines located in areas they control as a means to obtain funds for arms purchases and operational costs for their wars. Rogue states also profit heavily from the illegal diamond industry. For example, Liberia, governed for the past forty years by U.S.-supported dictators, is a major supporter of the war in Sierra Leone waged by the RUF.

Liberian government officials share in the profits from illegal diamond mining in Sierra Leone, which is the major impetus for their participation in that war. Most of the diamond-rich areas of Sierra Leone were under the control of RUF rebels in late 1990s. In Angola, UNITA rebels, the recipient of considerable military and economic assistance from the United States, stole $300 million of the $500 million in diamonds mined in Angola in 1998. In 1998, in the Democratic Republic of the Congo, at least $338 million in rough cut diamonds was stolen and smuggled by local militias.

BUSINESS RACKETEERING

Perhaps the most disturbing claim made against the more sophisticated organized crime groups is the one suggesting that these organizations are infiltrating and controlling large areas of legitimate business through **business racketeering**. Although it could be argued that some illicit enterprises, such as gambling, enjoy more public tolerance than others, there is widespread concern that underworld criminals are widely involved in the ownership of legitimate construction, solid waste disposal, food processing, and trucking businesses, as well as restaurants, bars, racetracks, and casinos.

Of great concern is that syndicates are using profits generated from their legitimate enterprises to expand their illicit undertakings. Another concern is that organized criminals, by combining their illicit and licit businesses, will make it difficult if not impossible for legitimate businesspersons to compete with them. Furthermore, the assumption by many law enforcement officials that the Mafia is a single, unified, national criminal consortium makes this suggestion even more disturbing, since it implies that much criminal involvement in legitimate businesses cannot be controlled.

Wealthy criminal organizations need new areas in which to reinvest newly made profits and thus have legitimate businesses. Buying, muscling into, or starting legitimate businesses also permits organized criminals not only to evade their income tax obligations, but also to continue their illicit operations discreetly behind seemingly innocent fronts. These assumptions are based on the premise that criminal syndicates operate like any other legitimate business. That is, they are designed to maximize profits through diversification of their activities.

Case Study

Mobstocks

As early as 1992, Gordon Hall used bribery to induce securities brokers to use high-pressure sales tactics to sell Eagle Holdings, Inc., stock shares to customers. This illegally inflated the price of the common stock shares. In 1996, he began to conspire with members of the Bonanno and Genovese crime families in New York to pump up the price of common stock issued by Health Tech International, Inc. Hall had been the chairman of Eagle Holdings and was now the chairman and CEO of Health Tech. Hall made an agreement with stock promoters Irwin Schneider, Claudio Iodice, and Eugene Lombardo, an associate of the Bonanno crime family in New York. In exchange for artificially inflating and supporting the stock price and volume of Health Tech common stock, Hall would pay Lombardo, Schneider, and Iodice with shares of the stock. Health Tech common stock and warrants, which are high-risk corporate securities similar to stock options, traded on the NASDAQ small-capital market under the trading symbols GYMM and GYMMW. Hall paid these shares of stock to Lombardo, Schneider, and Iodice under the guise of consulting agreements.

Well-placed informants reported this activity to government agents and, after some preliminary investigation, telephone calls from the group were intercepted via a wiretap. For almost a year, working with the U.S. Securities and Exchange Commission and officials from NASDAQ, agents and detectives conducted surveillance, intercepted conversations, analyzed complex business and trading records, and interviewed witnesses and experts to determine the extent of the conspiracy and develop the evidence necessary to indict and convict those involved.

Lombardo, Schneider, and Iodice paid bribes to brokers under them who manipulated the price of the securities by artificially creating demand for them. These brokers made false claims to customers to induce them to buy Health Tech stock that so the price would rise. The trading activity increased the price of the stock so that conspirators could sell their shares at a profit, or *dump* them. When customers decided to sell the Health Tech stocks, brokers would refuse to take their calls or make unauthorized trades in the customers' accounts. In January 1997, sales of Health Tech shares increased almost four times over sales in December 1996. By the end of February, the stock price had risen to a high of $2.813 per share, from its $0.87 close on December 31. This "pump and dump" scheme made millions of dollars for the conspirators at the expense of unsuspecting customers.

The investigation showed that as the scheme continued the Bonanno and Genovese crime families took control of two branches of Meyers, Pollack and Robbins, a major brokerage firm, and tried to expand the scheme to include other small-capital companies. Italian organized crime members sought to control which brokers worked at the branch offices to avoid detection by law enforcement and to control who would receive profits from the scheme. As disputes arose in these matters, OC members resorted to their classic methodology to maintain control. They made threats of violence against individuals who were not backed by other OC members and held "sit downs" or meetings, to resolve disputes with individuals who were backed by OC members.

In mid-January, Jonathan Lyons, who managed one of the branch offices being used by the group, complained that the office was functioning solely for the conspirators to sell Health Tech and tried to keep Lombardo's brokers from working in the office. Lombardo sent a Bonanno soldier and an associate to threaten Lyons. Lyons in turn sought protection through a friend from a Bonanno capo and another Bonanno soldier. Lombardo then contacted Frank Lino, a Bonanno family capo who met with other Bonnano members to resolve the dispute. When the resolution did not satisfy Lombardo, he contacted Rosario Gangi, a Genovese family capo to assist. Another meeting was held, which included Gangi and Ernest Montevecchi, a Genovese crime family soldier, and Lombardo prevailed. Gangi and Montevecchi were also instrumental in helping Lombardo control a second branch office of the firm.

At one point, Lombardo, Schneider, and Iodice became dissatisfied with the method and timeliness of Hall's payments. Lombardo, Iodice, and another individual met with and threatened Hall and his senior vice-president to ensure their continued cooperation and payment for the services of Lombardo and the others. Several telephone calls were intercepted in which Lombardo and others discussed their intent to hurt Hall.

When interviewed by agents and detectives, victims of the scheme reported that they were told by brokers that they had hundreds of people working under them, and had invested heavily in the stock themselves, and they made promises as to the future performance of the stock. One customer had even recorded a sales call in which a broker falsely claimed to have 250 other brokers working under him and that he had purchased 1 million Health Tech warrants himself.

Late in the conspiracy, Lombardo, Iodice, and others attempted to take over a third brokerage firm and use it to manipulate the stock of another small-capital company. The principal of that company refused to go along with the scheme and was told, "You are either with us or you are not with us," and, "If you are not with us, you will have a problem." When these statements were made, he was also threatened with a blunt metal object.

As a result of the investigation, thirty-three people were indicted on charges of extortion, securities fraud, stock manipulation, and commercial bribery. The defendants included several members and associates of the Genovese and Bonanno crime families, as well as the principals of Health Tech and Meyers, Pollack and Robbins. Twenty-eight defendants pled guilty and five were convicted after two separate jury trials.

Source: FBI, 2006

Organized crime groups seek both profitable and safe investments. Therefore, these groups make calculated moves into a community's commercial life through ownership of legitimate businesses. Anderson (1979) suggests that participation in legitimate business serves several needs. First, this participation offers concealment opportunities for illegal activities, such as pickup points for gambling operations and disposal points for stolen goods. Second, these businesses provide money-laundering opportunities for illegal profits. The Pennsylvania Crime Commission (1980: 227–230) provides evidence of laundering operations involving banks, beer distributorships, car dealerships, bars, and nightclubs. Third, legitimate businesses are excellent sources of reportable and legitimate income. Organized crime groups regularly use bars and restaurants as legitimate reporting mechanisms because their high cash volumes are ideal for concealing illegal profits (Pennsylvania Crime Commission 1984).

Reasons to Seek Legitimacy

Finally, active participation in legitimate businesses enhances the integration of crime group members with members of the business community. Chambliss (1978) reported that distinctions between organized crime and legitimate businesses in Seattle were nearly impossible to discern. In his Morrisburg study, Potter (1994) reported intense intertwinement of legal and illegal businesses serving as gambling collection points, pornographic film distribution points, fencing and loan-sharking operations, and street-level prostitution operations.

Organized crime provides lucrative services to some businesspeople in a community. This does not imply that all businesses deal with organized crime or that all organized crime activities are favorable for business but that, in a significant number of specific situations, businesses avail themselves of the services of organized crime. Relationships between fences and retail establishments are particularly good examples. In fact, in her classic study of fencing, Walsh (1977) estimated that about two-thirds of the fences active in the purchase and resale of stolen goods were also legitimate business proprietors.

Organized crime's racketeering services provide businesses with potent weapons for harassing competitors or securing favorable employee contracts (Chambliss 1978; Pennsylvania Crime Commission 1980; Block and Chambliss 1981; Potter and Jenkins 1985). The literature includes numerous examples of this symbiotic relationship: the automobile industry's attempts to suppress unionization (Pearce 1976), local industry's collusion with the Teamsters (Chambliss 1978), the activities of the Roofer's Union (Pennsylvania Crime Commission 1980), and corruption in the garment manufacturing industry (Block and Chambliss 1981). Business racketeering provides opportunities for management to collaborate in efforts to gain control of unions and their pension funds. The Teamsters union is an example of this relationship, as is organized crime's extensive influence in Philadelphia area union health care plans (Pennsylvania Crime Commission 1983).

Finally, businesses occasionally utilize organized crime's financial services in joint investment ventures. Numerous local case studies have reported instances of legitimate businesspeople openly engaging in partnerships with reputed organized crime figures, particularly in the trucking, construction, mining, and banking industries. This consensual relationship offers the advantage of stimulating quick capital accumulation for both parties.

Legitimate activity often fails to supply quick capital needs that can be secured through illicit sources. Morrisburg drug networks offered investment opportunities for legitimate business capital that could subsequently be converted into wholesale illicit drug purchases (Potter 1994). Furthermore, legitimate business holdings by Morrisburg gambling organizations have all but eliminated the need for layoff services and provide avenues for profitable investments in real estate and local service industries (Potter 1994).

Organized crime often supplies investment capital that would otherwise not be available from other sources. Developments in cities such as Las Vegas, Miami, Newport, Kentucky, and Saratoga Springs, New York, illustrate the power of organized crime's investment capital. As previously noted, Morrisburg gambling syndicates enhanced the survivability of small businesses that ultimately assisted in the revitalization of a sagging economy. The Pennsylvania Crime Commission (1980) states that mob-owned businesses employ approximately 2,000 persons in that state's garment industry. Clearly, the move into legitimate business is nothing more than a smart business decision enabling the criminal group to amass more profit while protecting its original investment in crime.

Labor racketeering is the use of union power for personal profit. At its heart, it relies on fear, both personal and economic. With the repeal of Prohibition in 1933, organized crime leaders were eager to identify new sources of revenue. One of the first to identify labor racketeering as a profitable venture in the early years of the twentieth century was New York racketeer Arnold Rothstein. Lepke Buchalter and Jacob Shapiro then developed labor racketeering into a major criminal enterprise in the 1930s and 1940s (Block and Chambliss 1981; Potter and Jenkins 1985). By the 1950s the Kefauver Committee was suggesting that organized crime groups played dominant roles in the labor unions of eight industries: the hotel and restaurant industry, baking, distilling of alcoholic beverages, trucking, garment manufacturing, carpentry, meat packing, and construction (Moore 1974: 68–79).

Organized crime initially infiltrated the international labor unions, specifically the International Longshoreman's Association (ILA) and the International Brotherhood of Teamsters (IBT). To many, the ILA has been a virtual synonym for corruption in the labor movement. In 1937, Albert "the Executioner" Anastasia muscled his way into six Brooklyn, New York, waterfront locals. Anastasia, who headed the Italian organized crime's death squad, Murder, Inc., was the boss of what later became known as the Gambino Cosa Nostra family until his death in 1957.

The Teamsters union was a logical union for organized crime domination. After all, a teamsters' strike could virtually cripple the nation, which depends heavily on the trucking industry. Organized crime took control of the Teamsters when Jimmy Hoffa, relying on his mob ties, gained the presidency. Hoffa later became the subject of investigation by the McClellan Committee in the late 1960s and was finally imprisoned in 1967, succeeded by Frank Fitzsimmons, who also had ties with known mob figures. Hoffa tried to regain control of the Teamsters after his release from prison, and his 1975 disappearance and presumable murder were thought to be the work of the Mafia.

Today, labor racketeering continues to be a major business of organized crime. The three major activities by which organized crime realizes illicit profits are (1) **sweetheart contracts,** (2) the misuse of union benefit funds, and (3) extortion, or **strike insurance.** A sweetheart contract is a contract that an employer and union officials devise with substandard terms for union

Ready-Mix Concrete Industry

As of the preparation of this text, the Ready-Mix Concrete Industry in New York City is an area of investigative focus by the federal government due to its history of being controlled by Italian organized crime groups through labor racketeering activities. At one time, Italian organized crime effectively regulated the concrete industry through its control of the two unions involved in manufacturing and delivering most of the concrete utilized in Manhattan construction projects. These two unions are the Teamsters Local 282 and the Cement and Concrete Workers Union. The Colombo crime family extorted a 1 percent kickback on all pouring contracts up to $2 million. Contracts from $2 million to $15 million were reserved for certain contractors that were approved by the Commission and resulted in a 2 percent kickback to Italian organized crime, and contracts over $15 million were reserved for a company controlled by the Genovese crime family.

members. This contract does immeasurable damage to the interests of union members. In return for a bribe paid to corrupt union officials, the company is able to negotiate a highly beneficial contract with its workers. Union demands for higher wages, better working conditions, and stronger benefit packages are reduced to benefit the company. It increases its profits at the expense of workers.

The only winners in the negotiation of a sweetheart contract are the company and the mob-controlled union officials themselves. In addition to reducing workers' legitimate economic benefits, a sweetheart contract also usually allows the company to use nonunion labor in specific circumstances, thereby reducing the opportunity for employment of union members.

Union pension and benefits funds offer the opportunity for the misuse of enormous cash reserves. All union contracts contain various benefit packages, such as health insurance, life insurance, and retirement benefits. Sometimes these benefit funds are managed by private insurance companies that take their cut of the workers' benefits in the form of administrative fees and profits. Sometimes the funds are administered by the employer, who is most likely to consider the company's profit margin and economic health before workers' health problems or retirement prospects.

Because of their history with private insurers and company-run benefit funds, many unions administer their own benefit funds. The vast majority of these funds are managed responsibly, return greater benefits to the workers than do the other options, and have been more reliable and solvent than the alternatives. However, in an organized crime–dominated union, these funds can be misused and workers' benefits endangered by risky investments determined by the financial needs of criminal syndicates, rather than the fiduciary responsibility to the workers.

Workers' benefit funds can be abused in several ways. The first is by making irresponsible, unsecured, and illegal loans to organized crime groups. The history of the International Brotherhood of Teamsters' Central States Pension Fund is dotted with such questionable investments. This pension fund was administered from the mid-1960s by Allen Dorfman, who made massive real estate loans to organized crime interests in Las Vegas, Florida, and other sunbelt states. Teamsters' money was used to help Kansas City and Chicago organized crime interests acquire casinos in Las Vegas. Additional casino and real estate speculation by major organized crime figures, such as Moe Dalitz, Meyer Lansky, and Ed Levinson, was financed in a similar way.

Mob-controlled benefit funds have also been used to provide organized crime figures with no-show jobs, leased automobiles, vacation properties, and homes. The benefit funds have also been used to pay debts to crime syndicates by contracting with mob-controlled companies for services that are never delivered. A prime example of such a relationship was the $1.3 million Teamster contract with the Hoover–Gorin advertising company, an organized crime-controlled business that never did any advertising or public relations work for the Teamsters union.

Finally, organized crime can profit from illegal control of a labor union through extortion, most frequently related to the selling of strike insurance, an extortion racket in which a union leader demands money in return for labor peace. It simply guarantees companies such as construction companies that their work will not be interrupted by workers' strikes even if the grievances are justified. A prime example of this type of extortion is the 2 percent organized crime tax imposed on construction contracts in New York City. Failure to pay this extortion demand means work stoppages and interruptions and an inability to get services from organized crime–controlled subcontractors. In particular, construction projects find it virtually impossible to get concrete poured at construction sites in New York City without paying this tax.

HIGH-TECH CRIME

High-tech crimes targeting computer networks are becoming an increasing problem because of the growing reliance of government entities, public utilities, industries, businesses, and financial institutions on electronic data and information storage, retrieval, and transmission. The creation of complex computer networks on which many of these entities depend has created opportunities for unintended access, disruption, and destruction of information by a wide range of hackers. Although most computer attacks are conducted by disgruntled employees and independent hackers, international criminal organizations have increasing capability to penetrate and exploit computer-based information and data systems. Penetration of computer systems provides criminals the ability to access and manipulate personal, financial, commercial, and government data. The introduction of computer viruses can compromise data system integrity. Hostile hackers could potentially disrupt critical public-sector assets (Denning and Baugh 1998; Finckenauer 2000; Grabosky et al. 2001),

The significant dependence on computer systems for daily business and administrative functions and the increasing interconnections between computer networks have increased both the vulnerability and potential costs of systems penetration. Many critical public infrastructure industries, including power and energy, telecommunications, and transportation systems, are operated or managed by computer networks. According to the U.S. Customs Service, all major international industries, businesses, and financial institutions rely on interconnected computer systems for commercial and financial transactions to remain competitive. Attacks on computer and information systems of U.S. corporations, financial institutions, universities, and government agencies by employees and external system penetration ranged from denial of service and sabotage to financial fraud and theft of proprietary information, according to surveys jointly conducted by the FBI and the Computer Security Institute.

Illegal intrusion and exploitation of computer networks in the United States have increased over the last several years, causing millions of dollars in losses to U.S. businesses and potentially threatening the reliability of public services. According to the joint 2000 FBI–Computer Security Institute Survey of security managers of U.S. corporations, financial institutions, universities, and government agencies, 273 respondents cited financial losses of $265.5 million from computer crime, almost double the reported losses of $136.8 million in 1998. The number of U.S. businesses reporting computer intrusions through Internet connections rose from 37 percent in 1996 to 70 percent in 1998, according to the joint survey.

As worldwide dependence on technology increases, high-tech crime is an increasingly attractive source of revenue for organized crime groups, as well as an attractive option for them to make commercial and financial transactions that support their criminal activities. With few of the risks associated with traditional criminal activity, high-tech crime allows criminals to operate in the relative security of computer networks, often beyond the reach of law enforcement.

International criminals, including members of traditional organized crime groups, are increasingly becoming computer literate, enabling them to use cutting-edge technologies for illicit gain. These criminals rely on publicly available sources to obtain information on system vulnerabilities. E-mail services routinely distribute information that can be used to exploit computer systems. In addition, public access to sensitive information is available in books, magazine and newspaper articles, electronic bulletin board messages, and websites. Such information provides potential hackers the latest methodology for staging computer attacks.

Criminal groups can also exploit businesses and government agencies by using programmers, many of whom are low-paid foreigners, to make software fixes or write new programs to gain access to computer systems and the information they contain. Press reports indicate that a Russian-speaking crime group in the United States recruited unemployed programmers in Russia to hack into other syndicates' computer systems, embezzle funds, and create programs to protect its funds in U.S. banks.

International criminals are using computers to support a wide range of criminal activity. Computers allow criminals to more securely and efficiently orchestrate and implement crimes without regard to national borders. Drug traffickers, for example, are using encrypted e-mail and the Internet to avoid detection and monitoring of their communications over normal telephone and communications channels.

The Internet has also become the primary means that international child pornography rings use to disseminate their material worldwide. These rings are operating in dozens of countries, peddling their illicit wares through the Internet and other global distribution networks. Modern technology allows child pornographers to store vast quantities of digital images on small portable computers easily smuggled into the United States and elsewhere.

Moreover, criminal commercial and financial transactions via computers occur amid countless legitimate public, business, and personal uses of computer networks, making them especially difficult to identify. Virtually any commodity, including weapons of mass destruction and their component parts and delivery systems, is being offered for international sale on Internet sites. U.S. Customs Service investigations show that many Internet sellers of contraband materials openly advertise that they have been in operation for many years without being caught by law enforcement. In December 1999, there were about 100 ongoing U.S. Customs Service investigations involving the sale of counterfeit goods over the Internet.

Computers are also exploited by international criminals to facilitate a wide range of economic crime, particularly targeting U.S. commercial interests. High-tech financial fraud through illicit access to credit card numbers and commercial accounts has the potential to cause serious losses for U.S. businesses conducting electronic commerce over the Internet. According to the joint FBI–Computer Security Institute survey in 1998, 241 U.S. business respondents reported $11.2 million in losses caused by computer financial frauds. Telecommunications fraud from computer attacks cost these companies an additional $17.2 million in losses. In March 1999, hackers pleaded guilty to breaking into U.S. phone companies for calling-card numbers that eventually made their way to organized crime syndicates in Italy. United States law enforcement information indicates that this high-tech theft cost U.S. phone companies an estimated $2 million.

Intellectual property rights violations through the penetration of computer networks also represent an increasing threat to U.S. businesses. Those responding to the 1998 survey reported losses of $33.5 million in theft of proprietary information from computer attacks.

International criminals may be using computer hacking and related methods for financial gain. Industry and law enforcement reports indicate that high-tech criminals are using advances in technology to target banks and other financial institutions. The anonymity and speed of electronic transactions could encourage criminal exploitation of these technologies. The following are examples of illegal access to computers that led to crimes.

- In October 2000, according to press reports, Italian authorities dismantled a Sicilian Mafia-led crime group that was planning to steal as much as $900 million in European Union (EU) aid earmarked for Sicily. Employing corrupt officials from the targeted bank and a telecommunications firm, the crime syndicate broke into the bank's computer network, created a virtual banking site linked to the interbank payments network, and was able to divert $115 million of the EU aid to Mafia-controlled bank accounts in Italy and abroad before they were discovered.

- In China, a computer hacker was convicted in November 1999 of breaking into the Shanghai Securities Exchange, where he changed transaction records that cost two Chinese companies more than $300,000, according to Chinese press reports.

- In South Africa in November 1999, an unidentified crime syndicate stole hundreds of thousands of dollars from local banks by using the Internet and bank-by-telephone services to hack into financial institutions, according to press reports.

- In 1994, individuals in St. Petersburg, Russia, aided by insider access, attempted to steal more than $10 million from a U.S. bank by making approximately 40 wire transfers to accounts around the world.

INTELLECTUAL PROPERTY RIGHTS VIOLATIONS

Intellectual property rights (IPRs) crimes involve the theft of trade secrets and copyright, trademark, and patent violations. The explosion of digitization and the Internet have further enabled IPR violators to easily copy and illegally distribute trade secrets, trademarks, and logos (Silk 1988; Smith 1999).

Because the United States leads the world in the creation and export of intellectual property, particularly motion pictures, computer software, sound recording, and book publishing, U.S. corporations are especially vulnerable to counterfeiting and other forms of copyright, trademark, and patent infringement. The film, computer software, sound recording, and publishing business represent almost 4 percent of the gross domestic product of the United States, or about $270 billion a year. In fact, these industries make up the largest export sector in the U.S. economy, bigger than the steel, automotive, aerospace, chemical, and plastics industries combined.

The largest market for illegal IPR products is the foreign market. Counterfeit or copied products are in direct competition around the world with U.S.-manufactured products, often at a much lower price. Some foreign markets are virtually completely closed to U.S. firms because of the cheaper counterfeit products available.

Copyright violations entail the illicit production and sale of computer software, recorded music, and videos. In 1998, trade losses suffered by U.S.-based industries due to copyright violations totaled nearly $12.4 billion, with losses to the motion picture industry of $1.7 billion, the sound recording and music publishing industry at $1.7 billion, the business software industry at nearly $4.6 billion, the entertainment software industry at $3.4 billion, and the book publishing industry at $685 million. In 1996, law enforcement raids around the world resulted in the seizure of nearly 5.1 million unauthorized copies of motion picture videocassettes, as well as more than 25,000 VCRs with an estimated production capacity of almost 33 million pirate videos per year.

Globally, one in every three compact discs (CDs) sold is a counterfeit copy, according to an estimate published in 1998. In 1999, worldwide sales of pirated sound recordings totaled more than $4 billion. Stolen software costs the industry $12 billion globally and topped $59 billion during the last five years. The average global piracy rate for software is 38 percent of total sales, with a U.S. rate of about 25 percent. Of the 523 new business software applications sold worldwide in 1997, 225 were pirated copies.

Counterfeit trademarked products account for approximately 8 percent of world trade, roughly $200 billion annually. A survey of 10 leading apparel and footwear companies indicated annual losses of nearly $2 billion due to sales of counterfeit goods. Online sales of such goods exceed $25 billion annually worldwide, according to ICC estimates. In 1999, U.S. Customs Service seized a record $98.5 million in counterfeit imported merchandise, an increase of $22 million from the previous year. The commodities most commonly seized were computer parts, sunglasses, and clothing, as well as audiocassettes, videocassettes, and CDs.

Patent violations involve the illegal manufacture of products using production processes, designs, or materials that are protected by patents, which give the holder the right to exclude others from making, using, or selling an invention for a specified period of time. The Pharmaceutical Research and Manufacturers Association estimates that the pharmaceutical industry loses more than $2 billion annually due to counterfeit medications sold on the open market. United States nongeneric pharmaceutical sales totaled $110.8 billion worldwide in 1997; estimated sales for 1998 were $124.6 billion.

IPR crimes threaten consumer interests in the United States and elsewhere by producing counterfeit products using inferior materials and poor-quality controls that can affect public safety and health. Since 1990, U.S. authorities have identified or seized nonconforming parts in U.S.-produced automobiles and commercial airplanes and substandard materials in household products and consumables such as infant formula and pharmaceuticals. The World Health Organization estimated in 1997 that at least 7 percent of the medicines sold worldwide are counterfeit products. United States authorities have confiscated misbranded and counterfeit pharmaceuticals, including birth control pills, medication to treat AIDS, heart disease, diabetes, cancer, and weight-loss preparations.

East and Southeast Asia are primary regions that violate IPR regulations, causing significant losses to U.S. businesses. China and Hong Kong harbor major duplicators of Western toys and clothing; firms in Malaysia, Singapore, and Taiwan copy U.S. audio, video, and software products. According to the U.S. Customs Service, 56 percent of U.S. IPR seizures (mostly music CDs, computer software packages, and movies) in the first half of 1999 were from China and Taiwan.

In Eastern Europe, Ukraine has emerged as the leading producer of pirated optical disc products, distributing them throughout the world. Israel remains a key distribution hub in a regional network for pirated optical media products that extends into Russia and Eastern Europe.

Latin America is the third-largest market for illegally duplicated CDs, videos, and cassettes. Illegal production of these products is centered in Brazil and Argentina. Paraguay continues to be a regional center for pirated goods, especially optical media, and serves as a shipment point for large volumes of products from Asia to the larger markets bordering Paraguay, particularly Brazil.

Although many IPR crimes are committed by ostensibly legitimate foreign manufacturing, business, and import–export enterprises, to enhance their competitiveness, criminal organizations are becoming common players in all stages of IPR crime, from manufacture to distribution. Product piracy and counterfeiting are attractive to criminal organizations because of the absence of strong criminal counterfeiting laws and the potential for large profits. Moreover, some criminal organizations use the proceeds from producing and selling counterfeit brand name consumer goods to fund other types of criminal activity, both in the United States and elsewhere.

In New York City, ethnic Chinese crime syndicates are increasingly counterfeiting consumer products as a source of tax-free income. The Vietnamese gang Born to Kill reportedly relies on the sale of counterfeit Rolex and Cartier watches to fund gang activities. The group's founder has claimed earnings exceeding $35 million from counterfeit product sales. In 1995, law enforcement officials in Los Angeles discovered several Chinese criminal groups, including the Wah Ching, the Big Circle Boys, and the Four Seas triad, engaged in counterfeiting floppy discs and CD-ROMs. Assets of more than $17 million in illicit products and manufacturing equipment, plastic explosives, TNT, and firearms were seized.

TRAFFICKING IN NUCLEAR MATERIAL

At the end of 2001, there were no indications that any organized crime group has tried or planned to steal or obtain weapons-grade nuclear material (uranium with greater than 90 percent uranium 235 concentration and plutonium). In fact, even in the wake of massive antiterrorist investigations in 2002, no information that terrorist organizations have ever been able to obtain weapons-usable nuclear material exists.

The few instances in which criminal entrepreneurs have obtained weapons-usable nuclear material have been crimes of opportunity made possible by insider knowledge of storage facilities and practices. As of the beginning of 2002, no such theft had ever occurred with potential buyers identified prior to the theft. Worldwide there have been 14 theft cases involving a total of 15.3 kilograms of weapons-usable uranium at various enrichments and 368.8 grams of plutonium. These cases, which represent all known attempts to traffic in nuclear material, have cumulatively involved quantities of weapons-grade material far, far less than what is necessary to build even a small nuclear weapon (Mueller 1994; Williams and Woessner 1996; Albini et al. 2000).

TRAFFICKING IN WOMEN AND CHILDREN

Arguably the most significant crime problem among the new growth industries for organized crime is trafficking in human beings, particularly women and children, across international borders. These individuals are usually sold for forced agricultural or industrial labor. A robust market also exists for women and children as objects of sexual exploitation. Endemic to human trafficking enterprises are conditions of abuse and exploitation, including sexual slavery and forced prostitution, sweatshop labor, domestic servitude, and coerced agricultural labor.

Both the logistics of human trafficking itself and the exploitative nature of the enterprises in which trafficked human beings are destined to participate make extreme forms of violence, including the use of rape as a means of control, common. Relatively conservative governmental estimates suggest that 700,000 women and children are smuggled across international borders by human trafficking groups every year. Other estimates emanating from nongovernmental agencies place the numbers much higher. Human trafficking specifically to service organized crime's worldwide brothel industry nets that industry $4 billion in annual profits (Ruggerio 1997; O'Neill 1999; Richard 2000; Erez 2001).

About 50,000 women and children trafficked, or 7 percent of the international total, come to the United States every year. The vast majority of these women and children are from Southeast Asia and Latin America. The major ports of entry used by human traffickers moving women and children into the United States are New York, Miami, Chicago, Los Angeles, and San Francisco. Secondary ports of entry are the District of Columbia, Cleveland, Orlando, Atlanta, and Houston. A few women from the United States have been trafficked abroad, particularly to clients in Japan and the Middle East.

The illicit traffic in women and children into the United States is an important component in maintaining illegal support structures for the U.S. prostitution industry. In Florida, police arrested a brothel operator who had paid to smuggle women and children from Mexico and then forced each into prostitution to pay off her $2,000 smuggling fee.

The exploitation of children smuggled across borders for sexual purposes is a growing international problem. There has been a significant and dramatic increase in travel by U.S. citizens to foreign countries to have sex with children. Often these children are caught in the human trafficking web and are paying off their smuggling fees. Less commonly they have been kidnaped for sale to prostitution operators. Perhaps the most disturbing fact is that most children forced into prostitution have been sold to traffickers by their parents.

What is most surprising about traffickers in women and children is how openly and boldly they operate their enterprises. Traffickers usually select source countries with three primary characteristics: (1) poor economic and employment prospects for women, (2) well-defined and organized extant criminal organizations, and (3) a culture that emphasizes a subordinate role for women in society. Trafficking organizations frequently recruit women who are hoping for a better economic life with advertisements promising jobs as maids, waitresses, dancers, and models.

Once women are in the trafficking pipeline, a variety of coercive tactics, often involving violence, is used to enslave them. Traffickers most commonly purchase underage girls from their relatives. About 225,000 women and children from Southeast Asia are trafficked across international borders each year, about one-third of the international total. Most of the women are under the age of 18, and about 60 percent of them are trafficked to Asian and Pacific markets, specifically, Thailand, Hong Kong, Singapore, Japan, and Australia. About 30,000 of them are trafficked to the U.S. market, making Southeast Asia the largest source for importation into the United States. About 150,000 women and children from the South Asian market are trafficked to the Middle East and other Asian destinations each year.

The second largest group brought to the United States comes from Latin America. About 10 percent of the 1 million women and children trafficked by Latin American organized crime groups go to the United States.

In recent years, the countries of Eastern Europe and the former Soviet Union have become increasingly important centers for the illicit trade in women and children. Traffickers move about 175,000 women and children from these countries across international borders each year. About 120,000 of them go to western European countries, most commonly Germany, Italy, and the Netherlands. About 4,000 of these women and children go to the United States.

Human traffickers moving women and children accomplish the task in various ways. But what is most surprising is how open and public this activity usually is. Traffickers in women and children invariably operate through legitimate business fronts such as employment agencies, travel agencies, entertainment companies, and marriage agencies. These businesses normally provide legitimate passports and visas to the women and children crossing international borders. Traffickers rarely use fraudulent or counterfeit travel documents to move women and children because corrupt officials from both countries of departure and entrance can provide legitimate documentation.

Equally surprising is the fact that human traffickers moving women and children often use commercial airlines operating from their home countries as primary modes of transportation. Women and children are moved in small groups, changing flights frequently to conceal their actual travel routes.

Human trafficking groups tend to be relatively small organized crime entities operating as loosely connected networks. Because women and children are renewable commodities, their sale is rapidly becoming a major income source for many organized crime groups.

Essential for all human trafficking organizations, especially those specializing in women and children, is the cooperation of corrupt officials in source, transit, and destination countries. The source country's law enforcement agencies widely ignore the recruitment process because they believe that the actual coercive acts in the trafficking scheme are most likely to take place in the destination countries. In 1997, four senior Bulgarian law enforcement officials, including two in charge of anticrime task forces, were fired because they were linked to an organized crime group involved in procuring women for forced prostitution. In Thailand, trafficking groups regularly recruit members of the military and police to act as escorts and guards for women and children who are being sent to foreign destinations for participation in the sex market.

Trafficking in women and children to the United States is likely to be a growth industry for organized crime, especially because it involves high profit margins, low risk of arrest, and relatively few convictions following arrest.

MONEY LAUNDERING

Organized criminal activity often requires considerable capital to purchase businesses to use as fronts for illegal enterprises and to transport, train, and pay corrupt public officials. The International Monetary Fund estimates that money laundering, used by drug traffickers to introduce the proceeds of their sales into the legitimate financial market, involves between 2 and 5 percent of the world's gross domestic product, about $600 billion annually.

Money laundering allows the true source of the funds gained through the sale and distribution of drugs to be concealed and converts the funds into assets that appear to have a legitimate legal source. The need to launder conspicuously large amounts of small-denomination bills, however, can render the traffickers vulnerable to law enforcement interdiction.

Money Laundering Defined

The Department of Justice defines **money laundering** in the following manner: "the process by which criminals conceal or disguise the proceeds of their crimes or convert those proceeds into goods and services. It allows criminals to infuse their illegal money into the stream of commerce, thus corrupting financial institutions and the money supply and giving criminals unwarranted economic power." It can be further described in the following manner: "A process . . . (a series of actions) through which income of illegal origin is concealed, disguised, or made to appear legitimate (Main objective); and to evade detection, prosecution, seizure, and taxation" (FBI 2006).

In any case, money laundering is the process by which criminal proceeds are made to appear to come from a legitimate source. Investigations into money-laundering activities typically use a two-prong approach:

1. The investigation of the underlying criminal activity, in simple terms, if there is no criminal activity, or "specified unlawful activity," that generates illicit proceeds, then there can be no money laundering.
2. A parallel financial investigation to uncover the financial infrastructure of the criminal organization. Following the money and discerning how the money flows in an organization in order to conceal, disguise, or hide the proceeds.

Current Money-Laundering Trends

Drug traffickers use various methods to launder their profits both inside and outside the United States. Presently, some of the more common laundering methods include the **Black Market Peso Exchange,** cash smuggling (couriers or bulk cash shipments), gold purchases, structured deposits to or withdrawals from bank accounts, purchase of monetary instruments (cashier's checks, money order, traveler's checks, etc.), wire transfers, and forms of underground banking, particularly the hawala system (discussed later in this chapter).

The money-laundering process usually involves three stages: placement, layering, and integration. The illicit gains enter into the commercial financial systems during the *placement stage*. Some methods for placement include cash smuggling (by couriers or bulk cash shipments); structuring bank deposits or withdrawals; wire transfers and remittance transfers to banks and shell companies; purchase of cashier's checks, money orders, traveler's checks, and securities; casinos; third-party checks (commonly used with the Black Market Peso Exchange); and electronic transfers. The method chosen for the placement depends on the trafficker's needs. At this stage the money-laundering operation is most vulnerable to law enforcement detection and seizure.

The second or *layering stage* involves a series of secondary transactions that move the funds from place to place to obscure their trail. In the *integration stage*, the proceeds are reintroduced or integrated into the economy as legitimately earned money that is available for utilization by the trafficker. In many drug source countries, the drug trafficker uses the laundered money to pay employees for services and buy properties and businesses. The money then contributes to the economic growth and stability of the microeconomies of the source countries, albeit only temporarily. The sophistication in obscuring the trail once the money has entered into the financial system has increased exponentially in recent years with technical advances in cyberbanking and e-cash.

The methods for laundering money are as numerous as the imagination allows, but they can be reduced to four categories:

1. Bulk movement strategy
2. Use of financial institutions
3. Use of nonfinancial and commercial businesses
4. Movement through the underground banking system.

Traffickers use several of these methods to integrate the drug money into the economy as licit profits. The following are some examples of common money-laundering methods.

Use of Bulk Movement Strategy

Overseas traffickers are likely to use the bulk movement strategy to withdraw their money from the United States. In countries such as the United States with the currency transaction reporting (CTR) requirements, cash transactions of more than $10,000 must be reported. Money launderers smuggle their cash out of these countries to one that does not have or does not enforce currency regulations. The methods used to smuggle the cash or monetary instruments are considered bulk movement whether on the person or in the luggage of couriers, in diplomatic pouches, in cargo, by mail, trucks, or private plane.

The enactment of the Uniting and Strengthening America by Providing Appropriate Tools Required to Intercept and Obstruct Terrorism (USA

Patriot Act), Title III, International Money Laundering Abatement and Anti-Terrorist Financing Act of 2001, Section 371, created a new criminal offense, the act of smuggling bulk cash or other monetary instruments in amounts of more than $10,000 out of or into the United States.

Use of Financial Institutions

Using financial institutions such as banks is still the safest and most efficient method of laundering money. Proceeds from street drug sales are almost invariably in cash and generally in small-denomination bills. The most convenient placement method is to deposit the money into a bank account and the next day transfer it out by wire to scores of other accounts. This alleviates the problem of transporting the voluminous cash and allows the trafficker to convert the currency into some other negotiable instrument or currency. Several wire transfers of funds can be accomplished within hours to hide the money trail. However, to use the banks, the reporting requirements need to be circumvented.

One way to circumvent the reporting requirements is to make numerous deposits under the $10,000 cash transaction reporting threshold, which is known as structuring or **smurfing.** Drug traffickers also purchase legitimate businesses, such as restaurants, bars, and flea markets, that take in large volumes of cash and then deposit drug profits as proceeds from these businesses. Because these businesses are cash intensive, they are exempted from the CTR requirements, enabling traffickers to deposit large amounts of cash without reporting their transactions. Of course, purchasing a bank or corrupting or coercing a bank official is another way that drug traffickers ensure a bank's assistance in structuring deposits. Using the Internet provides another more efficient, cheaper, and secure means of moving money, although it still requires financial institutions to transfer the funds. Identifying the customer is the main problem that arises from Internet usage.

Nonfinancial Institutions and Commercial Businesses

Traffickers commonly use front companies that conduct a legitimate business but have some illicit activity, such as money laundering, as the main business. Front companies are sometimes art dealers, precious metal companies, jewelry shops, real estate investors, car and boat dealerships, restaurants, hotels, and construction companies. The companies can also be *shell companies,* which are registered businesses with no legitimate business. Charities and religious organizations are unwittingly and sometimes wittingly used to collect drug money and deposit it into their accounts so that it can be moved overseas. Nonfinancial trades or businesses are subject to the same reporting requirements as financial institutions either when they deposit money in a financial institution or when they receive currency equal to or greater than the $10,000 threshold. In addition, although they are not money service businesses, casinos have extra services that include exchanging currency denominations, issuing checks for winnings, and even wire transferring funds to other casinos. Money launderers take advantage of these services.

Underground Banking System

The more formalized and secretive system of using ordinary businesses as fronts for money movement is called the **underground banking system** (UBS). It differs from the money service businesses because these companies on the surface are not in the business of moving money as are the remittance companies. A trafficker can bring the funds needed to purchase drug supplies or the proceeds from the sale of drugs to an underground banker and within hours have these funds transferred internationally with no official paper trail whatsoever. These systems charge very little for their services, much less than banks do. They are also faster, more efficient, more confidential, and more convenient.

Under the 2001 USA Patriot Act, section 373 amends 18 U.S.C. 1960 to prohibit unlicensed money-transmitting businesses from transferring funds for the public by any and all means, to include transfers within, but not limited to, this country or locations abroad by wire, check, draft, facsimile, or courier. Section 359 amends several regulations to include government regulation of informal money transactions. Section 365 creates 31 U.S.C. 5331, which imposes reporting requirements relating to currency received in a nonfinancial trade or business in an amount equal to or greater than $10,000 in one single transaction or in two related transactions and requires the filing of a report with the Financial Crimes Enforcement Network.

The **hawala system,** an international underground banking system that allows money to be deposited in bank accounts without any paper trail, bank charges, transmission delays, or foreign exchange regulations, is an alternative money remittance system used primarily in the Middle East. There are no contracts, bank statements, or transaction records, yet those who use the hawala system can move hundreds of thousands of dollars around the world in a matter of hours. The money transfer takes place between members of a network of hawaladars (hawala dealers) based on telephone, e-mail, and fax communications. Hawala requires only trust.

The **Black Market Peso Exchange** (BMPE), an alternative or parallel money system through which drug traffickers sell U.S. dollars to brokers for pesos, is another underground banking system that launders drug proceeds. The BMPE is estimated to be responsible for moving $5 billion worth of drug proceeds from the United States into Colombia. Money brokers utilize the black market in Colombia to purchase narcotics proceeds from the traffickers. The money broker pays the trafficker in pesos at the BMPE rate, a lower rate than the official exchange rate.

The broker then owns the narcotics proceeds in the United States and must find a way to move this currency. This is sometimes done through the purchase of **gold "shot"** (gold used to make jewelry) in the United States. The gold is smuggled out of the United States to Colombia and is then sold to legitimate gold depositories in Colombia. The broker is then paid in pesos at the official exchange rate. Another way to move money back to Colombia is through the use of a wire remittance business (e.g., Western Union). Narcotics proceeds are taken to a remitter who then breaks the money down into smaller transactions. For example, $100,000 U.S. might be broken down into 100 transactions of $1,000 each. The funds are then sent to Colombia under different names supplied by the broker.

WHAT HAVE WE LEARNED?

The sale of illegal goods and services to customers who are aware that these goods and services are illegal has long been a part of organized crime. Annual gross income for these activities has been estimated in the billions of dollars, and a majority of organized crime's income stems from rackets such as drug trafficking, prostitution, pornography, gambling, and labor and business racketeering. Additional billions are made by organized crime members who force or buy their way into legitimate business and utilize them to launder profits from the illegal businesses without a trail.

The most likely businesses to be affected by organized crime's business influence are low-technology businesses, such as garbage collection and the construction industry. Labor racketeering typically involves takeovers by mob figures who are aware that a mob-controlled work stoppage would destroy a product or delay a deadline.

DO YOU RECOGNIZE THESE TERMS?

arms trafficking
B-girls
Black Market Peso Exchange (BMPE)
bookmaking
business racketeering
call girls
contraband smuggling
corruption
counterfeiting
currency exchanges
drug trafficking
environmental crime
gambling
gold "shot"

hard-core pornography
hawala system
labor racketeering
loan-sharking
money laundering
shylocking
smurfing
soft-core pornography
sports betting
streetwalkers
strike insurance
sweetheart contract
underground banking system (UBS)
vigorish

POINTS OF DISCUSSION

1. Discuss why it is important for an organized crime organization to become involved in legitimate businesses.

2. List the different businesses in which organized crime is involved and identify the most lucrative.

3. Compare and contrast the various ways in which organized crime infiltrates and profits from the pornography and prostitution business.

4. In what ways do labor and business racketeering differ?

5. What is meant by the proceeds of a crime?

6. List and discuss three methods commonly used by criminals to launder illegally earned money.

SUGGESTED READING

BLOCK, A., and F. SCARPITTI. (1985). *Poisoning for Profit: The Mafia and Toxic Waste in America.* New York: William Morrow. The book presents information from undercover investigations, hearings, taped conversations, confessions, and suppressed official report documents of organized crime's involvement in illegal toxic waste dumping and the ineffectiveness of government agencies responsible for regulating toxic waste disposal.

COHEN, B. (1980). *Deviant Street Networks: Prostitution in New York City.* Lexington, MA: D.C. Heath. This book discusses the incidence, genesis, and persistence of visible street deviance and examines prostitution in New York City as an example of the problem.

COLEMAN, J. W. (1994). *The Criminal Elite: The Sociology of White Collar Crime*. New York: St. Martin's Press.

KING, R. (1969). *Gambling and Organized Crime*. Washington, DC: Public Affairs Press. This book examines illegal gambling and its interplay with organized crime and official corruption with a review of gambling law enforcement since colonial times.

MILLER, E. (1986). *Street Women*. Philadelphia: Temple University Press. The book describes life histories and interviews with sixty-four female street hustlers (prostitutes, con artists, and petty thieves) in Milwaukee, Wisconsin. It portrays today's typical female criminal as a young, poor, minority woman with limited education and skills and several children.

SIMON, C., and A. WITTE. (1982). *Beating the System: The Underground Economy*. Boston: Auburn House. This book provides a sector by sector microeconomic analysis of the underground economy—tax evasion and transactions involving payment in money or similar goods but not officially recorded in statistics or subjected to taxation—and suggests policy recommendations to reduce this siphoning of public revenues.

6

THE ILLICIT DRUG TRADE

This chapter will enable you to:

- Comprehend the origins and magnitude of the nation's drug problem
- Understand methods of measuring drug abuse
- Describe the causal relationship between drugs and organized crime
- View the drug business as a well-calculated, profit-generating enterprise

- Comprehend the structure and operating methods of the drug business
- Understand the role of foreign countries in the international drug trade
- Compare and contrast various drug control strategies

INTRODUCTION

Organized crime and drug trafficking are not mutually exclusive, for drug-trafficking organizations regularly engage in other criminal activities to support their operations. Similarly, organized crime groups, street gangs, and some terrorist organizations are involved in drug-related activities. For example, drug-trafficking organizations are engaged in the corruption of U.S. law enforcement officials, kidnappings, tortures, and murder to further their drug-trafficking operations. Mexican drug-trafficking organizations use street gangs to murder rivals and to distribute drugs throughout the United States. Russian organized crime groups, which distribute drugs in the United States, are also involved with the U.S. La Cosa Nostra in sophisticated financial fraud, money laundering, and other white-collar crime schemes. Colombian drug-trafficking organizations interact with terrorist organizations.

When major drug-trafficking organizations lose a load of drugs, they kidnap, torture, and often execute those involved. If the individual responsible for the loss flees, the organization kidnaps and threatens a close family member until the individual turns himself in to the organization.

Drug-trafficking organizations systematically engage in corruption to support their drug operations. This is particularly problematic along the southwest border of the United States, where U.S. law enforcement officials there have been convicted of participating actively in drug-related crimes, including waving drug-laden vehicles through entry sites in exchange for money, coordinating the movement of drugs across the border, using their official positions to transport drugs past checkpoints without being suspected, and disclosing drug intelligence information. In an eighteen-month period, an FBI-led public corruption task force in southern Arizona conducted a series of drug corruption investigations that resulted in the conviction of ten federal officers, two deputy sheriffs, three local police officers, and one local judge.

In January 1999 an FBI sting operation called Operation Ghostload illustrated the impact of drug-related corruption in the United States. As a result of this investigation, four Immigration and Naturalization Service inspectors who were assigned to the Nogales, Arizona, port of entry and seven drug traffickers were arrested. The inspectors were responsible for passing more than 20 tons of cocaine into the United States for which they received more than $800,000 in bribes. This demonstrates the corruption of U.S. law enforcement agencies by organized crime groups to protect their drug trafficking (McGraw 2000).

Most organized crime groups take advantage of the ease of international travel and the latest advances in telecommunications and technology to move large segments of their criminal enterprises into the U.S. market. For example, Oleg Kirillov, the leader of a Russian organized crime group based in Russia, established an operation in Miami, Florida, to launch a cocaine smuggling route between Peru and Russia. An investigation by the FBI in Miami determined that this group's network stretched from various locations in the United States to Russia, Europe, and South America. In addition to drug trafficking, group members were actively engaged in a variety of criminal offenses, including stock manipulation, credit card fraud, and motor vehicle theft. Kirillov and several of his associates were indicted and later convicted for their involvement in these criminal activities.

The interrelation of drug traffickers and violent street gangs has been well established. Street gangs continue to expand their illicit activities and build ties to domestic and international criminal organizations. While gangs are involved in a broad range of criminal activity, drug trafficking has remained a principal source of their revenue. These criminal organizations are firmly entrenched in regions near major transshipment points, freight terminals, or bulk warehouses. These groups are responsible for moving stolen cargo and high-technology commodities into other countries. These high-tech shipments are then available for exploitation by major criminal organizations.

In the aftermath of the 9/11 attacks on the World Trade Center and the Pentagon, the threat of terrorism continues. Its increasingly prominent role in international relations and business has increased the U.S. visibility and vulnerability. While there is no evidence per se of narcoterrorism within the United States, there are indications that some terrorist organizations, such as Colombia's FARC and, to a lesser extent, the National Liberation Army (ELN), support their activities through funds acquired as the result of their protection of drug traffickers or the distribution of drugs in Colombia. These terrorists also target U.S. interests in their own country. For example, in January 1993, three U.S. missionaries were kidnapped from a village in Panama by members of the FARC and remain missing. In February 2002, three U.S. citizens working in Colombia were kidnapped by suspected members of the FARC and were later executed in Venezuela.

DRUG CONTROL: A BRIEF HISTORY

Over the last 200 years, attitudes toward drugs and their use have vacillated considerably. During the nineteenth century, drugs containing cocaine and opiate extracts were considered as helpful compounds in everyday living. Shortly after the turn of the nineteenth century, these drugs were identified as potentially dangerous or addictive and therefore should be controlled under law. During the 1960s and 1970s, an era of social tolerance and antiestablishment sentiment resulted in a period when drug use flourished. Today, intolerance has reemerged because Americans have once again realized that some drugs are potentially dangerous and controls are necessary.

Prior to the nineteenth century, many drugs were used in their natural form. Cocaine and morphine, for example, were available only in coca leaves and opium poppy plants, which were chewed or dissolved in various solutions. With the introduction of organic chemistry in the nineteenth century, drugs such as morphine, heroin, and cocaine were isolated. The development of the hypodermic needle in 1856, which was soon adopted by physicians all over the world, facilitated drug use.

In addition, the astounding growth of the pharmaceutical industry in the late nineteenth and early twentieth centuries resulted in the development of amphetamines and barbiturates, which were widely consumed. As Musto (1991) points out, "during this time, because of a peculiarity of the U.S. Constitution, the powerful new forms of opium and cocaine were more readily available than in most nations. Under the Constitution, individual states assumed responsibility for health issues, such as the regulating of medical practice and the availability of pharmacological products." Nations with more restrictive drug laws, such as Great Britain, had a national drug policy that controlled the availability of certain dangerous drugs.

When the drug problem in nineteenth-century America is considered, we must remember that this was a time of widespread availability of drugs supported by unrestricted commercial advertising. During the last decade of the nineteenth century, as physicians arbitrarily used the hypodermic needle and addictive medications, the general public slowly became more concerned about drugs and their dangers. Also, there was a growing awareness of problems associated with alcohol abuse.

Early Drug Regulation

In 1906 the federal government enacted the Pure Food and Drug Act, which required medications containing drugs to state this on their labels. No laws existed at this point to restrict the availability of opium or its by-products. In February 1909, the International Opium Commission, made up of representatives from thirteen nations, gathered in Shanghai to discuss problems associated with opium and opiate use. However, the meeting failed to result in any international treaties or resolutions. The U.S. State Department's Opium Commissioner, Hamilton Wright, held the belief that, to control nonmedical consumption of opium in the United States, crop production in source countries should first be controlled, which would require a worldwide agreement and an international conference to do so.

In 1911 one such conference was convened at The Hague. Twelve nations signed a convention that required each country to enact domestic legislation controlling the narcotics trade. Accordingly, in 1914 the U.S Congress enacted the Harrison Narcotic Act, which relied on the government's ability to tax, rather than to interfere with the state-controlled prescribing methods of physicians. Essentially, the act required strict accounting for opium and coca and their derivatives from their entry into the United States through to their dispersal to a patient. To this end, a small tax was required for each transfer, and permits had to be obtained through the Treasury Department. Patients, however, paid no tax, nor did they require permits; in fact, they were not allowed to obtain one. For the most part during the 1920s and 1930s, opium and opiate product consumption in the United States declined drastically. Many middle-class drug users switched to other drugs, such as marijuana. The use that did occur was restricted to addicts in urban areas of larger cities.

Throughout the 1940s and 1950s, marijuana and cocaine use slowly gained popularity. The first U.S. president to declare war on drugs was Richard Nixon in 1971. At the time there were an estimated 1.5 million heroin addicts in the country, an increase from 50,000 during the 1960s (Treaster 1989). During the 1980s, cocaine gained considerable popularity among drug users and was transformed from a drug affordable only by the rich to crack cocaine, a cheap, smokable form of the drug. The Bureau of Justice Statistics (1992) says that there are an estimated 6.4 million cocaine users in the United States. In 1973 the federal government created the U.S. Drug Enforcement Administration (DEA), which is charged with enforcing the nation's federal drug laws. The military was given authority to aid in the drug control efforts during the 1980s and, late in that same decade, President George Bush appointed the nation's first drug czar to oversee federal and local drug control efforts. In 1993, Lee Brown assumed this position as the Director of the Office of National Drug Control Policy.

THE IMPACT OF DRUGS ON SOCIETY

Drugs play a multifaceted role in their effects on society. In addition to their more obvious effects on the physical and mental states of drug users, they prey on institutions and neighborhoods. Perhaps more insidious and destructive to the neighborhood is what could be termed the **cycle of disorder** created by drugs in society. The cycle typically begins with an overall fear of disorder by residents in a neighborhood, which leaves them feeling helpless and apathetic. Next, disorder increases and is easily identified by telltale signs, such as litter in the streets, growing numbers of vacant buildings, an increased number of groups of teens hanging out, broken windows throughout the neighborhood, and prostitutes working openly on the streets.

Residents who have lived in the neighborhood for years begin to move out, and those who stay are less likely to go out unless absolutely necessary. Because of divorce and unwanted pregnancies, new households are more likely to be single-parent families. Such an invasion of informal community control makes a neighborhood more susceptible to predatory and opportunistic offenders.

Indeed, policing the drug problem is no easy task. More and more inner cities look like war zones, where drug gangs seem to outnumber law enforcement officers by fifty to one. Arrests that are made do not seem to do much to deter future criminal activity; as a result, police feel trapped between rising crime rates and an angry, unappreciative citizenry who demand immediate results to unyielding problems.

In many U.S. cities, the use of drugs has become more pervasive. For example, according to the National Institute of Justice's Drug Use Forecasting, during 1989 in San Diego and Philadelphia, four out of every five males arrested tested positive for drugs. Accordingly, in other cities the incidence of arrestees testing positive for drugs was alarmingly high. For example, in 1989 in New York, 79 percent of arrestees tested positive for drugs; in Chicago the number was 74 percent, and in Los Angeles and Miami it was 70 percent.

In terms of numbers, drug arrests were also soaring nationally. For example, drug arrests by state and local police forces jumped from 559,000 in 1981 to 1,155,200 in 1988 (*U.S. News & World Report* 1990). Despite the increase in arrests, police see little measurable effect on drug use. Drug profits have also made the lure of corruption more tempting than ever. According to Sheldon Greenberg of the Police Executive Research Forum (PERF): "Ten or twenty years ago a bribe consisted of a $20 bill. Today, you have people in the drug culture saying 'there's ten grand in the bag . . . and its yours if you let me go'" (*U.S. News & World Report* 1990). In 1990 seven members of the Los Angeles County Sheriff's Narcotics Squad went on trial for skimming $1.4 million in seized drug money.

Measuring Drug Abuse

Although drug use is widespread in virtually all segments of society, the use of some drugs could be on the decline. Indications stem from national surveys of the drug problem. One, the Household Survey of Drug Abuse, was sponsored by the National Institute of Drug Abuse (NIDA), a branch of the U.S. Department of Health and Human Services. The survey, which consisted of approximately 100,000 respondents age 12 and older on a biannual basis, showed a significant drop in drug use nationwide between 1985 and 1990:

- Since 1985, drug abuse has declined 44 percent from the original 23 million reported drug abusers.
- Drug abuse by teenagers has dropped 13 percent from 1988 to 1990.

The household survey failed, however, to include people who live in jails, prisons, military bases, and other institutions, as well as the homeless.

In addition to the NIDA, a second national source of drug information from the Institute of Social Research at the University of Michigan surveyed approximately 15,000 high school students about their drug abuse. Results indicated that, although the incidence of drug use remained alarmingly high among youth, it decreased consistently over the preceding ten years or so. Many reasons are attributed for this decline, but it is difficult to point to any one variable. For example, drug abuse prevention programs such as **Drug Abuse Resistance Education (DARE)** have spread dramatically throughout the country since 1985. Social disapproval by peers is also no doubt a factor. In addition, the threat of contracting the AIDS virus may play a role in a person's decision not to use drugs.

The **Drug Use Forecasting (DUF)** program, sponsored jointly by the National Institute of Justice and the Bureau of Justice Assistance, also surveyed drug users to determine the extent of drug use and its impact on some forms of crime. The DUF provided data on the incidence of recent drug use by arrestees in selected cities across the nation, as well as trends in drug use among this segment of the population. Since its inception in 1987, the DUF program has conducted anonymous interviews and collected urine specimens numerous times each quarter from arrestees in twenty-four cities. With few exceptions, all cities cooperating in the data-collection process reported that significant numbers of arrestees tested positive for drug use, with cocaine topping the list as the major drug of choice. In addition to the preceding data, the DUF program provided important information that other drug abuse surveys cannot offer:

- Need for planning and allocating law enforcement resources
- Early detection of drug epidemics
- Ability to determine treatment and prevention needs

A shortcoming of the DUF program is the lack of a probability sampling plan that could be used to generalize test results to the total arrestee population in each participating city. The illicit drug trade and drug use present society with numerous problems. Succinctly put, two glaring threats are posed by the drug menace: drug-related crimes and income-generating crimes.

In July 1995, Eric Smith, while driving down a New Mexico highway, suddenly believed that his 14-year-old son was the devil. Smith killed and decapitated his son and threw his head out of the van window onto the highway. After capture, police learned that Smith was heavily under the influence of methamphetamine, a powerful stimulant that he had been manufacturing in a makeshift laboratory at his home. This is one of many examples of violence that over the years has become associated with drug abuse.

Drugs and Crime

Although the connection between drugs and crime appears evident, the extent of the relationship is debatable. Most discussions in this area revolve around one basic question: To what extent do drugs affect crime, or vice versa? To many people, the drug–crime connection is clear. For example, using or selling drugs is illegal, and those who choose to do so are subject to criminal sanctions. It also is clear that many crimes that do not involve drugs are a result of the exigencies of the illicit drug market:

- Some users steal to support their drug addictions.
- Prostitution is sometimes utilized to support drug use.
- Drug markets typically perpetuate violence by groups that attempt to gain a competitive advantage.

In attempting to understand the problem of drugs and crime, it is logical to consider that some drugs, due to their power to induce addictive use, are more likely than others to cause criminal activity. Examples are cocaine and heroin, which are both notable for their addictive qualities. Frequency of drug use is also a factor in the relationship between drugs and crime. A person who uses drugs several times a day is at a higher risk of involvement than is the occasional drug user. However, data provided by some studies attempting to measure the drug–crime relationship have been criticized. For example, one study in Miami indicated that 573 drug users were shown to have committed an astonishing 6,000 robberies and assaults and almost 7,000 burglaries in a twelve-month period (Bureau of Justice Statistics 1992).

A study conducted in Baltimore revealed that heroin users had high rates of criminal activity while they were addicted, but these rates dropped significantly when the users had been treated successfully. The 1990 DUF program, which tested the urine of persons in custody for the presence of ten different drugs, indicated that in most cities more than 50 percent of those tested were found to have used drugs recently (Bureau of Justice Statistics 1992).

In another study conducted by the U.S. Bureau of Justice Statistics (BJS) in 1991, more than three out of four jail inmates reported some drug use in their lifetime. More than 40 percent used drugs in the month before their offense, with 27 percent under the influence at the time of their offense. In a related BJS study, more than one-half of state prison inmates reported that they had been under the influence of drugs when they committed the offense for which they had been incarcerated.

The exact relationship between drugs and crime remains unclear, however. A generally accepted conclusion is that drug addiction does not cause crime, but it increases users' involvement in criminal activity.

Drugs and Violent Crime

Drug addiction and trafficking are closely related to violent crime in a number of ways. For example, some drug users commit violent criminal acts to acquire money for drugs. Both legal and illicit drugs can affect the user's physiological functions, cognitive ability, and emotions. Although no evidence exists to show a relationship between violence and drug use, many experts have concluded that a combination of direct and indirect factors may result in violent behavior. These include the type of drug, the user's personality characteristics, and environmental and cultural influences.

How Drugs and Crime are Related

Drugs and Crime Relationship	Definition	Examples
Drug-defined offenses	Violations of laws prohibiting the possession, use, cultivation, distribution, or manufacture Production of illegal drugs	Drug possession or use of marijuana Methamphetamine Cocaine, heroin, or marijuana sales
Drug-related offenses	Offenses performed under effect of drug, motivated by the user's need to support drug use, and connected with drug distribution itself	Violent behavior resulting from drug effects
Stealing to get money	Violence against rival drug dealers	
Interfactional	Drug use and crime are common aspects of a deviant life-style; the likelihood and frequency of involvement in illegal activity is increased because offenders are exposed to situations that encourage crime	A life orientation with an emphasis on short-term goals supported by illegal activities Opportunities to offend resulting from contacts with offenders and illegal markets Criminal skills learned from other offenders

Source: Bureau of Justice Statistics (1992).

Aggression among drug traffickers, also known as **intramural violence,** is common, and often erupts during disagreements about transactions. In addition, violence is used to protect or expand drug markets, intimidate competitors, and retaliate against sellers and buyers who are suspected of cheating. Another type of violence is aggression by drug traffickers against the police and police informants to avoid being arrested and punished for trafficking. This type of aggression is called **intermural violence** (Lyman 1990).

The following are situations in which drug-related violence can occur:

- Protection of drug-producing crops during harvest season
- Territorial disputes between rival drug dealers
- Enforcement of normative codes within drug-dealing hierarchies
- Robberies of drug dealers and their violent retaliation
- Elimination of drug informers
- Punishment for selling poor-quality, adulterated, or phony drugs
- Punishment for failing to pay drug debts
- Punishment for stealing, tampering with, or not sharing drug paraphernalia
- Retaliation for stealing, using without permission, or not sharing drug paraphernalia

Source: Bureau of Justice Statistics (1992).

Because of the clandestine nature of the drug trade and the desire of drug-trafficking participants to avoid the police, much, if not most drug-related violence goes unreported to police.

Drugs and Income-Generating Crime

Because drugs such as heroin and cocaine are both habit forming and expensive (primarily because of their illegal status), many drug users commit crimes to support their drug addiction. Property crimes such as burglary, larceny, arson, motor vehicle theft, and embezzlement are among the most common crimes committed by drug users. Other income-generating crimes include prostitution and the trafficking of the drugs themselves. These assertions are supported by data from the DUF program, which in 1990 showed that 60 percent or more of the males and 50 percent of the females arrested for crimes such as burglary, larceny, and stolen vehicles tested positive for drug use. Interestingly, property offenders were more likely to be drug users (Bureau of Justice Statistics 1992).

Drugs and Organized Crime

In July 1995, leaders of one of New York City's most notorious criminal gangs, the Latin Kings, were indicted on federal charges for attempted murder, racketeering, and cocaine and heroin trafficking. The indictments were aimed at the leaders of the gang, which boasts of chapters in five states and a membership of 3,000. High-ranking members wear beads and tattoos of the gang's emblem, a five-pointed crown. In his opening remarks during the case, Assistant U.S. Attorney Theodore Heinrich pointed out that the gang was founded in a Chicago jail during the mid-1940s as a self-protection organization for Hispanic inmates. The Latin Kings, along with its female counterpart, the Latin Queens, have chapters in Illinois, Florida, Massachusetts, Connecticut, and New York. For decades the group has focused on drug trafficking and the smuggling and trafficking of illegal firearms.

Although criminal gangs have plagued society for generations, only recently has the problem become so pervasive that it has affected most law-abiding people in one way or another. From New York to Los Angeles, from Chicago to

Envision yourself as the police chief in a medium-size East Coast city. The annual crime statistics show that drug abuse and related violent crime are on the increase. As a result, the media and public interest groups are calling for a reduction in drug-related crime. Design and explain your departmental crime-reduction strategy.

Miami, more than 45 major U.S. cities have identified some kind of a gang problem. Throughout recent history a mystique has surrounded the gangs, with Hollywood portraying gang antiheros in such films as *New Jack City, Good Fellows, The Warriors, The Outsiders, Colors,* and *South Central,* to name just a few. In addition, gangs have adopted colorful and intriguing names, such as the Mafia, Hell's Angels, the Crips, and the Shower Posse. However, regardless of their names or origin, most gangs of the 1990s have one common interest: the drug trade.

The Office of National Drug Control Policy (1994) suggests that drug-trafficking organizations can be characterized in one of three ways:

1. *Core organizations.* These tightly centralized and usually international organizations are involved with virtually all aspects of drug-trafficking operations, from drug manufacturing, distribution (wholesale and retail), enforcement, and money laundering. Examples of core organizations are the Mafia, the Colombian cartels, and the Chinese triads. Core organizations depend greatly on secondary organizations.

2. *Secondary organizations.* These operate much like subsidiaries of the core organizations and typically perform only one function, such as transportation, money laundering, or retail drug distribution within a specific geographical area. Because they are usually isolated from one another, one organization's destruction rarely disrupts the other. However, one key element to disrupting an entire trafficking network is the elimination of the secondary organization, because the core organization cannot survive without the services of the secondary organization.

3. *Local organizations.* The local organization distributes drugs within a localized area. Although these organizations usually consist of mid- to low-level dealers who are easily replaced, the local organization is also vital to the survival of the core. After all, the local organization furnishes the product to the drug users.

As discussed earlier, groups such as the Cali and Medellin cartels can be characterized as organized crime groups. These organizations have been credited with supplying up to 90 percent of the cocaine consumed in the entire world (Bureau of Justice Statistics 1992). Taken literally, all drug trafficking could be considered organized crime, but it might be helpful to distinguish between drug trafficking as organized crime and organized crime's involvement in drug trafficking. The illegal drug business is run with many of the same considerations as legal enterprises.

For example, those who produce and distribute illicit drugs need a means to conduct daily business in the open and with predictable hours. A system to transport the drugs is required along with the ability to extend credit to potential sellers in the field. In addition, as with legitimate business enterprises, business associates such as accountants, lawyers, and bankers are required to facilitate the drug-trafficking endeavor.

PLAYERS IN THE DRUG BUSINESS

As discussed in Chapters 7 and 8, many organized crime groups are involved in the illicit drug trade; however, a limited number of cocaine and heroin cartels control most trafficking aspects of these industries. On the manufacturing end, thousands of peasant farmers and tribespeople grow coca leaves and opium poppies in remote regions of the world. In addition, many are refiners and wholesale distributors. Each of these participants plays a significant role in the overall business of drug trafficking. The Sicilian Mafia is a major supplier of heroin to the United States, and the Cali cartel supplies most of the cocaine consumed on U.S. streets. Groups with similar backgrounds, including African American, Hispanic, Jamaican, Chinese, and Japanese groups, are also found among drug-trafficking organizations.

Adolescents and preteens are often used as lookouts for crack houses or drug couriers. Criminals are aware that preteens come under the jurisdiction of the juvenile court and are not subject to adult criminal penalties and thus exploit the juvenile justice system to their advantage.

Drug users themselves also make up a sizable portion of drug dealers in the United States. They do so to support their drug use. However, they barely make enough income to support their habits and are not considered the true financial beneficiaries of the drug trade. According to the Drug Use Forecasting Program (1993), 65 percent of those arrested and in jail for drug offenses who were tested voluntarily were found to test positive for cocaine.

At the bottom rung of the drug trade is the street dealer, who is subject to arrest, rip-offs, and calculated violence by competitors. This is especially true of crack dealers, the most visible target of law enforcement agencies in the largest U.S. cities. Contrary to most myths about the huge sums of money earned by street dealers, they actually earn only a modest income. Much of the confusion about how much street dealers earn probably stems from the discrepancy between large amounts of cash they are required to handle and the relatively small commissions they actually earn from these deals. It has even been suggested that, after factoring in the unusually long hours on the street, they realize only a few dollars more per hour than the minimum wage (Stone 1990). However, to compare street dealing to legitimate work may be missing the point, since most street dealers drift in and out of the drug business.

Because part-time jobs are so few in slum areas, the goal of many street dealers is simply to earn pocket money. However, for others who have proven street smarts or who are especially tough, a larger share of drug profits can be realized. In some cases street dealers have actually been put on salaries or commissions of 10 to 20 percent and have earned up to $1500 during an eight-hour shift.

THE BUSINESS OF DRUGS

To many, the cocaine trade evokes images of mountains of cash and white powder trafficked by powerful international cartel members and violent youth gang members. The street dealer and youth gang member are only the most visible aspects of the illegal drug trade. Behind the scenes are many unseen workers: middlemen, financiers, smugglers, chemists, pilots, bankers, attorneys, and enforcers.

The drug trade is a cold, calculating, money-driven business operating seven days a week all year long. Players in the trade are committed to processing, packaging, and distributing thousands of kilograms of heroin, cocaine, and marijuana to millions of drug users across the nation.

MONEY LAUNDERING IN MEXICO

In addition to being a major drug transshipment and producer nation, Mexico is also a conduit and repository for the laundering of drug proceeds generated in the United States. The country's 2,000 mile U.S.–Mexican border, close working relationships with Colombian drug-trafficking organizations, widespread corruption, and relative ease in absorbing large amounts of U.S. currency make Mexico an ideal location for money-laundering organizations.

Laundering drug proceeds for Mexican crime syndicates is commonly accomplished by shipping the bulk of currency back home. Tractor trailers and cars with hidden compartments are frequently used to smuggle drugs out of Mexico into the United States and then to return the proceeds to Mexico. The bulk movement of U.S. cash to Mexico has resulted in significant increases of financial seizures along U.S. roadways. During 1999, U.S. law enforcement seized more than $69.4 million on U.S. highways. From January 2000 to March 2001, police seized more than $19.2 million. Most of the currency seized likely was destined for Mexican drug-trafficking organizations.

Once the U.S. currency arrives in Mexico, a variety of laundering alternatives is possible. The U.S. currency is generally in small-denomination bills, such as tens and twenties. Money service businesses (MSBs), which include wire remittance services, cashier check companies, and casas de cambio (money exchange house) systems, readily transfer and exchange these small denominations of dollars to pesos. The MSBs function as a parallel banking system in Mexico, with the ability to exchange currency and transfer funds into any banking system worldwide. They provide currency conversion, exchanges, and money movement services for a fee. Legitimate businesses also seek the services provided by the MSBs. For example, Mexican immigrants have traditionally used wire remittance services to send U.S.-earned dollars back to Mexico to support their families. Chapter 5 discusses money laundering in more detail.

SOUTHEAST ASIA

In the 1990s many of the countries of Southeast Asia benefited from a sizable economic boom in the region. Lines of demarcation between legitimate business, law enforcement, politics, and organized crime have always been blurred at best in this region. But the economic surge of the 1990s created new bastions of wealth and political power that have benefited criminal organizations. In countries like Thailand and Singapore, governmental programs designed to stimulate economic growth and improve the economic infrastructure strengthened the upper-world economy. But these same business persons who accumulated wealth and power in response to these programs, also used the new wealth and power to establish growing and highly profitable criminal enterprises ancillary to their legitimate holdings (Thayer 1995; Lintner 1996; Renard 1996; Thai democracy: pass the baht 1996).

Many of these new criminal enterprises centered around arms trafficking, prostitution, illegal gambling, and contraband smuggling. But the vast majority continued to specialize in the cornerstone of Southeast Asia's illicit economy, drugs. In Burma, for example, major drug traffickers became heavy investors in infrastructure development, both as a profit-making enterprise in and of itself and as a means to facilitate drug smuggling and money laundering.

The opium-growing regions of Burma and Laos have made Southeast Asia the second largest source region for the world's supply of heroin. Cultivating and harvesting the opium poppy are the economic mainstays of the many hill tribes living in isolated, rural, impoverished areas of Southeast Asia. Poor weather patterns and climatic conditions negatively impacted opium cultivation from 1997 to 2000. Despite this fact, Burma alone accounted for 50 percent of the world's opium crop in 2000. But inefficiency in production and infrastructure problems resulted in Burma producing only 21 percent of the world's supply of opium, despite its high rate of cultivation. Laos accounted for about 4 percent of the world's opium production in 2000.

Ready recruits for drug-trafficking organizations can be found in both urban ghettos and impoverished rural areas of Southeast Asia. Heroin is often smuggled on fishing boats down the Gulf of Thailand and then transferred to the major international maritime shipping centers of Singapore and Hong Kong.

Massive criminal organizations, virtually immune from law enforcement interference because of widespread corruption in the governments and business communities of Southeast Asia, have been able to work in close collusion with police, the military, politicians and otherwise legitimate business people to spawn a massive drug and sex trade empire in the region. Drug trade profits are the source for most new commercial and business investment in the region. Outside investors, including Russian criminal organizations, have been enticed to invest in the prostitution and sex tourism industries, particularly in Thailand.

In addition to Thailand, Cambodia is now being increasingly utilized as a transshipment route for heroin. Cambodian government investments in economic development have greatly benefited the drug trade. For example, Teng Boonma, a major Cambodian shipping magnate and entrepreneur, is also a large-scale drug trafficker. He owns most of Kampong Saom, Cambodia's most important port city, and a key transit point for drugs.

Heroin and methamphetamine production in Southeast Asia is dominated by ethnic drug-trafficking armies operating mostly in Burma's remote opium-producing region. The drug-trafficking armies began as insurgent groups, often supported by the CIA, and still have an ethnically based political agenda. But over the years the biggest of these clandestine armies have become primarily engaged in the production and trafficking of heroin and methamphetamine and in other illicit and lucrative economic activities, including gem smuggling and illegal logging and timber smuggling. As a result of its continuing political repression directed at prodemocracy political groups, which began in 1988, the military regime in Burma has negotiated treaties with most of these ethnic armies in remote regions that have allowed the regime to fight any social or political changes in the country. In return, the Burmese government grants carte blanche to drug traffickers.

The arrest and subsequent retirement of heroin kingpin Khun Sa, for years a U.S. funded client warlord in the region, resulted in his Mong Tai

If you had to choose only one, which drug-control strategy do you feel is more critical: addressing the supply side or the demand side of the drug problem? Defend your response.

Army being broken up into smaller units. As a result, the United Wa State Army (UWSA) has become the largest drug producer in Southeast Asia. The UWSA is the largest regional producer of heroin and a major producer of methamphetamine, most of which is sold in Thailand.

Ethnic Chinese criminal organization and some Thai criminal networks act as brokers, financial backers, and transporters in the Southeast Asian heroin trade. Operating out of major regional commercial centers like Bangkok, Hong Kong, Singapore, and Taiwan and using a wide array of interchangeable front companies and legitimate businesses, Chinese and Thai criminal networks also arrange financing and transportation of drugs, routing drugs through many different ports, largely by commercial shipping, to their final destination.

AFGHANISTAN AND DRUG TRAFFICKING

The DEA estimates indicate that opium production in Afghanistan has increased 800 percent since 1990. Afghanistan now accounts for 72 percent of illicit worldwide global opium production. The Moslem fundamentalist government of Afghanistan, the Taliban, placed in power largely as a result of U.S. intervention in an Afghani civil war during the Reagan administration, allowed international drug traffickers to operate without interference in the country. Despite the Taliban's public condemnation of sin and particularly narcotics, including a vicious campaign of repression and murder directed at women, the illicit heroin industry continues unabated. In fact, virtually all of Afghanistan's opium poppy cultivation and morphine base and heroin-processing laboratories were located in Taliban-controlled territory. The Taliban profited from the Afghan drug trade by taxing opium production and drug movements (Rashid, 1995).

Since the overthrow of the Taliban by the U.S. military and Afghani warlords, most of whom were allied with the Taliban prior to U.S. intervention, the DEA has documented a massive increase in opium production. In fact, DEA has projected a 3,582-ton increase in opium production in Afghanistan in 2002. In addition, the per kilogram price of opium has skyrocketed from $30 a kilogram in 2000 to $333 a kilogram in 2002. The U.S.-backed regime in Afghanistan has encouraged the production of opium and with the help of the U.S. intelligence community has netted a first-year profit of over $525 million.

Iran is the major transshipment site for Afghan drugs being moved to drug markets in Western Europe. Traffickers use ancient trade routes to move drugs, as well as other contraband, from Southwest Asia through Iran to Turkey or to Iranian Persian Gulf coast seaports and harbors for shipment to the Arabian Peninsula. Pakistan and India are also key locales for smuggling. Karachi, Pakistan, is a major transshipment route for Afghan-produced opiates. India's well-developed transportation infrastructure, long coastline, and increased volumes of international trade have also made the Indian seaports of Mumbai, Goa, Chennai (Madras), and Calcutta prime locations for heroin smuggling.

TRENDS OF ORGANIZED DRUG TRAFFICKING

During the 1960s and 1970s in places such as Los Angeles and New York, the drug business could be considered in large part a cottage industry. That is, market entry was relatively easy and there was little monopolization of cocaine, heroin, and methamphetamine. Wholesalers cooperated with each other in a loose-knit, casual fashion. Street dealers were commonly supplied by more than one wholesaler, and the deals themselves were sporadic and not linked to any specific timetable. Those who endeavored to sell drugs did so at their own peril, risking arrest by police or being hijacked by competitors.

Organization

Today, however, drug distribution has become more **vertically integrated.** This occurs when a drug-manufacturing organization merges with an organization proficient in street-level distribution. For example, vertical integration occurs if a computer manufacturer buys a retail computer outlet. Accordingly, criminal trafficking organizations become vertically integrated in several stages with regional distribution and street sales. Vertical integration makes it difficult for drug operations to be detected through traditional police investigative methods such as "buy and bust" and informant operations. Each player in the organization has a specific role, and all work as a team to achieve a common goal. For instance, one person acts as a lookout while another steers customers to the crack house. Others run drug stash houses and money residences where cash is counted and then moved to a safe house. Still others provide protection and act as corruptors to gain influence in government. The emergence of the crack cocaine business during the mid-1980s and trafficking of it by Jamaican posses and California youth gangs is a good example of a vertically integrated drug distribution organization.

Similar to legitimate businesses, many trafficking organizations are becoming more **horizontally integrated.** This occurs when one crime organization absorbs another organization in the same drug market. In the drug trade the emergence of the Medellin Cartel during the 1970s is a good example. While serving time in a U.S. prison, cartel co-founder Carlos Lehder-Rivas was said to have collaborated with Jorge Luis Ochoa-Vasquez, who headed another drug-trafficking cartel. This merger played a significant role in consolidating Colombia's fragmented cocaine business into a well-organized drug-trafficking machine.

Popular Drug Trends

The U.S. drug scene has undergone several radical shifts in the past two decades. The most significant occurred in the mid-1980s, when phencyclidime (PCP) was considered one of the more widespread and dangerous drugs available. Street gangs learned, however, how to convert cocaine hydrochloride into a smokable freebase known as *crack*. Almost overnight, crack replaced PCP as the big moneymaker of the urban youth gangs. No single organized crime group could control the spread of crack cocaine.

An ounce of cocaine that could be purchased on the street for $1,000 yielded about 350 vials of crack (more if diluted) that sold for $10 each in some locations. Virtually anyone with several hundred dollars and a microwave oven could go into the crack cocaine business and triple his or her investment overnight. Crack turned the lower level of the cocaine trade from a moderately stabilized and discrete industry to a freewheeling, decentralized circus, with new groups emerging and established organizations expanding into huge trafficking enterprises.

In 1990, a new freebase form of methamphetamine called *ice* became available, and it was feared it would become the new drug rage and would be used in epidemic proportions. This never came to pass, as the popularity of ice remained predominantly in Asian communities located in Hawaii and Los Angeles. In the mid-1990s, the drug business is taking on yet another new complexion, with heroin regaining popularity.

The crack era of the mid- to late 1980s included violence and competition parallelled only by the gangsters of the Prohibition era. Thousands of cottage-industry operations existed side by side with many highly structured criminal conspiracies. The drug trade became an easy entry, equal opportunity employer. African American criminals in particular assumed more key roles in the drug trade in large cities such as New York and Los Angeles. Old taboos against selling drugs to minors became obsolete in the 1980s, with young entrepreneurial drug dealers allowing teens greater accessibility to drugs and more significant roles in crime organizations than ever before in history.

In September 1996 the Drug Enforcement Administration announced that Colombian drug traffickers had taken over the U.S. heroin market from Asia for the first time in history. Specifically, Colombian criminal groups, using existing cocaine-trafficking routes, were supplying an estimated 62 percent of the domestic supply of heroin, and the product was nearly 100 percent pure (Friend 1996).

Since the turn of the century, heroin, although not a new drug to the U.S. drug scene, has maintained a group of between 50,000 and 500,000 addicts. Beginning in the early 1990s, its use appeared to increase. For example, heroin seizures by police and the incidence of heroin-related hospital admissions increased in 1994 (Meddis 1994). Although the drug had the reputation as a drug of the poor, its popularity among middle- and upper-class drug users appeared to be increasing as well. Actor River Phoenix died in October 1993 of a heroin overdose in a posh Los Angeles nightclub. Six months later rock singer and heroin addict Kurt Cobain committed suicide.

Part of the attraction to heroin is its purity. Heroin purity on U.S. streets has increased to a shocking 40 percent, compared to 3 to 5 percent ten years ago. Colombian heroin has been documented as being as high as 90 percent pure, to win the existing U.S. heroin market.

Although everyone seems to agree that the drug business is big business, there is little agreement as to its exact size. One commonly quoted estimate from the National Narcotics Intelligence Consumers Committee (1989) is that national drug sales for 1987 totaled $150 billion. Other experts argue that this number is grossly inflated. A more conservative estimate was provided by the Office of National Drug Control Policy (1994) in the National Drug Control Strategy, which estimated that Americans were spending $49 billion annually on illegal drugs. A different assessment was provided by Rand Corporation drug expert Peter Reuter, who stated that "if New Yorkers are spending $80 billion a year on drugs, every man, woman, and child in the city would have a drug habit" (Stone 1990). Although debatable, some experts have even suggested that government statistics are purposely inflated to stimulate increased drug-control budgets.

In addition to criminal groups based abroad, domestic organizations cultivate, produce, manufacture, or distribute illegal drugs such as marijuana, methamphetamine, PCP, and lysergic acid diethyamide (LSD). By growing high-potency sinsemilla, domestic cannabis growers provide marijuana that easily competes with other illegal drugs. With demand for methamphetamine remaining high, especially in the west and midwest of the United States, the number of illicit laboratories that supply methamphetamine is increasing.

Cocaine

According to 2001 statistics, the use of both powder and crack cocaine has stabilized at high levels (DEA 2002a). The trafficking, distribution, and abuse of cocaine and crack cocaine have spread from urban environments in the United States to suburban areas and smaller cities, bringing a commensurate increase in violence and criminal activity. The level of violence associated with cocaine trafficking today, however, does not compare to the rampant violence of the 1980s when the crack epidemic was at its worst.

Trafficking of Cocaine by Colombian and Mexican Organizations

The U.S.–Mexican border is the primary point of entry for cocaine shipments being smuggled into the United States. The DEA estimates that approximately 65 percent of the cocaine smuggled into the United States crosses the southwest border and is available in nearly all major cities in the United States. Organized crime groups operating in Colombia control the majority of the worldwide cocaine business and use a sophisticated infrastructure to move cocaine by land, sea, and air into the United States. In the United States, Colombia-based groups operate cocaine distribution and drug money-laundering networks using a vast infrastructure of multiple cells functioning in many major metropolitan areas. Each cell performs a specific function within the organization (e.g., transportation, local distribution, or money movement). Key managers in Colombia oversee the overall operation.

During the 1990s, Colombian-based drug groups allowed Mexico-based trafficking organizations to play an increasing role in the U.S. cocaine trade. Throughout most of the 1980s, groups in Colombia used Mexican drug smugglers to transport cocaine shipments across the southwest border into the United States. After successfully smuggling the drugs across the border, Mexican transporters transferred the drugs back to the Colombian groups operating in the United States. However, the seizure of nearly 21 metric tons of cocaine in 1989 led to a new arrangement between transportation organizations operating from Mexico and the organized crime groups operating from Colombia.

This new arrangement radically changed the role and sphere of influence of the Mexican-based trafficking organizations in the U.S. cocaine trade. By the mid-1990s, Mexican-based transportation groups were receiving up to half the cocaine shipment they smuggled for the Colombia-based groups in exchange for their services. Both sides realized that this strategy eliminated the vulnerabilities and complex logistics associated with large cash transactions. The Colombia-based groups also realized that relinquishing part of each cocaine shipment to their associates operating from Mexico ceded a share of the Colombian wholesale cocaine market in the United States. Recent information suggests that other drug-trafficking organizations are playing a larger role in the distribution of cocaine in conjunction with the Colombian organizations. For example, Dominican drug-trafficking organizations have traditionally been responsible for the street-level distribution of cocaine. In New York City, Colombian, Dominican, and Mexican drug-trafficking organizations distribute multikilogram quantities of cocaine.

Today, traffickers operating from Colombia continue to control wholesale-level cocaine distribution throughout the heavily populated northeastern United States and along the eastern seaboard in cities such as Boston, Miami, Newark, New York, and Philadelphia.

The role of Mexico-based trafficking organizations is continuing to evolve as some major international criminals in Colombia are further distancing themselves from day to day wholesale-level cocaine distribution in the United States by turning this task over, at least occasionally, to the organizations operating from Mexico. A likely motivation for this change is the nonretroactive extradition law enacted by the Colombian National Assembly in December 1997. Accordingly, Colombian traffickers now face the prospect of extradition for overt acts committed on or after December 17, 1997, the date that the extradition amendment went into effect.

By distancing themselves from overt acts in the United States, Colombian drug lords hope to minimize the threat that the United States will gather sufficient evidence to support an extradition request. This shift does not mean that traffickers operating from Colombia will abandon the U.S. cocaine market en masse. Emerging drug lords who do not face the difficulties in micromanaging operations as do the jailed Cali criminal leaders have little reason to forgo the profits generated by the wholesale U.S. cocaine market.

Crack Cocaine Trafficking

While cocaine use in the United States has declined over the past decade, the rate of use in recent years still has stabilized at high levels. Crack, the inexpensive, smokable form of cocaine, continues to be distributed and used in most major cities. Crack cocaine usage also has stabilized and shows some indications of declining, although it also remains at a high level. Street gangs, such as the Crips and the Bloods, and criminal groups of ethnic Dominicans, Puerto Ricans, and Jamaicans dominate the retail market for crack cocaine nationwide. The directed expansion of these gangs to smaller U.S. cities and rural areas where street gangs imitate their urban counterparts has resulted in an increase in related crime. Gang members commit homicides, armed robberies, and assaults, including the use of physical violence, to maintain their drug distribution monopolies.

Cocaine prices in 2001 remained low and stable, suggesting a steady supply to the United States. Nationwide, wholesale cocaine prices ranged from $12,000 to $35,000 per kilogram. In most major metropolitan areas, however, the price of a kilogram of cocaine ranged from $13,000 to $25,000. Average purity for cocaine at the gram, ounce, and kilogram levels remained stable at high levels. In 2001, the average purity of a kilogram of cocaine was 73 percent. Typically, cocaine HCl is converted into crack cocaine, or *rock*, within the United States by the secondary wholesaler or retailer.

Crack cocaine is often packaged in vials, glassine bags, and film canisters. The size of a crack rock can vary but generally ranges from 1/10 to 1/2 gram. Rocks can sell for as low as $3 to as high as $50, but prices generally range from $10 to $20.

Heroin is readily available in many U.S. cities as evidenced by the unprecedented high level of average retail, or street-level, purity. As noted earlier, the heroin available in the United States comes primarily from South America (Colombia), Southeast Asia (principally Burma), Mexico, and Southwest Asia and the Middle East (principally Afghanistan). Virtually all heroin produced in Mexico and South America is destined for the U.S. market, but each of the four source areas has dominated the U.S. market at some point over the past 30 years. Over the past decade, the dominance of heroin suppliers to the United States has shifted from Southeast Asia to South America. In the West, black tar and, to a lesser extent, brown powdered heroin from Mexico have been and continue to be the predominant available form.

The increased availability of high-purity heroin, which can effectively be snorted, has given rise to a new, younger user population. While avoiding the stigma of needle use, this user group is ingesting larger quantities of the drug and, according to drug-treatment specialists, progressing more quickly toward addiction.

South American Heroin

The availability of South American (SA) heroin, produced in Colombia, has increased dramatically in the United States since 1993. It is available in the metropolitan areas of the Northeast and along the East Coast. Independent traffickers typically smuggle SA heroin into the United States via couriers traveling aboard commercial airlines, with each courier usually carrying from 500 grams to 1 kilogram of heroin per trip. These traffickers increased their influence in the lucrative northeastern heroin market, which has the largest demand in the United States, by pursuing an aggressive marketing strategy. They distributed high-quality heroin (of purity frequently above 90 percent), undercut the price of their competition, and used their long-standing, effective drug distribution networks. Investigations also indicate the spread of SA heroin to smaller U.S. cities.

Since the mid-1990s, Colombian heroin traffickers have diversified their methods of operation. Couriers still come into Miami, New York City, San Juan, Puerto Rico, and other U.S. cities on direct commercial flights from Colombia. Increasingly, however, Colombian traffickers are smuggling heroin from Colombia into the United States through such countries as Costa Rica, the Dominican Republic, Ecuador, Panama, Mexico, Argentina, and Venezuela.

In response to increased drug law enforcement presence at eastern ports of entry, some SA heroin traffickers have sought alternative routes. For example, they ship heroin through the Dallas–Fort Worth International Airport before it reaches its final destination at New York City's La Guardia Airport. Couriers often wear clothing impregnated with heroin. For example, in January 2002, U.S. Custom Service agents at the Miami International Airport arrested a courier who had arrived from Venezuela with 14 kilograms of heroin saturated in clothing. The following month, 18 kilograms of heroin saturated in clothing were seized in New York. Another method increasingly used to smuggle heroin is by sewing it into clothing. In New York in March 2002, two couriers were arrested at a hotel with approximately 8 to 10 kilograms of heroin sewn into 24 pieces of clothing. Also in New York that month, a Venezuelan married couple arrived at JFK International Airport on a flight from Caracas, with jackets in their luggage that had a combined total of 6 kilograms of heroin sewn into them.

Colombian heroin traffickers have also used commercial maritime transportation to move large amounts of their drug into the United States.

Some past maritime heroin shipments have been transported via cruise ships. Large shipments of heroin have also been smuggled via container-ized cargo, as evidenced by a May 2001 seizure of 54 kilograms of SA heroin in New York. Packaged in 1.5-pound bricks, the heroin was hid-den in false bottoms of 1,400 boxes, each of which contained 25 pounds of frozen plantains. This was the largest seizure of SA heroin in the United States up to that time.

Mexican Heroin

Mexican heroin has been a threat to the United States for decades. It is produced, smuggled, and distributed by polydrug-trafficking groups, many of which have been in operation for more than 20 years. Nearly all the heroin produced in Mexico is destined for distribution in the United States. Organized crime groups operating from Mexico produce, smuggle, and distribute the black tar heroin sold in the western United States. Tradition-ally, trafficking groups operating from Mexico have evaded interdiction efforts by smuggling heroin to the U.S. market as they receive orders from customers.

By keeping quantities small, traffickers hope to minimize the risk of losing a significant amount of heroin in a single seizure. Even large poly-drug Mexican organizations that smuggle multi-ton quantities of cocaine and marijuana generally limit the smuggling of Mexican heroin into the United States to kilogram and smaller amounts. Nevertheless, trafficking organizations are capable of regularly smuggling significant quantities of heroin into the United States.

Although illegal immigrants and migrant workers frequently smuggle heroin across the U.S.–Mexican border in 1- to 3-kilogram amounts for the major trafficking groups, seizures indicate that larger loads are being moved across the border, primarily in privately owned vehicles. Once the heroin reaches the United States, traffickers rely on well-entrenched polydrug-smuggling and distribution networks to deliver the product to the market, principally in the metropolitan areas of the midwestern, south-western, and western United States that have sizable Mexican immigrant populations. A traffic stop in April 2002 near Pleasanton, Texas, about 25 miles south of San Antonio, resulted in the seizure of 34 kilograms of brown powder heroin by Department of Public Safety troopers. The heroin bundles, placed inside metal boxes, were found in all four tires of a pickup truck headed for San Antonio.

Southeast Asian Heroin

High-purity Southeast Asian (SEA) heroin dominated the market in the United States during the late 1980s and early 1990s. Over the past few years, however, all indicators point to a decrease in this heroin. Significant investi-gations led to the incarceration in Thailand and extradition to the United States of more than a dozen high-level players in moving SEA heroin ship-ments to the United States.

SEA heroin trafficking links run from independent brokers and shippers in Asia through overseas Chinese criminal populations to ethnic Chinese criminal wholesale distributors in the United States. These ethnic Chinese criminals rely on local criminal organizations to distribute the heroin. Despite the recent decline in the trafficking of SEA heroin in the United States,

Chinese criminal groups remain the most sophisticated heroin-trafficking organizations in the world.

Trafficking groups composed of West African criminals also smuggle SEA heroin to the United States. Nigerian criminals have been the most active in U.S. cities and areas with well-established Nigerian populations, such as Atlanta, Baltimore, Houston, Dallas, New York City, Newark, Chicago, and Washington, D.C. Over the past several years, Chicago has become a hub for heroin trafficking controlled by Nigerian criminals who primarily deal in SEA heroin.

Southwest Asian Heroin

Traffickers operating from Middle Eastern locations smuggle Southwest Asian (SWA) heroin to ethnic enclaves in the United States. Criminal groups composed of ethnic Lebanese, Pakistanis, Turks, and Afghans are involved in supplying the drug to U.S.-based groups for retail distribution. These SWA heroin traffickers and wholesale distributors generally have been consistently cautious, rarely conducting heroin business with persons not of Southwest Asian or Middle Eastern ethnicity. Therefore, the ethnic aspect of SWA heroin importation and distribution has made it more prevalent in areas with large Southwest Asian populations.

West African traffickers, who primarily smuggled SEA heroin to the United States in the 1990s, now also deal in SWA heroin. In a particularly noteworthy seizure of approximately 24 kilograms of heroin in New York in May 2000, 90 percent of the seized heroin consisted of SWA heroin and the remaining 10 percent was SEA. While unusual, a shipment containing the two types of heroin is not unexpected. For the last several years, West African traffickers, based in Bangkok and who normally deal in SEA heroin, have been sending couriers to Pakistan to buy the cheaper Afghanistan-produced SWA heroin. Heroin in Pakistan is about half the price of SEA heroin in Bangkok, where the West Africans pay between $13,000 and $16,000 for a kilogram.

The most sizable seizure of SWA heroin occurred in New York City in September 2001 when city police officers confiscated approximately 50 kilograms of the substance. According to the Federalwide Drug Seizure System, this was one of the largest seizures of powdered heroin in the past five years.

Purity and Price

On the street, heroin purity and price often reflect the drug's availability. High purities and low prices, for example, indicate that heroin supplies are readily available. Data show that the nationwide average purity for retail heroin in 2000 from all sources was 36.8 percent. This number is significantly higher than the average of 7 percent reported two decades ago and higher than the 26 percent recorded in 1991. The significant rise in average purity corresponds to the increased availability of high-purity SA heroin, particularly in the northeastern United States (DEA 2002).

Nationwide, SA heroin ranged from $50,000 to $200,000 per kilogram in 2000. SEA and SWA heroin ranged in price from $40,000 to $190,000 per kilogram. Wholesale-level prices for Mexican heroin were the lowest of any type, ranging from $13,200 to $175,000 per kilogram. The wide range in prices reflects variables such as buyer–seller relationships, amount purchased, purchase frequency, purity, and transportation costs.

Methampheta-mine

Domestic methamphetamine production, trafficking, and abuse are concentrated in the western, southwestern, and midwestern United States. Methamphetamine is also increasingly available in portions of the South and eastern United States, especially Georgia and Florida. Clandestine laboratories in California and Mexico have been the primary sources of supply for methamphetamine in the United States.

Over the last decade, the methamphetamine trafficking and abuse situation in the United States changed dramatically. In 1994, ethnic Mexican drug-trafficking organizations operating superlabs (laboratories capable of producing in excess of 10 pounds of methamphetamine in one 24-hour production cycle) based in Mexico and California began to take control of the production and distribution of methamphetamine in the United States. Independent laboratory operators, including outlaw motorcycle gangs, had previously maintained control of methamphetamine production and distribution within the United States and continue to operate today on a lesser scale. The entry of ethnic Mexican traffickers into the methamphetamine trade in the mid-1990s resulted in a significant increase in the supply of the drug. Mexican criminal organizations based in Mexico and California provided high-purity, low-cost methamphetamine originally to cities in the Midwest and West with Mexican populations.

In 2001, approximately 8,000 clandestine methamphetamine laboratories were seized and reported to DEA's National Clandestine Laboratory Database. In 2001, 298 seized superlabs were reported. This represents a rise in the number of superlabs from 2000, in which the number totaled 168.

The supply of methamphetamine in the United States also comes from multiple small-scale laboratories, often operated by independent "cooks" who obtain the ingredients necessary from retail and convenience stores. Methamphetamine produced in these mom-and-pop laboratories is generally for personal use or limited distribution. A clandestine laboratory operator can use relatively common items, such as mason jars, coffee filters, hot plates, pressure cookers, pillowcases, plastic tubing, and gas cans to substitute for sophisticated laboratory equipment. The use of the Internet, which provides access to methamphetamine recipes, coupled with increased demand for high-purity product, has resulted in a dramatic increase in the number of mom-and-pop laboratories throughout the United States. In 2001, more than 7,700 labs had the capacity to produce 10 pounds at most.

Large clandestine methamphetamine laboratories in the United States usually use dosage-form pseudoephedrine or ephedrine drug products. Because of law enforcement attention and strong state precursor control laws in California, traffickers have now diversified to pseudoephedrine suppliers nationwide, buying at relatively lower prices in other parts of the country and trafficking the product to California, where the black market price can be as high as $5,000 per pound of product.

In addition, the use of methylsulfonylmethane (MSM) has been encountered as a "cut" in methamphetamine produced primarily by Mexican organizations. Legitimately used as a dietary supplement for horses and humans, MSM is readily available at feed and livestock stores, as well as health and nutrition shops. MSM can be used to add volume to the finished methamphetamine, thus increasing the profit. Increases in the use of MSM in producing methamphetamine could signal difficulty in obtaining precursors or a marketing method to meet demand while increasing profit.

The crystalline form of methamphetamine, known as *ice, glass,* or *crystal,* is gaining popularity. Converted from powder by criminal elements in Southeast Asia, Mexico, and the United States, ice traditionally was used in Hawaii and southern California.

Purity and Price

The DEA reports that the average purity of methamphetamine dropped from 71.9 percent in 1994 to 30.7 percent in 1999. The average purity of methamphetamine in 2000 rose slightly to 35.3 percent and 40.1 in 2001 (DEA 2002).

Methamphetamine prices vary throughout different regions of the United States. At the distribution level, prices range from $3,500 per pound in parts of California and Texas to $21,000 per pound in southeastern and northeastern regions of the country. Retail prices range from $400 to $3,000 per ounce.

Marijuana

Marijuana is the most widely abused and readily available illicit drug in the United States, with an estimated 11.5 million current users. At least one-third of the U.S. population has used marijuana sometime in their lives. The drug is considered a gateway to the world of illicit drug abuse. Relaxed public perception of its harm, popularization by the media and by groups advocating legalization, and the trend to smoke marijuana-filled cigars known as *blunts* have contributed to the nationwide resurgence in marijuana's popularity.

The Internet has also contributed to marijuana's popularity. Websites provide information and links extolling the virtues of marijuana. These sites provide group discussions and bulletin boards for posting documents and messages for public discussions. The sites also advocate the legal sale of marijuana. Several websites advertising the sale of marijuana and providing instructions on home to grow it have also been identified.

Marijuana smuggled into the United States, whether grown in Mexico or shipped from other Latin American source areas, accounts for most of the marijuana available in the United States. Marijuana produced in Mexico remains the most widely available, although high-potency marijuana comes from Canada. The availability of marijuana from Southeast Asia generally is limited to the West Coast. The availability of domestically grown marijuana has also increased.

Domestic Marijuana

According to the 2000 Domestic Cannabis Eradication/Suppression Program (DCE/SP), California, Florida, Oregon, Washington, and Wisconsin lead in producing indoor-grown marijuana. Statistics indicate that the major outdoor growing states in 2000 were California, Hawaii, Kentucky, and Tennessee; these states accounted for approximately three-quarters of the total of eradicated outdoor cultivated plants.

Mexican Marijuana

Organized crime groups operating from Mexico have smuggled marijuana into the United States since the early 1970s. These groups maintain extensive networks of associates, often related through familial or regional ties to associates living in the United States, where they control polydrug-smuggling and wholesale distribution from hub cities to retail markets throughout the United States.

Groups operating from Mexico employ a variety of transportation and concealment methods. Most of the marijuana smuggled into the United States is concealed in vehicles, often in false compartments, or hidden in shipments of legitimate agricultural or industrial products. Marijuana also is smuggled across the border by rail, horse, raft, and backpack. Shipments of 20 kilograms or less are smuggled by pedestrians who enter the United States at border checkpoints and by backpackers who alone or in groups (mule trains) cross the border at more remote locations. Jamaican organizations also appear to be involved in dispatching Mexican marijuana via parcel carriers.

Organized crime groups operating from Mexico conceal marijuana in an array of vehicles, including commercial vehicles, private automobiles, pickup trucks, vans, mobile homes, and horse trailers driven through border points of entry. Larger shipments ranging up to multithousand kilograms are usually smuggled in tractor trailers, such as the 6.9 metric tons of marijuana seized on April 3, 2001, by police from a tractor trailer in Otay Mesa, California. The marijuana packages had been wrapped in cellophane, coated with mustard, grease, and motor oil, and commingled in a load of television sets.

In addition to overland smuggling, drug traffickers use ocean vessels to move Mexican marijuana up the coast of Mexico to U.S. ports, drop-off sites along the U.S. coast, or rendezvous points with other boats bound for the United States. Law enforcement authorities in southern California indicate that marijuana is transferred from mother ships in international waters to Mexican fishing vessels. The smaller vessels then deliver the marijuana to overland smugglers on the Baja California Peninsula. From there, the marijuana is generally moved to border transit points and then carried to the Los Angeles metropolitan area for distribution to eastern markets.

Canadian Marijuana

Canada is becoming a source country for indoor-grown, high-potency marijuana of 15 to 25 percent, (THC) destined for the United States. Canadian law enforcement intelligence indicates that marijuana traffickers there are increasingly cultivating **cannabis** indoors. Such indoor-grown operations have become an enormous and lucrative illicit industry, producing a potent form of marijuana that has come to be known as *BC Bud* after its cultivation in British Columbia. Canadian officials estimate that cannabis cultivation in British Columbia is a billion-dollar industry and that traffickers smuggle a significant portion of the Canadian harvest into the United States.

Potency (THC Content) and Price

During the past two decades, marijuana potency has increased. According to the University of Mississippi's 2000 Marijuana Potency Monitoring Project (MPMP), commercial-grade marijuana THC levels rose from under 2 percent in the late 1970s and early 1980s to 6.07 percent in 2000. The MPMP reports that sinsemilla, a higher-quality marijuana usually grown domestically, also increased in potency, rising from 6 percent in the late 1970s and 1980s to 13.20 percent in 2000 (DEA 2002a).

Prices for commercial-grade marijuana have remained relatively stable over the past decade, ranging from approximately $400 to $1,000 per pound in U.S. southwest border areas to between $700 to $2,000 per pound in the Midwest and northeastern United States. The national price range for sinsemilla is between $900 and $6,000 per pound.

Commonly referred to as Ecstasy, XTC, Clarity, or Essence, 3,4-methylene-dioxymethamphetamine (MDMA) is a synthetic psychoactive drug that has stimulant and mild **hallucinogenic** properties. In the early 1990s, MDMA became increasingly popular among European youth. However, its use in the United States has increased at an alarming rate in the last five years.

MDMA is popular among middle-class adolescents and young adults and is becoming an abuse problem, because many users view it as nonaddictive and benign. MDMA is sold primarily at legitimate nightclubs and bars, at underground nightclubs sometimes called *acid houses,* or at all-night parties known as *raves.*

Although the vast majority of MDMA consumed domestically is produced in Europe, a limited number of MDMA laboratories operate in the United States. Law enforcement seized seventeen clandestine MDMA laboratories in the United States in 2001 compared to seven in 2000. These laboratories have limited drug production. Recipes for the clandestine production of MDMA can be found on the Internet, but acquiring the necessary precursor chemicals in the United States is difficult.

MDMA is manufactured clandestinely in Western Europe, particularly in the southeast section of the Netherlands near Maastricht and to a lesser extent in Belgium. Despite government efforts to curtail MDMA trafficking, the Netherlands remains a primary source country for the drug. International MDMA traffickers based in the Netherlands and Belgium and a significant number of U.S.-based traffickers who coordinate MDMA shipments to major metropolitan areas of the United States sometimes use Montreal and Toronto as transit points. In December 2000, the Royal Canadian Mounted Police (RCMP) seized approximately 150,000 MDMA tablets in Toronto that had been shipped via DHL International from Brussels, Belgium, by an Israeli MDMA trafficking organization. The shipment was destined for distributors in the United States.

Due to the availability of precursor chemicals in Canada, a number of MDMA laboratories have been discovered operating near metropolitan areas such as Vancouver, Toronto, and Montreal. Such laboratories continue to supply U.S.- and Canadian-based MDMA trafficking organizations. According to the RCMP, the total potential yield of MDMA from laboratories uncovered in Canada since 1999 is in excess of 10 million tablets.

Mexico is emerging as a transit zone for MDMA entering the United States. In April 2000, a shipment of 200,000 MDMA tablets was seized at the airport in Mexico City. The MDMA was discovered in an air cargo shipment manifested as aircraft parts sent from the Netherlands and destined for the United States (DEA 2002). Dutch authorities seized a 1.25 million-tablet shipment of MDMA destined for Mexico in September 2000.

In recent years, traffickers have begun to tap the potential of the Caribbean and South America as alternative routes for moving synthetic drugs, predominantly MDMA, from Europe to the United States. The region's numerous and established drug transportation groups, extensive network of commercial flights, abundance of couriers, and historic connections to Europe provide traffickers with the route to move synthetic drugs through South America and the Caribbean to the United States. Available seizure and investigative information indicates that practically all the MDMA transiting South America and the Caribbean comes from Europe on commercial flights. Thus far the Caribbean has overshadowed South America as a transit zone for European MDMA destined to the United States.

Purity and Price

MDMA tablets range in weight from 150 to 350 mg and contain between 70 to 120 mg of MDMA. The profit margin associated with MDMA trafficking is significant. It costs as little as 25 to 50 cents to manufacture an MDMA tablet in Europe, but its street value can be as high as $40; a tablet typically sells for between $20 and $30.

LSD Lysergic acid diethylamide (LSD) remains available in retail quantities in virtually every state in the United States. LSD production reportedly is centered on the West Coast, particularly in San Francisco, northern California, and the Pacific Northwest, but recently has been produced in the Midwest. Since the 1960s, LSD has been manufactured illegally within the United States. LSD production is a time-consuming and complex procedure. It is produced in crystal form that is converted to liquid and distributed primarily in the form of squares of blotter paper saturated with the liquid. LSD is less frequently sold as a liquid in breath mint bottles and vials, in gelatin tab form (*window panes*) of varying colors, and in pill form known as *microdots*. Several chemical recipes for synthesizing LSD are on the Internet, but clandestine production requires a high degree of chemical expertise. Chemists maintain tight control at the production level, but do not necessarily participate in the distribution of the drug. They usually sell the crystal LSD product to one or two trusted associates, insulating themselves from the wholesale distributors.

Few LSD laboratories have ever been seized in the United States because of infrequent and irregular production cycles. In 2000, the DEA seized one LSD laboratory in a converted missile silo in Kansas.

Distribution of LSD is unique within the drug culture. A proliferation of mail-order sales has created a marketplace in which the sellers are virtually unknown to the buyers, giving the highest-level traffickers considerable insulation from drug law enforcement operations. The vast majority of users are middle-class adolescents and young adults attracted by its low prices. Rock concerts continue to be favorite distribution sites for LSD traffickers; however, distribution at raves throughout the United States is becoming more popular. Contacts made at raves and concerts are used to establish future transactions and shipments of larger quantities of LSD.

You Decide

Should Drugs Be Legalized?

Any drug-control policy hinges on the aspects of the drug-trafficking problem that are deemed most important and the costs and efficacy of any particular policy. The policy option of outright legalization of dangerous drugs has been considered over the years. As the most radical approach to drug control, legalization means different things to different people. At one extreme it means complete elimination of any legal restrictions on the production, distribution, possession, or use of any drug. At the other extreme, it can mean allowing some limited uses of some drugs, producing the drugs only under government auspices, distributing them through tightly regulated distribution systems, and creating severe criminal penalties for the production or use of drugs outside the authorized system.

The goal of legalizing drugs is to bring them under effective legal control. If it were legal to produce and distribute drugs, legitimate businesspeople would enter the business, which should lessen the need for violence and corruption, since the industry would have access to the courts to settle disputes. Instead of absorbing tax dollars as targets of expensive enforcement efforts, the drug sellers should begin to pay taxes. Legalization might well solve the organized crime aspect of the drug-trafficking problem.

On average, legalized drug use might not be as destructive to users and to society as it is under the current prohibition because drugs would be less expensive, purer, and more conveniently available. However, by relaxing opposition to drug use and making drugs more freely available, legalization might fuel a significant increase in the level of drug use. It is not unreasonable to assume that the number of people who become chronic, intensive users would increase substantially. It is this risk, as well as a widespread perception that drug use is simply wrong, that mitigates against outright legalization.

An alternative is to choose a system more restrictive than outright legalization, but one that still leaves room for legitimate uses of some drugs. Arguably, such a policy would produce some of the potential benefits of legalization without accelerating growth in the level of drug use. The difficulty is that wherever the boundary between the legitimate and illicit use of drugs is drawn, an illicit market will develop just outside the boundary. Indeed, the more restrictive the boundary, the larger and more controlled by organized crime the resulting black market.

The existing drug laws in the United States establish a regulatory rather than prohibitionist regime. While most uses of heroin and marijuana are illegal, some research uses of these drugs are authorized under the current laws, and there is discussion of the possible use of these drugs for medical purposes, such as for the treatment of terminal cancer patients. Cocaine is legal for use as a local anesthetic and distributed through licensed pharmacists and physicians. But some legal use of these drugs has not eliminated illicit trafficking. For marijuana, heroin, and cocaine, the restrictions are so sharp relative to the current demand for the drugs that virtually the entire distribution system remains illicit and depends on drug trafficking. For amphetamines, barbiturates, and tranquilizers, the restrictions are fewer, so a larger portion of the demand is met by illegally diverting drugs from their legitimate sources of distribution. Distribution of these drugs takes the form of diversion from legitimate channels, rather than wholly illicit production and distribution.

Should drugs be legalized? You decide!

Source: M. Moore, *Drug Trafficking* (Washington, DC: National Institute of Justice, 1988).

DRUG-CONTROL STRATEGIES

One of the more important problems associated with the illicit drug problem is the violence that is associated with it. An unfortunate side effect of drug-related violence is that it often spills over into neighborhoods where innocent people may be injured or killed. Many other negative consequences can be observed. For example, some people fear that inner cities are becoming spawning grounds for the next generation of organized crime. In many areas drug-related street crimes, such as burglaries, robberies, and carjackings, are increasing. Furthermore, public health, economic well-being, and family stability are threatened due to the irresponsibility of drug users.

Various police departments around the country have implemented an array of enforcement initiatives to control the drug trade over the years. Some of these have proved more successful than others, but researchers Moore (1990) and Kleiman (1988) have developed six suggestions for alternative drug strategies in drug-infested neighborhoods.

Strategy 1: Expressive Law Enforcement

Essentially, **expressive law enforcement** is a law enforcement-oriented strategy, which suggests that more police resources be devoted to the drug problem, resulting in maximum arrests for drug offenses. This is accomplished by expanding the authority and resources of the Narcotics Bureau to the point that it becomes more productive. In addition, the patrol division should be equipped and encouraged to make more drug arrests.

Strategy 2: Mr. Big Strategy

The **Mr. Big strategy** emphasizes high-level distributors. The primary tactics are to employ sophisticated investigative procedures using wiretaps, informants, and undercover operatives. *Loose money* is also required to purchase drugs or pay informants. The premise for this strategy is that the immobilization of high-level traffickers will produce larger and more permanent results on the drug-trafficking networks than will arrests of lower-level, easily replaced figures.

Strategy 3: Gang Control

This strategy addresses one of the most urgent aspects of the current drug problem. Gangs are responsible for a significant increase in homicide rates in the cities in which they operate, and they use violence not only to discipline their own employees, but also to intimidate individual citizens who resist their intrusion. One way to address the gang problem is to view drug gangs as the same as youth gangs of the past and adopt similar enforcement strategies. The past strategy was not designed to eliminate gangs, but to take an aggressive stance against gang members, clubhouses, and activities. A second approach is to view gangs as organized criminal enterprises and to use all the techniques that have been developed to deal with more traditional organized crime. These techniques include the use of informants, electronic surveillance, witnesses, long-term undercover investigations, and special criminal statutes that create criminal penalties for conspiracy, extortion, or engagement in criminal enterprises.

Strategy 4: Citywide Street-Level Drug Enforcement

Another approach is to disrupt open dealing by driving it back indoors or forcing the markets to move so frequently that buyers and sellers have difficulty finding one another. Typical tactics include traditional buy-and-bust techniques, observation sale arrests, and arrests of users who appear in the market to buy drugs.

Strategy 5: Neighborhood Crackdowns

In the event that communities do not wish to commit to street-level enforcement alternatives, police can crack down on drug offenses in neighborhoods that are willing to join the police in resisting drug abuse. In some cases, neighborhoods are just beginning to be invaded by drug dealers, while others have long been occupied, but are now at a stage where they are determined to rid their streets of drugs and dealers. Crackdown areas could include a park that the police do not patrol frequently enough and from which other citizens are driven. Other areas could be abandoned houses converted to a shelter for both drug dealing and drug use or all but abandoned buildings whose owners are willing to have anyone pay the rent and who do not notice that the new tenants arrive with no furniture or clothes, but many guns.

Strategy 6: Drug Abuse Prevention

As a final strategy, drug abuse prevention focuses on the drug user rather than the dealer. Part of this effort consists of enforcement operations to suppress drug trafficking in and around schools. Another part consists of police-sponsored drug education designed to impart information and to discourage drug use. A third component includes an effort to create partnerships among police, parents, and schools to determine what the limits of acceptable drug use are and to establish a predictable community response to drug abuse.

It should be noted that not all strategies work well in all communities. Factors affecting the success or failure of any drug-control strategy hinge on elements such as the demographic makeup of the community; population density; urban, suburban, or rural settings; and so on. In addition, the manner in which the citizenry views the local police can also play a role in the degree to which many members of the community respond to or comply with

Discuss how an aggressive police crackdown can reduce the incidence of crime while recognizing the individual rights of community members.

local drug-control efforts. Hence, many police departments around the country are adopting a community-based approach to the drug problem.

OTHER CONTROL STRATEGIES

Other policy options have also been considered in combating drug abuse. Some have proved to be more effective in the short run, but others require more time to gauge their effectiveness. **Source country crop control** is one option. Many policy strategists have argued that the best way to control the production of illicit drugs is to limit the raw materials used to make them. Included in this strategy are controlling foreign production of opium and coca and restricting both foreign and domestic cultivation of marijuana.

Efforts generally take one of two forms: governments either try to persuade farmers to stop producing illicit crops or attempt to locate and destroy any illegal crops that can be found. In other cases, illicit crops are bought and destroyed before they reach illegal traffickers. Airborne spraying and ground-level search and destroy missions are also used to eradicate illicit crops. Problems arise in implementing these methods because there seems to be no shortage of areas where these crops can be grown, making it difficult if not impossible to reduce their production significantly. If one country ceases to produce an illegal crop, another country inevitably begins to do so to fill the market void. Moreover, foreign countries cannot always be relied on to pursue eradication policies vigorously. In many such countries, Myanmar and Thailand, for example, many growing areas are in remote locations outside governmental control. In other cases, the corruption of public officials stifles eradication efforts. Because of these problems, even when crop-control efforts are implemented, such actions can be counted on only as a short-term strategy.

Another control strategy is **interdiction.** It is based on the rationalization that foreign countries are not effective in preventing the production of illicit drugs and therefore the flow of drugs into the country must be stopped at U.S. borders. Theoretically at least, because U.S. agencies are given powerful search and seizure authority at the borders, it is likely that a significant percentage of illicit drugs smuggled into the country are detected. Agencies such as U.S. Customs Service, the Immigration and Naturalization Service, the U.S. Border Patrol, and the U.S. Coast Guard are involved in inspecting people, vessels, aircraft, automobiles, and cargo as they pass through ports of entry. One primary problem—the size of the task itself—can be identified with the task of interdiction. More than 12,000 miles of U.S. boundaries must be inspected daily, and more than 420 billion tons of goods and over 270 million people must be inspected every year.

WHAT HAVE WE LEARNED?

The illicit drug business provides organized crime operatives a considerable source of income, and much of the trade has been monopolized by larger crime syndicates. The most disturbing aspect of the drug business is that it represents both a crime and a public health problem. Most drug-control policy focuses on law enforcement and prosecution of violators of state and federal drug laws, while, in comparison, few public resources are dedicated to treatment and prevention efforts. Complicating the issue, drug trends change from time to time, and crime organizations respond accordingly. In many cases, crime organizations may actually influence the trends themselves.

Accordingly, the most glaring questions regarding the issue of drug trafficking and organized crime are these: What effect does organized crime have on drug trafficking? What effect does drug trafficking have on organized crime? These and other questions must be addressed by public policy planners, lawmakers, and law enforcement officials, who are often hampered by limited budgets, jurisdiction, and resources.

Although it could be argued that some success has been made against organized crime drug organizations, any true victories will be slow in coming because of their ever-changing nature. Thus it is imperative for police personnel to take full advantage of effective drug laws and procedures currently at their disposal. These resources are discussed in greater detail in Chapter 10.

DO YOU RECOGNIZE THESE TERMS?

cannabis
cycle of disorder
Drug Abuse Resistance Education (DARE)
Drug Use Forecasting (DUF)
expressive law enforcement
Golden Triangle
hallucinogenic

horizontally integrated
interdiction
intermural violence
intramural violence
Mr. Big strategy
source country crop control
vertically integrated

POINTS OF DISCUSSION

1. Discuss what lessons were learned from the Prohibition experience and drug-control efforts during the twentieth century.

2. Discuss what is meant by the *cycle of disorder* as it relates to the country's drug abuse problem.

3. Explain the ways in which we understand the magnitude of the drug problem.

4. Discuss the drugs and crime connection and to what extent the two are interrelated.

5. List and discuss Moore and Kleiman's six drug-control strategies.

6. Explain how the concept of community policing can be used to control drug abuse and trafficking in our communities.

7. Compare and contrast the different methods of conventional drug control and enforcement. Which of these methods seem to have the greatest impact?

SUGGESTED READING

KAPLAN, J. (1983). *The Hardest Drug: Heroin and Public Policy.* Chicago: University of Chicago Press. This book analyzes what the criminal justice system can and should do about heroin in the United States, and the author notes that existing policies harm criminal justice institutions, those who are addicted, and those upon whom addicts prey.

LEVINE, M. (1990). *Deep Cover.* New York: Delacorte Press.

LYMAN, M. D., and G. W. POTTER. (1996). *Drugs in Society: Causes, Concepts, and Control,* 2d ed. Cincinnati, OH: Anderson.

MUSTO, D. (1973). *The American Disease: Origins of Narcotics Control.* New Haven, CT: Yale University Press. The author traces attempts to deal with narcotics addiction from the end of the Civil War to the present, with an emphasis on 1900–1940 when official attitudes crystallized into lasting policies.

SHANNON, E. (1988). *Desperados.* New York: Viking.

WISOTSKY, S. (1986). *Breaking the Impasse in the War on Drugs.* Westport, CT: Greenwood. Using insider sources, such as diplomatic cables and internal law enforcement memos, the author examines the consequences of the Reagan administration's intensified war on drugs.

—7—
DOMESTIC ORGANIZED CRIME GROUPS

This chapter will enable you to:

- Understand the concept of domestic organized crime
- Recognize the interrelationships between various domestic organized crime organizations

- Understand the relationship between early black organized crime figures and contemporary youth gangs
- Realize the impact of rural organized crime

INTRODUCTION

In March 1996, eight members of the drug gang the Gangster Disciples were convicted of drug conspiracy in a widely publicized Chicago trial. Among them was an ex-police officer, Sonia Irwin, who had been previously assigned to the gang unit of the Chicago Police Department. Irwin, who became romantically involved with the gang's kingpin Larry Hoover, owned a small restaurant where national gang business was conducted. The case is meaningful because the gang was thought to be one of the largest in the nation with an estimated 25,000 members in 66 cities located in 22 states.

Few aspects of criminal activity inspire such fearful stereotypes in the public's overall perception of crime as gangs. Gang violence is nothing new in U.S. history. Even before the nation declared its independence, outlaw groups with names such as the Sons of Liberty formed in several colonial towns to express their opposition to British rule. A century later, ethnic gangs had become well entrenched in the urban areas of large U.S. cities, such as New York, Boston, and Chicago.

In the 1980s, a combination of factors fueled a dramatic increase in gangs and gang affiliation among the nation's youth. Gang violence grew to an unprecedented level as members waged war over turf for drug distribution, a trend that is continuing in the twenty-first century. In Los Angeles County, gang-related homicides increased over 250 percent, from 276 in 1979 to over 700 in 1990 (Brantley and DiRosa 1994). Despite the long history of gang violence in America, many neighborhoods remained unaffected until recently. Media portrayals of gang life in recent documentaries, movies, and television news magazines report intergang conflict, including drive-by shootings, senseless initiation rights, and the overall picture of the gang as a violent, predatory social phenomenon.

As we observed in Chapter 2, social scientists such as Thrasher (1927) and Shaw and McKay (1942) conducted scholarly ethnographic studies of gangs that illustrated gang members' chilling levels of alienation from society, the community, and each other. With few exceptions, the literature on gangs has focused on street youth gangs, with relatively little attention given to their adult counterparts in both urban and rural areas. This chapter discusses the various domestic criminal groups, which have characteristics of the organized crime unit. Indeed, these groups represent more than just youth gangs. Also discussed are black organized crime, outlaw motorcycle gangs, prison gangs, and the enigmatic rural organized crime groups.

PAST AFRICAN AMERICAN ORGANIZED CRIME

With the exception of historical data incorporated in Ianni's (1974) important work *Black Mafia,* no comprehensive history of the African American role in organized crime exists. What is available are snippets of vital information incorporated in other works. These fragmentary data indicate that African American organized crime has been in place for at least a century; was as important to its constituent community as Italian, Irish, and Jewish organized crime was to theirs; and has produced colorful leaders every bit as intriguing as Luciano, Genovese, and Costello. Numerous social commentators had already appreciated the importance of African American criminal organizations as early as the turn of the century. For example, W. E. B. Du Bois described the importance of black racketeers in his classic book *The Philadelphia Negro* in 1899. In his comprehensive study *An American Dilemma* published in 1944, Gunnar Myrdal, noted, "The policy game started in the Negro community and has a long history. During most of its history the policy racket in the Negro community has been monopolized by Negroes. Otherwise respectable businessmen have had a controlling interest in the numbers racket" (cited in Messick and Goldblatt 1976: 151). Ianni (1974) sets the date for a significant role by African Americans in Chicago's gambling enterprises as 1885. In fact, the evidence indicates that African Americans played a significant role in the early organization of crime in city after city.

By 1935 the Italian criminals in both Chicago and New York were realizing that black gambling operations were large and profitable enough to warrant takeover. Soon Italians moved in and made these operations part of their organizations. These takeovers did not mean, however, that blacks left the field of crime. Rather, they became representatives of organized crime in their neighborhoods, while relying on white syndicates for police and political protection. More recently, the method by which black criminals gain control of criminal rackets is through drug distribution. As we stated in Chapter 3, blacks depended on Italian criminals as drug suppliers until the mid-1970s, at which time they established working relationships with Colombian and Cuban traffickers.

Ianni (1974) found no evidence of a structure in black organized crime groups that resembles that of the Italian criminal hierarchy. He suggests that this might be by design, for if minority groups are perceived as being organized and strong, the major groups might consider them a threat and have them eradicated.

New York One of the most important organized crime groups of the 1930s and 1940s was the Forty Thieves (Ianni 1973, 1974; Peterson 1983), a loose coalition of numbers bankers under the leadership of the legendary Madame St. Clair (both a woman and a black, who clearly defies our stereotypes of organized criminals). The group, which operated in the area of 140th Street and Seventh Avenue in Harlem, started as an extortion ring in the 1930s but, by the end of that decade, it ran a series of major numbers banks in Harlem and had moved into the distribution of cocaine in a network that extended well beyond Harlem into New York's high society.

Out of the Forty Thieves came another major black organized crime figure, Ellsworth "Bumpy" Johnson (Gage 1971; Ianni 1974), a millionaire famous in organized crime folklore for flashing his sizable bankroll around Harlem. Johnson's career began as an enforcer for other organized crime groups in Harlem, but he soon graduated to narcotics distribution and served three prison terms for drug violations. In prison he attained a degree of celebrity rivaling his bad reputation on the street when he dedicated his energies to the study of philosophy, history, and poetry. Before his death in 1968, several of his poems were published in black literary reviews.

Chicago An equally interesting character was Edward P. Jones of Chicago (Irey and Slocum 1948: 187–188; Ianni, 1974: 100). Jones was born in Mississippi, the son of a Baptist minister who died shortly after his son was born. His mother moved him and his two brothers to Chicago. Using her meager inheritance, she set him up as a cab driver. To supplement his income, Jones began working the numbers game. He started as a runner, learned the intricacies of the business, and then borrowed $15,000 to start a numbers bank of his own.

By the early 1930s, the Jones bank was running a daily play of $15,000, which made it far and away the largest numbers bank in Chicago and led to black newspapers dubbing Edward Jones the city's "Policy King." One reason for Jones's, success was that he introduced a new element, business ethics, to the numbers game. The Jones bank was famous for paying off its winners quickly and honestly.

If Jones had any shortcoming (other than being a criminal), it was his fondness for personal extravagance. He boasted that he never wore the same suit twice, had elegant city and country homes, and wintered in Cannes, France. For a black in the racially repressed climate of the 1930s, such a display of wealth drew attention. The IRS took a long look at Jones and determined that between 1933 and 1938 he had paid taxes on $1,358,270, a remarkably high figure for any organized crime figure to report. In adding up his purchases in the same period, however, IRS investigators determined that he had spent $2,721,911. When the IRS put liens on Jones's holdings, they found that he had $204,000 in twenty different banks, $562,000 in government bonds, $133,000 in stocks, and $299,000 in real estate. His net worth was set at $1,600,000. Jones pleaded guilty to tax evasion and was sentenced to twenty-eight months in prison.

What is remarkable about the story of Edward Jones is that he is virtually ignored in the history of organized crime in general and Chicago organized crime in particular. His personal wealth probably dwarfed that of the more notorious crime figures and certainly ranked him with the three or four wealthiest organized criminals of his day. The fact that Jones has earned barely a footnote in the scholarly literature suggests a very distorted and inaccurate picture of the development of organized crime in the United States.

In Pittsburgh, as was the case in Chicago, African Americans played a key role **Pittsburgh** in the organization of gambling in the 1930s. Two black men in particular, William "Gus" Greenlee and William "Woogie" Harris, are credited with introducing the numbers racket to Pittsburgh in 1926 (*Pittsburgh Press* February 10, 1936). Greenlee was the owner of a black baseball team, the Pittsburgh Crawfords, and in cooperation with Harris ran one of the largest and most complex gambling networks of the period. They controlled almost 100 numbers banks, each with its own specified territory and own independent criminal organization (*Pittsburgh Post-Gazette* July 8, 1982). In total the Harris–Greenlee operation employed about 5,000 numbers runners in Pittsburgh's black community and had additional interests in bookmaking. In addition, the Harris–Greenlee operation, as did other gambling organizations in most other cities, had an ongoing contract with the politicians and police, which called for them to turn over 5 to 10 percent of their take to ensure immunity from law enforcement interference.

Haller (1979: 94) has reported the importance of black numbers operations in **Philadelphia** Philadelphia during the 1930s. He points out that these black-run banks had such an economic impact on the illicit market that a war broke out between them and Nig Rosen, a Philadelphia syndicate leader and Lansky emissary, when the black banks refused to join Rosen in lowering the payouts from 600 to 1 to 500 to 1. During the 1980s, black gambling rackets continued, and black numbers runners extorted money from white numbers bankers who were using black writers and subbankers in the black neighborhoods of Philadelphia. These white gamblers were forced to pay protection money to operate in the black neighborhoods.

There is probably no more famous open city in the annals of organized crime **Newport** than Newport, Kentucky where Moe Dalitz, Meyer Lansky, Gil "the Brain" Beckley, and Sam Tucker ran an empire for almost thirty years. Newport was and is a curious town. Directly across the Ohio River from Cincinnati, it apparently has served as Cincinnati's vice district since the 1930s. In the 1940s and 1950s, it was the site of lavish casinos, such as the Beverly Hills Club in Southgate and the Lookout House in neighboring Covington, legendary brothels such as the Hi-De-Ho Club in Wilder, a major layoff bank for bookmakers run out of the Tropicana, "bust-out" joints, and brothels too numerous to list.

It would be hard to conceive of a less likely place for black organized crime networks to operate than Newport. First, blacks made up only about 4 percent of the town's population. Second, Newport, a small southern town with a population of about 25,000, had a tight and incestuous political hierarchy and politically controlled law enforcement (such as it was). Nonetheless, there was a major African American presence in organized crime in Newport at the height of syndicate operations.

In the 1950s, Melvin Clark had a major share of the betting action in both Cincinnati and Newport and because, in his own words, he was "no Uncle Tom," he saw no reason to share the action with the most powerful white organized crime figures in the nation (Messick and Nellis 1973). Black criminal entrepreneurs also controlled several major nightclubs and casinos in Newport, including the Alibi Club and the Coconut Grove (Messick and Nellis 1973: 102–103). Clark, along with another black vice entrepreneur, "Bull" Payne, helped maintain an improbable but nonetheless major black presence in Newport organized crime through a brief war with Frank "Screw" Andrews, who was backed by the very powerful Levinson brothers, Edward and "Sleep-out" Louie, who would later become powers in Las Vegas. This black presence in the illicit markets of northern Kentucky survived the brief onset of conscience by local citizens in the late 1950s and early 1960s and an assault by the Kennedy Justice Department better than did its organized white counterparts.

So, at least in Harlem, Chicago, Philadelphia, Pittsburgh, and Newport, black organized crime is nothing new. In fact, it has existed and prospered for as long, if not longer, a period as its white counterpart. Its organizational structure and complexity were certainly the equal of more widely recognized white gangs. The rather sparse historical evidence available demonstrates that organized crime in the black community emerged right along with Italian, Jewish, and Irish mobs.

CONTEMPORARY AFRICAN AMERICAN ORGANIZED CRIME

The literature on the contemporary role of African Americans in organized crime is also sparse, but the information that is available points to a major black role in organized crime, which until very recently has not been the subject of extensive commentary in the literature. The role of black criminals was confined to their relationship with alleged Mafia-dominated rackets in drugs and ghetto gambling operations. Beginning in the 1970s, a notable departure occurred between black criminals and their Mafia counterparts. Since then several major drug-trafficking groups, established exclusively by blacks, have appeared in the ghettos, functioning for a time and then either dissolving or being broken up by the police. Experts believe that revenues from stolen goods along with the spoils of gambling operations provided the impetus for their autonomous drug ventures.

Eventually, black organized crime groups developed their own sources of supply, independent of the influence of other organized crime groups. In addition, they developed methods of importing, processing, and distribution. As did their white criminal counterparts, African American groups gradually sifted profits into legitimate businesses in the ghettos and black communities in larger cities. Some of the larger, more powerful drug organizations were those of Lerog "Nicky" Barnes, Frank Mathews, Jeff Fort, and Charles Lucas. These organized crime groups managed to spread far beyond the ghetto. The levels of sophistication and organization of drug trafficking varied among these groups, but investigations revealed that none of these organizations was hastily thrown together.

Leroy "Nicky" Barnes Barnes dominated the heroin distribution business in Harlem in the mid-1970s and could be the best-known black organized crime figure to the general public (Ferretti 1966: 106). Born in Harlem, Barnes became a drug dealer early in life and received a sentence for drug trafficking. While serving time in New York's Green Haven Prison, he became acquainted with organized crime figure Joseph "Crazy Joe" Gallo. When both men were released, they formed an alliance in which Gallo financed Barnes and set him up as the largest heroin dealer in Harlem. While cutting the Gallo brothers in on a percentage of the profits, Barnes went on to become a multimillionaire in the drug trade. Also known as the "King of Harlem," he was known to carry as much as $100,000 in his pockets and owned so many expensive cars that police had difficulty keeping track of him while under surveillance.

Because of Barnes's affluence in Harlem, rumors were that he was becoming the head of the first black Mafia. For years IRS investigators tried to convict him on tax evasion charges, but the sly Barnes claimed "miscellaneous income" and paid more than $250,000 on these ambiguous earnings, a claim that the IRS found difficult to disprove. Finally, in 1978, Barnes was caught red-handed and charged with drug distribution, resulting in a fine of $125,000 and a life sentence in prison.

Frank Mathews

Mathews began his organized crime career as a numbers runner in his hometown of Durham, North Carolina, and later moved to Philadelphia, where he established his own numbers bank; he eventually relocated to the Bedford–Stuyvesant section of New York (Goddard 1978: 104). In the 1960s in New York City, Mathews invested his profits from his numbers bank into the heroin industry. Mathews provided most of the local distribution apparatus for the famous **French Connection** operating out of Marseilles. In the three-year period from 1967 to 1970, Mathews expanded his heroin business into twenty states (Goddard 1978: 104–121).

Jeff Fort

Growing up in Woodlawn on Chicago's south side, Jeff Fort became involved in gangs at an early age, and although somewhat scrawny, he managed to become the leader of the Black P-Stone Nation, a gang referred to as America's most dangerous street gang in 1968. By the time Fort became a nationally known figure, he had already been convicted of armed robbery and assault. He was convicted in 1972 of defrauding the government of $1 million by convincing the Office of Economic Opportunity to fund a phony work program for keeping underprivileged youths out of gangs. When he was paroled in 1976, Fort joined the Moorish Science Temple of America in Milwaukee, Wisconsin, assuming the name of Chief Prince Malik. In 1978 he returned to Chicago and renamed his gang the El Rukins, which for years was the dominant organized crime group in Chicago's black community (Abadinsky 1985). The gang went on to become a major figure in drug smuggling on the city's south side.

In 1983, Fort was convicted of selling cocaine, and while serving time in a Texas prison, was tried on federal racketeering charges stemming from an alleged agreement with the government of Libya to commit terrorist acts. According to the testimony of former El Rukin general Trammel Davis, the Libyan government offered Fort $2.5 million to plant bombs on U.S. airplanes. Fort was convicted and sentenced to an additional eight years in prison.

Charles Lucas

Like many other African American organized crime figures, Charles Lucas began his career in the numbers racket (Shumach 1977: 37). The Vietnam War provided Lucas with the opportunity to become a major figure in his own right. He established a heroin importation and distribution network made up of black Vietnam veterans, primarily relatives, which enabled him to move heroin directly from Southeast Asia to the streets of the United States (Langlais 1978: 14). In addition to seeking control of wholesale drug markets in Indochina, the Lucas heroin network covered the Bronx, New Jersey, Chicago, North Carolina, and Los Angeles. All the trademarks of astute organization were apparent in the Lucas organization: Personnel were selected because they were trustworthy, not merely because of some sentimental friendship or childhood attachment; a division of labor among personnel was constructed such that each person knew only what was necessary to function; state of the art technologies in transport, processing, and packaging were used (Kelly 1987: 28).

YOUTH GANGS

The problem of youth gangs is not a new phenomenon in the United States. During the 1950s and 1960s, the fear of growing gang violence spread across the country. Newspapers and television stories regularly chronicled the spread of gangs, who adopted names such as the Vice Lords and Egyptian Kings. Movies of the time, such as *West Side Story, Blackboard Jungle,* and *The Wild Ones,* also addressed the nation's gang problem. Although the gang menace seemed to have all but disappeared in the late 1960s, it began anew in the early 1970s in major cities such as Los Angeles, Chicago, Detroit, and El Paso. In addition, other cities, including Milwaukee, Cleveland, and Columbus, Ohio, which had never experienced a gang problem, began to see considerable gang-related growth.

Although many reasons are given for the reemergence of the youth gang problem in the 1970s and 1980s, the most accepted explanation is the growing illicit drug market. The gangs of the 1950s relied on group loyalty, but modern-day gangs are lured by the easy profits of the drug trade, particularly crack cocaine. In addition, modern gangs are characterized by their adoption of lethal firearms, such as Uzi machine pistols and AK-47 assault rifles.

Today, frequent news accounts of gang violence are more than just media hype; they represent a violent and expanding segment of organized crime. Youth gangs find their genesis in neighborhoods where residents believe they have become hostage to intimidation. Competition over drug turf has resulted in increased recruitment of new gang members and escalated related killings and drive-by shootings. Law-abiding residents are often afraid to let their children outside to play in gang-occupied public parks. Neighborhood businesses suffer economically because residents are hesitant to leave the safety of their homes to shop. Police, juvenile justice officials, and juvenile courts find themselves frustrated over what to do about the problem.

Extent of Youth Gangs

It is difficult to determine the extent of gang activity in our cities. What is considered as a youth gang in one community is not considered as such in another. Attempts have been made to learn how many there are. In an effort to do so, in 1991 the National Institute of Justice surveyed police departments in seventy-nine of the nation's largest cities. More than 90 percent of reported gang activity consisted of 3,876 gangs with an estimated 202,981 members. Some estimates of gang involvement are even more disturbing. A 1991 report by the Los Angeles District Attorney's Office titled "Gangs, Crime, and Violence in Los Angeles," stated that more than half of LA's black population between the ages of 21 and 24 were involved in some type of gang activity (Brantley and DiRosa 1994). In many cases, the number of gang members easily exceeds the number of police officers in the community.

One of the first reports of disruptive youth gangs appeared in Philadelphia in 1791. In the nineteenth century, New York City experienced problems with youth campaigning for the Know Nothing Party and with Irish street gangs that started draft riots during the Civil War. Many Americans are familiar with the classic Broadway musical *West Side Story*, which depicts two twentieth-century street gangs.

Reasons for the Existence of Youth Gangs

Street gangs emerged in U.S. cities in the course of successive waves of migration, beginning with the movement from farms to cities and followed by waves of foreign immigration through to the present. Consequently, until the first third of the twentieth century, most street gang members were primarily white Europeans (e.g., Irish and Italian). By the 1970s, however, about four out of five street gang members were either African American or Hispanic. Today, the proportion of white and Asian youths in gangs appears to be increasing (*Orlando-Morningstar* 1997).

Street gangs exist for many reasons. Historically speaking, the primary influence has been socioeconomic factors such as race, social class, limited economic advantages, and immigration. In the 1980s another reason for gang proliferation, which was embraced by the public, the media, and politicians, was the rise of cocaine powder and crack. *Orlando-Morningstar* (1997) writes that some experts have traced the growth and migration of street gangs in the past thirty years to multiple causes, including these:

- Removal of manufacturing plants from the city, leaving behind service jobs that city youth are ill-prepared to handle because of inadequate education and family support systems
- Migration of middle-class minority families from urban centers to more affluent suburbs, destabilizing the middle-class neighborhoods in the city
- Increased density of segregated minority populations in the city
- Employer discrimination and wage gaps in service jobs in the city
- Loss of federal and state social services in the city
- Increases in the number of youths of gang age, without commensurate increases in community infrastructure for supervising these youths

Consequently, deprived of the traditional avenues for becoming productive members of society, many youths have turned to street gangs as a source of income, acceptance, identity, and status. There are, of course, many other risk factors that increase the likelihood of gang membership, including academic failure, low expectations of success, low neighborhood and community attachment, early antisocial behavior, favorable attitudes toward drug use, greater reliance on peers than parents, friendships with drug users, alcohol and tobacco abuse, and easy association with gangs.

How Street Gangs Are Organized

Virtually every gang evolves from a smaller group or clique. Cliques usually form around a particular concern, for example, racial or ethnic heritage, desire to guard territory, or need for protection from another group. They also can form around a particular money-making or criminal activity. Experts also report that many gangs have fairly short lives, often breaking up or drifting apart after a few months (Brantley and DiRosa 1994). Once formed, a street gang can range in size from ten members to as many as 1,000 or more. The term *supergang* was coined in Chicago in the late 1960s to describe a gang with thousands of members.

Members of the Crips, one of the largest California-based youth gangs.

As FBI agents and other criminal justice practitioners have observed, many gangs last only a short time before they weaken and wither away, either because of successful prosecution efforts or lack of interest by members. More successful gangs excel at extending their economic base and recruiting new members. As successful gangs flourish, they must extend their reach into legitimate businesses and begin laundering money and corrupting public officials, eventually coming to resemble established organized crime groups.

Derrick Hargress

Now in his 30's, Derrick "Vamp" Hargress was a member of a Crips gang set known as the Nine-Duce Hoovers (named after the streets where they hung out). Police think he was the mastermind of Crips's movement from Los Angeles to Seattle in the late 1980s. Hargress brought eight cohorts with him from southern California to Seattle in early 1987. Each week they transported 15 to 20 ounces of crack from Los Angeles while running three crack houses that generated $6,000 a day. According to Seattle prosecutors, "They also brought with them a level of violence and an element of organization previously lacking in drug distribution in this city." In early 1988, Hargress decided to branch out by sending several of his crew to operate a dozen crack houses in Oklahoma City. One gang member told Oklahoma City detectives that the gang had test marketed the area first. Hargress pleaded guilty in 1988 to selling crack near a school and using a gun to further his drug business. He was sentenced to twenty-five years in Leavenworth.

Source: U.S. News & World Report, August 19, 1991.

Understanding how gang organization progresses is important for several reasons, because those who are successful generally change their tactics as their criminal focus evolves. For example, there are indications that the Los Angeles-based Crips gang is attempting to unify all of its "sets" across the nation into one major organization, with a chief executive officer-style leadership structure (Brantley and DiRosa 1994). To protect such entrenched criminal enterprises from the scrutiny of law enforcement, leaders of these gangs often perform acts of violence. In fact, supergangs actually welcome the turf violence of other, less-entrenched gangs because it diverts the attention of law enforcement away from them.

Youth Gang Member Types

Research suggests that most street gangs are less sophisticated and hierarchical than traditional organized crime groups. Klein has argued that street gangs are "loosely knit and poorly organized groups that engage in cafeteria-style crime" (Klein et al. 1995). A gang's exact structure depends on size of its membership, extent of its illegal activities, and locale. Some gangs have leaders with formal titles, such as king, prince, prime minister, general, don, or chief. The higher levels of the organization change because of the death or imprisonment of the leaders or in-gang rivalry. The lower levels tend to be loosely organized. In some gangs, various factions or semi-independent groups share allegiance to the king or leader.

Street gang members often range in age from 8 to 25 years old. Generalizing about the interpersonal dynamics that characterize street gangs is difficult, but it is possible to classify members according to their level of involvement. In general, there are three types of street gang members: leaders, hard-core members, and fringe or marginal members. Leaders are usually the oldest members of the gang and have the most extensive criminal backgrounds. They direct the gang's criminal activity, sometimes even from prison. Studying the leader often provides insight into the culture and nature of the gang. A leader usually surrounds himself with trusted members and advisers, forming the inner circle. Leadership responsibilities are sometimes shared among various members of the inner group.

Hard-core gang members are usually the most violent and have committed the most serious crimes. Since the gang provides a sense of identity, the lives of these members often center on the gang. Law enforcement efforts are generally directed at the leaders and hard-core members. Fringe or marginal members are typically the newest and youngest members of the gang. They drift in and out of the gang, depending on its needs. Fringe or marginal members generally lack the direction either to be hard-core members or to leave the gang (Brantley and DiRosa 1994). Most of the nation's youth gangs have now developed their own terminology for member status. Police in Omaha, Nebraska, for example, have encountered the following terms:

- AG (gangster for life)
- BG (baby gangster)
- Foot soldier (lowest-ranking member)
- Homeboy (fellow gang member)
- Hoodsta (gangster)
- Killa (killer)

- **Wannabee** or mark (wants to be gang member)
- Queen (female gang member)
- Triple OG (third-generation gangster)

The MS-13: A New International Gang in the United States

In early November 2005, the Federal Bureau of Investigation and the Houston Police Department learned that six suspected members of Mara Salvatrucha, a violent Central American gang known as MS-13, were raiding a house on Liberty Street where a rival gang had stashed drugs. The MS-13 became the focus of the nationwide crackdown by the FBI and federal immigration agents and has gained notariety in recent years for home invasion robberies, drug dealing, and machete attacks on its enemies. But what happened in November 2005 heightened concerns that MS-13 members can be far more dangerous than originally thought.

MS-13 suspects swept through the house like a well-trained assault team using paramilitary tactics, including perimeter lookouts, high-powered weaponry, and the room by room sweep of the house that was notable for its precision and sophistication. When MS-13 suspects were confronted by authorities, the result was an intense shoot-out that killed two members.

The Houston shoot-out was significant in that it raised the question of whether its Los Angles members included people with paramilitary training who fled the Civil War in El Salvador during the 1980s and whether the gang was evolving into an organization formed in their image. American law enforcement investigations into the MS-13 extended all the way to El Salvador, where safe houses in Central America and Mexico were raided. More than 600 arrests resulted as well as the discovery of the gang's Constitution. Included in the materials seized were documents, most of which were crudely handwritten codes of conduct that listed a range of punishments from death to severe beatings for transgressions against the gang.

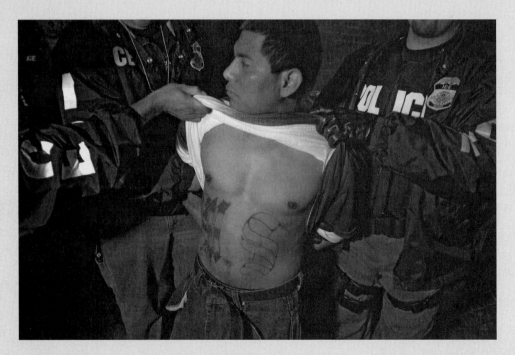

The M-13 gang is a well-trained paramilitary gang originating in Central America. American law enforcement has tracked their criminal activities in the United States. The group specializes in home invasions, and factions have been documented in Houston, Rhode Island, and Connecticut.

(*AP Wide World Photos*)

The MS-13 began in a low-income neighborhood in Los Angeles and slowly evolved into a loosely organized group of cells across the nation to an increasingly efficient and dangerous organization that has now become a significant concern for both the public and police. It is hard to know exactly how many members belong to the MS-13 gang, but estimates are as high as 10,000. MS-13 sales are most active in Los Angeles, the mid-Atlantic, Rhode Island, and Connecticut.

In addition to its efficient tactical capabilities, the group has also formed commerce routes across the nation for drug-trafficking operations that often include *theft crews* who steel over-the-counter cough and cold medicines from drugstores. These medicines can be abused or used to make other drugs and are sold to help finance MS-13 units.

In recent years, the MS-13's reputation as a particularly brutal gang became known by a series of incidents, several of them occuring in Northern Virginia. In one, a former MS-13 member who had become a police informant was fatally stabbed and her head almost severed. In another, MS-13 members used a machete to cut off several fingers of a rival gang member's hand. In Madison, Wisconsin, police arrested three MS-13 members who stole tens of thousands of dollars worth of over-the-counter medicines from 22 Walgreen drugstores throughout the Midwest. The drugs were being transported to a warehouse in Louisville, Kentucky, to be resold. Gangs members researched Walgreen stores and on a routine basis averaged $45,000 to $55,000 worth of stolen merchandise per day.

One prevailing problem in controlling juvenile gangs is the fact that the juvenile justice system is generally considered inadequate for dealing with hard-core street gang members who are minors. State juvenile codes were not designed for the type of serious violence that characterizes street gang crimes. On the other hand, laws addressing gangs generally do not cover juveniles, and many state and local prosecutors have expressed frustration at the lack of detention facilities for juveniles and the corresponding frequency with which juveniles receive probation for felony offenses. Of course, street gang members are very much aware of the significant differences between the juvenile and adult systems and often use juveniles to commit their crimes for them.

Laws Addressing Gang Violence

To address these concerns, in 1994 Congress broadened the federal court's jurisdiction over gangs in significant ways. Notably, provisions of the Violent Crime Control and Law Enforcement Act of 1994 are bringing more types of cases, including cases against street gang members, into the federal judicial system. Specifically, the act authorizes adult prosecution of those thirteen and older charged with serious violent crimes; prohibits the sale or transfer of firearms to, or possession of certain firearms by, juveniles; and triples the maximum penalties for using juveniles to distribute drugs in or near protected zones such as schools, playgrounds, video arcades, and youth centers.

Other significant provisions of the Violent Crime Control and Law Enforcement Act include the following:

- Bans on nineteen military-style assault weapons, assault weapons with specific combat features, "copy" models, and certain high-capacity ammunition magazines holding more than ten rounds
- Expansion of the federal death penalty to cover about sixty offenses, including murder of a federal law enforcement officer, large-scale drug trafficking, drive-by shootings resulting in death, and carjackings resulting in death
- Newer and stiffer penalties for violent drug-trafficking crimes committed by gang members

Since January 1997, twelve bills addressing youth violence or street gangs have been introduced in Congress. Some would expand a federal court role in prosecuting violent juvenile offenders. For example, the Anti-Gang Youth and Violence Act of 1997 provides for federal prosecution of serious and violent juvenile offenders and detention of juveniles prior to sentencing.

The Juvenile Crime Control Act of 1997 re-forms the federal juvenile justice system, combats violent youth crime, and increases accountability for juvenile criminal offenses. The Federal Gang Violence Law defines juvenile delinquency as a gang crime and amends the sentencing guidelines to increase the offense level for activities committed in connection with a criminal street gang (Orlando-Morningstar 1997).

Characteristics of Youth Gang Members

Theorists have suggested that gangs are made up of lower-class youths who find it difficult to adjust to middle-class settings. As a means to achieve status and to develop opportunities, members make rational decisions to join the gang as a means to achieve personal goals. Most research on youth gangs suggests that they are made up of young adolescent males, although some female gangs have been documented. The majority of gang members are adolescents or in their early twenties. In general, gang members leave the gang by adulthood and pursue conventional life-styles. Those who remain in the gang do so as a means of survival in communities offering little or no legitimate opportunities for success.

Despite awareness that some gang members are over the age of eighteen, there are no data to indicate the extent of adult membership. Many police officials are concerned that the older members of youth gangs are also the leaders and are more worthy targets of investigation and prosecution than are their youthful counterparts.

Gangs exist in virtually all ethnic communities. Although African Americans and Hispanics predominate, many gangs with white and Asian members also exist. To some extent, gang behavior is determined by the cultural heritage of the group. For example, differences exist between Chinese gangs associated with the Tongs and those with predominantly Vietnamese membership. Tong-related gangs are involved in profit-making activities such as extorting money from local businesses, whereas Vietnamese gangs appear to be largely entrepreneurial in nature and not tied to any larger group or territory.

Black Youth Gangs

The most prominent black youth gangs today are the Bloods and the Crips (an acronym for Common Revolution in Progress), both originating in Los Angeles during the 1970s. Until recently it was thought that to join either group the prospect needed to be black. As a rule this is the case, but in some cities, such as Denver, Asians and Hispanics have been documented as belonging to these groups. The Crips originated at Washington High School in southwest Los Angeles. In a short time, Crips factions emerged in other high schools around the Compton area. By committing assaults and robberies in surrounding neighborhoods, the Crips gained a reputation as a violent, predatory youth gang. As the gang grew, others realized that they would be forced to either fight, flee, or surrender. As a result, rival gangs formed.

The Bloods, originating on Piru Street in Los Angeles, represent the most visible rival youth gang to the Crips. They originally referred to themselves as the Compton Pirus, but later became known as the Bloods. The Bloods were quick to retaliate against the Crips. Although the number of members of both gangs has risen, the ratio of Crips to Bloods is estimated at three to one. In 1990, authorities in Los Angeles estimated the total number of gang members for both groups combined as 80,000. Both Crips and Bloods incorporate **colors**—blue and red, respectively—into their clothing and accessories: shoelaces, belts, suspenders, athletic shoes, and so on. Designer clothing is commonly worn with white T-shirts and baggy trousers worn low on the hips. Athletic caps and jackets are also common.

Both Crips and Bloods have adopted their own rules for speaking or writing to their **homeboys**, a term used to refer to fellow gang members. When greeting each other, each group has its own hand signs, which they flash quickly at one another. By communicating in this silent manner, they demonstrate their gang allegiance and brotherhood and identify their rivals.

Young members must undergo initiation rights before being accepted into the gang. Typically, they are **jumped in**, which means that they must fight a selected member of the gang for a designated length of time, often resulting in serious injury. Others are asked to commit a crime witnessed by the gang, which can include stealing a credit card and making purchases for gang members or stealing a vehicle.

The expansion of both the Crips and Bloods occurred in 1986, when factions of the gangs were identified in thirty-two states and 113 U.S. cities. Although their expansion conjures images of a master plan, it is generally agreed to have been a matter of happenstance. Neither gang is rigidly hierarchcial, with their members being divided into small subgangs called **sets**. Each set has anywhere from 30 to 100 members. Experts believe that many gang members originally left California to flee detection and prosecution. Others, it has been suggested, merely took advantage of other cities where friends and family lived to set up branch drug-dealing operations. In some cases, members may have realized that police in smaller cities were less aware of crack operations and the operational practices of gangs, thereby making the cities ripe territory for mobile gang entrepreneurs. Expanding gang operations was also motivated by profit, especially in areas where the crack market was not saturated and prices could be higher than in Los Angeles.

Study

Gang Like a Franchisee

A recently published academic study provides a rare behind-the-scenes glimpse of the finances of a street gang, from the money made selling drugs to the cost of providing funerals for dead members. The study by economist Steven Levitt of the University of Chicago and sociologist Sudhir Alladi Venkatesh of Harvard University likens the gang to a franchisee and finds that many members—the foot soldiers who sell drugs on the street—earn at or below minimum wage.

The National Bureau of Economic Research paper draws on the books kept by the gang's leader in a loose-leaf notebook detailing monthly revenue and expenses over a four-year period from the late 1980s to the early 1990s. That was the height of the crack cocaine epidemic in the eastern United States. Over that time, the profits of the inner-city gang roughly doubled as it grabbed turf from a rival group and its crack market expanded. But costs for weapons, mercenary fighters, bribes, and the like, also rose.

The data were obtained from a former gang member who now has a legitimate job after serving in prison. Venkatesh, who has been studying gangs actively since 1991, has known the informant for years. "For obvious reasons, we have accommodated his request to remain anonymous," he and Levitt say in their study. Nor do they reveal where the gang was headquartered. The gang, which has since broken up because of arrests and infighting, comprised a leader, three officers—an enforcer, a treasurer, and a runner who transported large quantities of drugs and money—and twenty-five to seventy-five foot soldiers. An additional 60 to 200 were rank and file members who paid dues to the gang in return for

(continued)

---

protection and to ensure a reliable drug supply. The gang was one of about one hundred grouped under a multistate organization. Just like a franchisee, it paid a royalty to the parent group amounting to about 20 percent of revenue. This is the reason why Venkatesh thinks the books probably understate what was actually made by the gang leader and his members. He reckons that gang members skimmed roughly 15 percent of the drugs off the tip for their own use or for resale.

Among the paper's other findings are these:

- Active gang members had a roughly one in four chance of dying over the period studied.
- Drug demand and prices dropped sharply during gang wars.

- Wages in the gang were extremely skewed, probably far more so than in corporate America. The gang leader made from $50,000 to $130,000 per year, not counting the 10 percent extra he probably made "off the books."
- The gang employed mercenary fighters, or warriors, during turf wars at about $2,000 per month.
- The death of a foot soldier cost the gang up to $5,000 in family compensation and funeral services.
- The gang made money through extortion by charging grocery stores and local businesses street taxes for letting them operate on its twelve-square-block turf.

A Gang's Bottom Line

	Monthly Average	
	Year 1	Year 4
Revenue		
Drug sales	$11,900	$53,000
Dues	5,400	9,600
Protection money, street tax	1,200	5,800
Total	$18,500	$68,400
Nonwage costs		
Cost of drugs sold	$2,800	$11,900
Tribute to gang hierarchy	3,200	6,000
Mercenary fighters	1,000	1,200
Funerals, payments to families of the deceased	300	1,100
Weapons	300	1,800
Miscellaneous[a]	500	3,200
Total	$8,100	$25,200
Wages		
Net profit to leader	$4,200	$10,900
Wage per foot soldier	140	470

[a]Includes parties, community events, bribes, and legal fees.

Sources: An Economic Analysis of a Drug-Selling Gang's Finances. National Bureau of Economic Research; R. Miller, "Study: Gang Like a Franchisee," *USA Today*, July 13, 1996, p. 3A.

Hispanic Youth Gangs

Although much of the gang literature focuses on black youth gangs, Hispanic gangs also represent a significant number of organized youth gangs. As with black gangs, Hispanic youth gangs also compete for turf in the drug trade and commonly roam in packs in the larger U.S. cities. They have proved to be fluid in their structure, with both Hispanic and Mexican nationalists often belonging to the same gang, as is the case with LA's Inca Boys and NSM (North Side Mafia) gangs. Many Hispanic gangs have been influenced by the

A band of six or seven sixth-graders at a school in a small town routinely threatens to beat up younger children who do not surrender their lunch money to them. Are these sixth-graders members of an organized crime group? You decide!

dress code of the Crips and Bloods groups with black dress, hand signals, street language, and the use of graffiti to mark turf.

Mobility of Youth Gangs

According to some media accounts, youth gangs in small cities are frequently satellite operations of gangs in larger metropolitan areas. However, preliminary research has suggested that gangs emerge in smaller cities primarily because of family relocation and local gang evolution, not migration. In a 1996 gang migration study, numbers were low in the cities studied, and gang migration neither influenced the local drug market nor caused local gang problems. Of the cities in the study, 47 percent reported the arrival of ten or fewer migrants in the previous year. Only 5 percent estimated that they had experienced one hundred or more recent arrivals (Orlando-Morningstar 1997).

Many experts believe that gang migration is more a trend of street gang culture than the development of individual gangs with a national infrastructure. It is true that some street gangs have national scope, but the majority are local imitations of Los Angeles or Chicago gangs. Only in proximity to large metropolitan areas such as Chicago and Los Angeles has there been evidence of significant gang migration. Eight reasons have been identified to explain gang member migration:

1. To stay with relocating families
2. To avoid apprehension and prosecution
3. To avoid retribution from rival gangs
4. To participate in private and public training and rehabilitation programs
5. To take advantage of new criminal markets and higher illegal profits
6. To reduce street gang rivalry and competition
7. To find communities that are easier to initiate and manipulate
8. To take advantage of limited law enforcement resources and lack of recognition and awareness of the gang

The most likely gang candidates for migration are young African American and Hispanic males, who travel short distances and stay at least several months. They primarily migrate to stay with their relocating families (57 percent) or to expand a drug market (20 percent).

OUTLAW MOTORCYCLE GANGS

Outlaw motorcycle gangs (OMGs) originally formed during the late 1940s as loose-knit, rowdy groups made up of disgruntled World War II veterans. As the decades passed, the tough-guy image was perpetuated and their numbers and sophistication grew. Although not all such groups fit within the definition of organized crime, many of the estimated 800 motorcycle gangs operating in the United States do (U.S. Marshal's Service 1986). Over the years, four of these groups have emerged as being the largest and most sophisticated. These are the Hell's Angels, Outlaws, Pagans, and Bandidos. Of these, all but the Pagans have chapters in both the United States and foreign countries.

In 1985 the FBI estimated that the Hell's Angels alone had more than sixty-three chapters in thirteen countries. In addition to these four groups, many other sophisticated but smaller OMGs also operate in the United States. These groups include the Vagos, located in the West and Southwest; the Warlocks, operating in the tristate area of Pennsylvania, New Jersey, and Delaware; the Dirty Dozen in Arizona; the Gypsy Jokers in the Pacific northwest; and the Sons of Silence in Colorado.

Outlaw motorcycle gangs have become easily identifiable because of their colors or membership jacket. Great pride is taken in a biker's colors, which bear the official logo or emblem of the gang sewn to the sleeveless leather or denim jacket. Generally, the gang's logo is affixed to the center of the back of the jacket, and the name of the group is sewn to the top rocker, with the specific territory or region of the gang occupying the bottom rocker. Aside from the specific message conveyed by the OMG member's colors, a great deal of significance is attached to various gang-related patches also attached to the jacket. These include "1 percent" or "13" patches, which reflect many different things, but are usually related to the biker's antisocial life-style.

In addition to the colors worn by an OMG member, his motorcycle is a great source of pride and significance. Most outlaw motorcycle organizations require members to own a U.S.-made motorcycle consisting of at least a 900-cc engine. The motorcycle represents more than mere transportation for the biker. Indeed, it signifies the biker mystique of a free-living, vagabond, reckless life-style. Weapons are also a common staple of OMG members.

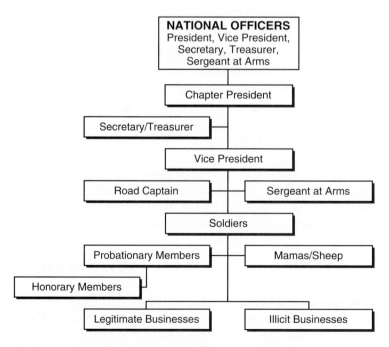

Outlaw motorcycle gang organizational structure.

In 1984, the U.S. Marshal's Service stated that OMG members are armed at nearly all times with concealed weapons located in pockets, boots, and belly bands. In addition, it is common to have female associates carry guns and knives and to remain close to their male counterparts at all times.

The OMG–Organized Crime Link

Chapter 1 discusses the various definitions and models of organized crime. When we apply outlaw motorcycle gangs to these definitions, it is clear that a close enough correlation exists to depict outlaw motorcycle gangs accurately as organized crime. Many gangs, such as the Hell's Angels and Pagans, evolved over the years to be considered organized crime organizations in their own right. Illustrating this point, Garner (1985) stated, "The organized crime scenario does not end with ethnic diversity, other factors are intimately involved. The role of outlaw biker gangs as enforcers and manufacturers of illegal drugs has been revealed by numerous indictments and arrests by federal and local law enforcement agencies. . . . This too is organized crime."

In his book *Theft of the Nation,* Cressey (1969) points out three positions absolutely necessary to an organized crime group: There is a position for a corrupter, whose function it is to establish relationships with public officials and other influential persons whose assistance is necessary to achieve the organization's goals. There is a position for a corruptee. There is also a position for an enforcer whose main duty it is to maintain organizational integrity by arranging for the maiming or killing of recalcitrant members.

Although it is true that not all outlaw motorcycle clubs are structured or organized sufficiently to be considered organized crime, many of the larger ones meet this definition. In fact, many small clubs have courted large ones in hopes that they will be absorbed as part of the larger organization. Such a move would provide the new members with all the clout, rights, resources, and privileges enjoyed by members of larger gangs. In addition, the larger group benefits by increased membership and organizational expansion.

Organizational Structure

OMGs have well-established organizational structures, with the positions of president and vice-president, along with other important ranks within the organization. The image of the biker is also undergoing some change. Some gang members are more likely to wear three-piece suits than the typical biker colors while conducting daily business deals. The president of the gang easily performs the role of the corrupter, essential to organized crime. The position of enforcer is filled by the sergeant at arms of a gang. Here is a brief discussion of the role and function of each position within the outlaw motorcycle gang unit.

Membership

National President.   Often the founder of the club, the national president is located near the national headquarters. In many cases he has a select group who answer only to him as bodyguards and enforcers. In most cases he possesses the authority to make final decisions over all club members and can override any voted decisions.

Territorial or Regional Representative.   In some cases, this person is also called the vice-president in charge of whatever region or district to which he is assigned. His duties are usually to handle all problems that local chapters are unable to resolve successfully at their level. As a rule, any problems that involve the club as a whole are handled at the national level.

National Secretary–Treasurer. This member handles the club's money and collects dues from local chapters. In addition, he drafts new club bylaws and makes changes to them, as well as recording the minutes of all meetings.

National Enforcer. Answering directly to the national president, this person sees to it that the president's orders are carried out. He could act as the president's bodyguard and handle special situations, such as punishing the club's rule violators or retrieving the colors from a member who has left the club. He has also been known to remove club-related tattoos from ex-members.

Chapter President. This person has claimed the presidency through a combination of personality, leadership skills, or personal strength or has been voted to it. He has final authority over all chapter business and its members.

Vice-President. As the second in command and the right hand of the chapter president, the vice-president presides over club affairs in the absence of the president. As a rule, he is hand picked by the president and is heir apparent to the club's leadership.

Secretary–Treasurer. Usually a person with the best writing skills, this member keeps the chapter roster, pays chapter bills, and maintains a crude accounting system for the chapter. He takes the minutes at all chapter meetings and collects any dues and/or fines.

Sergeant at Arms. Because of the unruly and violent nature of outlaw gangs, each chapter has one person whose principal duty is to maintain order at club meetings, functions, and runs. He is usually the strongest member physically and is completely loyal to the president. He can administer beatings to fellow members for violation of club rules. This person serves as the enforcer.

Road Captain. This person fills a unique position in the gang. He acts as the club's logistician and security chief for club-sponsored runs or outings. He maps out routes to be taken during runs and arranges for refueling, food, and maintenance stops. Road captains carry the club's money and use it for bail should a member be arrested. The road captain contacts local law enforcement agencies to express the club's intention while in their jurisdictions.

Members. The rank and file, fully accepted and dues-paying members of the gang, have sworn to live by the club's bylaws and implement the decisions of the club's leadership. As a rule, gangs have limited membership. This policy affords the president greater control over the affairs of the club, while ensuring that the gang's criminal efforts are not compromised by police organizations.

Probationary or Prospective Members. These persons are club hopefuls who spend from one month to one year in a probationary status and who must prove during that time that they are worthy to become club members. Most clubs require probates to commit felonies in the presence of their sponsoring member to weed out weak ones and police infiltrators. In addition to being nominated by a regular member for probationary status, new members must be voted in unanimously by club members at the end of their probationary period. While probates, they perform menial jobs at the clubhouse, carry weapons for members, and stand guard at parties. Probates are forbidden to

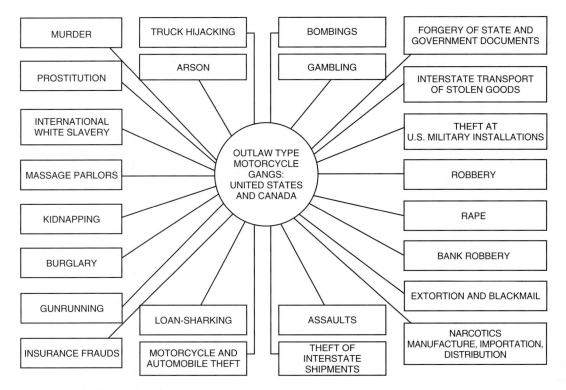

Criminal activities of motorcycle gangs

wear the club's colors, have no voting privileges, and must complete an initiation ceremony at which they are awarded their colors.

Associates or Honorary Members.   At the bottom of the hierarchy is the associate or honorary member. He is the person who has proved his worth to the club in some fashion. These persons are either professionals in the community who have supported the club or criminals with whom the gang has had a profitable relationship. Typically, these members are attorneys, bail bondspeople, motorcycle shop owners, and auto wrecking yard owners. They are allowed to party with the gang and go on runs, but are not voting members.

Over the years, important relationships between traditional organized crime and OMGs have been identified. For example, the New York Hell's Angels' chapter has been associated with a night club operated by members of the Gambino crime organization. Other links have also been observed between the Hell's Angels and Cleveland's organized crime groups in which the bikers have been employed as enforcers. The Pagans have also been associated with organized crime on the East Coast since the early 1980s.

Criminal Activity

The major outlaw motorcycle gangs have been involved in an array of criminal enterprises. In addition to drug trafficking, which is their largest money-maker, gangs have been involved in contract murder, extortion, arson for profit, prostitution, robbery, bombings, vehicle theft, mail fraud, and the systematic takeover of legitimate businesses for the purpose of laundering money. In many states, biker gangs virtually control the production and distribution of certain drugs, such as methamphetamine, a white-powdered stimulant.

Biker Constitution and Bylaws

All outlaw motorcycle clubs have bylaws or a constitution in one form or another that sets forth accepted standards of conduct for members and administrative procedures for gang operations. The larger the club, the greater the tendency and need to develop a written document. Typically, bylaws govern matters such as membership, requirements, fines for misconduct or breaking club rules, acceptable behavior during runs, and similar matters. Experts have found that bylaws for different clubs are the same. Here are some examples:

- All persons must be 18 years of age for membership.
- All prospective new members must be sponsored by a member.
- All prospective members must complete a probationary period.
- Each new member will pay the national headquarters initiation fee.
- Each member will pay monthly dues, set by the local president, to his chapter.
- No member shall transfer from one chapter to another without the permission of both presidents and the payment of a transfer fee to the national treasurer.
- When a member is in another chapter's jurisdiction, he will abide by its bylaws.
- Any member caught using the needle will lose his colors and everything that goes with them.
- Harley-Davidson or Indian motorcycles will be the only bikes used while in this club.

Involvement in the meth business is extensive and profitable. In 1986, the President's Commission on Organized Crime reported that an estimated 40 percent of the entire U.S. methamphetamine supply was controlled by motorcycle gangs. It has also been estimated that the Hell's Angels and other large outlaw gangs earn up to $1 billion a year from drug dealing, prostitution, gunrunning, theft, extortion, and murder. OMGs are involved in the cocaine trade as well. In 1992 the Bureau of Alcohol, Tobacco, and Firearms estimated that these groups control 50 percent of the illegal cocaine market in Oregon and 35 percent in North Carolina (Serwer 1992).

Over the years, biker gangs have adopted sophisticated technology as aids in their criminal pursuits. It is common for them to use walkie-talkies, cellular telephones, pagers, police scanners, scramblers, fax machines, personal computers, electronic eavesdropping equipment, and video-assisted surveillance.

The Hell's Angels

Formerly the Pissed Off Bastards of Bloomington, the Hell's Angels originated during the late 1940s. During that time, ex-World War II GIs who were unable to readjust to civilian life joined. Their chosen life-style was that of freedom of the road to ride motorcycles, live an outlaw existence, and compare themselves to famous western desperados such as Billy the Kid. The Hell's Angels were originally formed in Fontana, California, and were soon romanticized in the film *The Wild Ones,* starring Marlon Brando and Lee Marvin. Following the Korean War in the 1950s, membership increased, as it also did during the 1960s. A racist, sexist, and violent group, the Hell's Angels proudly wore the symbol of the death head—a winged skull—with Nazi insignias such as swastikas and iron crosses. In addition to U.S. chapters, the Hell's Angels are also located in many foreign countries, such as Canada, England, Switzerland, New Zealand, and Australia.

The Hell's Angels are one of the largest biker gangs, with an estimated 1,000 members. In addition, they are bureaucratically structured with a

Most members are from working-class backgrounds. Many are veterans, some work in blue-collar jobs, and others run small businesses such as bike repair shops and tattoo parlors. Many are rootless, with no links to the community in which they live. Hell's Angels think they are okay and that the rest of society is off track. Many are aging, approaching their late 40s and 50s. Blacks and women are not allowed to be members of the Hell's Angels. Members are an intensely bonded group with a strong code of mutual support. If one is attacked, the others must jump in to help. The club has written rules with strict penalties, from suspension for those who don't pay dues to expulsion for members caught dealing standard drugs, injecting drugs, or using crack. The typical Hell's Angel is obsessed with toughness and strength. Almost all the chapters own clubhouses, with some, such as those in California and New York, being large buildings or complexes. Most of them are outfitted with surveillance equipment and guards.

chain of command at both the national and local (chapter) levels. Positions of president, lieutenant, sergeant at arms, and treasurer are common in the organization. In the 1960s they moved into the drug-trafficking business, manufacturing and selling drugs such as LSD and meth.

One of the most widely publicized incidents involving the Hell's Angels happened at a free Rolling Stones concert in Oakland, California, in 1969. Despite their reputation for violence, the Angels were hired to provide security in return for $500 worth of beer. With 300,000 people in attendance, Hell's Angel Allen Passaro, 22, stabbed 18-year-old Meredith Hunter five times near the stage where the Rolling Stones were performing. The incident, filmed by a crew making the documentary *Gimme Shelter*, showed him trying to grab a revolver from Hunter. The clip was played several times for jurors at Passaro's trial. He was found not guilty. This case resulted in the Hell's Angels boasting that they were bigger than the law, resulting in stories of murders, drug dealing, and extortion. In fact, this incident resulted in an alleged murder contract being placed on singer Mick Jagger, which was reportedly canceled after the rock group paid $50,000 to the Hell's Angels (Serwer 1992).

In 1975 the federal government launched a two-year investigation into the illegal activities of the Hell's Angels, resulting in raids on several chapter hangouts. Among the thirty-two gang members charged with a wide range of felonies was Ralph "Sonny" Barger, 41, and his wife Sharon, 39. Their trial, one of the biggest in U.S. federal court history, began in San Francisco Federal Court in October 1979 and involved more than 300 defense attorneys. During the course of the trial, Judge Samuel Conti clamored, "I'd like to get this trial over with in my lifetime." Finally, on July 2, 1980, the eight-month multimillion dollar trial ended with a hung jury.

Another interesting case involving the Hell's Angels occurred in August 1983 when four members were convicted of conspiracy charges stemming from the Angel's war with the Mongols biker gang over a dispute about the common wording on their jackets. Two Mongols were machine-gunned to death and several others wounded because the Mongols dared to wear the word California on the bottom rocker of their leather jackets.

The grimmer side of the folk heroes: two Hell's Angels members stand handcuffed, faces to the wall, after arrest during a narcotics raid in southern California. "Berdeo" refers to the San Bernadino, California, branch of the Angels.

(*AP Wide World Photos*)

The Outlaws   The Outlaws began in Chicago during the 1950s, although they are now headquartered in Detroit. The organization has spread through the Great Lakes region with chapters in southeastern and southern United States. Outlaw members are most heavily involved in drug trafficking, particularly with regard to diazepam (Valium) and cocaine. Nondrug criminal activities include extortion, car theft, prostitution, and contract murder.

The Hollister, California, Incident

Hollister is a small town an hour's drive south of San Francisco. In 1946 over the July 4 weekend, the American Motorcycle Association sponsored the annual motorcycle Dirt Hill Climb Races, which drew hundreds of contestants and thousands of spectators. The seven-man police department watched apprehensively as the town filled with bikers.

During the evenings, drag races on Main Street were common, and fist fights grew to unmanageable proportions. One member of the Pissed Off Bastards of Bloomington (POBOB) motorcycle club was arrested for fighting, and the rest of his friends were so enraged at this that they descended on the jail and demanded his release. When local authorities refused, the estimated mob of 750 literally tore the town apart. This incident, highly publicized at the time, was the introduction of dangerous motorcycle gangs to society. Nevertheless, the Hollister incident contributed three very important biker traditions that survive to this day: the July 4 run, the one-percenter image, and calling anyone not part of the biker subculture "citizen." After the Hollister incident, the POBOB's membership increased, and new blood came in bringing new ideas, which included changing the gang's name to the Hell's Angels.

PHYSICAL MAKEUP OF A TYPICAL MOTORCYCLE GANG

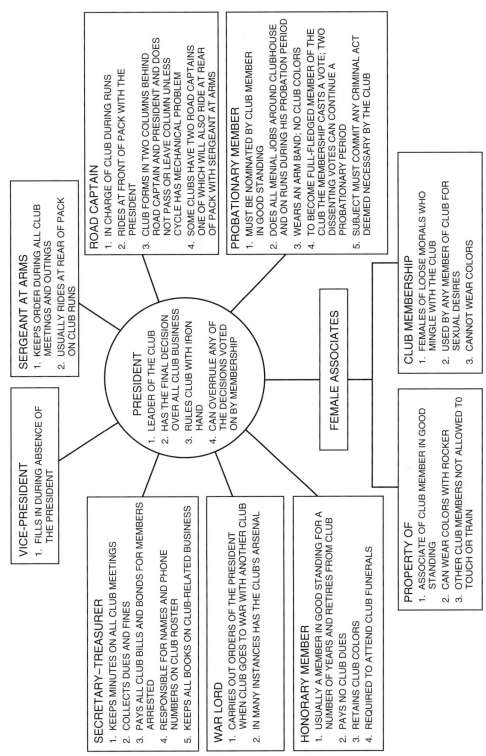

VICE-PRESIDENT
1. FILLS IN DURING ABSENCE OF THE PRESIDENT

SERGEANT AT ARMS
1. KEEPS ORDER DURING ALL CLUB MEETINGS AND OUTINGS
2. USUALLY RIDES AT REAR OF PACK ON CLUB RUNS

ROAD CAPTAIN
1. IN CHARGE OF CLUB DURING RUNS
2. RIDES AT FRONT OF PACK WITH THE PRESIDENT
3. CLUB FORMS IN TWO COLUMNS BEHIND ROAD CAPTAIN AND PRESIDENT AND DOES NOT PASS OR LEAVE COLUMN UNLESS CYCLE HAS MECHANICAL PROBLEM
4. SOME CLUBS HAVE TWO ROAD CAPTAINS ONE OF WHICH WILL ALSO RIDE AT REAR OF PACK WITH SERGEANT AT ARMS

PROBATIONARY MEMBER
1. MUST BE NOMINATED BY CLUB MEMBER IN GOOD STANDING
2. DOES ALL MENIAL JOBS AROUND CLUBHOUSE AND ON RUNS DURING HIS PROBATION PERIOD
3. WEARS AN ARM BAND; NO CLUB COLORS
4. TO BECOME FULL-FLEDGED MEMBER OF THE CLUB THE MEMBERSHIP CASTS A VOTE; TWO DISSENTING VOTES CAN CONTINUE A PROBATIONARY PERIOD
5. SUBJECT MUST COMMIT ANY CRIMINAL ACT DEEMED NECESSARY BY THE CLUB

PRESIDENT
1. LEADER OF THE CLUB
2. HAS THE FINAL DECISION OVER ALL CLUB BUSINESS
3. RULES CLUB WITH IRON HAND
4. CAN OVERRULE ANY OF THE DECISIONS VOTED ON BY MEMBERSHIP

SECRETARY-TREASURER
1. KEEPS MINUTES ON ALL CLUB MEETINGS
2. COLLECTS DUES AND FINES
3. PAYS ALL CLUB BILLS AND BONDS FOR MEMBERS ARRESTED
4. RESPONSIBLE FOR NAMES AND PHONE NUMBERS ON CLUB ROSTER
5. KEEPS ALL BOOKS ON CLUB-RELATED BUSINESS

WAR LORD
1. CARRIES OUT ORDERS OF THE PRESIDENT WHEN CLUB GOES TO WAR WITH ANOTHER CLUB
2. IN MANY INSTANCES HAS THE CLUB'S ARSENAL

HONORARY MEMBER
1. USUALLY A MEMBER IN GOOD STANDING FOR A NUMBER OF YEARS AND RETIRES FROM CLUB
2. PAYS NO CLUB DUES
3. RETAINS CLUB COLORS
4. REQUIRED TO ATTEND CLUB FUNERALS

FEMALE ASSOCIATES

CLUB MEMBERSHIP
1. FEMALES OF LOOSE MORALS WHO MINGLE WITH THE CLUB
2. USED BY ANY MEMBER OF CLUB FOR SEXUAL DESIRES
3. CANNOT WEAR COLORS

PROPERTY OF
1. ASSOCIATE OF CLUB MEMBER IN GOOD STANDING
2. CAN WEAR COLORS WITH ROCKER
3. OTHER CLUB MEMBERS NOT ALLOWED TO TOUCH OR TRAIN

Profile

On December 12, 1981, several members of the Outlaws motorcycle gang in Chicago abducted at gunpoint an Asheville, North Carolina, prostitute Betty Darlene Callahan and her boyfriend, Tommy Forrester. After breaking down the couple's motel room door, members bound and gagged them and took them to an abandoned mine shaft, into which they threw Forrester. Callahan was given the choice of joining him or going to Chicago to work as a prostitute to pay off Forrester's $1500 drug debt. Two days later, she arrived in Chicago where she was sold into white slavery. After a 44-day ordeal in which she was forced to engage in sex orgies at gunpoint, Callahan escaped and called the FBI. On November 5, 1982, five defendants, four of whom were members of the Outlaws motorcycle gang, were found guilty on federal kidnapping charges. All defendants were found guilty of weapons charges and violations of the federal Mann Act, which prohibits the interstate transportation of women for immoral purposes.

The Pagans The Pagans originated in Prince George County, Maryland, in 1959. Since then the group has expanded their numbers over the years by merging with other smaller outlaw motorcycle gangs. With their increasing size, they organized a Mother Club, which consisted of the founding thirteen members. The Mother Club sets policies for the club and plans its business dealings. Mother Club members enjoy a special status, shown by wearing a black 13 on their colors. The organization consists of several hundred members located in as many as twenty-six chapters across the country, extending as far west as Texas and California.

In addition to controlling methamphetamine manufacture in the northeastern United States, the Pagans are involved in marijuana, cocaine, hashish, and the distribution of diverted pharmaceutical drugs. For years, leaders avoided detection and prosecution by insulating themselves from their crimes. So many lower-level members were placed between the leaders and the crimes they managed that criminal investigations were difficult to conduct. More recently, several prosecutions successfully used federal racketeering laws. Unlike other outlaw motorcycle gangs, the Pagans run chapters directly under the control of its mother group.

As is the case in many organized crime groups, Pagan members cannot quit. In Pennsylvania, Pagan member Ralph "Lucifer" Yannotta tried to quit the club and join the Outlaws, a competing motorcycle club, during a power struggle. He was taken to a quarry, injected with a hypodermic needle filled with sulfuric acid from a car battery, stabbed dozens of times, and shot in the head. Miraculously, he recovered, but his wife and brother-in-law were later murdered.

The Pagans, originating in the northeastern United States, is one of the top four outlaw motorcycle gangs in the nation.

The Bandidos

The youngest but fastest growing of the four major outlaw motorcycle gangs is the Bandidos. Concentrated in Texas, the gang is bureaucratically structured with four regional vice-presidents, one of whom also serves as president. As with the other biker gangs, its revenue is generated by drug trafficking, prostitution, extortion, fencing, and welfare and bank fraud. Established in 1966, the gang began trafficking heroin as early as 1975. Today, methamphetamine is the group's mainstay with cocaine as a close second.

Profile

The Pagans

Police estimate that the Pagans have roughly 500 members on the street. Their colors feature a depiction of the Norse fire god. MC means motorcycle club, and PFFP means Pagans Forever, Forever Pagans. Over the years, successful RICO investigations have pruned the organization and sent many Pagans to prison.

Profile

PRISON GANGS

Little is known about **prison gangs** compared to other types of organized crime, partly because they base their operation within the confines of the prison and operate in considerable secrecy to shield their members from detection by prison authorities. In addition, there is reluctance on the part of prison administration to acknowledge the existence of such gangs. Therefore, the current literature on prison gangs is sparse, although these groups have grown to such an extent that they have become organized networks. Because most of these groups now operate both inside and outside the prison walls, many are considered powerful organized crime organizations in their own right.

During the Bourbon rule of Naples in the 1860s, a secret organization, the Camorra, was formed in the Spanish prisons. It was a criminal organization from its inception. Soon the Camorra moved its influence and control from the prisons into the city of Naples itself, where it ultimately gained control of a large faction of the local government. Like other organized criminal organizations, the Camorra was a highly structured and disciplined organization consisting of a hierarchy (chain of command) and a set of rules with which members were obligated to abide. Concentrating primarily on crimes such as theft and extortion, the Camorra frequently committed contract murder for profit, which closely parallels U.S. prison gangs of the past 50 years.

The Camorra enjoyed much of its influence between 1880 and 1900 and was managed by the capo'ntrine (unit head) and the capo in testa (head in chief). In addition, it had a charter or constitution that set forth the rules and expected code of conduct for all members. The charter was enforced by soldiers who would ensure that all members would abide by the rules.

In the last 40 years, some groups in the state and federal prison systems throughout the United States have evolved into highly structured, violent criminal gangs. These gangs commit crimes both inside and outside prison walls, presenting many serious problems for law enforcement and correctional officers.

Inside the walls, the gangs engage in extortion, smuggling of weapons and drugs, assaults, murder, protection of weaker inmates, management of fraud schemes (such as credit card and telephone toll frauds), gambling, and bribery of prison staff.

These activities normally do not cease when prison gang members are released on parole. Rather, the opportunities for criminal activities multiply.

Assume that you are a rural county sheriff who has discovered a small but organized prostitution ring operating in the county. With the public clamoring for results, how would you go about dealing with this problem?

On the outside, many prison gang members maintain their gang membership and loyalty, but expand their activities into narcotics and weapons trafficking, intimidation and murder of witnesses to crimes, policing corrections officers, contract killings, armed robberies, burglaries, rapes, extortion, blackmail, fraud, and cargo thefts. They also smuggle weapons, explosives, and narcotics into the prison for fellow gang members.

The advent of prison gangs can be traced to Washington State in 1950, with unrelated gangs developing in California in 1957 and Illinois in 1969. From these three bases, the gangs began to form in other nearby state prison systems in the 1970s, including Arizona, New Mexico, Texas, Michigan, Wisconsin, Kentucky, Missouri, and Pennsylvania. Gangs, both national and local, have now been reported in thirty-two state prison systems and in the federal prison system.

Prison officials throughout the nation have identified 114 gangs with a membership ranging between 13,000 and 15,000. While these gang members constituted only a small percentage of the overall 883,000 male inmates in state and federal prisons at the end of 1992, prison administrators say gang members were responsible for more than 50 percent of their problems with inmates. An example is the April 1993 eleven-day siege at the southern Ohio correctional facility in Lucasville, in which over 400 inmates held eight officers hostage, murdered one officer and nine inmates, and destroyed a cellblock by the time the standoff was negotiated to a peaceful conclusion. One of the two major groups leading the siege was the Aryan Brotherhood, a nationwide white supremist prison gang.

Prison gangs spread from one state to another by interstate transfers of inmate gang members or by rearrests of gang members in other jurisdictions. In some states, such as California, Arizona, Illinois, New Mexico, and Pennsylvania, there are several prison gangs with hundreds of members; in other states, particularly in the Southeast, New England, and the upper Rocky Mountain states, the gangs have recently taken root.

In 1986, the President's Commission on Organized Crime (1986b) issued a report that studied 114 gangs that prison officials identified as existing then, and concluded that 5 of the gangs appeared to meet the criteria for being an organized crime group.

1. *Continuity:* The criminal group carries out its purpose over a period of time and is able to survive changes in its leadership.
2. *Structure:* The criminal group is structured as a collective of hierarchically arranged independent offices devoted to a particular function. It can be either highly structured, like La Cosa Nostra, or more fluidly structured, like the Colombian drug-trafficking organizations. But no matter the structure, the group has ranks based on power and authority.

3. *Membership:* It is restricted and based on a common trait, such as ethnicity, race, criminal background, or common interest. All the groups demand absolute loyalty. Many require the potential recruits to murder on demand to prove their worthiness. In most organizations, membership is for life.

4. *Criminality:* The group pursues profits in its specialty areas. Crime is its reason for existence.

5. *Violence:* Violence and the threat of violence are an integral part of the organized crime group.

6. *Power and profit:* since the group's members work for the group's power and ultimate profit, group members realize that they must exhibit power over others. This results in political and police corruption and the use of violence against anyone who threatens the power of the group.

Nature of Prison Gangs

Some prison gangs are highly structured with a clear defined hierarchy, while others are more loosely organized. The major prison gangs have organizational charts with the gang leader at the top and associates or sympathizers at the bottom. Since the gang members are housed throughout the various institutions of the state Department of Corrections, organizational structures generally resemble those of the state government agency with several regional offices. For example, the Mexican Mafia, one of the nation's five major prison gangs, has the following structure: president (systemwide), vice-president (systemwide), generals (regional level), lieutenants (unit level), sergeants (unit level), soldiers, associates, and sympathizers (Camp and Camp, 1985).

To rise to the top of the prison gang hierarchy, a member must demonstrate physical prowess, commit violent acts, show leadership qualities, and gain seniority by serving for specific periods of time in the lower ranks. Leaders garner emotional support from followers by the deference paid to them, both in respect and in tribute.

The United States Bureau of Prisons in 1999 estimated that 130 gangs operate prison systems nationwide. The other gangs are more personal, operating as a family business. Some gangs prefer strong individual leaders, while others manage their operations with a leadership council. Most prison gangs have written rules, constitutions, bylaws, and an oath of allegiance. Some gangs have very structured rules, while others get by more on the whims of the leaders.

How does an inmate new to the prison system join one of the gangs? In most cases, his choice of gangs is determined by his race or ethnicity, since the gangs are rarely integrated along racial and ethnic lines (an exception is the powerful Consolidated Crip Organization, which has some Hispanics in the majority black southern California gang). The U.S. Department of Justice study (1985), in its survey of the 33 prison systems with gangs, found four types of admission requirements that gang candidates must meet:

1. Membership is based first on race or ethnicity and geography and usually is connected with racial superiority beliefs; for example, the Aryan Brotherhood nationwide is based on white supremist beliefs.

2. Prior association or affiliation with members in a location close to home; for example, the El Rukins in the Illinois prison system are a Chicago-based street gang.
3. Sharing of strong political and/or religious beliefs; for example, the Black Guerilla Family, a major California prison gang developed in 1966 from the Black Panthers and the Black Liberation Army, follows Maoist political beliefs.
4. Sharing of the motorcycle life-style; for example, the Avengers of the West Virginia State prison system and the Pagans of the Virginia and Maryland prison systems are outlaw motorcycle gangs.

New inmates can apply to join gangs in which they have past associations with current gang members or by stating that they accept the gang's values. In some gangs, however, membership is limited strictly to those who belong to the same street gang on the outside.

While some gangs use nonviolent initiation of new members, the *bloody entrance* is more common: candidates are required to commit a violent act against another inmate or a prison staff member. The five major national gangs all require murder or the drawing of blood as a prerequisite for membership.

When street gang members enter prison, they generally lose the power and autonomy they had in their communities and instead must succumb to the power of the prison gangs. As newcomers to the prison, they are sought after as recruits for the gangs, but when they take membership in the prison gang, they must abandon their previous rank in the street gang. Upon release, these prison gang members maintain their allegiance to the prison gang, but are usually able to exert influence over their old street gang, especially over the younger members. An exception to this rule are the Juartios, a violent street gang that originated in Mexico and now has a power base in Albuquerque; they keep their street gang name and rank while incarcerated.

Once initiated into a prison gang, it is not easy for a member to get out. Two-thirds of the gangs operate on the principle of **blood in, blood out,** believing that membership is for life. Leaving the gang is considered to be an active betrayal; its consequence can be harsh. In reality, though, some prison gang members mature behind bars or become informants and attempt to leave the gang when they are released. This often means moving to a new area to begin life over again far away from all past associates. Due to parole requirements in most jurisdictions, however, the majority of prison gang members return to their home communities. Since most of them are career criminals, they become a problem once again for the police.

Definition of a Prison Gang

A prison gang is an organization that operates within the prison system as a self-perpetuating, criminally oriented entity consisting of a select group of inmates who have established an organized chain of command and are governed by an established code of conduct. The prison gang usually operates in secrecy, and its goal is to conduct gang activities by controlling its prison environment through intimidation and violence directed toward nonmembers.

Recruitment   Firsthand information on the recruitment process practiced by prison gangs is sketchy, but prison officials believe many gangs have adopted a blood-in, blood-out policy by which prospective members are not considered for membership unless they first spill the blood of another inmate or a prison staff member. This ensures existing gang members that the recruit is not an undercover law enforcement officer and that the initiate possesses the forceful personality necessary to carry out the mission of the organization.

It is believed that once a member is accepted into the organization, he may not leave the gang without his own blood being spilled, so once a member, always a member. Relationships between gangs in prison and their street gang counterparts on the outside have been documented. For example, street gang members in Chicago commonly band together in the state prison system. New inmates who are part of a street gang are immediately accepted as members with no questions asked. Other examples are those of outlaw motorcycle gang members, who align in prison with groups such as the Aryan Brotherhood and gangs such as the Crips and who are accepted into the BGF (Black Guerilla Family) prison gang.

Other factors that seem to govern the selection process for prison gang membership include the ethnic background of the recruit and geography (the recruit's home turf). Because of racial considerations that underlie much of a prison gang's basic philosophies, a prospective member's race is one of the first recruitment variables to be considered by the gang. Other considerations include the following:

- The sharing of strong beliefs: political, religious, and so on
- The sharing of a particular life-style (e.g., gang members who ride motorcycles)
- Being a stand-up convict (tough) or one who has a physically imposing appearance and a propensity toward violence

In return for membership and status in the gang, the recruit enjoys the power, prestige, influence, and protection that the gang offers. Once in the gang, a member has the opportunity to move up through the ranks based on his physical and mental abilities, loyalty, and contributions to the organization, as well as on violent acts, physical stature, leadership qualities, and length of gang membership. Once a person is identified as a possible candidate for recruitment, the gang may require him to perform any number of initiation acts. The initiation varies from gang to gang, but in most cases requires the prospective member to perform a violent act against either another inmate or a correctional officer to prove his worthiness. Such initiation requirements serve two distinct purposes that benefit the gang: to take care of the gang's business and to provide the gang an opportunity to see the potential member in action so that abilities can be judged by existing members.

Some experts believe that some acts of prison violence are performed by inmates who wish to attract the attention of gangs so that the gang can consider the inmate for membership. For this reason and the fact that many inmates have a strong propensity for violence, prison officials face difficulties in determining with certainty the motive behind a specific violent act. Because gang rules prohibit leaving the gang, those who try are killed.

In reality, however, gang members have left prison without facing this harsh consequence. Others have chosen to leave the gang while still in prison, but seek safety in a protective custody unit. In other cases, some gang members holding leadership roles have even offered to exchange gang information for favorable treatment from prison officials. These *rollovers* frequently roam freely within the prison population by virtue of the status they have achieved in the leadership of the gang.

Prison Gang Structure

Prison gangs are usually controlled by an established system of leadership. In paramilitary fashion, many of these more sophisticated groups maintain control through an established chain of command. The hierarchy is established to better facilitate orders from the leader and to help insulate management from outside detection. Leadership is usually invested in a single strong leader, but can be a committee or council.

The tenure of a gang leader may be relatively short due to parole, transfers between prisons, and general dissatisfaction with a particular leader's performance. However, according to a 1983 U.S. Bureau of Prisons report, the longest time period that a prison gang leader was in power was between ten and fifteen years. Jeff Fort, mentioned previously, headed the Chicago-based prison gang, the El Rukins. Two Iowa-based groups, the Prison Motorcycle Brotherhood and the Vice Lords, kept their leaders for eleven years. The Aryan Warriors of Nevada and the Mexican Mafia of Arizona had single leaders for approximately nine years. A gang leader is usually succeeded by a member who is a strong personality within the gang or is elected democratically through an organization meeting.

Mexican Mafia

The oldest prison gang in the United States is the Mexican Mafia (EME), which originally consisted of Mexican American youth gang members who first organized in 1957 at the Deuel Vocational Institute in Tracy, California. The gang adopted its name by imitating the La Cosa Nostra. Its members came from the barrios of East Los Angeles, and after initially organizing to protect gang members, membership grew. The EME slowly gained control over drug trafficking, homosexual prostitution, debt collection (extortion), and gambling. Most of their criminal activities focused on victimizing African American and Caucasian inmates, while leaving Mexican prisoners alone. The EME's command structure is very similar to that of La Cosa Nostra as the government portrays it. For example, there are generals or godfathers who direct operations of the organization and supervise captains, lieutenants, and soldiers (soldados).

To be considered for membership, an inmate must be sponsored by an existing member who knows the prospect's abilities and talents. As is true for most prison gangs, a requirement for membership is for prospects to murder or draw blood. Once this preliminary act is completed, current members must vote for final approval. An indoctrination creed is commonly used by many Mexican American prison gangs.

Over the years the EME recruited some of the most dangerous and violent Mexican inmates. Penal institutions responded by transferring gang members from one institution to another, which served to expand the membership of the gang from the California prison system to the federal prison system.

The 1967 stabbing death of a Mexican American inmate at San Quentin was recorded as one of the first killings in the group. It resulted from a directive issued by leadership of the EME. The deceased allegedly gave law enforcement officers information about the gang's drug-trafficking activities. This killing of a brother Mexican American initially created much unrest throughout the prison population, but was generally thought to be justified under the circumstances. Shortly after this incident, other Mexican American inmates throughout California's prison system began forming another group to defend themselves against the violence-prone EME.

The new group, sometimes referred to as valley or northern Mexican Americans, adopted the name Nuestra Familia (NF), meaning "our family." In 1968 the EME assaulted two NF members in a disagreement over a pair of shoes. Resulting from this incident, several members of the NF ambushed some EME members in a cell block at San Quentin, which resulted in seventeen stabbings (one fatal). Since the 1968 incident, the EME has been in an all-out war with the NF, which as of 1978 had resulted in the murders of over thirty prisoners. Aligning with the EME against the NF is the white supremist group, the Aryan Brotherhood, which assists the EME in conducting various criminal activities, such as drug trafficking, robberies, and contract killings, both inside and outside prison walls. Today, the gangs have spread to at least seven other states, and although it is unclear how many members they have, it has been estimated that its numbers approach 600.

One goal of the EME, is to control drug trafficking in the areas of the country where EME influence is established, such as southern California. One method for achieving this is to identify a particular dealer operating in a neighborhood who is also known to an EME member. The member simply goes to the area, contacts the dealer, and advises him that from that point on he will be conducting business with the EME. If the dealer resists, he will be robbed and severely assaulted. If he then shows an unwillingness to cooperate, he will be killed and his drug business will be taken over by the EME. The creed of the Mexican Mafia (M-M) is "A member is to share all and everything."

Nuestra Familia   For some time, Nuestra Familia (NF), established in California's Soledad Prison in 1967, was smaller than its rival foe, the EME. During its early years the NF slowly gained an identity within the prison system by selling protection to other inmates who were fearful of the EME. By 1975 the NF had begun to establish *regiments* outside the prison system, using Fresno, California, as a national headquarters. Initially, NF membership was limited to Latin Americans, but with the current war with the EME, membership was extended to those of other ethnic origins, including Native Americans and, in some cases, whites. Additionally, the NF aligned with the Black Guerrilla Family in its war with the EME. The organizational abilities of the NF have always been superior to those of the EME. The gang has a constitution, which dictates that membership is for life and states that the organization comes before any member. In addition to the organization's constitution, the NF creed must be closely followed by each member.

NF membership is estimated at 750 to 800, with the organizational leadership consisting of a general with supreme power over all gang business. The NF headquarters is usually considered to be the prison in which the general is located, and directives are given from that location. The structure also consists of captains (a limited number), lieutenants (usually an unlimited number), and soldiers (soldados), as with the EME. The lieutenants generally

Indoctrination of Chicano Wards Known as Movidas

1. Stick with the raza (the gang), as you are Chicano.
2. Do not smoke or drink or eat after a white or black boy.
3. Do not ask the white or black boy for anything.
4. If you need something, ask a vato (a brother); if he has it, he will give it to you.
5. If you have food and frajos, you always share it with the rest of the vatos.
6. If you have a problem with another Chicano, this is what you do: You have a meeting with all the raza. If both of you want to box, take it in the blind and have someone keep an eye so you both don't get caught.
7. If a white or black boy starts talking shit to one of you, always fuck that puto up. But not right then and there. Just walk away, and get him later. This way you will not get busted. Make sure that you have a vato watching for you.
8. Always stay clean and have your clothes ironed. If a vato wants to walk around like a trampa, he has nothing to do with the rest of the raza.
9. If you have a problem, make sure that you have a meeting right away. This way, we could take a vote on what should be done about the problem.
10. Do not hang around whites or blacks. Talk to them once in a while, but don't make it a habit. If it's business, it's okay to talk to them as long as you want.

The Nuestra Familia Creed

- Life has one guarantee; you will always have me.
- You lead and I will follow.
- If I fall behind, you push me.
- If I betray you, kill me.
- I'll lead and you follow.
- If you fall behind, I'll push you.
- If you betray me, I'll kill you.

are responsibile for having available at least two weapons for each soldier in his regiment and for maintaining records of the names and addresses of all NF enemies.

Rank in the NF is usually achieved by the number of killings or hits the person commits. For example, a hit without a kill earns a member the title of warrior. A member earns a star for each killing; achieving the rank of lieutenant requires at least three stars. Because the NF maintains a ten-most-wanted list, any member killing one of the most wanted automatically earns the rank of lieutenant. Promotion to the rank of captain requires at least five stars and the assessment that the member has leadership ability.

Nuestra Familia's outside criminal activity is a protection racket directed toward owners of small businesses. It consists of harassing local businesspeople through vandalism, theft, and robbery and offering them protection against future acts. Usually, adolescent members of the NF are involved in this activity because the NF realizes that their treatment by the legal system will not be as harsh as it is on adults. In addition, kids are more impressionable and loyal to the gang.

Texas Syndicate

Since its 1974 emergence as a violent prison gang in Folsom Prison, the Texas Syndicate (ETsE) has gained considerable status within the prison system as one of the most violent of all gangs. ETsE is composed of Mexican American inmates originally from the El Paso and San Antonio areas.

Like the other prison gangs discussed in this chapter, ETsE membership is difficult to estimate but is thought to be nearly 175 in the state of Texas. Membership requirements are more secretive than for the other groups, but it is thought that, as with other gangs, membership is for life, and members must answer to an established chain of command. According to official sources within the Texas prison system, the ETsE has aligned with the Aryan Brotherhood in that state. The Texas Syndicate creed simply states, "Back your fellow Texas Syndicate member's play." Because of its growing numbers, ETsE members have begun criminal activities outside the prison walls in California, Texas, and other states. Like the EME and NF, the ETsE is involved in drug trafficking, assaults, extortion, and contract murder within the prison system.

The Mexikanemi

The Mexikanemi (also known as the Texas Mexican Mafia) was established in 1984. Its name and symbols cause confusion with the Mexican Mafia. As the largest gang in the Texas prison system, it is also emerging in the federal system as well and has been known to kill both outside and inside prison. The Mexikanemi fights with the Mexican Mafia and the Texas Syndicate, although it has been said that the Mexikanemi and the Texas Syndicate are aligning themselves against the Mexican Mafia. The Mexikanemi has established leadership positions of president, vice-president, regional generals, lieutenants, sergeants, and soldiers. The ranking positions are elected by the group and are based on leadership skills. Members keep their positions unless they are reassigned to a new prison. The Mexikanemi has a twelve-part constitution. For example, part five says that the sponsoring member is responsible for the person he sponsors; if necessary, a new person may be eliminated by his sponsor (Fleisher and Decker 2001).

The Nortenos and the Surenos are new Chicacano gangs in California, along with New Structure and Border Brothers. The origins and alliances of these groups are unclear; however, the Border Brothers are comprised of Spanish-speaking Mexican American inmates and tend to remain solitary. Prison officials report that the Border Brothers seem to be gaining membership and control as more Mexican American inmates are convicted and imprisoned.

The Crips and Bloods, traditional Los Angeles street gangs, are gaining strength in the prisons, as are the 415s, a group from the San Francisco area (415 is a San Francisco area code). The Federal Bureau of Prisons sites 14 other disruptive groups within the federal prison system that have been documented as of 1995, including the Texas Mafia, the Bulldogs, and the Dirty White Boys (Fleisher and Decker 2001).

Aryan Brotherhood

The Aryan Brotherhood (AB) is a motorcycle-oriented, white supremist group that began in the 1960s as the Diamond Tooth Gang at San Quentin Prison in California. It focuses on aggression against African American inmates. Members were easily distinguished by a piece of glass embedded in a front tooth. The gang later adopted the name Bluebird Gang, and each member was accordingly tattooed with a bluebird on his neck. Today the AB, which usually consists of members of outlaw motorcycle gangs, has prison-based branches around the country, but is most prominent in state prisions in California, Wisconsin, Arizona, and Idaho and throughout the federal prison system. The AB has about 500 members.

Criminal activity practiced by the AB is similar to that of other gangs and includes extortion of both inmates and their families outside prison, as well as robbery, protection schemes, drug trafficking, and contract murder. Like the NF and EME, a command hierarchy within the organization consists of a commission and a governing council. Members of the AB are promoted through the ranks by committing acts of violence. Other similarities with other prison gangs include establishment of a creed that must be sworn to at the time of initiation and subsequently adhered to by all members.

The AB has joined the EME in its war against the NF and the BGF. Becoming an AB member is somewhat difficult, because prospective members must be recommended by existing members who are in good standing with the organization. If even one member votes not to accept, the prospect is denied admission to the gang, a practice also used by many outlaw motorcycle gangs. Once admitted to the gang, membership is for life, and those who choose to leave it are usually killed. A tattoo of the organization's logo worn by each member is considered a prized possession. Tattoos of expelled members are removed by gang members, who cut or iron them off.

Black Guerilla Family

The late George Jackson, a former member of the Black Panther Party, founded the Black Guerrilla Family (BGF) in San Quentin in 1966. Its goal is the cultural unity and protection of African American inmates. It is a more politically motivated group than most other prison gangs and is closely aligned with the Black Liberation Army (BLA). The BGF has a chain of command that includes a chairman or supreme commander, central committee, field generals, captains of security, captains of arms, captains of squads, lieutenants, and soldiers. New recruits for the organization are frequently members of African American street gangs.

In fact, the youth street gang known as the Crips, with an estimated membership of 60,000, is closely aligned with the BGF, and it is thought that most Crips become automatic BGF members once they enter the prison system. A death oath commitment is required of new members, who frequently join the gang to share its criminal profits. Since the murder of George Jackson by prison officials, the BGF has been successful in recruiting

Rules of the Aryan Brotherhood

1. After reading these rules and you decide you would like to be in the AB and you are voted on and accepted: THERE IS ONLY ONE WAY OUT, THAT IS DEATH.

2. Once you enter into the AB, do not try to backslide in any way! You are not being given a free ride through this prison. If you do enter with these thoughts and you are found out, IT WILL MEAN YOUR DEATH!

3. After you are sworn into the AB, you will be advised of the social structure of the AB and will be expected to recognize it and abide with its decisions and orders!

4. The AB is exactly what it says, "A Brotherhood." When you see a brother involved in ANY sort of trouble or hassle, you go to his side. You may not be on the best of terms with the man, but he is your brother and will be treated as such. So back him! He is going to do the same thing for you when you need him.

5. A brother can sometimes be wrong. But in front of any nonbrother, he's right! Afterward, when you are alone, he can be dealt with, but NEVER in front of a nonbrother.

6. You will not bullshit or play games with a brother in front of a nonbrother so that everyone around you knows that the respect is there.

7. We take care of our own! We don't have time for the games that nonbrothers are involved in! You protect your brother, his property, and the interest of the AB as it were your own! Your brother will be doing the same for you.

8. If you are told to do something, there is a reason for you being told to do it. So do it!

9. You are in the AB for life! If you hit the streets and come back, you're still in it!! You must be willing to do for your brother what you want him to be doing for you! No matter where you are!!!

10. After a certain length of time it will be necessary to make a donation to a bank account in case any brother is placed on the adjustment center. A brother is to be taken care of to the fullest of the AB capacity!!! The donations will be reasonable.

11. The purpose of the AB is to bring back the respect that is long overdue in coming to this prison to the white race! AT ALL COST!!!

WE WILL STRIVE TO MAINTAIN THAT RESPECT.

The Constitution of the Texas Aryan Brotherhood

Section I: Title

The Texas Aryan Brotherhood is an independent organization of, by, and for Aryan Brothers of Texas. It is not affiliated with any other group or organization. Our organization is a White Supremacy group: no pretense is or will be made to the contrary.

Section II: Solidarity

1. The Texas Aryan Brothers are solidarity (brotherhood) among its members. Solidarity is our backbone; nothing is more paramount to the organization.

2. Each member is a mirror of his brother. Your actions reflect on all brothers, and breach of the brotherhood is a serious matter which will be handled as such.

3. Those brothers chosen for the organization are life term members, death being the only termination of membership.

4. Upon release from the TDC (Texas Deptartment of Corrections), a member will contact an incarcerated member to notify the organization of his place of residence. The member notified will contact a member of the steering committee, who will take note of the place of residence.

5. Upon release from the TDC, a member will contact a free-world member and, after taking note of each other's place of residence, will always maintain regular contact with each other.

6. Newly released members will have a six (6)-month grace period after they are released from the TDC or halfway house. The grace period will be used to readjust to the free world. After the six-month period the brother will establish and maintain regular contact with incarcerated members by whatever

means are possible. Incarcerated members for contact will be selected by the steering committee or by a committee member.

7. All incarcerated and free-world members will give each other full support and will follow their designated chains of command regardless of their place of residence.

Section III: Steering Committee

1. Will consist of five (5) charter members of the organization who will guide the organization in its policy making, chains of command, etc.

2. The members of the steering committee are the highest-ranking members of the organization and will be known only to the membership.

Section IV: Chairman

1. Each TDC unit will have one chairman, with the rank of captain, and one vice-chairman, with the rank of lieutenant, elected by the membership of that unit or appointed by the steering committee member who presides over that unit if election is not appropriate.

2. The captain is responsible for the family of his unit; the lieutenant is responsible for enforcing the captain's decisions. Each captain will maintain regular contact with his designated steering committee member, who will guide the unit in accordance with our policies.

Source: Missouri State Penitentiary

disenchanted members of other radical black organizations. California prison authorities assert that some BLA members who have been sent to prison have immediately become high-ranking officials of the BGF.

A strict code of discipline is enforced in the group. It consists of the following:

- The individual is subordinate to the family.
- The minority is subordinate to the majority.
- The lower level is subordinate to the higher level.
- The entire membership is subordinate to the central committee.

BGF members clash with members of the EME and the AB, but have occasionally worked with the NF. The goal of the organization is the cultural unity and protection of black inmates.

Gang Members in the Community

Members of prison gangs are generally 19 to 40 years old, highly mobile, and usually career criminals. For example, a 1990 study of New Mexico prison gangs by the Governor's Organized Crime Prevention Commission (1990) found that 58 percent of the 28 suspected prison gang members were classified as habitual criminals who committed multiple street crimes in short time frames.

Seeking to prove that most prison gang members are career criminals, the California Department of Justice conducted (1986) a study in 1984 that reviewed the recidivism patterns of 250 gang members following their release from prison. The gang members were randomly selected from the Aryan Brotherhood, Mexican Mafia, La Nuestra Familia, and the Black Guerilla Family, the largest prison gangs at that time. The review found the following:

1. During the three-year review period, 195 of the 250 gang members were rearrested.

2. After release, 14 of the 195 gang members were rearrested in one month; 179 were rearrested within the first year.

3. Of the 195 gang members rearrested during the three-year review period, 49 were rearrested once; 51 twice, 25 three or four more times, and 70 were returned to prison.
4. The repeated arrests of the 195 prison gang members included 65 misdemeanor violations and 340 felony arrests.
5. Included in the felony arrests were 24 for murder, 57 for robbery, 66 for burglary, 31 for drug offenses and 28 for assault with a deadly weapon.

Tie-ins between prison gangs and street gangs are becoming more common, particularly as arrests and incarceration due to intensified antidrug enforcement sends more street gang members into the prisons. As the New Mexico Governor's Organized Crime Prevention Commission discussed in its 1990 report, law enforcement intelligence analysis nationwide has found that prison gangs are exerting a greater influence on youth gangs in the communities. "Prison gangs' influence is increasing and is so powerful that many youth gang members expect to be in a particular prison gang," the commission stated. "The ongoing association of prison gang members with street gangs creates greater prison gang influence on younger youth gang members."

These influence patterns developed because parole policies often send prison gang members back to their communities, where many of them were once homeboy street gang members. Once back on their home turf, they are idolized by the younger street gang members, who look upon them as powerful, strong, experienced leaders. Taking advantage of the newfound idol status is relatively easy for the paroled prison gang members to do; they begin to use prison gang members to run drugs, commit burglaries and robberies, and sometimes kill for the prison gang. By committing crimes for the powerful prison gangsters, the youth gang members themselves gain increased prestige on the street and are treated with the same respect shown to the prisoner gangster. Thus, both sides profit from the relationship.

Of the 33 correctional agencies with prison gangs participating in the U.S. Department of Justice (1986) survey, 24 agencies reported that all or some of the gangs in their jurisdictions have counterpart gangs on the streets. These agencies are the state prison systems of Arizona, Arkansas, California, Connecticut, Florida, Georgia, Illinois, Iowa, Kentucky, Maine, Maryland, Massachusetts, Michigan, Minnesota, Missouri, Nevada, North Carolina, Ohio, Oklahoma, Pennsylvania, Utah, Washington, West Virginia, Wisconsin, and the federal prison system. While New Mexico did not participate in the Justice Department study, it now reports that many of its prison gangs have active street gang counterparts.

Studies have shown that prison gangs sometimes use the prison as the base of operations for crimes committed within communities. The Federal Bureau of Prisons reports evidence of this for its entire prison system, and state systems in Massachusetts, Pennsylvania, West Virginia, Kentucky, Georgia, Florida, Arkansas, Missouri, Iowa, Minnesota, Texas, Arizona, Nevada, and California also report prison-based gang leadership for crimes on the streets.

In addition to the ordinary crimes, there is recent evidence from various parts of the nation indicating that white supremist prison gang members, such as the Aryan Brotherhood, are in some instances joining forces with neo-Nazi and skinhead extremist and terrorist groups. These connections exist both behind the walls and on the streets.

Discussions of organized crime in the United States tend to focus almost exclusively on the activities of urban crime groups, with a particularly heavy emphasis on organized crime groups operating in New York and Chicago. Despite the urban slant of the scholarly and popular literature on organized crime, it is abundantly clear that criminal enterprises also operate in rural areas of the United States. Aside from the occasional reference to the **Dixie Mafia,** these rural criminal enterprises have escaped serious inquiry (Hunter 1983; Schmidt 1984; Abadinsky 1986: 210).

Rural organized crime, when discussed at all, is usually presented in terms of disorganized bands of fences, con men, strip-joint owners, and auto thieves. Occasionally, reference is made to the Dixie Mafia as a typical rural organized crime group (Hunter 1983; St. George 1991). This group is described as "a confederation of crooks who helped each other steal, murder, and swindle in towns and cities across the South" (St. George 1991). A member of the Florida Department of Law Enforcement is quoted as saying of the Dixie Mafia: "They remind me of Jesse James, cowboys riding up and down the roads looking for someone to steal from or kill" (St. George 1991). So while their urban brethren are depicted as suave, highly organized, intelligent, and cunning illicit businessmen in silk suits and shoes of fine Italian leather, rural organized criminals are presented as beer-guzzling rednecks, moving to and fro from stockcar races to strip joints, stealing cars, swindling widows, and murdering innocent victims or each other. The paucity of research has made it difficult to evaluate the utility of this view of rural organized criminals.

It is clear, however, that rural areas have drug dealers, bootleggers, prostitutes, gamblers, loan-sharks, auto thieves, and fences. These criminals provide illicit goods and services on a continual basis and do so with the accommodation of law enforcement. While this activity in rural settings has escaped much of the attention given its urban counterpart, it is nonetheless real and is becoming more public. Almost two dozen sheriffs and their deputies in rural counties of several southern states were charged with involvement in drug trafficking (Shenon 1988). In 1989 the sheriff of Henry County, Georgia, was sentenced to a thirty-five-year prison term for assisting drug smugglers. In Dawson County, Georgia, the sheriff was sentenced to thirty years for providing protection to drug smugglers (Coppola 1989). In 1988, the sheriff of Morgan County, Kentucky, along with the county judge and several local businessmen, was convicted on charges of protecting drug dealers and cocaine distributors (*Licking Valley Courier* 1989). In August 1991, the sheriffs of Wolfe, Lee, and Owsley counties (all in Kentucky), a deputy sheriff, and a police chief were convicted of bribery, extortion, and conspiracy to distribute cocaine and marijuana (Estep 1991). In 1991, the Newton County, Mississippi, sheriff pleaded guilty to charges that he failed to perform his duties, possessed gambling tables, and accepted bribes to protect bootlegging operations (Kelley 1989). While most of these revelations involve drug trafficking, the fact is that rural corruption is not new. It has a long, if unappreciated, history.

Studies of rural organized crime groups (Potter et al. 1990; Davis and Potter 1991; Potter and Gaines 1992) indicate that criminal enterprise can be classed in two major categories: (1) wholesale production and supply and (2) retail sales and service. The most profitable aspect of the crime industry is wholesale production and supply, including the growing and processing of high-grade marijuana crops and the transshipment of cocaine. The retail crime industry involves the provision of illicit goods to local residents and to transient customers and includes the illegal sale of liquor and drugs, prostitution services, and gambling.

The Wholesale Market

Much concern has been expressed about the growth of the wholesale drug market in rural areas and the criminal organizations that have been created to feed that market. Although no systematic and reliable accounting measure is available, there is widespread intersubjective agreement that the marijuana industry is the mainstay of many rural counties' farming economies. The attractiveness of cultivating marijuana is easy to understand; first and most obviously, it is a highly profitable crop. Two high-grade marijuana plants can earn as much money as an entire corn, soybean, or tobacco crop for the average farmer. Second, marijuana is one of the few crops that flourishes in poor agricultural conditions. Where the land is mountainous, rough, rocky, and virtually impossible to farm, only hardscrabble farming is possible, meaning small plots of vegetables, corn, or tobacco requiring intensive labor and care and yielding little profit. On the other hand, the same terrain is perfect for marijuana, which can be grown in small plots of about 60 square feet at a high profit. Rather than impeding the marijuana industry, the rugged terrain is a boon to the industry. It is easy to conceal marijuana plots "up the holler," intermingled with low mountain brush growth and covered by a high tree canopy. A marijuana garden of 60 square feet, if properly tended, will yield about $60,000 worth of high-grade marijuana.

The rural marijuana industry works very much like a truck farmers' cooperative. Buyers contract in advance with a grower for his or her crop and pick up the marijuana after processing, sometimes in tractor trailer-size loads. Buyers also can come to the county during the three harvests and visit the growers, evaluating their product and bidding for it in the same manner that tobacco companies bid for tobacco crops.

Marijuana is not the only drug-related wholesale business in rural markets, however. Moving cocaine has also become big business in rural areas. The most common method of moving cocaine is to bring a load to remote and temporary landing strips on light aircraft. The cocaine is then shipped by car or truck to its ultimate destination.

In many rural counties, the movement of cocaine depends on certain indigenous skills and knowledge in the local population. Years ago during Prohibition, local youth in Kentucky, for example, commonly ran moonshine liquor from rural areas to the major cities of the Midwest and South. Routes used invariably were small back roads (many of which are hardly roads at all) that stayed clear of major highways and population centers. These backwoods routes are still in operation. Today's cocaine runners are the descendants of the moonshine runners of a half-century ago. Many of them use the same combination of old logging roads, utility service roads, and "cow paths" to avoid major highways or cities and towns. One irony of this cocaine transport system is that the federal government has made money available to the states for setting up interdiction points along the major interstate highways. Although some cocaine is moved that way, most shipments never see a major highway. Although stopping Porsches with Florida plates could net a pound or two of cocaine every week or two, huge quantities likely are being moved by good-old country boys far from the prying eyes of state police.

The retail market in illicit goods and services in rural areas revolves around the basic human desires for liquor, sex, and gambling (drugs are available, but usually only as an ancillary service). Many rural areas have maintained liquor prohibition as an artifact of America's experiment with the Volstead Act at 1919–1932 (Davis and Potter 1991). The retail liquor trade takes three basic forms. First, individual entrepreneurs make a weekly run to a wet city, buy a truckload of liquor, and return to sell it to their friends and neighbors, exacting a considerable fee for the risks they are taking.

Second, but far more common, local residents have established illegal liquor stores in dry areas, invariably in private residences, retail businesses, or gas stations. Many of the private residences actually have installed circular driveways to facilitate a drive-in trade to keep their customers moving. These establishments buy liquor in quantity every week from legal dealers in the wet areas, usually at a prearranged price that benefits both the seller and buyer.

Liquor is also available by the drink in illegal roadhouses operating in rural areas. Most of these roadhouses are small establishments in which a single room in a house is set aside for drinking. These establishments commonly house a very small gambling operation and several prostitutes. Such places are known to the locals as **two-holers**. Occasionally, a few large roadhouses in rural areas rival the nightclubs in the wet cities. These establishments are often converted barns, warehouses, or old farmhouses. They feature a full-service bar, live bands, dancing, strippers, prostitutes, and casino-style gambling.

Gambling occurs in three formats in the rural areas. The most common is simply illegal machines located wherever a tourist, trucker, or other transient might stop. The second venue is a game room, which has pool tables, pinball games, and the like. The roadhouses described earlier also offer gambling. Most games feature $2 and $5 dollar bets, and the volume of business is brisk. At the larger roadhouses, tables are often reserved in advance for high-stakes games that go as high as $100 minimum bets in craps and blackjack. Many roadhouses will gladly make available a table, a dealer, refreshments, and hostesses for high-stakes poker games for a charge of 5 percent a pot.

Prostitution is a surprisingly common occupation for young women in very conservative rural counties often populated by dozens of fundamentalist Christian churches. These women work truck stops, restaurants, and local tanning salons, which are often fronts for prostitution, and at the roadhouses. The highway trade is the least sophisticated and is the rural equivalent of streetwalking in a major urban area. The tanning salon trade is very much like the massage parlor trade in major cities. Customers come in and pay for a tanning session, during which they are assisted by an employee. A massage might be suggested, or the customer might inquire about other services. Prices in these establishments range from $40 to $120 dollars, depending on the service requested. Prostitutes in roadhouses provide varied services. In the

Critical Thinking Project

Compare this chapter with theories of organized crime discussed in Chapter 2. Discuss in what ways society can best prepare for the emergence of future organized crime organizations.

small two-holers, the service is crude and the marketing strategy direct. Customers know why the women are present and little attention is paid to preliminaries or ambience. In the large roadhouses, however, the prostitutes are interesting crosses between urban America's B-girls and call girls. They are often paid a commission for the number of drinks they can get the customer to buy.

CHARACTERISTICS OF RURAL ORGANIZED CRIME GROUPS

The overwhelming majority of rural criminal enterprises involve small numbers of participants. A study of rural crime networks in eastern Kentucky (Potter and Gaines 1992) found that eleven of the twenty-eight enterprises (39.29 percent) studied encompassed the activities of individual entrepreneurs. Nine of the enterprises (34.14 percent) were limited partnerships managed by two to four people. The remaining eight enterprises were criminal networks involving between five and eleven participants. It is important to remember, however, that these numbers include only those in management positions, not the employees of these enterprises (Potter and Gaines 1992). Participants in rural criminal enterprises tended to be overwhelmingly male. In the Kentucky study only nineteen of the ninety-nine participants were female.

Despite the low percentage of females, this seems a high number since it counts only those in a management or coordination role in the enterprise. Traditional wisdom in the organized crime literature holds that organized crime is not an equal opportunity employer and that the participation of women is extremely rare. Although the Justice Department's report made no official count by gender, a quick survey of those mentioned as organized criminals in the 1980 Pennsylvania Crime Commission report (one of the most comprehensive statewide analyses of organized crime ever made) indicates that of 357 persons clearly identified as members of ongoing criminal enterprises only 2 (0.56 percent) were women. In addition to the gender makeup of criminal enterprises, the eastern Kentucky study also found that thirty-one of the ninety-nine participants were related by blood or marriage, clearly indicating the importance of familial ties to the organization of crime in rural settings.

WHAT HAVE WE LEARNED?

The image of the United States presented in civics courses is of a great melting pot of cultures, ideas, and traditions. The reality of the melting pot, however, is more akin to a pressure cooker where gang members view themselves as unintegrated parts of society. Local law enforcement agencies must respond to these gangs. These agencies should avoid strategies that simply displace gangs from one jurisdiction to another; indeed, policies that address the underlying causes of gang association and violence are needed. Finally, a great degree of coordination between police and social service organizations must occur to provide much needed resources.

DO YOU RECOGNIZE THESE TERMS?

blood-in, blood-out
colors
Dixie Mafia
French Connection
hard-core gang member
homeboys
jumped in

outlaw motorcycle gangs (OMGs)
prison gangs
rural organized crime
sets
two-holers
wannabee

POINTS OF DISCUSSION

1. Compare and contrast the unique dynamics of domestic organized crime in the United States.

2. Describe how each of the organized crime organizations fits the structural definitions discussed in Chapter 1.

3. Explain how the emergence of black organized crime parallels that of the outlaw motorcycle gangs.

4. In what ways do prison gangs and outlaw motorcycle gangs operate similarly?

5. Describe how the awareness of rural organized crime better prepares society for combating the problem of organized crime in general.

SUGGESTED READING

CAMP, G. M., and C. G. CAMP. (1985). *Prison Gangs: Their Extent, Nature and Impact on Prisons.* Washington, DC: U.S. Government Printing Office. This study provides a national overview of the nature and extent of prison gangs; examines the impact of gangs on prisons, inmates, and administrators; and determines strategies being used to counter prison gangs.

GRENNAN, S. (2003). *Gangs: An International Approach.* Upper Saddle River, NJ: Prentice Hall.

LAVIGNE, Y. (1987). *Hell's Angels.* New York: Carol Publishing Group (a Lyle Stuart book).

WOLF, D. (1991). *Rebels: A Brotherhood of Outlaw Bikers.* Toronto: University of Toronto Press. This book presents the author's descriptions and analysis of his experiences as a member of a Canadian biker gang known as the Rebels.

8

A COMPARATIVE PERSPECTIVE

This chapter will enable you to:

- Understand the organizational structure of emerging organized crime groups
- Compare and contrast the evolution of the most prominent Colombian cartels with that of other criminal groups
- Discover the differences between Chinese triads and tongs

- Compare and contrast Chinese and Japanese organized crime groups
- Determine the extent of the problem of Russian organized crime

INTRODUCTION

This book thus far has attempted to describe the origins, structure, and inner workings of organized crime in general and of several specific groups. This discussion indicated that the operation and structure of groups can differ. These differences are the essence of understanding the organized crime phenomenon. Chapter 7 presented information about youth, black, outlaw motorcycle, prison gangs, and rural organized crime. This chapter compares and contrasts some of the more prominent criminal organizations with foreign-based operations whose influence is considerable in the United States.

TRANSNATIONAL ORGANIZED CRIME

Without doubt the most compelling development in organized crime at the beginning of the twenty-first century is that of transnational organized crime groups and the suggestion that these groups are beginning to collaborate and cooperate in a systematic manner to facilitate the delivery of illicit goods and services on an international scale. Although organized crime scholars have been careful in their description of this phenomena, there is a real danger that a reconstructed and rehabilitated alien conspiracy theory of organized crime, emanating from the news media and the state, will replace the discredited Mafia model of years past.

Both the state and the media have clear interests in promoting a conspiracy model of organized crime. Certainly, this model explains the inability of governments to eradicate criminal syndicates without raising touchy issues of corruption. The media often replicate state doctrine and add their own touch of sensationalism and exaggeration in an attempt to attract viewers and readers. The danger is that the very real issues of transnational crime will be transformed into a comic book caricature resembling James Bond's *SPECTRE* or *SMERSH* or more likely, Maxwell Smart's *CHAOS*, headed by a series of cunning and powerful Dr. Nos or Fu Manchus.

Despite the internationalization of crime, little has changed in the organization of syndicates. They are still rather informal, loosely structured, open, flexible, and highly reactive to changes in the political and economic environments. The internationalization of organized crime has not resulted from some master plan by archcriminals. It is simply a reflection of the reactive, ephemeral, flexible characteristic of crime syndicates and that has allowed them to respond to technological advances in communications and transportation; to market adaptations resulting from the internationalization of investment capital, financial services, and banking; to internationalize manufacturing and increase the segmentation and fragmentation of production across international borders; and to increase emphasis on international and unrestricted trade across borders.

Organized crime syndicates are still rooted in local conditions, shielded by local politics, and limited by the need to control personnel at the local level. The European Union has weakened borders and encourages the free flow of people and goods. Russian, Italian, Rumanian, British, and Corsican syndicates respond to the new reality. The state and multinational corporations created these opportunities; not the Malina or the Mafia. For example, Nigerian drug traffickers are not responsible for the enormous recent increase in international trade or heightened flow of people across borders; they merely take advantage of the situation. Their collaboration with Asian heroin producers does not signify the birth of a new international criminal order; it merely reflects the same cooperation that is occurring in the worldwide business community. For example, collaboration by organized crime is as natural as a contract between U.S. car manufacturers and parts producers in Brazil or Mexico.

Nigerian smugglers use mechanisms to take efficient advantage of new technologies and opportunities, but the fact remains that the Nigerian syndicates are firmly rooted in economic inequality and pervasive patterns of corruption that are distinctly Nigerian.

The major issue is not collaboration between and among organized crime groups, but increased political corruption brought on by greater rewards from international commerce and weakened central governments whose powers have been surpassed and often usurped by multinational corporations. National sovereignty is not threatened by Colombian cartels, Southeast Asian warlords, Russian criminal entrepreneurs, or Zambian cattle poachers, but by the pervasive and growing corruption and increasing irrelevance of individual states in an international economy.

Organized crime has not changed very much from the system of patron–client relations described by Albini, which operates within the context of illicit entrepreneurship characterized by Smith, and which is facilitated by the businesspeople, law enforcement officials, and politicians of the crime networks, as Chambliss has portrayed. Organized crime syndicates are still localized, fragmented, and highly ephemeral entities. The only difference is that the world has changed and organized crime has adapted to the changes. Understanding the nature of these world changes is vital to understanding transnational organized crime in the twenty-first century.

INTERNATIONAL CHANGES AND ORGANIZED CRIME

As a complex social phenomena, organized crime has always been highly sensitive to developments in the economy, political environment, and social world. Recent dramatic changes in global politics and economics, such as the emergence and development of the *global village,* have affected both the opportunities and constraints confronting organized crime and, as a result, have initiated a series of organic changes in the way that criminal organizations do business. At the beginning of the twenty-first century, therefore, the contexts within which criminal organizations operate are undergoing fundamental change. Increased interdependence between nations, the ease of international travel and communications, the permeability of national boundaries, and the globalization of international financial networks have facilitated the emergence of what is, in effect, a single global market for both licit and illicit commodities (Williams 1994).

Certainly, recent years have seen a vast increase in transnational commerce as information, money, physical goods, people, and other tangible commodities move freely across state boundaries. This globalization of trade and a growing international consumer demand for leisure products have created a natural impetus for a fundamental change in the character of many criminal organizations, from essentially localized vice networks to transnational organized crime groups (Williams 1994). These opportunities have manifested themselves in five areas, all of which are outside the domain of organized crime groups, but each of which profoundly affects criminal organizations: (1) ease of international transportation, (2) growth of international trade, (3) new computer and communications technology, (4) rapacious growth of global financial networks, and (5) creation and opening of new markets.

International Transportation and Criminal Organizations

In the last half of the twentieth century, the ability of people to move easily across large distances increased dramatically, as did the ability to move materials across equally large distances. Between 1960 and 1974, "passenger volume on international commercial flights rose from 26 billion passenger miles to 152 billion. By 1992 the figure had increased to between 600 and 700 billion passenger miles" (Williams 1994). People are traveling farther, and more people are traveling. For example, in 1984 "288 million people entered the United States; by 1992 it had gone up to 447 million" (Williams 1994). The movement of vast numbers of people across international frontiers significantly increases the recruitment base for criminal organizations around the world (Godson and Olson 1995).

International Trade and Criminal Organizations

The growth of free trade and the gradual elimination of tariffs, restrictive covenants, and international barriers to commerce have resulted in an explosive growth in import and export markets. The same global trade network that facilitates legitimate import–export operations serves criminal organizations well. Global trade networks enhance the mobility of criminal organizations and create new markets for both illicit and licit services provided by criminal organizations (Williams 1994). The shift of some cocaine cartels to heroin as a product line and the entry of other cocaine cartels into the European market are prime examples of market mobility enhanced by international trade (Godson and Olson 1995).

Recent innovations in computer and communications technology also have important implications for criminal organizations, particularly with regard to their overall flexibility and adaptability in hostile environments (Godson and Olson 1995). Electronic fund transfer systems move billions of dollars around the world in the blink of an eye, making money laundering and the concealment of financial assets much easier than in the past. Encryption technology for faxes and cellular telephones has rendered electronic monitoring and tracing problematic at best. Signal interceptors, now readily available on aircraft, make it much easier for drug couriers to plot radar and avoid monitoring (Elliott 1993). Conducting business across state borders enhances the ability of criminal organizations to keep law enforcement at bay. Problems of coordination, security, and corruption often become insurmountable for state agencies. In addition, diversifying illicit operations and locales greatly enhances criminal organizations' ability to recover from losses resulting from social control activity or even the acts of competitors (Godson and Olson 1995).

Computer and Communications Technology and Criminal Organizations

Money is the most fungible of all commodities; it can be transmitted instantaneously and at low cost. It is chameleonlike in character, changing its identity easily. In the newly expanded global financial networks, money can be traced only with the greatest difficulty, if at all. Governments were already at an extreme disadvantage in the areas of taxation, regulation, and control of economic activities. The present-day global financial network makes the transfer of profits from illegal transactions easy, fast, and virtually immune from discovery. Money laundering, already an art form, is now conducted at warp speed. The internationalization of finance has rendered state law and state economic policy impotent (Williams 1994).

International Financial Networks and Organized Crime

The expansion of international trade, the globalization of financial networks, and the revolution in communications technology have led to the development of new markets in industrial and postindustrial mass-consumption societies. In addition, the heightened levels of integration brought about by the creation of a global economy have resulted in a degree of global transparency that has accentuated inequalities between societies and led to the emulation by developing countries of patterns of consumption in economically advanced societies. Combined with the ease of travel and the expansion in international communications, this has led to a convergence of consumer tastes in many societies around the world. Entrepreneurs, both criminal and noncriminal, have recognized the opportunities this presents for global markets and have tried to exploit them (Williams 1994).

Globalization and the Consumption Society

The creation of mass-consumer markets encourages the growth of organized crime in several ways. First, just like multinational corporations, these new transnational markets are open to criminal organizations. Second, criminal organizations can be better suited than legitimate corporations to exploit these opportunities. Criminal organizations have expertise in operating outside the law, regulations, and the norms of business practice, and

The Changing Character of Organized Crime in a Global Economy

they have few qualms about legal niceties in violating international borders. Criminal organizations operate outside the existing structures of authority and have already developed strategies for circumventing law enforcement both in individual nations and across international boundaries (Williams 1994).

Increasingly, criminal organizations are becoming transnational in nature, seeking only to penetrate new markets, not to acquire new turf, and conducting centrally directed operations in the territory of two or more nation-states by mobilizing resources and pursuing optimizing strategies across international borders. Unlike their multinational corporate counterparts, which seek to gain access to new territories and markets through negotiations with states, criminal organizations obtain access through circumvention, not consent. These groups engage in systematic activities to evade governmental controls, which is possible because the conditions that give rise to the emergence of organized crime also make it very difficult for governments to contain and control them (Williams 1994).

Criminal organizations continue to be extremely diverse in their structure, outlook, and membership. But in the postmodern world, what they have in common is that changes in technology, economy, and trade rules have made them highly mobile, even more adaptive than before, and have vested them with the ability to operate with ease across national borders. This is partly the result of the forces we discussed previously and partly because criminal organizations have always been constructed as informal social networks, rather than formal organizations, which increases immensely their flexibility and adaptability. It is a matter of more than passing interest that formal, legal organizations, including corporations and some agencies of the state, have been moving in the direction of more flexible, fluid, network structures in response to changes in the global economy. Not surprisingly, then, criminal organizations have a distinct advantage in that they have always operated covertly and have always deemphasized fixed structures as a rational response to their illegality (Williams 1994).

STRATEGIC ALLIANCES AND MODERN ORGANIZED CRIME

As a result of their increasingly transnational character and following the lead of transnational corporations, criminal organizations increasingly seek out strategic alliances with other criminal organizations. For multinational corporations, strategic alliances facilitate production where costs are low and allow corporations to take advantage of local knowledge and experience in marketing and distribution. Criminal organizations pursue strategic alliances for the same reasons (Williams 1994).

First, strategic alliances are simply rational responses to the emergence of global markets, and in particular to what is called the global–local nexus. The concept of a global market sounds forbidding. But, in fact, a global market is a composite of local markets that have become increasingly homogenized. Any corporation, legal or illegal, has two ways to increase profits in the marketplace: to gain entrance to new markets and to expand market share in existing markets. Multinational corporations and criminal organizations alike have found entering local markets that have been outside their purview or area of activity to be easier if they cooperate with organizations that are already entrenched in these markets. These local groups have better knowledge of local conditions and are more attuned to local problems, which is usually better for the organizations, who otherwise would be inserting themselves as competitors into unfamiliar territory. Linking with host criminal groups to facilitate access to new markets is the major impetus behind transnational strategic alliances among criminal organizations (Williams 1994).

Strategic alliances are also very useful as mechanisms to neutralize and/or co-opt potential competitors in a market. Cooperative strategies often offer a rational and effective response to a highly competitive situation. Cooperation with a strong competitor already enjoying high profitability in a market can lead to local market dominance. A foreign organization can offer a strong local competitor various incentives for entering into a strategic alliance. For example, the local organization's market share could be increased through the introduction of more diverse products. The promise of an entirely new market could be contingent on a strategic alliance or the exchange of some other valuable good or service (e.g., political contacts, ancillary services, specialized support). Whatever the reasons, the promise of mutual benefit is the foundation of transnational strategic alliances between criminal organizations (Williams 1995b).

Strategic alliances are effective means of circumventing restrictions, regulations, and barriers to markets. Where state regulations make it difficult to enter a market, the formation of an alliance with an organization that already has access is an attractive way to avoid such obstacles (Williams 1995).

The formation of a strategic alliance can be an indispensable way to minimize or spread risk. Multinational corporations know that expanding their activities and entering new markets require new investments and capital cost outlays. Being able to reduce or spread risks enables both corporations and criminal organizations to take advantage of opportunities that might otherwise have appeared to be too risky. The synergy inherent in a strategic alliance means that the participants are able to do things together that neither could do alone, at least not with nearly the same effectiveness or confidence (Williams 1995).

Strategic alliances between criminal groups are usually created in one five ways, depending on the objectives of the criminal organizations involved. The most common form is a *franchise alliance,* which is anchored by a large, well-developed, and highly stable criminal organization that does business with several smaller, independent, local criminal organizations. Another form is a *compensatory alliance,* in which two criminal organizations recognize that each, acting alone, has several inherent weaknesses that are offset by an alliance. The third type of strategic alliance is the *specialization alliance,* in which one criminal organization seeks an alliance with another to fulfill needs for specialized tasks that are beyond the purview and abilities of the first organization. Specialization alliances are contractual relationships covering specific tasks and responsibilities. *Countertrade alliances* are simple exchange relationships between criminal organizations in which goods or services are exchanged for other goods or services. Finally, a *supplier alliance* involves regularized relationships between various suppliers of basic raw materials and organizations that transform these materials into consumer products. Such alliances are common in the drug trade (Williams 1995b).

UNDERMINING CIVIL SOCIETY

Strategic alliances among criminal organizations operating on a transnational basis can pose serious threats to the security of both their host and home states. The willingness of criminal organizations to use force and violence in many areas, often against law enforcement agencies and the state itself, is a direct challenge to the existing state monopoly on organized violence. In many ways, the threat of violence from criminal organizations can be even more destabilizing than the activities of revolutionary or terrorist groups whose avowed aim is the destruction of state hegemony. Certainly countries, including Colombia, Myanmar, and Italy, have experienced extensive violence from criminal organizations resisting state control. Moreover, these challenges to the state's authority are usually unavoidable because they are inherent in both the character and activities of criminal organizations: "[E]ach crime network attempts to build a coercive monopoly and to implement that system of control through at least two other criminal activities—corruption of public and private officials, and violent terrorism in order to enforce its discipline" (Williams 1994). By their very nature, criminal organizations tend to undercut civil society, destabilize domestic politics, and undermine the state's legal authority (Williams 1994).

Impact on Local Economies

There is also considerable evidence that large transnational criminal organizations can have a profound impact on local economies. In the Andes, for example, the diversion of labor into illegal activities, the destruction of land and its use for the cultivation of coca leaves, and the generation of inflationary pressures work together to undermine the viability of local economies, which in such countries as Peru, Bolivia, and Colombia were already weak. An additional impact on local economies arises from the penetration of financial markets and the international banking system by organized crime. Corruption of basic financial institutions is now a major and growing concern, because transnational criminal organizations use international financial networks to launder money and in some cases to provide cover for ancillary illicit activities. Even financial institutions in major developed countries are not immune (Godson and Olson 1995).

Undermining State Legitimacy

The defiance of established authority and the corrupting of state officials and institutions in numerous countries are undermining the legitimacy of and public support for the state itself. In countries whose governments have been chronically unable to deliver needed and expected social services and whose economy is deteriorating, the government is often perceived of as a central problem, and the appeal of powerful, capable, and strong criminal organizations can overwhelm the respect for law (Godson and Olson 1995). Criminal organizations operating or seeking to operate on a transnational basis know that they can flourish in states with weak structures and dubious legitimacy.

Nations with severe economic inequalities, dominance by traditional oligarchies, and serious political, religious, or ethnic divisions are perfect targets for organized criminal activity. In these states the development of parallel political and economic structures is almost inevitable. In countries such as Peru, Bolivia, Laos, and Myanmar entire geographical areas are outside the control of the central government. In other countries, including

Mexico, Colombia, Nigeria, and Thailand, governmental institutions are so corrupt that they no longer have either the incentive or the capacity to reassert control (Williams 1994).

Where government authority is weak or absent, powerful criminal organizations may see themselves as legitimate political authorities. As criminal organizations begin to understand the extent of their influence and power, it is not too large a leap to assume that these organizations will realize that they may be able to do more than neutralize governments. They may be able to replace them (Godson and Olson 1995). In general, however, this seems unlikely. Criminal organizations do not wish to be sovereignty bound. Lacking the attributes of sovereignty is often an advantage, rather than a constraint for transnational actors: They are sovereignty free rather than sovereignty bound and use this freedom and flexibility to engage in activities that are difficult for states to regulate.

States within States

The issue is control versus autonomy: States want control, and criminal organizations want autonomy (Williams 1994). Transnational criminal organizations challenge aspects of state sovereignty and security that have traditionally been taken for granted. They prove the permeability of borders nominally under the control of states. Governments retain sovereignty, but if they are unable to control the importation of guns, drugs, and people into their territory, sovereignty loses much of its significance. Sovereignty may retain its utility as a basis for diplomacy in the international society of states, but it no longer reflects real control over territory (Williams 1994).

Criminal organizations obtain access to a state's territory through clandestine methods, minimize the opportunities for state control over their activities, and prevent the state from exercising real sovereignty. Although the main purpose of the criminal organization's activities is to make a profit, an inevitable by-product is an implicit challenge to authority and sovereignty. The threat to state sovereignty is insidious, rather than direct: It is a not a threat to the military strength of the state, but it is a challenge to the prerogatives that are an integral part of statehood (Williams 1994).

None of this should be taken to mean that all states oppose the activities of transnational criminal organizations. Alliances of convenience between states and criminal organization could pose serious security threats, especially from those trafficking in nuclear material (Williams 1994). As soon as a trafficking network is functioning effectively, product diversification is easy. Organizations that deal in drugs can also traffic in technology and components for weapons of mass destruction. Whether the recipients of such transfers are terrorist groups or states, the link between criminal activities and security is obvious (Williams 1994).

FUTURE TRENDS AFFECTING CRIMINAL ORGANIZATIONS

The character changes in organized crime initiated by rapidly expanding international travel and trade, developing communications technology, and the globalization of finance may well be accelerated in the coming years. A number of factors point to this acceleration.

Economics of Production

For poor farmers in many nations around the world, choosing to grow drug-related crops makes great economic sense. Markets for other commodities, such as coffee, rice, and gladiolus, are far less profitable and very unstable. In many places, even where the necessary marketing infrastructure and expertise exist, government controls make entry into these legitimate markets almost impossible for peasants. At the same time, drug entrepreneurs are expanding into new markets. Without dramatic and unlikely changes, raw materials for drug production will continue to be readily available (Godson and Olson 1995).

International Ungovernability

There is a global trend toward ungovernability, that is, the declining ability of governments to govern, manage a modern state, and provide adequate or effective services. In some cases, criminal organizations have been able to capitalize on the fact that large areas such as the Andes and Amazon regions in South America or much of the Golden Triangle in Southeast Asia were never under effective government control.

Criminal organizations have moved into these remote regions and have provided them with the major source of authority and social control. In other cases, criminal organizations have begun to contest local control of areas with the government. This situation provides favorable conditions for criminal groups to establish bases of operations and safe havens, particularly in areas key to drug trafficking and alien smuggling. Political geographers predict further continuing global fragmentation. Criminal organizations thrive where governments are weak (Godson and Olson 1995).

Immigration Streams and Organized Crime

Local criminal organizations often expand following immigration patterns. In the twenty-first century, economic pressures and widespread ethnic turmoil are likely to generate refugees and immigrants from regions where international criminal groups are based. Criminal organizations tend to exploit immigrant communities in a variety of ways for cover and concealment. Immigrant groups also provide a source of recruits. New immigrants, because of their recent experiences in their home countries, are often fearful of law enforcement, which makes them reluctant to cooperate with police. It is highly likely that increased organized criminal activity will accompany the immigration of Russians, East Europeans, Asians, Middle Easterners, Kurds, and others in coming years (Godson and Olson 1995).

Border Porosity

The long open borders between the United States and Mexico and Canada provide ready access for criminal and illegal goods. Tens of thousands of miles of U.S. coastline are virtually uncontrollable. The opening of free trade areas, such as the North American Free Trade Agreement (NAFTA), has lowered many existing controls and reduced customs inspections as well. Certainly, similar effects are anticipated in Europe as the European Union continues to open borders to free trade (Godson and Olson 1995).

Continued advances in technology and international transportation will facilitate growth in transnational criminal operations. The ease of modern communications makes contact among criminal organizations easy, fast, and more secure. New digital technologies make it more difficult for law enforcement agencies to intercept communications. The movement of trillions of dollars in wire transfers each day makes it possible for most actors to evade state monitoring (Godson and Olson 1995).

Preventing, disrupting, and prosecuting organized crime is difficult even under the best of conditions. The growth of transnational markets and the accompanying criminal organizations ready and willing to operate in these markets will make the task even more complex and immensely more difficult.

DRUG CARTELS AND THE INTERNATIONAL ORGANIZATION OF DRUG TRAFFICKING IN THE TWENTY-FIRST CENTURY

In terms of geographic reach, economic impact, and imperviousness to law enforcement, drug cartels became the dominant form of organized crime in the last two decades of the twentieth century. In the twenty-first century, drug cartels have taken advantage of the massive increases in international trade and commerce and have learned from the mistakes of earlier drug-trafficking organizations. The new cartels are more numerous, flexible, chameleon in their nature, and durable than any we have seen before.

Drug cartels are composed of independent drug-trafficking organizations that have pooled their resources and elected to cooperate with each other. Drug cartels are often incorrectly conceived of as single organized crime groups with thousands of members, wide geographical scope, and vertical control of the drug business from the point of harvest to the point of retail sales on the streets. Nothing could be farther from the truth. Drug cartels are merely associations of many smaller organized crime groups into a loose confederation of business associates. Some of the syndicates in a cartel may produce raw materials. Others may have well-established modalities for transportation. Still others may have money-laundering operations in place or may have important political and law enforcement connections to facilitate the creation of corrupt relations.

Drug-trafficking groups may decide to enter into a cartel relationship for any number of reasons. Most commonly, smaller, independent syndicates enter into a franchise relationship with a larger, better organized, and more stable syndicate. Another reason for the creation of a drug cartel is to bring together traffickers with differing strengths in the various aspects of the drug trade. In this arrangement, each independent syndicate realizes that it has a weakness that is compensated for by other syndicates. An organization with strong connections to the growers of a particular plant may need to align with another organization possessing skilled chemists to convert the plant into a high-quality drug. Still another organization may be skilled in smuggling and yet another criminal network may have access to buyers in another country. Occasionally, independent drug syndicates come together into a cartel because of a need for highly specialized services. For example, opium-growing warlords in the **Golden Triangle** (Burma, Laos, Thailand) of Southeast Asia established working relationships with various Chinese Triads because they needed to move their product to markets worldwide and to launder their profits. A financial structure adequate to the task was not available in the Golden Triangle. In these cases, drug cartels provide references and contacts for the establishment of contractual arrangements related to specific tasks. Finally, a more contemporary form of drug cartel operation involves a simple exchange between independent criminal organizations in which a good or service is exchanged for another. An example of this is the relationship between Colombian cocaine syndicates and drug trafficking organizations in

Mexico. The Colombians contract with the Mexicans to move their cocaine into the United States. In return for this service, Mexican organizations take half of the load they are smuggling as their fee and distribute it to smaller Mexican drug-trafficking organizations in the United States for retail sale.

COLOMBIAN COCAINE CARTELS

Colombian Traffickers and the Cocaine Market

Colombian drug-trafficking organizations handle the majority of the world's cocaine production. Three-quarters of the world's annual yield of cocaine is produced in Colombia. The cocaine base used to produce cocaine hydrochloride comes from Bolivia, Peru, and Colombia itself. In fact, there was a 28 percent increase in the amount of potentially harvestable coca plants in Colombia in 1998, indicating a concerted effort by Colombian traffickers to reduce their dependence on coca grown in more distant areas. Colombian cartels are also still quite active in the wholesale distribution of cocaine worldwide, but Mexican drug cartels have taken over a substantial portion of what used to be the Colombian share of wholesale distribution and even more of the responsibility for transportation and smuggling (Kline 1995; Schapiro 1997; Zabludoff 1998).

Colombia's role as a major cocaine producer is to a large part geographically determined because it shares borders with Peru and Bolivia, countries where substantial quantities of coca leaves are grown. Colombia's wholesale trafficking role in cocaine is also largely geographically determined. First, it is reasonably close to the United States, about a two-and-a-half hour flight from Miami. Second, Colombia is the only country in South America with both a Caribbean Sea and Pacific Ocean coastline, thereby opening up a variety of options and modalities for both maritime and air smuggling routes.

Coca leaves are transported to Colombia from Peru and Bolivia along a variety of routes, mostly overland and frequently along remote trails. The leaves are delivered to hundreds of locations, where the very rudimentary process of converting them into coca paste is accomplished. The coca paste is then carried over water, land, and often by air in light aircraft to concealed cocaine-producing facilities in the Colombian interior. The coca paste is then processed into cocaine hydrochloride, the white crystalline powder that, after being cut, is sold to cocaine users.

Colombian drug cartels transport the cocaine to the United States in every conceivable manner, sometimes using commercial maritime shipping, private and commercial aircraft, and even on occasion trains. It is generally conceded that the movement of the drug across large distances is the point of greatest vulnerability in the cocaine trafficking process.

While Colombian cartels did much of their own smuggling in the 1970s and early 1980s, by the late 1980s they had increasingly subcontracted the distribution of cocaine to Mexican drug traffickers. The cocaine was moved from Colombia to Mexico, where it was turned over to Mexican criminal organizations for transport to the United States. By the 1990s, most cocaine entering the United States was coming through Mexico. Mexican drug cartels, which had already established routes for the smuggling of heroin and marijuana into the United States, simply added cocaine to their polydrug-smuggling businesses. Mexican drug organizations also expanded the cocaine market in the United States by adding their own contacts to contacts previously developed by the Colombian cartels. Originally, the Mexican drug traffickers simply operated on a contract basis with the Colombians, charging a portion of the shipment as payment for their smuggling services. By the end of 1980s, Mexican smugglers were charging as much as 50 percent of the load for their services. It was at this point that the Mexican cartels began to evolve from mere logisticians in the cocaine trade into large-scale cocaine traffickers in their own right.

Common smuggling modalities involve the transportation of cocaine from Colombia through Mexico or Central America by air and then overland or by air to staging sites in northern Mexico. The cocaine is then broken down into smaller loads for smuggling across the U.S.–Mexico border. The primary cocaine importation points in the United States are in Arizona, southern California, southern Florida, and Texas. Typically, land vehicles are driven across the southwest border. Cocaine is also carried in small, concealed kilogram quantities across the border by couriers known as mules, who enter the United States either legally through ports of entry or illegally through undesignated points along the border. Colombian traffickers have also started using a new concealment method whereby they add chemical compounds to cocaine hydrochloride to produce *black cocaine*. The cocaine in this substance is not detected by standard chemical tests or drug-sniffing canines.

In addition to routes through Mexico, cocaine traffickers from Colombia have also established a series of smuggling routes throughout the Caribbean, the Bahama Island chain, and South Florida. They often hire traffickers from Mexico or the Dominican Republic to transport the drug. The traffickers use a variety of smuggling techniques to transfer their drug to U.S. markets. These include airdrops of 500 to 700 kilograms in the Bahama Islands or off the coast of Puerto Rico, midocean boat-to-boat transfers of 500 to 2,000 kilograms, and the commercial shipment of multiple tons of cocaine through the port of Miami. Bulk cargo ships are also used to smuggle cocaine to staging sites in the western Caribbean Gulf of Mexico area. These vessels are typically 150- to 250-foot coastal freighters that carry an average cocaine load of approximately 2.5 metric tons. Commercial fishing vessels are also used for smuggling operations. In areas with a high volume of recreational traffic, smugglers use the same types of vessels, such as ciagarette boats, as those commonly used by local recreational boaters.

Cocaine Wholesaling Structure

Nonetheless, some Colombian cartels continue to be active in the United States. Where this is the case, the cartels establish cells in a specific geographic areas. Most commonly, these cells are structured around familial relations or long-time, ongoing friendships. This arrangement makes any attempt by law enforcement to infiltrate or penetrate a cell virtually impossible. In addition, cells are structurally compartmentalized with a well-defined division of labor. Each cell specializes in a different aspect of the cocaine trade in the specific geographic location where it is found. Some cells transport drugs. Some cells are simply responsible for hiding cocaine and storing it for future sale. Some cells are engaged exclusively in money laundering and have no contact with the drug itself. Other cells are involved in the actual wholesale trading of cocaine to retail drug networks. On average, cells are made up of ten employees who have no knowledge about the membership, location, or activities of other cells in the area. If law enforcement activities are able to compromise one cell, none of the others is affected.

In addition, to compartmentalization, cell structure is characterized by a rigid chain of command. The head of each cell reports to a regional director for the cartel, and only to that individual. The regional director, in turn, reports to a designated individual in Colombia. Discretionary decisions in the United States are entrusted to only a handful of individuals, carefully insulated from the day to day drug operation, who answer directly to the cartel leadership in Colombia.

Colombian cartels make extensive use of the most sophisticated and up to date communications technologies. Particularly important to Colombian cartel operations are state of the art encryption devices, which, for all intents and purposes, considering the relatively short life of a drug transaction, translate communication into indecipherable codes. If the codes are ever broken, the transaction that they were related to is long over. In the 1970s, one of the best tactics available to law enforcement in dealing with Colombian cartels was wiretapping of frequent international phone conversations. These modern encryption technologies have made such telephone communications things of the past. Encryption technology not only hides information about drug transactions, but also hides financial information related to money laundering, making the building of criminal cases far more difficult than it was just a few years ago.

The Heroin Trade

One reason the Colombian cartels have passed off so much of their wholesaling business in cocaine to Mexican drug organizations is the increasing Colombian role in the production and sale of heroin. Starting in the late 1980s and steadily increasing in the 1990s, Colombian drug cartels have expanded into the growing and smuggling of high-grade heroin. Using their already existing retail sales contacts and their in-place cocaine organizations in the United States has enabled the Colombian cartels to become the dominant force in the U.S. heroin market. The heroin trade has also changed the economics of drug trafficking in South America. Because of climate, soil, and other factors, high-quality coca has a small and restricted cultivation area, with the best coca being cultivated outside Colombia. But the Colombians have found they can grow their own opium, thus eliminating their dependence on suppliers. The opium poppy, unlike the coca bush, grows exceptionally well along the eastern slopes of the Central Andean Mountain ranges in the central part of Colombia. Opium growers in Colombia work under contract to a drug cartel. The cartel supplies the locals with seeds and agricultural supplies, who in turn agree to sell the gum from the opium poppy pods to the cartels. Other growers operate independently, selling the opium gum to brokers who in turn sell it to chemists. The chemists then process the opium gum into morphine base and then into heroin. Chemists then either sell the heroin to trafficking organizations or operate under ongoing contracts with these organizations. The heroin is smuggled into the United States by the cartels.

Because heroin is smuggled in small quantities, the methods for smuggling are limited only by a smugglers imagination. Some smuggle heroin in hollowed-out shoes, some hide it in other shipments of commercial goods, some sew into the lining of their clothes, and others simply swallow it after wrapping it condoms.

The heroin trade from Colombia is primarily dominated by a series of new, smaller, drug cartels and syndicates. But the attractiveness of using already established smuggling and distribution channels dominated by the large cartels would seem to make increasing centralization of the heroin trade inevitable. Colombian traffickers have made such a huge impact on the U.S. for one simple reason: they sell higher-grade heroin than their competitors and they sell it at cheaper wholesale prices. Some Colombians introduced their new product line by simply including free samples in their cocaine shipments. By the end of the 1990s, Colombian trafficking groups in New York and Philadelphia had been so successful that their product brand names, No Way Out and Death Wish, became the most sought after heroin on the retail market, encouraging more and more retail syndicates to handle the products. At least on the East Coast of the United States, the Colombians have been able to create high name recognition for their products and intense customer loyalty, which has resulted in virtual domination of the market. As of 1998, the DEA was estimating that 65 percent of the heroin sold on the streets of the United States was grown and processed in Colombia.

The first of the great Colombian drug cartels surfaced in the mid-1970s. As the use of cocaine hydrochloride grew in the United States and law enforcement officers made more and more trafficking arrests, it became increasingly apparent that trafficking networks in the United States were operating in a common manner, using stash houses, laundering money, and developing trafficking networks in similar ways. It also became apparent that the actual smuggling of cocaine was being controlled from Colombia. The first cartel to be identified and the one that law enforcement alleges dominated early cocaine trade, was headquartered in Medellin, Colombia, and was led by the Ochoa brothers, Carlos Lehder, Pablo Escobar, and Jose Rodriguez Gacha. As the 1970s ended it appeared that the Medellin Cartel dominated the cocaine trade in both New York and Miami and therefore was probably the largest Colombian trafficking syndicate operating in the United States. It should be understood however, that the name Medellin Cartel is somewhat misleading. The Medellin Cartel was never a single drug trafficking organization, but rather a loose organizational confederation of many drug syndicates operating out of Medellin.

The Medellin Cartel

Carlos Lehder originally had the idea that cocaine could be smuggled to the United States in the same way that marijuana was being smuggled. Instead of continuing the traditional smuggling methods of hiding small quantities of cocaine in luggage on commercial flights, Lehder thought that cocaine could be moved on small, private aircraft in much larger quantities. To use light aircraft, he needed to establish a transshipment point. So, in 1976, Lehder bought a sizable portion of the Bahamian island of Norman's Cay, only 225 miles southeast of Miami. On Norman's Cay he built an airstrip as a refueling spot for the light aircraft he would use to fly cocaine from Colombia and then on to the United States. Lehder's idea worked spectacularly and was replicated in other locations throughout the Caribbean and Mexico.

Under pressure from the United States and in response to political instability within Colombia itself, the Colombian government agreed to extradite Lehder to the United States in 1987. Lehder was convicted of cocaine trafficking and sentenced to 135 years in a federal prison, a sentence that was subsequently reduced in return for his cooperation in the prosecution of Panamanian dictator Manuel Noreiga.

The Medellin Cartel's propensity for violence as the primary tool of dispute settlement eventually led to its downfall. The Cartel was responsible for the 1984 assassination of Rodrigo Lara Bonilla, Colombia's minister of justice and a subsequent attack on the Colombian Supreme Court. There is much dispute over who the prime mover was in planning and staging these attacks. There are good reasons to believe that the Ochoas and Lehder may have tried to mitigate the violence, rightly believing that it would interfere with their highly profitable cocaine business. There is little doubt, however, that Pablo Escobar was the prime instigator. Certainly, it was Escobar who was responsible for a 1989 bombing of an Avianca commercial airliner that killed 110 people. Allegedly, the bombing was cover for Escobar's real intent, which was to murder two people he suspected of being police informants who were passengers on the plane. Escobar also placed bounties of between $1,000 and $3,000 on police officers in Colombia. In Medellin itself as many as 2,000 police officers and civilians were murdered each year. In June 1991, Escobar turned himself in to Colombian authorities. But after only a year in confinement, he escaped in July 1992. From July 1992 to December 1993, Pablo Escobar was the subject of a massive manhunt. He was finally shot to death at a private residence in Medellin. Officially, the Colombian National Police are credited with Escobar's killing, although they were accompanied by U.S. military personnel and very likely CIA operatives in the operation. Who actually killed Escobar and under what conditions is a matter of considerable debate and speculation.

The Cali Cartel   With the slow process of incarcerating or killing the highly visible, extremely violent leaders of the Medellin Cartel proceeding in the late 1980s and early 1990s, drug-trafficking groups based in Cali, a city about 200 miles south of Medellin, began to gain more control of the cocaine market. Like the Medellin Cartel, the Cali Cartel was in reality not a single organizational entity, but rather a confederation of drug-trafficking syndicates sharing resources and cooperating with each other. Unlike the leaders of the Medellin Cartel, Cali Cartel members shunned publicity, avoided violence as much as possible, and posed as ostensibly legitimate businessmen.

Cali Cartel activities in the United States surfaced with the seizure of the largest clandestine cocaine laboratory ever discovered in the United States, on April 11, 1985, in the rural, upstate town of Minden, New York. The discovery of the laboratory was entirely accidental and occurred only because of a fire on the ten-acre farm. Evidence at the scene linked the labs operations to Jose Santacruz-Londono, one of the leaders of the Cali Cartel. The cocaine laboratory in Minden was capable of producing $700 million worth of cocaine a year.

The Cali Cartel's operation generated billions of dollars in cocaine-related revenue each year. The cartel used sophisticated business techniques to manage their operations and avoid interference by law enforcement. In the United States the cartel established a system of highly compartmentalized, insulated cells in major metropolitan areas. The cartel used thousands of contract employees as surrogates to handle the actual business of cocaine trafficking. Every aspect of the business was insulated from every other aspect. Cells that handled drugs were separate from cells that arranged car rentals. Other cells specialized in pager and cell phone purchases and disposal (the cartel allowed cellular phones to be used only once before being destroyed, making traces or taps impossible); drug storage and safe houses; and accountancy and bookkeeping. Cartel managers back in Cali accumulated extensive information about the families and relatives of employees operating in the United States that could be used to coerce employees into silence if they were arrested. Such information and the potential threats to family also kept employees from stealing or departing from Cali cartel protocols in the conduct of the cocaine business.

In the early 1990s the leaders of the Cali Cartel included the Rodriguez-Orejuela brothers, Jose Santacruz-Londono, Helmer "Pacho" Herrera-Buitrago, and Victor Julio Patino-Fomeque. While U.S. law enforcement agents had developed sufficient information to indict some of these individuals, the Colombian Constitution of 1991 outlawed extradition to the United States. Under pressure from the Clinton administration, however, the Colombian national police agreed to use information developed by U.S. investigations to indict the Cali Cartel's leadership in Colombia. During 1995–1996 the five major leaders of the Cali Cartel were arrested. Jose Santacruz-Londono died in March 1996. But, as we shall see, this did not end cocaine trafficking in Colmbia nor did it necessarily end the activities of cartel members.

At the turn of the century the Cali Cartel no longer had the market dominance over cocaine that it had in the last decade. But elements of the cartel were still very active in the cocaine trade and played an important role in the wholesale cocaine market.

Contemporary Colombian Drug-Trafficking Organizations

Ironically, successful law enforcement efforts against the Medellin and Cali cartels have had the effect of decentralizing the cocaine trade in Colombia, making it harder than ever to control. A number of veteran drug traffickers who had operated under the aegis of the Cali Cartel have now become significant powers in their own right.

Today much of the cocaine traffic in Colombia is centered in the northern Valle del Cauca region, of which Cali is the capital city, located on Colombia's southeast coast and on the Caribbean north coast. Cocaine traffickers in these regions have not repeated the mistakes of the Medellin and Cali cartels. They operate more independently of each other, and they have passed some of the major responsibilities for cocaine smuggling and wholesaling on to drug-trafficking syndicates in Mexico.

Arcangel de Jesus Henao-Montoya operates his cocaine-trafficking syndicate in the northern Valle del Cauca region. The Henao-Montoya syndicate appears to be the largest and most powerful of several independent trafficking groups that comprise the North Valle drug cartel. Until Arcangel's brother, Jose Orlando, surrendered to Colombian police to face money-laundering charges in September 1997, he led the syndicate. In November 1998, Jose Orlando was shot and killed in the maximum-security wing of Bogotá's Modelo Prison. The Henao-Montoya syndicate is closely allied with neofascist right-wing death squads and paramilitary units in the region under the control of Carlos Castano. Ironically, Castano is a close political and military ally of the United States in Colombia.

Diego Montoya-Sanchez left the Henao-Montoya syndicate to establish another of the major drug trafficking syndicates in the North Valle region. Montoya-Sanchez is responsible for multi-ton shipments of cocaine to Mexican drug syndicates, who then smuggle the cocaine into the United States. Montoya-Sanchez was the major supplier for Alejandro "Juvenal" Bernal-Madrigal and his Bogotá-based drug organizations (see below). Montoya-Sanchez operates large-scale cocaine-processing facilities in southern Colombia. He acquires the coca paste for his processing facilities directly from Peru.

Another major North Valle del Cauca drug syndicate is headed by Jairo Ivan Urdinola-Grajales and his brother, Julio Fabio Urdinola-Grajales. The Urdinolas are related to the Henao-Montoya family by marriage. Colombian officials arrested Jairo Ivan in April 1992 and later sentenced him to four-and-a-half years in prison on drug-trafficking charges. Julio Fabio surrendered to Colombian authorities in March 1994. In October 1997, a Colombian judge dismissed murder charges against Jairo Ivan Urdinola-Grajales. However, the Prosecutor General's Office has filed additional drug-trafficking charges against him. The Urdinola-Grajales brothers continue to run their drug syndicate from prison.

Victor Patino-Fomeque, the Cali Cartel leader who surrendered to Colombian authorities in June 1995, continues to direct a drug-trafficking syndicate from prison. Patino-Fomeque operated out of Buenaventura, Colombia, where he supervised maritime smuggling operations for the Cali Cartel. Despite a twelve-year prison sentence handed down in May 1996, Patino-Fomeque is out of prison.

The Ochoa brothers, Fabio, Juan David, and Jorge Luis, among the most notorious members of the Medellin Cartel, are back in the cocaine business. During 1990 and 1992 the Ochoa brothers voluntarily surrendered to Colombian authorities. In July 1996, Juan David and Jorge Luis were released from prison, and in September 1996 Fabio was released.

In March 1996, Juan Carlos "Chupeta" Ramirez-Abadia surrendered to Colombian authorities. In December 1996, Chupeta was sentenced to twenty-four years in prison, but actually served only seven-and-a-half years. While Chupeta was in prison, Jorge "El Monto" Orlando-Rodriguez took over management responsibilities for the Chupeta drug syndicate. Ramirez-Abadia, however, continued to make the major decisions about the syndicate's activities from prison. Chupeta's net worth is estimated to be in the neighborhood of $2.6 billion.

Alejandro "Juvenal" Bernal-Madrigal is a Bogotá-based transportation coordinator for Mexico- and Colombia-based traffickers. He was responsible for multi-ton shipments of cocaine from Colombia to Mexico. Juvenal also transported large amounts of drug money to Mexico. He was arrested in October 1999 by Colombian authorities.

Hugo Herrera-Vasquez heads a Cali-based trafficking organization that moves large quantities of cocaine from Colombia to the United States via Central America and Mexico. The Herrera organization also launders drug money destined for Colombia. Cash, wire transfers, and monetary instruments are used to move drug proceeds from the U.S. southwest border area to Colombia through Mexico and Panama.

MEXICAN DRUG SYNDICATES

While Mexican criminal syndicates have been involved in drug trafficking for decades, primarily marijuana and heroin, only recently have they made an important appearance in the cocaine market, first as surrogates for and then as partners of Colombian drug syndicates. Mexico's 2,000-mile-long border with the United States, much of which is in isolated rural areas with rugged terrain, makes it an obvious transshipment site for drugs. Its extensive coastal and inland mountain systems create perfect havens for growing marijuana and opium poppies (Schaffer 1996; Macko 1997; Eskridge 1998).

In addition, there is an enormous flow of legitimate commerce across the Mexican border every day. The number of commercial trucks legally making the border crossing has increased by 70 percent since 1993. Railway traffic has increased 60 percent in the same period. In 1999, 295 million people,

88 million automobiles, and 4.5 million trucks and rail cars entered the United States legally through the thirty-eight established points of entry. Every year Mexico does $100 billion worth of legitimate commercial trade with the United States. The opportunities for smuggling and concealment of drugs in this volume of traffic is obvious. Finally. Mexico is an attractive haven for drug trafficking because of widespread corruption in its law enforcement and judicial systems and the relative lack of resources available to Mexican police.

Early Mexican drug trafficking groups were primarily trans-shipment agents for larger drug organizations. In the 1980s, the Mexican drug organizations provided cross-border smuggling services, charging between $1,000 and $2,000 a kilogram for cocaine. Once the cocaine was safely inside the United States, it would once again be turned over to Colombian traffickers for wholesale distribution.

By the end of the 1980s, Mexican drug traffickers were demanding ever larger remuneration for moving Colombian drugs. Now the Mexican drug syndicates wanted payment in kind, a share of the cocaine being transported, up to 50 percent of the load, for their smuggling services. This new arrangement offered Mexican drug syndicates an opportunity to get into the wholesale cocaine-trafficking business themselves, thereby vastly increasing their profits. Eventually, this new arrangement with the Colombians resulted in not only dividing equally the cocaine shipments, but also of the United States. As the arrangement evolved over time, the Colombians retained the wholesale market in the eastern United States as their own, and Mexican drug cartels took over the wholesale market in the Midwest and West. By 1995 the Mexican syndicates had established themselves as major cocaine traffickers in their own right. Today this arrangement continues to evolve. Dominican traffickers have challenged Colombian hegemony in the East, particularly in New York and New Jersey, and Mexican syndicates have begun establishing cocaine-trafficking operations in New York, as well.

The structure and operations of Mexican drug syndicates are compartmentalized, but exhibit a stronger chain of command from their Mexican bases than other drug syndicates. Mexican drug cartels have representatives or surrogates located throughout the United States who are responsible for managing the day to day activities of the syndicate. But, unlike many other drug syndicates who have insulated their home country operations by granting greater autonomy to cells operating in foreign countries, the Mexican syndicates still retain a system whereby Mexican-based syndicate leaders provide specific instructions to their foreign-based syndicates on such issues as warehousing drugs, who to use for transportation services, and how to launder drug money. Despite the use of encrypted faxes, computers, pagers, and cellular telephones, this arrangement still leaves a longer trail of communications for law enforcement to follow and is considerably more risky than allowing foreign-based cells to operate with autonomy.

While arrest statistics are often a very misleading indicator of criminal activity, often reflecting law enforcement priorities, rather than the actual condition of the illicit market, DEA arrest numbers seem to reflect a rapaciously growing Mexican involvement in U.S. drug trafficking. For example, from 1994 to 1998, the number of Mexican citizens arrested at the border for drug smuggling increased by 800 percent. In addition, between 1993 and 1996 the number of Mexican nationals arrested within the United States by DEA increased by 65 percent. More striking is the fact that these arrests were not confined to

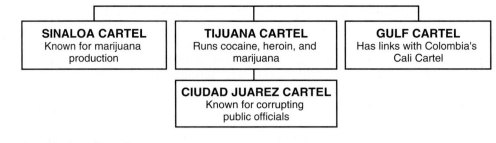

| SINALOA CARTEL
Known for marijuana
production | TIJUANA CARTEL
Runs cocaine, heroin, and
marijuana | GULF CARTEL
Has links with Colombia's
Cali Cartel |

CIUDAD JUAREZ CARTEL
Known for corrupting
public officials

Top Mexican Cartels

border areas or the southwest states bordering Mexico. A majority occurred in four cities far removed from the border: Des Moines, Iowa; Greensboro, North Carolina; Yakima, Washington; and New Rochelle, New York.

About two-thirds of the cocaine sold in the United States in transshipped over the Mexican border. Typically, large loads of cocaine come into Mexico from Colombia by air or boat. The cocaine is transported across land, usually in trucks, to a number of repository cities, such as Juarez or Guadalajara. From these warehousing sites, cocaine loads are usually driven across the U.S. border to repository sites in the United States, most commonly Los Angeles, Chicago, and Phoenix. Mexican trafficking syndicate representatives in these cities have contractual arrangements, usually with otherwise legitimate trucking companies, to move the cocaine across the country to smaller warehousing facilities closer to the point of sale. Individuals working in these *stash houses* guard the supplies and make arrangement for their distribution by cocaine wholesalers.

The size of Mexican cocaine operations is illustrated by a DEA investigation aimed at the U.S. operations of the Amado Carrillo-Fuentes organization, which resulted in the seizure of 11.5 metric tons of cocaine, over $18 million in U.S. currency, and almost 14,000 pounds of marijuana and the arrest of 101 defendants. This particular investigation also illustrated the point made earlier, that upper-echelon communications to local operatives in the drug market can be quite hazardous. These arrests were made through the interception and decoding of these communications.

In addition to their recently expanded role in cocaine trafficking, Mexican drug syndicates continue to play a large role in the U.S. methamphetamine market. Mexican drug syndicates are now engaged in the large-scale production of methamphetamine. The meth market was revitalized as consumer preferences shifted in the drug markets of the 1990s. The traditional control of the methamphetamine market by outlaw motorcycle gangs was broken by Mexican drug organizations operating in both Mexico and California.

Methamphetamine has a huge advantage over cocaine, heroin, and marijuana as a drug to be trafficked. Unlike the others, it does not depend on agricultural production. Methamphetamine is manufactured directly from precursor chemicals, and these chemicals are easily available to Mexican syndicates from chemical companies in India, China, and the United States. Mexico drug syndicates operate clandestine laboratories in Mexico and California capable of producing hundreds of pounds of the drug. From the labs, the meth is moved to traffickers across the United States for sale.

From the 1930s and certainly from the late 1940s and early 1950s, when Mickey Cohen struck a deal with the LAPD to allow him to traffick in Mexican heroin, the cultivation and refining of opium poppies has been an important source for the U.S. heroin market. Today about 29 percent of the heroin on the U.S. market comes from Mexico. Mexican drug syndicates produce about 6 metric tons of heroin a year for resale in the United States. Because of the crude refining methods used, Mexican heroin is frequently dark in color (black) and sticky or gummy (like tar), resulting in its name of *black tar heroin*. Black tar heroin is widely distributed through the Southwest, Northwest, and Midwest of the United States.

Mexico is the largest source of imported marijuana to the United States. At one time, in the 1930s through the 1960s, Mexico supplied as much as 95 percent of the marijuana consumed in the United States. Domestic U.S. production has cut that figure at least in half as of the 1990s, but Mexico retains its position as the largest foreign source for marijuana. This importing dominance was enhanced by the withdrawal of Colombian syndicates from the marijuana market in the 1970s, when the Colombians decided that marijuana was too bulky a commodity to be safely transported. In addition, the profit margin for cocaine vastly exceeds that of marijuana. In 1998, 742 metric tons of marijuana from Mexico was seized entering the United States. Today Mexican drug syndicates have begun to cultivate their marijuana in the United States. For example, in 1997 a group of people from Zacatecas, Mexico, was arrested in Idaho for cultivating 100,000 marijuana plants weighing almost 20 tons.

Like most criminal organizations in the early stages of establishing their control of a market share in prohibited substances, Mexican syndicates still cling to the excessive use of violence as a means of control. Like their centralized chain of command, this makes them particularly vulnerable, at least for the moment, to law enforcement intervention. Examples of this reliance on violence abound, for example, the 1998 killings of 22 people in Baja, California, carried out by rival drug traffickers, and 300 people in Tijuana, 75 percent of which were attributable to drug-trafficking disputes.

Mexican drug-trafficking organizations are still very much in the developmental stages. Their insistence on the heavy use of violence and centralized control from headquarters in Mexico makes them more vulnerable than other drug organizations. But, like the Colombian cartels, we can expect that these organizations will learn with time and restructure their operations accordingly. Today a variety of Mexican organizations operating from many major cities in Mexico dominate the Mexican drug trade.

The Arellano-Felix brothers organization is based in Tijuana and is one of the most aggressive of the Mexican trafficking groups. They move multi-ton quantities of cocaine and marijuana and smaller, but still significant, amounts of heroin and methamphetamine. Benjamin Arellano-Felix heads this syndicate, which operates in Tijuana, Baja California, and parts of the states of Sinaloa, Sonora, Jalisco, and Tamaulipas. Syndicate activities are coordinated through Benjamin's brothers, Ramon, Eduardo, and Javier. Ramon coordinates security operations for the syndicate and has a well-deserved reputation for the use of violence.

The Caro-Quintero syndicate is based in Sonora, Mexico, and specializes in trafficking in cocaine and marijuana. The syndicate was founded by Rafael Caro-Quintero, who has been incarcerated in Mexico since 1985 for his involvement in the murder of DEA Special Agent Enrique Camarena. Since Rafael's incarceration, his brother, Miguel has taken over day to day management responsibilities. Miguel is under indictment in the United States. He was arrested in 1992, but a Mexican federal judge in Hermosillo dropped all criminal charges and ordered his release from custody.

The Juarez Cartel was headed by Amado Carrillo-Fuentes until his July 4, 1997, death during surgery in Mexico City. The cartel is still heavily involved in the trafficking of cocaine, heroin, and marijuana. Following Amado's death, a power struggle broke out that resulted in sixty murders in the Juarez area between August 1997 and September 1998. Apparently, this violence was resolved with Vicente Carrillo-Fuentes, Amado's brother, taking control of the organization.

The Amezcua-Contreras organization, based in Guadalajara, is managed by three brothers, Luis, Jesus, and Adan Amezcua-Contreras. It is a massive methamphetamine-trafficking syndicate and a major supplier of precursor chemicals to other methamphetamine syndicates. This syndicate controls much of the legitimate trade in chemicals in Mexico as well. Jesus and Luis were arrested in June 1998, but all criminal charges were dropped by a Guadalajara judge. Adan, who was arrested in November 1997 on weapons charges and rearrested in March 1999 for money-laundering violations, was released from prison.

DOMINICAN DRUG-TRAFFICKING ORGANIZATIONS

The Dominican Republic is one of the poorest countries in the world. Dominican drug-trafficking organizations started out as retail cocaine dealers in emigrant communities in the United States. Perhaps the most famous of these communities was in the Washington Heights area of Manhattan in New York City. Starting in the mid-1970s, Dominican immigrants moved into this community and began handling Colombian-supplied cocaine. Soon their trafficking activities had spread into New Jersey, Connecticut, and some of the affluent suburbs of New York (Jackall 1997; Pellerano and Jorge 1997).

Dominican drug traffickers were mostly retail operators until the 1990s. At that time, many Colombian drug syndicates began to divest themselves of wholesale operations, passing them on to Mexican drug syndicates. The Mexicans were charging a transport fee of 50 percent of the drug shipment. Traffickers from the Dominican Republic saw this as an opportunity to get into the wholesale cocaine business. The Dominican Republic is closer to New York City than Mexico, emigrant Dominican communities had already been established in New York, and drug distribution systems had already been established in these communities. The Dominican trafficking syndicates made the Colombians an offer they could not refuse. For transportation of wholesale cocaine shipments to the New York City area, they would charge only 25 percent of the shipment as a fee, thereby undercutting the Mexican syndicates.

As a result of this business arrangement with Colombian cocaine traffickers, two major Dominican drug syndicates emerged. One syndicate, operating out of the Dominican Republic itself, provides stash sites for cocaine shipments from Colombia. This cocaine is transported into the Dominican Republic in small boats or by air drops. Traffickers from the Dominican Republic take it from there, smuggling the drugs into Puerto Rico in boats, repackaging the drugs, and shipping them to the continental United States by way of containerized maritime cargo ships or routine commercial air flights.

Once in New York City, the drugs are distributed by ethnic Colombian wholesalers or, increasingly, by a second syndicate, ethnic Dominicans, that now operates up and down the East Coast. Dominican drug syndicates also operate in smaller cities on the East Coast, including Fall River, Massachusetts, and Lewiston,

Maine. Many of these smaller cities have Dominican immigrants who work in low-wage, labor-intensive industries, such as garment manufacturing. Operations in these smaller cities have several advantages for Dominican syndicates. First, it expands their customer base. Second, they face virtually no competition from other established drug-trafficking organizations.

Dominican syndicates rotate members in the United States. Typically, they move operatives in for a two-year stay and then retire them to the island. Once back on Dominican soil, drug traffickers are protected by restrictive extradition laws to the United States.

Like many newly formed trafficking syndicates, the Dominicans employ violence to establish their reputation and protect their turf. One Dominican syndicate in New York City has been directly linked to seven murders, including the shooting of a police officer who was ambushed after responding to a fake 911 call. Another example is found in Lowell, Massachusetts, where in 1990 six people were found hogtied and choked to death as a result of a dispute with Dominican traffickers. In 1992, 146 houses in Lawrence, Massachusetts, were subjected to arson in a turf battle between several émigré Dominican gangs.

CUBAN ORGANIZED CRIME

The United States has experienced a tremendous influx of Cubans since 1959. Many of these immigrants chose to come to the United States to enjoy political and social freedom, but a significant percentage are criminals who are as opportunistic and entrepreneurial as their traditional organized crime counterparts. Cubans migrated in great numbers to the United States in three distinct historical periods.

1. In 1959, immediately before and after the fall of the Batista regime
2. Between 1965 and 1972, during the Camarioca boatlift or "freedom flotilla," when approximately 250,000 Cubans migrated to the United States
3. Between April 21 and November 10, 1980, when a boatlift from Mariel Harbor delivered approximately 125,000 new Cuban refugees into the country

The Marielitos

It has been conservatively estimated that 2 percent of the 1980 Mariel Harbor boatlift arrivals were classified as prostitutes, drug dealers, drug addicts, vagrants, or mentally ill. These **Marielitos** were much less sophisticated than the criminals in the two earlier groups and tended to exhibit a more violent nature than the earlier arrivals, partly because for two decades many Marielitos had been confined to brutal Cuban prisons. Fidel Castro denounced them as being the scum of Cuban society. Because so many Marielitos spent so much time in prison, upon release they had no legitimate business and consequently entered the drug market (see Chapter 6).

Since their arrival in the United States, many Marielitos have formed gangs that focus on drug trafficking. In cooperation with organizations such as the La Compania in drug-trafficking operations, the Marielitos were enforcers and executioners or performed other dirty work. The President's Commission on Organized Crime states: "The Marielito gangs are most often involved in cocaine trafficking, along with murders and assaults, which are usually a part of the illicit narcotics trade."

The profile of the Marielito is a poorly educated male, usually in his 30s with physical strength as his most marketable commodity. Many Marielitos are familiar with automatic weapons and guerrilla warfare, possibly because of previous military service in Angola or Central America. Ninety percent of the Marielitos have tattoos somewhere on their bodies depicting names, words, or symbols of criminal activities performed. Marielito gangs exist in Washington, D.C. (with membership as high as 500), Las Vegas, Los Angeles, and New York City. Other smaller gangs (ranging between five and ten members) have appeared in Connecticut, Florida, Indiana, Texas, Nevada, and California.

An Overview   Involvement by Latin American traffickers in the drug trade plays a major role in the influx of drugs to American streets. Heroin, cocaine, and marijuana are produced in many different Latin American countries and bring a handsome profit for foreign traffickers and their U.S. counterparts. Mexico has been active in drug production and importation for decades and still produces a significant percentage of the heroin and marijuana consumed in the United States. The groups controlling this activity are large organizations that employ native Mexicans as well as Mexican Americans who reside in the United States. Mexican traffickers have also been successful in the corruption of public officials, who provide protection of goods and intelligence information to the traffickers.

These traffickers have also been successful in establishing a working relationship with Colombian traffickers, who desire the use of Mexico as a transshipment point for Colombian cocaine in transit. South American countries such as Peru and Bolivia participate in global drug trafficking by producing the coca leaf for later use in cocaine manufacturing. The unstable economies of these countries serve as an incentive for involvement in coca leaf production, which offers the farmer a greater income than the growing of a legitimate crop.

Colombia is another South American country whose contribution to the drug business is not in growing coca leaves, but in converting them into cocaine hydrochloride (powder). For over a decade, one of the most powerful organized crime groups existed in this country, the Medellin Cartel. This group concentrates on the production of cocaine powder and uses violence and intimidation to facilitate the drug's subsequent delivery to the United States. In addition to Mexican and South American drug traffickers, many Cuban nationals residing in the United States are also involved in this illicit business. Since the late 1950s, huge numbers of Cubans entered the United States, many of whom were drug traffickers, such as the Marielitos and members of the La Compania, both of which demonstrate a propensity for violence. Although its official numbers are relatively small, the La Compania exerts influence in many major U.S. cities through hundreds of associate members.

A SMALL CORNER OF THE WORLD: ORGANIZED CRIME IN THE TRIBORDER AREA

The area where the borders of Argentina, Brazil, and Paraguay meet seems an isolated, very out of the way place for a major convergence of transnational organized crime groups. The Triborder Area (TBA) has become a major haven for drug- and arms-trafficking groups, money launderers, and sexual traffickers.

In the seemingly remote cities of Ciudad del Este and Foz do Iguacu, over $12 billion is laundered every year. Ciudad del Este is the commercial center of the TBA, generating $13 billion a year in commercial transactions, both legal and illegal. Much of this business is generated as a result of the city's position as a transshipment point in the robust drug- and arms-trafficking business.

The TBA hosts criminal organizations from around the world. It also has its own indigenous organized crime groups from Paraguay and Brazil. These native syndicates have helped to create a hospitable environment for organized crime groups from Chile, Colombia, Corsica, Ghana, Italy, Ivory Coast, Japan, Korea, Lebanon, Nigeria, Russia, and Taiwan. The importing of counterfeit CDs, CD-ROMs, and other pirated products links local syndicates with foreign partners in Asia and the Middle East.

Illicit commerce in the TBA is enhanced by virtually nonexistent immigration controls and pervasive governmental corruption. False identity documents, passports, and visas, particularly Paraguayan, are easily obtained in the TBA. Police and other government officials suffer from low pay, inadequate or nonexistent training, miserly funding from their central governments, bank secrecy laws, and very weak money-laundering controls. In an atmosphere of pervasive governmental corruption and human rights abuses, corruption flourishes.

Geography, Society and the Economy of Crime

The TBA region is defined geographically by three main population centers: Puerto Iguazu, Argentina; Foz do Iguacu, Brazil; and Ciudad del Este, Paraguay. Paraguayan economic planners tried to enhance the tourism business at Iguaza Falls by creating a free-trade zone in the Ciudad del Este area. The hope was that Argentinians and Brazilians would cross the border in search of inexpensive merchandise, particularly electronic products. The net result, however, was the creation of a free-trade zone for transnational organized crime groups.

Between 1971 and 2001 the population of the TBA increased dramatically from about 60,000 to more than 700,000, primarily as a result of the construction of the Itaipu Hydroelectric Dam (Junger 2002: 196). In addition, the TBA is a remarkably diverse little corner of the world. For example, Foz do Iguacu is populated by 65 different nationalities, including about 7,000 Lebanese, 30,000 Chinese, and 4,000 Koreans (Grinbaum 1996: Bartolome 2001; 25–26). In addition, the TBA has one of the largest Arab populations outside the Middle East. A 2001 report suggests that the TBA's population includes 23,000 Arabs of Palestinian and Lebanese descent (Daly 2001). The area was marked by a significant Lebanese emigration during the 1970s civil war in Lebanon. In Ciudad del Este and Foz do Iguacu, 90 percent of the Arab population is of Lebanese descent (Bartolome 2001: 4).

Ciudad del Este is a South American version of Casablanca in the 1940s. The city is populated with intelligence agents and their informants. Human traffickers, arms merchants, and drug traffickers are omnipresent. On the city's streets everything from the newest pirated computer software, to prostituted children, to AK-47s is easily obtainable. An AK-47 sells in the street bazaars for $375 (Goldberg 2002). The city is also a prominent banking and retail center. In fact, Ciudad del Este's retail economy is the third strongest in the world, ranking right behind Hong Kong and Miami. The city has a bigger retail economy than the rest of Paraguay combined (Rotella 1998; Rohter 2001). Lebanese and Palestinians operate many of the commercial enterprises in Ciudad del Este, although they tend to reside in the Foz do Iguacu area of Brazil.

In many ways it is difficult to determine which of the three countries of the TBA is the most corrupt. Carlos Menem, the president of Argentina, has resisted any attempts to reform the government and the courts. Menem has also been alleged to have been involved in a government cover-up of a bombing of a Jewish community center in Buenos Aires and arms trafficking (Rohter 2002a, 2002b, 2002c). Menem, whose parents were Syrian immigrants to Argentina, appointed a Syrian army colonel as the head of customs at the Buenos Aires Ezeiza International Airport, one of the prime smuggling entrepôts in South America (Anderson 2001).

In Brazil, an investigation by the Brazilian Congress in 2000 implicated congressmen, state governors, mayors, judges, and police officials in a series of criminal activities that included arms- and drug-trafficking and tax evasion (Downie 2000). The report suggested that Brazil's entire police structure had to be torn down and reconfigured because of the pervasive drug-related corruption. A congressional investigation in 2002 implicated over 100 politicians, police, and businessmen in a massive cargo theft enterprise (Colitt 2002).

Immigration fraud is abetted by pervasive corruption in the government of Paraguay. One investigation found that annually an average of 570 individuals enter Paraguay through the Ciudad del Este Airport with forged passports, visas, or identity documents. The investigation found that a bribe of $5,000 was sufficient to circumvent immigration controls (Bartolome 2001). More recent investigations have centered on the ease with which Lebanese citizens have been able to enter Paraguay with false documentation. Ahmad Assad Barabat, a regional Hizballah leader, entered Paraguay with a false visa issued in Panama (Bartolome 2001). The Paraguayan consul in Miami, Carlos Weis, sold more than 300 passports, visas, and bills of lading between 1999 and 2002 (Rohter 2001).

The fidelity, honesty, and effectiveness of police forces are key to controlling organized criminal activities. Police corruption is a prime precondition for large-scale organized crime activity. Many issues help explain the total lack of effectiveness of the Argentinian police against organized crime. First, the government is far more interested in repressing political dissent and maintaining public order than in fighting crime. Second, the Argentine judiciary moves with great deliberation at a snaillike pace, which is frustrating to many police. As a result, police frequently are engaged in brutality, framing suspects, and even murders and rapes (Delinquent: Tackling Crime Needs Police Reform 2002). Finally, Argentinian police are paid the equivalent of about $400 a month. For these reasons and many others, corruption is pervasive in the Argentinian security forces (U.S. Department of State 2001).

But problems with corruption only begin to describe the difficulties of the Argentine police. Since at least the 1970s the Argentine police have been integrally involved in organized crime activities, including prostitution, gambling, and kidnaping (Delinquent: 2002). The Brazilian police are similarly hampered by widespread corruption and human rights abuses. Brazilian state police forces have engaged in widespread murder, torture, and rape. They routinely detain people without arrest outside of the law. Death squad activity and vigilantism is epidemic in Brazilian policing. In addition, Brazilian police have been implicated in drug trafficking, kidnaping, and murder-for-hire schemes (Oviedo n.d.). Similarly, the Paraguayan police routinely engage in torture, death squad activities, the use of excessive force, illegal detention, and wanton violations of privacy rights (U.S. Department of State 2001). Paraguayan police also engage in large-scale extortion from both legitimate and illegitimate businessmen, particularly Arabs and others of foreign descent (Rogers 2001). The police force of Ciudad del Este is widely regarded as pervasively corrupt. Law enforcement largely depends on private security services. All 6,000 stores and shops, 36 banks, and 15 money exchanges in the city employ private guards (Grinbaum 1996).

The TBA is a perfect environment for thriving illicit enterprises and the operations of organized crime groups. Money laundering laws are lax. The governments and police forces are thoroughly corrupt. Unregulated commerce thrives. Immigration controls are easily circumvented. As a result, a confluence of both indigenous and transnational organized crime groups has set up operation in the area. Criminal organizations engaged in the trafficking of drugs, guns, children, and women flourish. Financial and business crimes are easily conducted. Smuggling of stolen goods and counterfeiting of other products occur without interference. While organized crime in the TBA may be thought of as in its developmental stages, the conditions for the success of these incipient enterprises are all present.

Organizing Crime in the TBA

One local organized crime group is headed by Luiz Fernando Da Costa. For years Da Costa ran a criminal organization in Brazil that traded arms for cocaine. Da Costa operated in the TBA until 2001. Since then he is rumored to have moved his base of operation to Colombia (Fernandino Is Shown to the Press 2001). Organized crime in Brazil has become much bolder and more violent in recent years. In 2002 the country narrowly averted an attempt by organized crime to bomb the Sao Paulo Stock Exchange. In 2003, drug organizations engaged in running battles with police in the streets of Rio de Janeiro, snarling traffic and paralyzing the city's business district, and organized crime groups assassinated two Brazilian judges. Additionally, Brazil's most prominent prison gang has close ties to both Da Costa and Italian organized crime figures. In the TBA, organized crime gunmen attempted the assassination of the Foz do Iguacu city council president (Lehman 2002; Colitt 2003; Muello 2003).

Cuidad del Este is, for all intents and purposes, a free-trade zone for organized crime. Money laundering, the theft of intellectual property, human trafficking, alien smuggling, and arms and drug trafficking all flourish. A significant portion of the illicit market revolves around the trade of drugs for arms by Colombian organized crime and political groups (Riyadh Alam-al-Din 2001). One of the largest criminal organizations in the Ciudad del Este area is the arms-trafficking syndicate run by Elvio Ramon Contero Aguero out of the town of Pedro Juan Caballero on the Brazilian border (Palacios and Florentin 2002). General Lino Cesar Oviedo, the head of the Paraguayan Cartel is also based in Ciudad del Este and Foz do Iguacu. The Paraguayan Cartel was responsible for multi-ton cocaine shipments originating in the TBA during the 1990s and for massive money-laundering operations in the TBA. Closely associated with the activities of the Paraguayan Cartel is Paraguayan General Jose Tomas Centurion (Lino Oviedo Case n.d.).

In addition to local generals and crime lords, criminal syndicates from around the world operate in the TBA, in close association with Paraguayan businessmen, politicians, the military, and the ruling Colorado Party. Colombian, Italian, and Nigerian organized crime groups all operate in the TBA (Silva 2000; Sweeney 2001).

The social demography of Ciudad del Este makes it a perfect location for the operations of Chinese organized crime groups, including the Fuk Ching,

Big Circle Boys, Flying Dragons, and Tai Chen (Rotella 1998). These crime groups run protection rackets in Ciudad del Este's Chinese community and engage in large-scale trafficking in counterfeit products (Bartolome 2001; Paraguay: Strong Ties Seen 2002). In addition, Korean organized crime groups with branches in Ciudad del Este, San Francisco, Buenos Aires, Sao Paulo, and Santa Cruz (Bolivia) are active in the region (Bartolome 2001). Two Canton-based Chinese organized crime groups, the Fu Shin and the Fei Jeii, are also active in Ciudad del Este and Foz do Iguacu (Milani 2001). These crime groups have been able to maintain virtual immunity from prosecution in the TBA because of bribes paid to Paraguayan judges (Bartolome 2001: 16). Several other Chinese organized crime groups in the TBA deal primarily in counterfeiting. The Sung-I and Ming groups have worked closely with the Egyptian Gamaa Islamiya (a group closely associated with Hizballah) in a product counterfeiting scheme (Hong Kong Mafia 2002).

Russian organized crime groups have initiated activities in Paraguay, primarily with the intention of trafficking cocaine to Europe, although they appear not to be setting up permanent operations in the TBA. These crime groups have also opened up contacts in Brazil with the intent of procuring Brazilian women for prostitution operations in Israel. The Russian groups may well be paying for drugs and women with arms. In the late 1990s, AK-47s and AR-15s have become more common as the weapons of choice for indigenous organized groups in the TBA and adjoining countries. Chechen organized crime groups have also made contact with drug traffickers and money launderers in the TBA from their base in Argentina. Presumably, the Chechens are attempting to open up another guns-for-drug conduit through the TBA (Russian Mafia in Latin America 2000).

Organized Crime Enterprises in the TBA

The three countries that converge in the TBA have similar characteristics with regard to the drug business. Argentina is not known as a drug-producing country, but it serves as a trans-shipment conduit for cocaine from Bolivia and heroin from Colombia. Brazil acts as a middleman in the trade between Western European nations and the United States in the precursor chemicals essential to the production of methamphetamine. Paraguay serves as a trans-shipment site for cocaine moving out of Peru (U.S. Department of State 2002). The TBA is primarily an area through which drugs destined for Argentina, Brazil, and Paraguay pass. The existence of more than 100 clandestine airstrips in the TBA enhances its utility as a transit point for both drugs and arms, particularly for cocaine, which is usually moved by small aircraft (Glock n.d.).

About $12 billion in illicit profits are laundered each year in the TBA (Oviedo n.d.). Money launderers use the banks and currency exchange businesses in Cuidad del Este and Foz do Iguacu to engage in fraudulent financial transactions (Bartolome 2001). Money-laundering activity is pervasive in the financial industry, particularly through Brazilian and Paraguayan banks operating in the TBA (Osava 1999). The Central Bank of Brazil estimates that 17 percent of the profits generated by Colombian drug cartels is laundered through the Brazilian bank system. Brazilian investigators estimate that 40 percent of the local businesses in Foz do Iguacu are nothing more than fronts established by organized crime groups for the purpose of laundering money. (Osava 1999; Oviedo n.d.). Paraguay is internationally recognized as a major money-laundering center (U.S. Department of State 2002). Almost all of Paraguay's $5 billion money-laundering activity occurs in Ciudad del Este (Oviedo n.d.).

The theft, smuggling, and transport of luxury cars is also a major business in the TBA. Cars that are stolen in Brazil and Argentina are moved to Paraguay, Bolivia, and other points of embarkation throughout the TBA. More than half of the 450,000 vehicles registered by drivers in Paraguay is acquired through illegal channels (Silva 2000). Stolen automobiles and other contraband passes along an illegally opened road cutting through the Iguau National Park. The Asuncion–Paranagua Highway is also a major conduit for contraband (Glock n.d.).

Counterfeiting and pirating commercial products is also a booming business in the TBA. More than half of all the business software utilized in Brazil is pirated. Forty percent of the cigarettes entering Brazil are illegal contraband smuggled into the country (Jones 2002). The large Arab community in the TBA seems to dominate the black market in counterfeit and pirated goods. Some investigators have suggested that bootlegged computer software and CDs are used to raise money for Hizballah and Hamas (Jones 2002). Ciudad del Este is the major transshipment point for counterfeit CDs and CD-ROMs entering South America from Hong Kong, Macau, Malaysia, and Thailand. About $1.5 billion worth of these counterfeits move through Ciudad del Este each year (Bartolome 2001). Estimates suggest that 90 percent of the commercial goods sold by stores, street vendors, and other agents in Cuidad del Este is counterfeit. Paraguayan law permits patents to be issued for international brand names by the National Brand Register, thereby facilitating the pirating of contraband merchandise (Bartolome 2001). Much counterfeiting activity is directly linked to organized crime groups operating in Korea, Lebanon, and Taiwan (Paraguay: 2002). The International Intellectual Property Alliance has identified Paraguay as its most serious problem nation (Nurton 2002).

Conclusion

Social, political, economic, and geographic variables have come together to create a perfect environment for sustaining organized crime in the TBA. The TBA is distant from other major population centers and far from the seat of state power in any of the three affected nations. Even if it were not geographically isolated, the pervasive political and law enforcement corruption in Paraguay, Brazil, and Argentina would still be a significant contributor to the creation of an organized crime entrepôt. Lack of banking regulations and extremely permissive banking enforcement in Brazil and Paraguay create a perfect environment for money laundering, which in turn fosters the drug and arms markets. The same preconditions that have sustained indigenous organized crime create an attractive environment for the operations of transnational criminal organizations.

The essential unanswered question is whether this set of circumstances is simply a happy coincidence for organized crime or whether its genesis has more sinister roots. It strains credulity to suggest that tens of thousands of Lebanese Arabs, Taiwanese, and Koreans simply happened to wander into this South American backwater on even to suggest that they knew of Ciudad del Este and Foz do Iguacu.

There is scant evidence as to how this organized crime boomtown came to pass. It is possible that transnational organized crime groups identified the potential for the area in the normal course of business, which, particularly in the case of the Taiwanese, may have involved Paraguay. It is harder to explain the Arab migration to the jungles of the TBA. The U.S. government seems to suspect that this may be part of a master plan to fund Islamic extremist groups through illicit enterprise. But the existence of many lawless states closer to the

Middle East makes it difficult to conclude that the obvious location for such a complex and sinister plot was a remote corner of Paraguay. Other speculations are also possible. We have seen over the decades the hidden hand of the CIA and the Mossad nudging some organized criminal enterprises into action for a specific purpose. The answer may lie in a combination of all these things. But for the moment the mystery of South America's twenty-first century Casablanca remains.

EMERGING TRANSNATIONAL CRIMINAL ORGANIZATIONS

Chinese Organized Crime

Chinese organized crime groups have always posed a particular difficulty for American law enforcement. Culturally and ethnically organized groups are among the most difficult to infiltrate and accumulate intelligence about. But the Chinese syndicates, operating primarily in ethnically defined, tightly organized Chinese communities of many major cities, have been virtually impossible to penetrate. The **triads, tongs** and Chinese street gangs operating in the United States are able to deflect most law enforcement efforts to control their activities. This problem became even more difficult as the twentieth century ended because a fourth Chinese organized crime entity, syndicates from mainland China, has now established a presence here (Chin 1996; Robinson 1999). The large, traditionally organized triads, headquartered in Hong Kong, Macau, and Taiwan, continue to be the largest Chinese organized crime groups operating worldwide. Triads, most of which trace their origins to seventeenth-century China, continue to control traditional illicit enterprises such as extortion, illegal gambling, gunrunning, and drug trafficking. But the newer mainland criminal organizations may be more aggressive and more difficult to control.

First, they are not encumbered by the traditional organizational structure of the triads, which is more ceremonial than functional in the world of organized crime. The newer groups tend to be more loosely organized and more flexible. They are therefore much more responsive to law enforcement pressure and to economic fluctuations and opportunities. Second, they have moved more aggressively than the triads into newer enterprises, such as software piracy, product counterfeiting, credit card fraud, and computer chip theft, allowing them to quickly build vast reserves to finance their forays into drug trafficking.

Traditionally, the triads established close working relationships with ethnic Chinese groups in major cities on the Pacific Rim of the United States and in Europe. Working with tongs and street gangs, they easily established local criminal structures to facilitate their enterprises and purchase drugs. The newer criminal syndicates from the mainland have apparently broken this monopoly and now deal directly with the tongs and the street gangs themselves. Like the more traditional triads, they now have a broad range of criminal contacts in many countries that can broker deals and provide logistical support.

Chinese organized crime groups have for decades had a strong presence in the many ethnic Chinese neighborhoods and urban enclaves around the world. Gambling operations, prostitution, loan-sharking and narcotics trafficking were the mainstay of these criminal organizations operating through the triads, tongs, and street gangs. What has changed is that another, newer type of criminal syndicate has been added to the milieu.

Chinese criminal organizations, no matter their origin, have always derived great strength from their ability to overlook ethnic differences and cooperate freely and openly with other groups around the world. In the United States and Europe, for example, Chinese organized crime groups have worked closely with Italian, Dominican, and even on occasion Mexican and Colombian drug traffickers in trafficking heroin. The well-established ethnic Chinese communities of Europe and North America have created established and relatively safe footholds for Chinese organized crime, thus making the United States and Europe major markets for illegal goods and services. In addition to the United States, Chinese organized crime activity is particularly prominent in the Netherlands, the United Kingdom, and Germany. But, since the late 1980s and early 1990s, Chinese criminal organizations have also established strong footholds in Central Europe, a major conduit for moving illegal Chinese immigrants to Western Europe.

The Triads

Although traditional triad societies are based in Hong Kong, Macau, or Taiwan, they also exercise great power in every country that has a sizable emigre Chinese community. Estimates are that the triads, collectively, have a worldwide membership that exceeds 100,000. The triads are traditionally organized associations of Chinese businessmen and Chinese organized criminals involved in a panoply of criminal enterprises. Most Hong Kong-based triads have evolved over the years from traditional cultural groups into loose-knit associations of illicit and licit businesspeople, cooperating with each other and sharing mutual business interests. Contrary to some perceptions, triad leaders neither dictate what criminal enterprises their members should pursue nor receive any direct monetary remuneration from these enterprises. They simply provide introduction and facilitate mutual association.

Case Study

Operation Hardtac

In 1997 the FBI began investigating Weng Keek Hoo, who had been recently released from prison and deported to Hong Kong for previous drug-trafficking convictions. The investigation revealed Hoo had successfully reestablished ties to heroin distributors in several United States cities and was now residing in New York City.

Using informants, electronic surveillance, records analysis, and undercover operatives, agents identified associates of Hoo in Philadelphia, Detroit, Atlanta, Los Angeles, and Gary, Indiana, as well as in Hong Kong, Macau, Singapore, Malaysia, Thailand, Peru, New Zealand, Nigeria, China, and Iran.

Agents also determined that large quantities of heroin were being shipped regularly from Southeast Asia to Vancouver, Canada, then on to Toronto, Canada, before being smuggled into the United States. FBI agents identified four distinct trafficking organizations directing the operations from Southeast Asia. These organizations were also linked to past heroin seizures in Canada and Australia and to another FBI investigation. The New York investigation was closely coordinated with the Royal Canadian Mounted Police, the Hong Kong Police, and the Australian Federal Police, and evidence was uncovered showing that several of the leaders of these organizations were members of the 14K Triad criminal enterprise based in Hong Kong.

In late 1998, after a 13-month investigation, federal grand juries in the eastern and southern Judicial districts of New York charged 21 members of the organization with drug trafficking and money laundering. Arrests were made in New York, Philadelphia, Atlanta, and Hong Kong, and heroin, semiautomatic and automatic weapons, vehicles, and more than $150,000 cash were seized.

Source: www.fbi.gov, 2006

Sixty different triad societies operate in Hong Kong alone. Hong Kong's largest triad is the Sun Yee On, which is also the only remaining triad with the traditional hierarchical structure. The 14K Triad, probably the second most influential in Hong Kong, has abandoned traditional hierarchies and is now a loose confederation of more that 15 separate groups. In addition to their drug-trafficking activities, the Hong Kong triads have been expanding their criminal enterprises into new ventures that include high-tech computer crimes and the manipulation of stock and futures markets. By the 1990s the Hong Kong triads were engaged in expansion that would have been unthinkable just a few years earlier, extending their criminal activities from Hong Kong into the Guangdong region of South China.

The largest triads, like Hong Kong's 14K and Sun Yee On and Taiwan's United Bamboo, have autonomous branches extending worldwide. It is important to understand that these are affiliated organizations, not extensions of one massive criminal organization into other countries. In addition, in response to the booming economy of the United States during the Clinton administration, the triads began investing heavily in legitimate businesses in the United States and Europe. The 14K and the Sun Yee On have made substantial real estate purchases in Canada according to the RCMP, and the FBI reports a vast expansion of 14K activity, both legal and illegal, in the United States.

Although triad groups frequently share resources and cooperate on specific projects, it is important to understand that there is no international triad organization and no centralized control of triad groups. Enterprises such as alien smuggling tend to center on small-scale, triad-affiliated organizations, whereas drug trafficking seems to involve more ad hoc collusion. The key point is that this is an ad hoc collusion based on mutual interests in a specific project or at a particular time, not an overarching criminal conspiracy.

Chinese Syndicates from the Mainland

Criminal syndicates based in mainland China (the People's Republic) are typified by the Big Circle Gang and the Fuk Ching. Both gangs have smaller cells operating in Chinese communities around the world. These cells cooperate

---

The Triad Hierarchy

The triads have a hierarchical style of authority within the organization, including the positions of first and second in command. Men holding these positions are not referred to by a title but by a number beginning with 4, a reference to the ancient Chinese belief that the world is surrounded by four seas. The triad organizational positions are as follows:

- The 489 is the shan chu or hill chief, the head of the triad society in a particular city or geographical area.
- The lung tau holds responsibilities as an adviser and counselor.

- The 438 is the incense master charged with ceremonial duties.
- The 426, the red pole or red rod, is the member most accomplished in the martial arts, or kung fu. He also acts as the enforcer or executioner of triad members and the organizer of attacks against the outside society.
- The 432, the grass sandal, is the messenger or liaison responsible for communications and interaction between other units.
- The 415 is an expert on administration or finance.
- A 49 is an ordinary member with no rank.

with each other and with the mainland organizations on an ad hoc basis. But the cells themselves operate autonomously without centralized authority or direction. Local cell leaders use their connections in Chinese ethnic communities and with mainland groups to mount what appear to be very complex criminal operations that are well planned and highly organized. Once again, this planning and organization are integral to the cell, not to the overall criminal organization. Because cells have contact with other cells worldwide, they are able to carry out large-scale drug-, arms-, and human-trafficking enterprises with surprising ease and success.

Canadian and U.S. law enforcement intelligence analysts report that the Big Circle Gang, the largest of the mainland groups, has become the most active Asian criminal organization in the world and achieved that status in less than a decade. By the end of the 1990s, the Big Circle Gang had established cells in Canada, the United States, and Europe and was extensively engaged in drug and human trafficking, vehicle theft and trafficking, financial fraud, product counterfeiting, and high-tech crimes. Big Circle Gang cells are highly sophisticated in their use of technology, which has made them virtually immune from electronic eavesdropping and surveillance. The Big Circle Gang first surfaced in the United States in the early 1990s; by the end of the decade it had major criminal organizations operating in New York, Boston, Seattle, San Francisco, and Los Angeles. The Fuk Ching is best known for its human-trafficking activities, but is also heavily involved in drug trafficking, particularly of heroin and methamphetamines.

The Fuk Ching Gang

The Fuk Ching is best known for its human-trafficking activities, but is also heavily involved in drug trafficking. It is regarded as one of the most powerful of the international and transnationally active Chinese organized crime groups in the United States. It is estimated to have approximately 35 members, with another 20 members currently in prison.

The Fuk Ching originally emerged in New York in the mid-1980s. As with other gangs, its main criminal activity in Chinatown was extortion. It was founded by a collection of young men, youths in their late teens and early twenties, from Fujian province in China, many if not all of whom had criminal records in China. Fuk Ching recruitment today continues to be among Fujianese teenagers.

One structural characteristic that makes Chinese organized crime different from other forms is the relationship between some of the street gangs and certain adult organizations. The Fuk Ching, for example, is affiliated with the Fukien American Association, an adult group or tong, that provides the Fuk Ching physical places to gather and hang out. They allow the gang to operate on the tong's territory, thus legitimizing them with the community. The tongs also provide criminal opportunities (such as protecting gambling operations) and supply money and guns.

Like the Fuk Ching, tong-affiliated gangs have an ah kung (grandfather) or shuk foo (uncle) who is the leader. The top gang position is the dai dai lo (big big brother). Communication between the tong and the gang occurs principally between these two individuals. Below the dai dai lo, in descending order, are the dai lo(s) or big brothers, the yee lo or saam lo (clique leaders), and the ma jai or little horses. A variety of norms and rules governs the gangs, such as respecting the ah kung, beating up members of other gangs for turf trespassing, not using drugs, following the orders of the dai lo, and not betraying the gang. Rules violators are physically punished or killed.

The Sicilian–Chinese Organized Crime (COC) Alliance

As we learned in Chapter 6, Mafia heroin originates primarily in Southeast and Southwest Asia and is then routed through Sicily before being smuggled into the United States. We now examine the development of a strong Asian relationship between the La Cosa Nostra and Asian nationals. In 1985, Hong Kong clothier Franklin Liu testified before the President's Commission on Organized Crime about his recruitment as a heroin courier for Sicilian criminals operating in New York. He was first contacted by Antonio Truano, a Sicilian organized crime figure, with regard to Truano's money-laundering operations. Liu had a four-year business visa allowing him to travel to and from the United States legally.

In one case, Truano gave Liu a suitcase with $400,000 in cash and instructed Liu to wire the money to a bank in Zurich, Switzerland. Because Liu had no drug-trafficking connections in the Far East, Truano arranged a connection and agreed to pay Liu $5,000 for each kilo (2.2 pounds) of heroin he brought into the United States.

Subsequent to this arrangement, Liu was contacted by a Thai woman who made arrangements to meet him at a hotel in New York City. Turano had given each of them one-half of a dollar bill so that each could identify the other. Liu gave the woman the keys to his car, which she returned the next day with heroin concealed in the trunk. The woman then exchanged the keys for a payment of $40,000 in cash and a $60,000 bank check. When Liu went to collect the money from Turano, he discovered that Turano had been arrested. Liu was subsequently arrested and convicted.

Enormous amounts of heroin were smuggled into the United States during early 1983. For example, one Sicilian operation had scheduled 1.5 tons of heroin for shipment to New York City, which had a wholesale value of over $333 million. Authorities estimate that the Pizza Connection was a worldwide operation encompassing countries such as Brazil, Canada, and Spain (see Chapter 1).

The Japanese Yakuza

When all the criminal organizations composing the **yakuza** are considered, it would have to be among the most powerful and largest of the world's many organized crime confederations. Yakuza organizations are extremely diverse in their criminal enterprises, and tend to be highly structured and well organized. Yakuza organizations not only dominate the Japanese underworld, but are also powerful actors in the legitimate economy. In fact, using their extortionate practice of *sokaiya,* they have successful penetrated all aspects of social, economic, and political life in Japan (Huang and Vaughn 1992; Song and Dombrink 1994; Shibata 1996).

There are at least 3,000 separate yakuza-affiliated criminal organizations in Japan, approximately 60 percent of which, with about 90,000 members, are housed under the aegis of three large yakuza organizations: the Yamaguchi-Gumi, Sumiyoshi-Kai, and Inagawa-Kai. These three associations control most gun, drug, and human trafficking; prostitution; illegal gambling; extortion; and white-collar criminal activity in Japan.

Scholars have estimated that yakuza activity in Japan yields an annual revenue of about $13 billion. Most yakuza criminal enterprises are based in Japan,

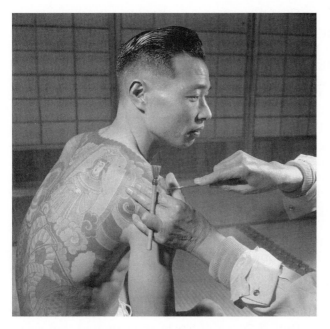

Yakuza gang members are known for extensive tattoos covering most of their body. Here a Japanese tattoo artist works on the shoulder of a yakuza gang member.

(*Horace Bristol, Corbis/Bettmann*)

although yakuza groups have a well-established presence, often in legitimate business activities, in Australia, the United States, and most of Asia. Transnational criminal activity engaged in by yakuza groups primarily involves drugs, guns, and trafficking in women for prostitution in the Japanese market.

Most yakuza organizations purchase their heroin and methamphetamine supplies from Chinese organized crime groups based in Taiwan and Hong Kong. Yakuza organizations have also established working relationships with South American drug traffickers to obtain cocaine to be sold in Japan. Chinese and Russian organized crime groups are primary yakuza sources for firearms. The arms-trafficking business is one of the most profitable for yakuza groups because of extremely restrictive Japanese laws regulating firearms. About 90 percent of the firearms in Japan originates from international sources.

Yakuza organizations are also heavily involved in the international trafficking of human beings, particular foreign workers for the Japanese construction industry and foreign women for yakuza-owned entertainment and prostitution businesses. Yamaguchi-Gumi affiliated groups are particularly active in the prostitution business and rely heavily on women imported from Russia, Southeast Asia, and Latin America. There is little or no evidence that yakuza groups traffic women to the United States.

Most yakuza transnational crime activities are used to supply or support criminal enterprises internal to Japan. In the 1990s yakuza organizations

---

Yakuza Organizational Design

- Kaicho: boss or father of the organization, who possesses absolute authority
- Wakato: deputy or captain
- Wakai shu: soldiers, who make up most of the membership of the organization

apparently began developing working relationships with Russian organized crime groups. In 1992 the Yamaguchi-Gumi established such a permanent working relationship with Russian organized groups as suppliers of firearms and prostitutes. The establishment of more open trade arrangements between Japan and Russia and the scheduling of regular flights between major cities in Russia and Japan have facilitated this relationship.

There is little evidence that yakuza groups are involved in drug trafficking in the United States. The real threats posed by the yakuza in the United States are in the area of legitimate business investment and money laundering. Yakuza groups are heavy investors in U.S. and Canadian real estate, with particularly heavy investments in golf courses and hotels. Yakuza groups also launder their criminal profits in the United States by playing the U.S. stock market, making substantial and potentially destabilizing investments. The Inagawa-Kai Yakuza confederation, which is involved in drug and arms trafficking, extortion, investment frauds, and money laundering, has invested heavily in Hawaii and the states on the west coast of the United States.

Vietnamese Gangs

In the first eight years after the nationalist victory in Vietnam, about 650,000 Indochinese emigrated to the United States. It has been estimated that about two-thirds of these were Vietnamese, Chinese Vietnamese, or Vietnamese American people with backgrounds in drug trafficking, prostitution, and other crimes. Vietnamese gangs formed in seven cities in California, four in Texas, three in Louisiana, two in Alabama, and one each in Washington, Colorado, Florida, Massachusetts, New York, Pennsylvania, Oregon, Virginia, and Hawaii. Many of these gangs have special training in firearms and explosives and are considered especially violent. Major Vietnamese gangs in California have long-established connections with former South Vietnamese military and governmental leaders.

The Shining Path

The cocaine industry in Peru has produced a large and extremely influential drug-trafficking terrorist group called Sendero Luminoso, or **Shining Path**. For years the organization has controlled the upper Huallaga Valley, a region that produces more than 60 percent of the world's coca. The group was founded in 1970 by Abimael Guzmán (known by followers as "Presidente Gonzalo"), a professor of Marxist philosophy at the University of Huamanga in Ayacucho who embraced Maoism during several visits to China.

Since Shining Paths' beginning, Guzmán was known to his followers as the Fourth Sword of International Communism. The ideology of the Shining Path is "Marxism–Leninism–Maoism, Gonzalo Thought." The comma is said to be meaningful because it indicates that Gonzalo's ideas are still in formation and that they are also the fullest, most scientific, most modern development of communist ideology (Robbins 1989). The President's Commission on Organized Crime (1986a) has also recognized the Shining Path as an organized crime organization:

The Shining Path seeks a rural-based revolution to rid the predominantly peasant population of the imperialistic influences of the United States and other foreign governments. Although existing evidence is insufficient to link the Shining Path to the drug trade, the group has incited peasants, many of whom make their living from coca cultivation, to rebel against anticoca projects in major growing areas. During 1984 several anticoca projects, including a United States–supported crop substitution program, were attacked by armed mobs, resulting in many injuries.

Shining Path tactics have included converging on a town for the purpose of driving out or murdering local officials and imposing a puritanical new order. This is accomplished by holding people's trials and by redistributing livestock and land. Although many believe that Sendero's activities seem unorganized and random, many assert that they are systematically tearing down the structures of authority by removing influential and wealthy citizens from communities.

A Drug Enforcement Agency (DEA) official based in Peru who spoke with one of the authors suggested that the Shining Path has been responsible for numerous violent murders of police officers and high-ranking government officials in an effort to deter government interference in drug-trafficking operations. An example is the January 1990 assassination of Peru's former defense minister, Enrique Lopez-Albujar.

According to DEA sources, the guerrilla methods of operation used by the Shining Path are those used by the North Vietnamese during the Vietnam conflict. Experts who have studied the Shining Path fear that the group's level of violence and number of victims will soar greatly in the neár future.

The strength of the Shining Path was lessened by the 1992 arrest of Guzmán in Peru. Although some experts have argued that his removal has seriously reduced the movement's prospects for seizing power, the Shining Path is still thought to carry out extensive operations, but most are terrorist rather than strictly military or paramilitary in nature (Rosenau 1994).

Before perestroika, organized crime was never officially acknowledged in the Soviet Union. Following the dissolution of the Soviet Union, however, the situation changed. By the end of 1991, government sources estimated that some 3,000 to 4,000 active organized crime groups existed in the Commonwealth of Independent States alone (Volobuev 1989). The fact that organized crime exists in Europe should come as no surprise. Block and Chambliss (1981) noted that "European cities had [forms of] organized crime that predated the Industrial Revolution." Organized crime has long existed in the French ports of the Mediterranean. In Italy, the 1992 assassinations of Giovanni Falcone and Paolo Borsellino, two leading investigators, illustrate the strength and capabilities of organized crime.

European Organized Crime

Eastern and Central Europe

In recent years, several significant changes have occurred in Europe, particularly those of a political nature. One-party governments have given way to multiparty democracies. In addition, the former Soviet Union and Yugoslavia have experienced political changes that resulted in the formation of several new states. In addition to politics, economic changes are also profound, not the least of which is that, for the first time, unemployment is accompanied by rapid inflation. Shortages of personnel, training, equipment, and facilities are a few problems. Social changes are also having important effects on the complexion of Central and Eastern Europe. These are due largely to the attempt to adapt to new political freedoms, the impulses of the market, and the disintegration of the safety net formerly provided by socialism. Moreover,

We know that Italian Mafia influence in legitimate U.S. businesses provides opportunities for members to hide illicit earnings and operate in secrecy. In what ways do you think this technique will be duplicated by emerging organized crime groups in the United States, and how will traditional organized crime respond?

legal changes stem from the need to reform newly established justice systems and to restructure criminal and procedural laws.

Each basic change has affected crime in general and organized crime in particular. The current criminal justice system in Eastern Europe is ill-equipped to deal with the increasing crime problem.

Block and Chambliss (1981) point out that the traditional view of organized crime as a single giant infrastructure is incorrect and misleading. As discussed in Chapter 1, organized crime is really a loose network of criminal organizations that provide illegal goods and services to the public. The Western Europe (and North American) concept of organized crime generally includes the following characteristics:

- Stability
- Relatively definite infrastructure and division of labor
- Profit orientation
- Illegal activities
- Use of violence or the threat of violence
- Corruption of and protection by public officials

Until recently, officials in European countries used the term organized crime to refer to ad hoc affiliations among a few offenders for the purpose of committing joint offenses. In Eastern Europe the concept of organized crime has changed rapidly. In fact, the ministry of the interior of the former USSR developed its own operational definition of organized crime, which essentially matches that used in the West (Volobuev 1989).

- Consolidation of criminal elements in a region or a county as a whole
- Development of a hierarchial chain of command
- Development of a group of leaders who are not implicated in the commission of specific offenses, but carry out organizational, administrative, and ideological functions
- Involvement of corrupted public officials in criminal activity
- Creation of a system of protection to neutralize all forms of social control

Europe's Shadow Economy

Despite claims by many European leaders that crime has virtually been eliminated from their countries, a great deal of petty crime, such as fraud, theft, smuggling, and loan-sharking exists. Much of what is now considered organized crime developed amid the **shadow economy** with wide support from the population. The shadow economy consists of two sectors: the **black market**, which was entirely illegal and dealt with smuggled goods, drugs, and so on, and the **gray market**, which provides goods and services in competition with the state-controlled market but at free-market prices.

For years, the shadow economy was lucrative, but increasing numbers of foreigners (businesspeople and tourists) with hard currency to spend raised the stakes. Fraud, theft, embezzlement, assault, and robbery against locals were supplemented by currency violations and prostitution targeted to foreigners. The international connections brought in the weapons trade, which thrived in contraband, gambling, and economic crimes (Jousten 1993). Although enterprising individuals continue to commit all these crimes, they have also become growth areas for organized crime, which seems to be expanding. Jousten (1993) discusses five illicit enterprises within the shadow economy that provide exceptional opportunities for emerging organized crime groups.

Drug Trafficking

One of the best growth areas for organized crime in Central and Eastern Europe is drug trafficking. Aside from alcohol, the most commonly abused drugs in the region are heroin and hashish. Heroin generally comes from Central Asian republics, but low-grade heroin also comes from home-grown poppies in Poland and some of the Baltic republics.

Home-grown opiates are thought to be a basically private enterprise with little organized crime affiliation. In Central Asia, however, organized crime, the narco-Mafia, controls the majority of heroin produced primarily in areas in the Near East such as the Golden Crescent. Selling drugs abroad is attractive for Central and Eastern European traffickers because it provides an opportunity to obtain hard currency and prized Western goods, which can be exchanged for a tidy profit in the shadow economy.

Corruption

It is clear that, in a time of economic scarcity, individuals rely on networks of friends and relatives to secure necessities. In this environment it is sometimes difficult to distinguish between gifts and bribes. A shop clerk will be bribed to set aside a few oranges from the next shipment, or a hospital clerk will be bribed to take in a patient requiring treatment past a long waiting line. Such corruption has become a way of life in Eastern Europe.

Internationally Organized Theft

The rate of theft is increasing dramatically throughout Central and Eastern Europe. Usually, this occurs on an individual basis and the role of organized crime is marginal. However, with regard to theft across borders, organized crime plays an important role, specifically for two particular targets: cultural artifacts stolen from homes and churches and expensive cars stolen from the

You Decide

Can Opportunistic Crime Be Characterized as Organized Crime?

Russian tax collectors apparently set tax rates for businesses arbitrarily, gouging some business owners for as much as they can get and offering sweetheart deals to others. Can such profiteering on the part of tax officials be characterized accurately as organized crime? You decide!

West for resale in the East. The primary link with organized crime rests with the international marketing of these items, a black market thought to be worth an estimated $6 billion annually.

Terrorism

The United States has long suspected Bulgaria of supporting international terrorism (Lupsha 1981). Bulgaria is ideally situated at a crossroads of East and West in a region where terrorism is well developed. In addition, terrorism is supported by the political, economic, and social instability of the region.

Trade in Firearms

Illicit trade in firearms was a direct result of the drastic reduction in the size of the army in the USSR, which resulted in a surplus of weapons. Records documenting the whereabouts of these weapons are either in disarray or have been destroyed. Compounding the problem, current military personnel are poorly paid, have low morale, and are tempted to supplement their pay by selling military-issue firearms to the black market. As a result, law enforcement officials have noticed a growing incidence of firearms being used in the commission of both street crimes and organized criminal activity.

By 1994, almost 6,000 separate organized crime groups were active in Russia, at least 200 of which were large and sophisticated enough to be operating outside Russia. In addition, the Georgian Mafia and Chechen and Azeri groups, operating in their own republics, took control of much of the black market. Several of these groups are active in the United States, including the Medessa Mafia in New York and California, Chechen groups, and the Malina, also in New York (Williams 1995a: 9). Further complicating the situation in Eastern Europe is the existence of organizations such as the Bulgarian company Kintex, which formerly provided espionage services, but is now totally devoted to the business of organized crime. In addition, Turkish drug-smuggling organizations expanded their traditional smuggling routes through the former Yugoslavia, taking advantage of the Croatian–Bosnian–Serbian conflict.

The changing economic situation in Central and Eastern Europe has lowered the standard of living for most of the population at a time when the market is becoming more consumer oriented. Centralized economic control has been decreased, and emphasis has been placed on free enterprise. As a rule, profits to be made in both the gray and black markets are tremendous, particularly on the international level. Because most if not all of the population is involved in the gray market, it is likely that organized crime will continue to flourish, and criminal recruits from the general population will be plentiful. Accordingly, the criminal justice system in Central and Eastern Europe is in a state of crisis and will indirectly create future problems for surrounding European countries.

Italy's Mafia Wars   As a result of the Italian Mafia's origin on the island of Sicily and its southern mainland provinces of Calabria and Campania, northern Italians viewed organized crime as primarily a regional problem. Today, few people believe that. With the European Union achieving full economic integration in the twenty-first century, it is feared that Italian organized crime groups will leap at the chance to extend their reach from one end of Europe to the other. Organized criminals in Italy have found it advantageous to take over legitimate enterprises. For example, in Sicily, these criminals have infiltrated the wine and citrus industries and assumed control of hospitals and soccer teams. As money-making entities in their own right, these acquisitions have enabled organized crime to increase their already considerable political clout.

As we observed in Chapter 3, the origins of what we know as the Mafia go back to the feudal past of nineteenth-century Sicily. It developed as a system of administration and justice when the oppressive government provided little of either. At the turn of the century, Mussolini thought he had dissolved the Mafia, but the invading allies in 1943 gave it new life. For decades, the Mafia thrived and flourished to become one of the most formidable crime organizations in world history. In December 1987, the maxitrial in Palermo resulted in the convictions of 468 mafiosi. A second trial one year later convicted an additional 40 people, but unfortunately, most were released on appeal (see Chapter 1).

Giovanni Falcone, a magistrate, was murdered with his wife and two bodyguards in a bomb attack outside Palermo in May 1992. In a book published shortly before his death, he explained how the Mafia's idea of honor was once tacitly shared by most Sicilians. But in the mid-1990s, this is no longer the case. Falcone's funeral was broadcast live on television and attended by thousands of mourners, who crowded Palermo's streets and cathedrals. Dignitaries present were heckled and booed by the crowd, which seemed to be an indictment against Italy's politically corrupt leaders. In November 1993, eighteen suspected mafiosi were arrested in connection with the murder of Falcone.

Only two months after Falcone's death, a second bomb killed Paolo Borsellino, a special Mafia prosecutor in Palermo. His police escort, four men and a woman, also died in the blast. As a result, the new government headed by Guiliano Amato ordered 7,000 troops to the streets of Palermo in an effort to demonstrate that the government was not turning a blind eye to its crime problems. The government also passed new anti-Mafia legislation, which give police special search authority, the power to tap telephones, and the right to use other forms of electronic surveillance. In addition, courts were given the power to seize the assets of those suspected of being Mafia members. More important, a full-scale U.S. style witness-protection program was implemented to encourage confessions from Mafia informers. Before their deaths, both Falcone and Borsellino had been asking the Italian parliament for such measures.

After Falcone's murder, several informers surfaced and provided authorities with information about the Palermo-based Mafia families. During the first part of 1993, a special Italian police squad, the DIA, arrested seventy suspected mafiosi. Over 300 mafiosi collaborated with authorities in return for promises of reduced sentences and a chance for them and their families to be relocated elsewhere to begin a new life. After the arrest of central Sicily mafioso Leonardo Messina, Operation Leopard was launched and another 241 mafiosi were arrested, and more than $2,000 billion lire ($1.4 billion) in Mafia assets was seized.

An important part of Messina's testimony was information on how the Mafia maintained its hold on public sector contracts in Sicily, which some experts suggest are the Sicilian Mafia's greatest source of income. Indeed, subsidies provided by Italy's central government to raise living standards in the impoverished south gave the Mafia a constant source of income. Year after year, money flows from Rome to finance development projects aimed at giving the backward region a modern infrastructure. More often than not, much of the money ends up in Mafia bank accounts, and the development projects often remain unfinished.

Mafia-linked companies enjoy a distinct advantage over those operating independently. Only companies willing to bow to the gangsters' conditions are

Judge Giovanni Falcone walking with Paolo Borsellino. Both were crusaders against the Mafia in Palermo, Sicily. They were killed in 1992 by hired Mafia killers due to their efforts against Italian organized crime.

allowed in on the deals. In addition to establishing prices, the Mafia imposes its own subcontractors, security men, and candidates for employment. To ensure compliance, it resorts to arson, bombings, and even murder. Between early 1992 and the end of 1993, more than 3,000 businessmen and politicians were arrested in connection with a billion-dollar corruption scandal. Prime Minister Giulio Andreotti was accused of consorting with the mob; secret service personnel were accused of manipulating slush funds and explosives, and judges were charged with having organized crime connections.

Italy's Mafia Structure

During the mid-1980s, a turncoat Mafia boss, Tommaso Buscetta, first gave Falcone his insight into the innerworkings of the mob. Another, Antonio Calderone, set forth its rules at great length.

> Cosa Nostra is a society of men of honor. According to estimates, these men number more than 1,500, divided among 67 families in the province of Palermo alone. The families are the basic units; each holds sway over a recognized territory. Each family has a chief, its *capofamigila,* chosen by its members, who is aided by a hand-picked *consiglieri* or counselor. Then are a number of deputies below, who are what could be called sergeants of the organization; each is known as the *capodecina* (head of ten) in charge of five, ten, twenty or even thirty soldati, the rank and file soldiers.
>
> Above the families lies the high command. The *capomandamento* is the colonel responsible for three families. In turn, he answers to a provincial

committee. Above that lies a regional committee, the government of the Cosa Nostra. Not even the Mafia claims national power. Instead, it has given affiliate membership to the heads of both the Calabrian 'Ndrangheta and the Neapolitan Camorra. We are the elite of crime. (Cramer 1993)

Sicilian mafioso are more than just criminals. They operate almost as a state within a state, which makes them a unique form of organized crime. The Mafia imposes its own laws (at gunpoint) and its own taxes. Extortion of owners of small businesses to pay protection money is common. In addition to extortion, the global heroin trade has provided Italy's Mafia families with considerable wealth. During the late 1970s, the Sicilian Mafia became a major force in the trade, and by the early 1980s its families were estimated to be supplying 80 percent of the heroin market in New York, using morphine base from Southeast Asia treated in secret laboratories around Palermo. During the early 1980s, competition in the drug trade resulted in countless murders of rival mafiosi and government officials alike. Between 1979 and 1982, the Sicilian Mafia murdered nine magistrates and over twenty police officers. Also among its victims were politicians, civil servants, journalists, trade unionists, and anyone else who was thought to hinder its activities.

Despite past successes in the global drug trade, the Sicilian Mafia seems to be losing ground. Italian and U.S. police estimate that Italian drug traffickers now supply less than 5 percent of the U.S. market, which is thought to be a decrease. One reason is a 1982 treaty between the two countries allowing close police collaboration and the exchange of prisoners and witnesses.

Russian Organized Crime

During the summer of 2002, Russian organized crime leader Alimzan Tokhtakhounov was arrested and charged with conspiring to commit wire fraud and bribery in connection with fixing the 2002 Summer Olympic figure skating competition. The case was developed by Italian investigators who, in wiretaps, overheard Tokhtakhounov put pressure on French Olympic Judge Marie-Renie Le Gougne to vote for the Russian pairs team of Elena Berezhnaya and Anton Sikharulidze, who did win the gold medal. In exchange, Tokhtakhounov said Russian skating officials would make sure that the French ice-dancing team won gold in that event, which they did (Brady 2002). This case illustrates Russian organized crime's ongoing influence in what appears to be a growing number of criminal enterprises (Dodd 2002).

The breakup of the Soviet Union in 1991 led to the precipitous introduction of capitalism and personal freedoms to the people of Russia and the fourteen other newly independent states. The change, unfortunately, had notable negative side effects. In particular, it created a platform for the growth of Russian organized crime. Reminiscent of the Prohibition era in the United States, hundreds, possibly thousands, of large and small gangs deal in drugs and raw materials, extort money, and steal, as the underpaid and often corrupt police look on (Hockstader 1995). High-ranking Russian government officials are also enriching themselves by aligning with known criminals. The term *Mafiya* (also called *organizatsiya*) has been associated with Russian organized crime most generally by the local media. In Russia, which is in the process of developing a free-market economy, a middle class, and the rule of law, virtually everything that has the appearance of criminality is labeled as Mafia. Schmid (1993) suggests that the term is overused in Russia, because whenever even the smallest merchant offers a product that is perceived as being too expensive, customers make a face and say "the Mafia."

The situation in Russia is complicated by the difficulty of running a legitimate business without breaking the law. Russian economic laws are generally unclear and contradictory in nature. Businesses that pay the legally required import and export tariffs often have no capital left to reinvest. So even though many smaller merchants acquire merchandise through questionable (and even criminal) sources, the Mafia may not be the culprit.

On the other hand, the many street markets have fallen victim to powerful Russian street gangs. Virtually anyone who attempts to earn money through production or trade is targeted and victimized. Farmers selling home-grown tomatoes in kolkoz markets are terrorized by competitors; prostitutes who have accompanied foreign visitors risk losing their entire earnings to thieves once they leave the hotel room. Shops that do not pay extortion money to gangsters often pay police or security firms to protect them from the gangs. In addition, Russian police claim that about 400 banks are controlled by organized crime groups, which explains, in part, why few bank robberies occur (Hockstader 1995).

More than 100 criminal syndicates have staked claim to the many emerging rackets in Russia. In fact, in an interview with *U.S. News & World Report* (1994), General Mikhail Yegorov, the first deputy interior minister of the Russian Federation and the overall director of Moscow's fight against organized crime, reported that 174 Russian crime organizations had been identified; they operate in every republic of the former Soviet Union and in twenty-nine countries, including the United States. Indeed, in 1994 the FBI had identified Russian crime groups operating in New York, Denver, Seattle, Cleveland, Minneapolis, Chicago, Dallas, and Boston. Russian mobsters who operate in the United States are entering into an array of criminal rackets, including heroin trafficking, prostitution, health-care fraud, billion-dollar gas tax scams, and money laundering (Frankel 1995a).

Russian mobsters are equipped with high-quality automatic weapons thought to be obtained from factories and military installations. Car bombs, homemade explosives, and even rocket-launched grenades have been detonated in Moscow, mostly attributable to gang wars and rivalries (Hockstader 1995).

Organized crime in Moscow is divided among eight criminal groups, although organized is rarely an accurate term to describe them. The most powerful of these groups are the Chechens, whose members originated in a tribe in the Caucasus Mountains and who have a long-time reputation of being brutal and fierce. Their specialty is bank fraud and extortion. Other groups include the well-armed Dolgoprudny group, which focuses on protection rackets; the Lyubertsy nationalist group, known for beating up any persons whom they view as being part of the counterculture; and the Solntsevo

---

The U.S. Mafiya's Gas Tax Scam

In September 1995, federal agents busted a diversified Russian crime gang. Fifteen Russian immigrants were indicted as part of a $140 million gas tax scam, the biggest in U.S. history. The scam involved members of the Mafiya who bought motor fuel from a supplier and then created an elaborate chain of companies to buy and sell it. One of these companies, the *burn*, supplied receipts showing that the motor fuel tax had been paid. When the government attempted to collect the taxes, the burn company, often nothing more than a postal box, had vanished.

group from southern Moscow, which runs slot machines rackets and taxi rings (Hockstader 1995). Other crime groups are organized geographically, with some claiming certain parts of cities, such as St. Petersburg and Odessa, and others with ties to small villages outside the larger cities.

All eight groups are involved in prostitution, drug trafficking, auto theft, and extortion (Duffy et al. 1994). More obscure groups focus on specialized crime, such as art theft and forgery. In short, Russian organized crime groups specialize in whatever market niche the local commerce affords. In all cases, turf wars between groups occur throughout Russia. In some quarters of Moscow, the sound of gunfire is a nightly occurrence, not unlike the Cicero suburb of Chicago, which served as Al Capone's base during Prohibition.

Organization and Structure

Crime groups in Russia are believed to lack the organization of other groups such as the Mafia. To aid in the understanding of Russian "organized" crime, the Financial Crimes Enforcement Network (1992) developed an organizational model. The structure is that of a cell, not unlike that of a Colombian cartel; its purpose is to minimize contact with other cells within the same organization to prevent the identification of the entire criminal enterprise.

The boss of a Russian organized crime cell, called a *pakhan,* controls *four* criminal cells through an intermediary called a *brigadier.* Bosses employ two spies to ensure the brigadier's loyalty and prevent his becoming too powerful. At the bottom of the structure are cells specializing in various types of criminal activity, such as drug trafficking, prostitution, political corruption, and enforcement. A similar structure places an elite leadership on top. Strategies and decisions are made only at the top of the echelon. Security personnel insulate the bosses from low-level street operators. Criminals on the lowest level of the echelon are not privy to the identity of the organization's leadership. Although this organizational structure represents a general idea of how Russian organized crime is structured, it is likely that after law enforcement became aware of the operating procedures of these groups, the groups adopted different structures.

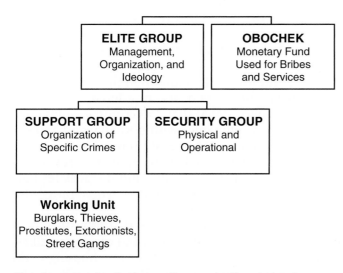

Russian organized crime cell: organizational structure.

Source: U.S. Department of the Treasury, Financial Crimes Enforcement Network (1996).

Case Study

Vyacheslav Kirillovich Ivankov, New York, New York

One of the first significant Eurasian Organized Crime (EOC) investigations in the United States occurred in 1993 with the targeting of Vyacheslav Kirillovich Ivankov, also known as Yaponchik, or Yaponets, a Russian "thief-in-law" (vor v zakone), who, according to the Russian Ministry of the Interior (MVD), had been dispatched to the United States to act as the coordinating authority for all EOC activity there. The investigation determined that Ivankov led an international criminal organization that operated mainly in New York, Toronto, London, Vienna, Budapest, and Moscow, but also in numerous other cities in the United States, Canada, and Europe.

Ivankov's organization specialized in extorting Russian business interests. The investigation proved that the Russian principals of Summit International in New York City were being extorted by Ivankov's organization. Summit International is an investment advisory firm for Russian émigrés in the United States. Ivankov and five of his subordinates were arrested by federal agents on June 8, 1995.

On July 8, 1996, in federal court in New York, Ivankov, Sergei Ilgner, and Valeriy Novak were convicted of extortion and conspiracy charges. Also, Vladimir Topko was found guilty of conspiracy charges, and Leonid Abelis and Yakov Volovnik pled guilty and cooperated with prosecutors. Roustam Sadykov fled to Russia, where the lack of an extradition treaty with the United States prevents him from being brought back for trial. Sentences imposed by the court ranged from four to almost twelve years.

This case is instructive because it marks the first time that the FBI and the MVD worked side by side on a criminal investigation. The Royal Canadian Mounted Police also furnished information critical to the investigation. Ivankov was the first head of an international EOC group to be brought to trial and convicted in the United States. This case is also significant in that it prevented Ivankov's organization from establishing a solid presence in the United States.

Source: FBI, 2006.

Operating Style

Russian organized crime groups, rather than focusing on the poor, prefer to victimize well-to-do people. For example, many Russian banks are partly or entirely controlled by organized crime. Organized crime groups launder their dirty money there and in Russia's new gambling casinos (Schmid 1993). In fact, banking is thought to be one of the most lucrative rackets of the Russian mafiosi and one of the most dangerous jobs for bankers. Nearly every banker in Moscow has been approached by at least one of the eight criminal groups (Duffy et al. 1994). In 1993, ten bankers were murdered in Moscow alone, with a total of thirty slain throughout Russia. In addition to the slain bankers, in 1993, ninety-four criminal entrepreneurs were also murdered.

A report issued by the Russian police stated that 150 criminal gangs control some 40,000 private and state-run companies within Russia, and an estimated 80 percent of all Russian businesspeople pay protection money to gangsters, the amounts ranging between 20 and 30 percent of gross revenues. This adds up to as much as half of a company's profits, and it translates into consumer prices that are almost 30 percent higher than they would otherwise be (Duffy et al. 1994).

Once the Russian organized crime group determines that a business is a success, six or so of its members dressed in business suits and carrying walkie-talkies visit it. The leader typically congratulates the owner for choosing to do business in Russia and for his or her newfound success. The owner will also be congratulated for doing business with the mob. In passing, a group member will mention that he knows the route that the businessperson's daughter takes to school. The rest is routine. By all indications, most citizens are unwilling to turn in organized criminals to the authorities. In St. Petersburg it is estimated that 70 percent of the police are corrupt. It is little wonder since they earn such low wages, but yet are given considerable police power.

Russian organized crime not only extorts and steals, but also has gone into business for itself, specifically in the areas of illicit drugs and illegal exports of substances such as magnesium, bronze, tin, titanium, aluminum, and petroleum. More alarming is the fact that police in Moscow are concerned that criminal organizations have stolen and sold nuclear bomb-making materials, such as enriched uranium and cesium 137, to international terrorists. In 1993, German officials arrested more than 100 people for smuggling nuclear components from the former Soviet Union (Frankel 1995b). Big profits can be made from the sale of these types of commodities. For example, on the black market, a kilogram (2.2 pounds) of chromium 50 sells for $25,000, a kilogram of cesium 137 may bring $1 million, and a kilogram of lithium 6 as much as $10 million.

Illegal income also comes from skimmed profits from factory managers, drivers, governmental officials, cabinet members, and customs officers. Organized crime also profits from the illicit arms trade. In fact, it has maintained an excellent working relationship with the Russian army, which explains why the arsenals of the Russian armed forces have dwindled rapidly in recent years.

Once realized, profits are used to finance other rackets in the United States, Canada, and Europe. Money travels in a loop from Russia to North America and back. In 1995, according to a Canadian police intelligence report, more than $1 billion a month came from Russia to the United States, Canada, and other money-laundering havens and then back to Russia. Officials in the United States have claimed that an unprecedented $20 billion in cash, most of it in crisp $100 bills, was shipped back to Russia in 1994 (Frankel 1995b). Much of the returned money is used either to bribe Russian officials, who help hide the counterfeiting of other $100 bills, or to aid in smuggling goods across the Russian border.

Both organized criminals and many governmental bureaucrats and private businesspeople get rich quick in Russia by exploiting the government's inability to protect the system. For example, Russian government officials can profiteer from citizens through tax levys. Although official tax rates exist, foreign companies often must negotiate directly with Russian tax officials regarding how much they must pay, and the rates can be as high as 40 percent.

Many small businesses are run off by tax officials who "renegotiate" tax terms at a rate much higher than the tax commissions set. It has been suggested that it is better to be victimized by organized crime than to be taxed by free-wheeling tax commissars who can effectively shut down a business with the stroke of a pen. However, not all businesses fall victim to organized crime or tax collectors. Indeed, the right gifts to the right people can allow businesses, especially large Western companies, to pay no taxes. In Moscow a large group of "consultants" sit on the board of directors of the Moscow branch of a prominent U.S. fast-food chain simply to keep the tax hounds away.

Privatization is a way to profit from the gray market while circumventing government regulations. Opportunistic businesspersons often take over chunks of government land on which they build dachas (country homes), often at government expense, and profit from their rental. For example, a Moscow hospital director, who now owns a dacha, rents private rooms to wealthy people at usurious prices (in hard currency) and puts the money in his own pocket.

The role of organized crime is strongly influenced by monopolists and corrupt government officials who profit from it. These are the players who fight against change and continue to resist the ongoing liberalization process. In this sense, criminals are the allies of the former communists and nationalists. At the same time, they have no desire to return to the old ways of authoritarian or totalitarian conditions under which criminals were restricted from maneuvering and manipulating the citizenry. Most experts agree that what is needed is to charge ahead with reforms that must also target corruption. Failure to do so will result in exploitation and autocracy in Russia.

Experts estimate that fifteen Russian organized crime groups are operating in the United States, but this figure is the subject of considerable debate. It is also thought that many of the Russian groups operating in the United States are not affiliated with their Russian counterparts (FinCEN 1992).

The literature comparing Russian and U.S. organized crime is scarce, and many misperceptions and inaccuracies exist. Many criminals are unorganized opportunists who are prone to violence. In almost all cases, Russian crime groups do not have a Mafialike structure. They pay percentages of their earnings to vori v' zakone, literally "thieves of the law," rather than being organized as a single family headed by a boss.

African Organized Crime

Africa is another important component of transnational organized crime. African organized criminals take advantage of social, economic, and political opportunities to expand their operations.

In his classic study of African organized crime, Opolet (1979) suggests that an appropriate definition of organized crime on the African continent is a criminal conspiracy to make a profit quickly and easily through the exploitation of political instability, disorganized and underfunded law enforcement, pervasive institutional corruption, and the exploitation of entrepreneurial opportunities. He identified three types of organized criminal entrepreneurs. One type includes established business and commercial leaders and high-ranking public officials who use their governmental and economic positions to personal advantage. Another involves less respectable, "shady" businesspeople who maintain working relationships with government officials and criminal entrepreneurs. The third group is composed of criminal operators engaging in drug trafficking, poaching, smuggling, and robbery (Opolet 1979). Implicit in Opolet's definition of illicit entrepreneurship are economic problems and the organization of law enforcement and criminal justice, coupled with illicit market opportunities that give rise to a set of social conditions conducive to the creation of organized crime syndicates.

Conflicts and inefficiency in law enforcement combined with political corruption and economic dislocation are major factors that lead to the creation of organized crime syndicates in Africa. The need for an illicit market for goods and services overrides all other needs in establishing criminal organizations. The activities of African organized crime syndicates are supported by several factors unique to the African situation: the ability to supply commodities such as ivory and coffee beans that are in high demand outside the continent and shortages of essential goods, such as sugar, soap, and motor vehicle parts, that can be obtained from outside sources (Kibuka 1979). Modern transportation has made the smuggling of goods out of and into Africa much easier, because smuggling activities can be hidden in normal commerce and tourism activities.

The core of syndicate activity in Africa revolves around black market business crimes that invite participation by highly educated but frequently unemployed or underemployed young people. Young people often find that their jobs fail to guarantee financial security (Kibuka 1979), and therefore black market entrepreneurship is attractive. In economies marked by high levels of surplus labor, unemployment, poverty, and an egregiously poor distribution of wealth and power, crime creates opportunity, and opportunity creates organized crime.

A highly diverse array of crime syndicates handling a variety of goods and services dominates the African scene. West African diamond and cattle smugglers, Ugandan and Kenyan coffee smugglers, and Somali poaching bands represent just some of the various criminal entrepreneurships on the African continent (Opolet 1979). New syndicates created in recent years are often involved in money laundering and the drug trade. In many ways, drug trafficking has been the key developmental variable in modern African organized crime. It has both augmented and reorganized traditional smuggling and poaching operations and has created an anomaly on a continent where the indigenous drug market has been decidedly weak and unprofitable.

A major weakness in the illicit market, however, is the apparent absence of a strong, high-profit, consumer-driven illicit drug market. Drug use as a social problem is a relatively new phenomenon in Africa that seems to postdate the establishment of its drug-trafficking syndicates. With the notable exceptions of khat chewing among the Sufis in eastern Africa and the use of cannabis products in both the northern and southern African regions, there is little historical evidence of the widespread use of psychoactive substances on the African continent (Asuni and Pela 1986). However, a study of 300 university students in Benin City, Nigeria, in the mid-1980s found ready availability and widespread use of indigenous psychoactive substances, such as coffee, cola nuts, cannabis, alcohol, and cigarettes (Nevadomsky 1985).

This survey also found some utilitarian use of diazepam and diazepoxide by students during examination periods. Even with these substances, recreational use was rare, and any use outside the pressures and stresses of the university system was very uncommon. Students' passing knowledge of cocaine was suspect; researchers found that students frequently confused cocaine with codeine. Cocaine use was not in evidence, and the drug itself was not reported to be readily available (Nevadomsky 1985). The study found no instances, whatsoever, of heroin use (Pela 1989), despite the already well-developed role of Nigeria as a transshipment point for Southwest and Southeast Asian heroin bound for the United States (Wankel, 1996). A similar study among fourteen- to twenty-five-year-olds found that alcohol, tobacco, indigenous stimulants, cannabis, and sedative–hypnotics were the most commonly used psychoactive substances in Nigeria.

The origin of African drug use appears to differ markedly from that found in Western industrial societies and plays a key role in explaining the slow development of wholesale and retail drug markets in Africa. Drug use in Europe and the United States is frequently recreational and social in nature, with personal pleasure playing a large role in the decision to consume. African drug use seems to be constrained within structural and political boundaries. For example, self-medication is a common and indeed necessary social response to the inadequacy of medical services in most African countries (Seck 1991). In addition, knowledge and familiarity with psychoactive substances has been constrained by lack of official concern with drug use.

Efforts in Africa to control drugs were slow to develop. Officials in the customs services and law enforcement were unfamiliar both with which

Case Study

Operation Pepsi Student Loans

In 1999, federal agents revealed that fraudulent student loan checks were being obtained by and mailed to individuals located in the Newark, New Jersey, metropolitan area. Some of the stolen identities utilized in this scheme were taken from stolen payroll records of Pepsi employees, which were processed by an outside vendor.

A criminal enterprise, composed of both Nigerian and Ghanian subjects, was linked to thirty-three fraudulent student loans. This enterprise had applied for fraudulent loans totaling nearly $700,000. All thirty-three loans were requested from Norwest Bank of South Dakota and managed for Norwest Bank by Servus Financial Corporation. Subjects of this criminal enterprise requested loan applications over the phone and then mailed the completed loan application and supporting documents back to Servus Financial Corporation.

Twenty-three of the applications using stolen identities were successful in obtaining loans. Of these, ten used the identities of Pepsi employees. The investigation found that the subjects were using stolen microfilm to obtain the employees' identifying information needed to complete the loan applications.

Over seventy different identities were used during this fraudulent operation. Once a loan application was requested, a member of the organization produced supporting documents to be mailed back with the application. The documents included false W2 forms, pay stubs, driver's licenses, and class schedules. Many false documents were produced on a personal computer located at the residence of one of the members of the enterprise.

Once the loans were approved, the checks were mailed to twenty-nine different addresses prearranged by members of the group. These addresses included individual houses, mail boxes, vacant apartments, and businesses. Once the checks were received, the group leaders recruited additional members to cash the checks. The checks were deposited into personal checking accounts, some were opened with stolen identities and some used the actual name of the recruited individuals. The checks were cashed in ten different banks located in New Jersey, New York, Virginia, Florida, and Massachusetts. Six of the leaders of this criminal enterprise were indicted and four have been convicted. One subject is believed to be hiding in West Africa.

Source: www.fbi.gov, 2006

drugs were controlled and the drugs themselves. In addition, police and administrative agencies were unaccustomed to enforcing drug laws, and such enforcement was a low priority. Underfunded, poorly organized, and politically weak government ministries responsible for the control of drugs did not elevate public or official concern (Seck 1991). Major European and U.S. pharmaceutical manufacturers exploited this almost benign neglect by both consumers and enforcers; since the 1960s, they had been using Africa as a psychoactive dumping ground for their products.

Pharmaceutical manufacturers, either deliberately or as a most profitable oversight, failed to honor the 1981 Convention on Psychotropic Substances in most African states. The manufacturers were no doubt encouraged in their dereliction by a strong profit motive, but the fact remains that many African states never ratified the 1981 Convention. This provided an excuse for the pharmaceutical companies' abuse of the convention and relative immunity for violating the convention (Seck 1991).

Drug trafficking by criminal organizations in Africa has markedly increased (Asuni and Pela 1986). Related to increased drug trafficking are indications of increasing drug use among a wider cross section of the African population, and greater availability of nonindigenous substances has been noted. Although the most common drug of choice continues to be cannabis (Asuni and Pela 1986), these increases in drug use, although marginal, date from the early 1980s and initially involved substances produced in Europe and India (Seck 1991).

Although still a relatively new phenomenon, drug trafficking occurs in most African states today. Heroin from Southeast Asia and the Middle East moves through Tanzania and Mozambique, nations that have become major points of entry for heroin (Grove 1995). Cartels use African states increasingly as trans-shipment points for cocaine as they deemphasize the less profitable U.S. market and reroute cocaine to Europe and Japan. Colombian cocaine syndicates have set up operations in Nigeria and several other West African countries, capitalizing on ineffectual government efforts to monitor the importation of goods, secure the integrity of international borders, and monitor internal capital flow (Grove 1995). Nigeria has become a significant point of entry for cocaine destined for South Africa.

Both Zambia and Zimbabwe have become increasingly important drug-trafficking centers, where mandrax (a sedative), dagga, or cannibus, cocaine, LSD, and heroin are moved along well-established traditional smuggling routes. In these countries, trading mandrax for automobiles and their spare parts stolen from South Africa is common. Zambia has become important as a cultivator of raw materials and a manufacturer of psychotropic drugs, particularly mandrax. Malawi, South Africa, and Zambia have also experienced an increase in the cultivation of dagga for both internal consumption and export (Grove 1995).

The social structures and political–economic factors that create a predisposition for organized crime obviously differ from one African state to another. Although addressing these elements for all African nations is outside the scope of this text, a short description of the Nigerian and South African situations will be useful, since both have been the subject of much international law enforcement and journalistic scrutiny.

Organized Crime in Nigeria

The key to understanding predisposing factors in the development of organized crime in Nigeria is the country's political economy. Nigeria has been under military rule for twenty-five of the thirty-five years since it gained independence. A 1996 survey of international business executives rated Nigeria's regime as the most corrupt government in the world (Farah 1996).

Nigeria is characterized by political instability, rampant inflation, and high rates of economic inequality. About 5 percent of the Nigerian population controls 40 percent of the nation's gross income (Kayode 1983). In its post-civil war era (1970–1977), Nigeria experienced a tremendous spurt in economic growth. Oil revenues increased dramatically, and the government encouraged foreign investment in the oil industry to the detriment of the agricultural sector of the economy, which was the cornerstone of the Nigerian economy to that time (Owomero 1984). Beginning in about 1958, the exploitation of petroleum reserves by ten major oil companies, including the Nigerian National Petroleum Corporation, began to be the major economic sector in Nigeria (Sokair-George and Mann 1987).

The petroleum industry generated skilled employment opportunities and revenue, but it also provided a windfall profit for wildcatter entrepreneurs in Nigeria, creating a huge opportunity for public corruption (Sokair-George and Mann 1987). In addition, investment in the oil industry brought about economic expansion in food importation, construction and manufacturing, and infrastructure development. This period of economic prosperity raised the wages of urban workers considerably, while depressing rural incomes and adding inflationary pressures to the money supply. A massive migration from rural to urban areas resulted (Owomero 1984).

The Nigerian government used an indigenization decree to effectively subsidize entrepreneurs who already possessed considerable wealth and financial resources, which strengthened their relations with government officials. The Nigerian government's economic policy decisions had the unintended effect of creating conditions conducive to a massive increase in crime and social deviance and widened the gap between the rich and poor and the urban and rural sectors of the country (Owomero 1984).

The rapid migration to the cities caused staggering rates of unemployment, and the ostentatious display of wealth by government officials and capitalist entrepreneurs signaled to the less advantaged that the best way to redistribute wealth was through criminal entrepreneurship, which was viewed as "illegal but permissible" (Owomero 1984). A cultural ethos of accumulation, economic dislocation, and instability created a climate in which criminal syndicates were established.

Nigerian law and its enforcement combined with the vestiges of British colonialism were also catalysts for criminal organization. The lack of integration between indigenous cultural values and the colonial Anglicized legal system rendered Nigeria's legal system incapable of controlling corruption and organized crime (Karabi-Whyte 1982). This problem is compounded by the fact that Nigeria is governed by two different criminal codes, one in the north and another in the south, both derived from English common law. Both impose legal values and a system inherited from British imperialism and fail to represent the culture, philosophy, and social realities of Nigeria (Karabi-Whyte 1982).

This conflict between colonial concepts of crime and justice and indigenous concepts extends to the definitions of crime itself. British mores and ethics define the context of criminality, but native culture measures deviance and legality differently; for example, indigenous culture accepts polygamous life-styles and the influence of the supernatural in criminal motivation (Karabi-Whyte 1982). On one level of rationalization, the definition of crime and corruption is confused by the distance between the realities of social life and cultural foundations and the precepts of British law. The law's failure to recognize a society's values and the existence of differences between legal prescriptions and acceptable standards of behavior presents an opportunity for criminal entrepreneurs.

The process of enforcing the law has also created opportunities for organized crime in Nigeria. Again, some of these difficulties emanate from Nigeria's colonial past. Nigeria's police force was originally responsible for advancing British principles of exploitation and coercion (Ahire 1990). The early Nigerian police were indigenous peoples placed in a bureaucratic structure imported to Nigeria from Britain. Rather than being instruments of indigenous order emanating from Nigeria's culture, the colonial police were based on the model of an occupation force designed to control and subjugate the population and extract British profits, not to protect the citizenry or prevent crime (Ahire 1990).

The Nigerian police face staggering problems in trying to cope with crime and corruption. Many of these problems are structural and organizational in nature. For example, the Nigerian police force has effective jurisdiction over only a small fraction of the population and geographic area of the country, and its efforts are generally ineffective and sporadic at best (Kayode 1983). In addition, the Nigerian police force faces a drastic shortage of well-trained and educated personnel, due primarily to a lack of adequate funding and the inability to offer competitive and attractive salaries (Igbinovia 1982). The lack of high-quality police personnel greatly reduces efficiency and effectiveness on the force, and the lack of adequate remuneration invites corruption at the most basic level of the Nigerian criminal justice system. Efficiency, effectiveness, and even police honesty have also been affected by a lack of modern equipment and supplies.

Corruption is easy to accomplish when crime detection and communications equipment are antiquated and unserviceable. In addition, public cooperation with the police in Nigeria has been abysmal, to a large degree because of a public perception of widespread corruption, but also because of a public fear of becoming involved with an incompetent police force (Igbinovia 1982).

Nigerian Drug Traffickers

Nigerian-based organized crime groups have been heavily involved in the smuggling of large quantities of Southeast Asian heroin to the United States since the mid-1980s. Early Nigerian drug trafficking revolved around a groups of Nigerian naval officers who were being trained in India and gained access to Southwest Asian heroin, which they subsequently moved on to the United States. Subsequently, Nigerian criminal organizations shifted their sourcing from Southwest to Southeast Asian heroin, primarily from Thailand. Nigerian traffickers obtain their heroin in Thailand and then pay couriers, usually fellow Nigerians, to smuggle small amounts of heroin to the United States on commercial aircraft. The fee paid to drug couriers is far in excess of what a Nigerian citizen could legitimately earn in a year (Rake 1995; Smith et al. 1999).

Nigerian drug couriers tend to use rudimentary and rather crude techniques to move drugs. Devices such as hollowed-out-shoes and false-bottom suitcases are common modalities of smuggling. Some couriers engage in a practice known as *swallowing,* which involves the ingestion of up to 150 condoms full of heroin, which will be expelled upon their arrival in the United States. This is a most dangerous practice in that the breakage of just one condom would result in a fatal overdose of high-purity heroin.

Because of law enforcement targeting of Nigerian citizens, Nigerian drug traffickers have increasingly turned to couriers of other nationalities, in particular, young women of European or U.S. citizenry who they believe are less likely to be selected for search. Members of the U.S. military traveling in uniform are also frequently recruited by Nigerian traffickers. Some Nigerian criminal organizations have set up courier training schools to instruct couriers in methods to avoid or divert the attention of customs officials and to instruct them on how to avoid drug courier profiling.

The usual pattern followed by Nigerian-employed couriers begins with the acquisition of the heroin in Bangkok. The courier then flies to a transit country, often Indonesia or Egypt, where the drugs are handed off to a second courier, who flies them to another transit country less likely to raise suspicions of U.S. customs officials, where the drugs are transferred to a third and last courier. The point of these complicated arrangements is to conceal the point of origin for the drugs, Bangkok, from U.S. officials.

Nigerian traffickers also frequently employ an additional smuggling technique known as *shotgunning,* which is the practice of placing many couriers on the same flight to the United States. The hope is to overwhelm customs officials upon arrival. If some couriers on the flight are detained, others will inevitably get through. The profit margin for heroin is so high that the loss of even a significant portion of a shipment still leaves the traffickers with immense profits. In addition to human couriers, some Nigerian trafficking syndicates have begun to use express mail as a means of getting the drugs to the United States.

Once in the United States, the heroin is sold by ethnic Nigerian wholesalers. Nigerian syndicates are especially active in cities with large Nigerian émigré populations, like Chicago, which is home to 200,000 Nigerian nationals. In Chicago the Nigerian wholesalers sell the heroin to street-level retailing organizations, particularly street gangs like the Blackstone Rangers and Vice Lords.

By the end of the twentieth century, Nigerian traffickers controlled 57 to 90 percent of the market for Southeast Asian heroin in the United States. During the 1980s, high-purity Southeast Asian heroin was the most common substance on the U.S. market. But the entry of Colombian drug syndicates into the heroin market in the late 1990s seriously undercut the Nigerian share of the market. Importing heroin from Southeast Asia is very expensive, while importing from Colombia is far cheaper. High-grade Colombian heroin is now available at a much less expensive price that Nigerian-imported Southeast Asian heroin. Competition from the Colombians has caused the Nigerians to begin to seek markets for their heroin in Europe.

Syndicated Drug Trafficking in South Africa

South Africa has for some time played a multifaceted role in drug trafficking. Prior to the end of apartheid rule, it had, as one of the wealthier African countries, a major consumer market, particularly among wealthy whites, for cocaine hydrochloride and hallucinogens. In addition, South Africa has been for some time a major source country for cannabis (dagga or marijuana), most of which it exported to Europe, North America, and Asia. Other drugs, such as opiates and hashish, had very small consumer markets in South Africa, but were transshipped by a number of trafficking syndicates around the world. South American, Asian, the United States, and European drug-trafficking syndicates have used South African gemstone, currency, ivory, automobile, and weapons smuggling syndicates on a contract basis. These firmly established South African syndicates have been able to use well-established routes and methods, simply adding drugs to the list of profitable contraband (Grove 1995).

The selection of South Africa as a drug transshipment entrepôt was not accidental. Nigerian heroin traffickers began capitalizing on the vulnerability of South African borders to create a new drug pipeline for heroin produced in Southwest Asia and destined for the United States. In fact, Nigerian syndicates found South African smuggling ventures so profitable that sizable numbers of Nigerian citizens began emmigrating to South Africa. In intelligence reports, the DEA also indicated that Colombian- and Brazilian-based drug organizations could be targeting South Africa as a transshipment point and potential wholesale customer for their cocaine.

Drug enforcement efforts, stricter laws, and the tightening of customs inspections in other countries in concert with high unemployment and the high cost of living in South Africa made the country an increasingly attractive site for drug syndicate operations. Internal political instability and the reorganization and reform of law enforcement services also made South Africa especially vulnerable at this time. Finally, the absence of a serious internal drug consumption problem has kept drug enforcement from becoming a major law enforcement priority. This lack of awareness and immediacy in all of Africa, particularly in South Africa, resulted in a slow and thus far reasonably ineffective response to the drug trafficking threat (Grove 1995).

When South Africa ended apartheid rule with its first all-races elections in 1994, it invited international investment and encouraged international trade. This invitation, along with other national characteristics, made South Africa attractive to criminal organizations (Duke 1996). These other characteristics included a relatively sophisticated physical infrastructure, well-developed financial institutions operating with few formal controls for money laundering, no currency reporting requirements for large cash transactions, and an underfunded, poorly trained law enforcement establishment that was spread thin and still contending with the predemocratic-era taint of corruption.

With local criminal organizations already involved in gunrunning, vehicle theft, and fraud, both U.S. and South African law enforcement agencies became increasingly concerned about the potential for the rapid growth of organized crime in a country still reforming its political and economic institutions. In fact, South Africa became so concerned about organized crime that it sent narcotics agents abroad to Brazil, Thailand, India, and Pakistan. United States concern was reflected in the DEA's decision to open offices in South Africa and the FBI's consideration of doing the same (Duke 1996).

South African law enforcement agencies also became concerned that indigenous consumption of cocaine and heroin was increasing and creating a lucrative local market. The strengthening local market was reflected in the drop in cocaine prices during 1996, from $55 per gram to $33 (Duke 1996). Intelligence analysts in South Africa identified Chinese, Japanese, Israeli, and Russian criminal syndicates operating in the country. The interest shown by the Nigerian criminal syndicates and the Cali Cartel in South African investment opportunities was particularly troubling (Duke 1996).

For several years, Nigerian organized crime groups moved substantial quantities of cocaine through Argentina or Brazil to Angola or Namibia for transshipment to Europe, North America, or South Africa. This strategy allowed smugglers to avoid points of heaviest surveillance and interdiction activity. These Nigerian syndicates have complemented their Angolan and Namibian smuggling by moving cocaine directly into South Africa. In August 1996, police in Bogotá arrested a group of couriers from Nigeria, Liberia, and Namibia preparing to move 44 pounds of cocaine into South Africa (Duke 1996).

The interdiction statistics for South Africa indicate the increasing importance of cocaine trafficking to criminal organizations there. In 1992, narcotics agents seized 24 pounds of cocaine, and by 1995 they had seized 411 pounds of cocaine. At South Africa's busiest airport, seizures of cocaine climbed from less than 9 pounds in 1992 to more than 249 pounds in 1996 (Duke 1996).

The heroin trade has also become an increasing problem in South Africa. Nigerians, Indians, and others move the drug from Burma, Thailand, Pakistan, and Afghanistan. Heroin seizures have raised the specter of an increasing local market. In 1992 and 1993, South African police seized less than 2 pounds of heroin, but by 1994 seizures had climbed to 59 pounds (Duke 1996).

A relatively unsophisticated drug distribution infrastructure exists within South Africa itself. It is built around a network of street gangs that has grown more sophisticated and become more entrenched with the heavy volume of cash associated with the retail and wholesale cocaine trade. Local gangs, such as the Hard Livings in Cape Town, have caused considerable community concern, which led to the shooting and burning of the Hard Livings leader, Rashaad Staggie, in September 1996 by local residents (Duke 1996).

South Africa has for some time been a major source of marijuana, a major local cash crop; it supplies markets as diverse as Western Europe and Australia. South Africa has also been home to a strong indigenous trade in mandrax, a drug similar to Quaalude in effect. Mandrax is manufactured in tablet form in the Durban area or is sent to Maputo, Mozambique, for manufacture (Duke 1996).

Political and economic reform in South Africa has also altered patterns of drug consumption in the country. During the years of white minority rule, for example, the cocaine market was limited to whites who could afford it. For the poor of South Africa's slums and townships, the drug of choice or economic necessity was *white pipe,* a mixture of mandrax and marijuana. Police engaged in drug enforcement have reported an increase in cocaine and crack use in some areas of the country as economic redistribution began (Duke 1996).

Investigations conducted by the South African Narcotics Bureau identified more than 100 drug syndicates operating in the country. The indigenous syndicates still specialize in dagga, mandrax, heroin, and LSD, but the importation of cocaine through Colombia and Brazil is becoming a major source of income for new and developing syndicates. The profitability of cocaine has pushed some established criminal organizations into replacing traditional recreational substances with cocaine (Grove 1995).

Issues Related to Organized Crime Facing Africa

The portrait of emerging and incipient organized crime groups in Nigeria and South Africa, as well as the snippets of information available about criminal organizations in other African states, indicates clearly that the 1990s were a time of opportunity for organized crime groups. They developed from loosely affiliated gangs of smugglers and rogues into full-blown syndicates with solid connections to the business and political communities. It was also a time of opportunity for African states to prevent that development and to ensure that smuggling and opportunistic criminal groups did not become permanent parts of the political landscape. Africa presents a series of unique problems and contradictions.

Economic instability and political corruption make the African continent ripe for cultivation by crime syndicates. On the other hand, the absence of strong indigenous markets, particularly in drugs, appears to mitigate against the formation of permanent and enduring organizations. The future of African organized crime rests on the response to several issues:

Will African states meet the economic challenges presented to them? Will these nations democratize both their political system and their economies? Will African states move past the era of individual corruption before it becomes institutionalized?

Syndicates in South America, Europe, Asia, and the United States await answers to these questions. If reform is not forthcoming, the syndicates will find Africa a solid investment for the future. Once an investment has been made and transnational crime organizations have secured working relations with indigenous organized crime syndicates, it will be too late to turn back and uproot them. As studies of criminal organization in the United States, Colombia, and elsewhere show, the real factors that attract organized crime are far removed from the criminal underworld. These factors are associated with corporate boardrooms and government ministries, not the bars and back alleys that are traditionally thought of as organized crime's domain.

Albanian Drug-Smuggling Networks

The breakup of Yugoslavia in the early 1990s and the subsequent local conflicts between ethnic Serbs, Croats, Bosnians, and Albanians have focused attention on small, highly localized, but increasingly important organized crime groups of Albanian decent, operating primarily from Kosovo or from Albania itself. Albanian crime groups tend to be tightly organized individuals related to one another as part of an ethnic clan system. These groups are primarily located in the Balkans and frequently associated with the Kosovo Liberation Front, but their drug-trafficking activities have resulted in a proliferation of small criminal organizations throughout Europe and now even in the United States (DeStefano 1985; Galeotti 2000). Albanian organized crime groups typically start out in partnership with larger Italian or Russian organized crime syndicates. Their criminal enterprises are varied but usually include smuggling drugs, arms, and cigarettes; alien smuggling; and trafficking women for the purpose of prostitution. Partly as a result of regional conflicts in the Balkans, Albanian émigré and refuge communities have sprung up in many large Western European cities. Using these communities as an organizing base, Albanian organized crime groups have followed.

Initially, drug smuggling was only an activity ancillary to arms trafficking. But in the mid-1990s Albanian organized crime groups began purchasing large amounts of heroin from Turkish wholesalers. In the years that followed, Albanian drug syndicates developed their own sources for Southwest Asian (Golden Crescent) heroin, moving the drug to central and northern Europe and becoming major competitors with their former Turkish partners. European law enforcement officials believe that by 1999 the Albanians had become the dominant suppliers of heroin to Norway, Sweden, southern Germany, and Switzerland. In addition, by 1999 Albanian crime syndicates were challenging the hegemony of Italian syndicates in heroin trafficking and alien smuggling in Italy. Indeed, Italian law enforcement sources believe the Albanians had taken over most of the prostitution enterprises in Italy by 1999 and were trafficking heroin, hashish, weapons, and cigarettes through Italy for shipment to other European destinations. According to Italian law enforcement, the Albanians had taken the illicit trade in women and children away from traditional Italian syndicates by the year 2000.

Although Albanian prostitution and heroin operations in the United States are still small scale, it is clear that Albanian syndicates have been moving into the cities of northeastern United States for the last several years.

WHAT HAVE WE LEARNED?

This chapter discussed international organized crime in various parts of the world. Probably the largest, best organized, and most powerful international groups are the Colombian cartels. The status of the Medellin Cartel, which was feared by Colombian nationals for more than a decade, has been the source of much speculation since Pablo Escobar's death in 1993. Some have suggested that it may no longer exist. Experts have theorized that the Cali Cartel, Colombia's second-largest cocaine cartel, has taken the lead in world cocaine production, but in a much more subdued manner than the Medellin Cartel. Cali's business manner is more like that of a large multinational corporation such as IBM or Coca-Cola. That is, despite its proclivity for excessive violence, it is well organized, compartmentalized, and careful to recruit only highly screened and highly skilled members.

Cuban organized crime typically involves criminals who came to the United States during any of several boatlifts over the last two decades. The Marielitos, who arrived during boatlifts in the 1980s, organized in southern Florida, but have systematically moved to other parts of the United States. They have gained a reputation for being excessively violent.

Among the more important changes to the organized crime scene have been the growth and expansion of Asian organized crime in the United States. With the newfound popularity of heroin in many parts of the United States and growing Asian populations in many of its cities, related gang activity is on the increase. The Chinese triads and their U.S. counterparts, the tongs, have been involved in a number of different criminal endeavors, including drug trafficking, extortion, and gambling. Drug trafficking links have been identified between known Mafia bosses and triad leaders. Other Asian organized crime groups have become well known in other parts of the world. Japanese yakuza groups, whose history dates back hundreds of years, are heavily involved in gambling, prostitution, and extortion rackets in Japan and many other countries.

Political changes in eastern and central Europe have also had an important impact on organized crime. In Russia, these groups are taking advantage of social, political, and economic conditions and are involved in extortion rackets, drug trafficking, trading in raw materials, and the corruption of public officials. Russia's new social order and its unstable economy have enabled Russian criminals to take advantage of criminal opportunities on a grand scale, and many groups are now competing for control of these rackets.

DO YOU RECOGNIZE THESE TERMS?

black market
calenos
caleta cell
Golden Triangle
doubling up
gray market

Marielitos
shadow economy
Shining Path
tongs
triads
yakuza

POINTS OF DISCUSSION

1. Explain the ways in which Colombian organized crime poses a greater threat to the United States than do traditional organized crime groups.

2. Discuss similarities in the evolution of the Italian Mafia and Russian organized crime groups.

3. Explain the emergence of eastern and central European organized crime groups.

4. Compare and contrast the new emerging Asian and Russian organized crime groups. How can experience with the traditional Mafia aid in combating the spread and influence of these new groups?

5. Explain the extent to which Russian organized crime organizations are gaining influence in the United States.

SUGGESTED READING

ALBANEESE, J. (2003). *Organized Crime: World Perspectives*. Upper Saddle River, NJ: Prentice Hall.

BOOTH, M. (1990). *Triads: The Growing Global Threat from the Chinese Criminal Societies*. New York: St. Martin's Press. This volume describes the history and current operations of the triads, the ancient Chinese criminal societies that now control 90 percent of the world's heroin trade and are increasingly involved in financial and computer crime.

GRINBAUM, R. (1996). In Paraguay, smuggler's paradise. *World* Press Review, 43, 1 (January): 25–26.

GUGLIOTTA, G., and J. LEEN. (1989). *Kings of Cocaine*. New York: Simon & Schuster.

KAPLAN, D., and A. DUBRO. (1986). *Yakuza: The Explosive Account of Japan's Criminal Underworld*. Reading, MA: Addison-Wesley. This study traces the yakuza, the principal organized crime society in Japan, from its beginning as a protector of the common people to its current worldwide network and considers how it has achieved a place of honor in Japan's popular culture.

KELLY, R., ed. (1986). *Organized Crime: A Global Perspective*. Totowa, NJ: Rowman & Allenheld. Thirteen essays examine the formations, structures, activities, methods, and social interactions of diverse criminal organizations in various countries and regions throughout the world.

SHANNON, E. (1988). *Desperados*. New York: Viking.

—9—

TERRORISM AS ORGANIZED CRIME

This chapter will enable you to:

- Compare and contrast international and domestic terrorism incidents
- Understand the ways in which some types of terrorist activity relate to organized crime

- Describe some of the more prominent terrorist organizations
- Understand the political, social, and financial motivations of terrorist groups

INTRODUCTION

Many Americans have a vivid recollection of the terrorist attacks on New York City and Washington, D.C., on September 11, 2001. The attacks involved members of the Islamic terrorist group al Qaeda, who infiltrated U.S. borders and coordinated the hijacking of four commercial jet planes, which were used as missiles to attack the Pentagon and the World Trade Center. The attacks resulted in an estimated 2,800 violent deaths. The events of September 11 illustrate the fact that terrorism can strike anywhere, and virtually anyone can become a victim. As a result of these attacks, U.S. citizens are learning more about terrorism and its causes, implications, and countermeasures. But the enigmatic nature of terrorism and terrorist groups make understanding it a difficult task.

Global terrorism is nothing new, but the extent to which it exists is overwhelming. For example, the FBI reports that more than 14,000 international terrorist acts resulting in more than 10,000 deaths have taken place worldwide since 1968. Domestically, between 1980 and 1999, 327 incidents of terrorism were recorded in the United States. Of these, 239 were committed by domestic terrorists and 88 by foreign terrorists. During this same period, 130 acts of domestic terrorism were prevented by law enforcement in the United States (FBI 2000).

AN OVERVIEW

Most acts of terrorism have three basic participants: the perpetrator, the victim, and the audience affected (or the target). Although the perpetrator often is difficult to identify, the victim of the attack is usually the most controversial. The issue of terrorism is clouded because it is commonly viewed as a form of low-intensity, unconventional aggression on the lower end of the warfare spectrum. In this unrealistic view, terrorism is an act of war rather than a criminal activity, which gives it a purpose and some sense of dignity. However, most people recognize that embassy bombings, political hostage taking, and aircraft hijackings are criminal terrorist acts. Accordingly, they understand that such acts are designed to shock and stun and are outside the warfare conventions.

This chapter discusses terrorism as a part of the examination of organized crime. Some will argue that because many terrorist acts are politically or ideologically motivated they do not qualify as a form of organized crime. Although this is partially true, the authors suggest that political agendas and profit motivation can be concurrent causes of many acts of terrorism. In 1986, the President's Commission on Organized Crime defined what constitutes an organized crime group. Because many terrorist acts are committed by persons working in a group with a designated leader or a division of command and with a certain amount of social support, perhaps many terrorist groups can accurately be termed organized crime. For example, Peru's Shining Path, which has an estimated 4,000 to 5,000 members, has controlled the coca leaf-growing fields for years to generate revenue to support its national political agenda. Similarly, many early anti-Castro Cuban refugee groups in the United States engaged in illegal acts, such as running gambling syndicates, importing cocaine, and committing extortion as a means of funding their political agendas. It could also be argued that the origins of the Southeast Asian heroin traffic can be found in the Cold War policies of the United States and its allies of providing logistical support and military aid to the many Kuomintang warlords of the Golden Triangle in an attempt to contain the influence of the Chinese communists.

TERRORISM DEFINED

Whether domestic or international, terrorism is pervasive throughout the world and remains one of the most complex and difficult issues facing law enforcement in the twenty-first century. Much like the term organized crime, there is no single, universally accepted definition of the word *terrorism*.

The Federal Code of Regulations defines **terrorism** as "the unlawful use of force and violence against persons or property to intimidate or coerce a government, the civilian population, or any segment thereof, in furtherance of social or political objectives" (28 CFR, Section 0.85). In comparison, the Federal Bureau of Investigation (2000) offers a more compartmentalized definition addressing both domestic and international terrorism:

Domestic terrorism: the unlawful use, or threatened use of force by a group or individual, based and operating entirely within the United States without foreign direction, committed against persons or property to intimidate or coerce a government, the civilian population, or any segment thereof, in furtherance of social or political objectives.

International terrorism: violent acts or acts that are a danger to human life that are a violation of the criminal law of the United States or any state or that would be a criminal violation if committed within the jurisdiction of the United States or any state. These acts appear to be intended to intimidate or coerce a civilian population, influence the policy of a government by intimidation or coercion, or affect the conduct of government by assassination or kidnapping. International terrorist acts occur outside the United States or transcend national boundaries in terms of the means by which they are to be accomplished, the persons they appear intended to coerce or intimidate or the locale in which the perpetrators operate or seek asylum.

The literature of terrorism has been closely associated with the word **guerilla**, which can be defined as "little war" (Friedlander 1982). Georges-Abeyie (1983) distinguishes the two by suggesting that terrorist groups have a more urban focus, usually attack innocent civilians and property, and operate in small groups or bands of three to five persons.

In many ways, terrorism is easier to describe than to define. Essentially, it is the unlawful use or threat of violence against persons or property to further political or social objectives. It is designed to intimidate or coerce a government, individuals, or groups to change their behavior or policies. The National Institute of Justice (1995) reported that state and local law enforcement organizations believed that terrorism was more widespread than official FBI statistics indicated. In fact, many agencies characterized neo-Nazis, antifederalist, animal rights, environmentalists, and antiabortion groups as terrorists. It becomes apparent that organized crime groups that have the wherewithal and commitment to practice terrorism possess a unique criminal resource.

Terrorist tactics take many forms: hostage taking, aircraft piracy, sabotage, assassination, hoaxes, and indiscriminate bombings or shootings. Ironically, most victims of terrorist acts have little to do with either causing or satisfying terrorists' grievances. The bombing of the Alfred P. Murrah Federal Building in Oklahoma City on April 19, 1995, could be considered a terrorist act that, at least from a perpetrator's standpoint, represents the epitome of success. In addition to killing 168 people, including 19 children, and instilling considerable public alarm, it attracted immense publicity to the terrorists themselves and their cause. We will take a closer look at the Oklahoma City bombing later in this chapter. Another unprecedented terrorist act in Tokyo, Japan, also took place in 1995. Members of a religious cult group used lethal nerve gas in the city's commuter train, killing twelve people and injuring thousands. These events are just two of many recent terrorist incidents that have occurred around the world. Since 1987, terrorist attacks, mainly by Middle Eastern groups, have left more than 400 Americans dead on American-owned properties abroad (Cooper 1995b).

WHO ARE THE TERRORISTS?

The political and social circumstances that lead to the creation of terrorist groups vary widely around the world. Persons who carry out such acts vary in age, race, and cultural background. In 1986, the President's Task Force on Combating Terrorism (PTFCT) reported that an estimated 60 percent of the Third World population is under twenty years of age and half are fifteen years or younger. This being the case, a volatile mixture of youthful aspirations coupled with economic and political frustrations tends to create a pool of possible terrorists in those countries. Today's terrorists have a deep-seated belief in the justice of their causes. They are tough and cunning and have little regard for their lives or the lives of others. Terrorists' weaponry often comes from the illegal international arms market and could originate with legitimate arms vendors, which are, to a great extent, unregulated. Through their expansive organizational structure, many terrorists have the ability to acquire timely information on potential targets and the security precautions for these targets. As governmental pressures become more effective against them, terrorists will simply focus on easier targets.

Terrorists can be a part of a large organization or can act with only a few persons who share similar beliefs. Examples of large terrorist organizations are the Palestine Liberation Front (PLF), which has an estimated 300 members operating among three factions. The Abu Nidal Organization (ANO) boasts a membership of 500 and has an international theater of operation. Many terrorist organizations have membership in the thousands. White (1991) points out that most terrorist groups have a membership of fewer than fifty people; under a command element, which usually consists of a few people, the group is divided according to specific tasks. For example, intelligence sections are responsible for accessing targets, support sections provide the means to carry out the assault, and tactical sections actually carry out the terrorist action. Organizationally and operationally, these groups are structured much like other organized crime groups.

In comparison, some terrorist acts are committed by loners who have strong social or political beliefs. One such terrorist, known as the Unabomber, was responsible for bombs that struck sixteen times since 1978, killing three people and injuring twenty-three others. In 1996, the FBI arrested the primary suspect in the Unabomber case. Theodore Kaczynski, a Harvard graduate and hermit in rural Montana, possessed evidence suggesting that he was responsible for the two-decade rein of terror. The Unabomber gained a reputation as an elusive law enforcement target. In late June 1995, he set off a nationwide scare by threatening to bomb an airliner in California. He then claimed it was a prank and promised to stop killing provided the *New York Times* or the *Washington Post* would publish his 35,000-word manifesto that he had sent to them. Both newspapers published excerpts on August 2, 1995. In the manifesto the bomber wrote, "The industrial revolution and its consequences have been a disaster. Almost everyone will agree that we live in a deeply troubled society. . . . it is necessary to develop and propagate an ideology that opposes technology and the industrial system."

The Unabomber case illustrates the power of domestic terrorism, even though the crimes in this case were most likely perpetuated by a lone individual. Whether acting in concert with a group or alone, the terrorist poses a considerable threat to public safety.

Experts agree that to best combat terrorism, law enforcement must learn about the motivations and organizational structure of terrorist groups and make prudent application of the law governing such acts.

FORMS OF TERRORISM

In his book *Terrorism: An Introduction,* White (1991) suggests that five distinct forms of terrorism can be considered: criminal terrorism, ideological terrorism, nationalistic terrorism, state-sponsored terrorism, and revolutionary terrorism.

Criminal terrorism involves the use of terror for profit or psychological gain (Wilkinson 1974). Criminal terrorism fails to merit the same attention as does nationalistic violence. The terrorists seem to lack the political sophistication and support of other types of terrorists (Bell and Gurr 1979). Thus, the control of criminal terrorist activity typically becomes a law enforcement matter.

Ideological terrorism is normally an effort to change the current political power. It has been argued that ideological terrorism involves a revolution, but this is not always the case. For example, some governments employ the use of death squads whose actions might appear to be part of a repressive government, but this could be an extension of revolutionary terrorism.

Nationalistic terrorism is characterized by activity that supports the interests of an ethnic or nationalistic group, regardless of its political ideology (White 1991). Nationalistic terrorists often align with either western or eastern ideologies. This could be viewed in terms of superpower support (food, supplies, weapons, etc.) for nationalistic interests. In other words, we could say that the West tends to supply our terrorists, while the East tends to supply theirs. Stated differently, the goals of democracy are opposed to those of Marxist socialism (White 1991).

State-sponsored terrorism occurs when governmental regimes use or threaten to use violence in international relations outside established diplomatic protocol. The term became somewhat popular during the Reagan administration in describing low-level violence used against U.S. diplomatic and military installations. This form of terrorism is typified by such events as the 1979 takeover of the U.S. embassy in Teheran and the bombings aimed against U.S. military personnel in the Middle East. Countries that support such activities are known as terrorist states. Iran, Syria, Afghanistan, Chile, Argentina, El Salvador, and Libya are among the most notorious state sponsors of terrorism.

States sponsor terrorism for many different reasons. One is to achieve foreign policy objectives that could not otherwise be achieved through political or military means. Sometimes states sponsor terrorism to create or expand their power and influence among ideological movements. Other state-sponsored incidents attempt to stifle domestic opposition through assassination of dissidents abroad. These types of terrorists are easy for a state to disavow. The use of state-sponsored terrorism represents a low-risk, low-budget method of conducting foreign policy. State-supported terrorists can benefit by receiving government assistance in arms or explosives, communications, travel documents, and safe havens for training operatives. Their actions are frequently difficult to trace, so the governments involved can maintain respectability and legitimacy in the international community while secretly financing and supporting terrorist activities to achieve their goals.

Revolutionary terrorism involves persons whose guerrillalike tactics invoke fear in those holding political power and their supporters. The goal is to overthrow the current power base and replace it with political leaders who share the terrorists' views. Common tactics used by revolutionary terrorists are kidnappings, bombings, and assassinations, all of which are skillfully designed to force the existing government to respond with repressive measures. The terrorist then uses media coverage to attempt to expose the government as being inhumane and in need of being overthrown. Examples of revolutionary terrorism are Mao Tse-tung's takeover of China from Chiang Kai-shek and Fidel Castro's successful takeover of the Cuban government from the Batista regime during the late 1950s.

These five forms of terrorism by no means represent all the forms that exist throughout the world. White (1991) points out that being defined as a terrorist is often a function of the perceived moral rightness of the factions involved. For example, are groups who use force and violence to overthrow a dictatorship revolutionary terrorists or freedom fighters? Is the employment of violence against a government's murderous policies justifiable self-defense or is it nationalistic terrorism? These areas are murky because each group involved believes that the use of violence to achieve its particular political end is justified under the circumstances.

RECENT CHANGES IN TERRORISM

Since the early 1900s, terrorists' motivations, strategies, and weapons have changed to some extent. The anarchists and the left-wing terrorist groups that succeeded them, such as the Red Armies that operated in Germany, Italy, and Japan in the 1970s, have vanished, and the extreme right has now adopted the initiative. However, most international and domestic terrorism is neither left nor right, but ethnic-separatist in nature. Ethnic terrorists have more staying power than ideologically motivated ones because they draw on a larger reservoir of public support.

Perhaps the most notable change in recent decades is that terrorism is by no means the militants' only strategy. Groups such as the Muslim Brotherhood, the Palestine Hamas, the Irish Republican Army (IRA), the Kurdish extremists in Turkey and Iraq, the Tamil Tigers of Sri Lanka, the Basque Homeland and Liberty (ETA) movement in Spain, and many others have had both political and terrorist wings from the beginning.

The political arm provides social services and education, runs businesses, and contests elections; the military wing engages in ambushes and assassinations. This division of labor has clear advantages. The political leadership can publicly dissociate itself when the terrorist component commits a particularly outrageous act or when something goes wrong. The claimed lack of control can be real, because the armed wing tends to become independent; the men and women with guns and bombs often lose sight of the movement's wider goals and can end up doing more harm than good.

Terrorist operations have also changed somewhat when we consider that airline hijackings have become increasingly rare. Hijacked planes cannot stay in the air forever, and few countries today are willing to let them land. Toward the end of the twentieth century, the trend was moving away from attacking specific targets (such as the other side's officials) and toward indiscriminate killing. Furthermore, the dividing line between urban terrorism and other tactics has become blurred, and the line between politically motivated terrorism and the operation of national and international crime syndicates is often impossible for outsiders to distinguish. One fundamental difference exists between international crime and terrorism, however. Organized crime groups who are profit motivated have no interest in overthrowing the government and decisively weakening society, but prefer that a prosperous economy host their parasitic existence.

State-sponsored terrorism has clearly not disappeared. Several Middle Eastern and North African countries still support it. Tehran and Tripoli, however, are less eager to argue that they have a divine right to engage in terrorist operations outside their borders; the 1986 U.S. air strike against Libya and the various boycotts against Libya and Iran had an effect. No government today boasts about surrogate warfare it instigates and backs. However, Sudan, without fanfare, has become for terrorists what the Barbary Coast was for pirates of another age: a safe haven.

Use of Chemical and Biological Weapons

The limited use of chemical weapons along with the almost nonexistent use of nuclear material by terrorists is for the most part technical. The scientific literature is replete with the technical problems inherent in the production, manufacture, storage, and delivery of each of the three categories of unconventional weapons.

The manufacture of nuclear weapons is not simple, nor is delivery to their target. Nuclear material, of which a limited supply exists, is monitored by the U.N.-affiliated International Atomic Energy Agency. Only governments can legally produce it, so even in this age of proliferation investigators can trace those abetting nuclear terrorists without great difficulty. Monitoring can overlook a more primitive nuclear weapon, such as a nonfissionable one, but not radioactive nuclear material. Iranian agents in Turkey and Kazakhstan have been known to attempt to purchase such material in the former Soviet Union.

Chemical agents such as nerve gases are relatively easy to produce or obtain, but not so easy to keep in stable condition, and their dispersal depends largely on climactic factors. The terrorists behind the 1996 attack in Tokyo chose a convenient target (a subway) where large crowds of people gather. Biological agents, on the other hand, are far and away the most dangerous; they can kill hundreds of thousands of people, whereas chemicals can kill only thousands. They are relatively easy to produce, but storage and dispersal are even trickier than for nerve gases. The risk of contamination for people handling bacterial weapons is high, and many of the most lethal bacteria and spores do not survive well outside the laboratory.

Given the technical difficulties, terrorists are probably less likely to use nuclear devices than chemical weapons and least likely to use biological weapons. But difficulties can sometimes be overcome, and the choice of weapons will in the end depend on terrorists' specialties and access.

Infoterrorism

Society has become vulnerable to a new kind of terrorism in which the destructive power of both the individual terrorist and terrorism as a tactic are infinitely greater. Previously, terrorists killed kings or high officials, but others only too eager to inherit their power quickly stepped in. However, the advanced societies of the twentieth and twenty-first centuries depend on the electronic storage, retrieval, analysis, and transmission of information. A country's national defense, local police, banking, trade, transportation, scientific research, and a large percentage of the transaction records of government and the private sector are now online. This exposes enormous vital areas of national life to sabotage by any computer hacker, which could render a country unable to function, resulting in the growing concern about *infoterrorism* and *cyberwarfare*.

Laqueur (1997) has suggested that with $1 billion and twenty knowledgeable hackers, a single terrorist could shut down the United States. There is little secrecy in the *wired* society, and protective measures have proved of limited value, as illustrated by teenage hackers' penetration of highly secret systems in many fields. The possibilities for creating chaos are almost unlimited now, and vulnerability will almost certainly increase in this new century.

Terrorists' targets are also changing. For example, why assassinate a politician or indiscriminately kill innocent people when a planned attack on electronic switching can produce a far more dramatic and lasting result? For instance, the switch at the Culpeper, Virginia, headquarters of the Federal Reserve's electronic network, which handles all federal funds and transactions, would be an obvious place for a modern-day infoterrorist to hit. If the new terrorism directs its energies toward information warfare, its destructive power will be considerably greater than any it wielded in the past.

The ability of states and societies will most likely be of less interest to terrorists of the future than to ordinary criminals and organized crime. Electronic thieves, whether engaged in credit card fraud or industrial espionage, are part of the system, using it rather than destroying it. After all, its destruction would cost them their livelihood. This takes us well beyond terrorism as we have known it in the past. New definitions and new terms may need to be developed for new realities, and intelligence services and policy makers must learn to distinguish among the various forms of terrorists and their emerging motivations, approaches, and goals.

To what extent does terrorism exist today, and how will it change in years to come? The answers to questions such as these are difficult because of the ever-changing complexion of terrorists themselves and their causes. In general, however, several observations can be made with regard to the nature and extent of terrorism today.

INTERNATIONAL TERRORISM

On August 7, 1998, two car bombs ripped through the U.S. embassies in Kenya and Tanzania, leaving more than 250 people dead and 5,500 injured. The incident was one of the decade's most lethal terrorist attacks. Shortly after the bombings, police in Tanzania and Kenya began rounding up suspects, but one person surfaced as the mastermind of the attack: Osama bin Laden. On August 20, 1998, acting on intelligence information that bin Laden was planning terrorist training at a secret complex in eastern Afghanistan, the United States fired 75 Tomahawk cruise missiles from Navy ships in the Arabian and Red Seas. The missiles, a retaliatory measure, landed on targets in both Afghanistan and Sudan.

According to intelligence reports, bin Laden's training complex in Afghanistan included a command center, an ammunition depot, and four training centers. At the camp, terrorists learned to handle explosives, run obstacle courses, practice on firing ranges, and operate armed personnel carriers and tanks. National Security Advisor Sandy Berger commented that "[t]his is the largest terrorist training camp in the world" (Wiseman 1998). Bin Laden, a Saudi-born terrorist, was known by terrorist experts to have assembled a large-scale international terrorism network and directed his followers to kill Americans, civilian or military, adult or infant. His goal was to get the United States to abandon its allies, friends, or interests in the Middle East, the Persian Gulf, and Africa.

Like many other terrorist leaders, bin Laden justifies his crimes by hiding behind the religious cloak of Islam. Ironically, however, Muslims have been among the most tragic victims of terrorism in Egypt, Israel, the West Bank, Algeria, Lebanon, and elsewhere. Ten of the 12 people killed in the Tanzania bombing were Muslims, as were many of the more than 260 killed in Kenya. Much of bin Laden's network has yet to be uncovered, but some of his past activities have been well documented. They occured in the following locations:

1. Sudan: bin Laden was expelled in 1996 under U.S. pressure, but may still own numerous businesses there, including interest in a drug plant.
2. Afghanistan: bin Laden fought in the country's U.S.-backed war against the Soviets in the 1980s; set up training camps, and helped to finance the Taliban.
3. Kenya and Tanzania: President Clinton cited "convincing information" that bin Laden plotted the August 7 bombings that killed 263 people.
4. Saudi Arabia: bin Laden's birthplace, and source of a multimillion-dollar inheritance, has stripped him of his passport. He has vowed to topple the ruling dynasty.
5. Pakistan: bin Laden led meetings of Islamic extremist groups in Peshawar and made the decision to "hit American interests."
6. Yemen: bin Laden formed alliances with tribal chiefs in his father's homeland and set up training camps.
7. Somalia: bin Laden supplied troops to fight U.S. forces in 1993. "We inflicted big losses on the Americans," he later boasted.
8. Egypt: bin Laden funded Egyptian extremists and was suspected of backing an attempt on President Hosni Mubarak's life in 1995.
9. Britain: bin Laden allegedly financed a London-based Algerian group suspected of numerous bombings in France.

In November 1998, the U.S. government charged bin Laden with the August embassy bombings in East Africa and offered an unprecedented reward of $5 million for information leading to his arrest. The 238-count indictment charged that bin Laden and others had financed, trained, and ordered terrorist attacks against the United States since 1991 (Katz 1998).

Revisiting September 11, 2001

On September 11, 2001, the nature of international terrorism took an alarming and desperate turn. Two hijacked airliners slammed into the twin towers of the World Trade Center in New York, killing more than 2,800 people. On the same day a third hijacked airliner crashed into the Pentagon in Washington, D.C., and a fourth crashed in Pennsylvania before reaching its target. The attack was allegedly coordinated by al Qaeda, a fundamentalist Islamic terrorist group led by Osama bin Laden operating out of Afghanistan under the protection of the Taliban regime that controlled the country (Zunes 2001b). Much has been written about the specific events of that day, but for our purposes the important points to be emphasized are that (1) large-scale international terrorist attacks had, for the first time, occurred within the borders of the continental United States and (2) the government of the United States responded by initiating massive new security measures domestically and a war on terrorism internationally.

Following the 9/11 attacks, the United States responded domestically by federalizing airport security, beginning a massive sweep that resulted in detaining thousands of immigrants and foreign citizens living in the United States, beginning a process of reorganizing U.S. intelligence services, and initiating the first comprehensive investigation of international money laundering ever undertaken by federal law enforcement. These developments had profound impacts on the organization of crime internationally and the commitment of U.S. government to pursuing types of organized criminality that previously had been largely ignored. Crimes such as arms trafficking, money laundering, alien smuggling, and the production of weapons of mass destruction suddenly became priority concerns (Klare 2001).

The U.S. government also responded internationally. An extended air campaign was launched against the Taliban government in Afghanistan that had harbored Osama bin Laden's al Qaeda organization. United States and British troops, allied with warlords of the Northern Alliance, an Iranian-backed group opposing the Taliban, occupied much of Afghanistan and deposed the Taliban regime. For much of the remainder of the fall of 2001, U.S. British and North Alliance troops pursued al Qaeda operatives and bin Laden in Afghanistan, finally trapping them in and around the mountain town of Tora Bora in early December. Heavy U.S. bombing supported an attack on Tora Bora by Northern Alliance troops, but the bombing sealed off only one of the two escape routes out of Tora Bora into Pakistan. Many of the al Qaeda troops, probably including bin Laden, escaped using the alternative route through the mountains on the Pakistani border. During January and February of 2002, al Qaeda reorganized itself in the Shahikot area and al Qaeda leaders probably escaped into the Waziristan tribal regions of western Pakistan (Nordland et al. 2002).

The 9/11 terrorist attack raises vital issues regarding organized crime, corporate crime, intelligence activities, and terrorism. It will be years before investigations of what happened and how it happened provide us with a comprehensive picture of the complex events that led up to the attacks, but sufficient information exists to raise three compelling issues (Zunes 2001a).

1. How much information did the U.S. government have before the attacks of 9/11 and what did intelligence agencies do with this information? For example, in 1998 Robert Baer, a CIA case officer in Saudi Arabia, warned of the existence of an al Qaeda cell in Saudi Arabia and produced a list of known al Qaeda terrorists operating there, which included many of the participants in the 9/11 attacks (*Financial Times of London* 2001).

In January 2001, the Bush administration told the FBI to back off investigations of the bin Laden family in the United States (BBC Newsnight 2001). On February 13, 2001, United Press International's terrorism expert, Richard Sale, reported that the National Security Agency had broken the encryptions used by

Search and recovery team at work on September 23, 2001, at Ground Zero of the World Trade Center, which was destroyed after terrorist hijackers crashed two planes into it on September 11, 2001.

(*Joel Meyerowitz, Getty Images/Time Life Pictures*)

bin Laden and his operatives. In May 2001, the U.S. State Department gave the Taliban $43 million in economic assistance for Afghani farmers (*Los Angeles Times* 2001). In June 2001, BND, the German intelligence service, warned the United States and Israel that terrorists were planning to hijack commercial aircraft and use them as weapons (*Frankfurter Allgemeine Zeitung* 2001).

In July 2001, Osama bin Laden was treated for kidney disease at the American hospital in Dubai and was interviewed by CIA officials (*Le Figaro,* 2001). In August 2001, the FBI arrested a member of an al Qaeda cell operating in Boston, which would hijack two of the 9/11 airplanes. The FBI reported that the suspect had been taking flying lessons and possessed Boeing aircraft flight manuals (Reuters, September 13, 2001). Also in August, Russian president Vladimir Putin ordered his intelligence agencies to warn the U.S. government of an impending attack (MSNBC, September 15, 2001). Finally, Daniel Sieberg reported on CNN (2001) that employees of Odigo, Inc., a large Israeli company, were warned two hours before the first plane hit the World Trade Center that an attack on it was imminent.

These incidents represent some of the thousands of anomalies and questions surrounding the activities of U.S. intelligence; they are important because they direct our attention to some compelling issues discussed throughout this book with regard to other incidents and controversies. How effective is law enforcement intelligence gathering and analysis in the United States? How often is intelligence work compromised by foreign policy initiatives and involvements? And, finally, when it comes to intelligence gathering, just who is working for whom?

2. How much of what happened on 9/11 is a result of **blowback** (unanticipated negative outcomes) from activities and policies of the U.S. government itself? For example, we know that many of the leaders of both al Qaeda

and the Taliban were trained, financed, and organized by elements of U.S. intelligence as part of the U.S. intervention in Afghanistan in the 1970s. The United States had experienced the devastating effects of blowback before, particularly in relation to U.S. policy toward Cuba. Was 9/11 another example of intelligence agencies not anticipating the potential impacts of their activities?

How much of what is occurring in fundamentalist Islamic terrorist groups directly results from U.S. foreign policy? How much terrorism is a response to the U.S. removal of the democratically elected government of Iran in the 1950s? How much is related to the two U.S. invasions of Lebanon, intervention against Iraq in support of the ruling family in Kuwait, or continuing military support of the royal family of Saudi Arabia and other middle eastern dictatorships? How great a role has the United States played in establishing fundamentalist regimes that support terrorism? United States policy from the 1950s to the 1980s supported conservative religious states in opposition to liberal secular states because fundamentalist governments were regarded to be more reliable supporters of U.S. economic interests.

3. Finally, what is the impact of the 9/11 attacks on international drug trafficking? We know that, following U.S. intervention in Afghanistan in the 1970s, new opium smuggling routes vastly increased the availability of heroin in the United States. Little has changed in Afghanistan since then. In its efforts to depose the Taliban, the United States allied with warlords of the Northern Alliance, traditional opium producers. Ironically, these same warlords were being financed and supported by the Iranian government, also considered enemies of the United States.

The benefits of U.S. intervention in Afghanistan to organized crime now appear to have been substantial. For example, on November 21, 2001, the British newspaper *The Independent* ran the story "Opium Farmers Rejoice at the Defeat of the Taliban." The story reports a massive increase in opium cultivation in Afghanistan. In November 25, 2001, another British newspaper, *The Observer,* ran the story "Victorious Warlords Set to Open Opium Floodgates." It reported that warlords allied with the United States were encouraging farmers to drastically increase opium cultivation. Finally, Ayub Afridi, a convicted Afghani drug trafficker, was released from prison and recruited by the CIA to help in unifying the many Pashtun tribe warlords in support of the new Afghani government (*Asian Times* 2001).

When information to answer these questions becomes public, the answers will likely reveal the close collaboration among governments, terrorists, corporations, and organized crime in an increasingly transglobal world.

The United States has responded to the September 11, 2001, attacks on numerous fronts. For example, many states passed antiterrorism legislation and established security procedures to deal with possible future attacks. Security in U.S. airports has been federalized with the establishment of the Transportation Security Agency (TSA) to standardize security procedures and deal with airport security concerns.

Responding to September 11, 2001

Perhaps the most sweeping response to national concerns about terrorism occurred on November 25, 2002, when President George W. Bush signed legislation creating a cabinet-level Department of Homeland Security. Its creation is the largest reorganization in the federal government since the Department of Defense was created in 1947.

Governor Thomas Ridge of Pennsylvania, who had been director of the White House Office of Homeland Security, was appointed to head the department. Former Navy Secretary Gordon England was selected as Ridge's deputy, and Asa Hutchinson, the former administrator of the Drug Enforcement Administration, became undersecretary for border and transportation security.

The Department of Homeland Security is an intelligence clearinghouse dedicated to protecting the United States from the terrorist attacks that had exposed security lapses and intelligence failures and had led to calls for changes to the nation's defense, intelligence, and law enforcement sectors. It combines about 170,000 federal workers from 22 agencies with an annual budget approaching $40 billion. The department will bring together intelligence analysis and infrastructure protection, border protection and immigration, and a comprehensive response and recovery division. Its personnel came from preexisting agencies. At its creation, the department dispersed responsibilities for homeland security among more than 100 different organizations. The new department is to be a point of contact for homeland security issues for state and local agencies.

The department is divided into four divisions: Border and Transportation Security; Emergency Preparedness and Response; Chemical, Biological, Radiological, and Nuclear Countermeasures; and Information Analysis and Infrastructure Protection. Existing agencies placed under the department's authority are the Immigration and Naturalization Service, U.S. Coast Guard, Customs Service, Border Patrol, Federal Emergency Management Agency, Secret Service, Transportation Security Administration, and the border inspection part of Animal and Plant Health Inspection Service.

The new department is not designed to become a domestic intelligence agency, but it will analyze intelligence and "legally accessible information" from multiple sources such as the CIA, National Security Agency, FBI, Drug Enforcement Administration, Department of Energy, Customs Service, and Department of Transportation. Civil libertarians are concerned that virtually anyone could be targeted as a suspected terrorist and become the object of a domestic intelligence inquiry.

Critics of the new Homeland Security Department, however, say it creates overlap by taking employees from twenty-two existing agencies such as the Immigration and Naturalization Service, Coast Guard, and the Border Patrol, departments that critics believe should simply be strengthened. Others have argued that creating the new department serves only to divert resources from the fight against terrorism and gives citizens a false sense of security.

MIDDLE EASTERN TERRORISTS

A substantial amount of international terrorism takes place in the Middle East and, accordingly, numerous groups operate in this geographic region. Most terrorist activity revolves around the issues of a Palestinian homeland,

You Decide

Israel's existence and military occupation of Arab and Palestinian lands, Arab states jockeying for regional power, and Islamic religious extremism. The rise of terrorism in this area is a good example of the steady growth of state-supported terrorism. Over the decades, Middle Eastern groups have acquired sophisticated arms, extensive logistical resources, accurate intelligence information, and a safe haven from which to operate as a result of their alliances with governments in the region.

For decades, most of the terrorist activity in this region has been associated with the Palestine Liberation Organization (PLO), which has focused most of its violence against Israel. Splintering away from the PLO are a number of related groups, such as the Popular Front and the Abu Nidal Organization (ANO), both of which are more violent than their parent organization. In addition, Jewish terrorist organizations have been formed. One of these is the Jewish Defense League (JDL), which had its beginnings in New York and originally focused on Soviet targets in an effort to convince the former USSR to allow the emigration of Jews. Since then the group has moved to Israel and focused on expelling Arabs from the country and integrating occupied lands into Israel.

One of the region's most notable terrorists is Libyan military dictator Colonel Mu'ammar al-Gadhafi, who has employed terrorism to lash out against political opponents and to further his own policy agenda within the Arab political arena. Although located in North Africa, Libya has called on a number of Middle East terrorist groups and organizations to commit terrorist acts. These groups include the Libyan People's Bureaus abroad, Revolutionary Committees, and the Anti-Imperialism Center in Triploi. Today, Libya is rumored to host one of the most extreme Palestinian terrorist groups, the ANO.

The Khomeini regime in Iran viewed terrorism as a basic tactic to be used against the United States and other sources of Western influence and as a tool to promote the Islamic Fundamentalist revolution. Iran's most notable terrorist group, the Hizballah movement in Lebanon, has carried out numerous kidnappings and hijackings since the early 1980s. As with Libya, Iran uses its government apparatus to recruit, train, finance, and deploy terrorists, especially in Lebanon.

Among the most long-standing and well-known practitioners of terrorism in the Middle East is the Palestine Liberation Organization (PLO), founded in 1964 as a nationalist organization dedicated to the establishment of an independent Palestinian state. In 1969, Yasir Arafat became the chairman of the PLO's executive committee. In general, it has an umbrella organization including a number of differing constituent groups, the most powerful of which is the Palestine Liberation Front.

Profile

Al Qaeda International

Al Qaeda ("The Base"), a recently established group with expansive resources, has targeted the United States and other nations. Osama bin Laden and others originally established al Qaeda in the early 1980s to support the war effort in Afghanistan against the Soviets. The resulting victory in Afghanistan gave rise to the overall jihad (holy war) movement. Trained Mujahedin fighters from Afghanistan began returning to Egypt, Algeria, and Saudi Arabia, with extensive terrorist training and the desire to continue the jihad. This antagonism began to be refocused against the United States and its allies. Members of al Qaeda issued **fatwahs** (rulings on Islamic law) indicating that such attacks were both proper and necessary.

Sometime during 1989, al Qaeda dedicated itself to continue to oppose non-Islamic governments with force and violence. The group grew out of the mekhtab al khidemat (the Services Office) organization that maintained offices in various parts of the world, including Afghanistan, Pakistan, and the United States. Al Qaeda began to provide training camps and guesthouses in various areas for the use of its groups and affiliated ones. Al Qaeda attempted to recruit U.S. citizens to travel throughout the western world to deliver messages and engage in financial transactions for the benefit of al Qaeda and its affiliated groups and to help conduct operations. By 1990, al Qaeda was providing military and intelligence training in various areas, including Afghanistan, Pakistan, and Sudan, for its use and that of its affiliated groups, including the Al-Jihad (Islamic jihad) organization.

A principal goal of al Qaeda was to drive the U.S. armed forces out of Saudi Arabia (and elsewhere on the Arabian peninsula) and Somalia by violence. Al Qaeda opposed the United States for several reasons. The United States was regarded as an infidel because it was not governed in a manner consistent with the group's extremist interpretation of Islam. Al Qaeda viewed the United States as providing essential support for other *infidel* governments and institutions, particularly those of Saudi Arabia, Egypt, Israel, and the United Nations, which were regarded as its enemies. Al Qaeda opposed the involvement of the U.S. armed forces in the Gulf War in 1991 and in Operation Restore Hope in Somalia in 1992 and 1993, which it viewed as pretexts for preparations for a U.S. occupation of Islamic countries. In particular, al Qaeda opposed the continued presence of U.S. military forces in Saudi Arabia (and elsewhere on the Arabian peninsula) following the Gulf War. Finally, al Qaeda opposed the U.S. government because of the arrest, conviction, and imprisonment of persons belonging to al Qaeda or its affiliated terrorist groups or with whom it worked, including Sheik Omar Abdel Rahman, who was convicted in the first World Trade Center bombing.

From its inception until approximately 1991, the group was headquartered in Afghanistan and Peshawar, Pakistan. The group relocated in 1991 to Sudan where it was headquartered until approximately 1996, when bin Laden, Mohammed Atef, and other members of al Qaeda returned to Afghanistan. During its years in Sudan, the network continued to maintain offices in various parts of the world and established businesses to provide income and cover to al Qaeda operatives.

Al Qaeda Ties to Other Terrorist Organizations

Although al Qaeda functions independently of other terrorist organizations, it also uses some of the terrorist organizations that operate under its umbrella or with its support, including the Al-Jihad; the Al-Gamma Al-Islamiyya, an Islamic group led by Sheik Omar Abdel Rahman and later by Ahmed Refai Taha ("Abu Yasser al Masri"); Egyptian Islamic Jihad, and a number of jihad groups in other countries, including Sudan, Egypt, Saudi Arabia, Yemen, Somalia, Eritrea, Djibouti, Afghanistan, Pakistan, Bosnia, Croatia, Albania, Algeria, Tunisia, Lebanon, the Philippines, Tajikistan, Azerbaijan, the Kashmiri region of India, and the Chechen region of Russia.

Al Qaeda also maintained cells and personnel in a number of countries to facilitate its activities, including Kenya, Tanzania, the United Kingdom, Canada, and the United States. By banding together, al Qaeda proposed to work against the perceived common enemies in the West, particularly the United States, which al Qaeda regards as an infidel state that provides essential support for other infidel governments.

The Fatwahs of al Qaeda

At various times from about 1992 until about 1993, Osama bin Laden, working with members of the fatwah committee of al Qaeda, disseminated fatwahs to members and associates directing attacks on U.S. forces stationed in the Horn of Africa, including Somalia. Indeed, bin Laden claimed responsibility for the deaths of 18 U.S. servicemen killed in Operation Restore Hope in Somalia in 1994.

On February 22, 1998, bin Laden issued a fatwah stating that it is the duty of all Muslims to kill Americans: "in compliance with God's order, we issue the following fatwah to all Muslims: the ruling to kill the Americans and their allies, including civilians and military, is an individual duty for every Muslim who can do it in any country in which it is possible to do it." This fatwah appears to have provided the religious justification and to have marked the start of logistical planning for the U.S. embassy bombings in Kenya and Tanzania.

In February 1998, bin Ladin and one of his top lieutenants and leader of the Al-Jihad organization in Egypt, Ayman Al Zawahiri, endorsed a fatwah under the banner of the International Islamic Front for Jihad on the Jews and Crusaders. This fatwah appeared in the publication *Al-Quds al-Arabi* on February 23, 1998, and stated that Muslims should kill Americans, including civilians, anywhere in the world where they can be found. In April 1998, one defendant in the East Africa trial, Mohamed Sadeek Odeh, discussed the fatwahs issued by bin Laden and al Qaeda against the United States with another defendant, Mustafa Mohamed Fadhil. This discussion took place in Kenya.

The Trial in New York City

As was revealed at the trial that took place in New York, a former member of bin Laden's al Qaeda network began working with the U.S. government in 1996. This witness revealed that al Qaeda had privately declared war on the United States and was operating both on its own and as an umbrella for other terrorist groups. The witness revealed that al Qaeda had a close working relationship with Al-Jihad. The witness also recounted that Bin Laden and al Qaeda were seeking to obtain nuclear and chemical weapons and that the organization engaged in sophisticated training. He revealed that al Qaeda obtained specialized terrorist training from and worked with Iranian government officials and the terrorist group Hiezballah.

A Closer Look

Becoming a Member of Al Qaeda

Becoming a member of al Qaeda is as difficult as entry into many other organized crime groups. Its recruitment officers for the organization that carried out the September 11, 2001, attacks used rigorous selection techniques that included background checks, interviews with relatives and friends, and one on one meetings to test the recruit's commitment to the cause. Membership for al Qaeda is limited; only Muslim men are considered. Information comes from interrogation of captives from the U.S. campaign in Afghanistan, documents from al Qaeda camps, testimony in past terrorism cases, and experience gained from efforts by U.S. intelligence to penetrate the terrorist organization with human sources.

As with many other criminal groups, al Qaeda takes precautions to make sure that it is not recruiting an enemy agent. Recruits must meet minimum standards, and they move from undergraduate to graduate levels of training while getting perks along the way, such as welcome ceremonies and audiences with senior leadership. A fundamental rule of recruiting for al Qaeda is that volunteers are never accepted. It searches to identify recruitment prospects whom leaders believe will further the organizations goals. Recruiters for al Qaeda look for the following:

1. Muslim men from late teens to early 30s
2. Willingness to die if necessary
3. Ability to follow orders
4. Patience and discipline

As with many organized crime groups, al Qaeda has established a sworn oath of allegiance and secrecy. Al Qaeda's code of silence is called *bayat,* a signed pledge to follow al Qaeda leadership even to the point of martyrdom. The penalty for breaking the oath is death.

Organizational safeguards, such as not sharing major terrorist plots widely within the organization, have made al Qaeda an exceptionally difficult target for U.S. intelligence.

Estimates are that there are thousands of sympathizers and low-level al Qaeda operatives around the world. The core of the organization, however, is surprisingly small, fewer than 200 full-fledged members.

Sensitive to the risk of penetration by U.S. agents, al Qaeda selects prospects from Islamic centers, schools, and mosques around the world. For example, a first step might be to encourage the prospect to enroll in a more conservative or militant mosque. Unless the person being interviewed is known and trusted, the al Qaeda officer conceals his affiliation. Prior to the U.S. military campaign in Afghanistan, a typical first step for recruits was attendance at a radical Islamic school in Pakistan. From there, recruits went on to an al Qaeda guest house and then on to one of at least a half-dozen camps in Afghanistan.

Following a welcoming ceremony, replete with celebratory gunfire, new recruits are assigned to basic training that could last up to six months and lead to more advanced study. Courses include kidnapping, assassination, downing aircraft, hijacking buses, handling plastic explosives, encrypting computerized communications, moving money through secret bank accounts, and clandestine surveillance, which is especially useful in identifying possible targets for terrorist attacks.

As with many organized crime groups, the penalty for betraying al Qaeda is death, and the organization is suspicious about the accidental deaths of senior members. For example, in 1996 Abu Ubaidah al-Banshiri, the group's military commander, died in a ferry that sank in Africa's Lake Victoria. Al Qaeda leaders, concerned that al-Banshiri could have defected, dispatched operatives to verify his death.

Al Qaeda responded to the presence of United States armed forces in the Gulf and the arrest, conviction, and imprisonment in the United States of persons belonging to al Qaeda by issuing fatwahs indicating that attacks against U.S. interests, domestic and foreign, civilian and military, were both proper and necessary. These fatwahs resulted in attacks against U.S. nationals in locations around the world, including Somalia, Kenya, Tanzania, Yemen, and now the United States. Since 1993, thousands of people have died in these attacks.

Sources: Statement for the Record of J. T. Caruso, Acting Assistant Director Counter Terrorism Division Federal Bureau of Investigation on al Qaeda International before the Subcommittee on International Operations and Terrorism Committee on Foreign Relations, United States Senate, Washington, DC; J. Diamond and T. Lacy (2002). "Al Qaeda has small, selective core," *USA Today*, September 19, p. 3A.

Thereafter, in August 1996, two years prior to the bombings of the embassies in East Africa, bin Laden issued a public declaration of jihad against the U.S. military. This was followed by a series of other statements, including the previously mentioned February 1998 fatwah. These public statements corroborated the information supplied by the witness. In a May 1998 press interview, bin Laden threatened U.S. interests and complained that the United States was using its embassies overseas to track down terrorists.

On August 7, 1998, the bombings of the embassies in Nairobi, Kenya, and Dar es Salaam, Tanzania, occurred roughly simultaneously. The persons responsible for these attacks have since been identified publicly as principal participants of al Qaeda and/or the affiliated terrorist group

Exiled Saudi dissident Osama bin Laden is seen in this April 1998 picture in Afghanistan. American officials said they are looking at bin Laden for involvement in the Friday, August 7, 1998, Kenyan and Tanzanian U.S. embassy explosions and the September 11, 2001, terrorist attacks. He has threatened a holy war against U.S. troops and citizens, and is suspected of backing other terrorist acts, including the 1996 attack in Saudi Arabia.

(*Courtesy of Wide World Photos*)

Egyptian Islamic Jihad (EIJ). Mohamed Rashed Daoud al-Owhali, a Saudi who admitted he was in the bomb truck used in Nairobi, confessed that he had been trained in al Qaeda camps, fought with the Taliban in Afghanistan (with the permission of bin Laden), had asked bin Laden for a mission, and was thereafter dispatched by others to East Africa after undergoing extensive specialized training at camps in Afghanistan. Another defendant, Mohamed Sadeek Odeh, in whose residence was found a sketch of the area where the bomb was to be placed, admitted he was a member of al Qaeda and identified the other principal participants in the bombing as al Qaeda members. Odeh admitted that he was told the night prior to the bombings that bin Laden and others he was working with in Afghanistan had relocated from their camps because they expected the U.S. military to retaliate.

There was independent proof of the involvement of bin Laden, al Qaeda, and EIJ in the bombings. First, the would-be suicide bomber, al-Owhali, ran away from the bomb truck at the last minute and survived. However, he had no money, passport, or plan by which to escape Kenya. Days later, he called a telephone number in Yemen and thus arranged to have money transferred to him in Kenya. The telephone number in Yemen was contacted by Osama bin Laden's satellite phone on the same day that al-Owhali was arranging to get money. Moreover, al-Owhali and Odeh both implicated men named Harun, Saleh and Abdel Rahman, now all fugitives, as organizing the Nairobi bombing. All three have been conclusively shown to be al Qaeda and/or EIJ members.

Indeed, documents recovered in a 1997 search of a house in Kenya showed Harun to be an al Qaeda member in Kenya. The house where the Nairobi bomb was assembled was located and proved to have been rented by that same al Qaeda member Harun. Moreover, records for the telephone located at the bomb factory show calls to the same number in Yemen that al-Owhali contacted for money after the bombing. Telephone records confirmed that the Kenya and Tanzania cells were in contact shortly before the bombings.

Additional proof of the involvement of al Qaeda and EIJ in the East Africa bombings came from a search in London of several residences and business addresses belonging to al Qaeda and EIJ members. These searches found a number of documents, including some with claims of responsibility in the name of a fictitious group. Al-Owhali, the would-be suicide bomber, admitted that he was told to make a videotape of himself using the name of a fictitious group, the same name found on the claims of responsibility. The claims of responsibility were received in London on the morning the bombings occurred, likely before the bombings occurred.

The trial record left little doubt that the East Africa embassy bombings had been carried out as a joint operation by al Qaeda and EIJ. The testimony in the trial confirmed the following:

- Al Qaeda has access to the money, training, and equipment needed to carry out successful terrorist attacks.
- The plan was made well in advance, but the group had the patience to wait to attack at the right time.
- Prior to carrying out the operation, al Qaeda conducted surveillance of the target, sometimes on multiple occasions, often using nationals to enter the

location without suspicion. The results of the surveillance were forwarded to al Qaeda headquarters as elaborate "ops plans" or "targeting packages" prepared using photographs, computer-assisted design and mapping software, and the operative's notes.

Terrorist Sleeper Cells

The 9/11 terrorist attacks resulted in one of the most comprehensive investigations of international money laundering ever undertaken by federal law enforcement in the United States. One pattern of terrorist financing that emerged involved al Qaeda cells operating in Europe that derived their income from legitimate employment and/or businesses within the country in which they existed. For example, one company run by cell members provided home repairs involving masonry, plumbing, electrical wiring, and so on; it hired mujahadin arriving from areas of conflict, such as Bosnia. Another enterprise operated by cell members purchased, repaired, and resold dilapidated automobiles.

Other cell members transferred money between accounts with little attempt to hide the transactions. Salaries, government payments to students, and family members supported the cell to some extent. Funds were deposited into accounts either by cash or wire transfer. Money for living and other expenses was withdrawn from ATMs.

The al Qaeda cell based in Germany included among its members Ramzi bin al-Shibh and hijackers Mohamed Atta and Marwin Al-Shehhi. This fact was instrumental in linking the hijackers to al Qaeda and determining the support they received for the events of September 11, 2001. It also established links between the German cell, the hijackers, and Zacarias Moussaoui which contributed to the 2002 indictment and 2006 conviction of Moussaoui for his role in the September 11 attacks.

Wire transfers were traced from Bin al-Shibh to Moussaoui. Links between Moussaoui and an al Qaeda cell in Malaysia have also been identified. In 2002, authorities in Malaysia arrested and charged a number of the members of this cell. Bin al-Shibh was one of the five terrorists appearing in videos recovered from an al Qaeda location in Afghanistan that were released by the Department of Justice after the 9/11 attacks.

U.S. State Department's Designated Foreign Terrorist Organization List

Name / Orientation	Primary Area(s) of Operation	Primary Goal(s)
Abu Nidal Organization (ANO), Palestinian nationalist	Middle East, Asia, Europe	Is anti-Israel, opposes moderate Arab regimes, seeks independent Palestinian state, rejects Middle East peace process
Abu Sayyaf Group (ASG), Islamic extremist	Philippines	Seeks Iranian-style Islamic state on one of the Philippines' southern islands
Al-Aqsa Martyrs Brigade, Palestinian nationalist	Middle East	Seeks establishment of independent Palestinian state; rejects Middle East peace process

(continued)

Name / Orientation	Primary Area(s) of Operation	Primary Goal(s)
Al-Gama'a Al-Islamiyya (IG),* (Islamic group), Islamic extremist	Egypt	Is anti-Egyptian government, seeks to establish Islamic state; responsible for attack on tourists at Luxor, Egypt (1997)
Al Qaeda*, Islamic extremist	Worldwide	Opposes non-Islamic regimes, strongly anti-Western, seeks to reestablish the Muslim state throughout the Persian Gulf; responsible for U.S. Embassy bombings in East Africa (1998), bombing of the U.S.S. *Cole* (2000), and attacks on the World Trade Center and Pentagon (2001)
Armed Islamic Group (GIA), Islamic extremist	Algeria, France	Is anti-foreign, anti-Algerian government, seeks to establish Islamic state; frequently massacres civilians
Asbat Al-Ansar, Palestinian nationalist	Middle East	Seeks establishment of independent Palestinian state; rejects Middle East peace process
Aum Shinrikyo (Aum Supreme Truth) cult	Japan, Russia	Seeks to bring about apocalypse; is responsible for 1995 sarin gas attack on Tokyo subway, resulting in 12 deaths and over 5,000 injuries
Egyptian Al-Jihad (EIJ), Islamic extremist	Egypt	Is anti-Egyptian government, seeks to establish Islamic state; original al-Jihad responsible for assassination of Egyptian President Anwar Sadat (1981)
Euzkadita Askatasuna (ETA) (Basque Fatherland and Liberty), separatist (Marxist–Leninist)	Spain, France	Is anti-Spanish government, anti-French government, seeks independent Basque state in northern Spain and southern France
Hamas, Islamic extremist	Israel, occupied territories, Jordan	Is anti-Israel, seeks to establish Palestinian Islamic state; tactics include large-scale suicide bombings; rejects Middle East peace process

Name / Orientation	Primary Area(s) of Operation	Primary Goal(s)
Harakat Ul-Mujahedin (HUM), Islamic extremist	Pakistan, Kashmir (northern India), Afghanistan	Is anti-Indian; seeks Islamic rule in Kashmir and throughout the world
Hizballah, Islamic (Shi'a) extremist, closely linked to Iranian government	Lebanon	Seeks to establish Islamic theocracy in Lebanon and to reduce non-Islamic influences in the Middle East; responsible for suicide truck bombings of U.S. Embassy and Marine barracks (1983) and U.S. Embassy Annex in Beirut (1984), among other terrorist acts
Kahane Chai,* Jewish extremist	Israel, West Bank	Seeks to continue Kach founder's rejectionist agenda, considered more militant than Kach party from which it sprang
Kurdistan Workers' Party (PKK), separatist (Marxist–Leninist)	Turkey, Europe, Middle East, Asia	Is anti-Turkish, seeks to establish independent Kurdish state in southeastern Turkey
Liberation Tigers of Tamil Eelam (LTTE), separatist insurgent	Sri Lanka	Is anti-Sri Lankan government, seeks to establish independent Tamil state in Sri Lanka
Mujahedin-E-Khalq Organization* (MEK or MKO), Marxist–Islamic, Iranian dissident	Iraq; worldwide operation	Seeks to overthrow Iranian government, has expressed anti-Western sentiment in the past
National Liberation Army (ELN), Marxist–Leninist	Colombia	Seeks removal of U.S. and other foreign businesses (especially petroleum industry) from Colombia and a revolution to establish Marxist–Leninist government
Palestine Islamic Jihad-Shiqaqi Faction (PIJ), Islamic extremist	Middle East	Is anti-Israel, rejects Middle East peace process, seeks to establish Islamic Palestinian state
Palestine Liberation Front (Abu Abbas Faction), Palestinian nationalist	Middle East, now based in Iraq	Is anti-Israel, rejects Middle East peace process, seeks to establish independent Palestinian state, responsible for seizure of *Achille Lauro* cruise ship (1985), during which an American was murdered

(continued)

(continued)

Name / Orientation	Primary Area(s) of Operation	Primary Goal(s)
Popular Front for the Liberation of Palestine (PFLP), Palestinian nationalist	Israel, occupied territories, Syria, Lebanon	Is anti-Israel, rejects Middle East peace process, seeks to establish independent Palestinian state
Popular Front for the Liberation of Palestine—General Command (PFLP-GC), Palestinian nationalist	Israel, occupied territories, Lebanon, Egypt	Is anti-Israel, rejects Middle East peace process, seeks to establish independent Palestinian state; broke from PFLP in 1968 because PFLP-GC founder believed PFLP too focused on diplomacy, not engaging in enough violence
Revolutionary Armed Forces of Colombia (FARC), Marxist–Leninist	Colombia	Seeks overthrow of current government and ruling class of Colombia
Revolutionary Organization 17 November, Marxist	Greece	Seeks to replace Greek government with communist system, rid Greece of U.S., EU, and NATO presence, end Turkish military presence on Cyprus; responsible for numerous assassinations, including several U.S. government officials
Revolutionary People's Liberation Party/Front (DHKP/C), Marxist	Turkey	Seeks to remove U.S. and NATO presence from Turkey and unite nonruling classes in revolution to overthrow Turkish government
Revolutionary People's Struggle (ELA), extreme leftist	Greece	Is anti-Greek government, seeks removal of U.S. military forces from Greece
Salafist Group for Call and Combat (Groupe Salafiste pour La Predication et Le Combat), Islamic extremist	Algeria	Is antiforeign, anti-Algerian government, seeks to establish Islamic state
Shining Path (Sendero Luminoso), Neo-Maoist	Peru	Is anti-Peruvian government, antiforeign, seeks peasant revolutionary regime; particularly brutal and indiscriminate

*Groups that have a presence in the United States.

Source: United States Department of State, 2002.

WEST EUROPEAN TERRORISTS

Although many dramatic terrorist acts have taken place over the years, some of the most spectacular have occurred in Europe. Most Western European terrorists belong to relatively small groups reminiscent of nineteenth-century anarchists, espousing a revolutionary philosophy dedicated to overthrowing the existing government and social order. Ironically, many such groups have not proposed a clear substitute social system. These groups include Northern Ireland's Provincial Irish Republican Army, Germany's Red Army Faction, and Italy's Red Brigades. The degree of organization of these groups varies from one group to the next, but can be very sophisticated. Most attack the state, its representatives, and other symbols of the established order, including attacks on the United States and NATO as representatives of imperialism. In comparison to Middle Eastern and Latin American terrorist groups, whose members are from the lower class, those who belong to West European groups are typically from the middle class and are often well educated.

LATIN AMERICAN TERRORISTS

Latin America has not been noted for political stability over the past two centuries (White 1991). Politics exist there in an extremely unstable climate and is marked by frequent military coups and highly repressive regimes in countries such as Guatemala, El Salvador, Chile, Argentina, and Nicaragua (prior to the Sandinista revolution of 1979). Acts of Latin American terrorism often indicate an impending full-scale guerrilla war. Many of these acts are used to demonstrate that the group continues to be a threat. For years Latin American terrorism did not pose a threat to U.S. citizens, but this changed toward the mid-1980s with the escalation of the cocaine wars between Latin American countries and drug traffickers.

Profile

The Basque Fatherland and Liberty

Formed in 1959, the Euzkadi Ta Askatasuna (ETA) is headquartered in the Basque provinces of Spain and France and has a membership of approximately 200 members. It is thought to be one of the oldest and most violent of the West European terrorist groups in operation and is headed by José Antonio Urruti-coechea-Bengoechea (José Ternera). Not known to have any state sponsorship, the ETA's goal is to establish an independent Marxist Basque nation, Euzkadi, through terrorism against Spanish interests. In addition, it strives to create an economic crisis in the Basque provinces by terrorizing businesses there.

The ETA regularly targets Spanish government officials and members of the military and security forces. In addition, the group has carried out numerous bombings against government facilities and tourist resorts. Millions of dollars of funds for ETA activities have been obtained from large ransoms for kidnappings, armed robberies, and extortion of so-called "revolutionary taxes."

The ETA's organizational structure is sophisticated. Most of its members (commandos) are organized into three- or four-member cells and are legal, that is, are not known to the police. Once they carry out an operation, they disappear into their surroundings. A large support group also exists, furnishing information, communications, and other items needed to maintain the group's infrastructure. ETA also has extensive ties with other terrorist groups. These include the Provisional Irish Republican Army and the Cuban government, which provide safe haven and training for members. ETA members have also been documented as being involved in attacks in Nicaragua against the Sandinista government.

Source: Public Report of the President's Task Force on Combating Terrorism (1986). Washington, DC: February.

Several Latin American terrorist organizations have become well known over the years. For example, in Cali, Colombia, the 19th of April Movement (M-19), with an estimated membership of 1,000, has fought the Colombian "bourgeoisie" and U.S. "imperialism" since its formation in 1974. M-19 activities include occupations and attacks on towns and army garrisons and assassinations of high-level military personnel. Fund-raising kidnappings of wealthy businessmen or employees of foreign companies and the hijacking of airliners are the signature of the M-19. Funds are also generated through drug-related activities, primarily by extorting money from coca leaf and marijuana growers in Colombia. One of the most notable events involving the M-19 was the 1985 seizure of Bogota's Palace of Justice, where it took 500 people hostage. Of these, fifty were killed, including eleven Supreme Court justices.

Another Colombian terrorist group is the Revolutionary Armed Forces of Colombia (FARC). Organized in 1966, today it is thought to be one of the largest terrorist groups there with a membership of 4,000 to 5,000. The FARC has a two-part strategy, combining terrorist operations with participation in legitimate Colombian politics. Its objective is to overthrow the established government in Colombia and replace it with a leftist regime. As with the M-19, the FARC is a classic **narcoterrorist** organization, fostering a close working relationship with Colombian drug traffickers. A majority of FARC's work is in protecting the processing of coca. It uses earnings from this protection to purchase arms.

A third Latin American terrorist group is Peru's Sendero Luminoso (Shinning Path). Like the FARC, the Shining Path is a large and extremely dangerous organization with an estimated 5,000 members. In 1992 it was estimated that its members had been directly responsible for the killing of 25,000 people over a twelve-year period (Smolowe 1992). Formed in 1969 and headed by Abimael Guzmán (Presidente Gonzalo), the group vowed to overthrow the legitimate government through a rural-based insurgency and to install a leftist, ethnic Indian state by the year 2000.

The group's forte is to conduct urban terrorism and rural guerrilla warfare. It is funded through bank robberies and extortion schemes consisting primarily of a "war tax" similar to that of the Basque ETA. In 1992, the Peruvian government captured Guzmán. Even though speculation was that the organization could not function without its cult-figure leader, recent evidence indicates that it is still a strong terrorist organization in Peru.

STATE-ORGANIZED CRIME

In his presidential address to the American Society of Criminology, William Chambliss raised the issue of what he called **state-organized crime** (Chambliss, 1988: 327), defined as "acts committed by state or government officials in the pursuit of their job as representatives of the government." In his view, governments often engage in smuggling (arms and drugs), assassination conspiracies, terrorist acts, and other crimes to further their foreign policy objectives. These actions can be seen as having immediate benefits (despite their illegality), but they often have unanticipated and unintended outcomes, sometimes referred to in intelligence circles as blowback. This section examines the issue of state-organized crime as it relates to the United States and some of the blowback that law enforcement agencies have had to cope with as a result of these activities. Governments rarely make public their criminal acts or keep records on the number of illegal acts they have committed, but it is clear from both historical and contemporary perspectives that state-organized crime is neither new nor rare.

Any U.S. government operation that is shielded from the public and hidden from congressional oversight over a long period of time will inevitably rely on criminal activity for support and funding. Covert operations provide the perfect setting for organized criminal activity simply because they are state-sanctioned clandestine operations (Chambliss 1986). These organizations recruit people with the—mostly criminal—skills necessary to carry them out. Official channels can facilitate the passage of covert organization members and goods related to their activities through customs. Investigators from law enforcement agencies can be diverted by claims of national security. It is typical for covert operators to work with well-established criminal undergrounds and for the government sponsoring the covert operation to at least tolerate and often abet the criminal activities of its organized crime allies.

In recent years, intelligence agencies in the United States have sought and received assistance from drug traffickers. Although outrageously hypocritical for a government waging a drug war against its own citizens to seek assistance from drug traffickers, it is not surprising. After all, as Chambliss (1986) points out, the characteristics of successful drug trafficking are the same as those that are essential to successful intelligence operations: Both require the movement of bulky commodities, money, and couriers quickly and secretly; great discretion and allegiance from temporary workers employed for illicit and covert activities; and the use of force and violence to assure the security of the operation.

STATE-SPONSORED TERRORISM AND U.S. FOREIGN POLICY

Iran

The Central Intelligence Agency (CIA) engaged in a massive conspiracy to overthrow the democratically elected prime minister of Iran, Mohammed Mossedagh, in 1953 (Prados 1986; Simon and Eitzen 1986; Beirne and Messerschmidt 1991: 258–259). Following his election, Mossedagh had nationalized several foreign-owned oil companies. His government offered compensation to the oil companies, but the Eisenhower administration did not tolerate any independence by foreign leaders and began a campaign to overthrow the Mossedagh government and replace it with the monarchy of Shah Reza Pahlavi. In return for U.S. support for the coup d'état, the Shah promised U.S. oil companies control of over 50 percent of Iran's oil production.

After removing the democratic government in Iran and placing the Shah in power, the CIA helped create, train, and finance SAVAK, a vicious secret police force loyal to the Shah. It arrested more than 1,500 people a month during the Shah's reign. On June 5, 1953, SAVAK murdered about 6,000 Iranian citizens in one day (Simon and Eitzen 1986: 158). Torture was frequently used on prisoners, and Amnesty International declared, "No country in the world has a worse record in human rights than Iran" (Beirne and Messerschmidt 1991: 258).

Although U.S. oil companies and arms merchants profited from the Shah's reign (Iran purchased $17 billion in military equipment from the United States), the ultimate costs of the coup should be determined by considering the impact of the 1979 Islamic revolution, which replaced the Shah's regime. The government of the Ayatollah Khomeni, which took over, was virulently anti-American, heavily engaged in the sponsorship of terrorism, responsible for the seizure of U.S. hostages, and part of a bizarre conspiracy involving U.S. intelligence during the Reagan administration.

Guatemala Fresh from its dubious success in Iran, the CIA intervened in the internal affairs of Guatemala the following year. In 1954, the CIA orchestrated a military coup that removed the democratically elected leader of Guatemala, Jacobo Arbenz, from power (Herman 1982: 176; Beirne and Messerschmidt 1991: 259). Arbenz was committed to democracy and had received 65 percent of the vote in Guatemala's election. His crime, however, was that he favored land reform. In Guatemala, 3 percent of the landowners owned 70 percent of the agricultural land. After his election, Arbenz nationalized 1.5 million acres of arable land, including land owned by the U.S.-based United Fruit Company. United Fruit insisted that the U.S. government act against Arbenz, and the CIA financed a rebel army in Honduras. On July 8, 1954, Arbenz fled the country. The new U.S.-sponsored dictator immediately canceled the land reform program, ended literacy programs, fired teachers, ordered the burning of subversive books, and broke up the peasants' agricultural cooperatives. For the next thirty years, Guatemala was ruled by a vicious military dictatorship that had been imposed on the citizens and supported by U.S. military forces.

Cuba In 1959, Fidel Castro overthrew Cuban dictator Fulgencia Batista. Batista had been friendly to U.S. corporations and to U.S. organized crime interests, who had run massive gambling, prostitution, and narcotics operations out of Havana (Kruger 1980; Hinckle and Turner 1981; Beirne and Messerschmidt 1991: 259–261). Once again, the Eisenhower administration elected to use the CIA to try to resolve the problem. As a first step in what was known as Operation 40, the CIA began to train anti-Castro Cuban exiles in terrorist tactics. Operation 40 was involved in terrorist attacks on Cuba, attempted assassinations of Cuban leaders, and an alliance with organized crime figures Sam Giancana, Santo Trafficante, and Johnny Roselli in a series of assassination plots against Castro himself.

In April 1961, CIA-trained Cuban exiles attempted an invasion of Cuba at the Bay of Pigs. The invasion was a military disaster for the Kennedy administration, and much of the military force was captured or killed. The failure of the Bay of Pigs invasion forced a change in tactics against Cuba. Operation 40 was replaced by JM/WAVE, an operation involving some 300 CIA agents and 4,000 to 6,000 Cuban exiles. JM/WAVE engaged in a series of terrorist attacks on Cuban sugar and oil refineries and factories. It also continued the assassination campaign begun under Operation 40.

In 1965, JM/WAVE was disbanded as a direct result of the discovery that its aircraft were engaged in narcotics smuggling, leaving thousands of highly trained, politically fanatic Cuban exiles in place in the United States. The blowback from JM/WAVE was considerable. Some of these CIA-trained exiles turned to terrorism, engaging in twenty-five to thirty bombings in Dade County, Florida, alone in 1975 and assassinating diplomats around the world (Herman 1982). Other JM/WAVE participants, having been trained in smuggling techniques and violence by the CIA, turned to organized crime, creating large gambling syndicates in New Jersey and Florida and forming the infrastructure for massive cocaine trafficking by Cuban and Colombian organized crime groups.

In 1972 the CIA targeted another democratically elected government for overthrow, presumably as part of the U.S. foreign policy commitment to democracy around the world. This time the target was the elected president of Chile, Salvador Allende (Simon and Eitzen 1986; Beirne and Messerschmidt 1991: 263). In 1970, Allende had been elected president; IT&T, which had significant mining investments in Chile, and the CIA immediately worked to destabilize the economy and Allende's government. Their plans did great damage to the Chilean economy, but failed to bring down the Allende government.

Chile

In 1973, the tactics changed and the CIA conspired with the Chilean military to overthrow Allende in a coup d'état. Allende and 30,000 Chilean citizens were killed in the coup. The democratic institutions Allende had created were dismantled, and General Pinochet, a man who saw himself as the successor to Adolph Hitler, began an unprecedented regime of repression. The Pinochet regime incarcerated over 100,000 Chileans and murdered another 20,000.

In one of the most disturbing examples of state-organized crime involving the U.S. government, the CIA and secret police agencies from five Latin American countries entered into a conspiracy to identify, monitor, and assassinate political dissidents in those countries. The terror campaign was orchestrated by Pinochet's secret police, the DINA, but was abetted by the governments of Argentina, Bolivia, Brazil, Paraguay, Uruguay, and the United States. Hundreds of people were abducted and murdered during Operation Condor (Herman 1982).

Operation Condor

Active alliances between various organized crime groups and the U.S. government can be traced to World War II when the Office of Naval Intelligence asked New York organized crime figures Meyer Lansky, Albert Anastasia, and Lucky Luciano to assist it with counterintelligence operations on the New York waterfront. During World War II, underworld figures in control of the New York docks were contracted by Navy intelligence officials to ensure that German submarines and foreign agents did not infiltrate the area. Despite his arrest and conviction for compulsory prostitution in 1936, Luciano was granted parole and given exile for life in 1954 in exchange for the aid he had provided from his prison cell during the war (Simon and Eitzen 1986: 81).

U.S. Intelligence Agency Collaboration with Organized Crime

The military also sought assistance from organized crime in the invasion of Sicily during World War II. New York organized crime syndicates sent their members door to door in Italian neighborhoods, collecting recent letters, maps, photographs, and postcards from Sicily to assist military intelligence (Messick and Goldblatt 1976). In addition, Vito Genovese, who was living in self-imposed exile in Italy, decided to play both sides against the middle. He had spent a great deal of money and effort currying favor with Mussolini, but he saw an opportunity to ingratiate himself with the U.S. government. Genovese acted as an "unofficial advisor to the American military

The OSS in Italy and Marseilles

government" following the invasion (Pearce 1976: 149; Simon and Eitzen 1986: 81). He helped the military find and install right-wing politicians loyal to organized crime in official positions in Italy as a buffer against popular support for socialist political parties. This collaboration continued in the postwar 1950s when the government perceived a new threat from communism.

Both organized crime and U.S. foreign policy interests were well served by this alliance with Genovese. Italian politicians opposed to the socialists and communists were assisted by organized crime in maintaining power, and organized crime was virtually given a crime-committing license by the government for almost four decades.

In the early 1950s, the intelligence community again sought the assistance of organized crime figures for France, which was engaged in a war to prevent its colony of Vietnam from gaining independence. The refusal of socialist dockworkers in Marseilles to load ships with military supplies bound for Vietnam threatened U.S. foreign policy in two ways. First, the containment of communism would be impaired if the French did not resist Ho Chi Minh and the Viet Minh in Vietnam. Second, the government of France, a major U.S. ally, was itself threatened by a possible socialist–communist electoral alliance and communist party domination of the trade unions. Attacking the French longshoremen, one of the most powerful leftist unions, served both ends. United States intelligence officers sought assistance from Corsican organized crime syndicates heavily involved in prostitution and waterfront corruption in breaking the French dockworkers' union.

The Corsicans created goon squads, which attacked union picket lines, harassed and even assassinated union leaders, and eventually broke the union, thereby allowing France to resume its war in Vietnam and providing the prologue for U.S. involvement a decade later. The payoff to the Corsican gangsters was enormous: They were granted the right to use Marseilles as a center for heroin trafficking, not only giving them a new and very profitable enterprise, but also creating the infamous French Connection, which would supply much of U.S. heroin needs for the next twenty years (Pearce 1976: 150).

The CIA in Southeast Asia

Links between U.S. intelligence agencies and drug smugglers occurred at least as early as the 1950s. The CIA provided direct support to Kuomintang (Chinese Nationalist) opium growers in Thailand and Burma. Ostensibly, this aid was given in the hope that these small scattered armies would someday attack communist China. The CIA set up two front companies, Civil Air Transport and Sea Supply Corporation, to provide air support for the Kuomintang opium trade. These companies supplied military aid to the Nationalist Chinese and flew their opium out of the Golden Triangle to Thailand and Taiwan. CIA assistance for these opium-growing warlords was largely responsible for the explosion of heroin addiction in the United States in the 1960s, when the number of known addicts increased from about 65,000 to more than 500,000 (McCoy 1972; Kwitny 1987). The world's largest opium merchant, Chang Chi-fu, operated for several decades as a CIA client.

Another Golden Triangle heroin czar, Li Wen-huan, was given direct financial, military, and logistical assistance by the CIA. A third major heroin trafficker, Lu Hsu-shui, was protected from a DEA investigation on orders from the CIA (Mills 1986).

During the Vietnam War, the CIA supplied, financed, and supported a renegade Laotian army made up of members of the Hmong (or Meo) tribe.

General Vang Pao commanded this 36,000-man secret army in a war against the Pathet Lao in an attempt to disrupt North Vietnamese supply routes to Viet Cong guerrillas in South Vietnam. Vang Pao's army was under the command of veteran CIA officers and was totally supplied, financed, and equipped by U.S. funds. As part of his assistance to U.S. intelligence, Vang Pao's army carried out a brutal assassination program of village leaders. Traditionally, Vang Pao's Hmong tribesmen were opium poppy farmers. The war interfered with their opium trade, so the CIA supplied them with aircraft from a CIA proprietary company, Air America, to transport the farmers' opium from the Laotian hills to a massive CIA base at Long Tieng, Laos. At Long Tieng, Vang Pao had established a massive heroin refinery. The DEA's Far East regional director, John J. O'Neill, said, "I have no doubt that Air America was used to transport opium" (Kwitny 1987: 51). Some of the Laotian heroin was transported to South Vietnam, where it was sold to U.S. troops, 20 percent of whom came home addicted to heroin.

In the 1980s the CIA also began operations in support of the Mujahadeen, a fundamentalist Moslem group of rebels fighting Soviet troops in Afghanistan. Like his Nicaraguan freedom fighters, President Ronald Reagan's Mujahadeen allies financed their war through drug trafficking, in this case heroin. Mujahadeen leaders supervised the growing of the opium poppy and, with the assistance of the CIA, which had reopened trade routes to supply the Mujahadeen with weapons, smuggled the drug onto the world market. The net result of CIA assistance to the Afghani rebels was that the areas of Afghanistan and Pakistan they controlled had become "the world's leading source of heroin exports to the United States and Europe" by 1986, according to a State Department report.

The Cia in Southwest Asia

CIA associates in the Caribbean, including the paymaster of the ill-fated Bay of Pigs invasion, played key roles in the operations of Castle Bank, a Florida money laundry for organized crime's drug money. Another Florida bank with strong intelligence community connections, the Bank of Perrine, has been used by Colombians to launder money from their burgeoning cocaine business. In the early 1970s, the CIA and organized crime played a key role in establishing and operating the World Finance Corporation, a Florida-based company involved in laundering drug money and supporting terrorist activities (Lernoux 1984).

The Cia and Money Laundering in Florida and the Caribbean Basin

Much of the opium profits from CIA involvement with drug traffickers in the Golden Triangle was laundered through the Nugan-Hand Bank in Australia. A network of high-ranking U.S. military officers and intelligence officers had links to the Nugan-Hand Bank, which was charged with narcotics trafficking, gunrunning, money laundering, and massive fraud by an Australian commission of investigation (Kwitny 1987, *New York Times,* March 8, 1987). In his investigation of the Nugan-Hand Bank, Kwitny charges that the bank laundered billions of dollars, helped finance the heroin trade in the Golden Triangle, and engaged in tax fraud and theft (Kwitny 1987: 76). The officers of this heroin bank were retired U.S. Admiral Earl F. Yates, its president; and former CIA director William Colby, its legal counsel. Former deputy CIA director Walter McDonald, former National Security Council advisor Guy Parker, and Andrew Lowe, one of Australia's largest heroin traffickers, were its consultants.

The Nugan-Hand Bank in Australia

The Bank of Credit and Commerce International

The close relationship between the U.S. government, the financial community, and organized crime is nowhere clearer than in the activities of the Bank of Credit and Commerce International (BCCI) (Kappeler et al. 1993: 237–238). BCCI was the seventh largest privately owned bank in the world. It had more than 400 branch offices operating in seventy-three countries. Among its many criminal activities were laundering at least $14 billion for the Colombian cocaine cartels, facilitating financial transactions for Panamanian president Manuel Noriega and international arms merchant Adnan Khashoggi, funneling cash to the contras for illegal arms deals and contra-backed drug trafficking, and assisting President Ferdinand Marcos in transferring his personal fortune, accrued through corruption and graft, out of the Philippines.

Despite the enormity of BCCI's crimes and its vital role in drug trafficking, the U.S. Justice Department was more than reluctant to investigate. In fact, the Justice Department had complete information on BCCI's drug and arms operations and its illegal holdings in the United States for more than three years before it initiated an inquiry. Perhaps the reluctance of U.S. law enforcement to interfere with such a major organized crime entity can be explained by the presence of what some have perceived as BCCI's friends in the U.S. government who held high office.

Cuban Organized Crime Groups

When the Cuban dictatorship of Fulgencia Batista was overthrown by Fidel Castro in 1959, U.S. intelligence agencies began a massive covert operation to remove Castro from power. To assist in military and terrorist attacks on Cuba, the U.S. government recruited former Batista allies in the Cuban refugee community in the United States and members of organized crime. Organized criminals had a major stake in Cuba. Prior to the revolution, they had operated in a partnership with Batista that had made Havana a major haven for gambling, prostitution, and drug trafficking. After the revolution, organized crime figures were imprisoned and/or exiled from Cuba, thereby costing organized crime millions of dollars in illicit revenue.

The anti-Castro Cubans were used in several secret operations whose main objective was to conduct acts of terror aimed at Cuba. Oil refineries and sugar refineries were bombed, sugar shipments poisoned, and the Cuban infrastructure disrupted through terrorist attacks. The public participation of Batista allies and organized crime figures in these efforts was a source of major embarrassment to the U.S. government. In the early 1970s, the anti-Castro terror campaign was called off when one of the planes being used by the anti-Castro Cubans crashed in California with several kilograms of cocaine and heroin aboard (*New York Times,* January 1, 1975).

The Iran–Contra Affair

The presidency of Ronald Reagan is likely to be remembered for two overriding initiatives: (1) the War on Drugs in the United States and (2) the war in Central America directed at the overthrow of the Sandinista government in Nicaragua by a coalition of paramilitary groups that came to be known as the contras. During the Reagan administration, law enforcement efforts directed at drug trafficking and drug use were intensified, generously funded, and backed up with new and draconian laws designed to put drug users behind bars. The Reagan presidency saw massive attempts at drug interdiction, crop eradication, and street-level enforcement, all combined with a "Just Say No" public relations campaign headed by First Lady Nancy Reagan.

Considering all the money, energy, and time the Reagan administration put into its campaign against illicit drug use, it is rather startling to realize that, while federal law enforcers were waging a drug war at home, Reagan administration foreign policy administrators were waging a drug-financed war in Central America. In the years since Ronald Reagan left the White House, overwhelming evidence has been developed by researchers, journalists, and congressional committees that the covert war by the contras against the government of Nicaragua was financed in large part by (1) direct funding from major cocaine traffickers, (2) a guns-for-drugs scheme involving the cocaine cartels, and (3) direct drug trafficking by some of the contra leadership. In addition, it now appears that U.S. government funds appropriated for humanitarian aid to the contras were going directly to known drug traffickers.

The Iran–contra affair and its associated drug trafficking raise interesting questions about priorities in the U.S. government. Was the Reagan administration more interested in fighting what it perceived to be a communist threat than in containing drug trafficking? Did it believe it could achieve both ends? Was it interested primarily in protecting investment opportunities for U.S. corporations and the wealthy, thereby sacrificing the drug war to corporate greed? Or were contradictory policies pursued by a variety of people in a variety of governmental agencies because contradiction is an inevitable aspect of contemporary economic and political life (Chambliss 1986)? We cannot say for certain that anyone, including the president, understood the ramifications of the various policies that were pursued. What we can say with certainty is that U.S. foreign policy, whether aimed at the containment of communism or at corporate expansion, resulted in drug trafficking aided and abetted by the very government that was waging war on drug users at home.

Medellin Cartel Support of the Contras

The most direct connections between Reagan's secret war in Nicaragua and the cocaine cartels were exposed in testimony before a Senate Foreign Relations Committee subcommittee by Ramon Milian-Rodriguez. He was the chief money launderer for the Medellin Cartel. He had begun his career in accountancy and money laundering as part of the CIA's earlier efforts to depose Fidel Castro in Cuba. Milian-Rodriguez, who had been recruited by the CIA-sponsored leader of the anti-Castro Cubans in Florida, Manuel Artime, had been trained to set up elaborate financial procedures to hide funding sources for earlier efforts against Cuba. He later used these skills for Medellin's cocaine cartel. Milian-Rodriguez disbursed $10 million from Colombian drug lords to the contras through financial couriers in Honduras, Guatemala, Costa Rica, and Miami between 1982 and 1985.

Milian-Rodriguez testified that the Medellin Cartel agreed to help the contras in return for favors from Washington: "The cartel figured it was buying a little friendship. We're going to buy some goodwill and take a little heat off them. They figured [that] maybe the CIA or DEA will not screw around so much" (*Newsday*, June 28, 1987).

Milian-Rodriguez testified that the drug cartel's contribution to the contras was arranged by long-time CIA veteran agent (also a former member of Artime's anti-Castro network) Felix Rodriguez. Rodriguez arranged the actual sites and times for the money drops. As Milian-Rodriguez said, "Felix would call me with instructions on where to send the money" (Cockburn 1987: 155).

Rodriguez was stationed at the Illopango airbase in El Salvador, where he oversaw air supply operations for the contras. More important, he reported directly to and received assistance from the office of Vice-President George Bush. In fact, during the period that cocaine cartel money was flowing to the contras, Rodriguez met personally with the vice-president three times (Cockburn 1987: 155).

Drug Smuggling by the Contras

While the contras were receiving cash contributions from the Medellin Cartel, they were also heavily involved in other drug-financed activities. The Reagan administration's covert war had been severely impeded by the Boland Amendment, passed by Congress in 1986, which cut off all military aid to the contras. As a result, the Reagan administration's National Security Council set up a secret and illegal resupply operation for the contras utilizing private sources. This covert resupply operation was run from the National Security Council by Lt. Colonel Oliver North (who later retired from the military and was a failed Republican candidate for the U.S. Senate from Virginia). Some of this resupply fund raising involved contributions from wealthy right-wing business interests in the United States and wealthy foreign sources of finance, such as Arab oil sheiks. Some of the financing came from drug sales, which were converted into weapons shipments for the contras.

Key to this drugs-for-guns operation was a ranch in northern Costa Rica owned by John Hull, an American. A report from the Senate Foreign Relations subcommittee investigating this matter indicated that Hull received $10,000 a month from the National Security Council in 1984 and 1985 (Kerry 1986: 10). High-ranking intelligence officers claimed that Hull "was getting well paid and did what he was told to do" by the CIA (*Boston Globe*, July 20, 1986). Hull's ranch operations in Costa Rica were assisted by two right-wing Cuban Americans, Felipe Vidal and Rene Corbo. Planes carrying cocaine from Pablo Escobar and Jorge Ochoa were flown into the Hull ranch, where it was unloaded and then transshipped by air or sea to the United States. Escobar and Ochoa paid a fee in return for their use of the facilities on the Hull ranch and for labor supplied by Reagan's so-called freedom fighters. Considerable testimony confirmed these cocaine transshipment operations.

What Did They Know and When Did They Know It?

A major part of the contras strategy for financing the violent overthrow of the Nicaraguan government appears to have been cocaine trafficking. Did high-ranking U.S. government officials know about the drug trafficking and, if they did, what steps did they take to stop it? By all indications, U.S. officials did know. As early as May 1985, the DEA station chief in San José, Costa Rica, told journalists, "We have reports that certain groups, under the pretext of running guns to the [contra] rebels, are smuggling drugs to the United States" (*Tico Times*, May 31, 1985). In May 1986, ABC News reported that investigators for the Senate Foreign Relations Committee had developed evidence that the "contras [had] smuggled shipments of cocaine in commercial shrimp boats from [Central America] to the Miami area." On January 20, 1987, the *New York Times* reported, "Officials from several [U.S. government] agencies said that by early last fall [1986], the Drug Enforcement Administration office in Guatemala had compiled convincing evidence that the contra military supply operation was smuggling cocaine and marijuana."

In February 1986, Jack Blum, the chief counsel to the Senate Foreign Relations Subcommittee investigating the contra resupply operations, said,

In 1994, former Lt. Colonel Oliver North was narrowly defeated by the Democratic incumbent for one of Virginia's U.S. Senate seats. Many people see North as a hero who was tricked into helping a freedom-loving people earn their independence from a communist regime. Others view him as a criminal who broke the law, lied to Congress, and aided drug traffickers. In your opinion, should the ends justify the means when drug trafficking is involved? Which was the greater evil facing the Americans: cocaine or communism? How should Oliver North be judged? Did he participate in organized crime, or not?

"I believe that there is no question, based on things that we have heard, that contras and the contra infrastructure have been involved in the cocaine trade and in bringing cocaine into Florida." Finally, Congressman Charles Rangel's House Select Committee on Narcotics Abuse and Control received a report from U.S. Customs that named thirty-eight individuals and companies involved in the contra resupply operation who were also involved in drug trafficking.

Even more compelling evidence demonstrates that the drug-smuggling operation was known at the very highest levels of the Reagan administration. In fact, it is now clear from documentary evidence gathered by the Senate Foreign Relations subcommittee that Oliver North not only knew about drug trafficking, but also did nothing to interfere with it. On March 28, 1986, a message was sent to North from Lewis Tambs, the U.S. Ambassador to Costa Rica, using CIA back-channel communications conduits, saying that contra leader Adolfo Chamorro "is alleged to be involved in drug trafficking." On April 1, 1985, a memo from Rob Owen to Oliver North described Costa Rican contra leader José Robelo as having "potential involvement in drug running." The same memo noted that another contra military leader, Sebastian Gonzalez, was "now involved in drug running out of Panama." On February 10, 1986, a memo from Owen to North specifically identified a DC-4 being used in the resupply operation as "used at one time to run drugs, and part of the crew had criminal records. Nice group the Boys [the CIA] chose." Finally, in notes recorded during an August 9, 1985, meeting with Robert Owen, North wrote, "DC-6 which is being used for runs out of New Orleans is probably being used for drug runs into U.S."

Lt. Colonel North was eventually convicted of lying under oath to congressional committees about his role in the Iran-contra affair. In a telling irony, North's conviction was set aside by a federal appeals court on the basis of one of the legal technicalities that he later raged against during his Senate campaign.

DOMESTIC TERRORISM

Although much international terrorist activity has targeted businesspeople, tourists, and businesses abroad, the United States has been comparatively free of such crimes. In fact, to many, terrorism is something that happens only in Europe, the Middle East, or in places other than the United States. In reality, this is not the case. For years, the fear of domestic terrorism in the United States was just that, only fear. In the late twentieth and early twenty-first century we know that this has changed.

This section introduces the dilemmas and misunderstandings posed by domestic terrorism and places the subject within a general context. Before we begin our discussion of domestic terrorism, we should point out that no definition of domestic terrorism is generally accepted and, accordingly (as of this writing), no U.S. laws are currently designed to control domestic terrorist acts per se. This brings up some interesting questions. Should acts of domestic terrorism be defined in terms of the crimes, the perpetrators, or the persons or organizations sponsoring them? Can state-sponsored foreign nationals committing terrorist acts on U.S. soil be termed domestic terrorists?

More than a year before the 2001 terrorist attacks, the National Commission on Terrorism released a report identifying suspected terrorist nations such as Iran, Sudan, and Iraq and concluded that the government must take steps to reinvigorate the collection of intelligence about terrorist plans and activities (National Commission on Terrorism 2000).

Following the 2001 terrorist attacks, Congress enacted and the president signed the USA Patriot Act. The act, discussed in some detail in Appendix A, created a number of new crimes, such as terrorist attacks against mass transportation and harboring or concealing terrorists.

Robert Gurr, a professor of political science at Northwestern University, has attempted to analyze domestic terrorism. He and coauthor J. Bowyer Bell argue that terrorism is a tactic used by the weak to intimidate the strong and the strong to intimidate the weak (Bell and Gurr 1979). If this is so, the United States has a long history of terrorism, especially related to leftist political movements that have used forms of terrorism to seek political gains.

Much contemporary evidence suggests that domestic terrorism is a current problem in the United States, but history shows that it has been ingrained in our society for more than a century. Bell and Gurr (1979) suggest that one of the earliest forms of domestic terrorism was aimed at protecting the status quo and economic privilege. For example, as discussed in Chapter 4, the actions of private and company security police forces in the nineteenth century was terrorist in nature. These persons, who often worked as strike breakers, were hired to keep workers from exercising both their rights of free speech and their rights to organized unions. The southern slave patrols were outright terrorist groups, as were the vigilante justice posses of the western states, who took the law into their own hands and used terror to serve their own self-interest. Many have argued that the Ku Klux Klan, organized in 1865, is another example of early domestic terrorism in the United States.

You Decide

Is Terrorism Organized Crime?

For years, experts in the organized crime field have argued that terrorism is a separate and distinct form of criminality from that of organized crime. Organized crime, they argue, is profit motivated, among other things, and cannot be lumped with terrorist acts, which are often politically or ideologically inspired. It is true that many terrorist acts, such as the acts committed by the Unabomber, are purely inspired by ideology; by all indications he had no

identifiable profit motive. But examples of political and financial motives of other persons and groups should also be considered. Let's look back to our earlier discussions in this book, which focus on the rise of some well-known gangsters, such as Al Capone, who dominated not only Chicago criminal rackets but also local politics.

Could Capone have gained such a stronghold on crime in Chicago without the political support of local politicians such as "Big Bill" Thompson? For that matter, could Big Bill Thompson have won his election without Capone's support? Perhaps we should consider that while Capone had no apparent aspirations to enter politics per se, his desire for wealth necessitated his control of local politicians to avoid detection and for protection from prosecution. Also, we should consider that the rise to power of many well-known gangsters is surrounded by countless acts of public violence—the bombing or burning of small businesses whose owners fail to pay back illicit loans or of tavern owners who refused to do business with local gangsters. Certainly, the brutal killing of police informers (through public executions, car bombs, etc.) has always had an indisputable deterrent effect for others in the community who might be predisposed to turn on the mob.

For a decade Pablo Escobar's Medellin Cartel conducted a campaign of domestic terrorism against the people and government of Colombia in its fight against extradition agreements between Colombia and the United States. Can these public acts of violence, even though committed by organized crime, be characterized as acts of domestic terrorism as well?

Consider the other side of the equation. If the experts are correct and indeed terrorism is ideologically motivated rather then profit motivated, to what extent does illicitly gained revenue play a role in the commission of some of the world's most significant terrorist attacks? After all, even the most politically charged terrorist attack requires a degree of precision, planning, know-how, equipment, intelligence information, and so on.

Money is needed to finance training, purchase weaponry, recruit personnel, provide transportation, and realize many other aspects of the planned deed. For example, some well-known terrorist groups, such as Myanmar's Shan United Army, Colombia's M-19, and Peru's Shining Path, have utilized profits generated from the drug trade to finance their insurgent campaigns. The Mideast group al Qaeda has a firm financial base. Without this considerable source of revenue, many groups would lose momentum or simply disband. So profit motivation clearly interfaces with many ideologically charged incidents.

Should terrorist acts be characterized as organized crime? Conversely, do some organized crime rackets often necessitate the use of terrorist deeds? Is terrorism organized crime? You decide!

A few groups espousing violence from the left were visible during the 1960s. That decade marked a historical era of cultural and social change, with protests against military intervention in Vietnam accompanied by advances in the feminist movement. Perhaps more significant, however, was the civil rights movement, which gained considerable momentum during the decade, redefining social relationships between ethnic and racial groups in the United States. The lack of progress in achieving peace and justice in the United States and the slow pace of reform led to frustration among some activists, which was played out in acts of violence.

Although the 1995 Amtrak bombing was considered a serious act of domestic terrorism, three other events of an even more serious nature have heightened the awareness of domestic terrorism in the United States: the 1993 Bombing of New York's World Trade Center (which has also been characterized as state-sponsored terrorism); the serial mail bombings by the Unabomber, which had been ongoing since 1978, and perhaps the most sobering incident of all, the 1995 bombing of the Federal Murrah Building in Oklahoma City. We will first consider this most important event.

On April 13, 1995, at 9:02 A.M., a 4,000-pound bomb was detonated in front of the Alfred P. Murrah Federal Building in Oklahoma City, resulting in a virtual collapse of the structure and the deaths of 168 people, including children located in a day-care center on the building's first floor. The incident was especially shocking because it invaded the nation's heartland. Since the bombing, many questions have gone unanswered. In particular, why the

The Bombing in Oklahoma City

federal building? Why Oklahoma? It could be suggested that federal buildings offer a likely passive political target for terrorists. Moreover, a target in the heartland of the nation provided the terrorists with a low-profile target while generating high-visibility media coverage for the event.

Timothy McViegh and Terry Nichols, both charged with complicity in the Oklahoma City bombing, were former members of the U.S. military and allegedly members of the radical Michigan Militia, a heavily armed, antigovernment group that also opposed taxes, the authority of federal agents, and the power of the federal government in general. As of the preparation of this book, however, it is still unclear whether the Oklahoma bombing was an isolated act carried out by individuals with personal agendas or by a larger organization whose goals remain unidentified.

Other Incidents in the Late Twentieth Century

Another event that heightened the awareness of domestic terrorism for the American people was the February 26, 1993, terrorist bombing of the World Trade Center in New York City. In 1994, four men were convicted of participation in the planning and execution of the bombing, which resulted in the deaths of eleven people and injuries to more than 1,000 others. In December 1995, Sheik Omar Abdel-Rahman, part of a radical Islamic group, and nine of his followers were convicted of complicity in the bombing (Frankel 1995a). The group also planned to blow up the United Nations, the FBI's New York headquarters, two tunnels, and a bridge and to assassinate selected judges and political leaders.

Another domestic terrorist, dubbed by the media as the Unabomber, plagued U.S. society for almost two decades. Between 1978 and 1995 the Unabomber's attacks resulted in the deaths of three persons and injuries of twenty-three. Victims included engineers, computer programmers, and

The 1995 bombing of the Alfred P. Murrah building in Oklahoma City served as a wake-up call for all Americans concerned about domestic terrorism.

others who were thought to pose a threat to the Unabomber and his personal convictions. He mailed threatening letters to both would-be and former victims espousing his political and social concerns. In April 1996, suspect Theodore J. Kaczynski was arrested by the FBI in Lincoln, Montana, and charged with at least one of the Unabomber's bombings. He was found guilty and sent to prison in 1998.

The FBI is designated as the lead agency to investigate domestic terrorism in the United States. Its national resources and jurisdiction make it an ideal law enforcement entity for this purpose, especially since domestic terrorist groups operate in more than one state. Because the FBI plays a role in national security, it is a logical organization to deal with this type of criminal behavior. This view is not held by all terrorism experts. Some have suggested that, because local police agencies are always the first to respond to terrorist acts, the FBI may not in fact be the best agency to deal with domestic terrorism. This controversy points out a need to study and define the role of law enforcement and its response to terrorism in the United States.

THE IDEOLOGICAL LEFT

Groups that became prominent during the 1960s and 1970s were organized around civil rights, the Vietnam War, feminism, and other political themes. Such groups were well disciplined, highly trained, and had an ability to adjust to changing operational conditions. Included in these groups were the Symbinese Liberation Army (SLA), the Black Liberation Army (BLA), and the Weather Underground (formerly the Weathermen). Of these, the Weather Underground (WU) gained considerable national attention as a result of confrontations with police during demonstrations in some of the nation's largest cities. Their ideological philosophy said much about their organizational goals: "Our intention is to disrupt the empire . . . to incapacitate it, to put pressure on the cracks, to make it hard to carry out its bloody functioning against the people of the world, to join the struggle, to attack from inside" (Homer 1983).

After several violent confrontations with the police, the WU adopted a more paramilitary stance to attack police buildings and courthouses in California and New York (Trick 1976). Although the WU was very visible for a period of time, by the late 1970s it was generally thought that it was literally underground and no longer operational. However, in 1981, a series of violent robberies occurred in New York, in which two police officers were murdered. The investigation showed that the robberies and murders were linked to the Weather Underground, which was also associated with the Black Liberation Army.

When the WU was campaigning against society, other groups with similar ideological philosophies emerged. One such group was the New World Liberation Front (NWLF), originating in the San Francisco area. It adopted guerrilla techniques similar to those of the WU in carrying out attacks against major corporations or government buildings. Although it was not as well known as the WU, some experts credited it with being one of the most active domestic terrorist groups in the nation at the time (Trick 1976).

In the early 1980s, another terrorist group, the United Freedom Front (UFF), emerged. The group's membership was small, consisting of four white males, three white females, and one black male, most of whom were associated with similar groups during the 1970s (Harris 1987). In addition to a number of bombing incidents, the UFF was implicated in the murder of a New Jersey state police officer and the attempted murders of two Massachusetts state police officers.

In addition to these predominantly white leftist groups, black leftists have played a role in U.S. domestic terrorism. For the most part, prisons were the main spawning ground for many black leftist groups. Many black prisoners viewed themselves as political prisoners and blamed society for not providing them with adequate educational, housing, and employment opportunities. Although many prisoners shared this philosophy, most chose not to support revolutionary acts against society. A small group of blacks adopted a Marxist political ideology, which essentially says that racism is an economic scheme designed to maintain a pool of surplus labor and prevent the rise of the working class. No meaningful change can occur as long as the U.S. economic and political systems are based on capitalism (Vetter and Pearlstein 1991). Thus some militant black leaders, such as Huey Newton of the Black Panthers, viewed the black prison experience as akin to slavery, a sort of neoslavery. The Black Panther Party was one of the first black political groups to emerge in the late 1960s. Indeed, many inmates were disgruntled, embittered, and ripe for recruitment (Jacobs 1976).

In 1986, another black group, the El Rukins (discussed in Chapter 6) was implicated in a terrorist plot when a group member purchased an antitank weapon during an undercover operation. Some members of the group allegedly met with officials of the Libyan government, presumably to commit acts of domestic terrorism for hire (Vetter and Pearlstein 1991).

THE IDEOLOGICAL RIGHT

Violent ultraconservative terrorist groups, also known as **hate groups**, also emerged in the United States, especially during the 1980s. In addition to random acts of violence, such groups have been blamed for more substantial terroristic behavior. For example, between January 1995 and June 1996 arson fires were set at thirty-three black churches in the South, raising the question of racial motives. In one case, a letter claiming responsibility for one of eight Tennessee church fires threatened a "reign of terror," and in another, suspects in three arsons in Georgia were linked with the Ku Klux Klan (KKK) (Fields and Twigg 1996).

The fires of the late 1990s were reminiscent of a similar wave of fires during the summer of 1964 when the KKK torched more than thirty black churches in Mississippi alone. Whether members of the KKK or some other group are ultimately found to be responsible for the arsons, it is clear that the fires have succeeded in horrifying a substantial segment of the nation's black population. Many hate groups have earned the distinction of being characterized as organized crime due to their degree of sophistication and organization. The Anti-Defamation League has estimated that approximately seventy-one such groups are still active in the country. As a rule, these groups tend to be heavily armed and focus on themes such as white supremism, Nazism, and religious revisionism. One group originating shortly after the Civil War, the Ku Klux Klan, experienced its third revival during the 1950s in the aftermath of the Supreme Court's *Brown* v. *Board of Education* decision.

A member of the Ku Klux Klan taunts protesters at a rally in Greensburg, Pennsylvania, August 16, 1997. Police, who kept several hundred people from interfering with the rally, were unable to keep some protesters from throwing eggs, bottles, and debris at the Klan members.

(*AP Photo/Gary Tramontina*)

During the 1950s and 1960s, the Klan gained membership in many southern U.S. states. At its peak, there were about 700 klaverns with a membership of 17,000 (Vetter and Pearlstein 1991). The organization performed different types of terrorist acts, which included cross burnings, beatings, bombings, and murder, designed to intimidate and harass civil rights workers. Despite many successful federal prosecutions since the 1960s, the Klan continues to endure. In 1989, former KKK Imperial Wizard David Duke was elected to the Louisiana state legislature. A self-professed Nazi during his college days, Duke claimed to have left the Klan in 1979, but his home address still served as the local Klan office when he entered the Louisiana statehouse.

Domestic Terrorism: White Supremacist and Hate Groups

The popular image of hate groups in the United States is embodied in the stereotype of Ku Klux Klan nightriders dressed in white robes and hoods, burning crosses, and engaging in random acts of violence toward African Americans in the South. This image is no longer an accurate description of what has become a paramilitary, terrorist underground of the far right in the United States. (This section is summarized from the following sources: Antidefamation League 1988a, 1988b; Southern Poverty Law Center 1989.) In fact, in the 1970s and 1980s, Klan membership declined and new, highly volatile, white supremacist groups began to appear in such far-flung locations as California, Texas, Idaho, and Connecticut.

The new groups are united in their hatred for blacks and Jews, but they have added other ethnic groups, such as Mexican Americans and Vietnamese, to their target list. In addition, these groups picture themselves as engaged in an ongoing war with the federal government, which is usually referred to as the Zionist Occupational Government (ZOG). Although these groups formerly focused their rhetoric on simple racism, they have now expanded their agendas to include immigration policies, AIDS, crime, farm policies, and taxes.

The white supremacist terrorist underground has no identifiable leader. A multitude of small groups, most formed around a charismatic leader, are scattered across the country. These groups are difficult to monitor and investigate because they often come into existence, break up, and re-form as a new organization as soon as law enforcement attention has been directed their way. However, by broadening their issue base and their geographic areas while becoming less public in terms of mass demonstrations, they have become a greater terrorist threat than at any time in the past.

In the early 1980s, white supremacist extremist groups took a distinctly paramilitary direction in their activities. In Texas, Klan leader and Aryan Nations' ambassador Louis Beam initiated paramilitary training camps to train followers in terrorist tactics directed at Vietnamese immigrants and their participation in the Texas shrimp and fishing industries. In Alabama, the leader of the Invisible Empire of the Ku Klux Klan, Bill Wilkinson, was also training his followers in paramilitary tactics. Other Klan groups formed illegal, vigilante border patrol units to attack immigrants. Not far below the surface of all of this activity was a philosophy of violent revolution, which spread from the Klan to Posse Comitatus groups and to newer Christian Identity groups (discussed later in the chapter).

These nontraditional hate groups had some success in recruiting white males from the ranks of farmers and blue-collar workers who were caught in the economic downturn of the mid-1980s. The white supremacist movement exploited their fears by blaming these problems on immigrants, minority groups, and an alleged Jewish conspiracy in financial and political communities. Posse Comitatus groups, for example, argued that the federal government itself was an illegal entity, and the highest authority to which citizens were required to respond was the county sheriff. The Christian Identity movement argued that only pure-race whites were true Christians and began to advocate a migration of all Christian whites to the Pacific northwest in an attempt to found a white homeland. The radical Christian right sponsored tax resistance movements, formed paramilitary survivalist compounds, and began to ready themselves for violent revolution.

In the mid-1980s, a particularly violent group of Christian survivalists known as the Order engaged in an eighteen-month terrorist campaign that they believed would lead to a white revolution that would overthrow the ZOG. In this terrorist spree, the Order engaged in bombings, armored car robberies, and the murder of a state trooper, a sheriff, and two FBI agents. The Order's leader, Bob Mathews, was finally killed in a police shoot-out in Washington State. By 1985, twenty-three members of the Order had been convicted of various crimes and were serving long prison sentences.

The Order's influence was not completely diminished by the death of their leader and imprisonment of his more violent followers. Its members became martyr figures for the white supremacist movement, uniting Klan members, neo-Nazis, and ultraviolent Skinhead groups. The Order had also convinced law enforcement officials of the seriousness of the terrorist threat in the white supremacist underground, and in several areas law enforcement moved quickly against other groups. Three major Ku Klux Klan organizations in North Carolina and Alabama were decimated by convictions on criminal charges and civil suits brought by the Southern Poverty Law Center, and Order II, a new group emulating the original Order, was quickly discovered and suppressed.

The bombing of the federal building in Oklahoma City brought the awareness of a possible new component to the organized crime problem: paramilitary militias. Militia members harbor intense hatred toward the government and believe that the federal government is conspiring to disarm its citizens. According to the militias' conspiracy view, federal authorities are enacting gun-control legislation to prevent people from resisting the imposition of a tyrannical regime or a "one-world" dictatorship (Halpern et al. 1996). Consequently, militia organizers are preparing for what they believe is an armed showdown.

Two incidents involving armed camps that occurred in 1996 illustrated the fact that such groups exist in America and might possibly pose a terrorist threat—the Freemen in Montana and the Viper Militia in Arizona. On March 25, 1996, an 81-day standoff began in Jordan, Montana, between a small, heavily armed group calling themselves the Freemen and the FBI. Federal prosecutors had warrants for the arrest of several of the group's members, mostly on charges of forging financial documents. On June 13, all sixteen residents in the compound surrendered to FBI agents; of those, twelve were charged with federal violations.

The second sobering incident was the arrest of twelve members of the Viper Militia on July 1, 1996, in Phoenix, Arizona. Federal authorities charged the suspects with a plot to bomb Phoenix government offices of the Bureau of Alcohol, Tobacco, and Firearms, the Internal Revenue Service, the Immigration and Naturalization Service, and the Secret Service. The suspects, ten men and two women, had taken part in training exercises that detonated ammonium nitrate bombs similar to that used in the Oklahoma City bombing.

Most militias, which appear to permeate much of the rural United States, seem to have formed since the early 1990s, but to what extent they play a role in organized criminal activity is unclear. By most estimates, thousands of people have been associated with the militia movement. Some suggest that more than 15,000 people are involved in at least forty states (Stern 1996). In their relatively short existence, they have earned a unique reputation. Members have shot at police officers, threatened public officials, and been arrested in countless armed confrontations. Those who make up the membership ranks include truck drivers, housewives, lawyers, physicians, loggers, and barbers, all of whom are prepared to fight the government with the belief that their freedom is at stake.

For years some militias have been loosely associated with extremist groups such as the KKK, the Birchite Minutemen, the White Citizens Council, and neo-Nazi groups such as the Order. Because of the racist and anti-Semitic agendas of these earlier groups, their numbers were relatively small and their ability to expand was limited. However, in recent years, against a social backdrop of economic uncertainty and alienation from the political system, militias have made a radical turn toward mainstream society. Cooper (1995a) characterizes the militias as a movement that for some time has been waiting to happen and suggests that they were born in the backlashes against civil rights, environmentalism, gay rights, the prochoice movement, and gun control.

Richard Butler, center, founder of the Aryan Nations sect, and other members of the neo-Nazi group salute as a crowd of counter-demonstrators attempts to shout them down in 1999 at an Aryan Nations rally in Coeur d'Alene, Idaho. About 80 members of this neo-Nazi group were confronted by demonstrators from the Jewish Defense League and several human rights groups.

(*AP Photo/Jeff T. Green*)

TRIGGERING EVENTS

Although the literature on militias is of recent vintage, three specific events occurring during the early 1990s are often cited as catalysts for the growth of much of the U.S. militia movement. First was the 1992 standoff between federal agents and white supremacist Randy Weaver in Ruby Ridge, Idaho, resulting in the killing of Weaver's unarmed wife and teenage son by federal agents. Also killed in the incident was a U.S. deputy marshal. Weaver and his family, however, instantly became martyrs and icons of resistance to perceived federal repression, which even generated a Randy Weaver support group called the United Citizens for Justice (UCJ).

Next was the April 1993 federal siege at Waco, Texas, against the Branch Davidian cult, which culminated in the fiery death of seventy-eight people, including twenty children.

The third and perhaps most important event occurred in February 1994, with the passage of the Brady Bill regulating firearms sales, followed in September of that year by the assault weapons ban, which also generated considerable political debate. Together these events marked the link between the militias and the gun issue.

Also in 1993, Randy Trochman formed the Militia of Montana (MOM), one of the largest in the nation. The group warns of impending martial law and one-world socialism, which will be preceded by the confiscation of the personal armory of the citizenry (Cooper 1995a).

An understanding of the role of militias is confused by their antienvironmentalist connection. Militias confronted with local police, sheriffs, IRS agents, and others in the early and mid-1990s, and a majority of militia-related incidents involved people who, in one way or another, are associated with the environment. So, in addition to protesting taxes and government regulation, many militias (calling themselves wise-use activists) also advocate property rights while opposing land-use laws.

This stems from the belief that land-use planning equals socialism. In Washington State, for example, one such organization, the Snohomish County Property Rights Alliance (PRA), boasts a membership of 10,000 and advocates resistance to the government and its preservationist backers. As of late winter 1994, local environmental activists in Washington State, New Mexico, Texas, and Montana reported receiving death threats from militia members (Helvarg 1995). In addition to the **anti-enviros** recruitment frenzy is the Counties Movement, which insists that county sheriffs have the right to arrest federal land managers who fail to respect the customs and culture of logging, mining, and grazing on public lands (Helvarg 1995).

Other Domestic Terrorist Groups

It is difficult to keep track of all of the small groups comprising the white supremacist terrorist underground. These groups are constantly forming, splitting, and re-forming under new names and in new places, but we can generally classify these groups in the following eight broad categories.

Christian Identity Groups

Christian Identity movement followers believe that persons of Jewish descent are direct descendants of Satan and that only white Anglo-Saxons are the children of God. They advocate a race war in which they believe only true Aryans will survive. Identity movement organizations usually are organized around churches with rather traditional names, such as Church of Jesus Christ, Mountain Church of Jesus Christ, and Church of Christ. By the beginning of the 1990s, Christian Identity churches could be found in thirty-three U.S. states and in Canada, England, and South Africa. The Christian Identity movement has brought such diverse hate-group participants as Ku Klux Klan members, survivalists, neo-Nazis, and Skinheads together under its banner. They believe that they are not committing crimes, such as cross burnings and random assaults, but are engaged in the true work of God.

Among the most influential of the Christian Identity churches is Richard Butler's Church of Jesus Christ Christian, located at the Aryan Nations compound in northern Idaho. In Harrison, Arkansas, Thom Robb, the leader of the Knights of the Ku Klux Klan, runs another influential Christian Identity church group. Still other branches of this ideology can be found in Ben Klassen's Church of the Creator in North Carolina and William Pierce's Cosmotheist Church in West Virginia.

White Nationalists

White nationalist terrorist groups advocate the creation of a new and totally separate country for whites. Some of these groups, including Robert Miles's Mountain Church, favor the creation of a white homeland in the Pacific Northwest; others, such as Harold Covington of the Confederate National Congress, believe that whites should form a homeland in the Deep South. Still others, such as Californian Daniel Johnson, favor a constitutional amendment to deport all nonwhites from the United States. Each of these white nationalists has espoused the supremacy of the white race while denigrating other groups, such as "Jews and the nonwhite races they attempt to seduce" (Holden 1986).

Third-Position White Supremacists

A position espoused by Tom Metzger and his White Aryan Resistance (WAR) group rejects all traditional political thinking and argues that the federal government, which is dominated by Jews and "white-race traitors," is the primary enemy to be attacked. WAR has based its recruiting campaigns on virulent racism and has attacked Asians, Hispanics, blacks, and the U.S. government itself. A similar group, the Oklahoma White Man's Association headed by Joe Grego, has been encouraging whites to arm themselves for a revolution to reclaim the country.

Neo-Nazi Skinheads

By the end of the 1980s, the white supremacist underground was joined by a series of ill-defined, loosely organized but extremely violent groups called Skinheads. They are young people who shave their heads, embellish their bodies with swastika tattoos, dress like punk rockers, wear steel-toed boots, and idolize Adolf Hitler. Unlike the other white supremacist terrorist groups, Skinheads are primarily urban, and they began a campaign of urban terror in the late 1980s. They beat an elderly black woman in San Diego, and they killed black men in Tampa, Las Vegas, and Portland. The skinheads also engaged in violent assaults on other minority-group members and gays in many other cities. Many of the Skinheads were loosely confederated under the banner of Tom Metzger's WAR.

The neo-Nazi Skinheads are essentially nonideological haters who simply organize themselves around racism and see violence directed at minorities, gays, women, and the government as the only solution to their problems. Skinhead violence, although widespread and prevalent, has been more random and represents a smaller part of an overall design than violence by other groups.

Racial Survivalists

Racial **survivalists** are often also Identity Christians who believe in the inevitability of a massive race war. They have carried this ideology a step further by forming paramilitary communes and engaging in the study of terrorist and survivalist tactics and weapons training. The most infamous of these groups is The Covenant, the Sword, and the Arm of the Lord (CSA) led by James Ellison. It has stockpiled illegal weapons, explosives, and survivalist supplies in a number of camps. Many CSA followers were arrested for aiding and abetting the Order's terror campaign.

Fifth-Era Ku Klux Klan Groups

Fifth-era white supremacists are primarily former Ku Klux Klan members who believe that the Klan's public activities, media events, and mass education programs are a waste of time. They believe that rather than trying to create a mass popular hate group, believers should form small groups of well-trained, hard-core violent militants in preparation for a guerrilla-style war against the federal government. Robert Miles's Mountain Church has been a prime advocate group for this philosophy.

Profile

The Skinheads

Of the many white supremacist organizations in the United States, the Skinheads originated in England during the 1970s. Although originating in Europe, the Skinhead movement coincided with the white supremacist movement in the United States, in which the Skinheads found allies with groups such as the Aryan Nation and the Order. The real danger of the Skinheads seems to lie in the influence the older white supremacists have on them (White 1991). Given their youthful makeup, the Skinheads tend to be more prone to violence than their older white supremacist counterparts. By all indications, although an extremely violent group, the Skinheads lack an organized infrastructure, and because of that, may not technically qualify as an organized crime group.

Karl Wolf raised his arm in a Nazi salute as he marched through the streets of Coeur d'Alene, Idaho, July 18, 1998. Scores of police in riot gear stood between parading white supremacists and protesters who jeered Aryan Nations marchers. Hundreds of protesters and onlookers lined the main street in this lakeside resort city as about 90 members and supporters of the Aryan Nations marched.

(*AP Photo/Elaine Thompson*)

Posse Comitatus

Posse Comitatus groups argue that the only valid governmental authority is found at the county level, and therefore the county sheriff is the highest authority to which they must submit. They engage in survivalist and paramilitary training, many are Identity Christians, most refuse to pay federal taxes, and some Posse Comitatus groups have targeted federal judges and IRS agents for execution. Posse Comitatus groups attempted to recruit farmers in the Midwest during the 1980s in response to the financial difficulties that many family farmers were undergoing at the time.

Populists

A number of populist groups are primarily anti-Semitic and argue that Jews run the media and the government. These groups have formed particularly in the far western and some midwestern states; they share ideological themes with several right-wing organizations, including Posse Comitatus, the Order, and the Aryan Nations. All believe that the white race is superior to all others and that all nonwhites (including Jews) are mentally and physically inferior. Politically, such groups reject the authority of the federal government as being controlled by liberals, Jews, and blacks. Many also espouse a philosophy of survivalism, contending that their members should prepare to fight in the racial or nuclear Armageddon that is destined to occur.

The Reverend Richard Butler of the Aryan Nations, Church of Jesus Christ Christian in Idaho, is one of the leaders of the neo-Nazi movement. The Aryan Nations maintains contact with similar groups, who are known to wear swastikas, double lightning bolts, and other emblems worn by Adolph Hitler's Nazis. One of the more violent neo-Nazi groups of the 1980s was the Order, a splinter group of the Aryan Nations. The group was founded by Robert

Mathews, author of the book *The Turner Diaries*. Much of the group's philosophy relates to Mathews's book, which envisions racial warfare in the United States headed by an elite, clandestine battalion, the Order, that organizes the overthrow of the federal government to be replaced by a white supremacy–based government. Members of the Order have been involved in a number of criminal acts since the early 1980s. These include robbery, counterfeiting, bombings, assaults on federal officers, and the murder of a Denver talk show host.

Another important survivalist right-wing group is the Covenant, the Sword, and the Arm of the Lord (CSA), which organized around 1980. Its members have participated in numerous bombings, arsons, and shootings, including the murders of two state troopers. In April 1985, the CSA compound near Harrison, Arkansas, was raided by federal agents, who arrested five members, including four members of the Order. All those arrested were later convicted of criminal charges.

The Posse Comitatus organization, operating in the Midwest, represents another supremacist extremist group that has a strong Christian identity and opposes taxes. Posse Comitatus members have also been involved in the murders of police officers in Arkansas and Nebraska and have been known to confront persons who repossess farms. Posse Comitatus members share the belief that the U.S. government has been taken over by Jews and that the nation must return to its Anglo-Saxon origins. In this group's view, advocating nonpayment of taxes is one way to oppose the Jews and the existing government.

The views shared by these groups, as unorthodox as they are, continue to pose a substantial threat to public order. We must remember that one of the theories behind the Oklahoma City bombing is that antifederalist separatists are using terrorist acts as a forum of social protest. Once again we see that terrorist groups consist of much more than Islamic fundamentalists and, worse yet, may be difficult to identify in mainstream America.

The movement by white supremacist groups poses an important threat to U.S. law and order and, although law enforcement crackdowns seem to have suppressed their activities, many such groups are still active around the country. In addition to their racist and sometimes Marxist agenda, many view federal and state laws as unconstitutional, advocate the nonpayment of taxes, and view state and local police (with the exception of the sheriff) as having no legitimate authority.

SINGLE-ISSUE TERRORIST ACTIVITY

In addition to right-wing domestic extremist groups, Schmid and de Graaf (1982) identify what they call **single-issue terrorist activity**. This form of terrorism is committed by small groups or individuals who attempt to exert pressure on authorities in an effort to grant some privilege to a larger group with whom the terrorists identify. The following are some single-issue examples.

Antiabortion Activists In January 1998, a 22-year-old gunman walked into a Brookline, Massachusetts, abortion clinic and shot seven people. Two of the victims, both receptionists, died. After the arrest of the alleged gunman, John Salvi, an organized vigil in his behalf was held in Boston by members of the prolife movement. Although this incident shocked the nation, it was not unlike other abortion clinic murders of recent years. The first killing related to the abortion issue was of an abortion doctor in Wichita, Kansas, who was shot by Paul Hill, a prolife activist now serving a life sentence for the crime. In 1993, physician David Gunn and his volunteer bodyguard were shot several times as they sat in his car at the Pensacola, Florida, Women's Medical Services Clinic. Both died. Michael Griffin, an antiabortion activist, was later convicted of premeditated murder. Between 1982 and 1986, antiabortion terrorists bombed more than forty birth control and proabortion clinics (Hoffman 1987). In addition to the violence, terrorists rely on fear. They harass people who attempt to attend the clinics, as well as doctors and other workers who provide abortion services. In 1993 Congress enacted the Federal Freedom of Access to Clinic Entrances (FACE) that allows women to go to clinics without facing harassment.

It could be argued that the violent rhetoric commonly heard at abortion protests serves as a catalyst for violence. This issue involves a philosophical problem: The First Amendment (freedom of speech) protects even the most outrageous statements and some forms of symbolic speech, such as flag burning. Although some have argued that blanket constitutional protection for all types of expression, from TV violence to pornography to hate speech, spurs harmful acts and should be restricted (Mauro 1995), the Supreme Court has generally rejected efforts to censor these forms of speech. This has increased the heated verbal exchanges at abortion protest sites. This became especially evident in 1992, when the U.S. Supreme Court voted unanimously in *R.A.V. v. St. Paul* to strike down a St. Paul, Minnesota, hate crime ordinance (bias-motivated disorderly conduct) that had been used to prosecute a white teenager for burning a cross in the yard of a black family. The majority of justices agreed that the law impermissibly singled out for prosecution special types of expression: racial, religious, or sexual insults. They stated that "the First Amendment does not permit St. Paul to impose special prohibitions on those speakers who express views on disfavored subjects."

Crime-Related Events

Because the violence associated with the abortion issue is fairly new to society, experts are unclear as to whether it constitutes organized crime, although federal investigators are increasingly convinced that it does fall under the RICO statute's definition of a criminal organization. Many antiabortion activitists follow a philosophy of Christian fundamentalism. What confuses the issue is whether such acts represent organized crime behavior or whether they are simply isolated incidents perpetrated by lone fanatics. In 1993 the U.S. Supreme Court recognized that the organized crime statute RICO could be applied to control some forms of abortion-related behavior. Implicit is an organized element associated with such activities. Many violent acts committed by extremists appear to be the work of loners. However, Goodman (1995) observes, "if these acts of violence are simply acts committed by isolated deranged individuals, how many deranged individuals does it take to make a conspiracy? How many deranged individuals does it take to make a movement?"

During the 1980s, death threats and stalkings slowly evolved into firebombings. In virtually all cases, prolife advocates claimed that the killers were loners or outsiders. The mainstream prolife rhetoric claiming that abortion is murder has led many to the conclusion that the killing of a killer is justifiable homicide and that murder to prevent murder is morally right (Goodman 1995). Such views, of course, ignore the long-established constitutional principle of due process.

In March 1993, the *Washington Post* reported that the Right to Life Committee had reported an increase in both new membership and heightened involvement by members. Although the organization did not formally adopt picketing at doctors' homes as a strategy, it supports individual members who do picket. The violence that occurred in Boston in 1995 has not been condoned by any prolife group. It has, however, gotten support from some who support the prolife movement. For example, after the arrest of John Salvi for the Brookline shootings, one man attending a vigil announced through a megaphone, "Why is the life of a receptionist worth more than the lives of fifty innocent babies?" (Baldauf 1994).

It has been speculated that federal authorities have not ruled out a conspiracy linking cases of abortion violence. In fact, since mid-1993, the Justice Department has been investigating the possibility that growing abortion clinic violence is more than a gossamer of coincidence (Howlett 1995). The starting point for conspiracy theorists is the two-paragraph statement written by the Florida gunman Paul Hill and signed by twenty-nine other prolife activists. The statement says in part, "We the undersigned declare the justice of taking all godly action necessary to defend all human life, including the use of force . . . we proclaim that whatever force is legitimate to defend the life of a born child, is legitimate to defend the life of an unborn child" (Howlett 1995). The suggestion in this statement is that an organized mandate for violence has been adopted by at least some prolifers.

THE MEDIA'S ROLE IN TERRORISM

Terrorism, both international and domestic, requires some form of publicity to be effective. One suggested reason for the increase in terrorist acts is the wide range of publicity they receive, which influences a broad national and sometimes global audience. Terrorists view the role of the media as a way to convey their message worldwide. The bolder the act and the more spectacular the violence, the greater the media coverage.

Although many people believe that terrorists use the media to achieve their goals and that the media tend to exaggerate and sensationalize incidents, they also support the First Amendment right guaranteeing freedom of speech and of the press.

Acts of terrorism are usually newsworthy, and members of the media view coverage as a professional and highly competitive responsibility. Some members of the media have argued that coverage of terrorist incidents helps to resolve them and that placing hostages on television may actually save their lives. On the other hand, untimely or inaccurate information released by the media could impede the resolution of an incident, narrow the options for dealing with it, or actually provide terrorists with valuable intelligence information.

CONTROLLING TERRORISM

In 1972, President Richard Nixon organized the Committee to Combat Terrorism, the first official government effort to combat the problem of terrorism in the United States. With recent developments in counterterrorism, along with the passing of the 2001 USA Patriot Act, national and global efforts to control terrorism have increased. In addition to legislative and congressional measures to address terrorism, Americans have become considerably more aware of safety, security, and the possibility of terrorist attacks on American soil.

Antiterrorist squads have been developed by both U.S. federal law enforcement agencies and the military. One such squad is the renowned **Delta Force**, whose members come from the four military service areas. As a rule, the activities of the Delta Force are secret, but their service was seen in Iran (1980), Honduras (1982), Sudan (1983), and during the Grenada Invasion (1983), and they were prepared to take action against the hijacking of the ship the *Achille Lauro* in 1985 (Siegel, 1992). Although the Delta Force is not a public policing organization, perhaps public police of the twenty-first century will form new partnerships with certain components of the military to address international problems that have an impact on local peacekeeping.

THE 1996 ANTITERRORISM BILL

A triumph in the fight against terrorism occurred on April 24, 1996, when President Bill Clinton signed into law the Federal Antiterrorism Bill. The law, which was signed on the one-year anniversary of the Oklahoma City Bombing, contained important provisions. Among other things, the bill provided for strict limitations for the appeals process by both state and federal death-row inmates. In addition, the bill permits the federal government to deny entry to the U.S. by foreigners who belong to groups considered to be terrorist organizations. Also, the government's power to deport aliens suspected of having terrorist ties was expanded. Other provisions of the 1996 bill include the following:

- Anyone who raises funds for or contributes to groups deemed to be engaged in terrorism will be liable to prosecution.
- Plastic explosive manufacturers are required to put *taggants*, or detection agents, in their explosives so that they can be traced.
- Criminals convicted of federal crimes will in many cases be required to pay restitution to their victims.

Many people believe the 1996 legislation will help to combat domestic terrorism, but the growing number of occurrences of terrorism, both domestic and foreign, make others skeptical of the law's deterrent effect.

THE 2001 USA PATRIOT ACT

Following the 2001 terrorist attacks, Congress enacted and the President signed the USA Patriot Act. The law is officially known as the Uniting and Strengthening America by Providing Appropriate Tools Required to Intercept and Obstruct Terrorism Act of 2001 (from which the acronym USA Patriot is derived). The law dramatically increases the investigatory authority of federal, state, and local police agencies, although sometimes only temporarily. The police powers expanded under the legislation are not limited to investigations of terrorist activity, but apply to many different criminal offenses. In fact, the law created a number of new crimes, such as terrorist attacks against mass transportation and harboring or concealing terrorists.

The act also permits longer jail terms for certain suspects arrested without warrant, broadens "sneak and peak" search authority (searches conducted without prior notice and in the absence of the suspect), and enhances the power of prosecutors. The law also increases the ability of federal authorities to tap phones (including wireless devices), share intelligence information, track Internet usage, expand money-laundering investigations, and protect U.S. borders. Many of the new crime-fighting powers created under the new legislation are not limited to acts of terrorism, but apply to many different kinds of criminal offenses, many of which involve organized crime activities (see Appendix A).

The Patriot Act has led civil rights advocates to question whether the government unfairly expanded police powers at the expense of civil liberties. Immediately after signing the legislation, President George W. Bush assured the nation that such was not the case. "Today, we take an essential step in defeating terrorism while protecting the constitutional rights of all Americans," Bush declared. Prior to its passage, the American Civil Liberties Union (ACLU) had criticized the legislation on the grounds that it would substantially reduce the constitutional rights of individuals facing processing by the justice system. After the act became law, the ACLU pledged to work with the Bush administration and law enforcement agencies across the country "to ensure that civil liberties in America are not eroded."

WHAT HAVE WE LEARNED?

Terrorism is especially difficult to control because its nature is difficult to understand and because of the lack of consensus as to how to fight it. Aggressive government-sponsored responses to terrorist groups can have negative results, including increased terrorist activity. On the other hand, ignoring terrorist activities could be interpreted as a license to operate with impunity.

In the future, efforts must be made to encourage the United Nations to take a more hard-line stance against terrorist attacks. Accordingly, efforts should be made to encourage cooperation among countries throughout the world to unify against terrorist activities and to share police, military, and intelligence resources to achieve that end.

DO YOU RECOGNIZE THESE TERMS?

anti-enviros
blowback
criminal terrorism
Delta Force
fatwah
guerilla
hate groups
ideological terrorism

narcoterrorist
nationalistic terrorism
revolutionary terrorism
single-issue terrorist activity
state-organized crime
state-sponsored terrorism
survivalist
terrorism

POINTS OF DISCUSSION

1. In your opinion, how should the term *terrorism* be defined?

2. Compare and contrast the motivations of a Middle Eastern terrorist organization with those of a domestic terrorist group. What are the similarities and differences?

3. Discuss the ways state-organized crime can be characterized as terrorism.

4. Discuss the trends in terrorism that you envision for the upcoming decade.

5. In what ways can Americans help protect themselves from the threat of domestic terrorism?

SUGGESTED READING

COMBS, C. C. (2000). *Terrorism in the Twenty-First Century*. Upper Saddle River, NJ: Prentice Hall.

KEGLEY, C. W., Jr. (2003). *The New Global Terrorism: Characteristics and Controls*. Upper Saddle River, NJ: Prentice Hall.

WHITE, J. (2003). *Terrorism: An Introduction, 2002 Update*. Pacific Grove, CA: Brooks/Cole. The author discusses the structure and development of terrorism, terrorist events of the early twenty-first century, terrorist groups, terrorist causes in various countries and regions of the world, and related issues.

─10─

ORGANIZED CRIME'S POLITICAL AND CORPORATE ALLIANCES

This chapter will enable you to:

- Understand the reciprocal link between organized crime and the upperworld
- Compare instances of collusion between organized crime and political leaders
- Contrast the social roles of organized crime with those of their corporate counterparts

- Learn about the relationships between well-known politicians and mob bosses
- Understand how and why politicians compromise themselves in organized crime relationships

INTRODUCTION

On August 23, 1991, a tramp steamer called the *Mercandian Continent* pulled into the port of Miami and, upon docking, a team of Drug Enforcement Administration and Customs agents hopped on board to inspect its cargo. In the hold was a large supply of cement posts and cornerstones, and in their cores were 12,250 kilograms of cocaine with an estimated street value of $200 to $300 million. Rather than seize the drugs, the agents decided to watch where they went. For three months the agents secretly followed the cement posts and cornerstones as they traveled all the way to Texas. When members of Colombia's Cali Cartel tried to remove the drugs, the agents moved in and arrests were made.

In response to this seizure, the Cali Cartel began hiding its cocaine in loads of frozen broccoli and okra. Once again, federal agents intercepted the drugs. With information supplied by two highly placed informants, the two shipments were linked and numerous indictments were handed down.

As the case moved toward prosecution, however, the cartel's U.S. lawyers were nearly successful in thwarting the investigation by trying to prevent informants from talking. As it turns out, defense attorneys Michael Abbell, Donald Ferguson, and William Moran were charged with concealing drug profits, bribing witnesses, preparing bogus affidavits, and delivering death threats from cartel leaders to informants (Duffy and Witkin 1995). Abbell's involvement with the cartels was particularly disturbing because he had been a high-ranking attorney for the Justice Department.

Chapter 1 and subsequent sections discussed organized criminals as the corrupters of public officials. Corruption is essential to the efficient and profitable conduct of business by organized crime groups, and evidence supports this view of organized criminals as corrupters. A more accurate perspective, reflecting the empirical research on organized crime, is that organized criminals, legitimate businesspeople, and government officials are equal players in a marketplace of corruption. Each comes to the marketplace with goods or services the others want, and a rather routine and institutionalized series of exchanges takes place.

Organized criminals who are primarily purveyors of illicit goods and services wish to exchange their products, money, and influence for protection; selective enforcement against competitors; and favorable policy decisions by government authorities. Public officials, either out of greed, the need for political support and money, or the desire for recognition, put their policy-making and enforcement powers on the market. Who initiates such a deal depends on circumstances, and the initiator is as likely to be the "criminal" as the "legitimate" actor.

CORPORATE SCANDALS OF THE TWENTY-FIRST CENTURY

Some authors maintain that occupational and corporate crime have become a way of life in U.S. business. Examples abound. Government investigations in the late 1950s revealed that the General Electric Company was heavily involved in price fixing. In 1975, Allied Chemical Corporation was fined $5 million and agreed to donate another $8 million to a cleanup fund after it was revealed that former employees had arranged to establish a small, seemingly independent business to supply it with the highly toxic chemical kepone. Workers in the Kepone manufacturing plant became seriously ill, and the Saint James River near the plant became contaminated. In May 1999, two companies, Hoffman-LaRoche Ltd. and BASF AG, agreed to plead guilty to charges of fixing the prices of vitamins A, B2, B5, C, and E and beta-carotene. The companies agreed to pay $500 million as part of a plea bargain agreement.

In his book *Organized Crime*, Abadinsky (2002) draws an interesting parallel between the activities of the giants of U.S. industry and organized crime. He suggests that the robber barons of early U.S. capitalism invented and refined many of the criminal tactics and schemes that would later become cornerstones of organized crime groups. In this new century, it appears that we have come full circle.

In 2002, major U.S. corporations were found to be involved in massive organized criminality, behaving more like organized crime syndicates than ostensibly legitimate businesses. One consistent theme of this book has been that the lines of distinction between the state, the business community, and the mob have become increasingly blurred over the years and that overlaps between the interests and activities of these three social sectors have become more and more pervasive. Nowhere is this point driven home with more clarity than in a review of the corporate scandals of 2002.

Enron, one of the largest energy companies in the world, was caught artificially boosting profits and hiding debts totaling more than $1 billion.

In addition, the company bribed officials of foreign governments and illegally manipulated prices and supplies in the Texas power market. Arthur Andersen, the prestigious accounting firm, was convicted of obstruction of justice for destroying Enron documents that would have exposed this massive fraud. Enron itself filed for Chapter Eleven bankruptcy protection and will probably face more than $100 billion in libaility claims (Patsuris 2002).

Another major energy company, Halliburton, hid more than $100 million in costs to customers. Vice-President Dick Cheney of the United States and others face a huge accounting fraud lawsuit lodged against officers of the company (Patsuris 2002).

WorldCom illegally inflated its reported cash flow by $3.8 billion while loaning its founder $400 million in off-the-books loans. The company's former CEO and controller have both been indicted. WorldCom filed for bankruptcy with over $41 billion in debts (Patsuris 2002).

Adelphia Communications, one of the largest cable television providers in the United States, loaned $3.1 billion off-the-books to the Rigas family, who controlled the corporation. In addition, it hid its debts and inflated its capital expenses in another accounting scandal. Three members of the Rigas family were arrested for fraud (Patsuris 2002).

Other companies also committed financial fraud. In 2002, Tyco's ex-CEO Dennis Kozlowski was indicted for embezzling $170 million and obtaining an additional $340 million through fraud. He allegedly used the money, in part, to fund real estate purchases worth more than $50 million in Florida, Massachusetts, and New York and to finance a $1 million birthday party for his wife. AOL Time Warner came under investigation by the Department of Justice for fraudulently inflating its corporate revenues. The activities of other major corporations were investigated: Dynergy; Global Crossing; Kmart; Merck, the pharmaceuticals giant; Mirant; Qwest Communications; Reliant Energy; and Xerox Corporation (Patsuris 2002). It could be that since we entered the new millennium, organized crime has indeed become organized capitalism. Let's now consider some other examples of the organized crime–corporate link.

Examples of Recent Corporate Scandals

Adelphia Communications Corporation: The founding Rigas family collected $3.1 billion in off-balance-sheet loans backed by Adelphia; overstated results by inflating capital expenses and hiding debt. Founder John Rigas and his son Timothy were convicted in 2004 on federal charges of conspiracy, bank fraud, and securities fraud. John Rigas was sentenced to 15 years in prison and his son was sentenced to 20 years. Six Rigas family members have agreed to forfeit assets worth more than $1.2 billion to settle cases brought by federal regulators.

Adelphia Communications Corporation has been sold for more than $17 billion to Time Warner, Inc., and Comcast Corp.

Enron Corporation: Boosted profits and hid debts totaling over $1 billion by improperly using off-the-books partnerships; manipulated the Texas power market; bribed foreign governments to win contracts abroad; manipulated California energy market. In December 2005, former Enron Corporation chief accounting officer Richard Causey pleaded guilty to securities fraud and agreed to help federal prosecutors' case against former bosses Kenneth Lay and Jeffrey Skilling, who were charged with federal fraud and conspiracy charges.

Another executive, Finance Chief Andrew Fastow pleaded guilty in January 2004 on conspiracy charges and agreed to testify against his former co-workers. Former treasurer Ben Glisan pleaded guilty in 2003 and was sentenced to five years in prison.

Tyco Corporation: Ex-CEO L. Dennis Kozlowski was indicted for tax evasion. SEC charged that the company was aware of his actions, possible improper use of company funds and related-party transactions, and improper merger accounting practices. Kozlowski and Chief Financial Officer Mark H. Swartz were convicted on twenty-two counts of grand larceny, conspiracy, securities fraud, and falsifying business records. Prosecutors accused the two of conspiring to defraud Tyco Corporation of millions of dollars to fund extravagant life-styles. The two executives were given sentences of eight to twenty-five years in prison.

WorldCom, Inc.: Overstated cash flow by booking $3.8 billion in operating expenses as capital expenses; gave founder Bernard Ebbers $400 million in off-the-books loans. Ebbers was convicted in March 2005 of federal fraud and conspiracy charges for his part in a massive accounting fraud now estimated at $11 billion. He was sentenced to 25 years in prison. The company's former finance chief Scott Sullivan was sentenced to five years in prison.

THE CONNECTION

It has been common throughout the history of organized crime for a series of exchanges between the **underworld** and **upperworld** to develop into a long-term corrupt relationship. Empirical research has revealed that in some cases those who occupy positions of public trust are in fact the actual organizers of crime (Gardiner 1970; Chambliss 1978; Gardiner and Lyman 1978; Block and Scarpitti 1985; Potter and Jenkins 1985).

Investigations of police corruption in Philadelphia and New York, for example, have demonstrated how thoroughly institutionalized corruption can be among public servants. In the private business sector, respected institutions such as Shearson/American Express, Merrill Lynch, the Miami National Bank, Citibank, and others have eagerly participated in illicit ventures (Lernoux 1984; Moldea 1986; Organized Crime Digest 1986 President's Commission on Organized Crime 1986: 31–42). For example, the infamous Pizza Connection case involved the distribution of Southeast Asian heroin through a series of pizza parlors located in the United States, the laundering of tens of millions of dollars through New York City banks, and transfer of these funds by these banks to secret accounts in Switzerland, the Bahamas, and other countries.

In addition to using banks to launder money, the Pizza Connection heroin traffickers deposited $5 million (all in $5, $10, and $20 bills) with the brokerage firm of Merrill Lynch Pierce Fenner and Smith over a six-week period. Merrill Lynch not only accepted these highly dubious deposits, but provided the couriers carrying the money with extraordinary security for their transactions. At the same time, couriers from the Pizza Connection were laundering $13.5 million through accounts at another brokerage house, E. F. Hutton, which also provided protection for the couriers (President's Commission on Organized Crime 1986: 31–42). Contrary to the official portrait of organized crime, under- and upperworld criminals form close, symbiotic relationships. Public officials and businesspeople are not the pawns of organized crime, but are in fact an integral part of it.

It would be virtually impossible to try to catalog all the cases of official corruption in U.S. history. In fact, it would be impossible to outline all the corrupt relationships between law enforcement officials, businesspeople, politicians, and organized criminals in a single city. The discussion here is limited to some important illustrations of alliances between white-collar, occupational, political, and organized criminals. Specifically, we concentrate on six examples of organized criminal activity: (1) the mob and John Fitzgerald Kennedy, (2) organized crime's relationships with Richard Nixon, (3) the relationship between organized criminals and the Reagan administration, (4) Bill Clinton and the Whitewater scandal, (5) a historical view of Meyer Lansky's attempts to integrate organized crime and corporate America, and (6) the role of organized crime and the state in the great savings and loan scandals of the 1980s.

ORGANIZED CRIME AND THE POLITICAL SYSTEM

Chapter 6 noted that in 1994 newspapers across the nation revealed that a clear political link was likely to exist between leaders of the Cali Cartel and Colombia's President Ernesto Samper. In 1996 a Colombian news magazine, *Semana*, revealed that in a taped conversation President Samper was said to have been joking with the wife of a known cocaine trafficker about his campaign treasurer Santiago Medina, who had claimed that the president accepted $6 million from the Cali Cartel during the 1994 presidential race. Samper publicly denied the charge. The trafficker, Jésus Sarria, had been under investigation for six months after the seizure of 5.9 tons of cocaine in El Salvador, which Sarria supposedly dispatched. This event pressured Samper to step down in Colombia's ongoing battle with drug trafficking. Although the allegation was never proved, it left doubt about the Colombian government's credibility.

One major point raised throughout this book has been that organized crime must be viewed as an integral part of society's political, economic, and social structure. In fact, a basic characteristic of all organized crime is that it must, of necessity, emphasize **collusion** among criminals, the police, and politicians. As Chambliss (1976: 182) argued in his study of Seattle, the cabal "that manages the vices is composed of important businessmen, law enforcement officers, political leaders, and a member of a major trade union." Political corruption is critical to the survival of organized crime. In fact, organized crime could not operate at all without the direct complicity and connivance of the political machinery (Hills 1969). As stated in Chapter 3, virtually every study of organized crime has commented on the close symbiosis between the machine and ward leader and organized criminals at the turn of the century (Block and Chambliss 1981; Peterson 1983; Potter and Jenkins 1985). In addition, investigations have consistently demonstrated the close relationship between political organizations and organized crime.

A 1937 grand jury in Philadelphia exposed collusion between a gambling syndicate and the city's mayor and district attorney (Potter and Jenkins 1985). The entire Seattle crime network was held together by political collusion (Chambliss 1978), as was the Reading, Pennsylvania, gambling syndicate (Gardiner 1967). In Pennsylvania, any major organized crime trial of the 1940s or 1950s included a list of public officials (judges, city councilmen, legislators) appearing as character witnesses for the defense (Potter and Jenkins 1985).

This is a **symbiotic relationship**. In return for official favors, organized crime is able to provide public officials campaign money, private graft, investment opportunities, and direct assistance in some types of bargaining and negotiations. For example, a comprehensive study of corruption in Morrisburg found that organized crime syndicates make above the board legitimate political contributions to candidates and considerable under the table cash contributions to political parties, which are primarily used as "street" money to encourage efforts to bring out voters. In addition, organized crime had a business relationship, particularly in a series of real estate transactions, with county officials, including two sitting judges (Potter 1994). The Pennsylvania Crime Commission (1980: 95–108) exposed several classic cases of massive political involvement with organized crime, including the following:

- State Senator Frank Mazzei, Lackawanna County Democratic Chairman Patrick Cummings, and others had a series of dealings with organized crime figures relating to kickbacks for state contracts, extortion, liquor licensing, and bail bond reform legislation.
- Anthony Grosso, a major Pittsburgh bookmaker, made payoffs to the city's district attorney, an alderman, and a constable.
- Widespread corruption was reported in state regulatory agencies, particularly in the Cigarette Tax Bureau and the Liquor Control Commission.
- The mayor of Chester, Pennsylvania, major Republican party officials, and the chief of police were implicated in Frank Miller's massive southeastern Pennsylvania gambling network.
- Organized crime networks in Reading, Pennsylvania, established a case-fixing system with the courts, actually setting a price list for the dismissal of cases.
- Investigation of gambling operations in Carbondale, Johnstown, Phoenixville, and other cities in Pennsylvania revealed close collaboration and cooperation between public officials in these cities and organized criminals.
- In Philadelphia, the major pornography distributors and Sam Rappaport, landlord for much of the vice district, actively engaged in fund-raising efforts for political candidates. They even went so far as to throw a cocktail party for former Philadelphia District Attorney Emmett Fitzpatrick, whose long association with loan-sharking syndicates was fully documented.

It has been estimated that since the late 1960s, organized crime figures have given $2 billion annually to public officials (King 1969: 286). Allowing for inflation, this figure had probably quintupled by 1995. Haller summed up the situation well in saying, "It is not so much that gambling syndicates influenced local political organization; rather gambling syndicates were the local political organizations" (Haller 1979: 88). Although Haller was writing about the great political machines of the 1930s and 1940s, his words also describe the situation today. Chambliss (1986) points to the role of organized crime as a very important source of political corruption at all levels of government. In commenting on organized crime in Seattle, he said;

> Money is the oil of our present-day machinery, and elected public officials are the pistons that keep the machine operating. Those who come up with the oil, whatever its source, are in a position to make the machinery run the way they want it to. Crime is an excellent producer of capitalism's oil. Those who want to affect the direction of the machine's output find that the money produced by crime is as effective in helping them get where they want to go as is the money produced in other ways. Those who produce the money control the machine. Crime is not a by-product of an otherwise

effectively working political economy: It is a main product of the political economy. Crime is, in fact, a cornerstone on which the political and economic relations of democratic–capitalist societies are constructed.

In virtually every U.S. city, criminal organizations sell sex and drugs, provide an opportunity to gamble and to watch pornographic films, or offer a loan, an abortion, or a special favor. The profits of these organizations are a mainstay of the U.S. electoral process, and their business is an important (if unrecorded) part of the gross national product. The business of organized crime in the United States may gross as much as $100 billion annually—or as little as $40 billion. Either way, the profits are immense, and the proportion of the gross national product represented by money flowing from crime cannot be gainsaid. Few nations in the world have economies that compare with the economic output of criminal activities in the United States (Chambliss 1978: 1–2).

A basic characteristic of organized crime is that it depends on the corruption of government officials for survival and continued profitability. Bribery, campaign contributions, delivery of votes, and other favors are used to influence legislators, city council members, mayors, judges, district attorneys, and others. It is not possible to understand organized crime or to place it in a social context outside its relationships with the political system.

THE MOB AND JOHN F. KENNEDY

Decades after the death of President John F. Kennedy, speculation still rages about who was responsible for his assassination and why the alleged assassin was killed. In 1979 the last official investigation of the Kennedy assassination, conducted by the House Select Committee on Assassinations, stated that organized crime could have been responsible for it. The compelling question was what connection, if any, Kennedy had with Italian organized crime. Perhaps his association with the mob can be traced to his father.

Joseph P. Kennedy, one of the wealthiest and most influential Irish-Americans of his time, made his fortune on Wall Street. Although never formally charged with criminal activity, banker Joseph Kennedy was suspected of being a bootlegger during Prohibition and working with New York mob bosses Frank Costello and Meyer Lansky. After the repeal of Prohibition, the elder Kennedy was thought to have maintained his contacts with known mob bosses, whose nightclubs he frequented in both New York and Miami.

Joseph Kennedy's political career was launched at a fund raiser for Franklin D. Roosevelt, who named him ambassador to Great Britain in 1938. Although many experts have suggested that Joseph Kennedy might have had ambitions to become president one day, he was forced to resign his post as ambassador in 1942 after publicly sympathizing with the Nazis. Although Joseph Kennedy's chances for a political career were clearly over, his son John became a likely contender for national office because of his military hero status. In 1947 the son entered the House of Representatives and six years later the Senate. In 1956 he sought the Democratic nomination for the position of vice-president of the United States.

By most accounts John Kennedy was an idealist. This became apparent in his work on the Senate's McClellan Committee, which focused on organized crime's influence on labor. Through 1960, both the president and his younger brother Robert relentlessly investigated some of the most powerful mob

John F. Kennedy enjoyed his celebrity friends. He is seen here with Frank Sinatra.

bosses in the United States, such as Chicago's Sam Giancana, Carlos Marcello of New Orleans, and one of the mob's strongest allies in organized labor, Jimmy Hoffa. It has been argued that many mob bosses were insulted that the son of one of their cronies, Joseph Kennedy, was now pursuing them.

In 1960, Kennedy was elected president of the United States, and his relationship with the mob changed. Indeed, many mob bosses viewed the president as owing them political debts. The first of these involved the 1960 West Virginia presidential primary. Much speculation existed that Joseph Kennedy had colluded with organized crime to stack the deck in favor of his son's candidacy.

A New Jersey mobster named "Skinny" D'Mato claimed that a political deal was struck with Joseph Kennedy whereby votes were bought by mobsters, who then paid off local sheriffs responsible for vote counting. One of D'Mato's close friends, Frank Sinatra, soon also became close friends with President Kennedy. Through Sinatra, he met Judith Campbell, who maintained an intimate friendship not only with Kennedy, but also with Chicago's mob boss Sam Giancana. Campbell, now known by her married name, Judith Campbell-Exner, has since testified that she acted as a courier for Kennedy to deliver cash to Giancana to use in the 1960 presidential campaign. Indeed, Illinois was a key state in determining Kennedy's presidential victory, and Giancana's influence over Chicago's political machine was thought by many

John F. Kennedy's Political Debts

to be a decisive factor in Kennedy's victory. Mob bosses felt that they had provided the difference in Kennedy's win by a close margin.

Once in office, Kennedy found himself embroiled in political turmoil over Castro's expanding power and the threat of communism spreading to the northern hemisphere. Desperate to rid Cuba of Castro, the CIA called on organized crime to facilitate his assassination. Three mob bosses took charge of the contract. The mob was amenable to the removal of Castro because, after assuming power in Cuba, Castro had closed all mob casinos in Havana, which were significant sources of mob revenue. Although the CIA–organized crime plot to kill Castro continued under the Kennedy administration, experts differ regarding exactly how much the president and the attorney general actually knew about it. In fact, many historians have suggested that the president knew nothing about the plot until 1962, at which time, upon learning of it, he halted it. Judith Campbell-Exner has stated, however, that she personally arranged meetings between President Kennedy and Sam Giancana to work out details of Castro's assassination.

The John Kennedy Assassination and the Mob: Is There a Link?

"Gangsters have always operated in a shifting, layered, shadowy world," Stephen Fox asserted in *Blood and Power,* his 1989 study of the history of organized crime. "They leave inscrutable histories replete with accident and misdirection, the imponderables of personality, appearances that correspond to no realities, and many surprises." He could have been writing about the organized crime's interaction with the Kennedy family.

Several authors of books on the assassination of John F. Kennedy concluded that the president set the stage for his own murder by compromising himself with the mob. He had used the mob's services in a plot to kill Cuban Premier Fidel Castro, they reasoned, all the while backing the Justice Department's unrelenting assault on organized crime. "It's understood by prosecutors and police," G. Robert Blakey and Richard N. Billings wrote in *The Plot to Kill the President* (1981), "that there is a line that must not be crossed. You are alright . . . just as long as you do not 'sleep with them,' that is, you do not take [Mafia] favors, either money or sex. The prosecutor or cop or government official who does cross the line and takes action against them . . . invites violent retribution." This, Blakey and Billings argued, is precisely what happened in Dallas.

John H. Davis took a similar tack in *Mafia Kingfish,* in which he advanced the theory that New Orleans organized crime chieftain Carlos Marcello played a pivotal role in John Kennedy's death. Davis ended his book, however, by acknowledging that he had failed to prove his case: "Despite the overwhelming web of circumstantial evidence suggesting the complicity of the Marcello organization in the assassination . . . and despite the fact that the President's murder did bear, in thinly disguised form, the fingerprints of a traditional Mafia execution, we are still uncertain about the precise details and extent of Carlos Marcello's suspected involvement in the crime."

A recent movie portrays organized crime as the prime force behind the president's assassination (with an assist from the CIA). In docudrama fashion, *Ruby* tells the story of Jack Ruby, the Dallas nightclub owner who gunned down accused Kennedy assassin Lee Harvey Oswald in the basement of Dallas's municipal building. The film argues that the mob, furious at Kennedy for not showing appreciation for its alleged help in swinging the 1960 election his way, killed the president out of revenge.

Director Oliver Stone, whose film *JFK* suggested that the Kennedy assassination was the product of a broadly based conspiracy, dismisses the Ruby premise. It is a myth concocted by "a bunch of New York tabloid writers who have always glamorized the mob and given them powers they do not possess," says Stone. "These people do not have one-tenth of the power ascribed to them by writers, and the people who've made *Ruby*." The real danger, Stone adds, is that "if push comes to shove and the government is forced to accept a conspiracy theory, they're going to try and lay it off on the mob. I guarantee that's what they'll do."

Be that as it may, the great majority of Americans believe the Kennedy assassination involved some kind of conspiracy. Only 11 percent of the respondents to a December 1991 Time–Cable News Network poll said they accepted the official Warren Commission explanation that Oswald, acting alone, killed the president. Asked to name one or more groups that might have been involved in an assassination conspiracy, 50 percent cited the CIA and 48 percent cited organized crime.

Sources: Stephen Fox, *Blood and Power: Organized Crime in 20th Century America* (New York: William Morrow, 1989), p. 11; G. Robert Blakey and Richard N. Billings, *The Plot to Kill the President* (New York: Time Books, 1981), p. 339; John H. Davis, *Mafia Kingfish: Carlos Marcello and the Assassination of John F. Kennedy* (New York: St. Martin's Press, 1989), p. 527, quoted by Jeffery Wells of Rolling Stone, in *Entertainment Weekly,* February 7, 1992, p. 12. The three other groups of possible conspirators listed in the Time–CNN poll were Cuban exiles (19 percent), U.S. military leaders (18 percent), and the Dallas police (13 percent).

In late 1960 President Kennedy announced his intention to appoint his brother Robert to the position of attorney general. Robert subsequently declared a virtual war on organized crime, an initiative that history has proved to be the most effective assault on the mob ever conducted by a U.S. attorney general. The paradox is that the Kennedys were pursuing the very mob bosses who were close to their father Joseph and who perhaps helped John win the presidential election. Gradually, more and more mob bosses believed that the Kennedys should not be hounding the mob when it had done and was doing favors in the plot against Castro for the Kennedys. In fact, Robert Kennedy had established a "most wanted" list of known organized crime figures and labor racketeers. First on the list was Jimmy Hoffa, followed by New Orleans mob boss Carlos Marcello.

Marcello first clashed with Robert Kennedy in 1959 at the McClellan Committee hearings, when he stalled a deportation order filed against him six years earlier. Because Marcello had never sought U.S. citizenship, Kennedy successfully deported him to Guatemala, where Marcello had established citizenship. Two months after his deportation, Marcello returned, claiming that the deportation was illegal and that Guatemala had never agreed to accept him. This exchange only fueled the ongoing resentment Marcello had for the Kennedys.

Carlos Marcello, mob boss of New Orleans.

Most evidence since John Kennedy's assassination has pointed to Lee Harvey Oswald as the assassin. It has been suggested that the mob carefully chose Oswald to do the shooting because he had no clear links to mob bosses. Oswald was born and raised in New Orleans and had close ties with his uncle, who was a bookmaker working for Carlos Marcello. Although the connection exists between Oswald and Marcello, it is not clear exactly how or whether Oswald was recruited for the assassination. What is more apparent, however, is Marcello's motive to kill the president and effectively neutralize his brother at the same time. In any case, Marcello was never charged with the crime and outlived the president by thirty years. Although this theory cannot be proved, it raises questions of possible mob involvement with the highest political office in the United States.

ORGANIZED CRIME AND RICHARD NIXON

When former President Richard Nixon died in 1994, President Bill Clinton, Senate Minority Leader Robert Dole, and others paid glowing tribute to him. The public pronouncements and news media coverage of Nixon's death made no mention of his ties to organized crime. Despite such a short public memory, there is no question about Richard Nixon's links to organized crime syndicates. Any debate centers only on how early in Nixon's career his cozy relationship with organized crime began.

One researcher suggests that Nixon's collaboration with the underworld began when he was working for the Office of Price Administration in 1943 (Kohn 1976). While in that position, Nixon met and became lifelong friends with Cuban-American Bebe Rebozo, who later made a fortune in Florida's real estate market, and a soon-to-be Democratic Senator from Florida, George Smathers, often referred to as the "Senator from Cuba." In 1943, Nixon was responsible for controlling the wartime market in rubber goods and overseeing the rationing of rubber, Smathers was a lawyer for an organized crime front company smuggling auto tires from Cuba, and Rebozo owned a gas station that sold the tires on the black market (Kohn 1976).

Other sources suggest that the Nixon–organized crime alliance took place in 1946 when Nixon was running for Congress in California. His campaign manager was Murray Choitner, a top organized crime defense attorney, and the campaign received considerable financial assistance and help with campaign "volunteers" from California gangster and heroin trafficker Mickey Cohen (Kohn 1976). Whatever the starting point of this relationship, it is clear that Nixon's social, business, and political friends included many people with curious ties to organized crime. For example, Nixon enjoyed deep-sea fishing with his friend Rebozo as the guest of Tatum "Chubby" Wofford and Richard Danner. Danner later managed the Sands Casino in Las Vegas, and Wofford was a business and gambling associate of Meyer Lansky. In fact, according to the Kefauver Committee investigation, Lansky's largest casino operation in Florida was in the Wofford Hotel.

Through these close friends, Nixon became acquainted with other organized crime figures, particularly ones with interests in Cuba. In 1952, Nixon and Danner traveled to Havana to visit a new syndicate hotel and casino (Kohn 1976). At least one researcher asserts that Nixon, Rebozo, and Smathers invested in Cuban enterprises during the 1950s (Kohn 1976).

In the 1960s Nixon profited handsomely from these associations. He acquired land on Key Biscayne and Fisher's Island off the Florida coast. His associates were already profiting in land development through two Lansky-created real estate companies, the Cape Florida Development Company and the Major Realty Company. Cape Florida Development was run by Rebozo and Donald Berg, who worked closely with associates of the infamous "Cleveland Four" (Dalitz, Rothkopf, Tucker, and Kleinman). The controlling shareholders at Major Realty were Senator Smathers and Lansky associates Max Orovitz and Ben Siegelbaum. He was the official greeter for the opening of organized crime Bahamas casinos, appearing first at the Nassau Bay Club in 1967 and then in 1968 at the opening of Resorts International's casino on Paradise Island, managed by long-time Lansky casino operator Eddie Cellini. Resorts International was a Lansky-inspired enterprise accomplished through the activities of the General Development Corporation, run by two more Lansky fronts, Wallace Groves and Lou Chesler. The board of directors of the General Development Corporation included Lansky's associate and stockbroker, Max Orovitz, and gangster "Trigger Mike" Coppola. General Development bought up half of Grand Bahama Island for later syndicate development and contracted with Nixon's legal client, National Bulk Carriers, to build a harbor there.

The Teamsters Endorsement

Nixon would later become the first Republican candidate for president to get the endorsement of a major labor union. In his case it was the mob-controlled Teamsters union. Jailed Teamsters boss Jimmy Hoffa had been little more than a functionary operating as a front man for Lansky and others at the head of the union. Organized crime had borrowed hundreds of millions from the teamsters **Central States Pension Fund**. Hoffa had been pursued relentlessly by Attorney General Robert F. Kennedy's Justice Department and had been sentenced to thirteen years in jail for jury tampering and misusing union funds. Hoffa's successors, Frank Fitzsimmons and Anthony "Pro" Provenzano, committed the union to Nixon's campaign, and in 1971 Nixon pardoned Hoffa.

In addition to Hoffa, Nixon also intervened on behalf of organized crime figures Leonard Bursten, Carl Kovens, and Morris Shenker, all Nixon campaign supporters. Bursten, a Miami National Bank director, had been sentenced to fifteen years for a fraudulent bankruptcy in a Beverly Hills housing development financed with $12 million of Teamsters money. His sentence was reduced to probation after the intervention of Nixon's campaign manager and lawyer, Murray Choitner. Carl Kovens was a Florida Teamsters union official convicted in the same pension fraud case as Hoffa and was released from prison as a result of Senator Smather's intervention. Kovens later collected $50,000 for the Committee to Re-elect the President.

A Justice Department investigation of Morris Shenker, an attorney for the Teamsters Union and Kansas City organized crime interests, for tax violations was quashed by Nixon's attorney general, Richard Kleindienst (Moldea, 1978). Moreover, Nixon fired Robert Morgenthau, the U.S. Attorney for the southern district of New York, who began investigating organized crime money laundering through Switzerland and went on to convict Max Orovitz of violation of stock registration laws.

ORGANIZED CRIME AND RONALD REAGAN

In the years since Ronald Reagan left the White House, sufficient time has passed for congressional committees, journalistic exposés, and even criminal prosecutions to reveal a pattern of high-level corruption in Reagan's administration. Indeed, in his first term, forty-five presidential appointees resigned as a result of criminal or ethics investigations (Simon and Eitzen 1986: 6–7).

Revelations surrounding the arming of U.S.-backed guerrillas in Nicaragua, drug trafficking by these same **contras**, arms shipments to the Middle East, government collusion with money-laundering entities such as the Bank of Credit and Commerce International (BCCI), and foreign policy decisions benefiting countries facilitating drug trafficking, particularly Panama and the Bahamas, heightened the perception of a "sleaze factor" in the Reagan administration.

Although the Reagan White House was clearly scandal ridden, the underlying malignancy of his presidency has not been as clearly articulated. Information that has been developed in the many investigations of unethical and criminal activities in the Reagan presidency has, with the passage of time and distance, revealed a most disturbing fact. Ronald Reagan, the law and order, get tough with criminals president, was from the inception of his presidency involved with organized crime.

Strong indications of an association surfaced in 1980 when Reagan's campaign received the endorsement of the International Brotherhood of Teamsters. This endorsement was quickly followed by additional support from other crime organization sources, which played a major role in putting Ronald Reagan in the White House. He received support from organized crime, and his administration reciprocated and gave organized crime's representatives seats on the highest councils of U.S. government. Persons with clear and compelling connections to organized crime were appointed to important governmental positions. Reagan's closest adviser and his best Washington-based friend throughout his presidency was a man whom Las Vegas FBI agents had called "a tool of organized crime," Senator Paul Laxalt.

Senator Paul Laxalt

Paul Laxalt, a former governor and the senator from Nevada, was Ronald Reagan's "closest friend and most trusted adviser" (*Wall Street Journal*, June 20, 1983: 1). Laxalt, who met with Reagan two or three times a week, was described in the press as the "first friend" and as Reagan's "eyes and ears" in the U.S. Senate (Condon 1983; Friedman 1984; Waas 1984). Senator Laxalt had served as Reagan's campaign manager in 1976, 1980, and 1984 and had delivered the nominating speeches for Reagan at the Republican national conventions in those years (Friedman 1984: 34; Hamill 1984).

While Laxalt's White House connections suggested he was a man of great respectability and power, his other associations were less than savory. Particularly troubling was Laxalt's long-time friendship and political association with Allen Dorfman, the man who had supervised the use of the Teamsters' Central States Pension Fund as a private bank for organized crime figures (*Time*, August 8, 1977: 28; Brill, 1978: Chap. 6; Moldea, 1978: 7; *Washington Post*, January 21, 1983: 1). Laxalt made no secret of his association with Dorfman or his actions on Jimmy Hoffa's behalf, as indicated in a letter Laxalt sent to Richard

Nixon asking that the incarcerated former Teamsters Union president, Jimmy Hoffa, be pardoned (Moldea 1986: 260):

Dear President Dick:
The other day I had an extended discussion with Al Dorfman of the Teamsters, with whom I've worked closely for the past few years. . . . This discussion, which described in detail the personal vendetta that Bobby Kennedy had against Hoffa, together with other information provided me over the years, leads me to the inevitable conclusion that Jim is a victim of Kennedy's revenge.

Laxalt went on to describe Hoffa as a "political prisoner" and called attention to his friendship with Dorfman, the man who had been named by the Justice Department's Organized Crime Strike Force as the person "most responsible for turning the Teamster pension fund into a series of mob loans" (Walsh 1983a): "While I don't know Mr. Hoffa personally, I have had the occasion to have a great deal of contact with Mr. Dorfman. . . ." (Moldea 1986: 260). Dorfman's role in organized crime was immortalized for all when he was shot down by ski-masked killers in a Chicago parking lot in 1983; accompanying Dorfman at the time of his murder was major Chicago organized crime figure Irwin Weiner, who escaped unscathed from the attack (*Washington Post,* January 21, 1983: 1).

Another major political supporter of Laxalt was the late Moe Dalitz, famous as the head of the notorious Cleveland Four during Prohibition and one of the leading organized crime figures in Las Vegas. When Laxalt was first elected to the U.S. Senate in 1974, Dalitz boasted that "Laxalt is my boy, I put him there" (Friedman 1984: 36). In his two campaigns for the Senate, Laxalt received $50,000 in direct campaign contributions from Dalitz and several of Dalitz's associates who were named by Department of Justice organized crime investigators as organized criminals (*Wall Street Journal* June 20, 1983: 1).

Both the depth of organized crime's political support for Laxalt and his personal business dealings reek of organized crime associations. In 1970, Paul Laxalt and his brother Peter built a gambling casino called the Ormsby House in Carson City, Nevada (Friedman 1984: A8). Their partner in the Ormsby House and source of most of the capital needed to build the casino was Bernard Nemerov, another organized crime figure, who at the time Laxalt had entered this business partnership was recognized as having "a long, documented history of association with some of the most notorious members of the national crime syndicate" (Friedman 1984: A1, A9). An IRS investigation revealed that organized crime was the beneficiary of a major **skimming** operation at the Ormsby House in the early 1970s (Friedman 1984: A1). The IRS charged that about $2 million a year was being skimmed from the gambling proceeds at the casino and funneled to organized crime (Friedman 1984).

Jackie Presser

Ronald Reagan's close relationship with Paul Laxalt only begins the task of cataloging Reagan's organized crime-associated advisors. One of the most blatant of these relationships was Reagan's choice of Teamsters Union president Jackie Presser as a senior economic adviser of his presidential transition team, despite Presser's impeccable mob credentials and although President Reagan was made aware of them by law enforcement officials. (Moldea 1986: 299). Presser was a long-time official of the Teamsters who became president of the union in 1983, even though he had never driven a truck in his life. Presser rose to prominence and power as what the Justice Department described as "a well known corrupt union leader" whose "fingers are out to pick whatever pockets he can" (*Washington Post* 1981: B13; Moldea 1983: 732).

Presser's appointment was arranged by Senator Laxalt and several senior Reagan advisers, including Attorney General Edwin Meese and Reagan campaign manager Ed Rollins. Even Reagan himself maintained frequent contact and friendly relations with Presser during his presidency (*New York Times* August 18, 1983: A21; *Friedman* 1984: 38; *Washington Post* November 14, 1985: A5 and September 17, 1987: A17; Moldea 1986: 343, 346–347).

Roy Williams

President Reagan's friendships with Teamster Union officials extended to Roy Williams, a Teamster president. Reagan began his pursuit of the presidency in 1980 with a speech to the Teamsters in Ohio following a private meeting with William Presser, Jackie Presser, and Roy Williams, then president of the Teamsters (Moldea 1983: 732). Williams had been described by a Senate investigating committee as "an organized crime mole operating at senior levels of the Teamster union" (Moldea 1983: 734). In fact, the day before his private meeting with Reagan, Williams had taken the Fifth Amendment repeatedly when interrogated by a Senate committee about his relationships with various organized criminals (Moldea 1983: 732). None of this seemed to bother Reagan, however. His first stop in Washington after winning the election in November 1980 was Teamsters Union headquarters, where he met again in closed session with Presser, Williams, and other members of the Teamsters directors (Moldea 1982: 7).

Reagan and the International Longshore-men's Association

Ronald Reagan's friendship with the Teamsters Union was not his only labor union alliance. In some respects, Reagan was no friend of organized labor: He crushed the Air Traffic Controller's Union, and he battled the AFL–CIO throughout his presidency. But when a union had strong organized crime connections, Ronald Reagan was able to overcome his antilabor bias.

In 1983, Ronald Reagan became the first U.S. president ever to address the national convention of the International Longshoremen's Association (ILA) (*Washington Post,* August 17, 1983: A4). Most politicians kept a significant distance between themselves and the ILA for very good reasons. Like the Teamsters union, the ILA had been expelled from the AFL–CIO for its organized crime connections. The AFL–CIO charged that the ILA was run by New York organized crime groups (Hutchinson 1970: 197). The President's Commission on Organized Crime, after its investigation of the International Longshoremen's Association, concluded that the ILA is "virtually a synonym for organized crime in the labor movement" (Hutchinson 1970: 197). In a journalistic investigation of the ILA, NBC reported that as a result of massive systematic hijacking operations "organized crime and the Longshoremen's Union have been able to put their tax on every item moving in or out of the ports they control" (NBC Evening News, September 6 and 7, 1977). More than thirty of the ILA's officials have been convicted on a wide variety of criminal charges (*Washington Post,* August 17, 1983: A4).

Former ILA president Thomas Gleason typified the union's leadership when he took the Fifth Amendment at a grand jury investigating corruption in the union (*Washington Post* August 17, 1983: A4). Gleason engaged in a series of highly questionable business deals, including selling warplanes to the Dominican Republic (Hutchinson 1970: 107).

Consider former President Ronald Reagan's associations with mob figures during the same period in which the First Lady counseled young people to "just say no" to drug dealers and gangsters. Was the president of the United States being duped by organized criminals, or was he a willing player in organized crime activity for his own political agenda? You decide!

When President Reagan addressed the International Longshoremen's Association on July 18, 1983, he portrayed Gleason with the same flowery language he usually reserved for his friend Paul Laxalt and his drug-running contra "freedom fighters." Gleason "sticks by his friends and he sticks by his country," Reagan said, "that kind of integrity and loyalty is hard to come by today" (Hutchinson 1970: 107). The president had neglected to mention a high-level briefing he had been given just before the speech from Justice Department lawyers attempting to dissuade him from giving the address, which detailed corruption within the ILA (Hutchinson 1970: 107).

In December 1980, Ronald Reagan appointed Raymond Donovan, the vice-president and labor liaison for Schiavone Construction Company, as secretary of labor. Donovan's name had been forwarded to the president by the Teamsters' leadership as their first choice for the job, even though he was virtually unknown to every prominent national labor leader (*Washington Post* December 17, 1980: A2; Moldea 1983: 733).

Raymond Donovan

Within a month the FBI presented the results of background investigation of Donovan to the Senate Labor Committee (Moldea 1982: 9). The FBI charged that Schiavone Construction was "mobbed-up" and that Donovan had extensive "social and business ties with organized crime figures" (*Washington Post,* January 28, 1981: A3). One FBI informant charged that Donovan had personally made a series of payoffs guaranteeing labor peace to an organized crime hit man (*Washington Post,* February 18, 1981: A2). In addition, the FBI's New York office submitted a second, secret report charging that Donovan's construction company had granted "preferential treatment on subcontracting projects" to William "Billy the Butcher" Masselli, a New Jersey organized crime figure; the FBI memo charged that Donovan and his associates had conspired with Masselli in "numerous, possibly fraudulent schemes" (*Washington Post,* May 30, 1985: A3).

Ronald Reagan's relationships with Paul Laxalt, labor racketeers, and Raymond Donovan were not the only cases of close associations between administration officials and organized crime. Although we may never know with certainty the true extent of organized crime's infiltration of the Reagan White House, these additional cases support that association:

Other Reagan Administration Ties to Organized Crime

- Reagan's first national security adviser, Richard V. Allen, had a series of business deals with organized crime figures, including Howard Cerny, who had been intimately involved in Robert Vesco's far-flung financial scams and who had also served as a liaison for the CIA with European organized crime groups (Sklar and Lawrence 1981: 1).

- Former CIA director William Casey was a partner of Carl Biehl in Multiponics, an agribusiness firm. Biehl was well known in the New Orleans underworld; federal wiretaps had recorded him in illicit ventures as early as the early 1950s. Multiponics went bankrupt in 1971 after deceiving its investors (Moldea 1982: 10).

- Max Hugel, the deputy director of the CIA, was forced to resign after his connections to organized crime became known. He had been executive vice-president of Centronics Data Computer Corporation, owned in part by Caesar's World, the casino company, which at that time was under federal investigation for hidden organized crime ownership related to Meyer Lansky's massive underworld empire. In addition, Centronics had a consultancy relationship with Moe Dalitz and his Las vegas casinos (Moldea 1982: 10–11).

- William McCann, Reagan's nominee as ambassador to Ireland, had to withdraw his nomination after it was learned that he was a business associate of Louis Oster, a convicted stock fraud and insurance swindler who had engaged in securities violations as part of illicit dealings with Santo Trafficante and Tony Accardo (Moldea 1982: 11).

- Reagan maintained very close political and personal relations with Walter Annenberg, whose father had been a partner of major organized crime figures in the Nationwide News Service, which in the 1920s had supplied race results to bookies throughout the country (Haller 1976: 122–123). In 1939, father and son had been indicted on charges of tax evasion and selling pornography illegally through the mails (Haller 1976: 123). Walter Annenberg's reward for pioneering the wire service and the pornography industry in the United States was his appointment as ambassador to Great Britain by Richard Nixon and his role as a regular host of Reagan's frequent vacation retreats to Palm Springs, California (Scott 1988).

- Ronald Reagan maintained a close relationship with Frank Sinatra, who was a frequent guest at White House functions and was awarded the Presidential Medal of Freedom. In addition, Reagan wrote him an absolutely glowing letter of recommendation for his casino license hearing in Nevada. Sinatra's extensive organized crime associations and dealings have been immortalized in a widely distributed nineteen-page Justice Department report (Gage 1971: 103, 110; Blakey and Billings 1981: 381; Moldea 1982: 7; *Washington Post* October 7, 1987: A19).

Payback   We will never know how many investigations and prosecutions have been compromised by the involvement of the White House with organized crime or how much insider information organized crime was given and subsequently made use of to enhance its profitability and avoid prosecution. With regard to the Reagan presidency, however, we can point with certainty to some very tangible and positive outcomes for the mob:

- In response to complaints from Paul Laxalt, the Reagan administration reined in federal investigations of organized crime in Las Vegas.

- The Reagan administration supported Laxalt's opposition to proposed regulations aimed at reducing the laundering of illicit drug profits through Las Vegas casinos (Moldea 1984a: 31; *Washington Post* December 12, 1985: A19).

- The Reagan administration supported Laxalt's attempt to divert the focus of federal criminal investigation efforts from organized crime to street crime (Moldea 1982: 6).
- Despite having the support of the attorney general, Laxalt was unable to get FBI director William Webster to close down the political corruption hotline in Las Vegas (Friedman 1984: 39).
- During Raymond Donovan's tenure as secretary of labor, prosecutions of union officials declined by 30 percent (Moldea 1986).
- The Reagan administration imposed a 33 percent cutback of the FBI's investigations of gambling, prostitution, arson for hire, pornography, and gangland murders. The president also announced that no new undercover operations would be authorized against organized crime or white-collar crime in his administration (Moldea 1986).
- The Reagan administration severely curtailed the investigative and enforcement abilities of the Securities and Exchange Commission, the Internal Revenue Service, and the Justice Department's Organized Crime Strike Force (Moldea 1986).
- One of the very first legislative proposals to come out of the Reagan White House was a bill that repealed two federal taxes on gambling (Moldea 1986).
- Attorney General William French Smith tried to persuade Congress to repeal the Ethics in Government Act and the Foreign Corrupt Practices Act (Moldea 1986).
- In his first term, Reagan received 588 commutation requests, but he granted only 10, all white-collar criminals with organized crime ties (*Washington Post* July 27, 1984: A3).

President Reagan's own Commission on Organized Crime publicly criticized his relationships with Teamsters Union officials and suggested that these associations had delayed federal prosecutions of labor racketeers. Reagan's friendship with Laxalt; his appointments of Presser, Donovan, Casey, Hugel, and McCann; and his glowing support of Gleason and the ILA cannot simply be ignored or dismissed as politics as usual.

The Reagan administration and its activities reveal the extent to which organized crime can and has integrated itself into the normal day to day workings of the highest levels of the U.S. government and, even more shockingly, the extent to which the highest-ranking U.S. officials nonchalantly accept organized crime as a partner in the business of government.

BILL CLINTON AND THE WHITEWATER SCANDAL

Allegations of criminal wrongdoing surfaced almost immediately after President Bill Clinton took office in January 1993. In particular, charges of improprieties in a crooked land development deal served as a perennial source of news for reporters during the president's first four years. Nevertheless, in the summer of 1995, investigations by House and Senate committees into President Clinton's alleged involvement in the Whitewater scandal revealed that, at least as far as Whitewater was concerned, Clinton had little connection with organized crime per se. As of the preparation of this book, however, individual

Given the numerous examples of collusion between politicians and organized crime figures, do you believe that it is possible for a presidential candidate to win the nation's highest office without making concessions to the mob? Predict the political consequences of various options regarding corruption that a candidate might take.

criminal involvement by the Clinton administration has not been ruled out. This became evident when in January 1996, Hillary Rodham Clinton was the first First Lady in U.S. history to be subpoenaed by a federal investigative grand jury for questioning in the Whitewater question.

By all indications, Whitewater was merely another of many bank disasters caused by deregulation of the banking industry during the 1980s and rapacious greed by opportunistic players in that industry. However, as we have seen, it often takes years after a president leaves office for information to surface about all aspects of an administration and for information collected by investigators to become public. For example, it has only been in the last year that journalists Pete Brewton and Edward Bainerman have published exposés linking former President Bush to organized crime operatives. With the present set of investigations ongoing, we will just have to wait to see what they uncover.

However, one tantalizing suggestion has circulated in various journalistic accounts and some scholarly writings on the savings and loan fiasco. The suggestion is that at the heart of Whitewater lies cooperation between Governor Clinton with efforts of Presidents Reagan and Bush in Central America, particularly the resupplying of the contras and drug smuggling by the contras. Allegations have been made that Clinton authorized the use of National Guard troops and a National Guard airport in Arkansas for the contra operations. However, if this is true, it is in the interests of neither Republicans nor Democrats to reveal information about such collaboration. It may be many years before we learn the real issue in Whitewater.

THE BUSH FAMILY: A CONTINUING CRIMINAL ENTERPRISE?

One major theme that has emerged in recent years as scholars have studied the globalization of organized crime has been the close interface between corporate criminality, political criminality, and organized crime. Most leading scholars now see these three types of criminal activity as blending together, overlapping, and often indistinguishable from one another. There is probably no clearer example of this blending and overlap than the activities of one of American's leading political families, the Bushs.

The S&Ls, the Mob, and the Bushes

During the 1980s hundred of savings and loan banks failed. These bank failures cost U.S. taxpayers over $500 billion to cover federally insured losses and much more to investigate the bank failures (Pizzo et al. 1989; Brewton 1992; Johnston 1990). More than 75 percent of the savings and loan insolvencies were directly linked to serious and often criminal misconduct by senior financial insiders (Pizzo et al, 1989: 305). In fact, less than 10 percent of bank failures were related to economic conditions; the rest were caused by mismanagement or criminal conduct (Pizzo et al. 1989: 305).

The influence of organized crime has reached to the highest levels of government. Shown here are George Bush Sr., President George W. Bush, and Florida governor Jeb Bush.

(*AP Wide World Photos*)

A good example of the savings and loan failures can be found in the activities of Mario Renda, a savings and loan insider who often worked in close collaboration with organized crime (Pizzo et al. 1989: 123–126; 302). Renda served as a middleman in arranging about $5 billion a year in deposits into 130 savings and loans, all of which failed (Kwitny 1992: 27). Many of these deposits were made contingent on an agreement that the savings and loan involved would lend money to borrowers recommended by Renda, many of whom were organized crime figures or people entirely unknown to the banking institution involved (Kwitny 1992: 27).

Equally good examples of financial misconduct in the **savings and loan scandal** are found in the activities of the Bush family. In some cases Bush family members helped skim savings and loan funds, which were delivered to outsiders as a part of deals involving lucrative payoffs to bank directors. In other cases, members of the Bush family intervened to influence decisions involving highly speculative and unsound investments requiring loans that would not be repaid if the venture was not profitable. And, finally, the Bush family's political connections served to protect those guilty of misconduct in the savings and loan scandal (Kwitny 1992: 24).

In 1990 federal bank regulators filed a $200 million lawsuit against the officers of Silverado Banking, including Neil Bush, brother of the current president. The lawsuit accused them of gross negligence that resulted in a loss of $1 billion by Silverado and the bank's ultimate collapse (*Los Angeles Times* 1990).

Neil Bush: Taking Down Silverado

According to the Federal Deposit Insurance Corporation, "Our conclusion is that Silverado was the victim of sophisticated schemes and abuses by insiders and of gross negligence by its directors and outside professionals" (Johnston 1990). Neil Bush was reprimanded by the Office of Thrift Supervision for pervasive conflicts of interest while serving as a paid director of the bank. Of particular concern was his role in a series of loans totaling $132 million from the bank to two businessmen, Bill Walters and Kenneth Good (*Los Angeles Times* 1990: 1; Isikoff, 1992: A1). Walters and Good, after securing the loans from Silverado, lent Neil Bush $100,000 and later forgave the loan entirely. In addition, Walters and Good owned a company which paid $550,000 in salaries to Neil Bush (Los Angeles Times 1990: 1; Isikoff 1992: A1). In the end, Walters and Good lost a total of $330 million loaned to them by Silverado. They also received instructions from a member of Silrverado's board of directors on the establishment of family trusts to prevent the government from seizing the money they owed the bank (Kwitny 1992: 32). The shutdown of Silverado was postponed from October to December 1988 so that it would happen after the first President Bush's election campaign had ended. Neil Bush had to pay only $50,000 to settle the federal lawsuit against him, and he was able to avoid any legal costs because a senior banking industry lobbyist formed a legal defense fund to pay the legal costs (Fritz 1992).

Neil Bush also profited enormously from another company on the verge of bankruptcy. Apex Energy paid him over $200,000 in salary and oil deed compensation payments while teetering on the edge of bankruptcy (Failing Firm Paid Neil Bush Big Salary 1992). Neil Bush's small oil company also seemed to profit from its political connections when it was awarded a 1987 contract to drill for oil in Argentina (Bush's Son Misses Deadline For Reporting "Inside" Sale 1991).

Jeb Bush: Influence Peddling for a "Bust-Out" Scam

But Neil Bush was not the only Bush brother involved in the savings and loan collapses. Jeb Bush's (the current governor of Florida) curious relationship with Miguel Recarey is another illustration. Recarey was a long-time business associate of Tampa organized crime figure Santos Trafficante. Recarey also fled the United States when facing three separate indictments for labor racketeering, illegal wiretapping and Medicare fraud (Freedburg 1988: A1). Recarey's business, International Medical Centers, was the largest health maintenance organization for the elderly in the United States and had been supported from $1 billion in payments from the Medicare program. International Medical Centers went bankrupt in 1988 (Freedburg 1988: A1; Royce and Shaw 1988: 4). When International Medical Centers went under it left $222 million in unpaid bills and was under investigation for $100 million in Medicare fraud (Freedburg 1988: A1; Frisby 1992: G1). The U.S. Office of Labor Racketeering in Miami referred to Recarey and his company as "the classic case of embezzlement of government funds . . . "a bust-out operation" (Freedburg 1988: A1)

Jeb Bush's role in this saga began in 1985 when Recarey's attempt to create his "bust-out scam" corporation ran into a federal regulation that said no HMO could get more that 50 percent of its revenue from Medicare (Freedburg 1988: A1; Royce and Shaw 1988: 4). Jeb Bush intervened on Recarey's behalf with Health and Human Services Secretary Margaret Heckler and one of her top aides by convincing them to waive the regulation in the case of Recarey's company (Freedburg 1988: A1; Royce and Shaw 1988: 4). In addition to Jeb Bush's intervention, Recarey had paid $1 million to senior Republican lobbyists in Washington, who were also working the staff of Health and Human Services in pursuance of a waiver (Freedburg 1988: A1; Royce and Shaw 1988: 4). In addition, Jeb Bush had contacted Secretary Heckler earlier about complaints from doctors over the quality of International Medical Centers' care and allegations that Recarey had embezzled funds from another hospital (Royce and Shaw 1988: 4). Jeb Bush told an aide to Secretary Heckler that "contrary to any rumors that were floating around concerning Mr. Recarey, that he was a solid citizen from Mr. Bush's perspective down there [in Miami], that he was a good community citizen and a good supporter of the Republican Party" (Royce and Shaw 1988: 4).

Not surprisingly, in 1988 Recarey's company gave Jeb Bush's real estate company $75,000 to help it find a site for a new corporate headquarters (Freedburg 1988: A1; Royce and Shaw 1988: 4). It was a bad investment because International Medical Centers had already selected a corporate headquarters location when it hired Jeb Bush (Royce and Shaw 1988: 4).

Jeb Bush had a role in yet another savings and loan fiasco when he defaulted on a loan from Broward Federal Savings and Loan (LaFraniere 1990: A24). Broward Federal loaned $4,565,000 to J. Edward Houston, a real estate developer, in February 1985. The loan was secured only by Houston's personal guarantee. On the same day, one of Houston's companies lent the same amount to a partnership made up of Jeb Bush and Armondo Codina for the purpose of purchasing a building in Miami. The Bush–Condina partnership was required to repay the loan only if revenues from the building were sufficient to cover the repayment. Bush and Condina made no payments on the loan at all, and in 1987 Houston defaulted on the Broward Federal loan and the bank sued both Houston and the Bush–Condina real estate partnership. In a sweetheart settlement with the Federal Deposit Insurance Corporation, Bush and Codina only had to repay $500,000 of the $4.5 million loan and got to retain ownership of the building, which had been the collateral on the loan. In 1991, the FDIC sued the officers and directors of Broward Federal, charging that the loan ultimately used by Bush and Codina was an example of the bank's negligent lending practices (Frisby 1992: G1). The Bush–Condina loan played a key part in the failure of Broward Federal, which cost taxpayers $285 million (LaFraniere 1990: A24).

George W. Bush: Insider Information, Oil, and Baseball

President George W. Bush has also reaped significant benefits from some highly questionable business practices. For example, Bush sold $828,560 worth of Harken stock on June 20, 1990, just one week before the company stock posted unusually poor quarterly earnings and Harken stock plunged sharply. Shares lost more than 60 percent of their value over six months. When Bush sold his shares, he was a member of a company committee studying the effect of Harken's restructuring, a move to appease anxious creditors. According to documents on file with the Securities and Exchange Commission (SEC), his position on the Harken committee gave Bush detailed knowledge of the company's deteriorating financial condition. The SEC received word of Bush's trade eight months late. Bush has said he filed the notice, but that it was lost (Hedges 1992: 57–59).

At the time of the stock sale, President Bush was fully aware that Harken Energy was in a serious cash flow crisis and was about to lose millions of dollars (Yost 2000). Bush was investigated for insider trading, but on October 18, 1993, Bruce A. Hiler, the SEC's associate director for enforcement, wrote a letter to Bush's lawyer stating that "the investigation has been terminated as to the conduct of Mr. Bush, and that, at this time, no enforcement action is contemplated with respect to him" (Lardner and Romano 1999: A1). Hiler's official letter went on to say that it "must in no way be construed as indicating that the party has been exonerated or that no action may ultimately result from the staff's investigation" (Lardner and Romano 1999:) It is instructive to note that the head of the SEC at the time of investigation was a supporter of then-president Bush, as was the SEC's general counsel (who later acted as George W. Bush's private attorney) (Yost 2000). In addition, Harken, despite its poor performance and large losses, paid unusually high salaries and benefits to President Bush (Hedges 1992: 57–59). Bush was allowed to purchase stock options at a 40 percent discount paid for by company loans that were frequently forgiven (Hedges 1992: 57–59).

Harken Energy was awarded a contract to drill offshore oil wells for the government of Bahrain in 1990. It was a curious contract, because Harken had never drilled an oil well in water. Although Bahrain government officials denied that the fact that the president's son was on Harken's board had any impact on the contract, the *Wall Street Journal* quoted an official of Harken Energy as saying there was "never any question" about George W. Bush's involvement (Morrison 1999: A26).

Harken Energy also had links to the infamous Bank of Credit and Commerce International (BCCI). BCCI was the seventh-largest privately owned bank in the world. It had over 400 branch offices operating in seventy-three countries. Among its many criminal activities was the laundering of at least $14 billion for the Colombian cocaine cartels; the facilitating of financial transactions for Panamanian president Manuel Noriega and international arms merchant Adnan Khashoggi; the funneling of cash to the contras for illegal arms deals and contra-backed drug trafficking; and the assisting of Phillipine president Ferdinand Marcos in transferring his personal fortune, accrued through corruption and graft, out of the Philippines. Despite the enormity of BCCI's crimes and its vital role in drug trafficking, the U.S. Justice Department was more than reluctant to investigate. In fact, the Justice Department had complete information on BCCI's drug and arms operations and its illegal holdings in the United States for over three years before it even initiated an inquiry. Perhaps the reluctance of U.S. law enforcement to interfere with such a major organized crime entity can be explained by the proliferation of what some have perceived as BCCI's friends in the U.S. government holding high office (Castro 1988; Beaty and Gwynne 1991).

The *Wall Street Journal* commented extensively on Harken's links to BCCI, saying "The mosaic of BCCI connections surrounding Harken Energy may prove nothing more than how ubiquitous the rogue bank's ties were . . . . But the number of BCCI-connected people who had dealings with Harken—all since George W. Bush came on board—likewise raises the question of whether they mask an effort to cozy up to a presidential son" (Morrison 1999).

President Bush's relationship with the Texas Rangers shows a similar pattern of curious business dealings. In investigating his purchase of the Texas Rangers, the *Wall Street Journal* commented that following "a pattern repeated throughout his business career, Mr. Bush's play did not quite make the grade" (Morrison 1999: A26). In 1989, an investment group Bush led was given preferential treatment to buy the Texas Rangers baseball team by its seller, a friend of then-president George Bush, (Morrison 1999: A26; Sack 1999: 1). When they underbid for the team, baseball commissioner Peter Ueberroth brought another financier into the deal, "out of respect for his father," President Bush (Morrison 1999: A26; Sack 1999: 1). Bush later successfully promoted a controversial arrangement in which the city of Arlington provided a $135 million subsidy for a new ballpark, funded by a sales tax increase, with an option for the team to repurchase the park at a vastly reduced price (Romano and Lardner 1999: A1; Milbank 2000, A1). The present President Bush realized $15 million on a $600,000 investment when he sold his share of the team in 1998 (Morrison 1999, A26).

Jonathan Bush rounds out this discussion of brotherly financial chicanery. Jonathan was cited for carrying out stock transactions without registering in the Commonwealth of Massachusetts. While he was settling the complaint against him, he continued to violate Massachusetts securities laws. Neal Sullivan, who handles security trading issues for the Massachusetts secretary of state expressed his concern: "That created great concern for us. We were dismayed . . .. Anyone who has been notified that he is violating state law and continues to do so certainly exemplifies a cavalier attitude toward the registration laws." Jonathan Bush is a veteran stockbroker who, of course, knows about registration requirements. As Sullivan went on to comment, "Any time you have 880 transactions over several years, I wouldn't characterize that as minor" (Phillips 1991: 1).

Jonathan Bush: An Unregistered Broker

Finally, and perhaps most seriously, the Bush family pioneered the practice that has now become commonplace of collaboration between corporate and organized criminals. Prescott Bush, uncle of the current president and brother of the former president, played a key role in helping the Japanese yakuza extend their financial and real estate holdings to the United States. In 1989, Prescott Bush made arrangements for a front company for Japanese organized crime groups to buy into two U.S. corporations and to make a sizable real investment in the United States (Helm 1991a: 1; Isikoff 1992: A1). West Tsusho, a Japanese corporation, was identified by Japanese police officials as a front company for one of that country's largest organized crime syndicates. Prescott Bush was paid a fee of $500,000 for his help in negotiating West Tsusho's purchase of a controlling interest in Assets Management, a U.S. corporation (Helm 1991a: 1; Isikoff 1992: A1). Bush also assisted the Japanese mob in investing in Quantam Access, a U.S. software company, which was ultimately taken over by the Japanese (Helm 1991b: 10; Isikoff 1992: A1). Both companies ultimately went into bankruptcy (Isikoff 1992: A1; Moses 1992).

Prescott Bush: The Yakuza's Frontman

Despite assessments from senior law enforcement officers and experts on organized crime that efforts to control organized crime would be crippled, in December 1989 the administration of George H. Bush abolished all fourteen regional organized crime strike forces (McAlister 1989: A21; Struck out 1990). The organized crime strike forces had been created as independent entities so that they would not be subject to political influences or bureaucratic wrangling within federal law enforcement. In the two decades of their operation, the strike forces had secured convictions of major organized crime figures in several U.S. cities (Struck out 1990). It is at the very least curious that the federal strike force in Miami had been responsible for indicting Miguel Recarey, the man for whom Jeb Bush had intervened with regulators. Organized crime strike forces had also indicted Mario Renda, the organized

George H. Bush: Shutting Down the Organized Crime Strike Forces

crime liaison to the S&Ls, as well as several other key figures in the savings and loan fiasco (Pizzo et al. 1989: 112, 120–123, 303, 337).

ORGANIZED CRIME AND THE BUSINESS COMMUNITY

Organized crime exhibits the same characteristics as do a great many legal businesses. In fact, Smith (1978: 164) argued that organized crime "represents, in virtually every instance, an extension of a legitimate market spectrum into areas normally proscribed. Their separate strengths derive from the same fundamental considerations that govern entrepreneurship in the legitimate marketplace: a necessity to maintain and extend one's share of the market."

As with any business enterprise, organized crime groups seek to make safe and profitable investments. As a result, organized crime networks invariably move into legitimate enterprises (e.g., vending, bars, nightclubs, food products, the garment industry, bank and finance, trucking). To a large degree, this ambition to find legitimate investments for organized crime capital is dictated by the constraints imposed on organized crime enterprises by the illegal market. These constraints make geographical expansion difficult and mitigate against the inclusion of too many employees in illegal enterprises (Reuter 1983). The need for control in illicit enterprises often outweighs the desire to expand and reinvest in additional illicit enterprises. The close relationships between legitimate and illicit businesses have been documented time and again in every local study of crime groups.

Reciprocity   Organized crime represents a series of **reciprocal relationships** and services uniting criminals, clients, and representatives of the government. The most important function of organized crime is to provide a bridge between the covert world of organized crime and the overt world of legitimate business, finance, and politics. This reciprocal relationship, the uniting of what Alan Black has called the underworld and the upperworld, is the primary task of an organized crime syndicate.

In Philadelphia, the Prohibition-era liquor syndicates openly did business with the Union National Bank, using a series of bogus accounts and laundering their money through real estate transactions arranged by the upperworld banking system. In addition, the liquor syndicate had an ongoing contract with the Reading Railroad to transport its illegal products (Potter and Jenkins 1985). In the 1980s in Philadelphia, at least one gambling syndicate used a local bank's loan officer, rather than a loan-shark, to clean up outstanding debts (Potter and Jenkins 1985). This interface with legitimate business provides five vital functions for organized crime syndicates (Anderson 1979b):

1. A means to conceal other illegal activities.
2. A means to launder profits from criminal activities. In Philadelphia, illicit money was laundered through a legitimate bank, an auto dealership, a commercial loan company, an oil company, a beer distributorship, and a series of bars, restaurants, and nightclubs (Potter and Jenkins 1985). Such money-laundering operations range from the simple (using vending machine companies) to the extremely complex

(the arrangement between the Exchange Bank of Geneva and other subsidiaries of Meyer Lansky) (Fried 1980; Lernoux 1984). One of the most complex money-laundering and business arrangements is the pornography syndicate, which uses a system of seven corporations, one layered on top of the other, to conceal the ultimate destination of pornography profits (Pennsylvania Crime Commission 1980).

3. A source of legitimate and reportable income. The use of bars and restaurants as legitimate reporting mechanisms for illicit profits is a common occurrence in Pennsylvania (Pennsylvania Crime Commission 1984).

4. Furtherance of and the already high degree of integration between organized crime and respectable businesspeople.

5. Stable and relatively safe investment opportunities.

Organized crime also provides useful and necessary services to the business community. A significant number of businesspeople avail themselves of the services of organized crime for several key reasons. First, organized crime groups provide stolen goods for resale by businesses. Second, businesspeople often use the racketeering services of organized crime syndicates to harass competitors or to secure favorable contracts with employees (Chambliss 1978; Pennsylvania Crime Commission 1980; Block and Chambliss 1981; Potter and Jenkins 1985). For example, Detroit automobile manufacturers used organized crime syndicates in the 1940s to suppress efforts to unionize the auto industry and to supply strikebreakers (Pearce 1976: 140). In Seattle, local businesspeople gladly chose the corrupt Teamsters Union of Dave Beck over Harry Bridges's more radical alternative (Chambliss 1978).

The relationship between organized crime and business is both functional and necessary to the continued existence and efficient operation of organized crime. The degree of integration between organized crime and the legitimate business community is summed up by Quinney (1975): "Organized crime and legitimate businesses may mutually assist one another, as in regulating prices on commodities or enforcing labor contracts. Interdependence between the underworld of crime and upperworld of business ensures that both systems will be maintained. Mutual assistance accompanied by the profit motive provides assured immunity."

THE WORLDS OF MEYER LANSKY

Organized crime has grown into a huge business in the United States and is an integral part of the political economy. Enormous amounts of illegitimate money are passed annually into socially acceptable endeavors. An elaborate corporate and financial structure is now tied to organized crime (Quinney 1975: 145). Nowhere is this symbiotic relationship between organized crime and the legitimate business community clearer than in the career of Meyer Lansky and the many opportunities that he and his associates provided for organized crime to move into business and for business to profit from organized crime.

Organized crime banks are similar to legitimate banks, but they provide a number of additional functions. Money, usually in used bills, enters the banking system from a great variety of illicit sources: the profits of gambling, vice, narcotics, and burglary. The system can launder the money through Las

Vegas, Miami, Mexico, Liechtenstein, Switzerland, and the Caribbean, among others. Profits can be invested and give the businessperson a level of return on profit unheard of since the heyday of the well-known robber barons. Drugs naturally help lubricate this system, but after half a century, organized crime enterprises have thoroughly penetrated legitimate businesses. Did even Meyer Lansky know all the ramifications of his multinational money-moving conglomerate? The scale of the enterprise is suggested by two things: the vast profits of gambling alone must go somewhere, and the tiny proportion of drug operations that actually come to light involve a substantial capital investment.

Cressey (1969: 234) describes the role of a **money mover** who hides illegally obtained cash and puts it to work "Importing, real estate, trust funds, books, stock and bonds, are his typical undertaking." Of course, money movers come in various shapes and sizes. Some are glorified loan-sharks; others are men of wealth and international prestige.

It is the latter category that we wish to describe here. Do these top-flight financiers constitute a board of directors of organized crime? There is really no way to know. All that can be done is to describe the workings of the awe-inspiring Meyer Lansky and speculate whether he was only a cog in a much larger wheel who merely happened to have had the misfortune to win public celebrity.

The remarkable career of Meyer Lansky has been retold frequently, most comprehensively by Messick (1973), but a brief recapitulation might be useful. Lansky was born in Grodno, Russia, as Maier Suchowljansky in 1902; with his family, he migrated to New York in 1911. By 1918 he had formed acquaintanceships with Bugsy Siegel and Lucky Luciano. As with many others, Prohibition gave him his greatest opportunity, and the Bugs and Meyer gang rose to celebrity as a bootlegger mercenary force. By the late 1920s, with Lepke and Lucky, he had pieced together the outlines of a bootlegging syndicate that would be the dominant influence in organized crime for the next two decades. After Prohibition, he and Siegel cast their eyes farther afield to the West, the Sunbelt, and the Caribbean. In Miami, Lansky initiated the Gold Coast, with its hotels and casinos; in Cuba he created Batista's leisure empire; in Nevada and California, he used syndicate money to create a network of enterprises. Siegel died in 1947, having tried to make himself an independent force, but Las Vegas lived on to flourish and prosper. Lansky's business enterprises were sufficiently far-flung to withstand a setback such as the one dealt him by Fidel Castro. If Havana fell, he could turn back to Las Vegas or open new enterprises in Haiti, the Bahamas, or even in London.

Attempting to describe Lansky's activities is an almost impossible task, even if we could be sure if he was in fact involved in all of the numerous ventures that he is credited with (some authors credit him with virtually every financial scam since 1945). With this caveat, we can begin to describe Lansky's activities on behalf of organized crime. First, let's take a look at the cast of characters that so frequently are participants in Lansky-inspired activities.

Lansky associates can be divided broadly into two categories: (1) the old-time veterans of the gangs of the 1920s and 1930s and (2) newer associates, usually relatively clean lawyers and businesspeople. Lansky appears to have preserved his friendships and business partnerships over many decades. For example, after the hit on Bugsy Siegel, control of the Flamingo Hotel passed to three old Lansky cronies: Moe Sedway from the lower eastside of New York, Morris

Rosen, and "Gus" Greenbaum from Phoenix (Fried 1980: 253–254). Other examples of these long-standing relationships are instructive:

- The Minneapolis mob headed by Isadore Blumenfeld in the 1920s provided Lansky with some of his most durable business partners. Blumenfeld's brother, "Yiddy Bloom," held substantial investments in Miami area real estate and controlled a large portion of the New York gambling market (in the supposed heartland of the Five Families). Probably his best known financial coup was the early 1970s stock fraud surrounding the artificial boosting of Magic Marker shares. Bloom was joined in this by his son Jerold and fifteen fellow conspirators. In the background, no doubt were Lansky and other mutual friends (Pennsylvania Crime Commission 1980: 195–198).

- Also from the Blumenfeld mob was John Pullman, long used by Lansky in his banking ventures for organized crime. Pullman had lived in Canada and Switzerland and was an expert in the use of numbered accounts and dummy corporations. He was the head of the Bank of World Commerce in Nassau (Bahamas) in the 1960s, a highly effective laundry for mob money (Fried 1980: 276–277; Pennsylvania Crime Commission 1980: 198).

- "Dandy" Phil Kastel was part of the 1930s move to the Sunbelt from the New York mobs. In New Orleans, Kastel bridges the years from the early bootlegging and gambling syndicates to Carlos Marcello and, through it all, he was never far from Lansky's interests (Messick 1969: 105, 205, 247).

- "Doc" Stacher (born 1902) emerged from New Jersey organized crime to become a leader in organized crime's western empire (Cook and Carmichael 1980: 281–282; Fried 1980: 62).

- Sydney Korshak (born 1907) was patronized early in his career by the Capone mob. He enjoyed a very successful career representing labor unions and directed the flow of Teamsters money into the Nevada casinos. Korshak apparently accumulated enormous wealth from legitimate sources (Fried 1980: 285–286).

- Harry Teitelbaum, a prominent figure in the New York gangs of the 1920s, was also associated with the Bugs and Meyer mob and the L & G gang. By the 1950s, Teitelbaum was associated with Nig Rosen in a Lansky-inspired heroin-trafficking operation (Cook and Carmichael 1980; Fried 1980).

- Sam Cohen was a Los Angeles bookmaker who was closely associated with the Flamingo Hotel in Las Vegas in the 1960s and accused with Lansky of operating a major skim operation at the Fremont and Riviera casinos. With his sons Alan and Joel, he was involved in interesting deals in both Florida and the Pocono Mountains of Pennsylvania. These real estate deals were conducted in association with Alvin Malnik, Lansky's supposed heir. Sam Cohen fits the pattern of continuity from the Prohibition gangs to the financial world of the 1970s and 1980s. He moved from New York to Florida in the 1920s and joined the exodus to Nevada in the 1950s (Messick 1969: 326–331, 363; Mollenhoff 1973: 186).

- Benjamin Siegelbaum, a financial manipulator very close to Lansky, was involved in a Swiss money-laundering operation in the 1960s called the Exchange Bank of Geneva. Siegelbaum had been a partner of Nig Rosen, John Pullman, Yiddy Bloom, and others in his career.

- Morris Lansburgh was a Lansky associate who was extremely powerful in Miami, where he controlled substantial hotel interests in Miami Beach. He was alleged to have been a partner with Lansky and Sam Cohen in the Flamingo skim (Mollenhoff 1973: 186).

Other prominent figures in the Lansky orbit were newer and more respectable figures. Delbert Coleman came to prominence in the late 1960s in the Parvin–Dohrman affair. In 1968, Coleman was associated with Korshak in an attempt to purchase the Parvin–Dohrman casinos in Las Vegas and to float that company's shares artificially. Coleman and Korshak were also involved in Bernie Cornfeld's IOS scam (Raw et al. 1971: 229; Fried: 1980: 282–286; Demaris 1981: 247). Alvin Malnik was picked by some observers of organized crime to be Lansky's probable successor. He first came to prominence in the early 1960s with the attempt to establish a gambling resort at Paradise Island in the Bahamas. He had already established himself in the banking and real estate businesses in Miami, but soon became Lansky's public front man. The Paradise Island venture led to the establishment of Resorts International, the entertainment and gambling conglomerate that was the subject of intense law enforcement scrutiny for years as charges of control by Lansky surfaced (Mahon 1980).

In the early 1970s, Malnik was also involved with Sam Cohen's sons in land deals in Florida and the Poconos. Their companies, COMAL and Cove Associates, dealt with Caesar's World and the Teamsters' pension fund, both institutions that have attracted a substantial amount of law enforcement attention (Fried 1980: 282–286; Pennsylvania Crime Commission 1980: 252–254). Finally, Allen R. Glick of Pittsburgh attracted a great deal of attention when his firm Argent seemingly came from nowhere to secure a vast Teamsters' loan (about $146 million). This enabled him to take over the Stardust Casino in Las Vegas and much of the plundered Parvin–Dohrman company. In 1979 he was implicated in a skimming operation, which led to his being forced to sell out for a comfortable profit (Fried 1980: 284–285; Demaris 1981: 318, 320, 365–366, 391, 445, 525–526). The operations that these and other organized crime moneymen were involved in recycled the profits of organized crime and in turn generated immense new profits—which are almost wholly clean.

More on Las Vegas

Bugs and Meyer pioneered Las Vegas on behalf of East Coast organized crime interests, investing money from New York, New Jersey, Philadelphia, Cleveland, and other areas. However, in each case it was Lansky who managed and coordinated the enterprises. It would be incorrect to suggest that other mobs, such as the Cleveland Four, were acting as Lansky servants or as members of some kind of Jewish Mafia, only that their move to Las Vegas was conditioned by Lansky's enterprises.

The first great hotel in Las Vegas was Siegel's Flamingo (1946). After his murder, the hotel passed to three old Lansky cronies: Sedway, Rosen, and Greenbaum. Gus Greenbaum would later manage the Riviera, but he fell out with his Chicago-based employers.

By the late 1950s, the casinos were doing an admirable job of making old-time gangsters respectable, particularly in the case of the old Cleveland Four. For instance, Cleveland Four veteran Lou Rothkopf's nephew Bernie was a legitimate businessman, director of the MGM Grand Hotel (Demaris 1981: 56–59). Moreover, the casinos provided wonderful opportunities for skimming to defraud the IRS. Lansky was indicted at the Flamingo in the 1960s, along with partners Morris Lansburgh and Sam Cohen, for skimming several million dollars a year. By the 1970s, the casinos were equally far from having purged themselves of mob interests. Nick Civella and the Kansas City mob apparently controlled the Tropicana and the Dunes, in the latter case through Jimmy Hoffa's attorney Morris Shenker. At the Aladdin, Delbert Coleman and Ed Torres were believed to be representing someone who wished to remain hidden.

Under Allen Glick's management, the Stardust tried too hard at the skimming game. Some $3.5 million was skimmed from its slot machines between 1974 and 1976, a scale that was regarded as much too blatant by Argent's entertainment director, Chicago-based gambler Frank Rosenthal. By 1979, the Nevada Gaming Commission ordered Glick to sell—which he did, to friends of Moe Dalitz. He sold for a $2 million down payment, the assumption of $92 million in debts, and another $66 million to be paid from the casino's earnings by 1991. Presumably, Lansky was behind at least some of this skullduggery, but by this stage, he was extremely adept at hiding his hand.

Organized crime's move into Florida came at least as early as the western migration. Al Capone himself was one of the first to see possibilities in Florida for gambling and tourism. By the 1930s, mob money was moving into real estate and into such ventures as Tropical Park Race Track in Coral Gables (a joint New York–Chicago operation) and, especially, Lansky's Colonial Inn. The development of Miami Beach coincided with that of Las Vegas. For instance, in the 1940s, the Wofford Hotel in Miami was the Florida base for both Lansky and Costello; and the proprietor, Tatum Wofford, was friendly with rising stars Richard Nixon and Bebe Rebozo. Rebozo himself was close to the Cleveland syndicate. By the 1950s, organized crime had a well-developed role in such Miami hotels as the Sands and the Grand. By the 1980s, some estimates claimed that roughly half of Miami Beach hotels were connected to mob money through Lansky or such associates as Lansburgh and Yiddy Bloom (Moldea 1978: 105–107).

The Move to Florida

Mob-Connected Casinos of the 1950s

- The Thunderbird (1948) was fronted by a former lieutenant governor of Nevada, but was really a Lansky operation.
- The Desert Inn (1950) was run by the Cleveland Four.
- The Sands (1952) was owned by an awesome list of organized crime backers, including Lansky, Adonis, Costello, Stacher, Ed Levinson, "Kid" Cann, and Frank Sinatra.
- The Sahara (1952) was backed by Chicago, Cleveland, and New York moneymen.

- The Riviera was backed by the Chicago mob.
- The Dunes was opened by representatives of Raymond Patriarca of Rhode Island.
- The Stardust (1958) was a Dalitz operation, as was the Sundance.
- The Tropicana (1957) was backed by Kastel and Costello.
- The Palace was opened by Patriarca, Chicago mob investors, Lansky, and Teamsters union money. Teamsters' money also flowed into Caesar's Palace, the Landmark, the Dunes, and the Fremont.

Source: R. Hammer (1975: 224–225).

Florida also provided an extremely valuable banking structure that could be used by organized criminals from all parts of the country. This was unraveled (at least in part) by investigations surrounding the Watergate affair of the 1970s. For example, the scandal of Nixon's Winter White House revealed some interesting connections concerning the Keyes Realty Company. This company had been named in the Kefauver hearings for its role as intermediary in bribes between organized crime and Dade County political officials. In the 1940s it played a major role in developing Miami gambling. In 1948 this company transferred a Key Biscayne property to ANSAN, a shadowy Cuban investment group in which syndicate money was allegedly involved. This linked the Cuban ancien regime (such as José Aleman) with Batista and Luciano allies. Later, control of this real estate passed to two new groups: the Teamsters' pension fund and Lansky's Miami National Bank. In 1967 this land passed to Nixon and Bebe Rebozo at bargain rates. One of the Watergate burglars, a Cuban exile, was a vice-president of Keyes Realty.

The Miami National Bank is an interesting case study in itself. In 1958 it was taken over for the Teamsters, using Lou Poller as a front. Poller specialized in laundering money and, not surprisingly, he owed his primary loyalty to Lansky. Organized crime money now reemerged in the form of real estate, apartment buildings, hotels, motels, and mobile home companies. The Teamsters acquired this bank through Arthur Desser, another link between Hoffa and Lansky; Desser made the 1967 Key Biscayne sale to Nixon and Rebozo (Scott et al. 1976: 356–358; Cook and Carmichael 1980; Hinckle and Turner 1981).

By the 1970s, a "subculture of banks in southern Florida" was linked by "interlocking directorates and major investors" (Fried 1980: 141). Besides the Miami National, there were the Bank of Miami Beach, International Bank of Miami, the Key Biscayne Bank, and Southeast First. Federal prosecutors linked Southeast First to the intelligence community and especially to the 1976 murder of Chilean exile Orlando Letelier. These banks have also been associated with the Lansky and Luciano mobs and the Cleveland, Boston, and Las Vegas crime organizations.

Cuba Cuba represented the first major international venture of organized crime (Messick 1967, 1973; Blakey and Billings 1981: 228–232; Hinckle and Turner 1981). Lansky had acquired the Hotel Nacional in Havana as early as 1937, and this gave his friends a foundation on which to build after Batista's coup of 1952. Casinos appeared rapidly: Lansky's Havana Riviera, run by the Cellini brothers; the Havana Hilton; the San Souci; the Capri; the Commodore; the Tropicana. Each provided opportunities for skimming. At the Nacional, Cleveland money was the key investment, but the operator was Jake Lansky. Castro's revolution was a disaster for U.S. organized crime, but Lansky's circle of investors was already on the lookout for other opportunities.

The Banks At least by the 1950s, organized crime was learning the importance of clean money; no longer could gangsters depend on the loyal silence of bankers as in the bootlegging days. Lansky learned the techniques of laundering profits, especially through Swiss numbered accounts. Nig Rosen used such Swiss bank accounts for his heroin connection in the 1950s. Soon Lansky and his associates established their own banks. Malnik established the Bank of World Commerce in Nassau. Mob money flowed into the Bahamas before passing to Tibor Rosenbaum's International Credit Bank in Switzerland.

Then it could return to the United States for reinvestment. At every stage in these operations are familiar faces: the Bank of World Commerce was headed by John Pullman and investors included Ed Levinson. In turn, Levinson and Siegelbaum were active in other Swiss laundry shops, such as the Exchange Bank of Geneva. We observed the growth of the Florida network earlier.

These banks could provide a clean base for further ventures. For instance, Rosenbaum's bank supported Cornfeld's IOS. Again, the Overseas Investors Corporation gave Robert Vesco his opportunity to plunder a fortune. Both the Vesco and Rosenbaum ventures collapsed by the 1970s. They certainly had their successors, although full details will become apparent only when they, in turn, reach their inevitable date with fiscal reality (Messick 1969: 201–209; Raw et al. 1971; Clark and Tigue 1975; Fried 1980: 276–286).

Summarizing the complex saga of gambling in the Bahamas is no easy task. In the 1950s, the success of Lansky's ventures in Cuba led to attempts to establish similar gambling enterprises elsewhere. The front men for the Lansky enterprise were Wallace Groves and Louis Chesler. They attempted to develop a "free port" in the Bahamas, and in the early 1960s, Lansky interests were established at the Freeport Monte Carlo casino. This casino was managed by two of Lansky's longest-established gambling technicians, Dino and Eddie Cellini (Mahon 1980).

The Bahamas

Also in the late 1950s, Huntingdon Hartford was attempting to found a casino at Hog Island, promptly rechristened Paradise Island. However, he found considerable difficulty in getting a gambling license from the governmental minister concerned, Sir Stafford Sands. At this point Alvin Malnik entered the picture. He made a very tempting offer: Paradise Island would be bought out by a firm called Mary Carter Paint, and Lansky would see to obtaining a gambling license. The dating of this deal in the early 1960s was important; obviously, Lansky was seeking another Caribbean haven to replace Castro's Cuba. He brought with him such old gambling partners as Max Courtney, "Trigger Mike" Coppola, Frank Ritter, and the Cellini brothers.

From the mid-1960s, events happened rapidly; in 1966 Hartford and his adviser, Seymour Alter, sold Paradise Island to Mary Carter Paint. In 1967 the Paradise Island casino opened with a glittering assembly of guests, including Richard Nixon, and in 1968 Mary Carter Paint changed its name to Resorts International. However, the pressure was also intensifying, especially after Sands's party was defeated in the 1967 election. Lansky involvement in the casino was blatant, represented as it was by the presence of Dino and Eddie Cellini, both veterans of gambling operations in Kentucky and Cuba.

In the United States, the Organized Crime Strike Force of the Justice Department was appalled by the Lansky operation and began to release information about it to the media. However, it was the Watergate affair that led to the greatest embarrassments. It was suggested that Resorts International had been linked to Bebe Rebozo, that Resorts and Robert Vesco had been laundering Nixon campaign money, and that Seymour Alter had been the bagman for Vesco, Rebozo, and Resorts. Clouds were gathering over Paradise Island, but not sufficiently to prevent Resorts International from acquiring a gambling license in New Jersey (Cook and Carmichael 1980; Mahon 1980).

Organized Crime, the CIA, and the Savings and Loan Scandal

The savings and loan (S&L) scandal of the 1980s has been called "the greatest . . . scandal in American history" (Thomas 1991: 30) and the single greatest case of fraud in the history of crime (*Seattle Times*, June 11, 1991). Some analysts see it as the natural result of the ethos of greed promulgated by the Reagan administration (Simon and Eitzen 1986: 50). Others believe that it was a premeditated conspiracy to move covert funds out of the country for use by the U.S. Intelligence Agency (Bainerman 1992: 275).

Each of these depictions of the S&L scandal contains elements of truth. To a large degree, however, the S&L scandal was simply business as usual. What was unusual about it was not that it happened or who was involved, but that it was so blatant and coarse a criminal act that exposure became inevitable. Its exposure demonstrated three basic but usually ignored truths about organized crime with startling clarity:

1. There is precious little difference between those people whom society designates as respectable and law-abiding and those people whom society castigates as hoodlums and thugs.
2. The world of corporate finance and corporate capital is as criminogenic and probably moreso than any poverty-wracked slum neighborhood.
3. The distinctions drawn between business, politics, and organized crime are at best artificial and in reality irrelevant. Rather than being dysfunctions, corporate crime, white-collar crime, organized crime, and political corruption are mainstays of U.S. political–economic life.

The outlandish salaries S&L executives paid themselves, the subsidies to the thrifts from Congress that rewarded incompetence and fraud, the land "flips" that resulted in real estate being sold back and forth in an endless *kiting* scheme, and the political manipulation designed to delay the scandal until after the 1988 presidential elections are immensely interesting and important, but they are subjects for others' inquiries. Our interest is in the S&Ls as living, breathing organisms that fused criminal corporations, organized crime, and the CIA into a single entity that served the interests of the political and economic elite in the United States. A brief summary presents the most blatant examples of collaboration between financial institutions, the mob, and the intelligence community.

First National Bank of Maryland

For two years, 1983 to 1985, the First National Bank of Maryland was used by Associated Traders, a CIA proprietary company, to make payments for covert operations. Associated traders used its accounts at First National to supply $23 million in arms for covert operations in Afghanistan, Angola, Chad, and Nicaragua (Bainerman 1992: 276–277; *Covert Action* Vol. 35, 1990).

The links between the First National Bank of Maryland and the CIA were exposed in a lawsuit filed in federal district court by Robert Maxwell, a high-ranking bank officer. Maxwell charged that he had been asked to commit crimes on behalf of the CIA. Specifically, he charged that he was asked to conceal Associated Traders' business activities, which by law he was required to specify on all letters of credit. Maxwell alleged that he had been physically threatened and forced to leave his job after asking that his superiors give him a letter stating that the activities he was being asked to engage in were legal. In responding to Maxwell's lawsuit, attorneys for the bank state that "a relationship between First National and the CIA and Associated Traders was classified information which could neither be confirmed nor denied" (Bainerman 1992: 276–277; *Washington Business Journal* February 5, 1990).

The Washington, DC–based Palmer National Bank was founded in 1983 on the basis of a $2.8 million loan from Herman K. Beebe to Harvey D. McLean, Jr. McLean was a Shreveport, Louisiana, businessman who owned the Paris (Texas) Savings and Loan. *Houston Post* reporter Pete Brewton linked Beebe to a dozen failed S&Ls. In their investigation of the S&L fiasco, Stephen Pizzo, Mary Fricker, and Paul Muolo called Beebe's banks "potentially the most powerful and corrupt banking network ever seen in the U.S." Altogether, Beebe controlled, directly or indirectly, at least fifty-five banks and twenty-nine S&Ls in eight states. Beebe's background makes his participation in these banks and S&Ls particularly interesting. Beebe had served nine months in federal prison for bank fraud and had impeccable credentials as a financier for New Orleans–based organized crime figures, including Vincent and Carlos Marcello (Bainerman 1992: 277–278; Brewton 1992a: 170–179).

Palmer National Bank

Harvey McLean's partner in the Palmer National Bank was Stefan Halper. Halper served as George Bush's foreign policy director during the 1980 presidential primaries. During the general election campaign, Halper was in charge of a highly secretive operations center, consisting of Halper and several ex-CIA operatives, who kept close tabs on Jimmy Carter's foreign policy activities, particularly Carter's attempt to free U.S. hostages in Iran. Halper was later linked both to the Debategate scandal, in which it is alleged that Carter's briefing papers for his debates with Ronald Reagan were stolen, and with the October Surprise, in which it is alleged that representatives of the Reagan campaign tried to thwart U.S. efforts to free the Iranian hostages until after the presidential election. Halper also set up a legal defense fund for Oliver North.

During the Iran–Contra Affair, Palmer National was the bank of record for the National Endowment for the Preservation of Liberty, a front group run by Oliver North and Carl "Spitz" Channell, which was used to send money and weapons to the contras.

Another bank with clear connections to the CIA was the Indian Springs Bank of Kansas City, Kansas (Bainerman 1992: 279–280; Brewton 1992b: 197–200). The fourth largest stockholder in Indian Springs was Iranian expatriate Farhad Azima, who was also the owner of the air charter company Global International Air. Indian Springs Bank had made several unsecured loans totaling $600,000 to Global International Air in violation of the bank's $349,000 borrower limit. In 1983 Global International filed for bankruptcy, and Indian Springs followed suit in 1984. The president of Indian Springs was killed in 1983 in a car fire that started in the vehicle's back seat and was regarded by law enforcement officials as of suspicious origin.

Indian Springs Bank

Global International Air was part of Oliver North's logistical network, which shipped arms for the U.S. government on several occasions, including a shipment of 23 tons of TOW missiles to Iran by Race Aviation, another company Azima owned. In his investigation of the Indian Springs bank collapse, Pete Brewton was told that the FBI had not followed up on Indian Springs because the CIA informed them that Azima was "off limits" (*Houston Post* February 8, 1990). Similarly, the assistant U.S. attorney handling the Indian Springs investigation was told to "back off from a key figure in the collapse because he had ties to the CIA."

Azima did indeed have ties to the CIA. His relationship with the agency went back to the late 1970s, when he supplied air and logistical support to Eatsco (Egyptian American Transport and Services Corporation), a company owned by former CIA agents Thomas Clines, Theodore Shackley, and Richard Secord. Eatsco was prominently involved in the activities of former CIA agent Edwin Wilson, who shipped arms illegally to Libya. Azima was also closely tied to the Republican party. He had contributed $81,000 to the Reagan campaign.

Global International also had other unsavory connections. In 1981, Global International made a payment to organized crime figure Anthony Russo, a convicted felon with a record that included conspiracy, bribery, and prostitution charges. Russo was the lawyer of Kansas City organized crime figures, an employee of Indian Springs, and a member of the board of Global International. Russo later explained that the money had been used to escort Liberian dictator Samuel Doe on a goodwill trip to the United States.

Global International's planes based in Miami were maintained by Southern Air Transport, another CIA proprietary company. According to Franck Van Geyso, an employee of Global International, pilots for Global International ferried arms into South and Central America and returned to Florida with drugs.

Vision Banc Savings

In March 1986, Robert L. Corson purchased Kleberg County Savings and Loan of Kingsville, Texas, for $6 million and changed its name to Vision Banc Savings (Bainerman 1992: 280–281; Brewton 1992b: 333–351). Harris County, Texas, judge Jon Lindsey vouched for Corson's character to obtain state regulatory permission for the bank purchase. Lindsey was the chairman of the Bush campaign in 1988 in Harris County and later received a $10,000 campaign contribution and a free trip to Las Vegas from Corson (*Houston Post* February 11, 1990).

Corson was well known to federal law enforcement agents as a money launderer and a mule for the agency, meaning that he moved large amounts of cash from country to country. When he purchased Vision Banc, it had assets in excess of $70 million. Within four months it was bankrupt. Corson was indicted on a series of charges related to a separate Florida real estate venture costing $200 million. Vision Banc engaged in a number of questionable deals under Corson's leadership, but none more so than its $20 million loan to Miami lawyer Lawrence Freeman to finance a real estate deal (*Houston Post* February 4, 1990). Freeman was a convicted money launderer who had cleaned dirty money for Jack Devoe's Bahamas-to-Florida cocaine smuggling syndicate and for Santo Trafficante's Florida-based organized crime syndicate. Freeman was a law partner of CIA operative and Bay of Pigs paymaster Paul Helliwell.

Hill Financial Savings

Vision Banc was not the only financial institution involved in Freeman's Florida land deals. Hill Financial Savings of Red Hill, Pennsylvania, put in an additional $80 million (Brewton 1992a: 346–348). The Florida land deals represented only one in a series of bad investments by Hill Financial, which led to its collapse, which cost the U.S. Treasury $1.9 billion.

Sunshine State Bank

The cast of characters surrounding the Sunshine State Bank of Miami included spies, White House operatives, and organized criminals (Bainerman 1992: 281; Brewton 1992: 310–312, 320–323). The owner of the Sunshine State Bank, Ray Corona, was convicted in 1987 of racketeering, conspiracy, and mail fraud. He purchased Sunshine in 1978 with $1.1 million in drug-trafficking profits supplied by José Antonio "Tony" Fernandez, who was subsequently indicted on charges of smuggling 1.5 million pounds of marijuana into the United States.

Among Corona's customers and business associates were Leonard Pelullo, Steve Samos, and Guillermo Hernandez-Cartaya. Pelullo was a well-known associate of organized crime figures in Philadelphia who had attempted to use S&L money to broker a major purchase of an Atlantic City casino as a mob frontman. He was charged with fraud for his activities at American Savings in California. Steve Samos, a convicted drug trafficker who helped Corona to set up Sunshine State Bank as a drug money laundry, had also helped set up front companies that funneled money and weapons to the contras. Guillermo Hernandez-Cartaya was a veteran CIA operative who played a key role in the Bay of Pigs invasion. He also had a long career as a money launderer in the Caribbean and Texas on behalf of both the CIA and major drug-trafficking syndicates.

Mario Renda, Lender to the Mob

Mario Renda was a Long Island money broker who brokered deposits to various S&Ls in return for their agreement to loan money to phony companies (Pizzo et al. 1989: 466–471; Brewton 1992a: 45–47, 188–190). He and his associates received finders fees of 2 to 6 percent on the loans, most of which went to people with strong organized crime connections who subsequently defaulted on them. Renda brokered deals to 160 S&Ls throughout the country, 104 of which eventually failed. He was convicted of embezzling $16 million from an S&Ls and for tax fraud.

Renda also served CIA and National Security Council interests as a money broker by helping arrange for the laundering of drug money through various S&Ls on behalf of the CIA. He then obtained loans from the same S&Ls that were funneled to the contras. An organized crime-related stockbroker, a drug pilot, and Renda were convicted in the drug money-laundering case.

Full-Service Banking

At least twenty-two of the failed S&Ls can be tied to joint money-laundering ventures by the CIA and organized crime figures (Pizzo 1989: 466–471; Glassman 1990: 16–21; Weinberg 1990: 33). If the S&L scandals of the 1980s reveal anything, it is that corruption linking government, business, and syndicates is the reality of the day to day organization of crime.

Investigations of organized crime in the United States, Europe, and Asia have uncovered organized crime networks operating with virtual immunity from law enforcement and prosecution. Chambliss's study of organized crime in Seattle exposed a syndicate that involved participation by a former governor of the state; the county prosecutor; the police chief; the sheriff; at least fifty law enforcement officers; leading businesspeople, including contractors, realtors, banks, and corporation executives; and, of course, a supporting cast of drug pushers, pimps, gamblers, and racketeers (Chambliss 1978). The Chambliss study is not the exception but the rule. Other sociological inquiries in Detroit, Texas, Pennsylvania, New Jersey, and New York have revealed similar patterns (Albini 1971; Block and Chambliss 1981; Block 1983; Block and Scarpitti 1985; Potter and Jenkins 1986, 1989; Potter 1994). As Chambliss comments, in the everyday language of the police, the press, and popular opinion, organized crime refers to a tightly knit group of people, usually alien and often Italian, that runs a crime business structured along the lines of feudal relationships. This conception bears little relationship to the reality of organized crime today. Criminologists have discovered the existence of organizations whose activities focus on the smuggling of illegal commodities into and out of countries (cocaine out of Colombia and into the United States and guns and arms out of the United States and into the Middle East, for example); other organizations, sometimes employing some of the same people, are organized to provide services such as gambling, prostitution, illegal dumping of toxic wastes, arson, usury, and occasionally murder. These organizations typically cut across ethnic and cultural lines, are run like businesses, and consist of networks of people including police, politicians, and ordinary citizens investing in illegal enterprises for a high return on their money (Chambliss 1986).

INTERNATIONAL ACTIVITIES

The affairs of Cuba and the Bahamas illustrate that the financial magnates of organized crime long ago went international. Their international scope can be demonstrated for other ventures as well.

Tax Havens

Organized crime learned long ago that it was useful to register companies and place investments in **tax havens**, foreign nations with fairly lenient laws on the transfer of money. Examples include Switzerland, Liechtenstein, the Bahamas, Panama, the Cayman Islands, and the Netherlands Antilles. There would certainly be other countries where investigators have been slow to look for front companies, such as the Irish Republic.

The Industrialized World

Organized crime money has flowed freely into Canada: Sturman money through Morton Goss in Toronto and Lansky's interests through John Pullman. Also, Canada's convenience for drug importation has made cities such as Montreal open organized crime territory. Quasi-political organizations such as the Quebec FLQ dabble in the Miami drug trade.

Britain has proved an equally tempting target since the legalization of gambling in 1960. Lansky, the Cellinis, Angelo Bruno, and others all made exploratory journeys there in the 1960s. The British government closed casinos because of alleged organized crime involvement: the Colony Club in 1966 and *Penthouse* magazine's interests in 1971. British gangsters such as the Krays also tried to link up with U.S. colleagues, apparently both Bruno and Lansky. In England as in Holland, Sturman has made major incursions into the pornography trade (Blum and Gerth 1978).

When Australia was discussing the legalization of gambling in the mid-1970s, the Bally Corporation attempted to gain a foothold, but extensive connections with Dino Cellini and Gerry Catena led to their exclusion (Blum and Gerth 1978). Bally was much more successful in its ventures in Sweden (Block and Chambliss 1981: 135–142).

South America, Central America, and Mexico

In Latin America we find the most consistent pattern, hardly surprising if we look at the prosperous cities frequented by Americans in the 1930s and 1940s: Rio de Janeiro and Buenos Aires. There is clear evidence of organized crime involvement in a number of South American countries.

Mexico

In the National Lottery scandal of 1947–1949, Mexican senators were bought by mob money. In 1970, Acapulco was the center for a meeting involving Lansky, Levin, Korshak, and Newton Mandell of Gulf and Western

Corporation, which was also associated with Michele Sindona, the Italian banker whose collapse in the late 1970s caused major damage to the Vatican's finances (Lernoux 1984: 240). Gulf and Western was the corporation that U.S. military intervention in 1965 brought to a dominant role in the small Dominican Republic, where it enjoys the rights of a feudal barony. It is also widely active, for instance, in Brazil.

Honduras

Leading army officers were involved with organized crime in making the country a bridge for the cocaine traffic.

Guatemala

Guatemalan government officials provided Carlos Marcello with phony nationality papers after his expulsion from the United States by the Kennedy Justice Department.

Costa Rica and Nicaragua

Both countries were CIA fiefdoms in the 1950s and 1960s and were heavily involved in anti-Castro plots. CIA ventures involved dabbling by organized crime, primarily through Marcello and Trafficante. Dictators such as Stroessner (Paraguay) and the Somozas (Nicaragua) were easy targets for organized crime blandishments.

Argentina

Lansky's South American drug trade was coordinated by August Ricord from Argentina (Chambliss 1978: 165).

OTHER FINANCIERS

Fascination with Lansky-related enterprises can blind us to the achievements of others who shared both his humble origins and his later achievements. Mere association with a Lansky corporation should not lead us to believe that a person is a Lansky creation, much less a front. There appears to be some evidence for this in the case of Malnik, but only ignorance could lead to the assumption credited to Jack Dragna that all main Jewish criminals were part of a Lansky family. There are many examples of independent magnates of organized crime other than Lansky.

Moe Dalitz

In an FBI wiretap, the New Jersey gangster "Gyp" De Carlo remarked, "There's only two Jews recognized in the whole country today. That's Meyer and . . . Moe Dalitz." We have already discussed Dalitz's role in the Cleveland Four and his move into Las Vegas, especially his involvement at the Stardust and the Desert Inn. However, in the mid-1960s, income tax trouble and heat from the Casino Control Commission forced him to sell his enterprises. With the help of a large Teamsters' loan ($57 million between 1964 and 1972), Dalitz established an extremely posh country club at La Costa, north of San Diego.

The club at La Costa is interesting. Many have seen it as a mob social club, but in 1982 the company successfully sued *Penthouse* for depicting La Costa in this light. Like Lansky, Dalitz has proceeded from the bootlegging underworld to very substantial prosperity. In 1980 a *Forbes* article estimated his wealth at $100 to $150 million, second only to Lansky among the alumni of organized crime. It also cited his extremely healthy investment portfolio, including Detroit Steel and the Rock Island Railroad (Cook and Carmichael 1980).

The Teamsters and the Dorfmans

Anyone studying organized crime will investigate the activities of the Teamsters' Central States Pension Fund. This fund, which passed the $1 billion mark in 1972, served as an organized crime bank. It largely financed the development of Las Vegas and of gambling and leisure in Florida and California; it financed the La Costa Country Club, the Cove Associates deal, and other real estate deals. It played a large role in the deals that resulted in removing President Nixon from office. From the 1950s to the 1970s, this fund was largely directed by Paul Dorfman and his stepson, Allen.

In the 1930s, the Teamsters secured its position by providing employers with a tame and amenable alternative to the radical CIO and the communists. From the early 1930s, the leadership was closely tied to gangsters, especially in Detroit, but by the late 1940s, Jimmy Hoffa had consummated the organized crime–Teamsters union alliance. Hoffa's former mistress became friendly with Moe Dalitz, and this contact gave him a series of mob friends, including the Pressers in Cleveland and the Chicago mob. Hoffa became close to Paul Dorfman, an associate of Anthony "Big Tuna" Accardo. Dorfman had a distinguished record in the Capone mob as a labor racketeer. In the 1920s and 1930s, he had led the corrupt Chicago Wastehandlers Union after the murder of a predecessor (allegedly carried out by Jack Ruby) (Moldea 1978: 49–50, 55–58, 86–88, 141–49; Demaris 1981: 321–326, 342, 378, 402).

In 1951 the Teamsters set up the Central States Health and Welfare Fund, the insurance portion of which was run through a company managed by Paul's inexperienced stepson, Allen Dorfman. Allen learned quickly. He guided the investments of both the Teamsters and Hoffa personally. They moved into oil, stocks, and especially real estate; one unusually corrupt deal involved the Sun Valley retirement community, a deal that would later result in legal trouble for Hoffa. In 1955 the union established a new Central States South-Eastern and South-Western Pension Fund, run almost entirely by the Dorfmans.

Allen did extremely well. His own Union Casualty Agency became a substantial conglomerate. It owned insurance companies, oil interests, and slum housing, and it held real estate including a resort in the Virgin Islands. From the 1950s, the alliance with Lou Poller's Miami National Bank gave the Dorfmans a laundry akin to Lansky's. The move into the sunbelt was reflected by friendship with Dave Yaras, Carlos Marcello, and Santo Trafficante. Allen Dorfman was a man of great importance, close to the Chicago and Cleveland syndicates, Las Vegas, and all the varied interests the Teamsters had funded. Allen himself was succeeded in the Teamsters by Alvin Baron as asset manager. Who had benefited from the Dorfmans' largess? When the old trustees relinquished their control of the Central States Pension Fund in 1976, the chief recipients were familiar faces (Cook and Carmichael 1980):

- Allen Glick, $140 million
- Morris Shenker, $135 million
- Moe Dalitz, $93 million
- Alvin Malnik, $20 million

Ed Levinson

In 1963 a Senate inquiry into misdeeds by Bobby Baker was interrupted by protests from Baker's attorney, Edward Bennett Williams. Apparently, Baker's conversations with a gambler named Levinson had been wiretapped, and Williams protested that this constituted a violation of Baker's civil rights.

However, he had misunderstood one major point: The target of the investigation was not the wayward politician; it was the powerful but little-known gambler.

Ed Levinson was born in Chicago and operated as a gambler in Detroit, Miami, and quasi-open cities such as Newport and Covington (both in Kentucky). In 1952 he joined the mob migration to Nevada. He bought into the Sands, then the Flamingo, and later the Fremont. He accomplished this with the help of a Teamsters' loan, and he began a sizable skim operation of between $1 and $2 million a year in the early 1960s. Meanwhile, his brother Louis kept a foothold in the Cleveland syndicate's territory of northern Kentucky (Messick 1969: 348–362; Mollenhoff 1973: 104, 114–116, 187–189).

Levinson was extremely well connected with both the legitimate and criminal worlds. His connections aboveground were so good that he could secure access to secret FBI wiretaps while he contributed generously to Nevada politicians at all levels of government. In the underworld, he was close to Lansky faithfuls Doc Stacher and Benjamin Siegelbaum, and he participated in the Bank of World Commerce and the Exchange Bank of Geneva.

In 1962 the IRS began a large-scale investigation of Las Vegas skimming. This resulted in 1967 in convictions for the Fremont and for the Riviera, a Sam Cohen operation. Levinson was fined a token sum, but his notoriety was due primarily to the Baker link. It is interesting that so major an organized crime figure should be revealed to public scrutiny only because of a friendship with a corrupt politician stupid enough to associate publicly with the likes of Levinson and Siegelbaum. How many other Levinsons are there who have avoided such a fatal mistake (Mollenhoff 1973)? In short, like Dalitz, Levinson seems to be another example of the rise from organized crime to corporate business.

Reuben Sturman

Reuben Sturman is a figure of considerable wealth and influence who frequent reports have linked to organized crime. This does not necessarily mean that he was himself a criminal, although his pornography trade floated on the margins of legality, and he was convicted on both RICO and tax charges in the late 1980s. Nor does it mean that he is in any sense a servant of organized crime. He is merely an interesting example of a rich and powerful figure who is extremely difficult to fit into traditional models of organized crime. By contrast, he can easily be reconciled with theories that emphasize the coordinating role of capital and finance.

Sturman was born in 1924. By the late 1970s, he owned perhaps 800 retail pornography stores in the United States, often through very complex patterns of concealed ownership. In England he worked in close collaboration with local organized criminals such as the Holloway family, a well-established pornography group. On the European continent, his chief foothold was through the firm Intex Nederland, a key distributor of pornographic videos. A subsidiary of Intex is Video-Rama, which distributed pornographic videos throughout Europe and to the extremely lucrative Middle Eastern market of Cairo, Beirut, Kuwait City, and Riyadh. Firms such as Intex, Video-Rama, and their associated companies are registered in the Netherlands Antilles, a territory whose laws of business secrecy make the Swiss look ostentatious (Pennsylvania Crime Commission, 1980: 118–121).

This is a worldwide pornography syndicate—not a monopoly perhaps, but an enormously powerful conglomerate—whose representatives were all but unknown to the general public. Who had ever heard of Sturman or his representatives, such as his son David Sturman, Scott Dorman, or Frank Bilitz of Baltimore? In the Miporn investigation (1977–1980), the FBI found that the older Sturman associated with mobsters such as Robert DiBernardo and Teddy Gaswirth (Pennsylvania Crime Commission 1980: 118).

Were There Others? Was Lansky the only operator on his level, or were there others? If so, how many? There seem to be others who command awesome wealth but are much less publicized. For instance, there is no doubt that when Doc Stacher fled to Israel, he retired a rich man (worth at least $100 million). John Pullman may well have accumulated the same sort of fortune over the years. Even if they were this wealthy, did they act as independent financiers? It seems that these are vital questions to answer to appreciate the nature and scale of organized crime. Certainly, the continuation of such massive criminal money-moving operations in contemporary U.S. society is obvious. The great savings and loan collapses of the 1980s represent only the most recent example of high-level business–government–mob collaboration.

WHAT HAVE WE LEARNED?

Organized crime cannot survive or prosper without the all-important reciprocal relationship between upper- and underworld players. The chapter presented some of the more important examples of this reciprocal relationship to show the power of the organized crime–business alliance. For example, even the office of the president of the United States has not been immune from allegations of organized crime involvement.

John F. Kennedy, who is thought by some to have been assassinated by the mob, developed clear associations with powerful mob leaders. His father, Joseph Kennedy, could probably be credited with establishing gangster and bootlegging connections before John was born. John Kennedy maintained many of these contacts after his election to the presidency, an election in which he was victorious because of mob financial support and corruption during the election. Kennedy's mob ties included associations with Chicago's Sam Giancana and Giancana associates such as Judith Campbell-Exner, a mob courier suspected of delivering White House money from the president to Giancana.

President Richard Nixon had clear ties with organized crime figures such as Bebe Rebozo, a Cuban American real estate broker and later Florida state senator. Rebozo was clearly associated with Moe Dalitz of the Cleveland Four, as well as with other mob-connected underworld figures. Nixon was also the first president to be fully endorsed by a mob-run union, the Teamsters. In 1971, Nixon pardoned mob union leader Jimmy Hoffa, who was serving time in a federal prison for jury tampering.

Ronald Reagan is also suspected of having close ties with known organized criminals. His associations with the mob-run Longshoreman's Association, Jackie Presser, Senator Paul Laxalt, and Roy Williams pointed to Reagan as being involved in shady dealings. The associations discussed illustrate the benefits for organized crime members to have even as much as a tacit relationship with those who occupy the highly influential White House.

No discussion of organized crime's business affiliations can be complete without a discussion of Meyer Lansky and how he, almost single-handedly, set up organized crime and merged organized crime interests with those of legitimate business. In doing so, Lansky was able to show legitimate business operators how they could profit from organized crime involvement, while demonstrating the benefits of involvement of the illegal rackets with legitimate business to his organized crime associates. Other business-savvy gangsters discussed in this chapter include Ed Levinson, Moe Dalitz, and Reuben Sturman, all criminal visionaries in the merger of national criminal enterprises and legitimate business.

Finally, the savings and loan scandal illustrates how seemingly legitimate and respectable individuals in our society walk the thin line of public corruption and manipulation in search of personal wealth. The discussion highlights some of the events leading to the S&L scandal and discusses specific banks that played important roles in the event.

DO YOU RECOGNIZE THESE TERMS?

Central States Pension Fund
collusion
contras
money mover
reciprocal relationship
savings and loan scandal

skimming
symbiotic relationship
tax haven
underworld
upperworld

POINTS OF DISCUSSION

1. Explain the significance of organized crime's alliance with politicians and business leaders.

2. List and discuss the specific ways in which politicians can benefit from a partnership with organized crime. In what ways is the reverse true?

3. Identify similarities between organized crime's connection with Presidents Nixon, Kennedy, and Reagan.

4. Discuss the ways in which organized crime has a reciprocal relationship with legitimate business.

5. Discuss Meyer Lansky's contribution to legitimatizing organized crime and how his involvement enables us to better understand organized crime and the corporate and political alliance.

6. In what ways does the savings and loan scandal represent collusion between organized crime and legitimate commerce?

SUGGESTED READING

BAINERMAN, J. (1992). *The Crimes of a President.* New York: SPI Books.

BLOCK, A. (1991). *Masters of Paradise: Organized Crime and the Internal Revenue Service in the Bahamas.* New Brunswick, NJ: Transaction. This narrative describes and analyzes the use of the Bahamas by white-collar criminals from the United States for tax evasion, money laundering, and other financial crimes from the mid-1950s to 1980, as well as the efforts of the U.S. Internal Revenue Service to address this criminal activity.

BRILL, S. (1978). *The Teamster.* New York: Simon & Schuster.

GARDINER, J. (1970). *The Politics of Corruption: Organized Crime in an American City.* New York: Russell Sage Foundation. This research examines the conditions that made it possible for a local syndicate to take over an eastern industrial city, called "Wincanton," and control it off and on for 40 years.

LACEY, R. (1991). *Little Man: Meyer Lansky and the Gangster Life.* Boston: Little, Brown.

SCOTT, P. D., and J. MARSHALL. (1991). *Cocaine Politics: Drugs, Armies, and the CIA in Central America.* Berkeley: University of California Press. This book presents an analytic perspective on the facts of the Central American drug connection and information to fill the significant gaps left by the Kerry report of the Senate Subcommittee on Terrorism, Narcotics, and International Operations.

SIMON, D., and D. EITZEN. (1986). *Elite Deviance.* Boston: Allyn and Bacon. This book describes wrongdoing—criminal, moral, ethical—by wealthy and powerful individuals in corporate and governmental organizations. It expresses concern for a lack of social scientific knowledge of high-level deviance and suggests social and economic solutions.

CONTROLLING
ORGANIZED CRIME

This chapter will enable you to:

- Understand the role of the police in organized crime investigations
- Contrast the various police methods used in organized crime investigations
- Learn about various legal initiatives used to combat organized crime

- Understand how society can improve its approach to the organized crime problem
- Consider policy options for controlling organized crime at the business and political levels

INTRODUCTION

Thus far this book has examined the numerous rackets of organized crime, both legal and illegal. It has also tried to identify the synergistic relationship between many of these rackets and the role they play in the survival of the organized crime organization. This relationship is important to understand. An example is that labor racketeering and extortion are often concurrent types of criminal behavior for many organized crime groups. Drug trafficking and money laundering also produce a synergistic effect; one tends to add sustenance to the other. The many different groups and criminal rackets employed clearly indicate that national crime policy must attempt realistically to control such activity. However, because of the complexity of the problem and scarcity of resources, easy solutions are not available. This chapter considers some of the more important variables in controlling organized crime, as well as the debate on public policy relating to organized crime. The discussion in this chapter begins by considering the role of the police in fighting organized crime. It then reviews legal initiatives for controlling organized crime and their ability to do so effectively. Finally, it discusses some of the most important areas in which organized crime policy can be both clarified and improved.

THE POLICE RESPONSE

When citizens learn of local crime incidents from news media accounts, one of the first community resources the citizens look to for assistance is the police. They ask the same questions: What are the police doing to control crime? Do they have sufficient resources to do so? How can the police make the community safer without overextending their authority and sacrificing personal freedoms? Although it could be argued that perhaps too much reliance is placed on police agencies and the criminal justice system to deal with major crime issues such as organized crime, it is human nature for citizens to seek answers from them initially, not from social services.

The role of police in a democratic society is deliberately structured in a fragmented, decompartmentalized manner. This prevents the development of a police state operating under one national police system, which occurs in many countries. Safeguarding against the threat of a police state involves the willingness of those living in a democracy to accept some compromises. For example, restriction of the power and authority of police agencies limits their ability to investigate crime.

Criminal lawyers and some criminals themselves are keenly aware of legal limitations placed on the police by the Constitution, federal and state laws, and the operating procedures associated with every law enforcement agency. Such limitations exist to help ensure that the police recognize the rights and privileges guaranteed to citizens by a democratic system. So a dichotomy exists concerning the social benefits of granting the police additional authority to investigate organized crime and the threat of infringing on everyone's constitutional rights.

Law enforcement agencies operate at municipal, county, state, and federal levels of government, each serving a distinct purpose. Accordingly, powers enjoyed by police agencies at each level vary according to the laws in each jurisdiction. For example, municipal police officers generally have the power to obtain and serve search warrants, while in some states highway patrol agencies do not have these powers. Most federal law enforcement agencies, on the other hand, are vested with this authority.

Police Jurisdiction

It is often the **jurisdiction** of a police agency that determines the extent of police authority. This becomes an important factor in examining the problem of organized crime. The word *jurisdiction* refers to both the geographical area designated as part of a police agency's territory and the types of crimes that the agency has authority over.

One example is the authority vested in municipal (city) police officers, which is generally quite broad in nature. However, if investigative leads in a criminal case require a police officer to go out of town for an interview, for instance, the officer no longer has the jurisdiction of the home location in the town being visited. To continue investigating the case, arrangements must be made for the officer to work with a police organization in the second jurisdiction. It is also common for more than one police agency to have jurisdiction over a particular type of crime. This is evident in concurrent jurisdiction over drug trafficking at the federal level by the Drug Enforcement Administration (DEA) and the Federal Bureau of Investigation (FBI).

Reputed members of the Luchese crime family are walked out of the 3rd Precinct Police stationhouse in Bay Shore, New York, November 14, 2002. Sixteen alleged members and associates of the Luchese crime family were arrested on charges of racketeering, illegal gambling, loan-sharking and other crimes, capping an investigation of the mob's takeover of a Long Island strip club.

(*AP Photo/Robert Spencer*)

But in the event that agents from both organizations focus on the same drug trafficker, a cooperative agreement is needed so that only one agency continues the investigation or both work together, sharing mutual resources. When investigating organized crime groups, these working relationships are common.

Suffolk County District Attorney Thomas Spota addresses members of the press behind a display of evidence at his office in Riverhead, New York, November 14, 2002.

Source: (AP Photo/Robert Spencer)

Controlling Police Actions

In a democracy such as the United States, it is important to have a balanced relationship between the government and the people it serves. In most societies, the limits of freedom and proscribed behavior are reflected in laws. Of course, laws governing people in the democracy must not only reflect the values and objectives of the society, but must also be based on rational rules to which the people of the society are able to subscribe and choose to subscribe. Most people would probably agree that something should be done about the growth of organized crime and the enterprises in which it is involved. However, much disagreement exists regarding the best way to approach this challenge.

As a rule, the police are called on to identify organized crime groups and those associated with them and to dismantle these organizations through investigation and arrest, but how much authority should be given to the police to accomplish this task? The following section discusses the delicate balance between personal freedoms and law and order in communities.

The Constitution and the Police

The U.S. Constitution is the most significant foundation of modern policing. One of its essential purposes is to control the government's ability to intervene in the personal matters of its people. The Constitution resulted from a long debate at the Constitutional Convention in Philadelphia in 1787, and today it serves as the final authority in virtually all questions affecting the rights of individuals, the limits of power afforded to police and governmental authorities, and the limits of punishments imposed for violations of the law. Of the many important provisions of the Constitution, Articles I, III, and IV of the ten amendments called the Bill of Rights are most influential in addressing the rights of the accused and those convicted of crimes. Of particular importance in protecting individual rights are the Fourth, Fifth, and Fourteenth Amendments, which include prohibitions against unreasonable searches and seizures, forced self-incrimination, and violations of procedural due process.

The framers of the Constitution were acutely aware that tyrannical governments had often used accusations of crime to rid themselves of political dissidents. They also recognized that in punishing crime the state intervenes to take the life, liberty, or property of its citizens. Hence, respect for the rights of even the most despicable criminals has been a cornerstone of U.S. criminal justice, at least in theory if not always in practice. As a result, when new technology or scientific knowledge is introduced into the service of policing, it is appropriate to inquire about its possible effects on constitutional safeguards.

Undercover Operations

Of the many organized crime initiatives employed over the years, the traditional hallmark has been the use of **undercover agents** in covert operations. Because criminal organizations depend on concealing information about their operations, getting information about these operations is difficult. One successful way to do so is to get the criminals to reveal how they operate by using undercover operations. Although undercover work is considered one of the most dangerous components of any enforcement operation, it provides police with an advantage that would otherwise be unobtainable.

Important Constitutional Amendments Relating to Police Power

Fourth Amendment (Search and Seizure)

- Guarantees against unreasonable search and seizure
- Prohibits arrest without probable cause

Policing issues discussed: search and seizure, search warrants, use of deadly force

Fifth Amendment (self-incrimination)

- Guarantees grand jury indictment
- Protects against double jeopardy
- Gives right to due process
- Provides protection against self-incrimination

Policing issues discussed: charging suspects, questioning and interrogation, double jeopardy

Fourteenth Amendment (due process, not part of the Bill of Rights)

- Applicability of constitutional rights to all citizens regardless of state law or procedures

Search and seizure, self-incrimination, and due process issues are crucial in addressing organized crime. Although it is important to provide police the legal authority to pursue organized crime organizations effectively, citizens must be aware of and cautious about the ramifications of a police system that is too powerful. It has been suggested that, instead of expanding the powers of police agencies, police should focus on the use of existing laws and methods that have been successful in the past. These methods include undercover agents and informants, the prudent application of intelligence operations, and the collection of information on suspected organized crime members and organizations.

Once in place, operatives are able to witness firsthand discussions and decisions made by organized crime figures. These discussions often result in committing crimes with the undercover agent poised for surreptitious observation, a **proactive** advantage not enjoyed by police in most conventional investigations. Although the technique enables direct and covert observation of criminal enterprises, operatives require considerable training in hand to hand combat, firearms, understanding of intricate legal issues such as entrapment and search and seizure, and the use of sophisticated surveillance equipment. Once inside the criminal operation, however, the undercover agent has the ability to do a number of things firsthand:

- Learn the role of persons involved in criminal rackets
- Learn the locations where criminal discussions take place
- Identify resources used by organized crime members

One of the most commonly used techniques for undercover officers is the **buy and bust**. In this procedure, the officer poses as a drug buyer and then, after making a purchase from a dealer, arrests the suspect. This is an economical way to arrest dealers and to save money that would otherwise be spent on drugs—and probably never recouped.

Drawbacks to the buy and bust method are that it is dangerous and that an officer's identity soon becomes known, making it difficult for him or her to continue in an undercover capacity. In addition to noting the danger associated with undercover work, many experts have questioned the ability of agents to successfully infiltrate the higher levels of crime organizations.

Informants   In 1992, Gambino family mob boss John Gotti was sentenced to life by a federal court in New York City. Probably the most important tool used in the prosecution was testimony from underboss-turned-snitch, Salvatore "Sammy the Bull" Gravano. Gravano, who himself pleaded to nineteen murders, is a good example of the role that informants play in the prosecution of high-level organized crime cases. Gravano was supposed to stand trial along with Gotti, but struck a deal with prosecutors. In return for a twenty-year sentence, which he is currently serving in a high-security cell-block, Gravano agreed to testify in Gotti's trial (and almost ten others since). Thus, he became one of the highest-ranking mafiosi ever to turn state's evidence since mob soldier Joe Valachi turned on his Genovese family boss in 1963 (Lacayo 1992).

An **informant** can be defined as anyone who provides information about a criminal case, but who is not a complainant, witness, or victim. Informants can be either concerned citizens or ruthless criminals, but in many cases they are seeking some benefit for their testimony, as in the case of Salvatore Gravano. The use of informants who are attempting to plea bargain, that is, have charges dropped or receive a lighter sentence, creates the most controversy regarding the use of informants.

In the absence of an undercover police officer, informants are typically used for infiltration; they will be more readily accepted by the criminal group being investigated than police officers posing as criminals. Undercover agents can also attempt to purchase drugs directly from members of the criminal organization either with or without the use of an informant. In either case,

Sammy "The Bull" Gravano was the underboss of New York's Gambino family and testified against his boss, John Gotti.

use of informants usually results in criminal charges being filed against the seller in addition to the likelihood of a search warrant being issued and served at locations where drugs are believed to be stored. Most police organizations employ informants, in one fashion or another, to solve cases. In 1992, the Bureau of Justice Statistics reported that the FBI has more than 3,500 informants, of which an estimated 1,700 report directly on drug matters (Bureau of Justice Statistics 1992). The number and type of informants largely depend on the mission of the particular law enforcement organization and budgetary considerations.

Management of informants has inherent problems. Many informants have a drifting allegiance, agreeing to work with the police on one day and, for whatever reason, changing their minds and returning to their criminal aliases the next—sometimes unbeknown to their law enforcement control agent. This places a law enforcement officer in considerable danger. Another problem in informant management is getting too close to criminal sources. The management of a criminal informant requires a working relationship that can sometimes get too close. For example, in September 2002, former FBI agent John Connolly was sentenced to more than 10 years in prison for tipping off two mobsters that were about to be indicted (Lavoie 2002). The jury in this case found that Connolly had simply gotten too close to his informers and went too far to protect them.

Although virtually anyone can be a police informant, persons arrested for vice crimes are usually the best candidates. Once arrested, prosecutors might give them a chance to plea bargain. This time-tested technique gives prosecutors an excellent tool to convict a bigger fish and make inroads toward dismantling the organization. This technique was used effectively in the conviction of mob boss John Gotti: His alleged underboss Salvatore "Sammy the Bull" Gravano was the prosecution's key witness.

One of the most comprehensive and compelling research analyses of undercover police operations was conducted by Marx (1988), who points to a number of what he calls paradoxes, ironies, and trade-offs associated with undercover work. Specifically, he argues that undercover police operations are based on deceit, trickery, and lies. Additionally, many undercover operations, particularly those involving drugs, involve the police actually facilitating or unintentionally increasing crime in an effort to reduce it.

Reviewing the research literature leads Marx (1988) to conclude that undercover operations frequently lead to role reversals, with police involved in criminal activity and criminals acting as police. His ultimate evaluation of undercover tactics is that they are probably a necessary evil, but should be utilized only as a last resort and should be subjected to stringent controls and oversight. Initiating these controls becomes even more important as powerful new surveillance technologies become available to police agencies.

INTELLIGENCE OPERATIONS

Because organized crime is a covert criminal activity, police often have a difficult time learning the identity of participants and the exact extent of the criminal enterprises. To this end, it is important for law enforcement to gather information on suspected members of organized crime for purposes of investigation. However, the process of intelligence collection is also a covert activity and is one of the least understood activities of the police function.

The collection of criminal **intelligence** can be traced to the military. For decades, armies of all nations have routinely collected information on the location of enemy troops and the number of opposing forces, weapons, and so on. As technology has developed, so has the science of intelligence gathering. Compared to military intelligence, criminal intelligence gathering is a fairly recent development. Although critics charge that intelligence gathering is reminiscent of Hitler's SS (secret police), they believe that if conducted properly it can be one of the most effective resources in the fight against organized crime. Practically, intelligence gathering is something most of us do on a day to day basis; that is, we learn specifics about people, organizations, and procedures in which we have a personal interest. Accordingly, the police often learn of people who are supposedly involved in criminal conduct, but sufficient evidence is not available to arrest them. As a result, temporary intelligence files are assembled for this purpose and, based on the information in these files, officers can attempt to verify allegations of criminal conduct. If officers are successful in documenting a person's criminal involvement, the intelligence operation can become a criminal investigation.

Intelligence Versus Criminal Investigations

Several important distinctions exist between intelligence and criminal investigations. First, criminal investigations are reactive in nature, whereas the intelligence investigation is proactive. Collection of information on specific persons, places, groups, and businesses is an ongoing activity.

Second, criminal investigation case files are open, and information is developed with the goal of eventually convicting persons in a criminal trial. Intelligence files, on the other hand, are closed files; that is, they contain information on ongoing criminal activity, but not all of the information can be validated as factual. Because of this distinction, police maintain intelligence files separately from criminal investigation files, and access to intelligence files is strictly limited to persons who have a need to know.

Another distinction between the two types of investigations is that the result of a criminal investigation is arrest (or case closure), but a successful intelligence operation does not necessarily result in an arrest, but in a report of activity. This report is often accompanied by charts, graphs, computer listings, and other data to support the information contained in the report.

Intelligence Agencies

Combating groups involved in drug trafficking requires much exchanging of information. To that end, the Drug Enforcement Agency's El Paso Intelligence Center (EPIC) has proved to be of considerable value. This system enables federal, state, and local law enforcement agencies to catalog and share information on suspected drug traffickers and their drugs, weapons, and equipment. Other federal intelligence systems include the Narcotics and Dangerous Drug Information System (NADDIS), which tracks drug investigations, and the Regional Drug Intelligence Squads (RDIS), which are used to profile the major organizations involved in drug trafficking to establish joint investigations with federal and local police.

The Regional Information Sharing System (RISS) program is an innovative, federally funded program created to support law enforcement efforts and to combat organized crime activity, drug trafficking, and white-collar crime.

The RISS project began with funding by the Law Enforcement Assistance Administration. Since its inception in 1980, the primary impetus of RISS projects has been to provide law enforcement agencies with intelligence information on criminal activities in their jurisdictions. It also provides services to member agencies regarding assistance in asset seizures, funds for covert operations, analysis of investigative data on organized criminals, loans to purchase investigative equipment, and training in the use of such equipment in criminal investigations. The RISS program operates within seven RISS projects throughout the United States.

Although agencies such as the FBI and the DEA routinely perform intelligence operations, the Financial Crimes Enforcement Network (FinCEN) was established to share information housed under the Department of Treasury. Established in 1990, FinCEN is a multiagency support unit that analyzes intelligence information that helps identify suspects in money-laundering schemes. FinCEN offers services to federal agencies and state and local police organizations investigating financial crimes, especially those associated with violations of the Bank Secrecy Act of 1970.

It could be argued that following the money trail rather than the perpetrator should be the impetus of effective organized crime investigations, because one often leads police to the other. By tracing the path taken by illicit profits, police can obtain valuable information on cash deposits, property transactions, fund purchases, real estate ownership, and foreign currency transfers. The point where illicit wealth accumulates is the point closest to the most powerful underworld operators. Law enforcement should invest more heavily in intelligence operations directed at offshore financial institutions.

Improving Intelligence Investigations

Obtaining useful intelligence on organized crime is admittedly difficult, but law enforcement agencies can vastly improve their understanding of organized crime by focusing on the development of an accurate picture of organized crime industries. Intelligence operations should use the processes of distribution, supply, manufacturing, and financing, regardless of who is involved or whether they reside in the under- or upperworlds. This approach would cause intelligence efforts to be less concerned with forcing data into predetermined organizational charts reflecting preconceived notions of corporate bureaucracies. Analysts should be more concerned with assessing the market, production, and the social conditions that shape the patterns of organized criminals' interactions.

In addition, intelligence-gathering operations must be separated from those designed to make arrests and obtain convictions. Intelligence gathering, when done correctly, is unlikely to result in quick arrests and certain convictions. Agencies under pressure to show results calculated by numbers of arrests might tend to choose the easiest cases and arrest the most obvious and usually the least important criminal operatives, thereby inflating their statistics, but contributing little information about organized crime. Intelligence gathering must be recognized as important on its own merits, and success must be measured by the quality of data produced, not prosecutors' batting averages. The reactive intelligence strategies now commonly employed must be replaced by proactive intelligence operations sensitive to shifts in law, enforcement patterns, technology, markets, and social trends.

Law enforcement agencies have become committed to the traditional tactics of fighting organized crime. Extensive electronic surveillance of top gang leaders has produced reams of irrelevant data about the intimate details of such things as old Italians' exasperation with young Italians (McFadden 1987), but has yielded relatively little useful intelligence. Using plea bargains and granting immunity can be useful in obtaining convictions, but such testimony is often not corroborated and therefore is of questionable validity from an intelligence viewpoint. The well-worn federal practice of selecting a Joe Valachi or a Jimmy "the Weasel" Fratianno as a prime informant and then massaging and refining his testimony and replaying it in case after case not only produces a series of self-fulfilling prophecies, but also violates the concept of justice. In fact, precisely this kind of federally sponsored orchestration swayed the juries in the cases cited earlier to acquit crime figures such as John Gotti and "Little Nicky" Scarfo.

Rather than pursuing the lower echelons of organized crime, it makes a great deal of sense to target legitimate institutions that often enable underworld figures to amass and use their great wealth. Organized criminals such as Meyer Lansky and Moe Dalitz could never have accumulated their vast sums of money and then recirculated them as venture capital throughout the underworld without the cooperation of banks, corporate executives, and, on occasion, the government itself. Targeting the upperworld gatekeepers to underworld wealth requires a complete reassessment of law enforcement priorities. At a minimum, the enforcement arms of regulatory agencies should receive considerably more resources than they do at present. Just like closing down opportunities for corruption, closing down legitimate business partners of the underworld will do more damage to organized crime than will jailing a thousand "Little Nicky" Scarfos.

Legal Initiatives against Organized Crime

In 1965, President Lyndon B. Johnson opened a new offensive against organized crime by establishing the President's Commission on Law Enforcement and the Administration of Justice. Headed by Attorney General Nicholas Katzenbach, the commission analyzed the federal failure to cope with organized crime, and in its 1967 final report offered more than 200 suggestions for combating crime. These recommendations prompted two major pieces of legislation. The Crime Control and Safe Streets Act of 1968 made it easier to gather evidence about organized crime enterprises by authorizing court-ordered electronic surveillance at both federal and state levels. Two years later, in 1970, President Richard Nixon signed into law the Organized Crime Control Act, which granted greater powers to grand juries, permitted the detention of unmanageable witnesses, and authorized the attorney general to protect cooperative federal and state witnesses and their families.

In the 1980s, much of crime control legislation focused on the illicit drug trade. The Crime Control Act of 1984 expanded the authority of criminal and civil asset forfeiture laws and implemented a federally determined sentencing system for convicted offenders. Two years later the 1986 Anti-Drug Abuse Act established mandatory prison sentences for large-scale distribution of marijuana and imposed strict sentences for money-laundering activities. Among other things, it added designer drugs to the list of controlled substances.

The 1986 Money Laundering Control Act has been especially useful in combating organized crime. It made it unlawful to engage in a number of financial transactions intended to accomplish the following:

The 1986 Money-Laundering Control Act

- Further criminal acts such as drug trafficking
- Conceal funds associated with these activities
- Avoid currency-reporting requirements of the 1970 Bank Secrecy Act

Investigations of organized crime organizations have revealed that many transactions, especially those involving drugs, are in cash. Criminals try to convert this cash into a number of different financial instruments designed both to hide its true ownership and to conceal it from seizure by police. Members of organized crime's criminal group and people associated with the criminal unit, such as attorneys, stockbrokers, accountants, bankers, and real estate brokers—virtually anyone who knowingly launders the proceeds of illegal activity—are subject to prosecution under this law. An estimated fifteen states have versions of money-laundering statutes similar to federal ones that require financial institutions to report all cash transactions over $10,000.

Because the drug trade represents such a large part of organized crime's illegal rackets, in 1988 the Chemical and Diversion and Trafficking Act was passed to control substances known as precursor chemicals. These chemicals are the much-needed solvents and compounds required for manufacturing many different types of drugs, such as cocaine, methamphetamine, and PCP. The law requires detailed reporting and record keeping of transactions involving regulated chemicals. Purchases that exceed a specific quantity or those that are otherwise suspicious must be reported to the DEA. As with the federal money-laundering law, thirty-seven states also elected to regulate chemicals under state law. Many of these states' penalties are similar to those under federal law (National Institute of Justice 1993). In some cases, states require companies that supply chemicals to be registered with a regulating state agency.

The 1988 Chemical and Diversion and Trafficking Act

An especially important tool in the law enforcement arsenal against crime is the federal USA Patriot Act of 2001, largely enacted as a legislative response to terrorism. The act essentially increases the investigatory authority of federal, state, and local police agencies. The expanded police powers created under the legislation are not limited to investigations of terrorist activity, but also apply to many different criminal offenses. The provisions of the Patriot Act of 2001 are presented in Appendix A. The law was enacted in response to the terrorist events of September 11, 2001, to give police and prosecutors greater power to combat terrorism.

The USA Patriot Act of 2001

One icon in organized crime investigations is the ability of government agents to prosecute high-level figures on tax evasion charges. One of the first such cases was the successful prosecution of Al Capone near the end of Prohibition. Money proved to have criminal origins can be used by government investigators to show that organized crime participants have not paid taxes on that income and are therefore answerable to criminal penalties. The acts for which this procedure can be applied include filing a false income tax return,

The Internal Revenue Code

failing to keep required records, hiding assets with the intent to defraud, and assisting others in evading income taxes.

As a rule, agents from the Criminal Investigation Division of the Internal Revenue Service pursue violations of tax laws. Once evidence is secured, prosecutions take place through the U.S. Attorney's office. The most common method of detecting offenders is a technique known as the **net worth theory**. Under this theory, investigators estimate a target's net worth at the beginning of the tax period. Then, at the end of the period, the original figure is deducted from its current net worth, and if the taxpayer has a net gain, he or she is subject to prosecution. In effect, the Internal Revenue Service reconstructs a person's total expenditures by examining his or her standard of living and comparing it with reported income (Abadinsky 1990). Prosecutors can then claim that the taxpayer failed to report his or her entire income. Interestingly, the government is not required to show the source of the person's extra income.

ELECTRONIC SURVEILLANCE

Since its passage in 1968, the federal **electronic surveillance** or wiretap statute has proved to be a valuable investigative tool in the fight against organized crime. The purpose of the electronic surveillance law [18 U.S.C. S 2516(2)] is to establish standards for both federal and state levels that govern interceptions and hold prosecutors accountable for their actions in court-ordered eavesdropping. The federal law, also known as Title III, allows for ex parte or third-party surveillance of persons suspected of some crimes. As of 1986, twenty-nine states had enacted laws authorizing electronic surveillance under state statutes. Examples are the states of California and Illinois, whose laws require a warrant for virtually any type of electronic monitoring, including pen registers and one-party consensual monitoring, for which state law is more restrictive than federal law. In these states, federal agencies can use the federal law, but local officers have no authority to conduct ex parte monitoring of conversations, which greatly inhibits success in the prosecutions of organized crime figures.

Many law enforcement agencies find lawful authorization of electronic surveillance too expensive to pursue; it is a high-cost method of investigation. Such costs are attributed to (1) the assignment of personnel to supervise the command post and conduct surveillance assignments (which usually pulls officers away from their regular assignments); (2) extensive overtime because most wires are staffed on a 24-hour basis; (3) the acquisition of expensive and highly technical equipment, such as pen registers, tape recorders, and radios with scramblers; (4) training for the use of the equipment; and (5) overtime for secretaries who must type numerous surveillance reports and transcribe recorded conversations.

Although electronic surveillance statutes generally address the use of third-party telephone interceptions, many state laws also allow the use of other electronic surveillance devices, such as concealed body transmitters worn by undercover agents or their informers. The federal Title III, for example, authorizes the warrantless use of a hidden transmitter by undercover agents for one-party consensual monitoring, but many states view the practice as unduly intrusive and require officers to obtain a court order for this purpose.

In virtually all aspects of organized crime, including bookmaking, drug trafficking, and prostitution, money changes hands and huge profits are made. By tracing this money and eventually seizing it, police hope to quash the trade in illicit goods and services. Without their illicit proceeds, organized crime organizations will presumably lose their profits and the cash and assets necessary to run their criminal rackets.

Asset forfeiture is defined as the loss of ownership of property derived from or used in criminal activities. The two types of forfeiture are civil and criminal.

1. **Civil forfeiture** is a legal proceeding against a specific type of property believed to be used in a criminal activity. Although the law is used frequently today to combat organized crime, it is nothing new. Forfeiture was originally authorized by the first Congress to seize vessels suspected of smuggling contraband into the country. Property subject to forfeiture can be virtually anything from vehicles to equipment to cash proceeds of an illegal enterprise. Procedurally, the government is required to post a notice of the forfeiture proceedings and notify registered owners of the property so that any person having an interest in the property can challenge the forfeiture. As a rule, if no one claims the forfeiture, the property is forfeited administratively. One interesting aspect of civil forfeiture is that, even if someone protests the forfeiture, no criminal conviction is required in order for government prosecutors to forfeit the property successfully. The following sections discuss civil forfeiture in more detail.

2. **Criminal forfeiture** was first authorized in 1970 and is part of the criminal action taken against a defendant accused of racketeering, money laundering, or drug trafficking, all occupational staples of organized crime. This type of forfeiture depends on the conviction of the defendant, at which time he or she must forfeit various property rights and interests relating to the offense.

Forfeiture programs use recent changes in federal law that allow police to confiscate the material rewards derived from organized crime activities and reduce their ability to continue in illegal enterprises. One recent case addressing the use of forfeiture laws is the March 1996 decision (*Tina B. Bennis* v. *Michigan*) by the U.S. Supreme Court that upheld the right of police to seize an automobile used by a man who was having sex with a prostitute in the vehicle. The court's 5 to 4 vote upheld the seizure, even though the man's wife was co-owner and had no idea how the vehicle was being used.

The newer civil statutes have the advantage of being relatively easy to enforce. Civil forfeiture requires proof by a preponderance of the evidence, rather than beyond a reasonable doubt, as in criminal prosecution. In civil proceedings based on federal statutes, there is no need to trace the proceeds in question to a specific criminal transaction, such as a narcotics transaction. Instead, it is sufficient to link the suspects to drug dealing in general.

The popularity of asset forfeiture was spurred initially by the enactment of Racketeer Influenced and Corrupt Organizations Act and Continuing

Criminal Enterprise (CCE) statutes in 1970, and these laws allow government agents to try to take the profits out of criminal enterprises. Although federal officers have been using this technique for years, state and local officials have more slowly realized the impact of such laws on criminals. As a result, many local and state police agencies have focused their forfeiture efforts solely on the seizure of cash and cars. However, those agencies who have learned the advantages of the forfeiture laws understand that benefits are worthy of consideration.

The federal government has been slow in recognizing the importance of forfeitures until just the last couple decades. For example, in 1983, more than $100 million in cash and property was seized and forfeited to the government by convicted criminals. The 1989 figures for forfeitures are more than double that of 1983 (Bureau of Justice Statistics 1992).

Advantages of Civil Forfeiture

Of the two types of forfeiture, civil forfeiture has the broadest power against organized crime. The 1984 Federal Comprehensive Forfeiture Act increased the government's ability to seize property of suspected drug traffickers under federal law. Although tracing an asset to a criminal endeavor can be difficult, the fact that it is a civil process makes the task much easier for government agents. As noted previously, the most obvious reason for this is that civil forfeiture laws have a lower burden of proof, a preponderance of the evidence, than that required in criminal cases, which is proof beyond a reasonable doubt. It is not essential for law enforcement officers to show absolute certainty in connecting assets with criminal activity. They need only show that the evidence suggests that a particular asset was acquired by or used in conjunction with a specific criminal activity. Moreover, if criminal prosecution was precluded by a poorly conducted investigation (e.g., where important evidence was thrown out under the exclusionary rule), civil forfeiture is still possible.

Another advantage of civil forfeiture is that prosecutors may resort to the discovery process to obtain information otherwise not available to them. In doing so, the claimant may be deposed and compelled to disclose his or her records. For the reluctant witness, perjury and contempt sanctions are available.

Forfeiture of Attorney's Fees

On March 6, 1996, famed defense attorney F. Lee Bailey was sent to prison for failing to hand over millions of dollars to the federal government. At issue was $25 million in stock Bailey acquired from a drug dealer he once defended. While the government claimed that Bailey reneged on a verbal agreement to return the stock to the government, he contended that the money was his legal fee for representing Claude Duboc, a hashish and marijuana trafficker whose business earned an estimated $165 million annually. This case exemplifies how new legal tools allow government agents the ability to seize cash earned through illicit enterprises but used as legal fees.

Because of the cash nature of most illicit criminal enterprises, government agents have recognized that some lawyers have benefited from cash payments from their criminal clients. In a criminal case, these payments are subject to forfeiture if they are paid with illegal drug money or acquired through illegal means. Two important U.S. Supreme Court decisions, *United States* v. *Monsanto* (1989) and the Caplin & Drysdale case (1989) set precedent in this area. In the latter case, the law firm Caplin & Drysdale represented Chris Reckmeyer, who was eventually convicted of operating a

Facts on Forfeiture

What is civil forfeiture?

Federal and state forfeiture laws empower governments to take property without charging a crime. Legally, the property is accused of a crime, not the owner.

What property can the government seize?

Property can be seized if police believe it was:

1. Bought with profits of illegal activity, or
2. Used to facilitate a crime; for example, a home where drugs were sold. The courts define *facilitate* broadly. In one case, two phone calls cost a man his home because the home facilitated a drug deal.

How much evidence does the government need to seize property?

Probable cause, the same standard required for a search warrant or arrest. Police seize millions of dollars in cash each year because police dogs indicate that money smells like drugs, even when no drugs are found and no arrests made. To show probable cause, police can use hearsay evidence, such as a tip from an informant whose name is not revealed. Hearsay is not allowed in criminal trials, in which a defendant has a right to question his accuser.

Can property seized be reclaimed?

A person can file a request with the law enforcement agency that seized the property to return it. It is seldom approved. Usually, a person must file a lawsuit to have the property returned. The government files suit in cases involving real estate or assets worth more than $500,000. At trial, the burden of proof is on the owner, not the government. The owner must prove that the property is innocent by a preponderance of the evidence, a higher standard than the probable cause standard used to seize the property.

Who gets the seized assets?

Law enforcement keeps these assets.

What if a person is found innocent in a criminal trial?

This is irrelevant to the forfeiture case, during which an owner must prove the money or property was legally obtained.

How do civil and criminal cases differ?

Important parts of the Bill of Rights do not apply or are severely limited in civil cases. For example, civil defendants have no Sixth Amendment right to an attorney; invoking the Fifth Amendment right against self-incrimination can be used against the person. The ban on cruel and unusual punishment and excessive fines generally do not apply. Forfeitures do not have to fit the crime: An estate could be seized if a small amount of drugs was sold on the property.

What can be seized?

In addition to many state laws addressing forfeiture of assets, the Comprehensive Forfeiture Act enables officers to seize automobiles, aircraft, vessels, bank accounts, securities, real estate holdings, and privately owned businesses. In addition, the act enhances penalty provisions of the 1970 Controlled Substances Act to include a twenty-year prison term and/or fines up to $250,000. Basically, the act works in this way: If a drug dealer uses her automobile to drive to a location to sell a quantity of drugs, her car then becomes the conveyance that the dealer uses to facilitate the crime. The car is therefore seizable under law. Along the same lines, if investigators can show that an automobile was purchased with drug money, it is also seizable under the law (Lyman and Potter 1991).

Federal law also contains a sharing provision whereby an *equitable* transfer of the property can be facilitated. This provision divides property and distributes it among participating law enforcement agencies. Subsequent to the seizure, a determination is made to assess the degree of involvement of each participating agency, and a proportionate distribution of the assets is then made among the agencies.

As a loyal citizen of the United States and a supporter of the Constitution, you are dismayed by the efforts of drug traffickers to contravene U.S. laws. Recently, you have learned that managers of your New York investment bank have been indicted for money laundering. Thus, you are faced with a dilemma: Your mutual funds have increased in value, yet you are concerned about the allegations against your bank. What should your attitude be? Should you close your investment portfolio? Are rumors of wrongdoing sufficient to warrant action on your part?

multimillion-dollar marijuana operation and sentenced to seventeen years in prison. United States attorneys were able to show that Reckmeyer paid his legal fees with the proceeds from his drug operation. The funds were secured under federal forfeiture laws. In a landmark decision, the Supreme Court supported the seizure in claiming that, while a defendant has a right to legal representation, he or she has no right to hire a lawyer with drug money. Through this decision, the Court held that the government not only has the ability to forfeit drug assets needed to pay attorney's fees, but also that such forfeitures are neither unethical or unconstitutional.

THE RICO STATUTE

For decades, prosecution of organized crime figures was based on specific criminal acts that were defined under various state and federal statutes. The problem with this strategy is that kingpins and bosses typically employ lower-level members to carry out the majority of crimes, leaving the management insulated from detection and prosecution. So the easily replaced, lower-level pawns in organized groups would go to prison while their superiors would remain free to manage the group's criminal endeavors. The Racketeer Influenced and Corrupt Organizations Act (**RICO**) **statute** changed that by enabling prosecutors to arrest and convict upper-level players in criminal organizations based on the activities of those working for them.

In 1970, Congress passed the Organized Crime Control Act, designed to give law enforcement organizations a more effective way to pursue managers of crime organizations. The act's most effective measure is Title IX, known as the Racketeer Influenced and Corrupt Organizations Act (RICO), which defines thirty-two *predicate offenses* as racketeering activities and makes it a crime to use profits from these activities to establish, acquire, or operate a legitimate business involved in interstate or foreign commerce. Under RICO, violations can be punished by up to a $20,000 fine and twenty years in prison, in addition to the forfeiture of any assets derived from the activity. Borrowing from federal antitrust law, RICO also includes a civil section. This section allows anyone "injured in his business or property" by racketeering activity to sue the persons responsible and recover triple damages plus a "reasonable attorney's fee."

Prosecutors were slow in using the RICO statute, probably due to their misunderstanding of its use. Gradually, FBI agents in the mid-1970s began to convince U.S. attorneys to be more willing to use this powerful tool against organized crime. Federal prosecutors were also persuaded by U.S. Supreme Court decisions that endorsed prosecutions against strictly illegitimate enterprises, such as organized crime groups, and upheld broad application of RICO's forfeiture provisions. These two rulings set the stage for RICO to become the prosecutor's tool of choice to combat organized crime. RICO's power lies in its creation of new categories of racketeering offenses, which are defined as two or more acts within a ten-year period. RICO's predicate offenses include the following:

White slavery	Hobbs Act violations
Kidnapping	Counterfeiting
Drug trafficking	Wire fraud
Sports bribery	Bankruptcy fraud
Arson	Contraband cigarettes
Extortion	Embezzlement of union funds
Obstruction of justice	

As with forfeiture and conspiracy laws and drug statutes, many states have elected to adopt their own versions of RICO. State versions of RICO give state prosecutors more flexibility in pursuing organized crime prosecutions on a state level.

RICO was designed to attack large-scale organized crime activity through both criminal action and civil lawsuits. The act (18 U.S.C. 1962) has four basic categories:

RICO Basics

1. 1962(a): It is unlawful for any person receiving income, directly or indirectly, from a pattern of racketeering activity to invest the income or proceeds of the income in acquiring an interest in or the establishment or operation of any enterprise whose activities affect interstate or foreign commerce.

2. 1962(b): It is unlawful for any person to acquire or maintain control of any enterprise whose activities affect interstate or foreign commerce by means of a pattern of racketeering activity.

3. 1962(c): It is unlawful for any person employed by or associated with any enterprise whose activities affect interstate or foreign commerce to conduct or participate, directly or indirectly, in the conduct of the affairs of the enterprise through a pattern of racketeering.

4. 1962(d): It is unlawful for any person to conspire to violate the provisions of sections (a), (b), or (c).

The terms *person*, *enterprise*, and *racketeering activity* are the most important concepts in RICO.

- *Person*. Under the statute, a person is any individual or entity capable of holding a legal or beneficial interest in property. The term refers to those accused of either criminal or civil RICO violations.
- *Enterprise*. This term includes individuals, partnerships, corporations, associations, and other legal entities, as well as any labor union or group of individuals associated in fact, that might not be considered a legal entity. Under the law, all the RICO violations require the showing of interaction between persons involved and the activities of the enterprise.

- *Racketeering activity*. The act designates a number of federal and state violations (known as predicate acts) as racketeering activity (see the preceding list).

A pattern of racketeering activity is central to successful prosecution under RICO because it indicates long-term criminal activity. To show such a pattern, the prosecutor must show at least two acts of racketeering activity by the culpable person within ten years of each other. The racketeering acts do not have to be the same type of violation, and the most recent criminal act must be within the five-year statute of limitations for criminal prosecution.

Another unique feature of the law is that it contains both civil and criminal penalties. Criminal convictions under RICO can result in twenty years in prison and a $25,000 fine; under civil provisions a defendant may be forced to forfeit any money or property acquired with illicit money or used to illegally earn money.

Disadvantages of RICO

Upon its enactment, the White House hailed the RICO statute as a fulfillment of President Nixon's campaign promise to restore the nation to law and order, but critics saw it as a threat to the rights of individuals, cautioning that safeguards were necessary to ensure that the new legal weapons would be used only to fight organized crime. Abadinsky (1994) points out four basic problems with RICO:

1. It is overreaching, leading to the prosecution of persons who, although they may have been involved in criminal behavior, are not by any stretch of the imagination connected to organized crime.
2. Invoking RICO can result in freezing assets before a trial begins, which can effectively put a company out of business. The threat of freezing assets can induce corporate defendants to plead guilty even when they believe themselves to be innocent.
3. A RICO action brings with it the stigma of being labeled a racketeer, which may be inappropriate given the circumstances at issue.
4. RICO permits lawsuits for treble damages when ordinary business transactions, not organized crime or racketeering, are at issue.

One of the most problematic aspects of the RICO statute is that it fails to provide operational definitions of the terms *organized crime* and *racketeering*.

Advantages of RICO

The ambiguities, along with the stiff penalties under RICO, have made it an appealing investigative and prosecutorial tool. Many aspects of RICO make it attractive to prosecutors who target organized crime enterprises. A number of aspects of the law contain more powerful provisions than most laws. For instance, the twenty-year sentence authorized under RICO is longer than sentences in most predicate offenses. RICO's forfeiture provisions open a new arena of punishment for criminals and, in combination with the long sentence, thus give prosecutors effective leverage in the plea bargaining process. Finally, the broad definition of enterprise gives the trial prosecutor freedom to present a more complete picture of a defendant's criminal activities and helps convince judges to allow trials with multiple defendants. Many prosecutors see RICO as their strongest legal tool in fighting organized crime.

THE CONTINUING CRIMINAL ENTERPRISE STATUTE

The federal Continuing Criminal Enterprise (CCE) statute (21 U.S.C. 848) was enacted as part of the Comprehensive Drug Abuse Prevention and Control Act of 1970 and is another strong statutory weapon against organized crime. Like RICO, this statute gives prosecutors the means to reach the organizers, managers, and supervisors of major crime organizations. Prosecution under this statute requires proof of five elements to sustain prosecution:

1. The defendant's conduct must constitute a felony violation of federal narcotics laws.
2. That conduct must take place as part of a continuing series of violations.
3. The defendant must undertake this activity in concert with at least five other people.
4. The defendant must act as the organizer, manager, or supervisor of this criminal enterprise.
5. The defendant must obtain income or resources from this enterprise.

In addition to its utility in prosecuting managers of crime organizations, the CCE provides for some of the most severe criminal penalties for criminal enterprises, which include imprisonment for a minimum of ten years with no possibility of parole. In addition, the court may impose a life sentence with no provision for parole and fines totaling $100,000. Moreover, under CCE, all profits and assets that afforded the defendant a source of influence over the illegal enterprise are subject to forfeiture.

CONSPIRACY LAWS

The use of conspiracy charges in drug enforcement has proved to be one of the most successful tactics used in the last decade. Although conspiracies have existed for quite some time, the use of laws regarding them by federal, state, and local authorities has now become common. Although state law in this area differs from one jurisdiction to another, the basic conspiracy principles are the same. **Conspiracy** is defined as an agreement between two or more persons who have the specific intent either to commit a crime or to engage in dishonest, fraudulent, or immoral conduct injurious to public health or morals. In studying this definition, the applications of such a law in the area of drug control are obvious.

Organized crime involves criminal rackets (crimes), which usually require more than one player (e.g., a grower sells drugs to a manufacturer, who contracts a smuggler for transportation). The smuggler then transports the drugs to a wholesale buyer, who in turn sells them to a retail distributor. The retail distributor then sells the drugs to numerous dealers and users on the street. Given the required documentation by investigators, conspiracy charges can be brought against all such players in a drug operation. Because most conspiracy cases involve numerous defendants, a degree of confusion can result. Generally, three types of conspiracy are commonly used to prosecute drug traffickers:

1. *Chain conspiracies.* These occur when a criminal endeavor depends on the participation of each member of the criminal organization. Each member represents a link in the chain, and the success of the criminal goal requires all participants. If one link in the chain is broken (i.e., one member fails to accomplish his or her particular task), the criminal act is incomplete. To prosecute a chain conspiracy successfully, each member must be shown to be aware of the intended goal of the operation.

2. *Wheel conspiracies.* These involve one member of a criminal organization who is the hub or organizer of the criminal plan and members who are the spokes. To qualify as a wheel conspiracy, all members who are spokes must be aware of each other and must agree with each other to achieve a common illegal goal. For this reason, the wheel conspiracy is difficult to prosecute because it is difficult to show a common agreement among the spokes.

3. *Enterprise conspiracies.* A person who has been shown to participate in two or more patterns of racketeering may be prosecuted for enterprise conspiracy. To conspire to commit any of the substantive offenses under RICO is a separate crime. Basically, an enterprise conspiracy requires an agreement to enter into an enterprise by engaging in a pattern of racketeering. The enterprise conspiracy recognizes that in some criminal organizations not all members have one common goal. Therefore, only a member's willingness to join a criminal organization, an enterprise, by committing two or more acts of racketeering must be proved.

THE COMPREHENSIVE DRUG ABUSE PREVENTION AND CONTROL ACT

Earlier we discussed some of the more important laws that were passed to address organized crime activities. However, we now consider another major legal tool that has become the cornerstone of U.S. federal drug control, the 1970 Comprehensive Drug Abuse Prevention and Control Act, Title II of which is also known as the Controlled Substances Act (CSA). This federal measure updated all previously existing drug laws and gave uniformity to federal drug control policy. The CSA has the following four provisions:

1. Mechanisms for reducing the availability of dangerous drugs
2. Procedures for bringing a substance under control
3. Criteria for determining control requirements
4. Obligations incurred by international treaty arrangements

The CSA places all substances that were in some manner regulated under existing federal law into one of five schedules based theoretically on the medical use of the substance, its potential for abuse, and safety or addiction (dependence) liability. In addition to scheduling dangerous drugs, the law imposes nine control mechanisms on the manufacture, purchase, and distribution of controlled substances.

The CSA has proved to be an effective aid in prosecuting organized crime figures because of its broad power to prosecute under both criminal and civil provisions. In addition to being used to pursue members of organized crime organizations, persons acting as associates of organized crime as well as those possessing and using controlled drugs can be prosecuted.

MULTIJURISDICTIONAL TASK FORCES

As a part of the Anti-Drug Abuse Act of 1986 and 1988, federal discretionary grant funds were made available to state and local agencies that wished to expand drug enforcement efforts. A majority of these funds resulted in the creation of approximately 700 **multijurisdictional task forces** that employ an estimated 10,000 officers (National Institute of Justice 1990). These units are special enforcement divisions made up of police personnel from five to seven different law enforcement agencies. Their function is to respond to a number of special drug-trafficking problems within their collective geographical area. The strength of these units is that they can legally cross jurisdictional boundaries. The goal is to disrupt drug trafficking by the arrest, prosecution, and conviction of drug traffickers.

The Organized Crime Drug Enforcement Task Force

In 1984 under the Reagan administration, a federal task force concept, dubbed the Organized Crime Drug Enforcement Task Force (OCDETF), was operationalized. The task force, operating in most major U.S. cities, is charged with targeting major national and international drug-trafficking organizations at the highest levels of importation and wholesale distribution. These task forces are highly organized ongoing initiatives that are housed in U.S. attorneys' offices. The composition of investigators in a particular OCDETF investigation is determined by the initiating agency; for example, in one case the lead could be the FBI and in another, Customs or DEA. Assistant U.S. attorneys become involved early in the investigations to help the initiating law enforcement agency establish electronic surveillance, convene grand juries, administer asset forfeiture, and participate in other activities usually required in complex drug investigations.

Since the inception of the task force concept, the program has had considerable success, with the primary focus being the detection and prosecution of leaders of large criminal organizations who control illicit drug importation and distribution. OCDETF participating agencies include the U.S. attorney's office, DEA, FBI, Customs, ATF, IRS, the U.S. Marshal's Service, and the Coast Guard, as well as state and local police agencies. OCDETF task forces operate in thirteen core cities throughout the United States and, in addition to initiating investigations, they provide financial support for local law enforcement.

Particularly important to the success of the OCDETF program is the sustained use of the investigative grand jury, which prosecutors employ in more than 60 percent of all task force cases (Lyman and Potter 1991). Investigators use undercover techniques extensively in developing cases that subsequently result in indictments. This technique is particularly suited to the OCDETF mission since there is a need for a long-term, complicated investigation requiring agents to follow all leads in pursuit of all major dealers, be they manufacturers, suppliers, or money launderers.

The use of the **investigative grand jury** has proved effective in organized crime investigations because of the broad range of power that grand juries enjoy. Some of the more powerful rights granted the grand jury are the authority to subpoena persons and documents, punish, grant immunity, issue indictments, and maintain secrecy of the proceedings.

The grand jury has been used successfully at both the federal and state levels. In the case of the states, the authority to call a grand jury may rest with the governor, the state attorney general, or the local prosecutor. The ability of the grand jury to grant immunity broadens the powers of this investigative body, which is particularly useful considering that many witnesses are criminals who have intimate knowledge of the criminal operation. Most criminals are aware that under the Fifth Amendment they cannot be compelled to give testimony against themselves. When a criminal is reluctant to testify, prosecutors can pursue testimony using one of several options:

1. The prosecutor can compel the testimony by seeking a contempt citation if the prosecutor can prove that the testimony will not incriminate the witness.
2. The prosecutor can release the witness and continue the proceedings without the benefit of the witness's testimony.
3. A plea bargaining agreement could be reached providing the witness's testimony with the understanding that testifying can result in a lesser charge or sentence for any crime the witness committed.
4. The prosecutor can give the witness total immunity from prosecution in exchange for the testimony. A witness who is given total immunity can be compelled to testify. Refusal under these circumstances can result in punishment of the witness.

Two kinds of immunity may be granted to witnesses in organized crime prosecutions.

1. *Transactional immunity.* A witness given **transactional immunity** for testimony about a criminal act is literally immune from ever being prosecuted for that particular crime in the future. Some witnesses have in the past attempted to blurt out additional crimes connected with the primary offense in an attempt to take an "immunity bath" and be free from all responsibility for those crimes. In fact, immunity is not attached when the witness purposely mentions additional crimes. It is extended to other crimes, however, when the prosecutor chooses to mention them during examination of the witness in court.

2. *Derivative-use immunity.* When **derivative-use immunity** is granted to a witness, the witness is immune only from having his own testimony used against him at a later time. If evidence of an independent nature is uncovered, however, the witness may be prosecuted on the basis of this evidence.

The statewide grand jury is the functional equivalent of the special grand jury at the federal level. It conducts investigations of organized crime involvement that are not confined to a particular area or jurisdiction. Both have proved effective in focusing resources on large criminal organizations. States that have authorized the empaneling of a grand jury have experienced its effectiveness as a sound investigative tool against organized crime. As with the investigative grand jury, one of the most effective features of the grand jury is its authority to subpoena persons and documents, punish contemptors, grant immunity, issue indictments, and maintain secrecy of proceedings. In addition, the statewide grand jury enables a more concentrated investigation into widespread criminal enterprises.

The Witness Security Program

Prior to the inception of the **federal witness protection program**, witnesses who testified on behalf of the government were sometimes harassed, assaulted, intimidated, and even murdered. Until 1970 the protection of government witnesses was left to each individual law enforcement agency. Because of limited resources and inconsistent services, the need arose for a single federal program. The WITSEC program was implemented in 1971, and since then more than 5,000 witnesses have entered it and have been protected, relocated, and provided new identities by the U.S. Marshal's Service. The program is the first of its kind in the United States and has served as a prototype for similar programs in other countries.

The WITSEC has proved to be one of the most significant prosecution tools in cases involving major organized crime figures. It offers lifetime protection to witnesses who testify against organized crime figures. Such a program is necessary because of criminal conspiracies, secretive and clandestine drug operations, and the general covert nature of organized crime. The WITSEC program is considered a successful program because, in eight of every ten cases in which a protected witness has testified, ten defendants are convicted and receive substantial prison sentences. In addition, WITSEC boasts a 97 percent success rate in protecting witnesses under its supervision.

EVALUATING EFFORTS TO CONTROL ORGANIZED CRIME

The federal government's efforts to battle organized crime are often based on a conspiratorial view of organized crime as a highly structured entity. Under this assumption, the boss or godfather is at the top of a criminal corporation and is the most important target for police. In such a highly structured organization, successfully targeting the leader can (but not always) incapacitate the organization. This strategy of going after crime bosses is **headhunting**. It is the motivating force behind the laws, the enforcement practices, and distribution of resources making up the federal response to organized crime. This strategy has been used for decades in investigations, resulting in the arrest and conviction of such mob bosses as Al Capone, Lucky Luciano, and John Gotti.

THE HEADHUNTING STRATEGY

Since the earliest days of Prohibition, federal enforcement efforts against organized crime have been predicated on identifying and prosecuting group leaders and members of any applicable offense. These offenses are often unrelated to illicit entrepreneurship and comparatively minor infractions of law. But arresting a known member of organized crime for even a small offense gives prosecutors leverage to undertake other investigations of the group. The headhunting strategy is based on the assumption that organized crime operations are too well organized and too complex to be proved in court. In the headhunting strategy, success is calculated by a body count.

Arrests, indictments, and convictions are used for the all-important tool of flipping an offender. **Flipping** is the time-honored practice of arresting a low-level offender on a relatively minor charge with the goal of using his or her testimony against either the boss or another higher-up in the organization. Because conspiracy places a high premium on the arrested person's position in the organized crime hierarchy, the farther up that hierarchy an arrest goes, the more disruptive it is to the business of organized crime.

Because organized crime groups are tightly structured and disciplined, the incapacitation of a boss should be debilitating to the organization. Of course, because of the notion of an insulated hierarchy, the culture of violence, the code of silence, and the intense loyalty of conspirators acting out feudal ties emanating from foreign cultures, successful headhunting requires an enormous array of law enforcement powers that must be expanded and updated continually. New laws creating new crime categories, such as drug kingpin or racketeer, must be enacted so that even stiffer sentences can be imposed on those convicted in organized crime prosecutions. Simply getting convictions on the basis of the crimes charged would not be a sufficient deterrent; additional penalties must be included.

As often happens with law enforcement initiatives, no rigorous assessments or evaluations of the headhunting strategy are available for inspection (President's Commission on Organized Crime 1986b: 205). Critics complain that when organized criminals are arrested and prosecuted successfully the government sees this as evidence that its policies are working. When arrests fail to lead to convictions or the penalties received are mild, police agents often complain that weak laws and a lenient court system hindered their efforts and that additional resources and more legal authority are needed to implement the headhunting strategy.

The Effectiveness of Headhunting

The government keeps no comprehensive statistics on how many organized criminals have been arrested, convicted, and incarcerated. Some fragmentary data suggest the wide scope of the government's headhunting strategy. For example, a 1986 *Fortune* magazine listed the top fifty alleged Mafia bosses in the United States (based on interviews with law enforcement officials). The *Fortune* article demonstrated that fifteen of the fifty were in jail, ten were under indictment, and one was a fugitive (Rowan 1986). Eight of the top ten had been incapacitated by law enforcement. Of the five mob families of New York, the top leaders of three, the Colombo, Bonanno, and Lucchese syndicates, and half of the Genovese syndicate leaders were incapacitated. From 1981 to 1985, seventeen of the twenty-four alleged Mafia bosses across the country were indicted or convicted (President's Commission on Organized Crime, 1986b: 47). In 1984 alone, organized crime indictments totaled 2,194, almost exclusively consisting of alleged Mafia group members.

Additionally, conviction rates and the length of sentences increased. The General Accounting Office (GAO) estimated that the conviction rate for organized criminals rose from 56 to 76 percent between 1972 and 1980 (Albanese 1985). The GAO also noted an increase in jail terms for those convicted. The problem with all this activity is that the government has failed to produce evidence that any of these prosecutions have resulted in a diminution of organized crime's illicit ventures. The federal government simply has no way to measure the impact on organized crime (President's Commission on Organized Crime 1986a: 203).

Other indicators seem to suggest that organized crime is alive and healthy despite these law enforcement efforts. For example, prosecutions of a major gambling syndicate in Philadelphia in the early 1980s spawned at least two dozen other crime networks in the same neighborhood to replace the target crime group (Pennsylvania Crime Commission 1974; 1986). Major enforcement efforts directed at syndicate heads in Seattle and Wincanton resulted in minimal restructuring of street-level operations and no discernible impact on the provision of illicit goods and services at all (Gardiner 1970; Chambliss 1978). Accordingly, major prosecutions in New York directed at labor racketeering and drug trafficking weeded out inefficient and highly well-established operators, leaving more viable organized crime groups in their wake (Block and Chambliss 1981).

Prosecutions aimed at the pornography syndicate resulted in the creation of at least six new major organized crime groups and the revival of one group that had been closed down a decade ago by successful prosecution (Potter 1986). Studies of the organized role of vice consistently showed that prosecutions had only a negligible impact on the operations of organized crime syndicates (Albini 1971; Reuter 1983; Reuter et al. 1983).

Problems with Headhunting

Perhaps one reason that the headhunting strategy results in little impact on organized crime is that the policy itself is based on misunderstandings of the workings of organized crime. Organized crime syndicates long ago learned that to be successful in a threatening legal environment they must be prepared to adapt their structures and practices. The irony of the situation is that the more successful federal investigators and prosecutors become in incarcerating organized crime leaders, the more the industry responds by decentralizing and maintaining temporary and ephemeral working relationships. Because the headhunting approach never disables more than a small proportion of the total number of organized crime entrepreneurs at any given time, it can actually strengthen some organized crime groups by weeding out their slothful and inefficient competitors.

Another aspect of the headhunting strategy is that it often involves targeting the easiest cases. Successful prosecutions of highly visible and public but not overly influential crime figures are good press, but they have very little impact on the criminal organizations. The selection of "Little Nicky" Scarfo, the alleged boss of Philadelphia's Cosa Nostra family, for special federal treatment left the field open for far more powerful and dangerous crime figures. The relative immunity of major figures in organized crime, such as corrupt public officials, money launderers, and others who serve as bridges between the underworld and the upperworld, clearly demonstrates the deficiencies in the headhunting strategy.

Furthermore, headhunting is not always successful. For example, charges against Jack Nardi, Jr., a Teamsters' official, were dismissed on October 9, 1985. In May 1986, all six defendants were acquitted in the celebrated RICO trial of "Matty the Horse" Ianniello. On March 13, 1987, John Gotti and six alleged accomplices were acquitted on racketeering charges.

Some argue that the idea that vigorous prosecution and stiff criminal penalties will win the war against organized crime is at variance not only with current research on organized crime, but also with historic precedent. Literally thousands of cases in which organized crime figures have been arrested, convicted, and imprisoned in the last five decades could be discussed here. The fundamental question remains—So what? There is little evidence that these prosecutions have negatively affected or altered the activities of organized criminal entrepreneurial groups in illicit markets.

FIGHTING CORRUPTION

It is axiomatic that organized crime cannot flourish without a favorable political environment in which systematic abuses of the public trust occur. Although there is no reason to believe that the customers of organized crime can be deterred from seeking illicit goods and services, there is every reason to believe that corruption can be deterred. Instead of wasting valuable resources on surveilling criminals with a bad reputation or collecting urine samples in a campaign to isolate drug consumers, governments might focus their attention on people in a position to serve as corrupt links between the underworld and the upperworld.

At a minimum, increased and more comprehensive reporting of assets and sources of income by public officials in key decision-making positions should be required. Mayors, city managers, governors, attorneys general, prosecuting attorneys, and police officers should be required to file personal financial reports annually. Law enforcement could monitor tax returns more closely. Increased restrictions on contributions to political candidates must be enacted to outlaw political action committees and limit contributions to $100, or public financing of political campaigns must be adopted as a national policy.

Corruption can be made more difficult by eliminating special police squads, such as vice and narcotics squads. Having investigatory activities located in one place just makes the job of organized crime's corrupters easier. They have to buy their crime-committing license from only one source, rather than from numerous enforcement units.

CLEANING UP MONEY LAUNDRIES

The increase in drug-trafficking profits has focused attention on the critical role of financial institutions in laundering illicit incomes. Organized crime groups have become dependent on bankers, stockbrokers, lawyers, realtors, and others close to the financial community (Lernoux, 1984; Demaris, 1986; Moldea, 1986). Proactive steps to make it difficult for money laundering to take place should be considered. Corporations should be required to provide sufficient information to allow investigators to follow money trails with greater ease: Reports should list (1) all corporate officers; (2) all stockholders or other investors; (3) all sources of investment capital, including those emanating from foreign corporations and offshore banks; and (4) all bank accounts, both foreign or domestic. Silent partnerships and fronts should be outlawed.

Existing requirements to report large sums of money transferred between and among banks should be enforced. This should apply to trust accounts, and the following should be reported: the names of everyone who has access to the money, the sources of income in the accounts and the allocation of withdrawals. Businesses presently excluded from reporting requirements, such as restaurants, bars, and other cash-intensive entities, should be included. Interbank transfers and wire transfers to foreign banks and corporations should be reported.

Foreign currency transactions should be limited and subjected to requirements detailing where the money is going and why. Perhaps the money should be taxed as a way to discourage this practice (a type of preventive financial measure). Certainly, criminal and civil penalties for what are euphemistically called white-collar crimes should be increased drastically. Corporate executives should be licensed by the state, and those convicted of crimes should be barred from participation in public corporations, corporations engaged in interstate commerce, and so on. Surely, if the federal government can justify putting labor union locals into receivership based on the criminal records of their officers, the same should hold for brokerage houses. Independent auditing of all corporations should be mandated. The auditors should be employed by the state and paid for by a state-imposed fee on corporations.

Finally, federal prosecutors (and jurors alike) should recognize that a corrupt organization is a corrupt organization, whether it is the Mafia or a national brokerage firm. The seizure of corporate assets under the RICO statute for criminal activities in pursuit of racketeering should become as common as the confiscation of a drug dealer's ill-gotten gains.

DRUG DECRIMINALIZATION

Some people have suggested that since the first objective of control policies aimed at organized crime should be reducing the size of the illicit market and the profits emanating from that market, **decriminalization** of some activities should be considered. They argue that it is the very existence of these laws against consensual crimes that creates such a remarkable opportunity for criminal entrepreneurs. Those advocating decriminalization argue that although vice-type crimes require cooperation between buyer and seller, there is no victim to call the police, and there is no complainant to instigate an investigation. As a direct result, these laws are enforced in a highly selective and discriminatory manner.

People who are unlucky enough to be arrested under the gambling, drug, and prostitution statutes are almost always the most visible and easiest to catch. Their convictions fill the prisons with junkies and streetwalkers. The fact is that the enforcement of these laws serves to strengthen organized crime rather than control it. Because those who will be apprehended are those with the least organization, the least power, the least expertise, and very probably the smallest operators, the law weeds out inefficient organized crime players.

Opposing Decriminalization

Despite the cries of those advocating decriminalization, the issue has its opponents. For example, national polls have shown that 80 percent of people surveyed do not favor the decriminalization–legalization option (Bureau of Justice Statistics 1992). A 1995 Gallup Poll revealed that 85 percent of those sampled rejected legalization of any form (Pena 1995). Furthermore, if we are to take seriously the principles of a democratic government, it can be argued, the laws should reflect what the people want.

Students of history have already learned the decriminalization lesson. For example, if we take time to consider the history of drug control policy, we will see that for the most part drugs have been perfectly legal and readily available for most of our country's history. Only in the last eighty years or so have

You Decide

What Is the Best Approach for Attacking Organized Crime?

Organized crime is an insidious form of criminality that permeates virtually all society. The U.S. Constitution ensures citizens personal freedoms and protection from oppressive police actions, but it has become clear that the police might need expanded authority to combat organized crime more effectively. Some have suggested that more police be added to existing police forces to fight the organized crime scourge. Accordingly, additional prisons could be needed if more emphasis is placed on fighting organized crime. Are more police, more laws, and more prisons the answer? Others have argued that these options are too reactionary and that a more proactive, innovative approach is warranted. Because of organized crime's interface with politicians, government officials, and legitimate businesspeople, the best way to combat organized crime could be tighter scrutiny of relationships between these people and regulation of legitimate business's partnerships with suspected organized crime groups. What do you think would work best: more traditional police enforcement of organized crime or new approaches for regulation of organized crime connections in legitimate society? You decide!

we moved from a philosophy of total tolerance of drugs to regulation of them and, finally, to total prohibition of them in many cases. Our own history, as well as that of other civilized countries in the world, tells us that there are reasons for this growing intolerance of dangerous drugs. People behave irresponsibly under the influence of drugs, and most people do not want to live or work in a drug-abusing environment.

The decriminalization experience in Alaska is illustrative. Between 1975 and 1990, the Alaska Supreme Court (not a vote of the people) forced decriminalization of marijuana on its citizens. After drug abuse among school-aged children there soared compared to national averages, Alaska's voters were finally successful in restoring prohibition on the drug. The victimless crime argument can also be rebutted. After all, most victimless crimes are committed against the public morality despite the mutual complicity of its participants. It has been argued that the morality issue of enforcing vice offenses might be the most sensible argument of all to preserve a wholesome, healthy, and responsible community for everyone.

Of course, in actuality law enforcement efforts against organized crime figures involve more than just arresting street walkers and small-time junkies. Agents in all levels of government regularly pursue large-scale players in the drug-trafficking scene. Cases focusing on kingpins such as John Gotti, Manual Noriega, and Medellin Cartel cofounder Carlos Lehder are only a few. Each of these was the manager of a large criminal organization that is now either defunct or seriously defrayed. Aggressive enforcement efforts in conjunction with innovative laws, such as RICO, CCE, and forfeiture sanctions, can in fact make a difference.

EFFECTIVENESS OF ORGANIZED CRIME PROSECUTIONS

The effectiveness of efforts to control organized crime must be determined. Since President Ronald Reagan declared war on organized crime in the United States in 1982, literally hundreds of mafiosos were arrested, prosecuted, and imprisoned. In 1996, seventeen members of Detroit's Tocco family were arrested by federal agents. The arrests, which literally encompassed the entire crime family, linked the Detroit mob to thirty years of extortion, racketeering, illegal gaming, and violence. The family's boss, Jack Tocco, was sixty-nine at the time of the arrest and was considered by the FBI as one of the most powerful Mafia bosses in the United States (Johnson 1996).

In 1995, mob bosses in Boston, New Orleans, Chicago, Philadelphia, Cleveland, Newark, and New York City were convicted or indicted. Other mafiosi arrested in recent years include Philadelphia's "Little Nicky" Scarfo and "Crazy Phil" Leonetti, Louis Gatto of Fair Lawn, New Jersey, and John Gotti of New York City. Furthermore, over the years government agents have electronically monitored businesses, homes, and cars of suspected mobsters, forced the first fair national Teamsters Union elections, and stemmed the flow of skimmed cash from mob-owned Las Vegas casinos. It could be argued that government efforts have accomplished just about everything except its primary goal: to extinguish organized crime.

Law enforcement has been predicting the end of organized crime for almost as long as they have known about it. It is not as though the government has not tried. Since the early 1980s, federal law enforcement agencies such as the DEA, FBI, and the U.S. Marshal's Service have hired more agents, conducted more wiretaps, and had more witnesses approved to enter the witness protection program than ever before. Federal prosecutors have used the powerful RICO statute in organized crime prosecutions since the late 1970s, allowing entire families of mobsters and organized gangs to be imprisoned while their assets are seized by the government. In fact, one main purpose of RICO was to free so-called captive institutions from mob control. Even this promise has left something to be desired, for example:

- In 1986, a trustee was appointed to end extortionate activities (including two murders) associated with Teamsters Local 560 in northern New Jersey. Members elected a mob-linked candidate in two federally supervised elections. When the judge ousted Michael Sciarra from the local presidency, members elected his brother, who then appointed Sciarra business agent.

- In 1988, a federal administrator was appointed to clean up gangland activities associated with the nation's largest fish market, New York's Fulton Street Fish Market. Prior to the expiration of his term in 1992, the administrator admitted that a mob-enforced monopoly still unloads virtually every crate of fish, resulting in increased seafood prices and far-reaching control of the seafood industry.

WHY WON'T IT DIE?

Some have suggested that organized crime will not die because it is more than just people committing crimes. It is a process that exploits societies' weaknesses through criminal cooperation, rather than legitimate competition. As long as people are willing to gamble, borrow money with poor credit, or take illegal drugs, organized crime will be ready to serve them. Bookies whose identities will be protected, loan-sharks who collect loans, and drug dealers who sell their product will be provided, if not by the Italian mob, then by Colombians, Mexicans, Asians, Jamaicans, Chinese, and others. There will always be a thief looking for a fence or a public official willing to accept a payoff.

Organized crime is a social parasite, it relies more on victims and users than on coconspirators. The incarceration of one mobster or 1,000 mobsters will not address the root of organized crime because it is a flexible, loose-knit federation consisting of various criminals, some mafiosi, some not, who run their own rackets and pass up others.

If by some miracle law enforcement could jail all 1,700 suspected mafiosi in the nation and their associates (whose numbers, no doubt, range into the tens of thousands), other criminals would move in to fill the void.

Therefore, after more than a century of scrutiny by government officials and scholars, no final, workable solution to address organized crime has been found. Whether it will ever be purged from society completely is highly doubtful. Perhaps control of organized crime should be viewed as a perennial task likened to taking out the garbage: Every day you identify it, collect it, and throw it away.

THE FUTURE OF ORGANIZED CRIME

For more than a century, perhaps the only predictable thing that can be said about organized crime is that it is highly unpredictable. Groups are fluid and ever changing, and they provide commodities and services not provided by legitimate governments. One way to consider the future of organized crime could be by considering its current situation.

Albanese and Pursley (1993) offer some suggestions about which current issues are the most relevant in predicting the future of emerging criminal groups.

- *Language barriers.* Although efforts to combat organized crime have been somewhat consistent since the mid-1980s, officials are now hampered by a lack of understanding of the language and cultures of some emerging foreign organized crime groups such as Asian, Jamaican, and Caribbean groups.
- *Distrust by ethnic communities.* Newly arriving immigrants often distrust police because in their countries of origin the police were corrupt and self-serving.
- *New criminal groups.* Despite depictions by filmmakers and the media, Italian American groups are not the dominant groups in organized crime. Recent trends suggest that groups originating from countries such as Colombia, Jamaica, Vietnam, and Hong Kong are of much greater concern than the Mafia.
- *Reducing public demand.* Illegal markets for drugs, gambling, and prostitution are driven entirely by public demand. Police agencies will address the problem of demand in the future through improved education programs and more effective competition for these services from legitimate channels.

- Increased treatment. Many experts have suggested that by paying greater attention to treating those afflicted with gambling and drug addictions the market of those purchasing such goods and services will be drastically reduced.

Although it is difficult to predict future crime trends with any degree of certainty, we should use current trends as a barometer of possible future occurrences. We must also remember that organized crime is highly adaptive and often tries to profit from the weaknesses of individuals, institutions, and even countries. Recall our discussion in Chapter 7 about Russian organized crime members who have attempted to sell nuclear devices to countries hostile to the United States.

Probably the single most significant trend in legitimate society today is the advent of the computer age and the quest for power through the use of information. Let's consider some possibilities.

One thing is certain: For generations, organized crime has had the uncanny ability to identify social patterns and trends and find a niche in which to make money. For example, since the latter part of the twentieth century, information has become a stealable commodity. With twenty-first century satellites, telecommunications, microwave towers, and computers, the information highway seems to be open to virtually anyone and to **information theft**. As many corporate moguls have learned, the strategic use of information can be a source of power. Of course, organized crime organizations still practice violence and intimidation, but they use information to enhance the power they already possess. Does this mean that tomorrow's gangsters will be college educated and computer literate? Chances are that the answer is yes.

Information Theft

Moore (1994) predicts that the top target of twenty-first-century organized crime will be financial institutions. Clearly, financial revenues from drug trafficking have, over the years, made Colombian cartels international players in global finance. Many business losses, sometimes larger than the budgets of entire countries, are often blithely written off by drug cartels. Banks will probably be handling increased amounts of customer information, which will prove valuable not only to them, but to criminal organizations as well. As a result, criminal organizations will carefully place *moles* in financial institutions to provide information such as computer passwords and access codes, allowing criminals to infiltrate accounts without casting suspicions on their operatives.

Organized criminals will probably continue to employ highly skilled computer hackers in the twenty-first century to penetrate targeted institutions. In doing so, they will change bank records, credit card accounts, and reports and alter criminal, educational, and even military records. For that matter, it is possible that personal records will be subjected to deletion or alteration for criminal purposes. Some people have even suggested that with the advent of DNA technology, which has been touted as *the* method of identifying people in the twenty-first century, a criminal service could develop where one's genetic identity could be altered—for a price, of course.

More than anything else, the goal of organized crime leaders in the twenty-first century will be to make their organizations appear legitimate in the eyes

The Power of Legitimacy

of the public. Colombian cartels already have considerable stock holdings in some of the largest Fortune 500 companies in the world. In addition, Japan's premiere organized crime group, the yakuza, is thought to have major stock and real estate holdings in virtually all parts of the world.

As discussed in Chapter 6, many Italian American crime families have long since been successful in infiltrating large-scale industries, such as solid waste hauling, the restaurant business, and the garment industry. In the twenty-first century, large criminal organizations likely will have controlling interest in some of the world's largest multinational corporations. Industrial espionage will involve technology for stealing plans, strategies, formulas, and other valuable information possessed by competitors.

Satellite Technology

Moore (1994) predicts that since satellite-imaging services are becoming increasingly available on the commercial market, crime organizations of the future will own their own communications satellites. A communications network would enable large-scale crime organizations, such as those involved in drug trafficking or money laundering, to have their own secure information systems, free of surveillance or detection by police authorities. Other criminal enterprises, such as sports gambling and prostitution, could also be enhanced with the use of privately owned satellites. With such technology, criminal organizations could operate from sites where law enforcement agencies are sympathetic and would fix sporting events worldwide from horse racing to school sports. Such an operation was discovered in 1992 in the Dominican Republic, where a $1 billion gambling operation was fixing sporting events in the United States.

Indeed, there is no reason not to believe that the huge amounts of money earned by large-scale organized crime organizations will be put to use to purchase whatever they need to make themselves as invulnerable as possible. All the technology will serve one distinct purpose—to allow the organized crime organization to better provide illegal goods and services.

The Nuclear Mafia

Adding to future concerns is the very real threat of organized crime groups acquiring arms and nuclear materials and making them available to any governmental regime for a price. In recent years, Germany has become the global hub of nuclear smuggling (Moore 1994). It has been suggested that the task of nuclear smuggling for organized crime is not so farfetched. In 1996, *Time* magazine reported that anyone who wanted to destroy a medium-sized city such as New Orleans needs only two things: an understanding of the technology involved and actual fissionable material (e.g., 55 pounds of enriched uranium) (Waller 1996). With the increasing use of nuclear technology around the world and the destabilization of Russia, the formerly stringent controls on uranium and plutonium are increasingly being subverted.

If all this seems too farfetched, we must remember that in countries such as Colombia and Italy organized crime already rivals the legitimate government. Just how far could such organizations go with space-age technology designed to enhance productivity, effectiveness, and efficiency? Without a realistic, sensible public policy that deals with these issues, we will have no choice but to sit back and see for ourselves.

A review of policy options addressing organized crime must consider several important aspects of the problem. For example, organized crime is a continually changing phenomenon. Some groups, over time, gain influence and then fade into obscurity, while others rise into prominence in both the under- and upperworlds and over time become stronger and more ingrained in society. Many reasons can be cited for this. For example, law enforcement efforts are sometimes responsible for the demise of some seemingly well-established organized crime groups, such as the Medellin cartel, youth gangs, and Jamaican posses. Other groups, such as outlaw motorcycle gangs and big-city syndicates, have endured over time, possibly because of their expanding financial resources, sheer numbers, and ability to become entrenched in both legitimate and illicit industries. In other cases, changing ethnicity as well as social and political influences also play a role in a group's ability to endure through time. Still, the ability of a group to adapt to changing public demands and needs could contribute to their longevity.

The structure and application of laws addressing organized crime should also be considered. Many laws currently used to combat organized crime are dysfunctional, because they tend to focus on the individual offender, rather than on group or organizational involvement in criminal enterprises. Conversely, laws designed to focus on the group, such as RICO and Continuing Criminal Enterprise, are sometimes misapplied to persons who are not acting as members of a larger organization.

Organized crime's markets are enormous, thus ensuring a continual challenge for authorities to focus on both the demand and supply of its goods and services. Many policy options have been considered over the years to deal best with the growth and influence of organized crime. Some of these focus on identifying and arresting those involved in the supply of illegal goods and services; other options focus on arresting members of the public who demand these services.

Although some organized crime scholars have long argued that decriminalization or legalization is one way to reduce the market domain of organized crime (Albini 1971; Anderson 1979b; Smith 1980; Luksetich and White 1982; Albanese 1985), both public consensus and many high-ranking officials in the law enforcement community disagree. It has been argued that merely removing the criminal label from gambling, loan-sharking, prostitution, and drug trafficking, and even legalizing and regulating them, would not eliminate organized crime's involvement entirely. For instance, we know that legalized off-track betting in New York did not drive bookmakers out of business, although in some cases it did constrain their activity. Bookmakers must offer odds within the limits of those being offered by the state, and they must be restrained in their collection methods, but, most important, bookmaking profits appear to have stabilized at between 5 and 10 percent (Reuter 1983).

The argument that drug decriminalization and legalization will dissolve organized crime also loses ground when we consider that many of organized crime's most profitable enterprises focus on scams and schemes involving perfectly legal activities, such as labor racketeering and the extortion of money from persons in legitimate businesses (e.g., the solid waste, restaurant, and garment industries). It is true that as long as the profits are high and the risks diffuse, criminal entrepreneurs will continue to engage in these activities. The compelling question is this: How can we effectively reduce these profits and make the risk of doing business simply unattractive for both the providers and users of organized crime's rackets?

Although there are many examples of successful prosecutions of organized crime figures, our efforts to control and eradicate organized crime in its entirety have not been completely successful. This is so for two basic reasons: (1) the headhunting strategy, which is predicated on false assumptions about the importance of bosses to the illegal market, has failed, and (2) strict adherence to the alien conspiracy model, which suggests that organized crime consists solely of Italian criminals and fails to recognize the role of the many other ethnic, racial, and social groups making up organized crime in America is not accurate.

Organized crime groups operate in a complex web of interrelated and tangled environments. They are affected by the opportunities and constraints of the market, the legal system, politics, upperworld commerce, and the community in which they operate. Most attempts to analyze organized crime focus almost exclusively on the criminal aspects of organized crime. However, the organized aspects are reflected more fully in relations with other social institutions. Traditionally, analyses of organized crime have concentrated on the deviance of organized crime, rather than on its institutionalized and normative aspects. In Chambliss's words, this emphasis has "obscured perception of the degree to which the structure of America's law and politics creates and perpetuates syndicates that supply the vices in our major cities" (Chambliss 1978: 6).

Empirical research on organized crime suggests that to understand it we must understand its social context. This social context is defined by two recurring themes, two consistent threads running through the organization of crime: official corruption and the exigencies of the political economy. The evidence is compelling that organized crime should not be conceptualized as a dysfunction in society or as an alien force impinging on society, but as part and parcel of the political economic system. This point of view has compelling implications for policy. The argument advanced here suggests that policy makers have been attacking the wrong targets in their battle against organized crime.

Smith (1978: 162) observed that, traditionally, law enforcement strategy "has rested on the belief that acts of crime are the sole responsibility of the perpetrator, and that as a consequence of removing him from society, the criminal acts would disappear." However, the evidence suggests that the existence of illicit drug dealers, loan-sharks, gamblers, and other illegal entrepreneurs is due to the fact that the legitimate marketplace leaves a number of potential customers unserved. Control of organized crime can be achieved only with a greater understanding of organizational and market behavior by "learning how to reduce the domain of the illicit [entrepreneur] . . . and a wider appreciation of the entire market spectrum, and a deeper analysis of the dynamics that nurture its illicit aspects" (Smith 1978: 175–176). Smith argues that an understanding of the task environment of particular enterprises will promote a better and more comprehensive understanding of how such illicit enterprises emerge, survive, and make a profit from crime. A similar suggestion comes from Reuter, Rubinstein, and Wynn, who argue that investigators of organized crime need to be trained "in the detection of corporate crime, tax evasion, and the effect of government regulation . . . on the motivation of criminals to enter and remain in an industry" (Reuter et al. 1983: 30).

When we endeavor to rethink strategies to control organized crime, we must begin by conceptualizing it as a business, not just an alien conspiracy. Doing so will direct us to efforts that will improve our understanding of the causes of organized criminal behavior and the means used to organize illicit enterprises. In addition, this view directs our attention toward the elimination of arbitrary distinctions between legal and illegal goods and services, particularly in gambling, lending, drug distribution, and sexual services. This view also directs our attention to issues of corporate deviance and political corruption. Any control strategy that fails to recognize the importance of organized crime's political and economic links is doomed to failure. So, rather than directing enforcement efforts at specific individuals or groups, a realistic view of organized crime points to the importance of regulation and oversight in both the economic and political communities. Tighter restrictions on campaign financing, corporate registration, better monitoring of conflicts of interest, more comprehensive financial disclosure, and tighter reporting requirements for businesses would be among the minimal steps necessary to interrupt organized crime's relationships with the worlds of politics and commerce. Clearly, better control of corporate and political deviance would narrow the window of opportunity for organized crime and therefore make it more amenable to control.

The way we conceptualize and understand organized crime prescribes the means selected to control it. Detailed policy alternatives are beyond the scope of this discussion, but several thematic departures from present policy can be suggested from what we know about organized crime. Specific policies directed at corruption, money laundries, improved intelligence, and the strategic selection of law enforcement targets and policies directed at market demand can be suggested. None of these are necessarily new, but the debate and consideration of all alternatives are important in solving this monolithic social problem. Attacking white-collar criminals is not as politically satisfying nor as economically profitable as jailing highly visible and reasonably unimportant purveyors of vice on the street.

Furthermore, there is little reason to believe that powerful political and economic interests that profit handsomely from organized crime are suddenly likely to adopt effective measures to curtail what is a major source of wealth in America. But once these political and business entities can be kept in check through a system of regulation and scrutinization, control of organized crime will become more of a reality than an illusion.

DO YOU RECOGNIZE THESE TERMS?

asset forfeiture
buy and bust
civil forfeiture
conspiracy
criminal forfeiture
decriminalization
derivative-use immunity
electronic surveillance
federal witness protection program
flipping
headhunting

informant
information theft
intelligence
investigative grand jury
jurisdiction
multijurisdictional task force
net worth theory
proactive
RICO statute
transactional immunity
undercover agent

POINTS OF DISCUSSION

1. Discuss the role of the police in combating organized crime.

2. Explain in what ways organized crime investigations could encroach on the personal freedoms of U.S. citizens.

3. List and discuss the different ways in which undercover investigations and the use of informants pose special problems in controlling organized crime.

4. Explain the utility of intelligence operations in understanding organized crime.

5. Of all the legal initiatives discussed in this chapter, which do you believe are the most useful in combating organized crime?

6. In what ways can society improve its understanding of organized crime to formulate a more workable public policy toward it?

SUGGESTED READING

DINTINO, J., and F. MARTENS. (1983). *Police Intelligence Systems in Crime Control: Maintaining a Delicate Balance in a Liberal Democracy*. Springfield, IL: Charles C. Thomas. The authors explore the use of police intelligence systems to control organized crime, probing the essential dilemma of effectively enforcing the law versus upholding constitutionally protected civil liberties.

MARX, G. (1988). *Undercover: Police Surveillance in America*. Berkeley: University of California Press. Drawing on official records, unpublished documents, and interviews with the Federal Bureau of Investigation and local police, this study examines the variety of undercover operations and the ethical issues involved.

PASSAS, N. (1995). *Organized Crime*. Brookfield, VT: Dartmouth Publishing.

APPENDIX A

SELECTED PROVISIONS FROM THE 2001 USA PATRIOT ACT

Title II—Enhanced Surveillance Procedures Section 203. Authority to Share Criminal Investigative Information

(b.)AUTHORITY TO SHARE ELECTRONIC, WIRE, AND ORAL INTERCEPTION INFORMATION.—LAW ENFORCEMENT.—Section 2517 of title I8, U.S.C., is amended by inserting at the end the following:

"(6) any investigative or law enforcement officer, or attorney for the government, who by any means authorized by this chapter, has obtained knowledge of the contents of any wire, oral, or electronic communication, or evidence derived therefrom, may disclose such contents to any other Federal law enforcement, intelligence, protective, immigration, national defense, or national security official to the extent that such contents include foreign intelligence or counterintelligence (as defined in section 3 of the National Security Act of 1947 (50 U.S.C. 401(a)), or foreign intelligence information (as defined in subsection 19 of section 2510 of this article), to assist the official who is to receive that information in the performance of his official duties. Any federal official who receives information pursuant to this provision may use that information only as necessary in the conduct of that person's official duties subject to any limitations on the unauthorized disclosure of such information."

Sec. 213. Authority for Delaying Notice of the Execution of a Warrant

Section 3103 a. of Title 18, United States Code is amended—(1) by inserting "(a) IN GENERAL.—" before "in addition": and (2) by adding at the end the following:

"(b.) DELAY.—with respect to the insurance of any warrant or court order under this section, or any other rule of law, to search and seize any property or material that constitute[s] evidence of a criminal offense in violation of the laws of the United States, any notice required, or that may be required, to be given may be delayed in—"(1) the court finds reasonable cause to believe that providing immediate notification of the execution of a warrant may have an adverse result (as defined in section 2705); "(2) the warrant prohibits the seizure of any tangible property, any wire or electronic communication (as defined in section 2510), or, except as expressly provided in chapter 121, any stored wire or electronic information, except where the court finds reasonable necessity for the seizure; and "(3) the ward provides for the giving of such notice within a reasonable period of its execution, which period may thereafter be extended by the court for good cause shown."

What This Means

Prior to the enactment of the USA Patriot Act, government agencies already had the authority, in limited situations, to delay notification for searches of some forms of electronic communications that were in the custody of a third party. (Delayed notification searches are sometimes called "sneak and peak" searches.) Previous law, according to the U.S. Department of Justice,[1] was a

---

[1] References to the Department of Justice in this appendix are derived from U.S. Department of Justice Field Guidance on Authorities (Redacted) Enacted in the 2001 Anti-terrorism Legislation (Washington DC: DOJ, no date). Web posted at *www.epic.org/terrorism/DOJ guidance.pdf*. Accessed November 16, 2002.

mix of inconsistent rules, practices, and court decisions varying widely from jurisdiction to jurisdiction. The lack of uniformity was said to have hindered the investigation of terrorism cases and other nationwide investigations.

The U.S. Patriot Act attempts to resolve this problem by amending title 18, section 3103, of the U.S. Code to create a uniform standard authorizing courts to delay the provision of required notice if the court finds "reasonable cause" to believe that providing immediate notification of the execution of the warrant may have an "adverse result" (such as endangering the life or physical safety of an individual, flight from prosecution, evidence tampering, or witness intimidation) or might otherwise seriously jeopardize an investigation or unduly delay a trial. This section of the USA Patriot Act is primarily designed to authorize delayed notice of searches, rather than delayed notice of seizures.

Sec. 216. Modification of Authorities Relating to Use of Pen Registers and Trap and Trace Devices

(b) ISSUANCE OF ORDERS.—

(1) IN GENERAL.—section 3123 (a) of title 18, U.S.C., is amended to read as follows:

"(a) IN GENERAL.—"(1) ATTORNEY FOR THE GOVERNMENT.—upon application made under section 3122 (a) (1), the court shall interconnect apartheid order authorizing the installation and use of a pen register or trap and trace devices anywhere within the United States, if the court finds that the attorney for the government has certified to the court that the information likely to be obtained by such installation and use is relevant to an ongoing criminal investigation."

What This Means

Although Congress enacted a pen/trap statute in 1986 (which made possible the collection of noncontent traffic information associated with communications, such as the phone number dialed from a particular telephone), it could not anticipate the dramatic expansion in electronic communications that would occur in the next fifteen years. Thus, the 1986 statute (18 U.S.C. 3127) contains certain language that appeared to apply to telephone communications and that did not unambiguously encompass communications over computer networks.

Section 216 of the USA Patriot Act updates the pen/trap statute in three important ways: (1) the amendments clarify that law enforcement may use pen/trap orders to trace communications on the Internet and other computer networks; (2) pen/trap orders issued by federal courts have nationwide effect; and (3) law enforcement authorities must file a special report with the court whenever they use a pen/trap order to install their own monitoring device on computers belonging to a public provider.

Sec. 219. Single-Jurisdiction Search Warrants for Terrorism

Rule 41 (a) of the Federal Rules of Criminal Procedure is amended by inserting after "executed" the following: "and (3) in an investigation of domestic terrorism or international terrorism (as defined in section 2331 of title 18, U.S.C.), by Federal magistrate judge in any district in which activities related to the terrorism may have occurred, for the search of property or for a person within or outside the district."

What This Means

Under prior law, Rule 41 (a) of the Federal Rules of Criminal Procedure required that a search warrant be obtained within a district for searches within that district. The only exception was for cases in which property or a person within the district might leave the district prior to execution of the warrant. The rule created what some saw as unnecessary delays and burdens in the investigation of terrorist activities and networks that spanned a number of districts, since warrants had to be obtained separately in each district. Section 219 purports to solve that problem by providing that, in domestic or international terrorism cases, a search warrant may be used by the magistrate judge in any district in which activities related to the terrorism have occurred for a search of property or persons located within or outside the district.

Sec. 224. Sunset

(a) IN GENERAL—except as provided in subsection (b), this title and the amendments made by this title (other than Sections 203(a), 203(c), 205, 208, 210, 211, 213, 216, 219, 221, and 222, and the amendments made by those sections) shall cease to have an effect on December 31, 2005.

What This Means

None of the provisions shown here are scheduled to expire in 2005.

Civil Rights Implications

While many aspects of the USA Patriot Act have been criticized as being potentially unconstitutional, Section 213, which authorizes delaying notice of the execution of award, may be the most subject to challenge. The ACLU maintains that under this section, law enforcement agents could enter a house, apartment, or office with a search warrant while the occupant is away, search through his or her property, and take photographs without having to tell the suspect about the search until later.[2] The ACLU says that this provision will mark "a sea change in the way search warrants are executed in the United States." The ACLU also believes that the new provision is likely to be illegal because the Fourth Amendment to the Constitution protects against unreasonable searches and seizures and requires the government to both obtain a warrant and to give notice to the person whose property will be searched for conducting the search. The notice requirement enables the suspect to assert his or her Fourth Amendment rights. A person with notice, for example, might be able to point out irregularities in the warrant, such as the fact that the police are at the wrong address or that, because the warrant is limited to a search for a stolen car, the police have no authority to be looking in dresser drawers. In a covert search warrant, there are no clear limitations on what can be searched. According to the ACLU, Section 213 has taken what had previously been an extremely limited authority and expanded it so that it is now available in any kind of search (physical or electronic) and in any kind of criminal case.

The ACLU also questions the constitutionality of Section 216, "Modification of Authorities Relating to Use of Pen Registers and Trap and Trace Devices."[3] This section essentially says the courts shall use a search warrant whenever a qualified prosecuting attorney, acting in an official capacity, certifies that the warrant is needed. This requirement effectively eliminates judicial oversight in the issuance of such warrants and mandates that courts issue warrants under specified circumstances, rather than assess the lawfulness of warrant requests. The Supreme Court has yet to rule on the constitutionality of sneak and peak searches or on Section 213 requirements.

[2]Much of the information in this paragraph is taken from American Civil Liberties Union, How the Anti-Terrorism Bill Expands Law Enforcement "Sneak and Peek" Warrants.
[3]American Civil Liberties Union, How the Anti-Terrorism Bill Limits Judicial Oversight of Telephone and Internet Conversations.

Summary   Within weeks of the USA Patriot Act becoming law, U.S. Attorney General John Ashcroft announced that he was using the authority of his office to allow federal corrections officials and select others to listen in on certain telephone communications between jailed suspects accused of terrorism and their lawyers—without obtaining prior approval by a judge. The attorney general said that communications between inmates and their lawyers would be monitored when "reasonable suspicion exists to believe that a particular inmate may use communications with attorneys or their agents to further or facilitate acts of terrorism."[4] Ashcroft's decision, which raised questions in Congress, effectively ended the long-standing tradition of lawyer–client confidentiality for telephone conversations with federal prisoners. Following Ashcroft's announcement, President George W. Bush signed an executive order allowing secret military tribunals to try foreign terrorism suspects at home or abroad without many of the constitutional protections given to defendants in the federal court system. The president's order effectively removed suspected foreign terrorists from the jurisdiction of the federal court system. Bush said that the order was required to avoid having to prosecute accused terrorists under court rules that might result in the disclosure of state secrets or make the United States more vulnerable to terrorism.

---

[4]William Glaberson, Experts divided on new anti-terror policy that scuttles lawyer-client confidentiality." *New York Times,* November 12, 2002.

CHRONOLOGY OF WHITE SUPREMACIST DOMESTIC TERRORIST INCIDENTS IN THE 1980s

- May 14, 1980: J. B. Stoner of the Crusade Against Corruption is convicted for the bombing of a Birmingham, Alabama, church.
- August 20, 1980: Two black joggers are killed by sniper fire in a Salt Lake City park. Joseph Paul Franklin, a neo-Nazi with a long criminal record, is convicted for the crimes.
- January 1981: Texas Ku Klux Klan leader, Louis Beam, opens a paramilitary warfare training camp for white supremacists in the Dallas area.
- March 21, 1981: Nineteen-year-old Michael Donald is lynched by members of the United Klans of America in Mobile, Alabama.
- April 8, 1981: Louis Beam is indicted for conducting paramilitary maneuvers on federal land without a permit.
- May 14, 1981: The Texas Knights of the Ku Klux Klan are enjoined from harassing Vietnamese fishermen.
- May 20, 1981: Billy Riccio, grand dragon of the Alabama Invisible Empire of the Ku Klux Klan, is incarcerated for a parole violation after being photographed with a weapon at a Klan paramilitary training camp in Cullman, Alabama.
- Spring 1981: Members of the Posse Comitatus hold joint military training maneuvers with the Ku Klux Klan in the Sierra Nevada Mountains of California. The Posse Comitatus also sponsors a paramilitary training camp in Wisconsin, where more than 200 men are trained.
- Summer 1981: More than 1,000 people attend fifty-five classes in weapons training and survivalism at the Christian Patriots Defense League Summer Freedom Festival in Louisville, Illinois.
- June 18, 1981: Pennsylvania Invisible Empire of the Ku Klux Klan leader Terry J. Chidester is charged with murdering a 68-year-old black man.
- June 20, 1981: Knights of the Ku Klux Klan leader Don Black is convicted of conspiring to overthrow the government of Dominica. Seven others plead guilty to the same charges.
- August 21, 1981: Neo-Nazi leader Michael Canale is sentenced to four years in prison for the arson of a California synagogue.
- September 16, 1981: Six neo-Nazis are convicted of conspiracy in a plan to fire bomb buildings in Greensboro, North Carolina.
- February 1982: Five elderly black women were awarded $535,000 in damages after members of the Ku Klux Klan left a Klan meeting and fired shotguns from a passing car at the women.
- March 1982: Fifty Posse Comitatus members begin training killer teams in guerrilla warfare tactics in Weskan, Kansas. Classes are held in the use of explosives, booby traps, poisons, silencers, and hand to hand combat.
- May 1982: A Colorado Springs Ku Klux Klan member and six other people were arrested after selling ten bombs to an undercover agent. This incident

was part of a larger Posse Comitatus plot, which involved selling bombs, killing two federal judges, and blowing up the IRS headquarters in Denver.

- July 1982: Over 200 people representing thirteen Ku Klux Klan and neo-Nazi groups gather at Richard Butler's Aryan Nations' World Congress.
- September 1982: The Aryan Nations, the National Association for the Advancement of White People, and seven Ku Klux Klan splinter groups meet at Stone Mountain, Georgia, over the Labor Day weekend and announce the formation of the Confederation of Klans.
- December 1982: Carolina Knights of the Ku Klux Klan leader Glenn Miller leads 150 heavily armed Klansmen and Nazis in a rally at a Marine air station in North Carolina.
- 1983: Louis Beam proposes a point system for the white supremacist underground in which terrorists would get points for the assassinations of federal officials and civil rights leaders.
- 1983: Tom Metzger founds the White Aryan Resistance in California.
- 1983: Robert Miles of the Mountain Church publishes an essay urging hate groups to turn away from public activities and engage in secret, underground terror tactics. Thom Robb of the Knights of the Ku Klux Klan endorses the idea.
- January 4, 1983: Two hundred and fifty farmers battle police at the auction of a farm belonging to a Posse Comitatus member who had been active in paramilitary activities.
- February 17, 1983: Posse Comitatus member Gordon Kahl kills two federal marshals in North Dakota.
- April 21, 1983: Virgil Griffin and five other Ku Klux Klan members and six neo-Nazis are indicted by the federal government in relation to a riot in Greensboro, North Carolina, that killed five anti-Klan protesters.
- May 1983: As part of a harassment campaign initiated by Glenn Miller's Carolina Knights of the Ku Klux Klan, a cross is burned at the home of a black prison guard in North Carolina.
- June 3, 1983: Posse Comitatus member Gordon Kahl dies in a shoot-out after killing an Arkansas sheriff.
- July 28, 1983: The Klanwatch offices of the Southern Poverty Law Center are damaged by arson. Three members of the Knights of the Ku Klux Klan are arrested in the arson.
- September 1983: The Order is formed.
- December 3, 1983: Order member Bruce Pierce is arrested for passing counterfeit money in Union Gap, Washington.
- December 3, 1983: Tom Metzger of the White Aryan Resistance and Richard Butler of the Aryan Nations are arrested for an illegal cross burning in the San Fernando Valley of California.
- March 16, 1984: Order members rob an armored truck in Seattle, netting $43,345.
- April 23, 1984: Order members rob another armored truck in Seattle, netting $230,379.
- Spring 1984: Louis Beam sets up an Aryan Nations computer network.
- May 17, 1984: Nine Alabama members of the Invisible Empire of the Ku Klux Klan are indicted for civil rights violations as a result of an attack on civil rights marchers in Decatur, Alabama.

- June 18, 1984: Talk show host Alan Berg is murdered by Order members in Denver. Berg was on a hit list that contained a dozen other targets.
- June 1984: Richard Snell, a member of the Covenant, Sword, and Arm of the Lord murders Louis Bryant, an Arkansas state trooper.
- July 19, 1984: Members of the Order rob an armored truck in Ukiah, California, netting $3.8 million. The money is distributed to white supremacist groups across the nation, including Glenn Miller in North Carolina, Tom Metzger in California, and William Pierce in West Virginia.
- November 9, 1984: Three Georgia members of the Invisible Empire of the Ku Klux Klan are convicted of federal civil rights violations in connection with several racially motivated assaults.
- November 27, 1984: Alabama Ku Klux Klan members are enjoined by a federal court from further paramilitary training at the Klan's Camp My Lai in Cullman, Alabama.
- December 8, 1984: Order founder Robert Mathews is killed in a shoot-out with the FBI at Whidbey Island, Washington.
- January 17, 1985: Glenn Miller, the White Patriot Party, the Carolina Knights of the Ku Klux Klan, and the Confederate Knights of the Ku Klux Klan are ordered in federal court to cease paramilitary training in North Carolina and to cease the harassment of black North Carolina citizens.
- February 1985: Billy Riccio, an Aryan Nations and Ku Klux Klan member, is arrested on weapons charges. Police confiscate a hit list from Riccio during the arrest.
- April 9, 1985: Five members of the United Klans of America are arrested in Florida for conspiring to bomb properties owned by blacks and Jews.
- April 12, 1985: Twenty-three members of the Order are indicted on RICO charges, including charges of robbery, counterfeiting, bombing, arson, illegal weapons, and murder.
- April 15, 1985: Order member David Tate shoots and kills Missouri state trooper Jimmie Linegar. Tate is arrested on April 20.
- April 19, 1985: Federal agents and Arkansas police raid the survivalist compound of the Covenant, Sword, and Arm of the Lord. CSA leader James Ellison and four members of the Order are arrested. Illegal weapons, land mines, explosives, cyanide, a rocket launcher, and an armored car are seized in the raid. Ellison and six CSA members are indicted for weapons violations and on racketeering charges.
- June 7, 1985: Six Klan members and neo-Nazis and two city policemen are held civilly liable for assault and battery on anti-Klan demonstrators in Greensboro, North Carolina.
- June 24, 1985: Law enforcement officers raid the Posse Comitatus compound of James Wickstrom and dismantle it in rural Wisconsin.
- June 1985: Nine members of the White Patriot Party are arrested in connection with racial attacks and vandalism in Belle Glade, Florida.
- June 30, 1985: An internal investigation uncovers a Klan unit within the Louisville, Kentucky, police department called the Confederate Officers Patrol Squad.
- August 17, 1985: A raid on a Christian Identity survivalist compound led by Michael Ryan finds the bodies of a murdered 5-year-old boy and a 26-year-old man.

- September 23, 1985: Nine White Knights of Liberty members (a Ku Klux Klan splinter group) are indicted for harassing blacks in western North Carolina.
- October 1985: The FBI reports to Congress that it has uncovered 16 paramilitary training camps around the country, most of them in the South and West.
- November 1985: Identity Christian leader Larry Humphreys leads a heavily armed band of followers to a Georgia farm to prevent foreclosure on the farm.
- January 7, 1986: Twelve members of the White Knights of Liberty are indicted in relation to shootings, cross burnings, and harassment of blacks and interracial couples.
- April 1986: Ohio Knights of the Ku Klux Klan Grand Dragon Dale Reusch is convicted for the illegal transportation of weapons.
- July 25, 1986: Glenn Miller, Stephen Miller, and their White Patriot Party are held in contempt of court for violating an injunction against paramilitary training in North Carolina.
- August 8, 1986: Former White Student Union president Greg Withrow is beaten and his hands are nailed to a board after he renounces racism and exposes connections between his organization and white supremacist terrorists.
- September 15–29, 1986: A federal office building, a priest's home, and two local businesses in Kootenai County, Idaho, are bombed by Aryan Nations members.
- September 27, 1986: Three former White Patriot Party members, including Stephen Miller and Jack Jackson, are indicted for conspiracy to rob a restaurant, purchase stolen military explosives, and blow up the Southern Poverty Law Center.
- October 23, 1986: William Potter Gale and seven members of the Committee of the States, a Posse Comitatus front group, are arrested in a plot to assassinate a federal judge and IRS officials in Nevada.
- December 15, 1986: Six members of the Arizona Patriots are arrested for planning robberies and bombings.
- December 1986: Neo-Nazi Karl Hand is convicted of attempted murder in Louisiana.
- January 8, 1987: Five White Patriot Party members are indicted on federal charges of conspiring to obtain military weapons from Fort Bragg, North Carolina.
- January 17, 1987: Civil rights marchers are attacked by Klan members in Forsyth County, Georgia.
- January 17, 1987: Three men are killed and two others are injured in the shooting and arson of an adult bookstore in Shelby, North Carolina. Three White Patriot Party members are charged with the attack.
- February 13, 1987: A Mobile, Alabama, jury finds the United Klans of America liable for the murder of Michael Donald and awards his mother $7 million in damages.
- April 24, 1987: Ten white supremacists, including Richard Butler, Louis Beam, and Robert Miles, are indicted on seditious conspiracy charges in Fort Smith, Arkansas.

- April 30, 1987: Glenn Miller and three of his followers are arrested on fugitive warrants in Missouri.
- July 1987: White Aryan Resistance youth leader David Mazzella praises the Skinhead movement after Skinheads attack an elderly black woman on a bridge in San Jose, California.
- November 6, 1987: Aryan Nations ambassador-at-large Louis Beam is arrested in Mexico after having been placed on the FBI's Ten Most Wanted List.
- November 9, 1987: Chicago-area Skinheads vandalize several Chicago businesses and synagogues on the forty-ninth anniversary of Hitler's Kristallnacht attack on Jews in Germany.
- December 20, 1987: A black man is stabbed to death outside the Tampa Museum of Art in Florida by two Skinheads.
- July 25, 1988: Christian Identity minister and Posse Comitatus leader James Wickstrom is indicted for counterfeiting. Wickstrom and his accomplices intended to use the money to buy stolen weapons and establish a white supremacist paramilitary training camp in Pennsylvania.
- November 13, 1988: Mulgreta Seraw, an Ethiopian man, is beaten to death by Skinheads in Portland, Oregon.
- December 10, 1988: A black man is murdered by Skinheads in Reno, Nevada.
- January 14, 1989: About 400 Skinheads and Klan members march in Pulaski, Tennessee.
- May 19, 1989: Klan member Frank Cox is convicted for the murder of Michael Donald in Mobile, Alabama.
- September 1989: Six hundred Klan members and Skinheads rally at Stone Mountain, Georgia.
- September 30, 1989: Sixteen Skinheads are indicted on civil rights and weapons violations charges by Justice Department.
- October 23, 1989: Four Posse Comitatus members are arrested in North Carolina in connection with a $3 million real estate fraud.

Source: The Klanwatch Project of the Southern Poverty Law Center, Hate Violence and White Supremacy. (1989). Montgomery, AL: The Center.

REFERENCES

ABADINSKY, H. (1981). *The Mafia in America: An Oral History.* New York: Praeger.
———. (1985). *Organized Crime.* Chicago: Nelson-Hall.
———. (1990). *Organized Crime,* 2nd ed. Chicago: Nelson-Hall.
———. (1994). *Organized Crime,* 3rd ed. Chicago: Nelson-Hall.
———. (1997). *Organized Crime,* 5th ed. Chicago: Nelson-Hall.
———. (2002). *Organized Crime.* 7th ed. Belmont, CA: Wadsworth.
AHIRE, P. (1990). Re-writing the distorted history of policing in colonial Nigeria. *International Journal of the Sociology of Law* 18(1): 45–60.
ALBANESE, J. (1985). *Organized Crime in America.* Cincinnati, OH: Anderson.
———. (1989). *Organized Crime in America,* 2nd ed. Cincinnati, OH: Anderson.
ALBANESE, J. S., and R. D. PURSLEY. (1993). *Crime in America: Some Existing and Emerging Issues.* Upper Saddle River, NJ: Prentice Hall.
ALBINI, J. L. (1971). *The American Mafia: Genesis of a Legend.* New York: Appleton-Century-Crofts.
ALBINI, J. R., E. ROGERS, and J. ANDERSON. (2000). Russian organized crime and weapons of terror: The reality of nuclear proliferation. In D. Rounds, ed. *International Criminal Justice: Issues in a Global Perspective* (pp. 19–31). Boston: Allyn and Bacon.
ANDERSON, A. G. (1979a). *The Business of Organized Crime: A Cosa Nostra Family.* Stanford, CA: Hoover Institution Press.
ANDERSON, J. (1979b). Washington merry-go-round. *Washington Post,* April 12.
ANDERSON, M. E. (2001). Al-Qaeda across the Americas. *Insight on the News* 17, 44 (November): 20–21.
ANTHONY, I. (1929). *Paddle Wheels and Pistols.* Philadelphia: Macrae Smith.
ANTI-DEFAMATION LEAGUE OF B'NAI B'RITH. (1988a). *Extremism on the Right: A Handbook.* New York: B'nai B'rith.
———. (1988b). *Hate Groups in America: A Record of Bigotry and Violence.* New York: B'nai B'rith.
ASBURY, H. (1938). *Sucker's Progress.* New York: Dodd, Mead.
———. (1940). *The French Quarter: An Informal History of the New Orleans Underworld.* New York: Knopf.
ASUNI, T., and O. A. PELA. (1986). Drug abuse in Africa. *Bulletin on Narcotics,* 38(1–2): 55–64.
ATKINSON, G. (1981). *After the Moonshiners: By One of the Raiders.* Wheeling, WV: Steam Book and Job Printers.
BAINERMAN, J. (1992). *The Crimes of a President.* New York: SPI Books.
BALDAUF, S. (1994). Killings spur move to stem abortion clinic violence. *Christian Science Monitor,* December 30.
BARTOLOME, M. C. (2001). Threats to the Security of States: The Triborder Region as a "Grey Area" in the Cone of South America. November 29. *www.geocities.com/mvbartolome/triplefonteral.htm.*
BEATY, J., and S. GWYNNE. (1991). The dirtiest bank of all. *Time,* July 29: 42–47.
BEIRNE, P., and J. MESSERSCHMIDT. (1991). *Criminology.* New York: Harcourt Brace Jovanovich.
BELL, D. (1953). Crime as an American way of life. *Antioch Reviews,* 13, Summer: 131–154.

BELL, J. B., and T. R. GURR. (1979). Terrorism and revolution in America. In H. D. Gram and T. R. Gurr, eds., *Violence in America.* Newbury Park, CA: Sage.

BENNETT, D. H. (1988). *The Party of Fear: From Nativist Movements to the New Right in American History.* Chapel Hill: University of North Carolina Press.

BEST, J., and D. F. LUCKENBILL. (1994). *Organizing Deviance,* 2nd ed. Upper Saddle River, NJ: Prentice Hall, p. 60.

BLAKEY, G. R., and R. N. BILLINGS. (1981). *The Plot to Kill the President.* New York: Time Books.

BLAU, P., and J. BLAU. (1982). The cost of inequality: Metropolitian structure and violent crime. *American Sociological Review* 147, 154: 29.

BLOCK, A. (1978). History and the study of organized crime. *Urban Life* 6: 455–474.

———. (1979). The snowman cometh: Coke in progressive New York. *Criminology* 17, May: 75–99.

———. (1983). *East Side–West Side: Organizing Crime in New York, 1930–1950.* New Brunswick, NJ: Transaction.

———. (1986). A modern marriage of convenience: A collaboration between organized crime and U.S. intelligence. In R. Kelly, ed., *Organized Crime: A Global Perspective.* Totowa, NJ: Rowan & Littlefield.

———. (1991). *Masters of Paradise: Organized Crime and the Internal Revenue Service in the Bahamas.* New Brunswick, NJ: Transaction.

BLOCK, A., and W. J. CHAMBLISS. (1981). *Organizing Crime.* New York: Elsevier.

BLOCK, A., and F. SCARPITTI. (1985). *Poisoning for Profit: The Mafia and Toxic Waste in America.* New York: Morrow.

BLOK, A. (1974). *The Mafia of a Sicilian Village, 1860–1960.* New York: Harper & Row.

BLUM, H., and J. GERTH. (1978). The mob gambles on Atlantic City. *New York Times Magazine,* February 15.

BOOTH, M. (1990). *Triads: The Growing Global Threat from the Chinese Criminal Societies.* New York: St. Martin's Press.

BRADY, E. (2002). Russian charged in Olympic skating fix. *USA Today,* August 1: 1–A.

BRANTLEY, A. C., and A. DIROSA. (1994). Gangs: A national perspective. *FBI Law Enforcement Bulletin,* May: 1–19.

BREWTON, P. (1992a). *The Mafia, CIA and George Bush.* New York: SPI Books.

———. (1992b). *Untold Story.* New York: SPI Books.

BRILL, S. (1978). *The Teamster.* New York: Simon & Schuster.

BUENKER, J. D. (1973). *Urban Liberalism and Progressive Reform.* New York: Scribner's.

———. (1992). *Drugs, Crime, and the Criminal Justice System.* December.

BYNUM, T. S. (1987). Controversies in the study of organized crime. In T. Bynum, ed., *Organized Crime in America: Concept and Controversies.* Monsey, NY: Willow Tree Press.

CALIFORNIA DEPARTMENT OF JUSTICE, DIVISION OF LAW ENFORCEMENT. (July 1976). *Organized Crime Involvement in California Pornography Operations.* Sacramento, CA: The Department.

———. (July 1986). *Organized Crime in California.* Division of Law Enforcement. Sacramento, CA: Investigation and Enforcement Branch, Bureau of Organized Crime and Criminal Intelligence.

CAMP, G. M., and C. G. CAMP. (1985). *Prison Gangs: Their Extent, Nature and Impact on Prisons.* U.S. Department of Justice, Office of Legal Policy. Washington DC: U.S. Government Printing Office.

CARR, J. (1972). *The Second Oldest Profession: An Informal History of Moonshining in America.* Upper Saddle River, NJ: Prentice Hall.

CASTELLS, M. (1998). *End of Millenium, The Information Age: Economy Society and Culture.* Vol. 3. Oxford: Blackwell.

CASTRO, J. (1988). The cash cleaners. *Time,* October 24: 65–66.

CAVENDER, G., and L. BOND-MAUPIN. (1993). Fear and loathing on reality television: An analysis of America's most wanted and unsolved mysteries. *Sociological Inquiry* 63(3): 305–317.

CHAMBLISS, W. J. (1964). A sociological analysis of the law of vagrancy. *Social Problems,* 12 (Summer).

———. (1976). Vice, corruption, bureaucracy and power. In W. Chambliss and M. Mankoff, eds., *Whose Law? What Order?* New York: Wiley.

———. (1978). *On the Take.* Bloomington: Indiana University Press.

———. (1986). State-organized crime. Paper presented at the annual meeting of the American Society of Criminology, November.

———. (1988). *On the Take: From Petty Crooks to Presidents,* 2nd ed. Bloomington: Indiana University Press.

CHIN, K. (1996). *Chinatown Gangs: Extortion, Enterprise, and Ethnicity.* New York: Oxford University Press.

CLARK, T., and J. TIGUE. (1975). *Dirty Money.* New York: Simon & Schuster.

CLECKLEY, H. (1959). Psychopathic states. In S. Aneti, ed., *American Handbook of Psychiatry.* New York: Basic Books.

———. (1976). *The Mask of Insanity,* 5th ed. St. Louis, MO: Mosby.

CLOWARD, R. A., and L. E. OHLIN. (1960). *Delinquency and Opportunity: A Theory of Delinquent Gangs.* New York: Free Press.

COATES, R. (1930). *The Outlaw Years: The History of the Land Pirates of the Natchez Trace.* New York: Literary Guild of America.

COCKBURN, L. (1987). *Out of Control.* New York: Atlantic Monthly Press.

COHEN, A. K. (1965). The sociology of the deviant act: Anomie theory and beyond. *American Sociological Review* 30 (February).

COHEN, B. (1980). *Deviant Street Networks: Prostitution in New York City.* Lexington, MA: D.C. Heath.

COLITT, R. (2002). Brazil tracks down the real culprits behind surge in highway robberies. *Financial Times.* London: May 2: 10.

———. 2003. Another judge killed as drug crime alarms brazil. *Financial Times.* London: March 25: 11

CONDON, G., Jr. (1983). The power gamble: Paul Laxalt and the Nevada gang. *Washington Dossier:* September.

COOK, J., and J. CARMICHAEL. (1980). The invisible enterprise. *Forbes* 126, issues 7–11.

COOPER, M. (1995a). Montana's mother of all militias. *Nation,* May 22.

———. (1995b). Combatting terrorism. *Congressional Quarterly,* July 21: 1.

COPPOLA, V. (1989). Georgia's high sheriffs. *Newsweek,* August.

CRAMER, R. B. (1993). Men of honor. *Esquire,* June.

CRESSEY, D. R. (1967). The functions and structure of criminal syndicates. In *Task Force on Organized Crime.* Washington, DC: U.S. Government Printing Office, pp. 25–55.

———. (1969). *Theft of the Nation: The Structure and Operations of Organized Crime in America.* New York: Harper & Row.

———. (1972). *Criminal Organization: Its Elementary Forms*. New York: Harper and Row.

DABNEY, J. (1974). *Mountain Spirits: A Chronicle of Corn Whiskey from King James' Ulster Plantation to America's Appalachians and the Moonshine Life*. New York: Charles Scribner's Sons.

DALY, J. (2001). The suspects: The Latin American connection. *Jane's Terrorism and Security Monitor* 1, October.

DAVIS, R. S., and G. W. POTTER. (1991). Bootlegging and rural criminal entrepreneurship. *Journal of Crime and Justice*, 14(1): 145–159.

DEBORD, G. (1970). *The Society of the Spectacle*. Detroit, MI: Black and Red.

———. (1990). *Comments on the Society of the Spectacle*. New York: Verso.

Delinquent: Tackling Crime Needs Police Reform. (2002). *Economist*. London: October 5.

DEMARIS, O. (1981). *The Last Mafioso*. New York: Bantam.

———. (1986). *The Boardwalk Jungle*. New York: Bantam.

DENNING, D. E., and W. E. BAUGH. (1998). Encryption and evolving technologies: Tools of organized crime and terrorism. *Trends in Organized Crime*, 3(3): 44–75.

DeSTEFANO, A. (1985). Balkan connection: Brazen as the Mafia, ethnic Albanian thugs specialize in mayhem; active in the heroin trade, the faction is so violent, prosecutors need guards. *Wall Street Journal*, September 9: 1.

DODD, M. (2002). Kingpin's methods typical. *USA Today*, August 2: 10–C.

DONOVAN, F. (1966). *River Boats of America*. New York: Crowell.

DOWNIE, A. (2000). Corruption's roots deep and wide-reaching in Brazil. *Christian Science Monitor*. December 14: 6.

DRUG ENFORCEMENT ADMINISTRATION. (1989). *Drugs of Abuse*. Washington, DC: U.S. Government Printing Office, September.

———. (2002a). *Drug Intelligence Trend: Increase in Mexican Couriers Transporting Colombian Heroin to Mexico*. Washington, DC: DEA (December).

———. (2002b). *Anatomy of a Southeast Asian Heroin Conspiracy*. Washington, DC: DEA (August).

———. (2002c). *Mexico Country Brief*. Washington, DC: DEA (July).

———. (2002d). *Changing Dynamics of Cocaine Production in the Andean Region*. Washington, DC: DEA (June).

———. (2002e). *Burma Country Brief*. Washington, DC: DEA (May).

———. (2002f). *The Drug Trade in Colombia: A Threat Assessment*. Washington, DC: DEA (March).

DUFFY, B., J. TRIMBLE, and Y. SHCHEKOCHIKHIN. (1994). The wise guys of Russia. *U.S. News & World Report*, March 7: 41–47.

———, and G. WITKIN. (1995). The old man and the seizures. *U.S. News & World Report*, June 37.

DUKE, L. (1996). Drug trade moves in on S. Africa. *Washington Post*, September 1: A33.

ECHEVARRIA, V., and A. RAKE. (1993). Scramble for Africa's diamonds. *New African*, November: 24.

EREZ, E. (2001). Women as victims and survivors in the context of transnational crime. In N. Ollus and S. Nevala, eds. *Women in the Criminal Justice System: International Examples and National Responses* (pp. 136–146). Monsey, NY: Criminal Justice Press/Willow Tree Press.

ESKRIDGE, C. (1998). The Mexican cartels: A challenge for the 21st century. *Criminal Organizations*, 12: 1, 2.

ESTEP, B. (1991). If sheriffs don't resign, they face ouster proceedings. *Lexington Herald-Leader,* August 17: 10.

Failing firm paid Neil Bush big salary. (1992). *San Francisco Examiner,* September 15: A9.

FARRINGTON, D. (1988). Psychobiological factors in the explanation and reduction of delinquency. *Today's Delinquent,* 2(37): 51.

FEDARKO, K. (1993). Escobar's dead end. *Time,* December 13: 46.

———. (2000). *Terrorism in the United States: 1999: 30 Years of Terrorism: A Retrospective Perspective. Counterterrorism Threat and Warning Unit.* Washington, DC: U.S. Government Printing Office.

Fernandino Is Shown to the Press. (2001). *El Tiempo.* Bogota. April 21.

FERRETTI, F. (1966). Mister untouchable. *New York Times Magazine,* June 5: 15–17, 106, 108–109.

FIELDS, G., and B. TWIGG. (1996). More church fires set; girl arrested. *USA Today,* June 11: 1A.

FINANCIAL CRIMES ENFORCEMENT NETWORK. (1992). *Russian Organized Crime. U.S. Department of the Treasury.* Washington, DC: U.S. Government Printing Office.

FINCKENAUER, J. (2000). Meeting the challenge of transnational crime. *National Institute of Justice Journal.* July.

FIRESTONE, T. (1993). Mafia memoirs: What they tell us about organized crime. *Journal of Contemporary Criminal Justice,* 9(3): 197–220.

FLEISHER, M. S., and S. DECKER. (2001). An overview of the challenge of prison gangs. *Corrections Management Quarterly.*

FRANKEL, B. (1995a). Radical Islam, West face off again in NYC. *USA Today,* January 9: 2A.

———. (1995b). Extortion now the least of its illegal activities. *USA Today,* September 14: 1A.

FREEDBERG, S. (1988). Contras, "Bugs" and the Mob. *Wall Street Journal,* August 9.

FRIED, A. (1980). *The Rise and Fall of the Jewish Gangster in America.* New York: Holt, Rinehart and Winston.

FRIEDMAN, R. I. (1984). Senator Paul Laxalt, the man who runs the Reagan campaign. *Mother Jones,* August–September: 32–39.

FRIEND, T. (1996). Colombia now source of heroin. *USA Today,* September 4: 1A.

FRIMAN, H. R., and P. ANDREAS. (1999). *Illicit Global Economy and State Power.* New York: Rowman & Littlefield.

FRISBY, M. (1992). Bush sons' ventures expose him to scrutiny. *Austin American-Statesman,* May 17: G1.

FRITZ, S. (1992). Bush kin: Trading on the name? Evidence suggests the president's relatives may be exploiting their relationship. But they hotly deny impropriety, saying such accusations are spinoffs of the Bill Clinton scandals. *Los Angeles Times,* May 10: 1.

GAGE, N. (1971). *The Mafia Is Not an Equal Opportunity Employer.* New York: McGraw-Hill.

GALEOTTI, M. (2000a). Turkish organized crime: Where state, crime and rebellion conspire. *Transnational Organized Crime,* 1.

GALLANT, T. W. (1999). Brigandage, piracy, capitalism, and state-formation: Transnational crime from a historical world-systems perspective. In J. M. Heyman, ed. *From States and Illegal Practices* (pp. 25–61). New York: Berg Publishers.

GALLIHER, J., and J. CAIN. (1974). Citation support for the Mafia myth in criminology textbooks. *American Sociologist,* 9: 68–74.

GARDINER, J. A. (1967). Public attitudes toward gambling and corruption. *Annals of the American Academy of Political and Social Science,* 17: 374.

———. (1970). *The Politics of Corruption: Organized Crime in an American City.* New York: Russell Sage Foundation.

———, and T. R. LYMAN. (1978). *Decisions for Sale: Corruption and Reform in Land-Use and Building Regulations.* New York: Praeger.

GARNER, G. W. (1985). *Outlaw Motorcycle Gangs and the Drug Trade.* Special report. Washington, DC: U.S. Department of Justice, p. 3.

GEORGES-ABEYIE, D. (1983). Women as terrorists. *Perspectives in Terrorism.* Wilmington, DE: Scholarly Resources.

GLOCK, C. (N.D.) Brazil–Paraguay: A Full Plate for Journalists. *www.impunidad. com/atrisk/brasil_paraguay7_19_01E.html.*

GODDARD, D. (1978). *Easy Money.* New York: Farrar, Straus & Giroux.

GOLDBERG, J. (2002). In the party of God. *New Yorker,* 79, 32: (October).

GOODMAN, E. (1995). Pro-life fanatics have taken their rhetoric over the edge. *Boston Globe,* January 4: 6B.

GOVERNOR'S ORGANIZED CRIME PREVENTION COMMISSION. (1990). *New Mexico Prison Gangs.* Albuquerque, NM. New Mexico Department of Public Safety Organized Crime Bureau, July.

GRABOSKY, P., R. SMITH, and G. DEMPSEY. (2001). *Electronic Theft: Unlawful Acquisition in Cyberspace.* Oakleigh, Australia: Oxford University Press.

GRIFFITH, G. (1975). Life and Adventures of Revenooer No. 1. Birmingham, AL: Gander Publishers.

GRINBAUM, R. (1996). In Paraguay, smugglers' paradise. *World Press Review,* 43, 1 (January): 25–26.

GROVE, W. (1995). The drug trade as a national and international security threat. *CJ International,* May–June.

GUSFIELD, J. (1963). *Symbolic Crusade: Status Politics and the American Temperance Movement.* Urbana: University of Illinois Press.

HALLER, M. (1972). Organized crime in urban society: Chicago in the twentieth century. *Journal of Social History,* 5: 222.

———. (1979). Changing structure of American gambling in the twentieth century. In E. H. Monkkonen, ed., *Prostitution, Drugs, Gambling and Organized Crime, Part 1.* (pp. 313–340). New York: K. G. Saur.

———. (1990). Illegal enterprise: A theoretical and historical interpretation. *Criminology,* 28(2), May: 207–236.

HALPERN, T., D. ROSENBERG, and I. SUALL. (1996). Militia movement: Prescription for disaster. *USA Today Magazine,* January: 17–22.

HAMILL, P. (1984). With friends like these. *Village Voice,* August 21: 13.

HAMMER, R. (1975). *Playboy's Illustrated History of Organized Crime.* Chicago: Playboy Press.

———. (2002). Gotti dies with his legacy in ruins. *USA Today,* June 11, 7-A.

HARE, R. D. (1980). A research scale for the assessment of psychopathy in criminal populations. *Personality and Individual Differences,* 1: 111–119.

HARRING, S. L. (1977). Class conflict and the suppression of tramps in Buffalo, 1892–1894. *Law and Society Review,* 11, Summer.

———. (1983). *Policing a Class Society.* New Brunswick, NJ: Rutgers University Press.

HARRIS, J. W. (1987). Domestic terrorism in the United States in 1985. In P. Wilkenson and A. M. Stewart, eds. (pp. 230–240). *Contemporary Research on Terrorism*. Aberdeen, Scotland: Aberdeen University Press.

HAVIGHURST, W. (1964). *Voices on the River: The Story of Mississippi Waterways*. New York: Macmillan.

HEDGES, S. (1992). The color of money: The president's eldest son and his ties to a troubled Texas firm. *U.S. News and World Report,* March 16.

HELLMAN, D. A. (1980). *The Economics of Crime*. New York: St. Martin's Press.

HELM, L. (1991a). Japanese wise up to gangsters: Yakuza have long been tolerated and even romanticized. But with financial scandals and violent tactics, lawmakers and residents are saying enough is enough. *Los Angeles Times,* August 1: 1.

———. (1991b). Bush brother was a consultant to company under scrutiny in Japan finance: Prescott Bush gave investment advice to a firm lately suspected of gangland ties and of exchange violations, police investigators say. *Los Angeles Times,* June 11: 10.

HELVARG, D. (1995). The anti-enviro connection. *Nation,* May 22: 722.

HERMAN, E. (1982). *The Real Terror Network*. Boston: South End Press.

HESS, H. (1973). *Mafia and Mafioso: The Structure of Power*. Lexington, MA: D.C. Heath.

HILLS, S. L. (1969). Combating organized crime in America. *Federal Probation,* 33 (March).

HINCKLE, W., and W. TURNER. (1981). *The Fish Is Red: The Story of the Secret War against Castro*. New York: Harper & Row.

HINDUS, M. S. (1977). The contours of crime and justice in Massachusetts and South Carolina, 1767–1878. *American Journal of Legal History,* 21 (July).

HOBSBAWN, E. (1959). *Primitive Rebels*. New York: W. W. Norton.

HOCKSTADER, L. (1995). Crime atop chaos. *Washington Post,* March 20–26: 6–9.

HOFFMAN, B. (1987). Terrorism in the United States in 1985. In P. Wilkenson and A. M. Stewart, eds. *Contemporary Research on Terrorism* (p. 230). Aberdeen, Scotland: Aberdeen University Press.

HOLDEN, R. (1986). *Postmillennialism as a Justification for Right-Wing Violence*. Gaithersburg, MD: International Association of Chiefs of Police.

HOMER, F. D. (1983). Terror in the United States: Three perspectives. In M. Stohl, ed., *The Politics of Terrorism* (pp. 145–177). New York: Marcel Dekker.

Hong Kong mafia linked to Hizballah in tri-border region. 2002. *ABC Color.* Asunción. November 22.

HOSER, R. (1993). *Smuggled: The Underground Trade in Australia's Wildlife*. Doncaster, Australia: Kotabi Publications.

———. (1996). *Smuggled-2: Wildlife Trafficking, Crime and Corruption in Australia*. Doncaster, Australia: Kotabi Publications.

HOWLETT, D. (1995). Incidents, reports spark FBI probe. *USA Today,* January 10: A1.

HUANG, F., and M. VAUGHN. (1992). A descriptive analysis of Japanese organized crime: The Boryokudan from 1945 to 1988. *International Criminal Justice Review,* 2: 19–57.

HUNTER, J. M. (1983). All organized crime isn't Mafia: A case study of a non-traditional criminal organization. Paper presented at the meeting of the Academy of Criminal Justice Sciences, San Antonio, Texas, March.

HUTCHINSON, J. (1970). *Imperfect Union: A History of Corruption in American Trade Unions*. New York: Dutton.

IANNI, F.A.J. (1973). *Ethnic Succession in Organized Crime*. Washington, DC: U.S. Government Printing Office.

———. (1974). *Black Mafia: Ethnic Succession in Organized Crime*. New York: Simon & Schuster.

———, and E. REUSSO-IANNI. (1972). *A Family Business: Kinship and Social Control in Organized Crime*. New York: Russell Sage Foundation.

IGBINOVIA, P. E. (1982). Police in trouble: Administrative and organizational problems in the Nigeria police force. *International Journal of Public Administration*, 28(2): 334–372.

INCIARDI, J. A. (1975). *Careers in Crime*. Chicago: Rand McNally.

———, BLOCK, and L. HALLOWELL. (1977). *Historical Approaches to Crime*. Beverly Hills, CA: Sage.

IREY, E., and W. J. SLOCUM. (1948). *The Tax Dodgers*. New York: Greenberg.

ISIKOFF, M. (1992). As race heats up, so does scrutiny of Bush's family; relatives' business affairs become target. *Washington Post*, July 14: A1.

———. (1995). A turncoat in the drug war. *Newsweek*, June 26: 26.

JACKALL, R. (1997). Wild cowboys: Urban marauders and the forces of order. Cambridge, MA: Harvard University Press.

JAMES, J. (1976). Motivations for entrance in prostitution. In L. Crites, ed. *The Female Offender*. Lexington, MA: D. C. Heath.

———. (1977). Prostitutes and prostitution. In E. Sagarin and F. Montanino, eds. *Deviants: Voluntary Actors in a Hostile World*. Morristown, NJ: General Learning Press.

———. (1980). *Perspectives on Prostitution*. Seattle, WA: Judicial Advocates.

JENKINS, P., and G. W. POTTER. (1986a). Organized crime in London: A comparative perspective. *Corruption and Reform*, 1(2): 165–187.

JOHNSON, K. (1996). Feds say 17 leaders of Detroit's underworld indicted and arrested. *USA Today*, March 15: 2A.

JOHNSTON, O. (1990). Seidman puts S&L bailout at $500 billion. *Los Angeles Times*, July 31: 1.

JONES, P. M. (2002). Pirated goods cripple Brazil's economy, but solutions seen as weak. *Chicago Tribune*, November 4: 1.

JOUSTEN, M. (1993). Organized crime in Eastern Europe. *Criminal Justice International*, March–April: 11–18.

JUNGER, S. (2002). Terrorism's new geography. *Vanity Fair*, 508 (December).

KAPPELER, V., M. BLUMBERG, and G. POTTER. (1993). *The Mythology of Crime and Criminal Justice*. Prospect Heights, IL: Waveland Press.

KARABI-WHYTE, A. G. (1982). Cultural pluralism and the formulation of criminal policy: A comparative criminology report. *Revue Internationale de Criminologie et de Police Technique*, 35(4): 339–352.

KATZ, L. M. (1998). U.S. offers $5M for bin Laden. *USA Today*, November 5: 1A.

KAYODE, P. (1983). Nigeria. In E. J. Johnson, ed. *International Handbook of Contemporary Developments in Criminology* (pp. 473–493). Westport, CT: Greenwood Press.

KEFAUVER, E. (1951). *Third Interim Report*. Washington, DC: U.S. Government Printing Office.

KELLNER, E. (1971). *Moonshine: Its History and Folklore*. Indianapolis, IN: Bobbs-Merrill.

KELLY, R. J. (1987). The nature of organized crime and its operations. In *Major Issues in Organized Crime*. Washington, DC: National Institute of Justice.

———. (1989). 40% in the country said to grow weed. *USA Today*, July 11.

KENNEY, D., and J. FINCKENAUER. (1995). *Organized Crime in America*. Belmont, CA: Wadsworth.

KERRY, J. (1986). *Interim Report. Subcommittee on Narcotics, Terrorism, and International Operations, United States Senate*. Washington, DC: U.S. Government Printing Office.

KIBUKA, E. P. (1979). Crime in African countries. *International Review of Criminal Policy*, 35: 13–23.

KING, R. (1969). *Gambling and Organized Crime*. Washington, DC: Public Affairs Press.

KIRK, S., P. MANCUST, T. PALMER, and M. E. MALONE. (1983). A rift within organized crime. *Boston Globe*, February 16.

KLARE, M. (2001). How the war on terrorism could escalate. *Foreign Policy in Focus*, September.

KLEIMAN, M. A. R. (1988). Crackdowns: The effects of intensive enforcement on retail heroin dealing. *NIJ Issues and Practices*, September.

KLEIN, M., C. L. MAXON, and J. MILLER, eds. (1995). *The Modern Gang Reader*. Los Angeles, CA: Roxbury.

KLINE, H. (1995). *Colombia: Democracy under Assault*. Boulder, CO: Westview.

KNAPP COMMISSION. (1972). *Report of the Commission to Investigate Alleged Police Corruption*. New York: Braziller.

KOBLER, J. (1958). King of the moonshiners. *Saturday Evening Post*, August 2.

KOHN, H. (1976). The Nixon–Hughes–Lansky connection. *Rolling Stone*, May 20: 41–50, 77–78.

KOOISTRA, P. (1989). *Criminals as Heroes: Structure, Power and Identity*. Bowling Green, OH: Popular Press.

KRUGER, H. (1980). *The Great Heroin Coup*. Boston: South End Press.

KWITNY, J. (1987). *The Crimes of Patriots: A True Tale of Dope, Dirty Money, and the CIA*. New York: Norton.

———. (1992). The real S&L scandal: How Bush's pals broke the banks. *Village Voice*, October 20: 24.

LACAYO, R. (1992). Why is Sammy the Bull singing? *Time*, March 16: 31.

LA FRANIERE, S. (1990). S&L bailout involved Jeb Bush partnership: Federal government paid $4 million on an investment loan issued by Florida thrift. *Washington Post*, October 15: A24.

LANDESCO, J. (1929). *Organized Crime in Chicago*. Chicago: University of Chicago Press.

LANGLAIS, R. (1978). Inside the heroin trade: How a star double agent ended up dead. *Village Voice*, March 13: 13–15.

LAQUEUR, W. (1997). Postmodern terrorism. *Foreign Affairs*, September–October: 24–36.

LARDNER, G., and L. ROMANO. (1999). The life of George W. Bush: The turning point; After coming up dry, financial rescues. *Washington Post*, September 30: A1.

LASWELL, H. D., and J. McKENNA. (1971). *The Impact of Organized Crime on an Inner-City Community*. New York: Policy Sciences Center.

LAVOIE, D. (2002). Ex-FBI agent sentenced in mob tip-off. *USA Today*, September 17, 3-A.

LEHMAN, S. (2002). Brazilian police thwart bomb plot. *Columbian*, October 22: A5.

LERNOUX, P. (1984). *In Banks We Trust*. Garden City, NY: Doubleday.

LEWIS, N. (1964). *The Honoured Society*. New York: Putnam's.

Licking Valley Courier. (1989). Former sheriff begins jail term. January 1.

LIGHT, I. (1992). Numbers gambling among blacks: A financial institution. In E. Monkkonen, ed. *Prostitution, Drugs, Gambling and Organized Crime, Part 2.* New York: K. G. Saur.

LINEDECKER, C. (1981). *Children in Chains.* New York: Everett House.

Lino Oviedo Case and Its Connection with Argentina. N.D. *Página.* Buenos Aires: www.pagina12.com.ar/2001/suple/carrio/cap11.pdf

LINTNER, B. (1996). Narcopolitics in Burma. *Current History,* 95(602): 432–437.

LUKSETICH, W. A., and M. D. WHITE. (1982). *Crime and Public Policy: An Economic Approach.* Boston: Little, Brown.

LUPSHA, P. A. (1981). Individual choice, material cultures, and organized crime. *Criminology,* 18: 3–24.

———. (1990). Minimizing danger in drug enforcement. *Law and Order,* September: 21.

———, and G. W. POTTER. (1991). *Drugs in Society.* Cincinnati, OH: Anderson.

———, and ———. (1996). *Drugs in Society: Causes, Concepts, and Control,* 2nd ed. Cincinnati, OH: Anderson.

MACKO, S. (1997). Today's Mexican drug cartels. *ERRI Daily Intelligence Report—ERRI Risk Assessment Services,* 3, 338; December 4.

MAHON, G. (1980). *The Company That Bought the Boardwalk.* New York: Random House.

MARSHALL, T., and G. EVANS. (1939). *They Found It in Natchez.* New Orleans, LA: Pelican Publishing Co.

MARTENS, F., and M. CUNNINGHAM-NIEDERER. (1985). Media magic, Mafia mania. *Federal Probation,* 49(2): 60–68.

MARX, G. (1988). *Undercover: Police Surveillance in America.* Berkeley: University of California Press.

MASTROFSKI, S., and G. W. POTTER. (1986). Evaluating law enforcement efforts to control organized crime: The Pennsylvania Crime Commission as a case study. *Policy Studies Review,* 6: 1.

MCALISTER, B. (1989). Organized crime fighters losing independence in Thornburgh plan. *Washington Post,* December 28: A21.

MCCAGHY, C. H., and S. A. CERNKOVICH. (1987). *Crime in American Society.* New York: Macmillan.

MCCOY, A. (1972). *The Politics of Heroin in Southeast Asia.* New York: Harper & Row.

MCFADDEN, R. D. (1987). The Mafia of the 1980s: Divided and under siege. *New York Times,* March 11: A1.

MCGRAW, S. (2000). Statement for the Record of Steven C. McGraw, Deputy Assistant Director Investigative Services Division Federal Bureau of Investigation, December 13, 2000 (*www.fbi.gov*).

MEDDIS, S. V. (1993). Declaration of war on Mafia. *USA Today,* December 13: 3A.

———. (1994). Smack's back. *USA Today,* May 25: 3A.

MERTON, R. (1938). Social structure and anomie. *American Sociological Review,* 3.

———. (1957). *Social Theory and Social Structure.* New York: Free Press.

MESSICK, H. (1967). *The Silent Syndicate.* New York: Macmillan.

———. (1969). *Secret File.* New York: Macmillan.

———. (1972). *The Mobs and the Mafia.* New York: Ballantine.

———. (1973). *Lansky.* New York: Berkeley.

MESSICK, H., and B. GOLDBLATT. (1972). *The Mobs and the Mafia: An Illustrated History of Organized Crime.* New York: Gallahad.

———, and ———. (1976). *The Only Game in Town.* New York: Thomas Y. Crowel.

MESSICK, H., and J. L. NELLIS. (1973). *The Private Lives of Public Enemies*. New York: Dell.

MIECZKOWSKI, T. (1986). Geeking up and throwing down: Heroin street life in Detroit. *Criminology*, 24(4): 645–666. *biondi.fcl.com.br/facasper/jornalismo/esquinas/noticia.cfm?secao=4&codigo=87*.

MILIBANK, D. (2000). Dispelling doubts with the rangers. *Washington Post*, July 25: A1.

MILLER, E. (1986). *Street Women*. Philadelphia. Temple University Press.

MILLER, W. (1991). *Revenuers and Moonshiners: Enforcing Federal Liquor Law in the Mountain South, 1865–1900*. Chapel Hill: University of North Carolina Press.

MILLER, W. B. (1958). Lower class culture as a generating milieu of gang delinquency. *Journal of Social Issues*, 14.

MILLS, J. (1986). *The Underground Empire*. New York: Doubleday.

MOLDEA, D. E. (1978). *The Hoffa Wars: Teamsters, Rebels, Politicians and the Mob*. New York: Paddington.

———. (1982). Reagan administration officials closely linked with OC. *Organized Crime Digest*, February: 6–10.

———. (1983). More than just good friends. *Nation*, June 11: 732.

———. (1986). *Dark Victory: Ronald Reagan, MCA, and the Mob*. New York: Viking.

MOLLENHOFF, C. R. (1973). *Strike Force: Organized Crime and the Government*. Upper Saddle River, NJ: Prentice Hall.

MOORE, M. (1987). Organized crime as a business enterprise. In H. Edelhertz, ed. *Major Issues in Organized Crime Control*. Washington, DC: National Institute of Justice.

MOORE, M. H. (1990). Supply reduction and drug law enforcement. *Crime and Justice*, 13.

MOORE, R. H. (1994). Wiseguys: Smarter criminals and smarter crime in the 21st century. *Futurist*, September–October: 33–37.

MOORE, W. (1974). *The Kefauver Committee and the Politics of Crime, 1950–1952*. Columbia, MO: University of Missouri Press.

MORASH, M., and D. HALE. (1987). Unusual crime or crime as usual? Images of corruption at the Interstate Commerce Commission. In T. Bynum, ed. *Organized Crime in America: Concepts and Controversies* (pp. 129–148). Monsey, NY: Criminal Justice Press.

MORRIS, N., and G. HAWKINS. (1970). *The Honest Politician's Guide to Crime Control*. Chicago: University of Chicago Press.

MORRISON, M. (1999). Vetting the frontrunners I — George W. Bush: From oil to baseball to the governor's mansion. *Wall Street Journal*, September 28: A26.

MOSES, J. (1992). Prescott Bush faces inquiry over pay received in arranging investment deal. *Wall Street Journal*, September 9: C15.

MUELLER, H. (1994). Fissile material smuggling: German politics, hype and reality. *Arms Control Today*, 24: December: 7–10.

MUELLO, P. (2003). Brazilians outraged by slayings of judges: Organized-crime groups unleash wave of violence. *Houston Chronicle*. March 27: 27.

———. (1991). Opium, cocaine and marijuana in American history. *Scientific American*, July: 40–47.

MYERS, W. H. III. (1995). The Emerging Threat of Transnational Organized Crime from the East. *Crime, Law and Social Change*, 24(3): 181–222.

NATIONAL COMMISSION ON TERRORISM. (2000). *Countering the Changing Threat of International Terrorism*. Washington, DC: U.S. Department of State.

National Criminal Intelligence Service. (2005). UK Threat Assessment Report. Home Office, London, UK: Paragraph 1.1.

National Institute of Justice. (1989). Illicit Drug Wholesale/Retail Price Report, United States. July.

———. (1990). Multijurisdictional drug law enforcement strategies: Reducing supply and demand. *Issues and Practices.* NIJ-126658: December: 7–9, 22.

———. (1993). Preventing illegal diversion of chemicals: A model statute. U.S. Department of Justice, Research in Brief. November: 2.

———. (1995). Update: State and local responses to terrorism. Washington, DC: U.S. Department of Justice, June.

National Narcotics Intelligence Consumers Committee. (1989). The NNICC Report 1988: The Supply of Illicit Drugs to the United States. June.

Nelli, H. (1976). *The Business of Crime: Italians and Syndicate Crime in the United States.* New York: Oxford University Press.

Nevadomsky, J. (1985). Drug use among Nigerian university students: Prevalence of self-reported use and attitudes to use. *Bulletin on Narcotics,* 37(2–3): 31–42.

Nordland, R., S. Yousafzai, and B. Dehghanpisheh. (2002). How Al Qaeda slipped away. *Newsweek.* August 19: 34–41.

Nurton, J. (2002). Goodbye to a difficult year: The world's leading IP practices. *Managing Intellectual Property.* London, June: 56–70.

O'Brien, J., and A. Kurins. (1991). *Boss of Bosses.* New York: Simon & Schuster.

Office of National Drug Control Policy. (1994). National Drug Control Strategy, Executive Summary. Washington, DC: U.S. Government Printing Office.

Office of Technology Assessment. (1995). Money Laundering. U.S. Congress Information Technologies for Control of Money Laundering. OTA-ITC-630. Washington, DC: U.S. Government Printing Office.

O'Neill, A. (1999). International trafficking in women to the United States: A contemporary manifestation of slavery. Washington DC: Central Intelligence Agency, Center for the Study of Intelligence.

Opolet, J. S. E. (1979). Organized crime in Africa. *International Journal of Comparative and Applied Criminal Justice,* 3(2): 177–183.

Orlando-Morningstar, D. (1997). Street Gangs. Special Needs Offenders Bulletin. Federal Judicial Center: August, pp. 1–16.

Osava, M. (1999). Cities of Latin America/Brazil: Laundering and Flight of Capital on the Border with Paraguay. Inter-Press Service report. *ips.org/Spanish/mundial/indices/Correo/cor0606051.htm.*

Oviedo, N. D. In the Triborder Area US $12 billion Is Laundered per Year from Narcotics Trafficking, According to an Official Report. *misionesonline.net/paginas/action.lasso?-database=noticias3&layout=web&-response=noticia.html&id=11349&autorizado=si&-search.*

Owomero, B. (1984). Crime and development: The Nigerian experience. *Canadian Criminology Forum,* 7(1): 41–56:

Palacios, C. and O. Florentin. (2002). Paraguay: Police confiscate arsenal from gangster's home. *Notcias.* Asuncion: December 6.

Paoli, L. (2002). The paradoxes of organized crime. *Crime Law and Social Change* (37)1: 51–97.

Paraguay: "Strong Ties" Seen between Hong Kong Mafia, Tri-border based Hizballah. (2002). *ABC Color.* Asunción: November 22.

Patsuris, P. (2002). The corporate scandal sheet. *Forbes Magazine,* August 5 (*www.forbes.com*).

PEARCE, F. (1976). *Crimes of the powerful: Marxism, crime and deviance*. London: Pluto Press.

PELA, O. (1989). Patterns of adolescent psychoactive substance use and abuse in Benin City, Nigeria. *Adolescence*, 14(95): 569–574.

PELLERANO R., and E. JORGE. (1997). Money laundering rules in the Dominican Republic. *Banking Law Journal*, 114(2): 136–141.

PENA, P. (1995). Drug war, crime on many minds. *USA Today*, December 12: 1A.

PENNSYLVANIA CRIME COMMISSION. (1974). *Report on Police Corruption in Philadelphia*. Harrisburg, PA: Commonwealth of Pennsylvania.

———. (1980). *A Decade of Organized Crime*. St. David's, PA: Commonwealth of Pennsylvania.

———. (1983). *Annual Report*. St. David's, PA: Commonwealth of Pennsylvania.

———. (1984). *Annual Report*. Harrisburg, PA: Commonwealth of Pennsylvania.

———. (1986). *Report*. Conshohocken, PA: Commonwealth of Pennsylvania.

———. (1987). *Annual Report*. Conshohocken, PA: Commonwealth of Pennsylvania.

———. (1990). *Organized Crime in Pennsylvania: A Decade of Change*. Conshohocken, PA: Commonwealth of Pennsylvania.

PETERSON, V. W. (1983). *The Mob: Two Hundred Years of Organized Crime in New York*. Ottawa, IL: Green Hill.

PHILLIPS, F. (1991). State fines Bush's brother in stock case. *Boston Globe*, July 26: 1.

PIZZO, S., M. FRICKER, and P. MUOLO. (1989). *Inside Job: The Looting of America's Savings and Loans*. New York: McGraw-Hill.

POTTER, G. W. (1986). *The Porn Merchants*. Dubuque, IA: Kendall/Hunt.

———. (1990). Black organized crime. *IASOC Notes*, 2(2): 3–8.

———. (1994). *Criminal Organizations: Vice, Racketeering and Politics in an American City*. Prospect Heights, IL: Waveland Press.

———, and L. K. GAINES. (1992). Country comfort: Vice and corruption in rural settings. *Journal of Contemporary Criminal Justice*, 8(1): 36–61.

———, L. GAINES, and B. HOLBROOK. (1990). Blowing smoke: marijuana eradication in Kentucky. *American Journal of Police*, 9.

———, and P. JENKINS. (1985). *The City and the Syndicate: Organizing Crime in Philadelphia*. Lexington, MA: Ginn.

———, and V. KAPPELER. (1998). *Constructing Crime*. Prospect Heights, IL: Waveland Press.

PRADOS, J. (1986). *President's Secret Wars*. New York: Morrow.

———. (1986a). *The Impact: Organized Crime Today*. Washington, DC: U.S. Government Printing Office.

———. (1986b). *America's Habit: Drug Abuse, Drug Trafficking and Organized Crime*. Washington, DC: U.S. Government Printing Office.

QUINNEY, R. (1975). *Criminology*. Boston: Little, Brown.

RABIN, A. (1979). The anti-social personality: Psychopathy and sociopathy. In Hans Toch, ed. *The Psychology of Crime and Criminal Justice*. New York: Holt, Rinehart and Winston.

RAKE, A. (1995). Drugged to the eyeballs. *New African*, June: 16–19.

RANKIN, H. (1969). *The Golden Age of Piracy*. New York: Holt, Rinehart & Winston.

RASHID, A. (1995). Nothing to declare: the political void in Afghanistan has spawned a vast smugglers' market that is crippling Pakistan's economy and threatens those of other nations in the region. *Far Eastern Economic Review*, 158: 58–60.

Raw, C., B. Page, and G. Hodgson. (1971). *Do You Sincerely Want to Be Rich?* New York: Viking.

Reiman, J. (1998). *The Rich Get Richer and the Poor Get Prison,* 5th ed. New York: Macmillan.

Renard, R. (1996). *The Burmese Connection: Illegal Drugs and the Making of the Golden Triangle.* Boulder, CO: L. Rienner.

Resendiz, R., and D. M. Neal. (1998). International auto theft: The illegal export of American vehicles to Mexico. In Delbert Rounds, ed. *International Criminal Justice: Issues in a Global Perspective* (pp. 7–18). Boston: Allyn and Bacon.

Reuter, P. (1983). *Disorganized Crime: The Economics of the Visible Hand.* Cambridge, MA: MIT Press.

————, J. Rubinstein, and J. Wynn. (1983). *Racketeering in Legitimate Industries: Two Case Studies.* Washington, DC: National Institute of Justice.

Richard, A. O. (2000). *International Trafficking in Women to the United States: A Contemporary Manifestation of Slavery and Organized Crime.* Washington, DC: United States Central Intelligence Agency.

Riyadh Alam-al-Din. (2001). Washington begins the war on Hizballah in the border triangle. *Al-Watan al-Arabi,* Paris: December 21: 18–19.

Robinson, J. (1999). *The Merger: How Organized Crime Is Taking Over Canada and the World.* Toronto, Canada: McClelland and Stewart.

Roe, C. (1910). *Panderers and Their White Slaves.* Chicago: Revell.

Rohter, L. (2001). Terrorists are sought in Latin smugglers' haven. *New York Times,* September 27: A3.

————. (2002a). Iran blew up Jewish center in Argentina, defector says. *New York Times,* July 24: A9.

————. (2002b). Slow-motion justice in Argentina. *New York Times,* March 11: A24.

————. (2002c). World briefing Americas: Menem acknowledges Swiss bank account. *New York Times,* July 25: A9.

Romano, L., and G. Lardner. (1999). Moving up to the major leagues; Father's campaign, baseball provide foundation for own run. *Washington Post,* July 31: A1.

Rosen, R. (1982). *The Lost Sisterhood: Prostitution in America, 1900–1918.* Baltimore: Johns Hopkins University Press.

Rosenau, W. (1994). Is the Shining Path the "New Khmer Rouge"? *Journal of Studies on Conflict and Terrorism,* 17: 305–322.

Rotella, S. (1998). Jungle hub for world's outlaws. *Los Angeles Times,* August 24: 1.

Rothert, O. (1924). *The Outlaws of Cave-in-Rock.* Cleveland, OH: Arthur H. Clark.

Rowan, R. (1986). The 50 biggest Mafia bosses. *Fortune,* November 10: 24–38.

Royce, K., and G. Shaw. (1988). The Jeb Bush connection: Bush son steered funds to Miami businessman. *Newsday,* October 3: 4.

Rubinstein, J., and P. Reuter. (1978). Fact, fancy and organized crime. *Public Interest,* 53.

Ruggiero, V. (1996). War markets: Corporate and organized criminals in Europe. *Social and Legal Studies,* 5(1): 5–20.

————. (1997). Trafficking in human beings: Slaves in contemporary Europe. *International Journal of the Sociology of Law,* 25(3): 231–244.

Ryan, P. (1995). *Organized Crime.* Santa Barbara, CA: ABC-CLIO.

Saba, R. P. et al. (1995). The demand for cigarette smuggling. *Economic Inquiry,* 33: 189–202.

SACK, K. (1999). George Bush the son finds that oil and blood do mix. *New York Times,* May 8: 1.

SATCHELL, M. (1979). The big business of selling smut. *Parade,* August 19.

SCHAFFER, E. (1996). Mexico's internal state conflict over the war on drugs. *Criminal Organizations,* 10(3).

SCHAPIRO, M. (1997). Doing the wash: Inside a Colombian cartel's money-laundering machine. *Harper's,* February: 56–59.

SCHELLING, T. (1976). What is the business of organized crime? In F. Ianni and E. Reuss-Ianni, eds. *The Crime Society—Organized Crime and Corruption in America* (pp. 69–96). New York: Times–Mirror.

SCHMID, A. P., and J. DE GRAAF. (1982). *Violence as Communication: Insurgent Terrorism and the Western News Media.* Beverly Hills, CA: Sage.

SCHMID, U. (1993). *Russia and the Plague of Organized Crime.* Zurich: Swiss Review of World Affairs, September: pp. 6–8.

SCHMIDT, W. E. (1984). New era, new problems for South's sheriffs. *New York Times,* September 10: 1, 15.

SCHUR, E. M. (1965). *Crimes without Victims.* Upper Saddle River, NJ: Prentice Hall.

SCOTT, P., ET AL. (1976). *The Assassinations.* New York: Random House.

SCOTT, W. (1988). Personality parade. *Parade,* October 30: 2.

SECK, I. (1991). Traffic in psychotropic substances in Africa. *International Criminal Police Review,* 429: 30–34.

SELLIN, T. (1938). *Culture, Conflict and Crime.* Bulletin 41. New York: Social Science Research Counsel.

SERWER, A. E. (1992). The Hells Angels' devilish business. *Fortune,* November: 118.

SHANNON, E. (1991). New kings of coke. *Time,* July 1: 29–36.

SHAW, C., and H. D. McKAY. (1942). *Juvenile Delinquency and Urban Areas.* Chicago: University of Chicago Press.

SHENON, P. (1988). Enemy within: Drug money is corrupting the enforcers. *New York Times,* April 11: A1, A12.

SHERRY, E. (1986). *Raiders and Rebels.* New York: Hearst Marine Books.

SHIBATA, Y. (1996). Quaking lenders: How gangsters complicate Japan's banking crisis. *Global Finance,* 10: 40–41.

SHUMACH, M. (1977). 30 indicted in Queens heroin crackdown. *New York Times,* April 15: 1, 37.

SIEGEL, L. (1992). *Criminology.* St. Paul, MN: West Publishing.

SILBERMAN, C. E. (1978). *Criminal Violence, Criminal Justice.* New York: Random House.

SILK, M. A. (1988). Economic crime in China: Despite strict definitions and harsh punishments for economic crime, many offenders are slipping through the net. *China Business Review,* 15 January/February: 25–29.

SILVA, R. (2000). Effective Measures to Combat Transnational Organized Crime in Criminal Justice Processes. Paper presented at the 116th International Training Course, Asia and Far East Institute for Prevention of Crime and Treatment of Offenders, Tokyo, November 2000. *www.unafei.or.jp/pdf/103.pdf.*

SILVER, G. (1979). *The Dope Chronicles 1850–1950.* San Francisco: Harper & Row.

SIMON, C. P., and A. D. WITTE (1982). *Beating the System: The Underground Economy.* Boston: Auburn House.

SIMON, D. R., and D. S. EITZEN. (1986). *Elite Deviance.* Boston: Allyn and Bacon.

SKLAR, H., and R. LAWRENCE. (1981). *Who's Who in the Reagan Administration.* Boston: South End Press.

SMITH, D. C., JR. (1974). *The Mafia Mystique.* New York: Basic Books.

———. (1978). Organized crime and entrepreneurship. *International Journal of Criminology and Penology,* 6.

———. (1980). Paragons, pariahs, and pirates: A spectrum-based theory of enterprise. *Crime and Delinquency,* 26.

———. (1990). *The Mafia Mystique.* Lanham, MD: University Press of America.

SMITH, R., M. HOLMES, and P. KAUFMANN. (1999). *Nigerian Advance Fee Fraud.* Canberra, Australia: Australian Institute of Criminology.

SMITH, R. G. (1999). *Defrauding Governments in the Twenty-First Century.* Canberra, Australia: Australian Institute of Criminology.

SMOLOWE, J. (1992). His turn to lose. *Time,* September 11: 47–48.

SOKAIR-GEORGE, E., and C. MANN. (1987). Petroleum industry and white-collar crime in Nigeria. *Indian Journal of Criminology,* 15(1): 56–66.

SONG, J., and J. DOMBRINK. (1994). Asian emerging crime groups: Examining the definition of organized crime. *Criminal Justice Review,* 19(2): 228–243.

SOUTHERN POVERTY LAW CENTER. (1989). *A Decade of Hate.* Montgomery, AL: The Center.

STERN, K. S. (1996). Militia mania. *USA Today Magazine,* January: 13–14.

STONE, M. (1990). Coke Inc.: Inside the big business of drugs. *New York Times,* July 16: 20–29.

Struck out. (1990). *San Diego Union Tribune,* January 1: B8.

SUTHERLAND, E. H. (1973). In Karl Schuessler, ed. *Edwin H. Sutherland: On Analyzing Crime.* Chicago: University of Chicago Press.

SUTTLES, G. D. (1968). *The Social Order of the Slum.* Chicago: University of Chicago Press.

SWEENEY, J. (2001). DEA boosts its role in Paraguay. *Washington Times,* August 21.

TAYLOR, I., P. WALTON, and J. YOUNG (1973). *The New Criminology.* New York: Harper & Row.

Thai democracy: pass the baht. (1996). *Far Eastern Economic Review,* 159, November 28: 16–19.

THAYER, A. (1995). Cambodia: Asia's new narco state? *Far Eastern Economic Review,* 158 (23): 24–27.

THOMAS, M. (1991). The greatest American shambles. *New York Review of Books,* January 31: 30.

THRASHER, F. M. (1927). *The Gang.* Chicago: University of Chicago Press.

TREASTER, J. (1989). A nice place: Just ask the drug barons. *New York Times Magazine,* May 23:

TRICK, M. M. (1976). *Chronology of Incidents of Terroristic, Quasi-terroristic, and Political Violence in the United States. National Advisory Committee on Criminal Justice Standards and Goals.* Washington, DC: U.S. Government Printing Office, March.

TURKUS, B., and S. FEDER. (1951). *Murder, Inc.* New York: Farrar, Straus and Young.

UNITED NATIONS. (2002). *Results of a Pilot Study of Forty Selected Organized Crime Groups in Sixteen Countries.* New York: United Nations: Office of Drugs and Crime.

U.S. DEPARTMENT OF STATE. (2001). *Country Reports on Human Rights Practices 2001. www.state.gov/g/drl/rls/hrrpt/2001/wha/8278. htm;www.state.gov/g/drl/rls/hrrpt/2001/wha/8297.htm.*

————. (2002). *International Narcotics Control Strategy Report 2002.* *www.state.gov/g/inl/rls/nrcrpt/2002/html/17952pf.htm.*

U.S. MARSHAL'S SERVICE. (1986). *Motorcycle Gangs.* Washington, DC: U.S. Department of Justice, June.

VETTER, H. J., and G. R. PEARLSTEIN. (1991). *Perspectives on Terrorism.* Pacific Grove, CA: Brooks/Cole.

VILLANO, A. (1978). *Brick Agent.* New York: Ballantine.

VOLOBUEV, A. (1989). Soviet Union: Combating organized crime. Problems and perspectives. *Criminal Justice International,* 5(6): 11–15.

WAAS, M. (1984). The Senator and the Mob. *City Paper.* Washington, DC, May 25: 14.

Wall Street Journal. (1991). Bush's son misses deadline for reporting "inside" sale. April 4: A4.

WALSH, D. (1983a). Agents say casino "skimmed" during Sen. Laxalt's ownership. *Sacramento Bee,* November 1: A9.

WALSH, M. (1977). *The Fence.* Westport, CT: Greenwood Press.

WARREN, R. L. (1973). *The Community in America.* New York: Rand McNally.

WEEMS, C. (1992). *A Breed Apart.* Tabor City, NC: Atlantic Printing.

WHITE, J. R. (1991). *Terrorism: An Introduction.* Pacific Grove, CA: Brooks/Cole.

WHYTE, W. F. (1961). *Street Corner Society.* Chicago: University of Chicago Press.

WILKINSON, P. (1974). *Political Terrorism.* New York: Wiley.

WILLIAMS, P. (1994). Transnational criminal organizations and international security. *Survival,* 36(1): 96–113.

————. (1995a). Transnational criminal organizations: Strategic alliances. *Washington Quarterly,* 18(1): 57–72.

————. (1995b). Transnational organized crime. *Criminal Organizations,* 9(3): 1–8.

————, and P. N. WOESSNER. (1996). The real threat of nuclear smuggling. *Scientific American,* 274 (January): 40–44.

WILSON, J. Q. (1975). *Thinking about Crime.* New York: Basic Books.

WISEMAN, P. (1998). Missiles hit Sudan, Afghanistan: Chemical plant terrorist camps were targeted. *USA Today,* August 21: 3A.

WISOTSKY, S. (1986). *Breaking the Impasse in the War on Drugs.* Westport, CT: Greenwood Press.

YOST, P. (2000). Crisis at Bush's Oil Company. Associated Press Online (September 7). www.ap.org.

ZABLUDOFF, S. (1998). Colombian narcotics organizations as business enterprises. *Transnational Organized Crime,* 3(2).

ZUNES, S. (2001a). International terrorism. *Foreign Policy in Focus,* September.

————. (2001b). The war in Afghanistan is far from over. *Foreign Policy in Focus,* November.

Chicago, 92–97, 104, 224, 244, 309
Chicago Commission of Inquiry (1915), 18, 40
Chicago White Sox, 105
Chile, 328, 347, 351
China
  contraband market, 164
  drug trafficking, 161, 203
  environmental crime, 171
  Fuk Ching, 297–298
  heroin, 210–211
  high-tech crime in, 181
  illicit gems and gold markets, 172
  immigrants, 295
  intellectual property rights (IPRs) violations, 172, 183
  mainland syndicates, 294, 296–297
  organized crime, 294–295
  revolutionary terrorism, 329
  Sicilian connection, 298
  street gangs, 294
  tongs, 294
  Triborder Area, 291–292
Chinese Triads, 5, 50, 73, 195, 200, 275, 294–296
Chlorofluorocarbons (CFCs), 164
Choitner, Murray, 386, 387
Christian Identity, 364, 367
Christmas, Annie, 140
Church of Jesus Christ Christian, 367, 369
Church of the Creator, 367
CIA (Central Intelligence Agency), 333, 349–353, 407, 408–412
Ciccio, Don, 23–24
Cigarettes, 164
Citibank, 379
Civella, Nick, 405
Civil forfeiture, 431–433
Clarity (MDMA), 215–216
Clark, Melvin, 225
Classical school of criminology, 61
Cleveland Four, 389, 405, 413
Clines, Thomas, 410
Clinton, Bill, 332, 373, 380, 386, 393, 394
Clinton, Hilary Rodham, 394
Clustered hierarchies, 12–13
Cobain, Kurt, 206
Cocaine (See also Crack; Drug abuse; Drug control; Drug trafficking)
  Colombian and Mexican trafficking of, 160–161, 207–208, 276–278
  crime and, 197, 199
  history of, 194–195
  Mexican syndicates and, 282–286
  natural use of, 194
  rural distribution channels and, 262
  South African, 319
Cock Group, 10–11
Codina, Armondo, 397
Coe, Blackie, 139
Cohen, Mickey, 284, 386
Cohen, Sam, 403, 404, 405, 415
Colby, William, 353
Coleman, Delbert, 404, 405
Coll, Peter, 106–107
Coll, Vincent, 106–107
Collaboration. See Strategic alliances

Collusion (See also Corporate crime; Corruption; Law enforcement; Politics)
Colombia
  Cali Cartel, 122–124, 200, 201, 280–281, 376
  contemporary syndicates, 281–282
  contraband smuggling and, 164
  corruption and, 273c
  counterfeit currency and, 160
  drug trafficking, 192, 207–208
  Juvenal Group, 13–14
  marijuana, 161
  Medellin Cartel, 59, 279–280
  money laundering, 189
  nontraditional organized crime, 122–124
  as source of cocaine and heroin, 160, 161, 209–210, 276–279
  terrorism and, 347
Colombo, Joe, 19, 38, 112–114, 442
Colors, 235, 238
Colosimo, "Big Jim," 93, 97
COMAL, 404
The Commission (criminal), 7, 121 (See also Crime commissions)
Committee to Combat Terrorism, 372
Communications technology, 6, 8, 13, 278
Community-based drug control, 219
Community history theory (Suttles), 67
Community/social theory, 74–81
Compensatory alliances, 271
Comprehensive Drug Abuse Prevention and Control Act, 438–439
Compton Pirus, 234
Computer technology. See Technology
Confederate National Congress, 367
Congo. See Democratic Republic of the Congo
Congressional hearings, 3
Connolly, John, 425
Consiglieres, 43
Consolidated Crip Organization, 250
Conspiracies, 17, 73, 437–438 (See also Alien conspiracy theory)
Construction industry, 17, 38, 177
Contero Aguero, Elvio Ramon, 291
Conti, Samuel, 243
Continuing Criminal Enterprise (CCE) statutes, 432, 437
Contraband smuggling, 163–164, 289, 293, 303–304
Contract services, 42
Contras. See Iran-contra affair
Contreras, Juan, 140
Controlled Substances Act (CSA), 438–439
Convention on Psychotropic Substances, 314
Cook, James, 149
Cooperative strategies. See Strategic alliances
Copeland, John, 132
Coppola, "Trigger Mike," 387
Corbo, Rene, 356
Core groups, 13–14
Cornfeld, Bernie, 404, 407
Corona, Ray, 410, 411

Corporate crime
  banking and, 406–407
  contemporary scandals, 377–380
  in Cuba, 406
  in Florida, 405–406
  international organized crime and, 412–413
  in Las Vegas, 100–103, 404–405
  major organized crime figures and, 413–416
  Meyer Lansky and, 401–404
  reciprocity and, 400–401
  and the savings and loan scandals, 408–412
Corruption (See also Corporate crime; Law enforcement; Politics)
  African organized crime, 312
  of business persons, 18, 53
  Central and Eastern Europe, 303
  and the community social control function, 78–80
  drug trafficking and, 192–193, 196
  human trafficking and, 185–186
  international organized crime and, 267, 272–273
  Juvenal Group and, 13–14
  of law enforcement, 12, 13, 18, 44, 53, 150, 283
  of political structures, 18, 41–42, 44, 53, 78–81, 150, 283
  public view of, 151
  rural, 261
  Russian organized crime, 311–312
  South African, 319
  Triborder Area and, 289, 290
  undermining of civil society, 272
Corson, Robert L., 410
Cosa Nostra, 33, 34, 43–45, 120–121, 306–307 (See also Mafia)
Cosca, 20–21
Cosmano, James "Sunny Jim," 103
Cosmotheist Church, 367
Costa, Luiz Fernando Da, 291
Costa Rica, 209–210, 413
Costello, Frank, 31, 32, 106, 120, 121, 382, 405
Counterfeiting, 165–166, 182, 289, 292–293
Countertrade alliances, 271
Countess Piazza, 140
Counties Movement, 367
Coupe, Bras (Squire), 132
Court files, 4
Cove Associates, 404
The Covenant, 368, 370
Covington, Harold, 367
Crack, 205, 208, 320
Crackdowns, 218
Crime commissions, 18, 19–21
Crime Control Act of 1984, 428
Crime Control and Safe Streets Act of 1968, 428
Crime networks, 9, 14–15, 48, 52–53, 72, 267
Criminal behavior categories, 16–18
Criminal forfeiture, 431–432
Criminal groups, 7–9, 40–41
Criminal terrorism, 328
Criminological theories. See Theories